READER'S DIGEST
BARTHOLOMEW

ATLAS
OF THE
WORLD

READER'S DIGEST
BARTHOLOMEW
ATLAS

OF THE WORLD

The Reader's Digest Association, Inc.
Pleasantville, New York / Montreal
Cape Town / Sydney

Cartographic Director
John C. Bartholomew

List of Contributors

The publishers wish to thank the following
for their valued assistance in preparing
the thematic section of this atlas:—

Dr Mary T. Brück
Mr Michael Burns
Prof. John Erickson
Prof. Iain MacGibbon
Prof. Aubrey Manning
Dr Derek S. Miller
Prof. Rosalind M. Mitchison
Dr J. Andrew Tweedie
Prof. Brian G. J. Upton
Dr Stephen Wyn Williams

Design of thematic section:—
Graphic Partners - Design Consultants
Photographs. Title page:—
NASA/Woodmansterne Ltd
Exploring the Solar System:—
NASA

Copyright © John Bartholomew & Son Ltd. 1983.

1st Edition 1983
Reprinted 1984

Originally published in Scotland as
Bartholomew Family Atlas of the World

Library of Congress Catalog Card Number 83-61162
ISBN 0-89577-172-1

Printed in Scotland by
John Bartholomew & Son Ltd.

Contents

IV   List of Contributors

THE WORLD

VIII   Exploring the Solar System

x   The Earth Takes Shape

XII   Dynamic Earth

XIV   Global Climate

XVI   The Natural Habitat

XVIII   Energy for Mankind

XX   Famine and Plenty

XXII   Man in Society

XXIV   Rich World, Poor World

XXVI   Co-operation and Confrontation

XXVIII   Transport Networks

XXIX   The World in Figures

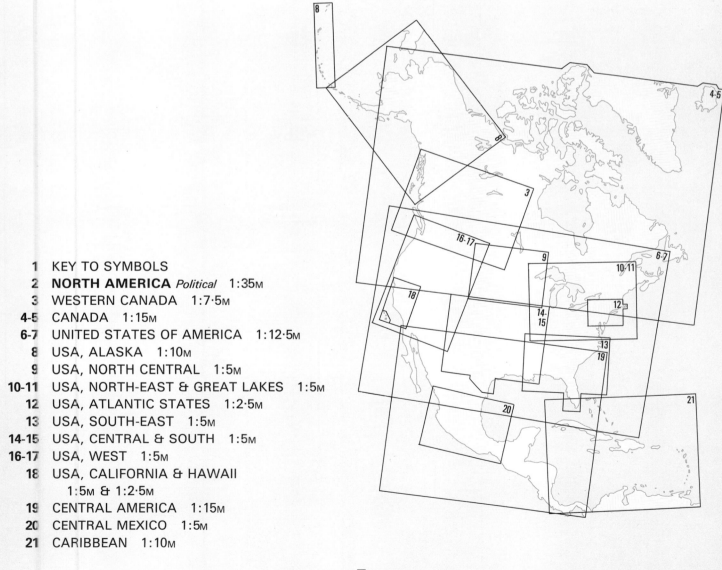

1   KEY TO SYMBOLS

2   **NORTH AMERICA** *Political*   1:35M

3   WESTERN CANADA   1:7·5M

4-5   CANADA   1:15M

6-7   UNITED STATES OF AMERICA   1:12·5M

8   USA, ALASKA   1:10M

9   USA, NORTH CENTRAL   1:5M

10-11   USA, NORTH-EAST & GREAT LAKES   1:5M

12   USA, ATLANTIC STATES   1:2·5M

13   USA, SOUTH-EAST   1:5M

14-15   USA, CENTRAL & SOUTH   1:5M

16-17   USA, WEST   1:5M

18   USA, CALIFORNIA & HAWAII
        1:5M & 1:2·5M

19   CENTRAL AMERICA   1:15M

20   CENTRAL MEXICO   1:5M

21   CARIBBEAN   1:10M

22 SOUTH AMERICA *Political* 1:35M
23 SOUTH AMERICA, SOUTH 1:15M
24-25 SOUTH AMERICA, NORTH 1:15M
26 CENTRAL CHILE - ARGENTINA &
    URUGUAY 1:7·5M
27 SOUTH-EAST BRAZIL 1:7·5M
28 EUROPE *Political* 1:15M
30 SCANDINAVIA 1:7·5M
31 GREAT BRITAIN & IRELAND 1:5M
32-33 UNITED KINGDOM 1:2·5M
34 LONDON-PARIS-BONN · 1:2·5M
35 ALPS 1:2·5M
36 FRANCE 1:5M
37 SPAIN 1:5M
38-39 ITALY & THE BALKANS 1:5M
40-41 NORTH CENTRAL EUROPE 1:5M
42-43 EUROPEAN RUSSIA 1:10M

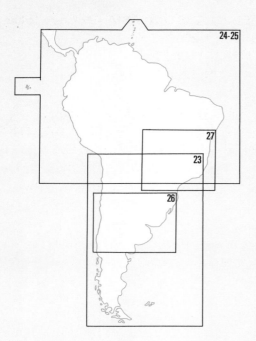

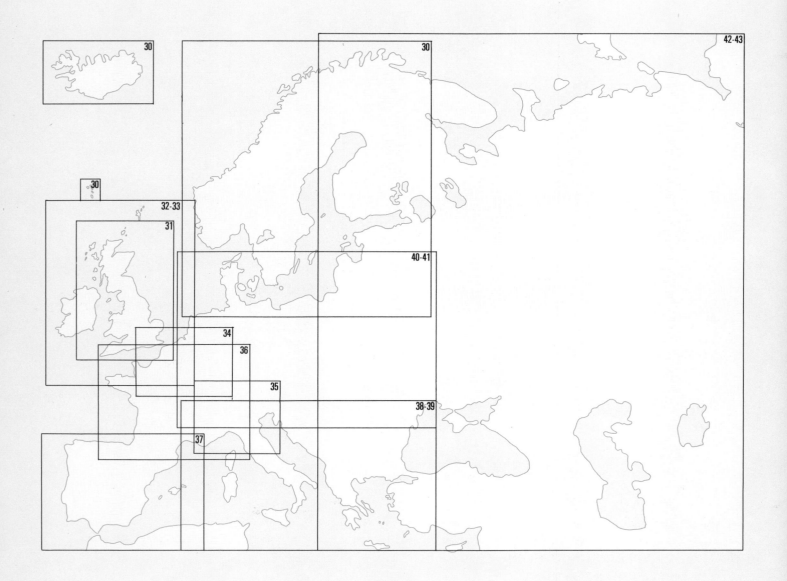

44-45 ASIA & AUSTRALASIA - *Political* 1:40ᴍ

46-47 USSR 1:20ᴍ

48-49 FAR EAST 1:20ᴍ

50 CENTRAL CHINA 1:10ᴍ

51 JAPAN & KOREA 1:10ᴍ

52 CENTRAL JAPAN-KOREA 1:5ᴍ

53 SOUTH-EAST ASIA, PENINSULAR 1:10ᴍ

54 MALAYSIA & INDONESIA, WEST 1:10ᴍ

55 INDONESIA, EAST & PHILIPPINES 1:10ᴍ

56-57 SOUTH ASIA & MIDDLE EAST 1:20ᴍ

ASIA & AUSTRALIA (continued)

58 INDIA, NORTH-WEST & PAKISTAN 1:7·5ᴍ

59 INDIA, NORTH-EAST & BANGLADESH 1:7·5ᴍ

60 INDIA, SOUTH & SRI LANKA 1:7·5ᴍ

61 IRAN & AFGHANISTAN 1:7·5ᴍ

62 TURKEY, SYRIA & IRAQ 1:7·5ᴍ

63 ISRAEL, LEBANON & CYPRUS 1:2·5ᴍ

64-65 ARABIAN PENINSULA & NILE VALLEY 1:7·5ᴍ

66 AFRICA *political* 1:40ᴍ

67 AFRICA, NORTH-EAST 1:15ᴍ

68 AFRICA, WEST 1:15ᴍ

69 NORTH & WEST AFRICAN COASTS 1:7·5ᴍ

70-71 AFRICA, CENTRAL & SOUTHERN 1:15ᴍ

72 SOUTH AFRICA 1:7·5ᴍ

73 ATLANTIC OCEAN 1:60ᴍ

74-75 INDIAN & PACIFIC OCEANS 1:60ᴍ

AUSTRALIA

76-77 AUSTRALIA & SOUTH-WEST PACIFIC 1:20ᴍ

78 AUSTRALIA, SOUTH-EAST 1:7·5ᴍ

79 NEW ZEALAND 1:5ᴍ

80 POLAR REGIONS 1:40ᴍ

1-64 ABBREVIATIONS & INDEX

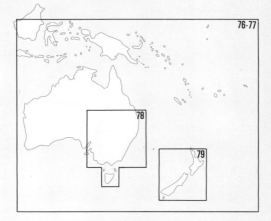

EXPLORING THE SOLAR SYSTEM

Solar systems are probably very common in the Universe, but the one we know is made up of the Sun, the planets and their satellites, comets, asteroids, meteoroids, interplanetary dust and gas. In this 'Space Age', the main aim of exploration has been to understand the history and origin of the Solar System. Our achievements have been many and remarkable, sending men to the Moon and back, projecting spacecraft to the outermost planets and developing new materials for everyday use (non-stick pans); but so far, no sign of life has been found beyond Earth itself.

Space Missions

The idea of space travel can be said to have begun as early as 1895. Sputnik 1, launched by the Russians in 1957, paved the way for manned space flights. The table summarises the most significant of recent space missions.

Voyager 2
This probe was launched on 20 August 1977. Already its route has taken it past Jupiter (1979) and then on to Saturn (1981). If all goes well it will encounter Uranus in 1986 and Neptune in 1989, thus taking advantage of the favourable line-up of the four largest planets, which will not happen again for another 150 years.

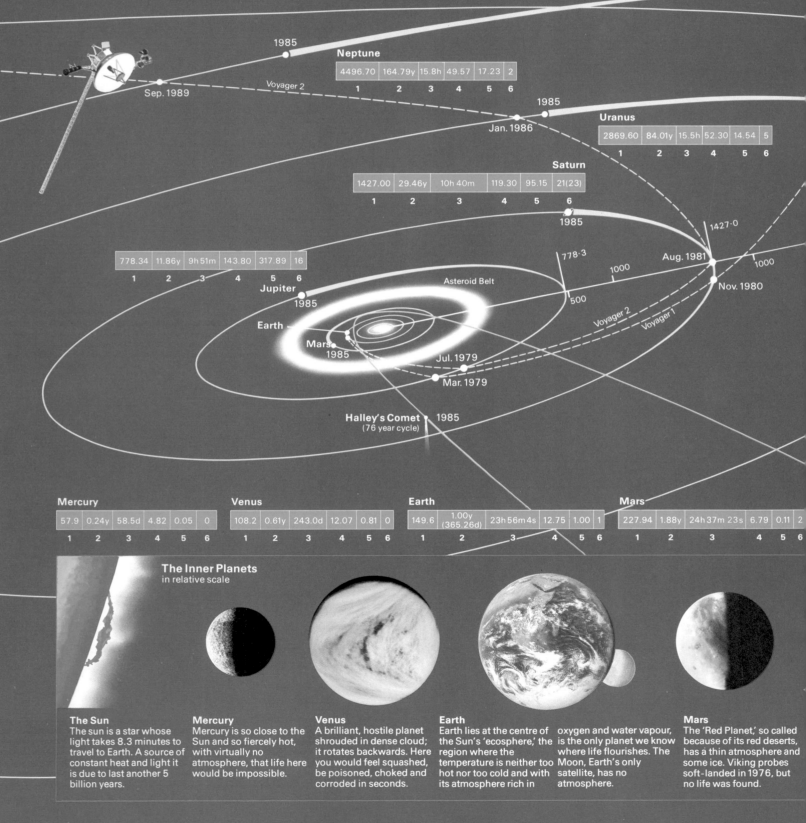

Neptune
| 4496.70 | 164.79y | 15.8h | 49.57 | 17.23 | 2 |
| 1 | 2 | 3 | 4 | 5 | 6 |

Uranus
| 2869.60 | 84.01y | 15.5h | 52.30 | 14.54 | 5 |
| 1 | 2 | 3 | 4 | 5 | 6 |

Saturn
| 1427.00 | 29.46y | 10h 40m | 119.30 | 95.15 | 21(23) |
| 1 | 2 | 3 | 4 | 5 | 6 |

Jupiter
| 778.34 | 11.86y | 9h 51m | 143.80 | 317.89 | 16 |
| 1 | 2 | 3 | 4 | 5 | 6 |

Asteroid Belt

Earth

Mars

Halley's Comet (76 year cycle)

Voyager 2 / Voyager 1

Sep. 1989 / 1985 / Jan. 1986 / Aug. 1981 / Nov. 1980 / Jul. 1979 / Mar. 1979

1427·0 / 778·3 / 1000 / 500 / 1000

Mercury
| 57.9 | 0.24y | 58.5d | 4.82 | 0.05 | 0 |
| 1 | 2 | 3 | 4 | 5 | 6 |

Venus
| 108.2 | 0.61y | 243.0d | 12.07 | 0.81 | 0 |
| 1 | 2 | 3 | 4 | 5 | 6 |

Earth
| 149.6 | 1.00y (365.26d) | 23h 56m 4s | 12.75 | 1.00 | 1 |
| 1 | 2 | 3 | 4 | 5 | 6 |

Mars
| 227.94 | 1.88y | 24h 37m 23s | 6.79 | 0.11 | 2 |
| 1 | 2 | 3 | 4 | 5 | 6 |

The Inner Planets in relative scale

The Sun
The sun is a star whose light takes 8.3 minutes to travel to Earth. A source of constant heat and light it is due to last another 5 billion years.

Mercury
Mercury is so close to the Sun and so fiercely hot, with virtually no atmosphere, that life here would be impossible.

Venus
A brilliant, hostile planet shrouded in dense cloud; it rotates backwards. Here you would feel squashed, be poisoned, choked and corroded in seconds.

Earth
Earth lies at the centre of the Sun's 'ecosphere,' the region where the temperature is neither too hot nor too cold and with its atmosphere rich in oxygen and water vapour, is the only planet we know where life flourishes. The Moon, Earth's only satellite, has no atmosphere.

Mars
The 'Red Planet,' so called because of its red deserts, has a thin atmosphere and some ice. Viking probes soft-landed in 1976, but no life was found.

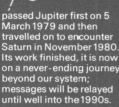

Voyager 1

The Voyager missions are perhaps the most ambitious yet as their aim is to 'see' the four 'giants' of the solar system, Jupiter, Saturn, Uranus and Neptune. Voyager 1 was launched a few days after its 'twin' on 5 September 1977. It by- passed Jupiter first on 5 March 1979 and then travelled on to encounter Saturn in November 1980. Its work finished, it is now on a never-ending journey beyond our system; messages will be relayed until well into the 1990s.

Spacecraft	Launch date	Launch objective: Date reached	Nearest approach	Comments
Sputnik 1 (USSR)	Oct. 1957	Earth orbit	215km from Earth	Its radio signals were picked up all over the world.
Lunik 1,2,3 (USSR)	Jan. 1959	Moon bypass; Jan. 1959	6437km from Moon	2 crash-landed Sep 1959; 3—first pictures of farside of Moon Oct 1959.
Vostok 1 (USSR)	Apr. 1961	Earth orbit	327 km from Earth	First manned space flight. Lasted 1 hour 48 min.
Gemini 6/7 (USA)	Dec. 1965	Space docking; Dec. 1965	290 km from Earth	Successful space docking operation between two manned spacecraft.
Apollo 11 (USA)	Jul. 1969	Moon; Jul. 1969	Landed at Sea of Tranquility	Armstrong and Aldrin landed and walked on the Moon.
Pioneer 10 (USA)	Mar. 1972	Jupiter; Dec. 1973	528 000km from Jupiter	Sent pictures and information about Jupiter.
Skylab (USA)	1973	Siting space station; Jul. 1973	427 km from Earth	Skylab damaged on ascent. Repaired in orbit.
Mariner 10 (USA)	Nov. 1973	Venus + Mercury; Feb. '74, Mar. '75	5790km (Venus) 327km (Mercury)	Bypassed Venus—sent back pictures. Later approached Mercury.
Viking 1/2 (USA)	Aug. 1975	Mars; Jul.and Sep. 1976	Chryse and Utopia regions	Unmanned landing—sent pictures. Viking 2 sent surface samples.
Voyager 1/2 (USA)	Sep.+Aug. 1977	Jupiter, Saturn, Uranus and Neptune; both passed Jup. '79, 1 passed Sat. '80 and 2, '81	2– 722 000km (Jupiter); 1–124 000km (Saturn)	1 launched second on a more direct orbit—reaching destinations first.

Sep. 1988

1985

Pluto

5900.00	247.70y	6d 9h	3.00	0.002	1
1	2	3	4	5	6

4496.

2869·6

4000

3000

2500

2000

1500

2000

million kilometres
million miles

Average distance from Sun (million km)
Revolution period round Sun ('Earth' years)
Rotation period round own axis (days, hours, mins, secs)
Equatorial diameter: (1000km)
Mass (Earth=1)
Number of known satellites

1	2	3	4	5	6

Other Moons Revealed

Since 1610, when Galileo spotted four of Jupiter's moons, many more have been seen. Information received from both Voyagers would indicate that Saturn certainly has 21, but possibly as many as 23. From what we know so far, most of the moons belonging to these two planets are icy, inhospitable places, unable to support life. Several are irregular in shape and some rotate backwards. Titan, Saturn's largest moon, with an atmosphere similar to Earth's, is the only one where there might be life, but at such low temperatures growth would be very slow.

Io (Jupiter)
It lies 413 000km from Jupiter and has a red, sulphury surface, which is changed constantly by its active volcanoes.

Ganymede (Jupiter)
The largest of all the moons in the solar system it is 1070 000km from Jupiter. Its surface is icy and grooved.

Callisto (Jupiter)
An icy, crater-pitted moon, it lies 1883 000km from Jupiter. Its largest crater (Valhalla), a ring basin, may be very ancient.

Mimas (Saturn)
The crater, Herschel (walls-5km; central peak-6km), covers a third of this moon, which lies 186 000km from Saturn.

Dione (Saturn)
The surface is covered with craters, the largest of which is Amata. This moon is 377 000km from Saturn.

Titan (Saturn)
Very distant from Saturn at 1222 000km, Titan is featureless, has a hazy orange sphere and a bluish polar collar.

Satellites of Jupiter

Satellites of Saturn

relative scale

The Solar System
in relative scale

The Inner Planets

(see facing page)

Uranus

Neptune

Pluto

Jupiter
Everything about Jupiter is big. It is the largest planet; has a hydrogen-rich atmosphere and a ring system (discovered by Voyager 1).

Saturn
Noted for its rings, Saturn is next in size and position to Jupiter. Pioneer 11 (1979) and the Voyagers have confirmed that Saturn has a liquid gas surface.

Uranus
This planet, which appears as a greenish disc, has a system of nine rings. Unlike the other planets it rotates at a steep angle.

Neptune
Neptune was discovered in 1846. Through the telescope it appears bluish with two parallel equatorial belts.

Pluto
Pluto and its moon, Charon, are recent discoveries. This icy planet has an exceptional orbit which brings it inside Neptune's path.

THE EARTH TAKES SHAPE

Man has dominated earth for only 2 million years. Compared to the planet's 4·4 billion year history, that is a tiny fraction of a vast period of time impossible to imagine. But we can form some idea of the relative duration of the history of life from the Earth Time Whorl.

Earth Time Whorl

The infinite variety of life as we know it originated and evolved in close conjunction with the evolution of earth's atmosphere, continents and oceans. Evidence comes from scientists who have traced back the earliest forms of life by simulating primitive earth conditions and examining rocks and fossils. Life emerged slowly. The simplest forms of algae appeared 3·3 billion years ago in the Precambrian period, followed by more complex soft-bodied sea animals and the first vertebrates. About 570 million years ago the pace increased as fish, land plants, amphibians, insects, spiders, ferns, swamp forests and reptiles evolved, many to be wiped out by a major life extinction 225 million years ago. Dinosaurs and mammals appeared 210 million years ago, followed by the first birds and flowering plants. It was a time of violent mountain building, extremes of climate and fluctuating sea-levels; then a catastrophic change during the Cretaceous period, around 65 million years ago, ended the dinosaurs' domination. Man is a descendant of the first monkeys and man-like apes which emerged 35 million years ago.

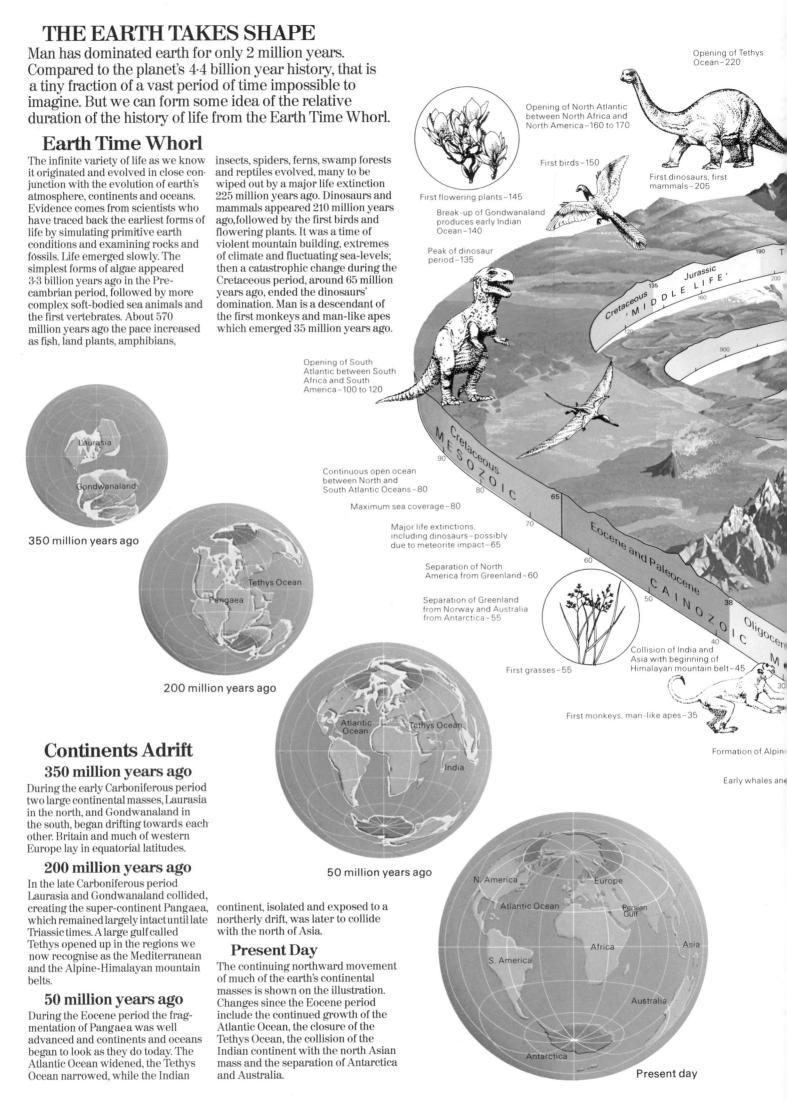

Opening of Tethys Ocean – 220

Opening of North Atlantic between North Africa and North America – 160 to 170

First birds – 150

First dinosaurs, first mammals – 205

First flowering plants – 145

Break-up of Gondwanaland produces early Indian Ocean – 140

Peak of dinosaur period – 135

Opening of South Atlantic between South Africa and South America – 100 to 120

Continuous open ocean between North and South Atlantic Oceans – 80

Maximum sea coverage – 80

Major life extinctions, including dinosaurs – possibly due to meteorite impact – 65

Separation of North America from Greenland – 60

Separation of Greenland from Norway and Australia from Antarctica – 55

First grasses – 55

Collision of India and Asia with beginning of Himalayan mountain belt – 45

First monkeys, man-like apes – 35

Formation of Alpine

Early whales an

350 million years ago

200 million years ago

Laurasia

Gondwanaland

Pangaea

Tethys Ocean

Atlantic Ocean

Tethys Ocean

India

50 million years ago

Continents Adrift

350 million years ago

During the early Carboniferous period two large continental masses, Laurasia in the north, and Gondwanaland in the south, began drifting towards each other. Britain and much of western Europe lay in equatorial latitudes.

200 million years ago

In the late Carboniferous period Laurasia and Gondwanaland collided, creating the super-continent Pangaea, which remained largely intact until late Triassic times. A large gulf called Tethys opened up in the regions we now recognise as the Mediterranean and the Alpine-Himalayan mountain belts.

50 million years ago

During the Eocene period the fragmentation of Pangaea was well advanced and continents and oceans began to look as they do today. The Atlantic Ocean widened, the Tethys Ocean narrowed, while the Indian continent, isolated and exposed to a northerly drift, was later to collide with the north of Asia.

Present Day

The continuing northward movement of much of the earth's continental masses is shown on the illustration. Changes since the Eocene period include the continued growth of the Atlantic Ocean, the closure of the Tethys Ocean, the collision of the Indian continent with the north Asian mass and the separation of Antarctica and Australia.

N. America

Europe

Atlantic Ocean

Persian Gulf

Africa

Asia

S. America

Australia

Antarctica

Present day

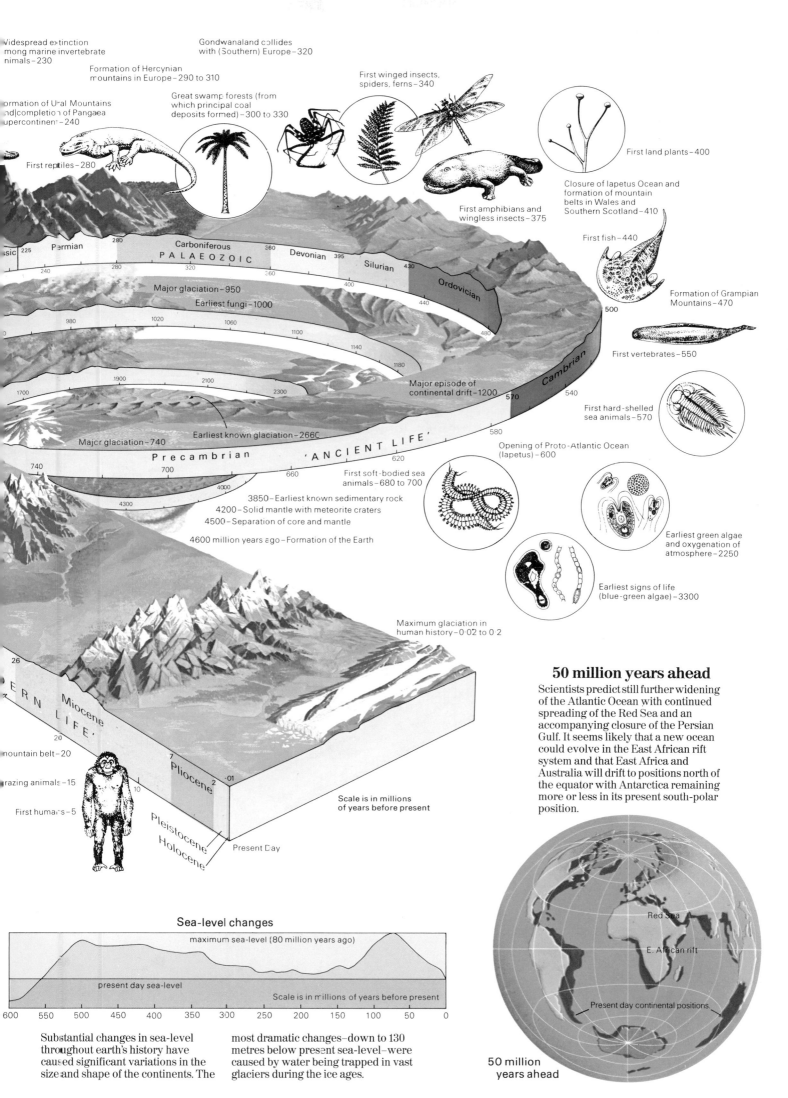

Widespread extinction among marine invertebrate animals – 230

Gondwanaland collides with (Southern) Europe – 320

Formation of Hercynian mountains in Europe – 290 to 310

First winged insects, spiders, ferns – 340

Formation of Ural Mountains and completion of Pangaea supercontinent – 240

Great swamp forests (from which principal coal deposits formed) – 300 to 330

First reptiles – 280

First land plants – 400

First amphibians and wingless insects – 375

Closure of Iapetus Ocean and formation of mountain belts in Wales and Southern Scotland – 410

First fish – 440

Permian 280   Carboniferous 360   Devonian 395   Silurian 430
225   Ordovician
240   280   320   360   400   440   480

P A L A E O Z O I C

Major glaciation – 950
Earliest fungi – 1000
980   1020   1060   1100   1140   1180

Formation of Grampian Mountains – 470

500

First vertebrates – 550

1700   1900   2100   2300

Cambrian   540
570

First hard-shelled sea animals – 570

Major episode of continental drift – 1200

580

Major glaciation – 740   Earliest known glaciation – 2660

Opening of Proto-Atlantic Ocean (Iapetus) – 600

Precambrian   'ANCIENT LIFE'   620

740   700   660   4000
4300

First soft-bodied sea animals – 680 to 700

3850 – Earliest known sedimentary rock
4200 – Solid mantle with meteorite craters
4500 – Separation of core and mantle
4600 million years ago – Formation of the Earth

Earliest green algae and oxygenation of atmosphere – 2250

Earliest signs of life (blue-green algae) – 3300

Maximum glaciation in human history – 0·02 to 0·2

26

Miocene

mountain belt – 20

grazing animals – 15

First humans – 5

20
7
10
Pliocene   2   ·01

Pleistocene
Holocene

Present Day

Scale is in millions of years before present

50 million years ahead

Scientists predict still further widening of the Atlantic Ocean with continued spreading of the Red Sea and an accompanying closure of the Persian Gulf. It seems likely that a new ocean could evolve in the East African rift system and that East Africa and Australia will drift to positions north of the equator with Antarctica remaining more or less in its present south-polar position.

Red Sea

E. African rift

Present day continental positions.

50 million years ahead

Sea-level changes

maximum sea-level (80 million years ago)

present day sea-level

Scale is in millions of years before present

600   550   500   450   400   350   300   250   200   150   100   50   0

Substantial changes in sea-level throughout earth's history have caused significant variations in the size and shape of the continents. The most dramatic changes–down to 130 metres below present sea-level–were caused by water being trapped in vast glaciers during the ice ages.

DYNAMIC EARTH

Unlike our neighbours, Moon, Mars and Venus, Earth is a dynamic and
'living' planet. Turbulent motions within the interior bring about
large-scale crustal movements which actively determine
the size and shape of our oceans and continents,
and give rise to earthquakes and volcanoes.

The Unstable Crust

The Earth is made up of three main
layers, crust (or lithosphere), mantle
and core. The thickness of the crust
ranges from a few kilometres beneath
mid-ocean ridges to 100 km under
mountains such as the Alps. The mantle
makes up 82% of the Earth's volume
and reaches a temperature of 3700°C
while the core reaches 4300°C.

These high internal temperatures
are responsible for the Earth's crustal
instability. As material in the mantle is
hot and therefore in a plastic state, it
circulates in a convecting pattern. The
upwelling produces new crust at mid-
ocean ridges, the sea floor is drawn
apart horizontally and subsequently
descends beneath the continental rim
to be re-absorbed in the mantle.

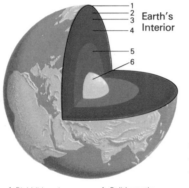

Earth's
Interior

1 Rigid lithosphere   4 Solid mantle
  (to 100 km)   (to 2900 km)
2 'Soft' upper mantle   5 Liquid outer core
  (to 250 km)   (to 5000 km)
3 Transition zone   6 Solid inner core
  (to 700 km)   (to 6371 km)

Plate Tectonics

The theory of Plate Tectonics explains
how the Earth's crust is moving in
vast, rigid sections or 'plates', and is a
modern revolution in our understanding of the planet. The plates float
on the plastic upper mantle and move
continously against one another at
rates of up to 20 cm a year.

The relation of inter-plate movement is defined by the type of plate
margin, Constructive, Destructive or
Conservative (see right). Constructive
plate movement is well illustrated in
the Atlantic Ocean. At the mid-ocean
ridge, new ocean floor is continually
being produced as the Americas
move further apart from Europe and
Africa. Destructive plate movement is
found on all sides of the Pacific Ocean,
as the various plates slide down
beneath the surrounding lithosphere.
Conservative plate movement can
cause the most destructive earthquakes. It arises where adjacent
plates slide past one another along
transform faults, such as the San
Andreas fault in California.

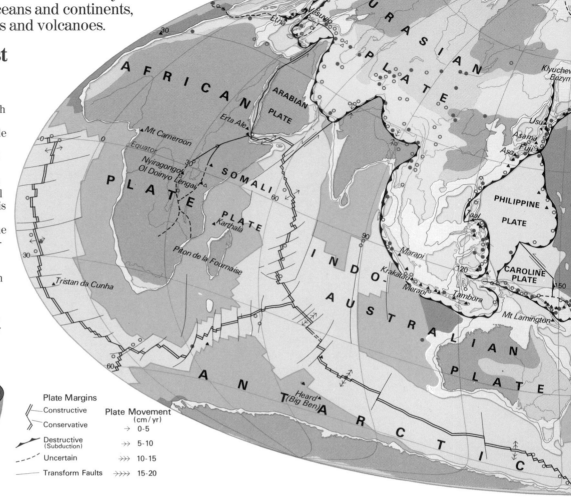

Plate Margins
— Constructive
— Conservative
— Destructive
  (Subduction)
- - Uncertain
— Transform Faults

Plate Movement
  (cm/yr)
→   0-5
→→   5-10
→→→   10-15
→→→→   15-20

Island-Arc
Volcanoes protrude in long,
narrow island chains parallel to
ocean trenches, as around the
Pacific Ocean

Mid-Ocean Ridge
(Constructive Plate Margin)
Axis of sea-floor spreading
(crustal extension). Zone of
submarine volcanism and
earthquake activity

Ocean floor

New lithosphere
being formed

Continental
crust

Continental
lithosphere

Volcano Chain
Volcano erupted above Hot Spot
is borne away by the spreading
lithosphere. As subsequent
volcanoes form, a chain of
undersea or island volcanoes
develops across the ocean floor

Hot Spot
Column of hot, rising mantle
supplies magma which erupts
as an oceanic volcano

Magma (molten ro
wells up to fill ga
created by sea-flo
spreading

Convection curren

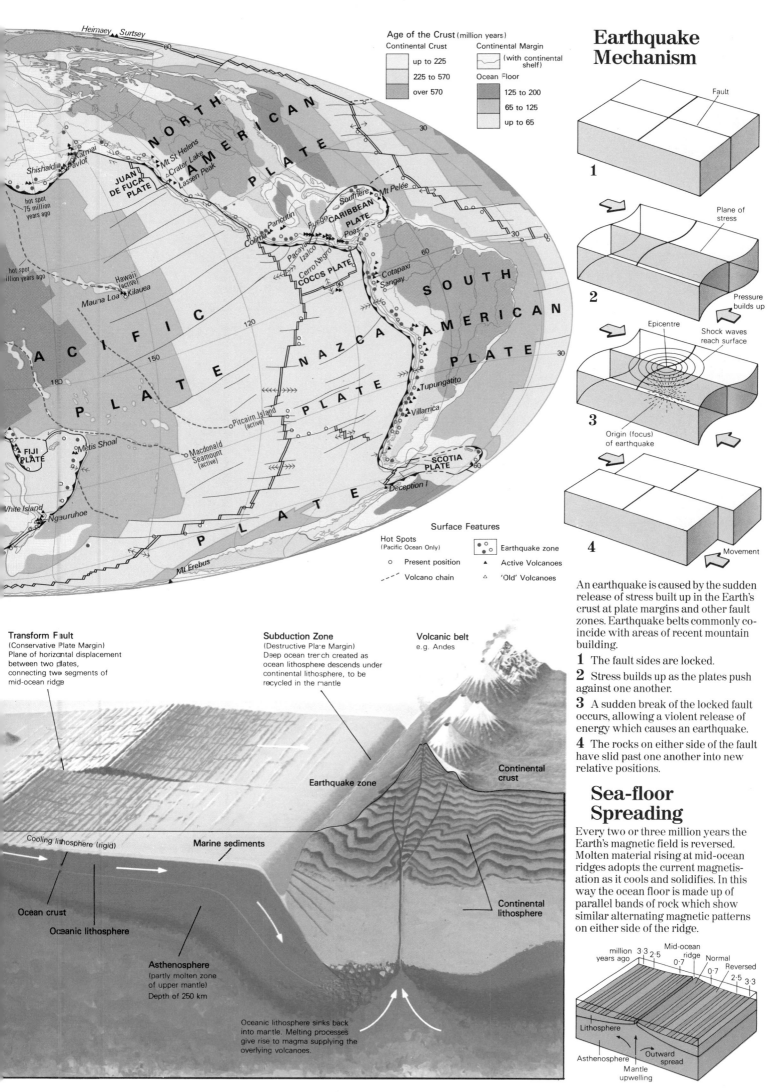

Earthquake Mechanism

1

2 Plane of stress — Pressure builds up

3 Epicentre — Shock waves reach surface — Origin (focus) of earthquake

4 Movement

An earthquake is caused by the sudden release of stress built up in the Earth's crust at plate margins and other fault zones. Earthquake belts commonly co-incide with areas of recent mountain building.

1 The fault sides are locked.

2 Stress builds up as the plates push against one another.

3 A sudden break of the locked fault occurs, allowing a violent release of energy which causes an earthquake.

4 The rocks on either side of the fault have slid past one another into new relative positions.

Sea-floor Spreading

Every two or three million years the Earth's magnetic field is reversed. Molten material rising at mid-ocean ridges adopts the current magnetisation as it cools and solidifies. In this way the ocean floor is made up of parallel bands of rock which show similar alternating magnetic patterns on either side of the ridge.

million years ago 3·3 2·5 0·7 — Mid-ocean ridge — Normal 0·7 — Reversed 2·5 3·3

Lithosphere — Asthenosphere — Mantle upwelling — Outward spread

Age of the Crust (million years)

Continental Crust
- up to 225
- 225 to 570
- over 570

Continental Margin (with continental shelf)

Ocean Floor
- 125 to 200
- 65 to 125
- up to 65

Surface Features

Hot Spots (Pacific Ocean Only)
- ○ Present position
- --- Volcano chain

- Earthquake zone
- ▲ Active Volcanoes
- △ 'Old' Volcanoes

Transform Fault
(Conservative Plate Margin)
Plane of horizontal displacement between two plates, connecting two segments of mid-ocean ridge

Subduction Zone
(Destructive Plate Margin)
Deep ocean trench created as ocean lithosphere descends under continental lithosphere, to be recycled in the mantle

Volcanic belt e.g. Andes

Earthquake zone

Continental crust

Continental lithosphere

Cooling lithosphere (rigid)

Marine sediments

Ocean crust

Oceanic lithosphere

Asthenosphere (partly molten zone of upper mantle) Depth of 250 km

Oceanic lithosphere sinks back into mantle. Melting processes give rise to magma supplying the overlying volcanoes.

GLOBAL CLIMATE

Climate is of vital concern to man. Constantly variable, it affects his environment, his ability to grow food, his mobility and well-being.

The Rhythm of the Seasons

The combined effects of rainfall patterns and temperature variations form the main climate characteristics.

As the earth revolves around the sun the tilt of its axis gives rise to the summer season in the hemisphere facing the overhead sun and the winter season in the hemisphere further from the sun. Solar radiation, winds and ocean currents, together with latitude, altitude and the effects of land relief, determine the main types of climate, examples of which are shown by the graphs.

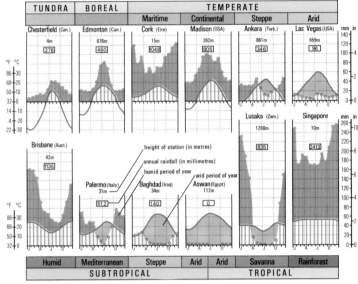

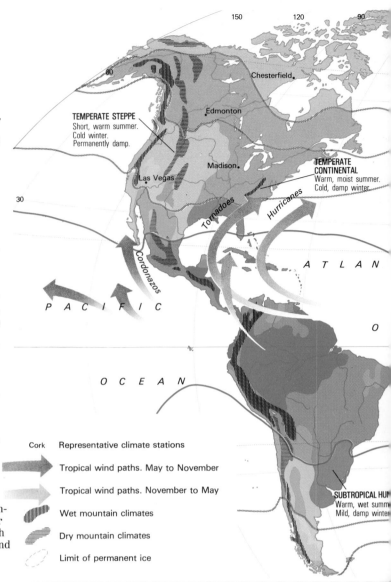

Cork — Representative climate stations

Tropical wind paths. May to November

Tropical wind paths. November to May

Wet mountain climates

Dry mountain climates

Limit of permanent ice

The Restless Atmosphere

All weather is confined to the lower part of the atmosphere (as shown on the accompanying global maps) where the air is in a state of perpetual unrest. This movement sometimes has tremendous force, eroding land and depositing rain and snow. Illustrated is the Intertropical Convergence Zone (ITCZ) where trade winds converge and force air to rise leading to torrential rainfall. The circulation of the air makes up three distinct 'cells' in each hemisphere where warm air rises and cold air sinks–the Polar, Ferrel and Hadley cells.

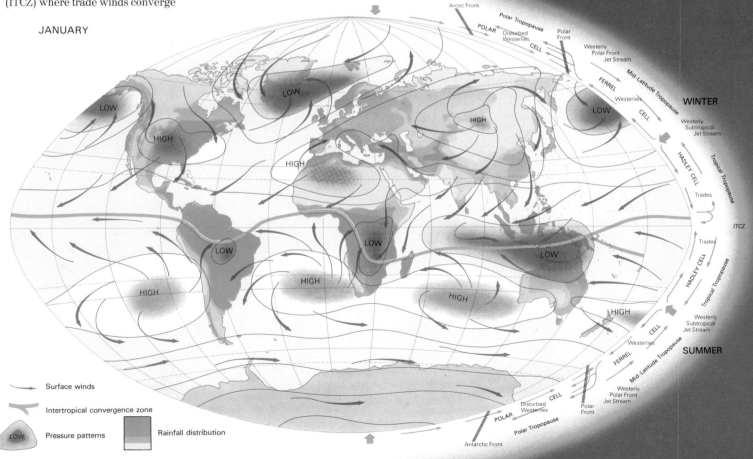

Surface winds

Intertropical convergence zone

LOW — Pressure patterns

Rainfall distribution

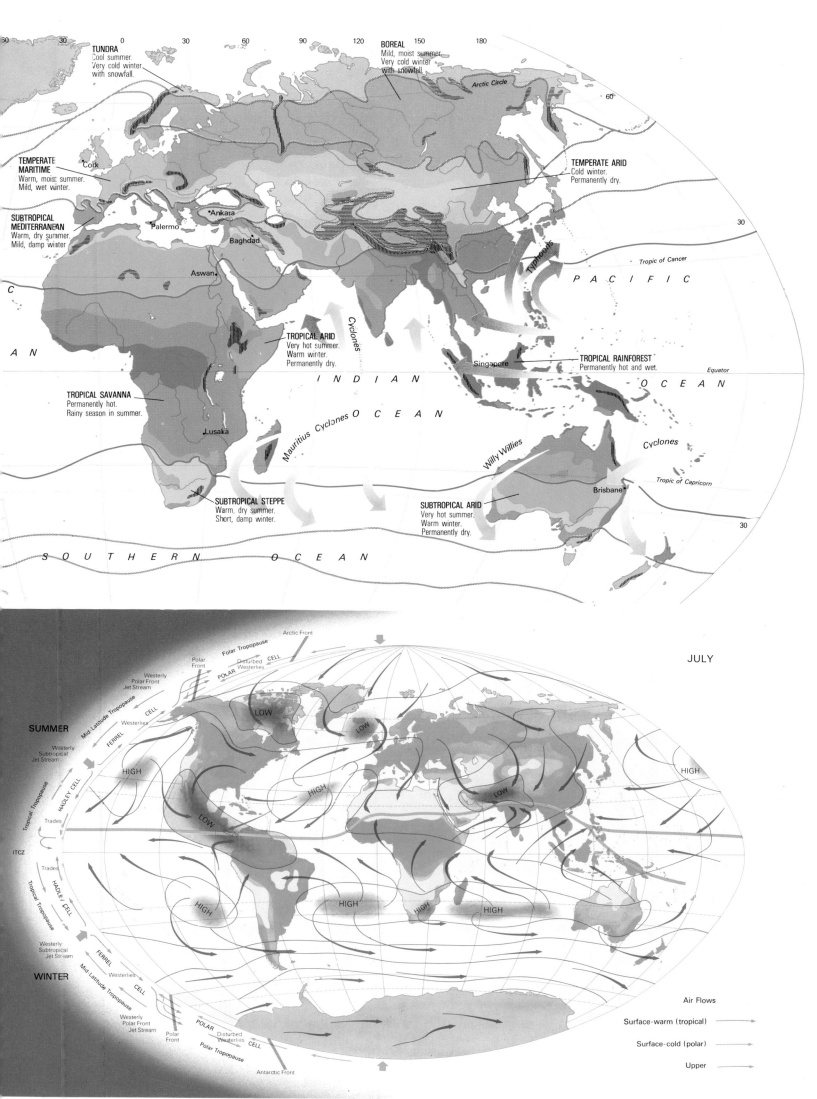

TUNDRA
Cool summer.
Very cold winter
with snowfall.

BOREAL
Mild, moist summer.
Very cold winter
with snowfall.

Arctic Circle

TEMPERATE ARID
Cold winter.
Permanently dry.

TEMPERATE MARITIME
Warm, moist summer.
Mild, wet winter.

•Cork

SUBTROPICAL MEDITERRANEAN
Warm, dry summer.
Mild, damp winter.

Palermo

•Ankara

Baghdad

Aswan

P A C I F I C

Tropic of Cancer

C

A N

TROPICAL ARID
Very hot summer.
Warm winter.
Permanently dry.

Cyclones

TROPICAL RAINFOREST
Permanently hot and wet.

Singapore

Equator

I N D I A N

O C E A N

Typhoons

TROPICAL SAVANNA
Permanently hot.
Rainy season in summer.

•Lusaka

Mauritius Cyclones O C E A N

Cyclones

Willy Willies

Brisbane•

Tropic of Capricorn

SUBTROPICAL STEPPE
Warm, dry summer.
Short, damp winter.

SUBTROPICAL ARID
Very hot summer.
Warm winter.
Permanently dry.

S O U T H E R N   O C E A N

JULY

Arctic Front

Polar Tropopause

Polar Front

Westerly Polar Front Jet Stream

Disturbed Westerlies CELL

POLAR

SUMMER

Mid-Latitude Tropopause

CELL

Westerlies

FERREL

Westerly Subtropical Jet Stream

HADLEY CELL

Tropical Tropopause

Trades

ITCZ

Trades

Tropical Tropopause

HADLEY CELL

Westerly Subtropical Jet Stream

FERREL

Mid-Latitude Tropopause

Westerlies

CELL

WINTER

Westerly Polar Front Jet Stream

Polar Front

POLAR

Disturbed Westerlies CELL

Polar Tropopause

Antarctic Front

LOW

LOW

HIGH

HIGH

LOW

LOW

HIGH

HIGH

HIGH

HIGH

HIGH

Air Flows

Surface-warm (tropical)

Surface-cold (polar)

Upper

XV

THE NATURAL HABITAT

Within each broad climatic zone plants and animals have become adapted to local environments. Adaptation means that they have adjusted to a particular climate, are able to find food, escape predators and reproduce.

Highest Mountains to Deepest Ocean Trenches

Climate and altitude combine to cause vertical zones of habitat types in a pattern which is broadly similar throughout the world.

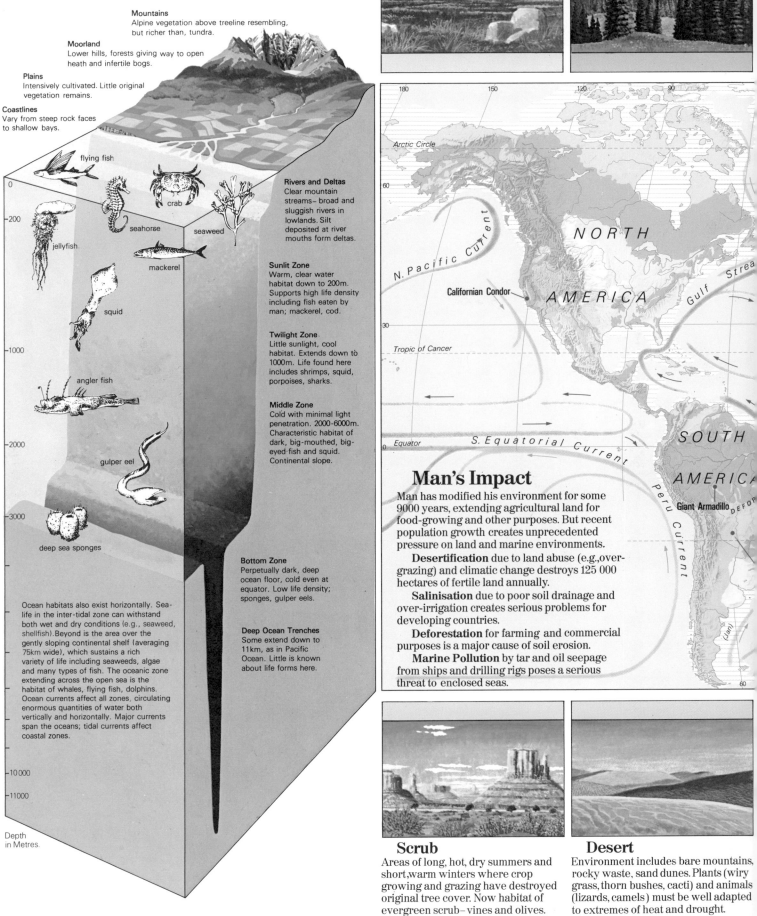

Mountains
Alpine vegetation above treeline resembling, but richer than, tundra.

Moorland
Lower hills, forests giving way to open heath and infertile bogs.

Plains
Intensively cultivated. Little original vegetation remains.

Coastlines
Vary from steep rock faces to shallow bays.

flying fish

seahorse   crab   seaweed

jellyfish

mackerel

squid

angler fish

gulper eel

deep sea sponges

Rivers and Deltas
Clear mountain streams– broad and sluggish rivers in lowlands. Silt deposited at river mouths form deltas.

Sunlit Zone
Warm, clear water habitat down to 200m. Supports high life density including fish eaten by man; mackerel, cod.

Twilight Zone
Little sunlight, cool habitat. Extends down to 1000m. Life found here includes shrimps, squid, porpoises, sharks.

Middle Zone
Cold with minimal light penetration. 2000-6000m. Characteristic habitat of dark, big-mouthed, big-eyed fish and squid. Continental slope.

Bottom Zone
Perpetually dark, deep ocean floor, cold even at equator. Low life density; sponges, gulper eels.

Deep Ocean Trenches
Some extend down to 11km, as in Pacific Ocean. Little is known about life forms here.

Ocean habitats also exist horizontally. Sea-life in the inter-tidal zone can withstand both wet and dry conditions (e.g., seaweed, shellfish). Beyond is the area over the gently sloping continental shelf (averaging 75km wide), which sustains a rich variety of life including seaweeds, algae and many types of fish. The oceanic zone extending across the open sea is the habitat of whales, flying fish, dolphins. Ocean currents affect all zones, circulating enormous quantities of water both vertically and horizontally. Major currents span the oceans; tidal currents affect coastal zones.

Depth in Metres.

0
-200
-1000
-2000
-3000
-10 000
-11000

Tundra
Flat areas frozen over except during brief summers when flooding occurs. Habitat of compact, wind resistant plants; lichens and mosses: animals ; lemmings and reindeer.

Northern Forest
Extensive coniferous forest area where winters are severe, summers brief. Conifers include spruce, fir, giant redwoods. Habitat of beavers, squirrels and red deer.

Arctic Circle

N. Pacific Current

NORTH AMERICA

Californian Condor

Tropic of Cancer

Gulf Stream

SOUTH AMERICA

Giant Armadillo   DEFOR

Peru Current

Equator   S. Equatorial Current

(Jan)

Man's Impact

Man has modified his environment for some 9000 years, extending agricultural land for food-growing and other purposes. But recent population growth creates unprecedented pressure on land and marine environments.

Desertification due to land abuse (e.g., over-grazing) and climatic change destroys 125 000 hectares of fertile land annually.

Salinisation due to poor soil drainage and over-irrigation creates serious problems for developing countries.

Deforestation for farming and commercial purposes is a major cause of soil erosion.

Marine Pollution by tar and oil seepage from ships and drilling rigs poses a serious threat to enclosed seas.

Scrub
Areas of long, hot, dry summers and short, warm winters where crop growing and grazing have destroyed original tree cover. Now habitat of evergreen scrub–vines and olives.

Desert
Environment includes bare mountains, rocky waste, sand dunes. Plants (wiry grass, thorn bushes, cacti) and animals (lizards, camels) must be well adapted to extremes of heat and drought.

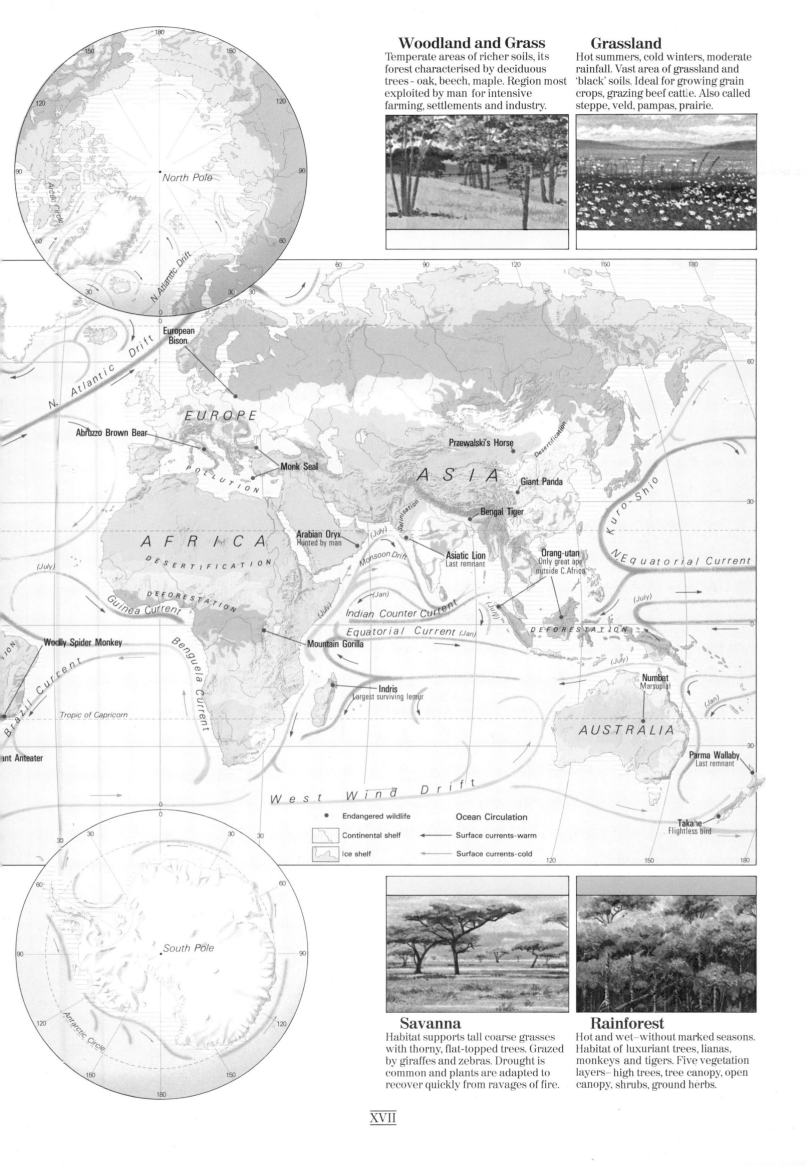

Woodland and Grass

Temperate areas of richer soils, its forest characterised by deciduous trees - oak, beech, maple. Region most exploited by man for intensive farming, settlements and industry.

Grassland

Hot summers, cold winters, moderate rainfall. Vast area of grassland and 'black' soils. Ideal for growing grain crops, grazing beef cattle. Also called steppe, veld, pampas, prairie.

180
150   150
120   120
90   90
North Pole
60   60
Arctic Circle
30   Drift   30
0

N. Atlantic Drift

European Bison

EUROPE

Abruzzo Brown Bear

POLLUTION

Monk Seal

AFRICA

DESERTIFICATION

DEFORESTATION

Guinea Current

Arabian Oryx
Hunted by man

(July)

Monsoon Drift

ASIA

Przewalski's Horse

Desertification

Giant Panda

Salinisation

Bengal Tiger

Asiatic Lion
Last remnant

Orang-utan
Only great ape
outside C.Africa

Kuro-Shio

N.Equatorial Current

(July)

(July)

DEFORESTATION

Woolly Spider Monkey

Brazil Current

Benguela Current

(July)

(Jan)

Indian Counter Current

Equatorial Current (Jan)

Mountain Gorilla

(Jan)

(July)

Numbat
Marsupial

Indris
Largest surviving lemur

Tropic of Capricorn

AUSTRALIA

Parma Wallaby
Last remnant

ant Anteater

West Wind Drift

Endangered wildlife

Continental shelf

Ice shelf

Ocean Circulation

Surface currents-warm

Surface currents-cold

Takahe
Flightless bird

180
150   150
120   120
90   90
South Pole
60   60
Antarctic Circle
30   30
180

Savanna

Habitat supports tall coarse grasses with thorny, flat-topped trees. Grazed by giraffes and zebras. Drought is common and plants are adapted to recover quickly from ravages of fire.

Rainforest

Hot and wet–without marked seasons. Habitat of luxuriant trees, lianas, monkeys and tigers. Five vegetation layers– high trees, tree canopy, open canopy, shrubs, ground herbs.

ENERGY FOR MANKIND

Energy driven machines support modern life. 75% in value of mineral exploitation goes towards energy production. In the 1970s fears that oil and gas were running out triggered a world-wide energy crisis with an initial quadrupling of oil prices.

World Minerals (by value of production)

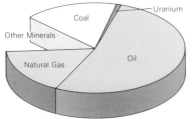

Uranium
Coal
Other Minerals
Natural Gas
Oil

Energy Balance

World energy use has trebled in the last 30 years, industrially developed countries using far more than developing countries. However, energy consumption, particularly of fossil fuels, is increasing at a faster rate in the developing world where, traditionally, bio-mass fuels are used–wood, charcoal, animal dung, plant alcohols. The concentration of energy resources in developing countries results in massive transportation of fuels to areas of use. Coal is more widely available than oil, but is more costly to transport.

Energy Reserves

Estimates of reserves of fossil fuels depend on how much we are prepared to pay for their recovery and transportation. From the map it can be seen that in many countries coal is most important. However, in the Middle East oil predominates.

Since industry prefers to use oil, supplies from the Middle East have greatly increased its economic importance and power.

Profiles of Change

At present there are three main sources of energy: fossil fuels, hydro-power and nuclear power. Of the fossil fuels coal has been the most important in the past: the use of oil and gas increasing throughout the 20th century. But, in anticipation of declining oil supplies, coal has re-gained importance. The harnessing of hydro-power, the second major source, is limited by topography, rainfall and conflicting land-use requirements. The development of nuclear power, the third major source, is controversial. Curtailment has arisen from fears of safety, pollution and military mis-use. The hope is now that uranium fission will be replaced by hydrogen fusion (the release of energy through the joining of nuclei of pairs of hydrogen atoms in rapid succession) with its promise of a longer future.

With the depletion of fossil fuels attention has turned towards the development of renewable sources such as solar, wind, tides, waves and heat from deep in the earth (geothermal).

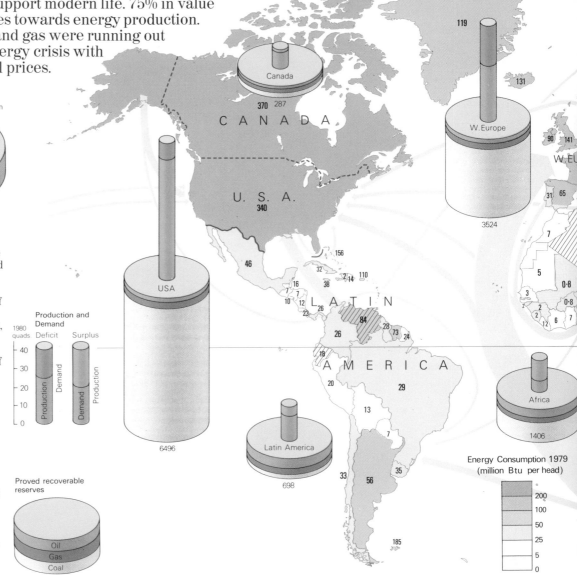

Production and Demand

1980 quads. Deficit   Surplus
Demand / Production

Proved recoverable reserves

Oil
Gas
Coal
total (quads.)

Energy Consumption 1979 (million Btu per head)

200
100
50
25
5
0

One quadrillion (quad.) of energy = 1 million billion British thermal units (Btu) and is equivalent to 25 million metric tons of oil fuel.

The cost of oil (in US $ per barrel)

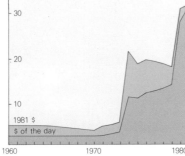

1981 $
$ of the day

The high prices which Middle Eastern countries now obtain for their oil severely affects industry, especially in developing countries.

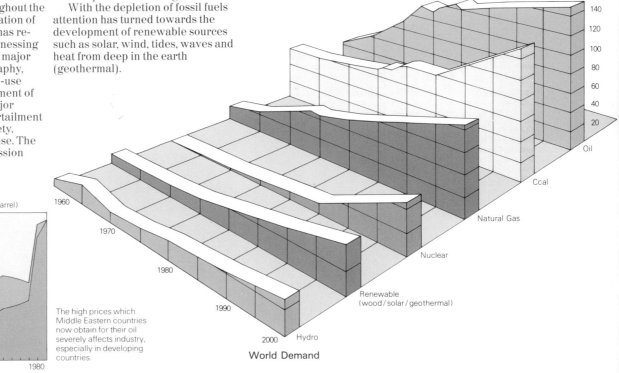

quads.
140
120
100
80
60
40
20

Oil
Coal
Natural Gas
Nuclear
Renewable (wood / solar / geothermal)
Hydro

1960
1970
1980
1990
2000

World Demand

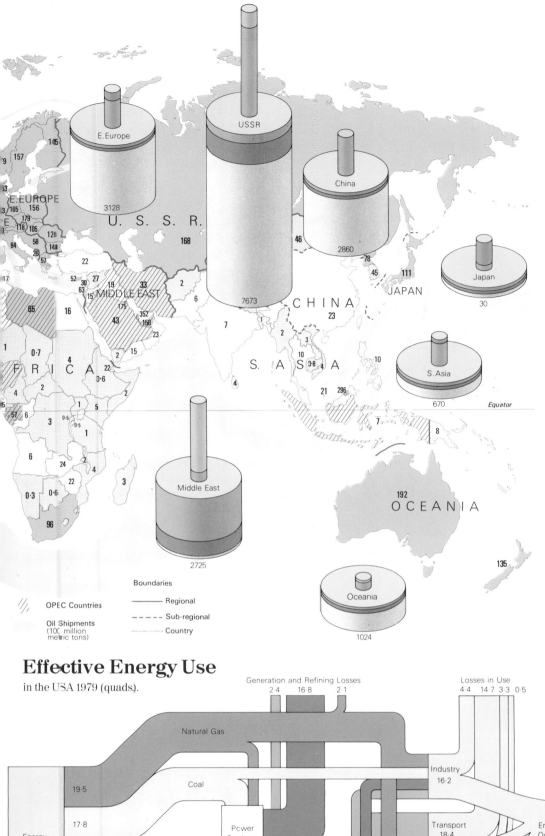

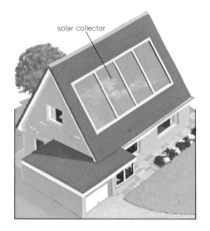

Renewable Energy

Problems of cost, storage and conversion to usable power remain to be resolved. Tidal power has emerged as a proven source and experiments with waves and ocean currents are being carried out.

Solar

Solar energy which is good for heating, air conditioning, crop drying and water pumping can be converted by the individual user.

solar collector

Wind

Wind, though changeable and seasonal, is a good winter source of energy in temperate areas.

generator

Geothermal

There are 20 geothermal power stations in operation today and domestic usage of heat from hot springs and geysers is well-established in Iceland and New Zealand.

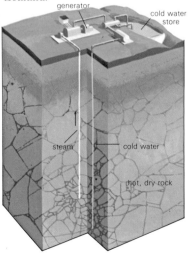

generator
cold water store
steam
cold water
hot, dry rock

Boundaries

— Regional
--- Sub-regional
...... Country

/// OPEC Countries

Oil Shipments
(100 million metric tons)

E. Europe 3128
USSR 7673
China 2860
Japan 30
S. Asia 670
Middle East 2725
Oceania 1024

Equator

U.S.S.R. • CHINA • JAPAN • S. ASIA • OCEANIA • MIDDLE EAST • AFRICA • E. EUROPE

Effective Energy Use

in the USA 1979 (quads).

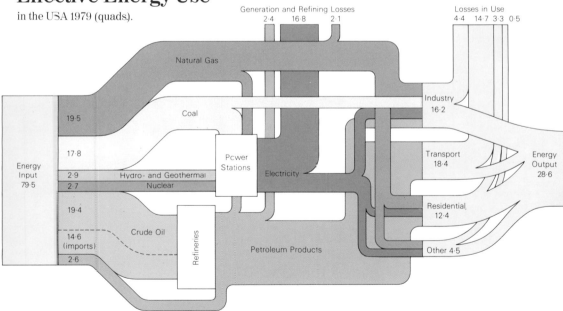

Generation and Refining Losses
2·4 16·8 2·1

Losses in Use
4·4 14·7 3·3 0·5

Natural Gas
Coal
Hydro- and Geothermal
Nuclear
Crude Oil
Petroleum Products
Electricity
Power Stations
Refineries

Energy Input 79·5
19·5
17·8
2·9
2·7
19·4
14·6 (imports)
2·6

Industry 16·2
Transport 18·4
Residential 12·4
Other 4·5
Energy Output 28·6

At present much energy is wasted by inefficient and extravagant uses developed when fuels were cheap and plentiful, although since 1974 significant improvements have been made with smaller cars and improved building design. Energy is lost in the conversion of fuels to usable power such as electricity: power stations being very inefficient. Energy wastage also occurs in transport, being only 20% efficient and consuming about $\frac{1}{3}$ of all primary energy—a picture reflected by the United Kingdom. Another important use of energy is for heating and cooling processes. Many experiments and developments are taking place in the area of energy conservation such as preventing heat loss by insulation and recycling waste heat generated in industry.

FAMINE AND PLENTY

One of the most critical problems facing mankind is that while millions of people, particularly in the industrialised world, are overfed, some 500 million are undernourished and about 5 million die from starvation or hunger-related diseases every year.

Massive population growth and the wasteful use of food resources contribute to this growing catastrophe. Current production of grain alone could provide everyone with ample calories if evenly distributed, but this would require political will and a global strategy.

A Sufficient Diet

The sufficiency of a diet can be measured by calorific content which, if expressed as a percentage of energy requirements for each country, brings out the striking inequality of world food distribution (see map).

The North-South division is further emphasised when diet is linked to income (see diagram below). In countries at the $200 level (A) diet is typically made up of natural carbohydrates such as grains, traditionally the diet in industrialised countries. However, increasing affluence in these countries has brought about marked changes and today a typical diet at the $10,000 level (B) includes a high proportion of fats and processed carbohydrates.

It is increasingly believed that these dietary patterns contribute to the major health problems of the industrialised world, notably heart disease and cancer. A change in diet in favour of more fish, poultry, fresh fruit and vegetables and cereal grains would be advantageous from a medical point of view.

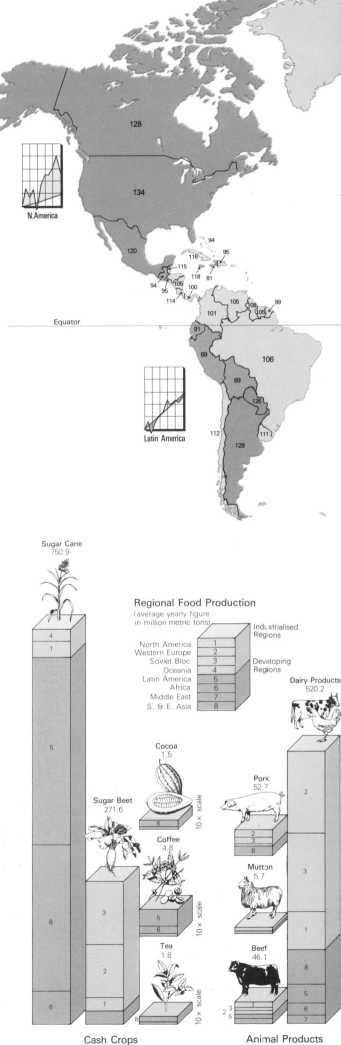

Diet and National Wealth

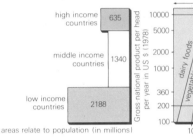

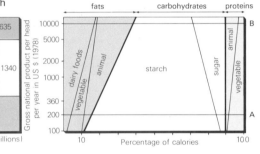

high income countries 635
middle income countries 1340
low income countries 2188

areas relate to population (in millions)

Gross national product per head per year in US $ (1978)

fats   carbohydrates   proteins

dairy foods / vegetable / animal / starch / sugar / animal / vegetable

Percentage of calories

The Food Providers

For most food products there are only a few major suppliers, often exclusive to particular regions. Most countries are therefore dependent on the equitable distribution of food supplies. Areas where food production fails to increase at the same rate as population growth become increasingly vulnerable, as in most of Africa and large parts of South Asia and Latin America.

More land could be brought under cultivation in needy areas, although there is little scope for this in the Middle East and South-East Asia, while crop yields could be significantly increased by the appropriate use of fertilizers, pesticides and high-yielding seeds.

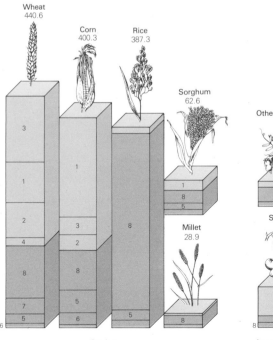

Wheat 440.6
Corn 400.3
Rice 387.3
Sorghum 62.6
Millet 28.9
Other Legumes 48.6
Soybean 83.8
Potatoes 261.5
Cassava 120.8
Sugar Cane 750.9
Sugar Beet 271.6
Cocoa 1.5
Coffee 4.8
Tea 1.8
Dairy Products 520.2
Pork 52.7
Mutton 5.7
Beef 46.1

Grains   Legumes   Root Crops   Cash Crops   Animal Products

Regional Food Production
(average yearly figure in million metric tons)

	Industrialised Regions
North America	1
Western Europe	2
Soviet Bloc	3
Oceania	4
Latin America	5
Africa	6
Middle East	7
S. & E. Asia	8

Developing Regions

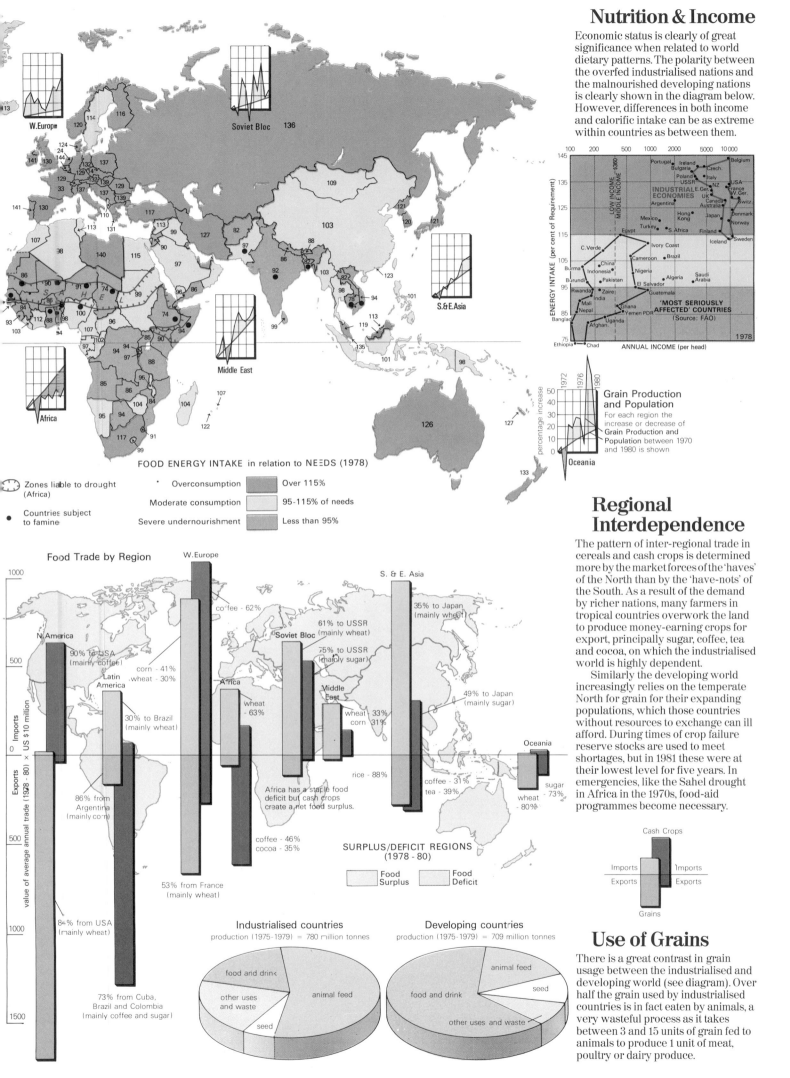

Nutrition & Income

Economic status is clearly of great significance when related to world dietary patterns. The polarity between the overfed industrialised nations and the malnourished developing nations is clearly shown in the diagram below. However, differences in both income and calorific intake can be as extreme within countries as between them.

FOOD ENERGY INTAKE in relation to NEEDS (1978)

Zones liable to drought (Africa)

Countries subject to famine

- Overconsumption — Over 115%
- Moderate consumption — 95-115% of needs
- Severe undernourishment — Less than 95%

ENERGY INTAKE (per cent of Requirement) vs **ANNUAL INCOME (per head)** — 1978

LOW INCOME · MIDDLE INCOME · INDUSTRIAL ECONOMIES

'MOST SERIOUSLY AFFECTED' COUNTRIES (Source: FAO)

Grain Production and Population

For each region the increase or decrease of Grain Production and Population between 1970 and 1980 is shown

W.Europe · Soviet Bloc · S.& E.Asia · Middle East · Africa · Oceania

Food Trade by Region

value of average annual trade (1978 - 80) × US $10 million

Imports / Exports

N.America — 90% to USA (mainly coffee)
86% from Argentina (mainly corn)
84% from USA (mainly wheat)

Latin America — 30% to Brazil (mainly wheat)
73% from Cuba, Brazil and Colombia (mainly coffee and sugar)

W.Europe — coffee - 62%, corn - 41%, wheat - 30%
53% from France (mainly wheat)

Africa — wheat - 63%, coffee - 46%, cocoa - 35%
Africa has a staple food deficit but cash crops create a net food surplus.

Soviet Bloc — 61% to USSR (mainly wheat), 75% to USSR (mainly sugar)

Middle East — wheat - 33%, corn - 31%, rice - 88%

S. & E.Asia — 35% to Japan (mainly wheat), 49% to Japan (mainly sugar), coffee - 31%, tea - 39%

Oceania — sugar - 73%, wheat - 80%

SURPLUS/DEFICIT REGIONS (1978 - 80)

- Food Surplus
- Food Deficit

Regional Interdependence

The pattern of inter-regional trade in cereals and cash crops is determined more by the market forces of the 'haves' of the North than by the 'have-nots' of the South. As a result of the demand by richer nations, many farmers in tropical countries overwork the land to produce money-earning crops for export, principally sugar, coffee, tea and cocoa, on which the industrialised world is highly dependent.

Similarly the developing world increasingly relies on the temperate North for grain for their expanding populations, which those countries without resources to exchange can ill afford. During times of crop failure reserve stocks are used to meet shortages, but in 1981 these were at their lowest level for five years. In emergencies, like the Sahel drought in Africa in the 1970s, food-aid programmes become necessary.

Cash Crops
Imports / Exports
Grains

Use of Grains

There is a great contrast in grain usage between the industrialised and developing world (see diagram). Over half the grain used by industrialised countries is in fact eaten by animals, a very wasteful process as it takes between 3 and 15 units of grain fed to animals to produce 1 unit of meat, poultry or dairy produce.

Industrialised countries
production (1975-1979) = 780 million tonnes

food and drink · animal feed · other uses and waste · seed

Developing countries
production (1975-1979) = 709 million tonnes

animal feed · seed · food and drink · other uses and waste

MAN IN SOCIETY

The world's population is unevenly spread; most
people live in big cities, while others live in
isolated communities.

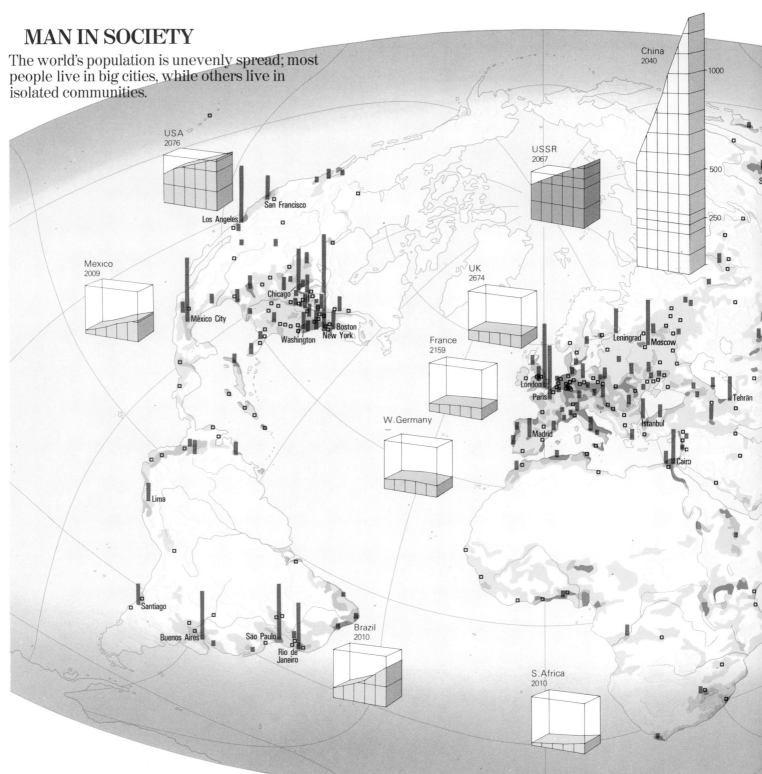

Urbanisation

In developed countries most towns and
cities have grown rapidly, mainly as a
result of better sanitation and health.
While mechanisation of agriculture
has reduced the need for farm labour in
rural areas, factory and service
developments have created jobs in
urban areas, which, combined with
easier access to education and medical
services have attracted people to live
in towns and cities. Although the most
highly industrialised countries are
currently the ones most densely
urbanised, there is evidence of a
growing trend to decentralise industry from these population centres.
This is well illustrated in the UK and
by the rural industrialisation policies
of Norway and Switzerland.

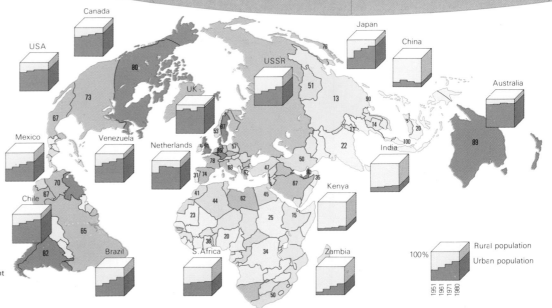

Urban Population Levels 1980

| 0 | 20 | 40 | 60 | 80 | 100 per cent |

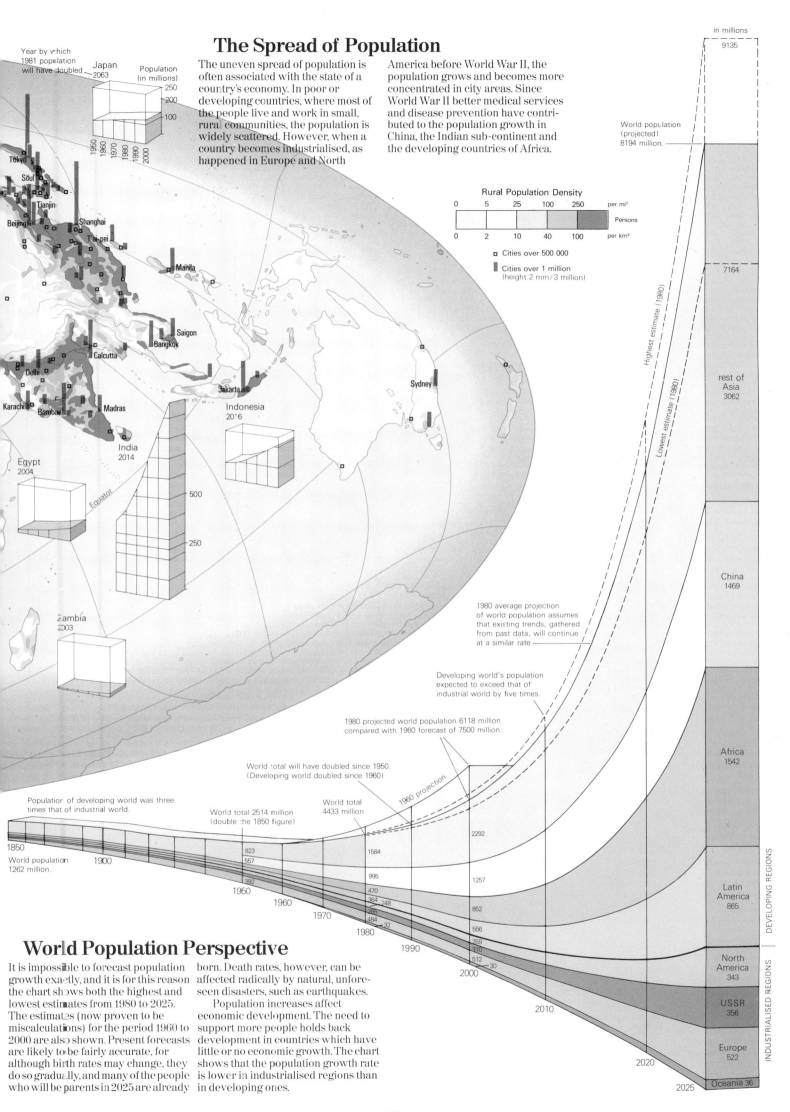

The Spread of Population

The uneven spread of population is often associated with the state of a country's economy. In poor or developing countries, where most of the people live and work in small, rural communities, the population is widely scattered. However, when a country becomes industrialised, as happened in Europe and North America before World War II, the population grows and becomes more concentrated in city areas. Since World War II better medical services and disease prevention have contributed to the population growth in China, the Indian sub-continent and the developing countries of Africa.

Year by which 1981 population will have doubled

Japan 2063

Population (in millions)

Rural Population Density

| 0 | 5 | 25 | 100 | 250 | per mi² |

Persons

| 0 | 2 | 10 | 40 | 100 | per km² |

□ Cities over 500 000

▮ Cities over 1 million (height 2 mm/3 million)

Egypt 2004

India 2014

Indonesia 2016

Zambia 2003

Sydney

in millions

9135

World population (projected) 8194 million.

7164

rest of Asia 3062

China 1469

1980 average projection of world population assumes that existing trends, gathered from past data, will continue at a similar rate.

Developing world's population expected to exceed that of industrial world by five times.

Africa 1542

1980 projected world population 6118 million compared with 1960 forecast of 7500 million.

World total will have doubled since 1950. (Developing world doubled since 1960)

Latin America 865

Population of developing world was three times that of industrial world.

World total 2514 million (double the 1850 figure)

World total 4433 million

North America 343

USSR 356

1850
World population 1262 million.

1900

1950

1960

1970

1980

1990

2000

2010

2020

2025

823
557
392
470
364 248
265
484 32

1584
995

2292

1257

852

556

259
310
512
30

1960 projection

Highest estimate (1980)

Lowest estimate (1980)

Europe 522

Oceania 36

DEVELOPING REGIONS

INDUSTRIALISED REGIONS

World Population Perspective

It is impossible to forecast population growth exactly, and it is for this reason the chart shows both the highest and lowest estimates from 1980 to 2025. The estimates (now proven to be miscalculations) for the period 1960 to 2000 are also shown. Present forecasts are likely to be fairly accurate, for although birth rates may change, they do so gradually, and many of the people who will be parents in 2025 are already born. Death rates, however, can be affected radically by natural, unforeseen disasters, such as earthquakes.

Population increases affect economic development. The need to support more people holds back development in countries which have little or no economic growth. The chart shows that the population growth rate is lower in industrialised regions than in developing ones.

RICH WORLD, POOR WORLD

The populations of different countries show several patterns of linked characteristics such as age distribution, employment structure, population density, income per capita and change of wealth. Wealthy countries include both mineral-rich states and the colonies of these wealthier countries and for the most part enjoy a temperate zone climate.

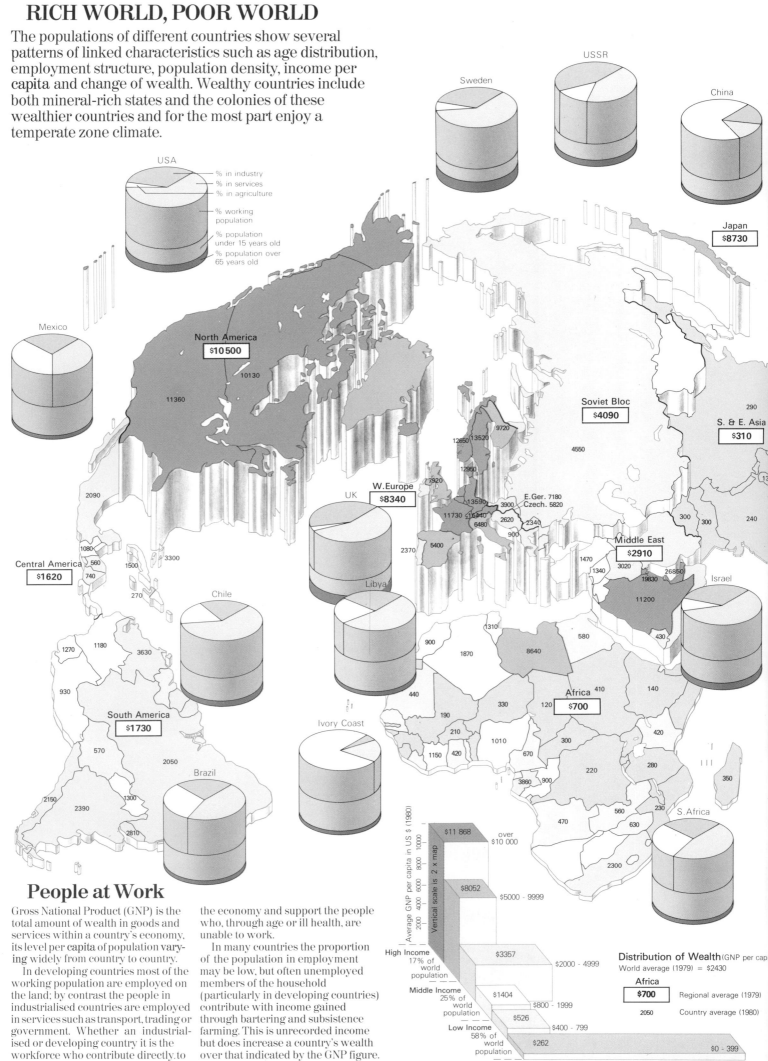

USA

- % in industry
- % in services
- % in agriculture
- % working population
- % population under 15 years old
- % population over 65 years old

Sweden

USSR

China

Japan
$8730

Mexico

North America
$10 500

10130

11360

Soviet Bloc
$4090

290

S. & E. Asia
$310

UK

W.Europe
$8340

9720

12650 13520

12950

7920

13590

E.Ger. 7180
Czech. 5820

3900

2090

11730 16340
6480

2620

2340

900

Middle East
$2910

1470

3020

Israel

1340

19830 26850

11200

430

Libya

2370

5400

Central America
$1620

1080 560
1500 3300
740
270

Chile

1310

900

580

1870

140

8640

1270 1180
3630

1010

Africa 410
$700

120

930

Ivory Coast

440

330

300

South America
$1730

190

210

420

570

2050

1150 420

670

280

Brazil

2150
2390

1300

2810

3860 900

220

350

470

560

230

S.Africa

630

2300

People at Work

Gross National Product (GNP) is the total amount of wealth in goods and services within a country's economy, its level per capita of population varying widely from country to country.

In developing countries most of the working population are employed on the land; by contrast the people in industrialised countries are employed in services such as transport, trading or government. Whether an industrialised or developing country it is the workforce who contribute directly to

the economy and support the people who, through age or ill health, are unable to work.

In many countries the proportion of the population in employment may be low, but often unemployed members of the household (particularly in developing countries) contribute with income gained through bartering and subsistence farming. This is unrecorded income but does increase a country's wealth over that indicated by the GNP figure.

Average GNP per capita in US $ (1980)

Vertical scale is 2 x map

$11 868 over $10 000

$8052 $5000 - 9999

High Income
17% of world population

$3357

$2000 - 4999

Middle Income
25% of world population

$1404

$800 - 1999

Low Income
58% of world population

$526

$400 - 799

$262

$0 - 399

0 1000 2000
Population in millions (1980)

Distribution of Wealth (GNP per cap
World average (1979) = $2430

Africa
$700 Regional average (1979)

2050 Country average (1980)

XXIV

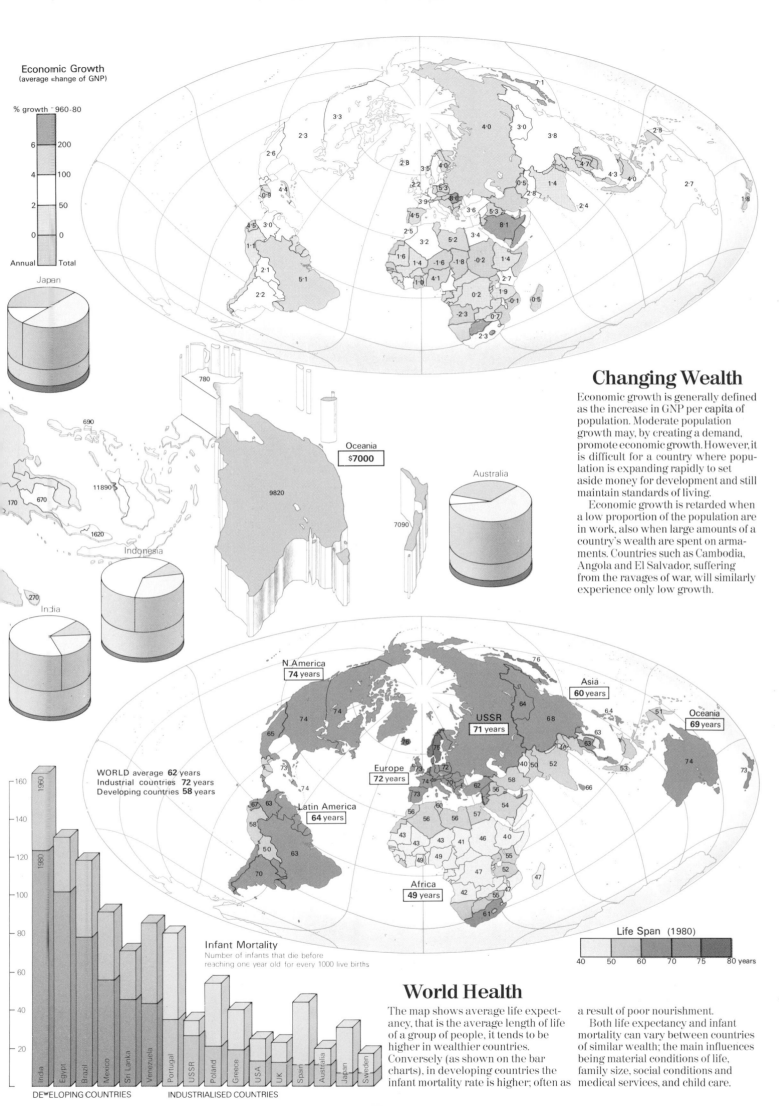

Economic Growth
(average change of GNP)

% growth 1960-80

6 — 200
4 — 100
2 — 50
0 — 0

Annual   Total

Japan

7·1

4·0   3·0   3·8   2·8

2·6   2·3

2·8   3·5   4·0   0·5   1·4   4·7   4·3   4·0   2·7

0·9   4·4   2·2   5·3   8·6   3·6   5·3   2·4   1·8

4·5   3·0   4·5   2·5   5·2   3·4   8·1

1·1   3·2   -1·6 -1·8 -0·2 1·4

1·6   1·4   1·0   4·1   2·7

2·1

2·2   5·1   0·2   1·9 -0·1 0·5

2·3   0·7

2·3

690

780

170   670   11890

1620

270   Indonesia

India

9820   Oceania
       $7000

7090   Australia

Changing Wealth

Economic growth is generally defined as the increase in GNP per capita of population. Moderate population growth may, by creating a demand, promote economic growth. However, it is difficult for a country where population is expanding rapidly to set aside money for development and still maintain standards of living.

Economic growth is retarded when a low proportion of the population are in work, also when large amounts of a country's wealth are spent on armaments. Countries such as Cambodia, Angola and El Salvador, suffering from the ravages of war, will similarly experience only low growth.

N.America
74 years

Asia
60 years

76

74   74   64

65   USSR
      71 years   68   64   Oceania
                              69 years

76   63   51

73   Europe   75   40 50   63

WORLD average **62 years**   **72 years**   72   52   53

Industrial countries **72 years**   74   70   58   66   74

Developing countries **58 years**   73   56   73

67   63   Latin America   56   60   54

58   **64 years**   56   56   57   40

50   43   43   43   41   46   55

63   49   49   47   52   47

70   Africa   42   55   47

49 years   61

160   1960

140

120   1980

100

Life Span (1980)

80   40   50   60   70   75   80 years

60

Infant Mortality
Number of infants that die before
reaching one year old for every 1000 live births

40

20

India | Egypt | Brazil | Mexico | Sri Lanka | Venezuela | Portugal | USSR | Poland | Greece | USA | UK | Spain | Australia | Japan | Sweden

DEVELOPING COUNTRIES   INDUSTRIALISED COUNTRIES

World Health

The map shows average life expectancy, that is the average length of life of a group of people, it tends to be higher in wealthier countries. Conversely (as shown on the bar charts), in developing countries the infant mortality rate is higher; often as a result of poor nourishment.

Both life expectancy and infant mortality can vary between countries of similar wealth; the main influences being material conditions of life, family size, social conditions and medical services, and child care.

CO-OPERATION AND CONFRONTATION

During the first half of this century much of the world was still colonised, and indirectly controlled by Europe. In the last fifteen years some 50 nations have achieved independence, bringing the total number of independent nations to some 180.

Regional Grouping

Independent nations have for centuries formed associations for purposes of trade, military assistance or mutual security. Political segmentation since the Second World War has led to the withdrawal of support to former colonies, thus compounding the need for international co-operation. As a result innumerable bilateral agreements have been formed, as well as larger regional groupings with which we are concerned here.

Furthermore, the wish to reach mutual understanding and agreement on a wider and even global scale led to the founding of the League of Nations in 1919. This was superseded by the United Nations in 1945, an ambitious concept, as its membership includes most independent nations

The extent to which individual nations have given up their sovereignty to join an international organisation varies significantly. Most have sacrificed very little independence, but membership can involve acceptance of the jurisdiction of an international commission or court of law over certain internal affairs.

COMECON, however, is an involuntary organisation of sovereign nations whose policies are shaped by decisions made in the USSR.

Global Military Balance

At present, eight major regional military groupings are identifiable. Four of these are formal organisations, and these are shown on the map. The global military balance, however, is dominated by the two superpowers (USA and USSR), who account for half of the total world military expenditure and a fifth of the world's armed forces. Their dominance in terms of conventional weapons can be seen clearly in the diagrams. Although the USSR possesses more weapons than the USA, the latter's weapons tend to be technologically superior.

An important feature of the 1970s and early 1980s has been the increased spending on weapons by developing countries; three-quarters of the world's arms trade found its way to the Third World (particularly the Middle and Far East).

Currently the 'nuclear club' has five members, and is dominated by the two superpowers. Both have large stockpiles of strategic weapons, but the USSR has a clear advantage in 'theatre' (intermediate range) weapons, like the SS-20. The introduction by the USA of Cruise and Pershing II missiles should redress the balance during the 1980s.

Many people are concerned about the enormous amount of money being spent on maintaining the military balance when millions of people still lack basic social needs. Lasting solutions to this problem seem unlikely to be found in the foreseeable future.

Economic Groups

- Latin American Integration Association (LAIA)
- Central American Common Market (CACM)
- Caribbean Community and Common Market (CARICOM)
- British Commonwealth Members
- British Commonwealth Dependencies

Military Groups

- Organization of American States (OAS)
- Warsaw Treaty (WTO)
- North Atlantic Treaty (NATO)
- ANZUS Pact

Nuclear Confrontation

- Missile Fields (SS-20)
- Arcs of Threat:
  Soviet SS-20
  NATO Cruise Missile

World Distribution of Military Power

Tanks

0 10 000 20 000 30 000 40 000 50 000 60 000 70 000

1. USA
2. USSR
3.
4. USA
5.
6. USA
7.
8.

1. NATO   5. S. & E. Asia
2. WTO   6. ANZUS
3. China   7. Middle East
4. OAS   8. Africa

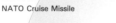

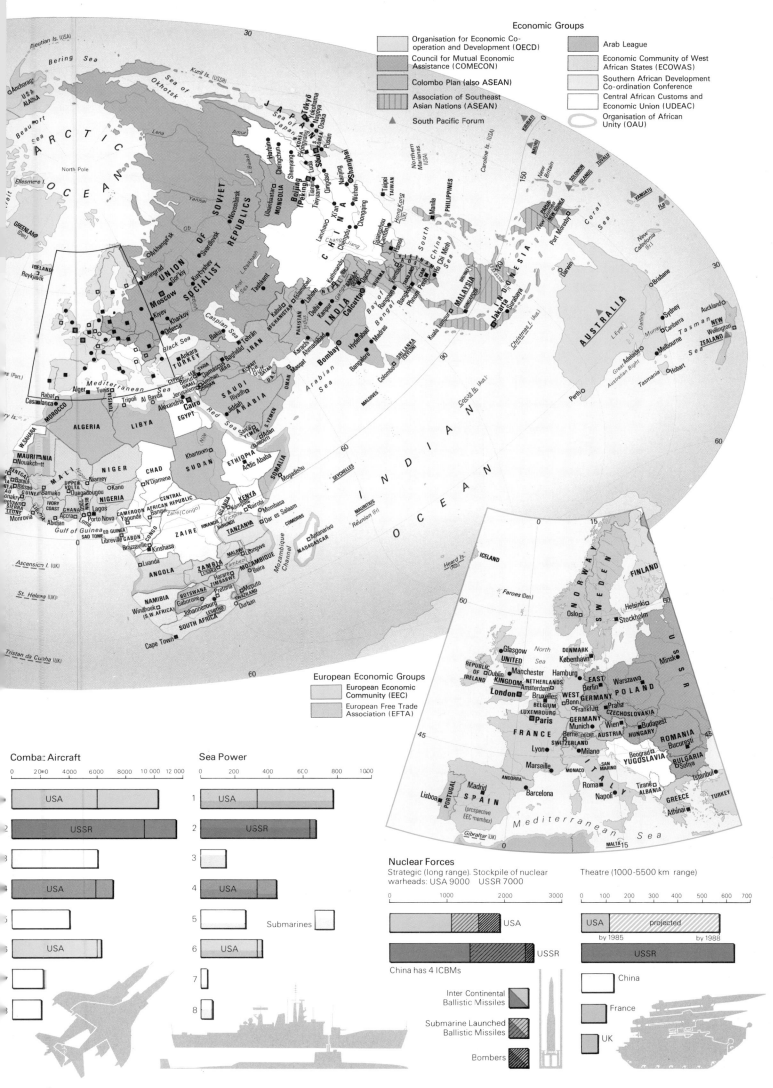

Economic Groups

- Organisation for Economic Co-operation and Development (OECD)
- Council for Mutual Economic Assistance (COMECON)
- Colombo Plan (also ASEAN)
- Association of Southeast Asian Nations (ASEAN)
- ▲ South Pacific Forum
- Arab League
- Economic Community of West African States (ECOWAS)
- Southern African Development Co-ordination Conference
- Central African Customs and Economic Union (UDEAC)
- Organisation of African Unity (OAU)

European Economic Groups

- European Economic Community (EEC)
- European Free Trade Association (EFTA)

Combat Aircraft

0 2000 4000 6000 8000 10 000 12 000

1. USA
2. USSR
3.
4. USA
5.
6. USA
7.
8.

Sea Power

0 200 400 600 800 1000

1. USA
2. USSR
3.
4. USA
5. Submarines
6. USA
7.
8.

Nuclear Forces

Strategic (long range). Stockpile of nuclear warheads: USA 9000   USSR 7000

0 1000 2000 3000

USA

USSR

China has 4 ICBMs

- Inter Continental Ballistic Missiles
- Submarine Launched Ballistic Missiles
- Bombers

Theatre (1000-5500 km range)

0 100 200 300 400 500 600 700

USA   projected
by 1985   by 1988

USSR

- China
- France
- UK

TRANSPORT NETWORKS

Trade and travel is indispensable to civilisation, with the ship as the main carrier of the world's commerce. The continuous development of routes and modes of transport aids economic progress and mobility.

Road and Rail

Integrated road and rail networks are the basis of industrialised society. Containerisation and the extension of modern highway systems have increased flexibility and reduced the emphasis on railways transporting freight.

Roads – comparative lengths (Log scale)

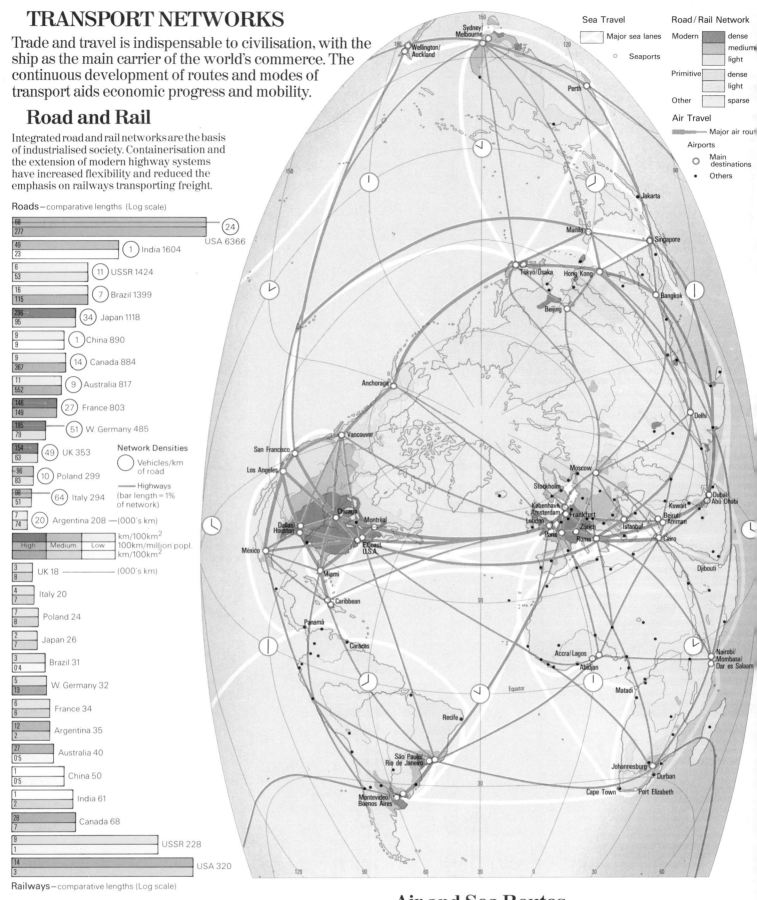

68 / 277	(24)	USA 6366
49 / 23	(1)	India 1604
6 / 53	(11)	USSR 1424
16 / 115	(7)	Brazil 1399
296 / 95	(34)	Japan 1118
9 / 9	(1)	China 890
9 / 367	(14)	Canada 884
11 / 552	(9)	Australia 817
146 / 149	(27)	France 803
195 / 79	(51)	W. Germany 485
154 / 63	(49)	UK 353
96 / 83	(10)	Poland 299
98 / 51	(64)	Italy 294
7 / 74	(20)	Argentina 208 — (000's km)

Network Densities

○ Vehicles/km of road

— Highways (bar length = 1% of network)

High	Medium	Low	km/100km²
			100km/million popl.
			km/100km²

3 / 8	UK 18 — (000's km)
4 / 7	Italy 20
7 / 8	Poland 24
2 / 7	Japan 26
3 / 0·4	Brazil 31
5 / 13	W. Germany 32
6 / 6	France 34
12 / 2	Argentina 35
27 / 0·5	Australia 40
1 / 0·5	China 50
1 / 2	India 61
28 / 7	Canada 68
9 / 1	USSR 228
14 / 3	USA 320

Railways – comparative lengths (Log scale)

Journey Time

The Suez Canal cuts 3600 n.miles off the London-Singapore route, while Concorde halves the London-New York journey time.

Air and Sea Routes

A great-circle network of primary air routes centred on the Northern Hemisphere provides rapid transit across the globe for mass travel, mail and urgent freight.

Bulk carriers, also following great-circle arcs, ply the oceans between major ports to supply the commodities of world trade.

Sea Travel
Major sea lanes
○ Seaports

Road / Rail Network
Modern — dense / medium / light
Primitive — dense / light
Other — sparse

Air Travel
— Major air rout[e]
Airports
○ Main destinations
• Others

Sail (via Cape) 164 days
Steam (via Cape) 43 days
Steam (via Suez) 30 days
Supertanker (via Cape) 28 days
Diesel (via Suez) 15 days

Concorde 3½ hours
Jet 7 hours
Propeller 12 hours
First Flight 4½ days

Singapore ◄— London —► New York

THE WORLD IN FIGURES

MOUNTAIN HEIGHTS

Metres	Feet		Metres	Feet	
8848	29 028	Everest (Qomolangma Feng) *Nepal-Tibet*	6908	22 664	Ojos del Salado *Chile-Argentina*
8611	28 250	K2 (Godwin Austen) *Kashmir-Singkiang*	6870	22 541	Bonete *Bolivia*
8586	28 168	Kangchenjunga *Nepal-India*	6800	22 310	Tupungato *Argentina-Chile*
8475	27 805	Makalu *Tibet-Nepal*	6770	22 211	Mercedario *Argentina*
8172	26 810	Dhaulagiri *Nepal*	6768	22 205	Huascarán *Peru*
8126	26 660	Nanga Parbat *Kashmir*	6723	22 057	Llullaillaco *Argentina-Chile*
8078	26 504	Annapurna *Nepal*	6714	22 028	Kangrinboqê Feng (Kailas) *Tibet*
8068	26 470	Gasherbrum *Kashmir*	6634	21 765	Yerupaja *Peru*
8013	26 291	Xixabangma Feng (Gosainthan) *Tibet*	6542	21 463	Sajama *Bolivia*
7890	25 885	Distaghil Sar *Kashmir*	6485	21 276	Illampu *Bolivia*
7820	25 656	Masherbrum *Kashmir*	6425	21 079	Coropuna *Peru*
7817	25 645	Nanda Devi *India*	6402	21 004	Illimani *Bolivia*
7780	25 550	Rakaposhi *Kashmir*	6310	20 702	Chimborazo *Ecuador*
7756	25 447	Kamet *India-Tibet*	6194	20 320	McKinley *USA*
7756	25 447	Namcha Barwa *Tibet*	6050	19 850	Logan *Canada*
7728	25 355	Gurla Mandhata *Tibet*	5895	19 340	Kilimanjaro *Tanzania*
7723	25 338	Muztag (Ulugh Muztagh) *Sinkiang*	5700	18 700	Citlaltepetl *Mexico*
7719	25 325	Kongur Shan (Kungur) *Sinkiang*	5642	18 510	El'bruz *USSR*
7690	25 230	Tirich Mir *Pakistan*	5452	17 887	Popocatepetl *Mexico*
7590	24 903	Gongga Shan (Minya Konka) *China*	5200	17 058	Kenya *Kenya*
7546	24 757	Muztagata (Muztagh Ata) *Sinkiang*	5165	16 946	Ararat *Turkey*
7495	24 590	Pik Kommunizma *USSR*	5140	16 864	Vinson Massif *Antarctica*
7439	24 407	Pik Pobedy (Tumor Feng) *USSR-Sinkiang*	5110	16 763	Stanley *Zaire-Uganda*
7313	23 993	Chomo Lhari *Bhutan-Tibet*	5030	16 500	Jaya (Carstensz) *Indonesia*
7134	23 406	Pik Lenina *USSR*	4810	15 781	Mont Blanc *France*
7010	23 000	Ancohuma *Bolivia*	4508	14 790	Wilhelm *Papua New Guinea*
6960	22 834	Aconcagua *Argentina*	4201	13 784	Mauna Kea *USA*

RIVER LENGTHS

Km	Miles		Km	Miles	
6695	4160	Nile *Africa*	2850	1770	Danube *Europe*
6570	4080	Amazon *South America*	2820	1750	Salween *Asia*
6380	3964	Yangtze *Asia*	2780	1730	São Francisco *South America*
6020	3740	Mississippi-Missouri *North America*	2655	1650	Zambezi *Africa*
5410	3360	Ob-Irtysh *Asia*	2570	1600	Nelson-Saskatchewan *North America*
4840	3010	Huang He (Yellow River) *Asia*	2510	1560	Ganges *Asia*
4630	2880	Zaïre (Congo) *Africa*	2430	1510	Euphrates *Asia*
4500	2796	Paraná *South America*	2330	1450	Arkansas *North America*
4440	2760	Irtysh *Asia*	2330	1450	Colorado *North America*
4416	2745	Amur *Asia*	2285	1420	Dnepr *Europe*
4400	2730	Lena *Asia*	2090	1300	Irrawaddy *Asia*
4240	2630	Mackenzie *North America*	2060	1280	Orinoco *South America*
4180	2600	Mekong *Asia*	2000	1240	Negro *South America*
4100	2550	Niger *Africa*	1870	1160	Don *Europe*
4090	2540	Yenisey *Asia*	1859	1155	Orange *Africa*
3969	2466	Missouri *North America*	1799	1118	Pechora *Europe*
3779	2348	Mississippi *North America*	1609	1000	Marañón *South America*
3750	2330	Murray-Darling *Australia*	1410	876	Dnestr *Europe*
3688	2292	Volga *Europe*	1320	820	Rhine *Europe*
3240	2013	Madeira *South America*	1183	735	Donets *Europe*
3058	1900	St. Lawrence *North America*	1159	720	Elbe *Europe*
3030	1880	Rio Grande *North America*	1094	680	Gambia *Africa*
3020	1870	Yukon *North America*	1080	671	Yellowstone *North America*
2960	1840	Brahmaputra *Asia*	1014	630	Vistula *Europe*
2896	1800	Indus *Asia*	1006	625	Tagus *Europe*

LAKE AND INLAND SEA AREAS

Areas are average and some are subject to seasonal variations.

Sq. Km	Sq. Miles		Sq. Km	Sq. Miles	
...000	142 240	Caspian *USSR-Iran (salt)*	22 490	8680	Nyasa (Malawi) *Malawi-Mozambique*
82 900	32 010	Superior *USA-Canada*	19 400	7490	Ontario *USA-Canada*
68 800	26 560	Victoria *Kenya-Uganda-Tanzania*	18 390	7100	Ladoga *USSR*
65 500	25 300	Aral *USSR (salt)*	17 400	6700	Balkhash *USSR*
59 580	23 000	Huron *USA-Canada*	10-26 000	4-10 000	Chad *Nigeria-Niger-Chad-Cameroon*
58 020	22 480	Michigan *USA*	9600	3710	Onega *USSR*
32 900	12 700	Tanganyika *Tanzania-Zambia-Zaire-Burundi*	0-8900	0-3430	Eyre *Australia*
31 330	12 100	Great Bear *Canada*	8340	3220	Titicaca *Peru-Bolivia*
30 500	11 800	Baykal *USSR*	8270	3190	Nicaragua *Nicaragua*
28 570	11 030	Great Slave *Canada*	6410	2470	Turkana (Rudolf) *Kenya-Ethiopia*
25 680	9910	Erie *USA-Canada*	5780	2230	Torrens *Australia (salt)*
24 390	9420	Winnipeg *Canada*	5580	2160	Vänern *Sweden*

GREATEST OCEAN DEPTHS

Metres	Feet	Location	Metres	Feet	Location
		PACIFIC OCEAN			**ATLANTIC OCEAN**
11 022	36 160	Marianas Trench	9220	30 249	Puerto Rico Trench
10 882	35 702	Tonga Trench	8264	27 113	South Sandwich Trench
10 542	34 586	Kuril Trench	7856	25 774	Romanche Gap
10 497	34 439	Philippine Trench	7500	24 600	Cayman Trench
10 047	32 962	Kermadec Trench			
9810	32 185	Izu-Bonin Trench			**INDIAN OCEAN**
9165	30 069	New Hebrides Trench	7450	24 442	Java Trench
9140	29 987	South Solomon Trench	7440	24 409	Weber Basin
8412	27 598	Japan Trench	7102	23 300	Diamantina Trench
8066	26 463	Peru-Chile Trench			
7822	25 662	Aleutian Trench			**ARCTIC OCEAN**
6662	21 857	Middle America	5570	18 274	Nansen Fracture Zone

NATIONS AND DEPENDENCIES

COUNTRY	Area (sq. miles)	Population ('000)	Capital
North and Central America			
Anguilla (UK)	35	6	—
Antigua and Barbuda	171	75	St. John's
The Bahamas	5353	210	Nassau
Barbados	166	249	Bridgetown
Belize	8867	145	Belmopan
Bermuda (UK)	20	60	Hamilton
Canada	3 851 794	23 937	Ottawa
Cayman Is. (UK)	100	17	George Town
Costa Rica	19 652	2213	San José
Cuba	44 218	9859	La Habana (Havana)
Dominica	290	83	Roseau
Dominican Republic	18 703	5437	Santo Domingo
El Salvador	8056	4540	San Salvador
Grenada	133	110	St. George's
Guadeloupe (Fr.)	687	329	Basse Terre
Guatemala	42 042	7007	Guatemala
Haiti	10 714	5009	Port-au-Prince
Honduras	43 277	3691	Tegucigalpa
Jamaica	4411	2188	Kingston
Martinique (Fr.)	425	325	Fort-de-France
Mexico	759 529	67 458	México
Montserrat (UK)	39	12	Plymouth
Netherlands Antilles (Neth.)	383	257	Willemstad
Nicaragua	53 668	2672	Managua
Panama	29 208	1939	Panamá
Puerto Rico (USA)	3435	3675	San Juan
St Kitts-Nevis (UK)	100	50	Basseterre
St. Lucia	238	120	Castries
St. Vincent	150	124	Kingstown
Trinidad and Tobago	1980	1060	Port of Spain
United States of America	3 615 108	228 959	Washington
South America			
Argentina	1 072 515	27 740	Buenos Aires
Bolivia	424 160	5570	La Paz
Brazil	3 286 474	119 025	Brasília
Chile	292 256	11 487	Santiago
Colombia	439 732	26 670	Bogotá
Ecuador	175 851	8357	Quito
French Guiana (Fr.)	35 135	66	Cayenne
Guyana	83 000	865	George Town
Paraguay	157 046	3062	Asunción
Peru	496 222	17 625	Lima
Surinam	63 251	441	Paramaribo
Uruguay	72 172	2924	Montevideo
Venezuela	352 142	14 602	Caracas
Europe			
Albania	11 101	2732	Tiranë (Tirana)
Andorra	175	35	Andorra-la-Vella
Austria	32 374	7559	Wien (Vienna)
Belgium	11 781	9833	Bruxelles (Brussels)
Bulgaria	42 823	9007	Sofiya (Sofia)
Cyprus	3572	629	Nicosia
Czechoslovakia	49 371	15 282	Praha (Prague)
Denmark	16 614	5122	Kobenhavn (Copenhagen)
Faroes (Den.)	540	41	Tórshavn
Finland	130 128	4863	Helsinki
France	212 741	54 085	Paris
Germany, East	41 645	16 854	Berlin (East)
Germany, West	95 957	60 931	Bonn
Gibraltar (UK)	2	30	Gibraltar
Great Britain and N. Ireland, see United Kingdom			
Greece	50 948	9329	Athínai (Athens)
Greenland (Den.)	840 000	52	Godthåb
Hungary	35 919	10 754	Budapest
Iceland	39 702	231	Reykjavík
Ireland	27 136	3308	Dublin
Italy	116 311	56 940	Roma (Rome)
Liechtenstein	62	25	Vaduz
Luxembourg	999	364	Luxembourg
Malta	122	315	Valletta
Monaco	·7	28	Monaco
Netherlands	13 104	14 284	Amsterdam/'s-Gravenhage
Norway	125 181	4079	Oslo
Poland	120 727	35 805	Warszawa (Warsaw)
Portugal	35 394	9836	Lisboa (Lisbon)
Romania	91 699	22 268	Bucuresti (Bucharest)
San Marino	24	22	San Marino
Soviet Union, see USSR			
Spain	194 882	37 746	Madrid
Sweden	173 664	8322	Stockholm
Switzerland	15 941	6466	Bern
United Kingdom	94 249	55 886	London
USSR	8 649 421	266 674	Moskva (Moscow)
Vatican City	·2	1	Vatican City
Yugoslavia	98 766	22 328	Beograd (Belgrade)
Asia			
Afghanistan	250 000	15 940	Kabul
Bahrain	255	422	Al Manāmah
Bangladesh	55 606	90 199	Dhaka (Dacca)
Bhutan	18 000	1296	Thimbu
Brunei	2226	220	Bandar Seri Begawan
Burma	261 788	35 289	Rangoon
Cambodia	69 898	5760	Phnom Penh
China	3 691 506	1 008 000	Beijing (Peking)
Hong Kong (UK)	410	5106	Victoria
India	1 269 341	683 810	New Delhi
Indonesia	741 028	146 243	Jakarta
Iran	636 364	38 126	Tehrān
Iraq	167 924	13 072	Baghdād

COUNTRY	Area (sq. miles)	Population ('000)	Capital
Israel	8019	3876	Jerusalem
Japan	143 243	116 551	Tōkyō
Jordan	37 737	3244	Amman
Korea, North	46 814	17 892	P'yŏngyang
Korea, South	38 010	38 455	Sŏul (Seoul)
Kuwait	9382	1353	Kuwait
Laos	91 428	3426	Vientiane
Lebanon	4015	2658	Beirut
Macau (Port.)	6	315	Macau
Malaysia	127 671	13 436	Kuala Lumpur
Maldives	115	154	Malé
Mongolia	604 247	1669	Ulaanbaatar (Ulan Bator)
Nepal	54 600	14 288	Kathmandu
Oman	82 000	891	Masqat (Muscat)
Pakistan	310 402	83 782	Islamabad
Philippines	115 739	48 098	Manila
Qatar	4416	231	Doha
Saudi Arabia	927 000	8960	Rïyadh
Singapore	238	2414	Singapore
Sri Lanka	25 332	14 815	Colombo
Syria	71 498	8977	Dimashq (Damascus)
Taiwan	13 892	17 480	T'ai-pei
Thailand	198 269	46 961	Bangkok
Turkey	301 381	45 358	Ankara
United Arab Emirates	32 278	1040	Abū Dhabi
Vietnam	127 245	54 175	Hanoi
Yemen	75 290	5812	San'ā'
Yemen, South	128 586	1903	Aden ('Adan)
Africa			
Algeria	919 587	18 919	Alger (El Djezair)
Angola	481 349	7078	Luanda
Benin	43 483	3530	Porto Novo
Botswana	224 710	800	Gaborone
Burundi	10 747	4110	Bujumbura
Cameroon	183 590	8444	Yaoundé
Cape Verde	1557	324	Praia
Central African Republic	240 539	2294	Bangui
Chad	495 753	4455	N'Djamena
Comoros	719	353	Moroni
Congo	132 046	1537	Brazzaville
Djibouti	8378	352	Djibouti
Egypt	386 197	39 773	Cairo
Equatorial Guinea	10 830	363	Malabo
Ethiopia	471 783	31 468	Addis Ababa
Gabon	103 346	657	Libreville
The Gambia	4127	603	Banjul
Ghana	92 100	12 244	Accra
Guinea	94 925	5425	Conakry
Guinea-Bissau	13 948	793	Bissau
Ivory Coast	124 503	8637	Abidjan
Kenya	224 959	15 865	Nairobi
Lesotho	11 716	1396	Maseru
Liberia	43 000	1858	Monrovia
Libya	679 355	3100	Tripoli
Madagascar	226 657	8714	Antananarivo
Malawi	36 332	5951	Lilongwe
Mali	478 819	6940	Bamako
Mauritania	397 954	1634	Nouakchott
Mauritius	720	958	Port Louis
Morocco	177 220	20 182	Rabat
Mozambique	303 074	10 473	Maputo
Namibia	318 260	1009	Windhoek
Niger	489 189	5318	Niamey
Nigeria	356 668	84 732	Lagos
Réunion (Fr.)	969	525	Saint-Denis
Rwanda	10 169	5098	Kigali
São Tomé and Principé	372	113	São Tomé
Senegal	75 954	5661	Dakar
Seychelles	171	66	Victoria
Sierra Leone	27 699	2735	Freetown
Somalia	246 154	3914	Muqdisho (Mogadishu)
South Africa	471 443	29 285	Pretoria
Sudan	967 487	18 371	Khartoum
Swaziland	6705	557	Mbabane
Tanzania	363 707	18 141	Dar es Salaam
Togo	21 925	2476	Lomé
Tunisia	63 378	6354	Tunis
Uganda	91 134	13 201	Kampala
Upper Volta	105 839	6040	Ouagadougou
Western Sahara	102 703	165	—
Zaire	905 361	29 270	Kinshasa
Zambia	290 586	5680	Lusaka
Zimbabwe	150 698	7730	Harare
Oceania			
American Samoa (USA)	76	32	Fagatogo
Australia	2 966 139	14 927	Canberra
Fiji	7055	615	Suva
French Polynesia (Fr.)	1621	148	Papeete
Guam (USA)	212	106	Agaña
Kiribati	309	59	Tarawa
Nauru	8	7	Yaren
New Caledonia (Fr.)	7376	140	Nouméa
New Zealand	103 736	3268	Wellington
Niue (NZ)	100	4	Alofi
Pacific Is., Trust Terr. (USA)	502	121	Kolonia
Papua New Guinea	178 259	3200	Port Moresby
Solomon Islands	11 500	229	Honiara
Tonga	270	97	Nuku'alofa
Tuvalu	10	8	Funafuti
Vanuatu	5700	117	Vila
Western Samoa	1093	156	Apia

URBAN POPULATIONS
(Populations in thousands)

North and Central America

	'000
New York USA	16 120
México Mexico	14 750
Los Angeles USA	11 496
Chicago USA	7868
Philadelphia USA	5549
San Francisco USA	5182
Detroit USA	4618
Boston USA	3448
Houston USA	3102
Washington USA	3060
Toronto Canada	2999
Dallas USA	2975
Cleveland USA	2834
Montréal Canada	2828
Miami USA	2640
Guadalajara Mexico	2468
St. Louis USA	2355
Pittsburgh USA	2264
Baltimore USA	2174
Minneapolis USA	2114
Seattle USA	2092
Atlanta USA	2030
Monterrey Mexico	2019
San Diego USA	1862
La Habana Cuba	1861
Cincinnati USA	1660
Denver USA	1620
Milwaukee USA	1570
Tampa USA	1569
Phoenix USA	1508
Kansas City USA	1327
Vancouver Canada	1268
Buffalo USA	1242
Portland USA	1242
New Orleans USA	1187
Indianapolis USA	1167
Columbus USA	1093
San Juan Puerto Rico	1084
San Antonio USA	1072
Sacramento USA	1014
Rochester USA	972
Salt Lake City USA	936
Providence USA	919
Memphis USA	913
Louisville USA	906
Nashville-Davidson USA	851
Birmingham USA	847
Oklahoma City USA	834
Dayton USA	830
Greensboro USA	827
Santo Domingo Dominican Rep.	818
Norfolk USA	807
Albany USA	795
Guatemala Guatemala	793
Toledo USA	792
Honolulu USA	763
Jacksonville USA	738
Hartford USA	726
Ottawa Canada	718
Port-au-Prince Haiti	703
Orlando USA	701
Tulsa USA	690
Puebla Mexico	678
Edmonton Canada	657
Panamá Panama	655
Kingston Jamaica	655
Syracuse USA	642
Scranton USA	640
Charlotte USA	637
Allentown USA	637
Richmond USA	632
Grand Rapids USA	602
Ciudad Juarez Mexico	597
Calgary Canada	593
León Mexico	590
Winnipeg Canada	585
Québec Canada	576
West Palm Beach USA	573
Omaha USA	570
Greenville USA	569
Hamilton Canada	542
Austin USA	536
Tijuana Mexico	535
Youngstown USA	531
Tucson USA	531
Raleigh USA	531
Springfield USA	531

South America

	'000
Buenos Aires Argentina	9910
São Paulo Brazil	8584
Rio de Janeiro Brazil	5184
Santiago Chile	4039
Lima Peru	3969
Bogotá Colombia	3831
Caracas Venezuela	2576
Belo Horizonte Brazil	1815
Salvador Brazil	1526
Medellín Colombia	1442
Fortaleza Brazil	1339
Montevideo Uruguay	1314
Recife Brazil	1241
Brasília Brazil	1203
Pôrto Alegre Brazil	1159
Nova Iguaçu Brazil	1094
Curitiba Brazil	1054
Cali Colombia	990
Belém Brazil	949
Barranquilla Colombia	825
Guayaquil Ecuador	823
Rosario Argentina	807
Maracaibo Venezuela	792
Córdoba Argentina	791
Campinas Brazil	663
La Paz Bolivia	655
Manaus Brazil	635
Valparaíso Chile	620
São Gonçalo Brazil	615
Quito Ecuador	600
Duque de Caxias Brazil	576
Asunción Paraguay	565
Santo André Brazil	553
Goiânia Brazil	516
Concepción Chile	513
La Plata Argentina	479

Europe

	'000
London UK	12 075
Paris France	8613
Moskva USSR	8099
Leningrad USSR	4638
Madrid Spain	3188
Berlin E Ger.-W Ger.	3056
Roma Italy	2830
Birmingham UK	2748
Manchester UK	2687
Kiyev USSR	2144
Athínai Greece	2101
Budapest Hungary	2064
București Romania	1934
Tashkent USSR	1779
Barcelona Spain	1755
Glasgow UK	1728
Hamburg W Germany	1664
Milano Italy	1634
Lisboa Portugal	1612
Warszawa Poland	1596
Wien Austria	1590
Baku USSR	1550
Khar'kov USSR	1444
København Denmark	1396
Stockholm Sweden	1393
Gor'kiy USSR	1344
Porto Portugal	1315
Novosibirsk USSR	1312
München W Germany	1297
Minsk USSR	1276
Kuybyshev USSR	1216
Sverdlovsk USSR	1211
Napoli Italy	1210
Lyon France	1186
Praha Czechoslovakia	1182
Torino Italy	1103
Marseille France	1077
Dnepropetrovsk USSR	1066
Tbilisi USSR	1066
Odessa USSR	1046
Chelyabinsk USSR	1031
Donetsk USSR	1021
Yerevan USSR	1019
Rotterdam Netherlands	1017
Bruxelles Belgium	1016
Omsk USSR	1014
Sofiya Bulgaria	1014
Perm' USSR	999
Kazan' USSR	993
Köln W Germany	977
Ufa USSR	969
Amsterdam Netherlands	965
Lille France	944
Rostov-na-Donu USSR	934
Volgograd USSR	929
Alma Ata USSR	910
Helsinki Finland	882
Saratov USSR	856
Łódź Poland	836
Riga USSR	835
Krasnoyarsk USSR	796
Voronezh USSR	783
Zaporozh'ye USSR	781
Beograd Yugoslavia	774
Genova Italy	760
Valencia Spain	752
Kraków Poland	716
Zürich Switzerland	707
Palermo Italy	699
Göteborg Sweden	694
's-Gravenhage Netherlands	672
L'vov USSR	667
Antwerpen Belgium	659
Essen W. Germany	658
Sevilla Spain	654
Krivoy Rog USSR	650
Oslo Norway	645
Frankfurt W Germany	631
Bordeaux France	622
Wrocław Poland	618
Dortmund W Germany	613
Düsseldorf W Germany	600
Yaroslavl USSR	597
Zaragoza Spain	591
Stuttgart W Germany	584
Karaganda USSR	572
Zagreb Yugoslavia	566
Leipzig E Germany	563
Duisburg W Germany	563
Krasnodar USSR	560
Bremen W Germany	559
Thessaloníki Greece	557
Poznań Poland	553
Irkutsk USSR	550
Vladivostok USSR	550
Izhevsk USSR	549
Sheffield UK	547
Dublin Ireland	544
Novokuznetsk USSR	541
Hannover W Germany	538
Liverpool UK	537
Barnaul USSR	533
Frunze USSR	533
Khabarovsk USSR	528
Toulouse France	521
Dresden E Germany	516
Tula USSR	514
Kishinev USSR	503
Zhdanov USSR	503
Tol'yatti USSR	502
Dushanbe USSR	493
Nürnberg W Germany	486
Penza USSR	483
Bologna Italy	481
Vilnius USSR	481
Samarkand USSR	476

Asia

	'000
Tōkyō Japan	11 696
Shanghai China	10 820
Calcutta India	9166
Beijing China	8626
Bombay India	8203
Sŏul South Korea	6879
Manila Philippines	5901
Jakarta Indonesia	5849
Delhi India	5277
Bangkok Thailand	5154
Tehran Iran	4496
Tianjin China	4280
Madras India	4277
Karachi Pakistan	4000
Shenyang China	3600
Dhaka Bangladesh	3459
Saigon Vietnam	3420
Baghdād Iraq	3206
T'ai-pei Taiwan	3050
Bangalore India	2914
İstanbul Turkey	2773
Yokohama Japan	2729
Osaka Japan	2700
Ankara Turkey	2624
Hanoi Vietnam	2570
Hyderabad India	2566
Ahmadabad India	2515
Pusan South Korea	2450
Singapore Singapore	2414
Chongqing China	2400
Kowloon Hong Kong	2378
Lahore Pakistan	2148
Wuhan China	2146
Nagoya Japan	2086
Phnom Penh Cambodia	2000
Guangzhou China	1840
Nanjing China	1750
Kanpur India	1685
Pune India	1685
Harbin China	1670
Lüda China	1650
Xi'an China	1600
Rangoon Burma	1586
Surabaya Indonesia	1556
P'yŏngyang North Korea	1500
Kyōto Japan	1467
Lanzhou China	1450
Chittagong Bangladesh	1388
Kobe Japan	1371
Taiyuan China	1350
Sapporo Japan	1337
Taegu South Korea	1309
Qingdao China	1300
Nagpur India	1298
Haiphong Vietnam	1279
Chengdu China	1250
Tel Aviv-Yafo Israel	1220
Bandung Indonesia	1202
Changchun China	1200
Damascus Syria	1142
Kao-hsiung Taiwan	1115
Kunming China	1100
Jinan China	1100
Fushun China	1080
Kita-Kyūshū Japan	1068
Fukuoka Japan	1055
Anshan China	1050
Zhengzhou China	1050
Kawasaki Japan	1041
Lucknow India	1007
Jaipur India	1005
Hangzhou China	960
Tangshan China	950
Beirut Lebanon	939
Baotou China	920
Aleppo Syria	878
Hiroshima Japan	859
Zibo China	850
Victoria Hong Kong	849
Changsha China	825
Faisalabad Pakistan	822
Shijiazhuang China	800
Inch'on South Korea	797
Sakai Japan	783
Qiqihar China	760
İzmir Turkey	758
Coimbatore India	736
Suzhou China	730
Jilin China	720
Chiba Japan	712
Madurai India	711
Xuzhou China	700
Hyderabad Pakistan	700
Fuzhou China	680
Nanchang China	675
Rawalpindi Pakistan	673
Esfahān Iran	672
Ammān Jordan	672
Mashhad Iran	670
Riyadh Saudi Arabia	667
Guiyang China	660
Wuxi China	650
Semarang Indonesia	647
Medan Indonesia	636
Agra India	635
Hefei China	630
Sendai Japan	628
Khulna Bangladesh	623
Colombo Sri Lanka	616
Davao Philippines	611
Varanasi India	607
Kwangju South Korea	606
Huainan China	600
Benxi China	600
Tabriz Iran	599
Kabul Afghanistan	588
Palembang Indonesia	583
Luoyang China	580
Adana Turkey	575
Jiddah Saudi Arabia	561
Indore India	561
Nanning China	550
Multan Pakistan	542
Okayama Japan	536
Jabalpur India	535
Hohhot China	530
Amagasaki Japan	528
T'ai-nan Taiwan	513
Allahabad India	513
Taejön South Korea	506
Higashiosaka Japan	501
Hsining China	500
Ürümqi China	500
Kumamoto Japan	498
Surat India	493
Patna India	491
Kagoshima Japan	490
Hamamatsu Japan	485

Africa

	'000
Cairo Egypt	6588
Alexandria Egypt	2320
Kinshasa Zaire	2008
Casablanca Morocco	1753
Johannesburg South Africa	1536
Alger Algeria	1503
Lagos Nigeria	1477
El Giza Egypt	1247
Addis Ababa Ethiopia	1133
Cape Town South Africa	1108
Dar es Salaam Tanzania	870
Durban South Africa	851
Abidjan Ivory Coast	850
Ibadan Nigeria	847
Nairobi Kenya	835
Dakar Senegal	799
Accra Ghana	738
Kananga Zaire	704
Harare Zimbabwe	686
Tunis Tunisia	648
Lusaka Zambia	599
Rabat Morocco	597
Pretoria South Africa	563
Tripoli Libya	551
Conakry Guinea	526
Port Elizabeth South Africa	476

Oceania

	'000
Sydney Australia	2874
Melbourne Australia	2578
Brisbane Australia	943
Adelaide Australia	883
Perth Australia	809
Auckland New Zealand	766

CLIMATE INDICATORS

Listed, from north to south, is a selection of places from different climate zones of the world (see pp xiv/xv), indicating their mean monthly temperatures (in °C and °F) and rainfall (in mm and inches). Also shown are their average temperatures and total rainfall for the year.

REYKJAVIK Iceland 64·1°N 21·9°W *TUNDRA*

	J	F	M	A	M	J	J	A	S	O	N	D	Year
°C	-0·2	0·2	1·5	3·5	6·7	9·7	11·3	10·8	8·5	5·2	3·0	0·4	5·0
°F	32	32	35	38	44	49	52	51	47	41	37	33	41
mm	89	64	62	56	42	42	50	56	67	94	78	79	779
ins	3·5	2·5	2·4	2·2	1·6	1·6	2·0	2·2	2·6	3·7	3·1	3·1	30·7

ANCHORAGE U.S.A. 61·2°N 150·0°W *BOREAL*

	J	F	M	A	M	J	J	A	S	O	N	D	Year
°C	-10·4	-7·6	-4·8	2·0	7·7	12·2	14·1	13·1	8·7	1·8	-5·6	-10·2	1·7
°F	13	18	23	36	46	54	57	56	48	35	22	14	29
mm	20	18	13	11	13	25	47	65	63	47	26	24	372
ins	0·8	0·7	0·5	0·4	0·5	1·0	1·8	2·6	2·5	1·8	1·0	0·9	14·6

STOCKHOLM Sweden 59·3°N 18·1°E *TEMPERATE Continental*

	J	F	M	A	M	J	J	A	S	O	N	D	Year
°C	-3·0	-3·1	-0·5	4·6	10·2	15·0	18·5	16·6	12·3	7·1	2·7	0·0	6·6
°F	27	26	31	40	50	59	65	62	54	45	37	32	44
mm	43	30	25	31	34	45	61	76	60	48	53	48	554
ins	1·7	1·2	1·0	1·2	1·3	1·8	2·4	3·0	2·4	1·9	2·1	1·9	21·8

EDINBURGH U.K. 55·9°N 3·2°W *TEMPERATE Maritime*

	J	F	M	A	M	J	J	A	S	O	N	D	Year
°C	3·3	3·5	5·1	7·4	9·9	12·9	14·8	14·4	12·5	9·4	6·4	4·6	8·6
°F	38	38	41	45	50	55	59	58	54	49	43	40	47
mm	57	39	39	39	54	47	83	77	57	65	62	57	676
ins	2·2	1·5	1·5	1·5	2·1	1·8	3·3	3·0	2·2	2·6	2·4	2·2	26·6

MOSKVA U.S.S.R. 55·7°N 37·6°E *TEMPERATE Continental*

	J	F	M	A	M	J	J	A	S	O	N	D	Year
°C	-12·7	-9·6	-3·8	5·7	13·3	15·8	17·8	16·9	11·8	5·9	-0·9	-7·0	4·4
°F	9	15	25	42	56	60	64	62	53	43	30	19	40
mm	39	38	36	37	53	58	88	71	58	45	47	54	624
ins	1·5	1·5	1·4	1·5	2·1	2·3	3·5	2·8	2·3	1·8	1·8	2·1	24·6

VANCOUVER Canada 49·2°N 123·2°W *TEMPERATE Maritime*

	J	F	M	A	M	J	J	A	S	O	N	D	Year
°C	2·8	4·1	6·4	9·4	12·6	15·5	17·8	17·2	14·4	10·3	6·3	4·2	10·0
°F	37	39	43	49	55	60	64	63	58	50	43	40	50
mm	214	161	151	90	69	65	39	44	83	172	198	243	1529
ins	8·4	6·3	5·9	3·5	2·7	2·6	1·5	1·7	3·3	6·8	7·8	9·6	60·2

PARIS France 48·8°N 2·3°E *TEMPERATE Maritime*

	J	F	M	A	M	J	J	A	S	O	N	D	Year
°C	3·4	4·3	7·9	11·0	14·6	17·8	19·5	19·1	16·5	11·7	7·2	4·3	11·5
°F	38	40	46	52	58	64	67	66	62	53	45	40	53
mm	56	46	35	42	57	54	59	64	55	50	51	50	619
ins	2·2	1·8	1·4	1·6	2·2	2·1	2·3	2·5	2·2	2·0	2·0	2·0	24·3

BUCUREŞTI Romania 44·5°N 26·0°E *TEMPERATE Steppe*

	J	F	M	A	M	J	J	A	S	O	N	D	Year
°C	-4·2	-1·5	6·2	12·4	17·3	21·2	23·5	22·9	18·2	13·0	6·4	0·6	8·2
°F	24	29	43	54	63	70	74	73	65	55	43	33	47
mm	46	26	28	59	77	121	53	45	45	29	36	27	592
ins	1·8	1·0	1·1	2·3	3·0	4·8	2·1	1·8	1·8	1·1	1·4	1·1	23·4

NEW YORK U.S.A. 40·7°N 74·0°W *TEMPERATE Continental*

	J	F	M	A	M	J	J	A	S	O	N	D	Year
°C	0·7	0·8	4·7	10·5	16·3	21·2	24·1	23·3	19·8	14·3	8·1	2·2	12·2
°F	33	33	40	51	61	70	75	74	68	58	47	36	54
mm	89	74	104	89	91	86	102	119	89	84	89	84	1100
ins	3·5	2·9	4·1	3·5	3·6	3·4	4·0	4·7	3·5	3·3	3·5	3·3	43·3

TŌKYŌ Japan 35·7°N 139·8°E *TEMPERATE Continental*

	J	F	M	A	M	J	J	A	S	O	N	D	Year
°C	3·3	4·2	7·2	12·5	16·9	20·8	24·7	26·1	22·5	16·7	10·8	5·8	14·4
°F	38	40	45	54	62	69	76	79	72	62	51	42	58
mm	48	74	107	135	147	165	142	152	234	208	96	56	1565
ins	1·9	2·9	4·2	5·3	5·8	6·5	5·6	6·0	9·2	8·2	3·8	2·2	61·6

TANGER Morocco 35·8°N 5·8°W *SUBTROPICAL Mediterranean*

	J	F	M	A	M	J	J	A	S	O	N	D	Year
°C	11·9	12·5	13·6	14·4	17·2	20·0	22·2	23·0	21·4	18·6	14·7	12·4	16·7
°F	53	54	56	58	63	68	72	73	70	65	58	54	62
mm	114	107	122	89	43	15	2	2	23	99	147	137	897
ins	4·5	4·2	4·8	3·5	1·7	0·6	0·1	0·1	0·9	3·9	5·8	5·4	35·3

JERUSALEM Israel 31·8°N 35·2°E *SUBTROPICAL Steppe*

	J	F	M	A	M	J	J	A	S	O	N	D	Year
°C	8·9	9·4	13·0	16·4	20·5	22·5	23·9	24·1	23·0	21·1	16·4	11·1	17·2
°F	48	49	55	61	69	72	75	75	73	70	61	52	63
mm	132	132	63	28	2	1	0	0	1	13	71	87	528
ins	5·2	5·2	2·5	1·1	0·1	0·1	0·0	0·0	0·1	0·5	2·8	3·4	20·8

NEW ORLEANS U.S.A. 30·0°N 90·2°W *SUBTROPICAL Hum*

	J	F	M	A	M	J	J	A	S	O	N	D	Yea
°C	12·5	13·9	16·3	19·9	23·5	26·7	27·6	27·7	25·7	21·3	15·5	13·0	20·
°F	54	57	61	68	74	80	82	82	78	70	60	55	68
mm	97	102	135	114	112	112	170	135	127	71	84	104	136
ins	3·8	4·0	5·3	4·5	4·4	4·4	6·7	5·3	5·0	2·8	3·3	4·1	53·

BAHRAIN 26·2°N 50·5°E *SUBTROPICAL Ar*

	J	F	M	A	M	J	J	A	S	O	N	D	Yea
°C	16·9	18·0	20·5	25·0	29·4	31·7	33·3	33·6	31·4	28·0	24·2	18·6	25·
°F	62	64	69	77	85	89	92	92	88	82	75	65	78
mm	8	18	13	8	1	0	0	0	0	0	18	18	79
ins	0·3	0·7	0·5	0·3	0·1	0·0	0·0	0·0	0·0	0·0	0·7	0·7	3·

HONG KONG 22·3°N 114·2°E *SUBTROPICAL Hum*

	J	F	M	A	M	J	J	A	S	O	N	D	Yea
°C	15·5	15·0	17·5	21·7	25·5	27·5	28·0	28·0	27·2	25·0	20·8	17·5	22·
°F	60	59	63	71	78	81	82	82	81	77	69	63	72
mm	33	46	74	137	292	394	381	361	256	114	43	30	216
ins	1·3	1·8	2·9	5·4	11·5	15·5	15·0	14·2	10·1	4·5	1·7	1·2	85·

MIAMI U.S.A. 25·8°N 80·3°W *TROPICAL Savan*

	J	F	M	A	M	J	J	A	S	O	N	D	Yea
°C	19·3	19·9	21·4	23·4	25·3	27·1	27·6	27·9	27·4	25·4	22·4	20·1	23·
°F	67	68	70	74	77	81	82	82	81	78	72	68	75
mm	51	48	58	99	163	188	170	178	241	208	71	43	151
ins	2·0	1·9	2·3	3·9	6·4	7·4	6·7	7·0	9·5	8·2	2·8	1·7	59·

BANGKOK Thailand 13·7°N 100·5°E *TROPICAL Savan*

	J	F	M	A	M	J	J	A	S	O	N	D	Yea
°C	25·8	27·5	28·9	30·0	29·4	28·6	28·3	28·3	28·0	27·5	26·4	25·3	27·
°F	78	81	84	86	85	83	83	83	82	81	79	77	82
mm	8	20	36	58	198	160	160	175	305	206	66	5	139
ins	0·3	0·8	1·4	2·3	7·8	6·3	6·3	6·9	12·0	8·1	2·6	0·2	55·

COLOMBO Sri Lanka 6·9°N 79·9°E *TROPICAL Rainfore*

	J	F	M	A	M	J	J	A	S	O	N	D	Yea
°C	26·1	26·4	27·2	27·7	28·0	27·2	27·2	27·2	27·2	26·6	26·1	25·8	26·
°F	79	80	81	82	82	81	81	81	81	80	79	78	80
mm	89	69	147	231	371	223	135	109	160	348	315	147	234
ins	3·5	2·7	5·8	9·1	14·6	8·8	5·3	4·3	6·3	13·7	12·4	5·8	92·

NAIROBI Kenya 1·3°S 36·8°E *TROPICAL Savan*

	J	F	M	A	M	J	J	A	S	O	N	D	Yea
°C	18·6	19·4	19·4	19·2	17·7	16·4	15·5	16·1	17·5	18·6	18·3	18·0	18·
°F	65	67	67	67	64	61	60	61	63	65	65	64	64
mm	38	63	124	211	157	46	15	23	30	53	109	86	95
ins	1·5	2·5	4·9	8·3	6·2	1·8	0·6	0·9	1·2	2·1	4·3	3·4	37·

LIMA Peru 12·1°S 77·0°W *TROPICAL A*

	J	F	M	A	M	J	J	A	S	O	N	D	Yea
°C	23·3	23·8	23·6	21·9	19·4	17·2	16·7	16·1	16·9	18·0	19·4	21·1	20·
°F	74	75	74	71	67	63	62	61	62	64	67	70	68
mm	1	1	1	1	5	5	8	8	8	2	2	1	41
ins	0·1	0·1	0·1	0·1	0·2	0·2	0·3	0·3	0·3	0·1	0·1	0·1	1·

RIO DE JANEIRO Brazil 22·9°S 43·2°W *TROPICAL Savan*

	J	F	M	A	M	J	J	A	S	O	N	D	Yea
°C	25·8	26·1	25·3	23·6	21·9	21·1	20·5	21·1	21·1	21·9	23·0	24·7	23·
°F	78	79	77	74	71	70	69	70	70	71	73	76	73
mm	124	122	130	107	79	53	41	43	66	79	104	137	108
ins	4·9	4·8	5·1	4·2	3·1	2·1	1·6	1·7	2·6	3·1	4·1	5·4	42·

JOHANNESBURG S. Africa 26·2°S 28·1°E *SUBTROPICAL Step*

	J	F	M	A	M	J	J	A	S	O	N	D	Yea
°C	20·0	19·7	18·3	16·1	12·5	10·3	10·5	13·0	15·8	18·3	18·9	19·7	16·
°F	68	67	65	61	54	50	51	55	60	65	66	67	61
mm	114	109	89	38	25	8	8	8	23	56	107	124	70
ins	4·5	4·3	3·5	1·5	1·0	0·3	0·3	0·3	0·9	2·2	4·2	4·9	27·

PERTH Australia 31·9°S 115·8°E *SUBTROPICAL Mediterrane*

	J	F	M	A	M	J	J	A	S	O	N	D	Yea
°C	23·3	23·3	21·7	19·2	16·1	13·9	13·0	13·3	14·7	16·4	19·2	21·7	17·
°F	74	74	71	66	61	57	55	56	58	61	66	71	64
mm	8	10	20	43	130	180	170	145	86	56	20	13	88
ins	0·3	0·4	0·8	1·7	5·1	7·1	6·7	5·7	3·4	2·2	0·8	0·5	34·

WELLINGTON New Zealand 41·3°S 174·8°E *TEMPERATE Maritir*

	J	F	M	A	M	J	J	A	S	O	N	D	Yea
°C	16·9	16·9	15·8	13·9	11·4	9·7	8·6	9·2	10·8	12·2	13·6	15·8	12·
°F	62	62	60	57	52	49	47	48	51	54	56	60	55
mm	81	81	81	97	117	117	137	117	97	102	89	89	120
ins	3·2	3·2	3·2	3·8	4·6	4·6	5·4	4·6	3·8	4·0	3·5	3·5	47·

This page explains the main symbols, lettering style and height/depth colours used on the reference maps on pages 2 to 80. The scale of each map is indicated at the top of each page. Abbreviations used on the maps appear at the beginning of the index.

BOUNDARIES

———————	International
— — — —	International under Dispute
· · · · · · · ·	Cease Fire Line
———————	Autonomous or State
———————	Administrative
— — — —	Maritime (National)
— — — —	International Date Line

COMMUNICATIONS

———————	Motorway/Express Highway
━━━━━━━	Under Construction
———————	Major Highway
———————	Other Roads
— — — —	Under Construction
- - - - - - -	Track
⇒——⇐	Road Tunnel
- - - - - - -	Car Ferry
———————	Main Railway
———————	Other Railway
— — — —	Under Construction
—→——←—	Rail Tunnel
- - - - - - -	Rail Ferry
·——·——·——	Canal
✈	International Airport
✦	Other Airport

LAKE FEATURES

	Freshwater
	Saltwater
	Seasonal
	Salt Pan

LANDSCAPE FEATURES

	Glacier, Ice Cap
	Marsh, Swamp
	Sand Desert, Dunes

OTHER FEATURES

	River
	Seasonal River
⇌	Pass, Gorge
	Dam, Barrage
	Waterfall, Rapid
	Aqueduct
	Reef
▲4231	Summit, Peak
·217	Spot Height, Depth
○	Well
↓	Oil Field
▲	Gas Field
—— Gas/Oil ——	Oil/Natural Gas Pipeline
Gemsbok Nat. Pk	National Park
∴UR	Historic Site

LETTERING STYLES

CANADA	Independent Nation
FLORIDA	State, Province or Autonomous Region
Gibraltar (U.K.)	Sovereignty of Dependent Territory
Lothian	Administrative Area
LANGUEDOC	Historic Region
Loire **Vosges**	Physical Feature or Physical Region

TOWNS AND CITIES

Square symbols denote capital cities   *Population*

▣	⬤	**New York**	over 5 000 000
▪	●	**Montréal**	over 1 000 000
▫	○	Ottawa	over 500 000
▪	•	**Québec**	over 100 000
▫	○	St John's	over 50 000
▫	○	Yorkton	over 10 000
▫	○	Jasper	under 10 000

Built-up-area

Height

	6000m
	5000m
	4000m
	3000m
	2000m
	1000m
	500m
	200m

0 — 0 — Sea Level

	200m
	2000m
	4000m
	6000m
	8000m

Depth

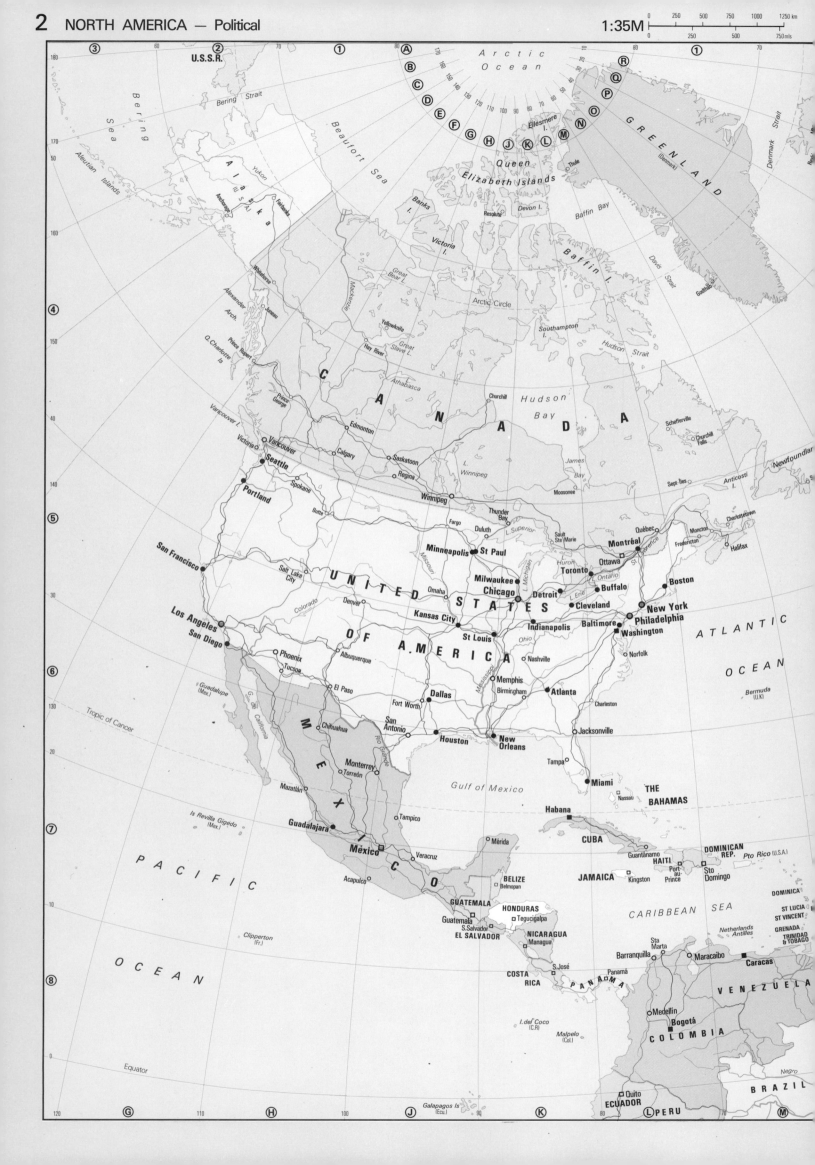

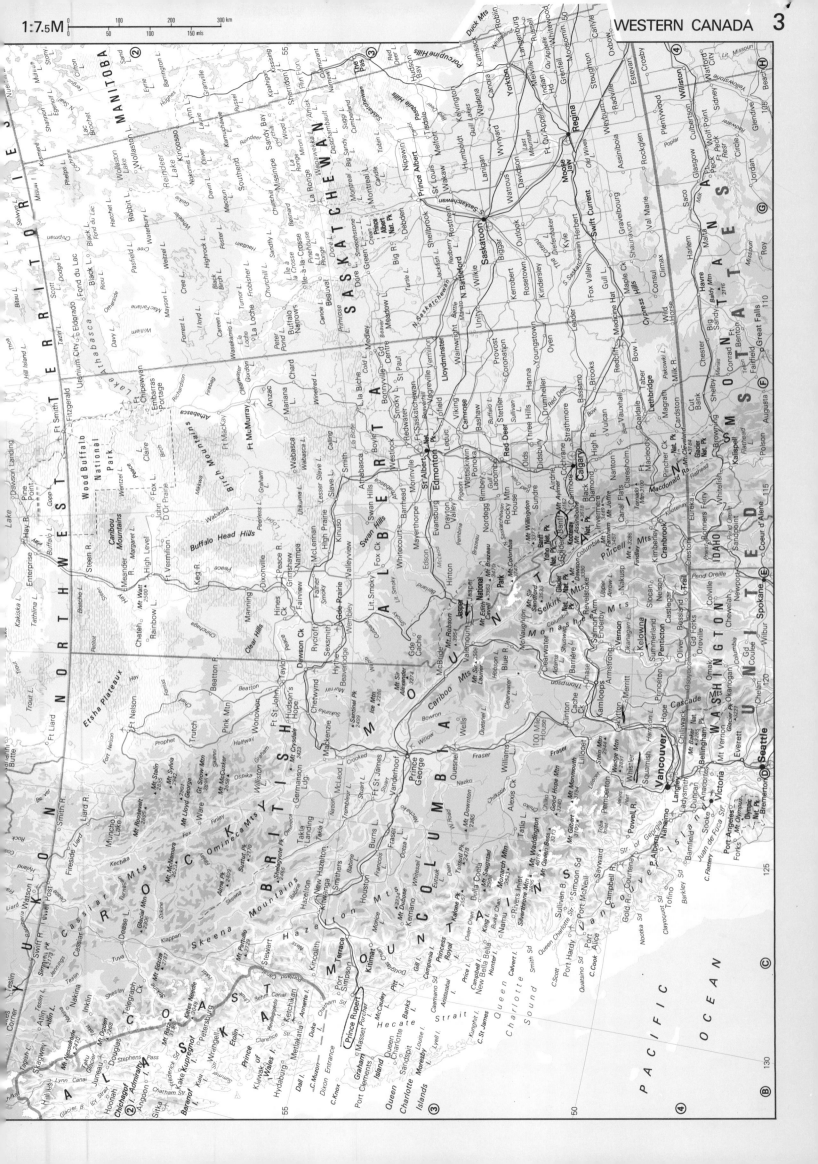

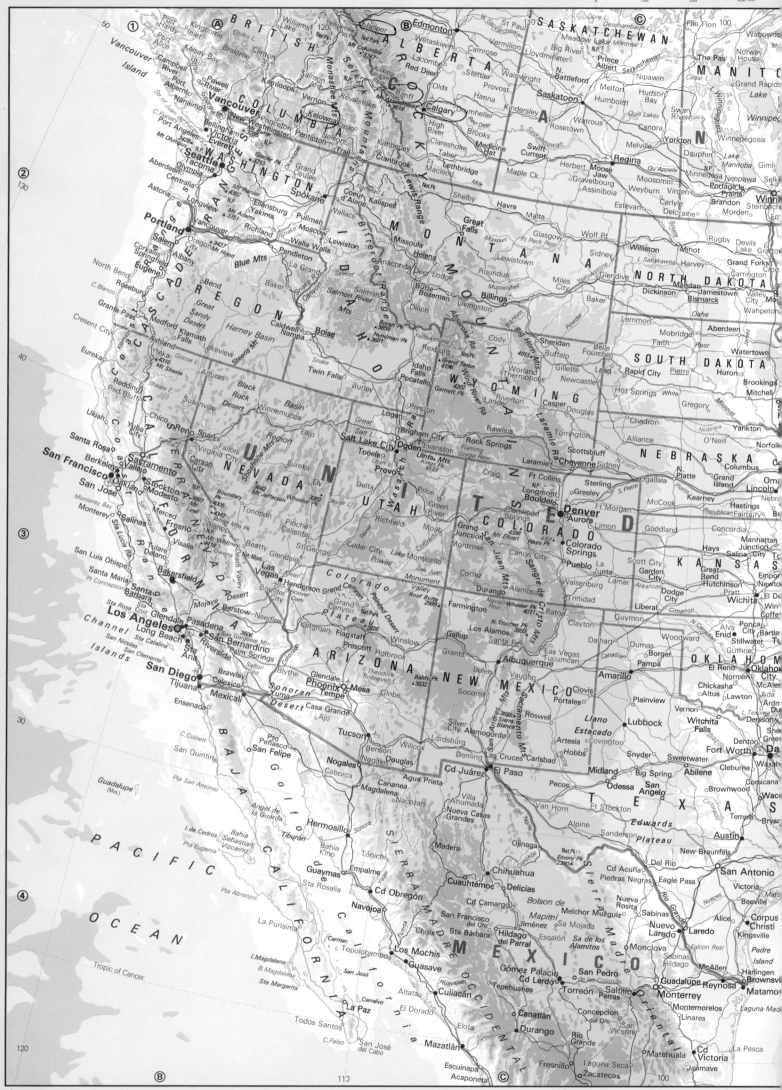

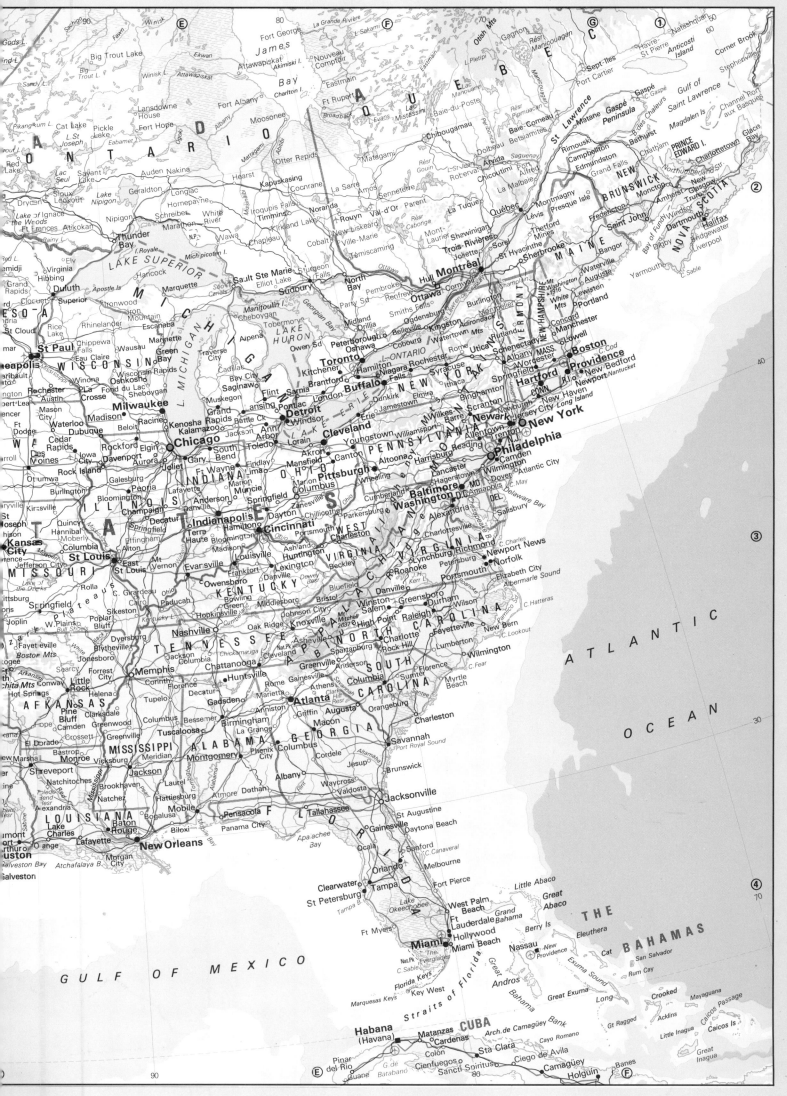

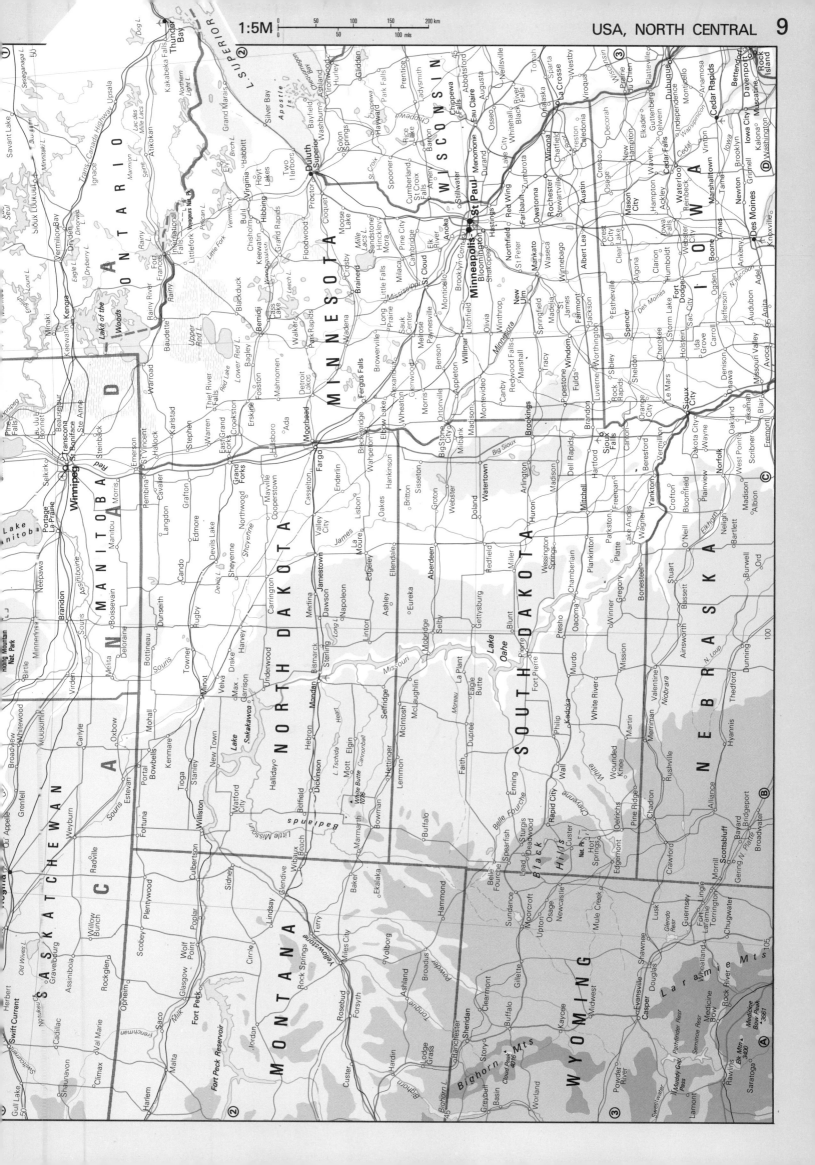

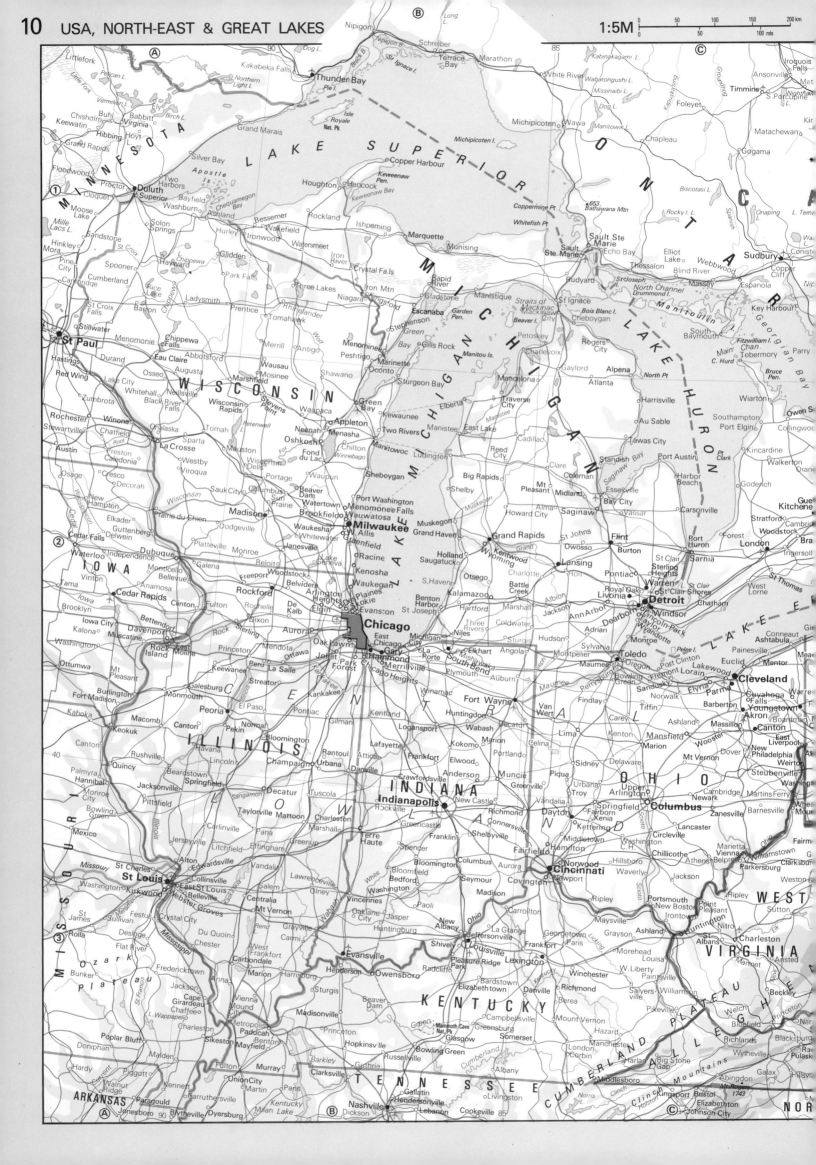

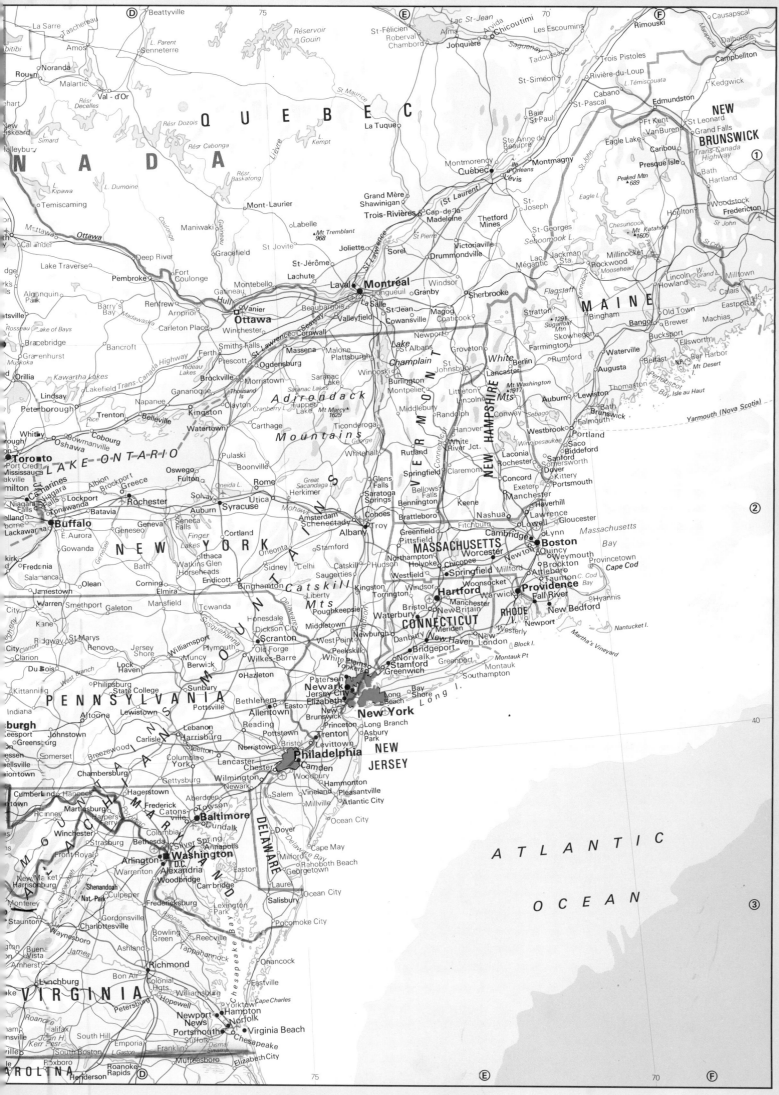

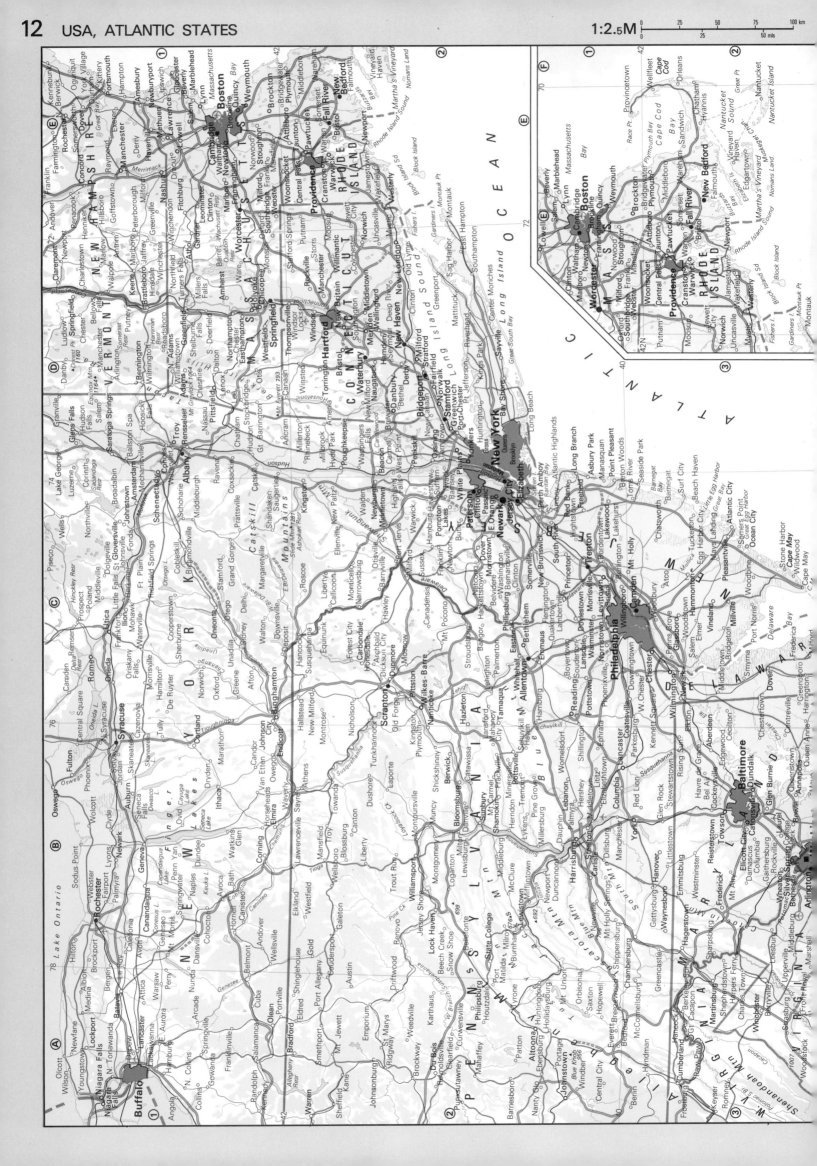

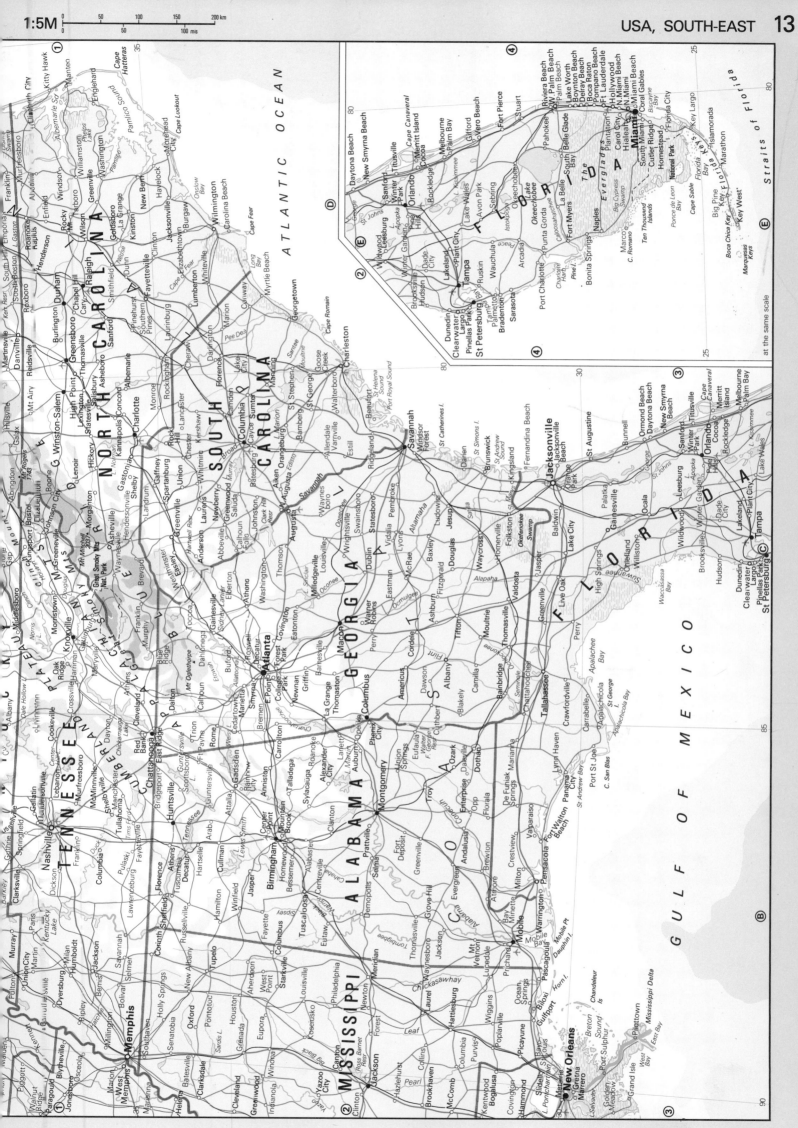

1:5M

50   100   150   200 km
50   100 mls

NEBRASKA

Kings Peak
4114

① Uinta Mts

Flaming Gorge Resr

Manila

Broadwater   Ⓑ

Oshkosh   L. McConaughy   Stapleton   Broken Bow
Medicine Bow Pk
3661
Bridger Peak   Laramie
3662   Foxpark   Kimball   Sidney   Ovid   Ogallala   Paxton   Sutherland   Ansley   St Paul
Baggs   Pine Bluffs   Chappell   BigSprings   North Platte   Gothenburg   Grand Island
Medicine Bow Mts   Cheyenne   Potter   Julesburg   Cozad   Lexington   Gibbon
Wellington   Platte   Maywood   Kearney   Has

Vernal   Yampa   Steamboat   Sterling   Holyoke   Imperial   Arapahoe   Holdrege
Roosevelt   Craig   Hayden   Springs   Fort Collins   Greeley   S. Platte   McCook   Alma   Red Cloud
Dinosaur   Meeker   Kremmling   Fall River Pass   Loveland   Brush   Otis   Culbertson   Norton   Lebanon   Republican
Rangely   White   Rocky Mtn   Estes   Fort   Wray   Benkelman   Phillipsburg
40   Nat. Park   Park   Longmont   Morgan   Cope   St. Francis   Oberlin   Stockton
Roan Plateau   Granby   Longs   Boulder   Byers   Colby   Hill City   Smoky Hill
Eagle   Berthoud Pass   Peak   Idaho   Lafayette   Arikaree   Goodland   Oakley   Saline   WaKeeney   Wilson
Grand   Rifle   Glenwood   Minturn   Loveland Pass   Springs   Denver   Kanorado   Hays
Valley   Springs   Leadville   Tennessee   Mt   Lakewood   Aurora   Limon   Burlington   Smoky   KAN
Mack   Fruita   Pass   Evans   Littleton   Englewood   Kit Carson   Cheyenne   Weskan   Russell
Palisade   4348   Castle Rock   Wells   Scott City   Ness   Great Bend   Hosin
Green   Grand   COLORADO   City

Bre del   Junction   Mt Elbert   Buena Vista   Manitou   Simla   Tribune
Moab   Delta   4399   Springs   Colorado   Tribune   Jetmore   Larned   Ste
Mt Harvard   Monarch   Salida   Pikes Peak   Springs   Lamar   Garden City   Kinsley   Lewis
35   Montrose   4378   Pass   4301   Pueblo   Syracuse   Lakin   Arkansas   Dodge   Pratt
Uncompahgre   Gunnison   Florence   Boone   Ordway   John Martin   Wiley   Montezuma   City
Plateau   Saguache   Canon City   Rocky   Resr   La Junta   Ulysses   Greensburg
Mt Peale   Uravan   Ouray   Arkansas   Fowler   Ford   Las Animas   Plains
3857   Monticello   Dove Creek   Silverton   Mt Wilson   South Fork   Monte   Blanca Peak   Walsenburg   Delhi   Springfield   Hugoton   Meade   Ashland   Red Hills
Abajo   Blanding   4342   Wolf Creek   Vista   4364   Purgatoire   Liberal   Medicine
② Mts   Cortez   Pass   Alamosa   Trinidad   Lodge

Bluff   Mexican   Mesa   Durango   Pagosa   Antonito   Raton   Boise   Hooker   Forgan   Alva
Hat   Verde   Springs   Des Moines   City   Guymon   N. Canadian   Cherokee
N.P.   Shiprock   Aztec   Chama   Cimarron   Texhoma   Fort   Fairview
Ganado   Bloomfield   Navajo   Tierra Amarilla   Springer   Clayton   Stratford   Perryton   Woodward   Supply
Farmington   Resr   Canjilon   Wheeler Peak   Dalhart   Cactus   Spearman   Seiling
PLATEAU   Caliente   4011   Taos   Hartley   Dumas   Arnett   Wat
Mentmore   Gallup   Thoreau   Espanola   Las Vegas   Mosquero   Canadian   Canadian
35   Ft   Los Alamos   Conchas L.   Logan   L   Borger   Washita   O
Wingate   Zuni   Mt Taylor   Jemez   Santa Fe   Meredith   Pampa   Weathe
Zuni   3444   Pueblo   Watrous   Panhandle   Clinton
Mts   Grants   Albuquerque   Santa Rosa   Tucumcari   Vega   Amarillo   Groom   Shamrock   Fort Cobb
St   Laguna   Bernalillo   Newkirk   San Jon   Adrian   Canyon   Resr
Johns   Moriarty   Pecos   Santa Rosa   Hereford   Wellington   Memphis   Hobart   Anada
Belen   NEW MEXICO   Vaughn   Friona   Tulia   Mangum   Wichita
Quemado   Los Lunas   Corona   Clovis   Hollis   Mts
Springerville   Polvadera   Farwell   Childress   Altus   Lawton
Magdalena   Portales   Muleshoe   Earth   Plainview   Quanah   Frederick
Alpine   South Baldy   Socorro   Kenna   Littlefield   Floydada   Vernon   Red   W F
3288   San Antonio   Llano   Morton   Dickens   Paducah   L   Wichita   Henr
Glenwood   Carrizozo   Levelland   Guthrie   Kemp   Double Mtn Fork
Elephant   Sacramento   Estacado   Lubbock   Seymour   Olney   Jacks
Gila   Butte Resr   Roswell   Tatum   Brownfield   Post   Aspermont   Haskell   Stamford   Anson   Breckenridge
Silver City   Truth or   Salinas   Hondo   Tahoka   Double Mtn Fork
Hillsboro   Consequences   Peak   Dexter   Lovington   Lamesa   Snyder   Merkel   Cisco
③ Tyrone   Central   Caballo   Tularosa   Mayhill   Hobbs   Seminole   Colorado   Sweetwater   Abilene
Bayard   Resr   Mts   Artesia   Andrews   City   Tuscola   Stephen
Lordsburg   San Andres   Alamogordo   L. McMillan   Eunice   Big Spring   Santa
Deming   Mts   Fairacres   Carlsbad   Anna   Cor
Las Cruces   Carlsbad Caverns   Malaga   Midland   TEX   Brownwoo
Columbus   University Park   N.P.   Jal   Kermit   Odessa   Coleman   Ballinger
Anthony   Red Bluff L.   Sterling   Colorad   Goldthw
Animas Peak   El Paso   Guadalupe Pk   Guadalupe   City   Carlsbad   San Angelo   Eden   Brady   San Saba
2597   Ciudad   Senecu   2667   Mtns N.P.   Monahans   Twin Buttes   Eldorado   L. Buchanan
Juárez   Fort Hancock   Toyah   Crane   Resr   Mason   Llano
Lag. de   Guadalupe   Sierra Blanca   Pecos   Big Lake   McCamey   Barnhart   Sonora   Edwards   Fredericks
30   Guzmán   El Porvenir   Kent   Van Horn   Balmorhea   Fort   Junction
Lucero   Rio Bravo del Norte   Eagle   Stockton   Sanderson   Rocksprings   Kerrville   Guad
Lag de   Villa   Peak   Mt Livermore   Plateau   Leakey
Sta María   Ahumada   San Antonio   2554   Fort Davis   Ozona   Comfort   Medina L.   Scher
de Bravo   Alpine   Langtry   Sando   Heights
Nueva   Galeana   Marfa   Marathon   Del Rio   San
Casas   MEXICO   Pecos   Sanderson   Amistad   Devils L.   Brackettville   Hondo   Anton
④ Grandes   Buenaventura   El Sueco   Ojinaga   Presidio   Chinati Pk   Resr   Uvalde
Madera   Gallego   2357   Big Bend   Boquillas   Ciudad   Bra
Matachic   CHIHUAHUA   Nat. Park   COAHUILA   Acuña   Jiménez   San
Ⓐ   Chihuahua   105   Aldama   Emory Pk   Manuel   100   Anton
2389   Benavides   Ⓑ

110   ⒶA   105   Ⓑ

30

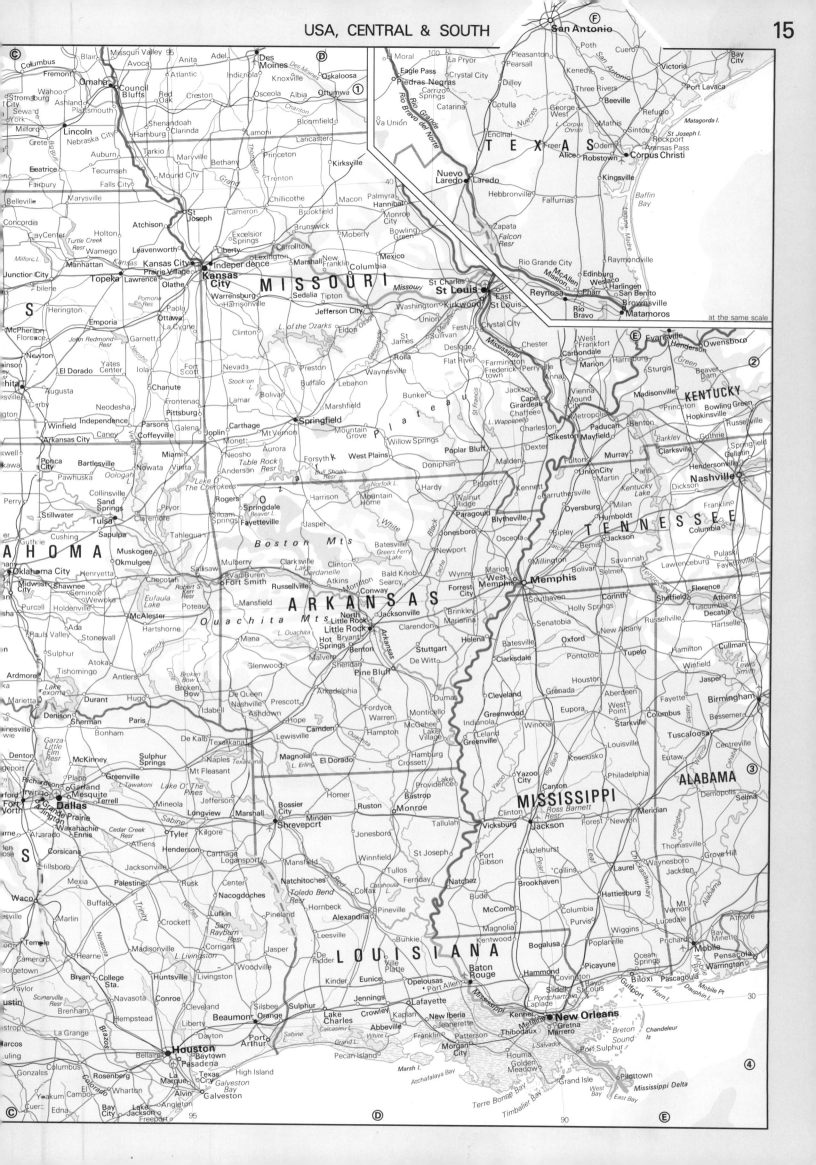

1:2.5M

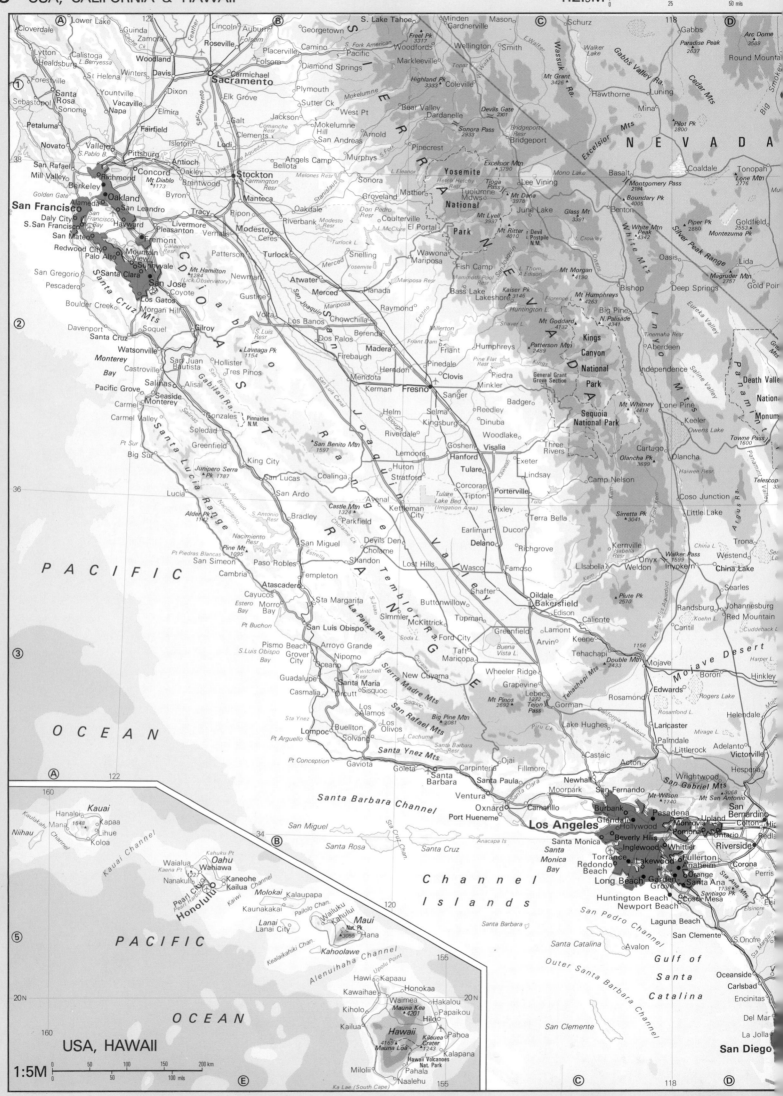

USA, HAWAII

1:5M

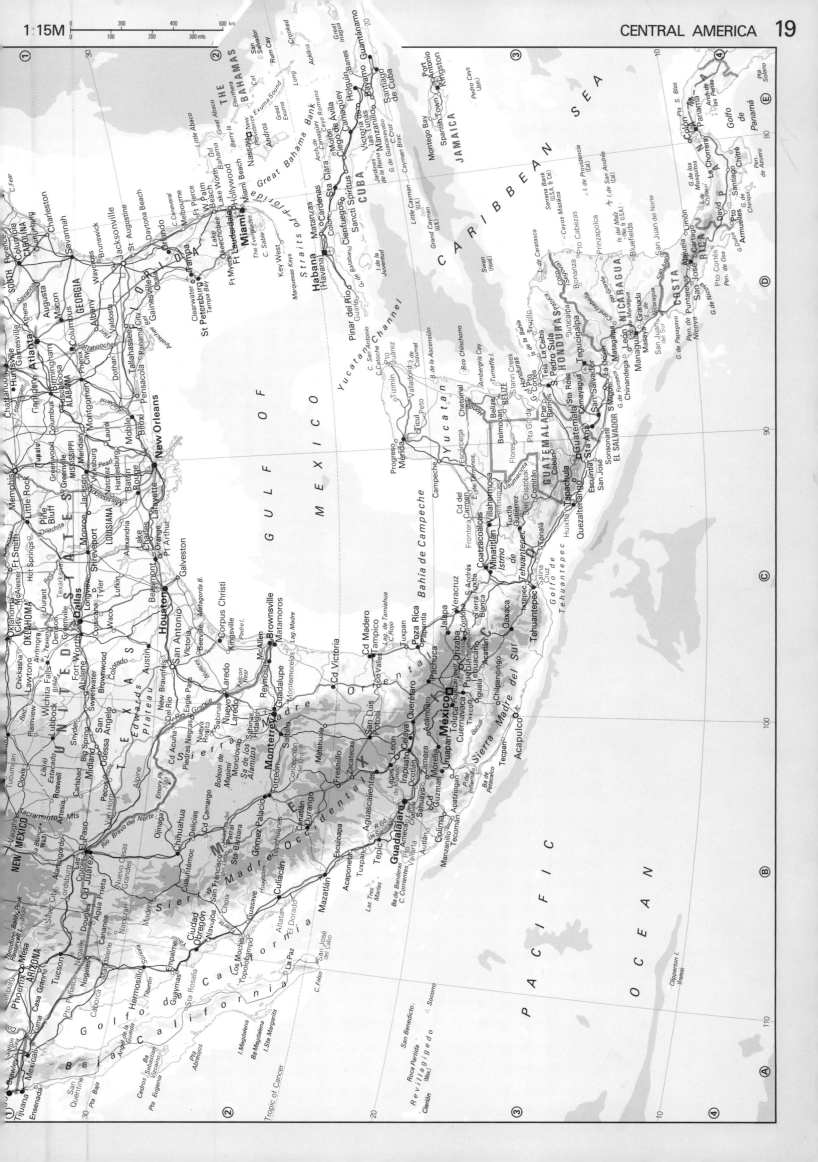

1:5M

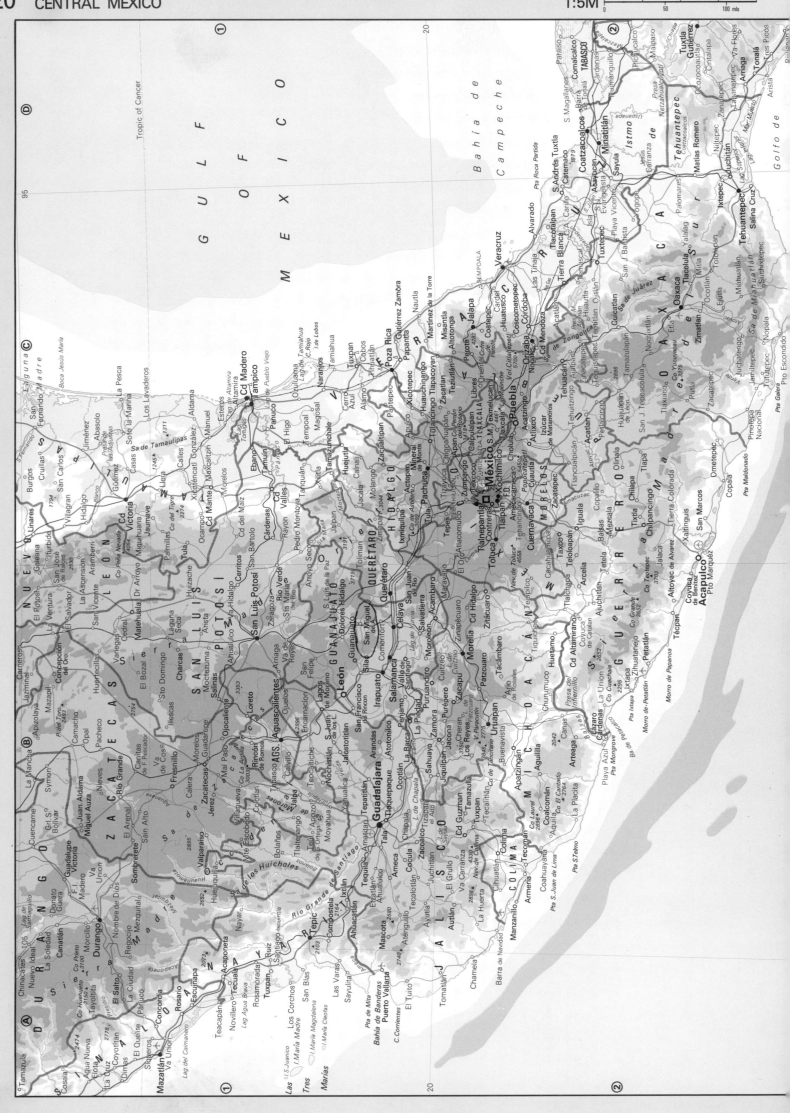

0   100   200   300   400 km
100   200 mls

Inset maps

TRINIDAD AND TOBAGO 1:2.5M
Galera Pt, Matelot, Northern Range, Mt Aripo 940, Tunapuña, Arima, Matura Bay, Cocos Bay, Pt Radix, St Joseph, Pt of Spain, San Juan, Princes Town, Upper Manzanilla, Rio Claro, Debé, Siparia, Guayaguayare, Moruga, Guayaguayare, Pt Galeota, Galeota Pt, Chupara Pt, Chaguanas, San Fernando, Gulf of Paria, Paria, Point Fortin, Point Fortin, Fullarton

DOMINICA 1:2.5M
C. Melville, Portsmouth, Marigot, Morne Diablotin 1447, Rosalie, Roseau, Grand Bay, 15°30', 61°30'

BARBADOS 1:2.5M
North Pt, Speightstown, Holetown, Bridgetown, Bathsheba, Mt Hillaby, Blackman's 340, South Pt, 13°15', 59°30'

ST LUCIA 1:2.5M
Gros Islet, Cap Pt, Castries, Soufrière, Mt Gimie 950, Vieux Fort, C. Moule à Chique, Dennery, 14°, 61°

ST VINCENT 1:2.5M
Porter Pt, Georgetown, Barrouallie, Kingstown, Soufrière 1234, 13°15', 61°15', Johnston Pt

GRENADA 1:2.5M
Bedford Pt, Sauteurs, Grenville, St George's, Mt St Catherine 840, Pt Salines, Prickly Pt, 12°, 61°45'

JAMAICA 1:2.5M
Montego Bay, Lucea, Savanna la Mar, S. Negril Point, Great Pedro Bluff, Black River, Southfield, Mandeville, May Pen, Mt Denham 986, Spanish Town, Kingston, Port Royal, Blue Mtn Pk 2256, Annotto Bay, Pt Antonio, Buff Bay, Morant Pt, Morant Bay, Long Bay, Portland Pt, Port Maria, Ocho Rios, St Ann's Bay, Galina Pt, Chapeltown, Moneague, Wakefield, The Cockpit Country, The Cockpit Mts, Blue Mts, Portland Bight, Falmouth

Main map

ATLANTIC OCEAN

THE BAHAMAS — Grand Bahama, Freeport, Great Abaco, Nicholl's Town, New Providence, Nassau, Andros, Eleuthera, Cat, New Bight, San Salvador, Rum Cay, Long, Great Exuma, Kemps Bay, Deadman's Cay, Crooked, Acklins, Mayaguana, Caicos Is (U.K.), Turks Is. (U.K.), Great Inagua, Matthew Town, Lit. Inagua

FLORIDA — Naples, Miami, Hollywood, Ft. Lauderdale, Pompano Beach, Delray Beach, West Palm Beach, Key West, The Everglades, Marquesas Keys, Florida Keys, Florida Bay, Florida Straits, Straits of Florida

Tropic of Cancer

CUBA — Habana, Guanabacoa, S. Antonio, Güines, Matanzas, Cárdenas, Colón, Cienfuegos, Santa Clara, Sancti Spíritus, Ciego de Ávila, Morón, Sta Cruz del Sur, Victoria de las Tunas, Camagüey, Holguín, Banes, Nuevitas, Las Tunas, Bayamo, Manzanillo, Santiago de Cuba, Guantánamo, Baracoa, Pinar del Rio, Nueva Gerona, I.de Juventud (I.de Pinos), G. de Batabanó, Arch. de Camagüey, Jardines de la Reina, C. San Antonio, C. Cruz, Pico San Juan 1146, Sierra Maestra, Pico Turquino 2005

Cayman Islands (U.K.) — Little Cayman, Cayman Brac, Grand Cayman

JAMAICA — Montego Bay, Savanna la Mar, Mandeville, Spanish Town, Kingston, Port Antonio, Blue Mts, Pedro Cays (Jam.)

HAITI — Cap-Haïtien, Port-de-Paix, Port-au-Prince, Gonaïves, Jacmel, Les Cayes, Anse d'Hainault, Jérémie, Île de la Gonâve, Île de la Tortue, Massif de la Hotte, La Selle 2680, Windward Passage, Jamaica Channel

DOMINICAN REPUBLIC — Santo Domingo, Santiago, S. Francisco, Puerto Plata, Samaná, Montecristi, Miches, La Romana, Pico Duarte 3175, Cordillera Central, I. Beata, C. Beata, I. Saona

Hispaniola

PUERTO RICO (U.S.A.) — San Juan, Arecibo, Aguadilla, Mayagüez, Ponce, Caguas, Cerro de Punta 1338, Mona, Mona Passage

Virgin Is (U.S.A. & U.K.), St Croix (U.S.A.), St Thomas, Anguilla (U.K.), St Martin (Fr. & Neth.), St Kitts, Nevis (U.K.), Barbuda (U.K.), Montserrat (U.K.), I. Blanquilla (Ven.)

Lesser Antilles — **Leeward Islands** — **Windward Islands**

ANTIGUA & BARBUDA, **Guadeloupe (Fr.)**, Pointe-à-Pitre, Basse Terre, Marie Galante, **DOMINICA**, Roseau, **Martinique (Fr.)**, Fort-de-France, **ST LUCIA**, Castries, **ST VINCENT**, Kingstown, The Grenadines, **BARBADOS**, Bridgetown, **GRENADA**, St George's, Los Testigos, I. Margarita, La Asunción, Tobago, Scarborough, **TRINIDAD AND TOBAGO**, Port of Spain, San Fernando, Trinidad

PUERTO RICO TRENCH

CARIBBEAN SEA

Bonaire (Neth.), Curaçao (Neth.), Aruba (Neth.), Islas los Roques (Ven.), Isla Margarita, Los Testigos

VENEZUELA — Caracas, Maracay, Maiquetía, Pto Cabello, Valencia, Barcelona, Cumaná, Carúpano, Güiria, Maturín, Cd Guayana, Cd Bolívar, Ciudad Bolívar, El Tigre, Anaco, San Juan de los Morros, Calabozo, El Baúl, Barinas, San Cristóbal, Mérida, Valera, Trujillo, Barquisimeto, Acarigua, Guanare, Coro, Pta Fijo, Pen. de Paraguaná, G. de Venezuela, Lago de Maracaibo, Maracaibo, Cabimas, Ojeda, S. Felipe, Tinaco, Altagracia de Orituco, V. de la Pascua, Coloradito, Tucupita, Orinoco, Barrancas, Carúpano, Pampatar, Caripito, Guayana, Cerro 1990, Río Tigre

COLOMBIA — Barranquilla, Cartagena, Sta Marta, Ciénaga, Valledupar, Riohacha, Soledad, Sabanalarga, Sincelejo, Montería, Plato, El Banco, Ayacucho, Sta Nevada de Sta Marta 5715, Pico Bolívar 4807, G. de, Golfo del Darién

PANAMA — Panamá, Colón, La Chorrera, David, Penonomé, Panama Canal, Arch. de las Perlas, G. de los Mosquitos

COSTA RICA — San José, Cartago, Alajuela, Heredia, Limón, Cerro Chirripó 3820, Pto Armuelles, Viejo, B. de Coronado

NICARAGUA — Bluefields, Río Grande, Puerto Cabezas, Prinzapolca, Bonanza, Waspán, Cabo Gracias à Dios, La Luz, Lag. de Perlas, Is. del Maíz (Nic. & U.S.A.)

HONDURAS — Iriona, Brus Laguna, Caratasca, Lag. de Caratasca, Cayos Miskitos

Swan I. (Hond.), I. de Providencia (Col.), I. de San Andrés (Col.)

COLOMBIAN BASIN

CAYMAN TRENCH

1:35M

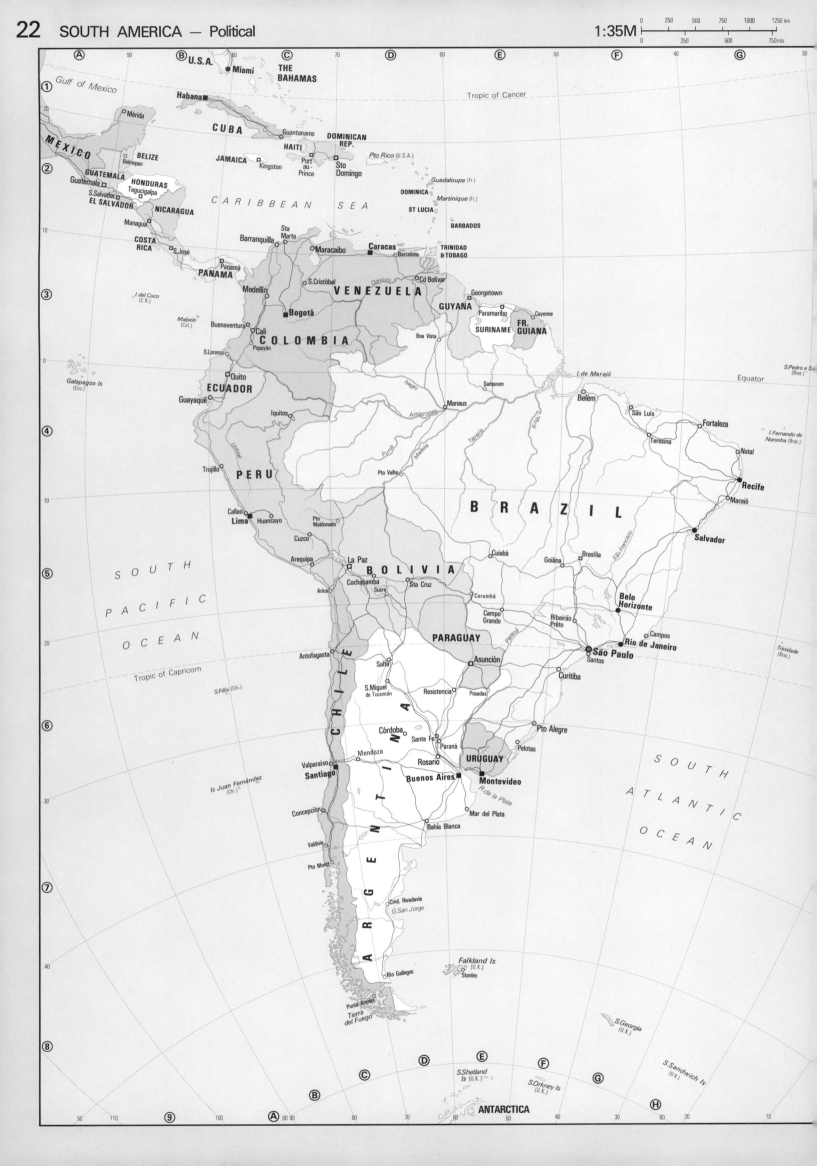

| 0 | 250 | 500 | 750 | 1000 | 1250 km |
| 0 | 250 | 500 | 750 | 1000 mls |

Ⓐ 90 Ⓑ U.S.A. 80 Ⓒ 70 Ⓓ 60 Ⓔ 50 Ⓕ 40 Ⓖ 30

① Gulf of Mexico • Miami

Tropic of Cancer

Habana ■
Mérida ○
20

CUBA
MEXICO
Guantanamo
THE BAHAMAS
BELIZE
Belmopan □
DOMINICAN REP.
② GUATEMALA
JAMAICA
HAITI
Pto Rico (U.S.A.)
Guatemala □
Kingston
Port au Prince
Sto Domingo
Guadaloupe (Fr.)
S.Salvador
HONDURAS
Tegucigalpa
DOMINICA
EL SALVADOR
NICARAGUA
Martinique (Fr.)
ST LUCIA
Managua
BARBADOS

COSTA RICA
○ S.José
CARIBBEAN SEA
TRINIDAD & TOBAGO

PANAMA
Barranquilla
Sta Marta
Maracaibo ○
Caracas ■
Barcelona

Panamá □
○ S.Cristóbal
Orinoco
Cd Bolivar
Georgetown
○ I.del Coco (C.R.)
Medellín ○
VENEZUELA
GUYANA
Paramaribo
Cayenne
③
Malpelo (Col.)
Bogotá ■
SURINAME
FR. GUIANA
Buenaventura ○
Cali ○
COLOMBIA
Boa Vista

Popayán ○
S.Pedro e S (Braz.)
S.Lorenzo ○
0
I. de Marajó
Equator
Galapagos Is (Ecu.)
Quito ●
Santarem
ECUADOR
Belém
Guayaquil ○
Negro
Manaus
São Luís
Iquitos ○
Amazonas
Fortaleza
④
I.Fernando de Noronha (Braz.)
Teresina
Natal
Purus
Madeira
Trujillo ○
Pto Velho ○
Recife ●
PERU
Maceió
10
B R A Z I L
Callao ○
Lima ■
Huancayo ○
Pto Maldonado ○
Salvador ●
Cuzco ○
Cuiabá ○
Goiãna ○
Brasília □
São Francisco
Arequipa ○
La Paz ●
⑤
BOLIVIA
Cochabamba ○
Sta Cruz ○
Arica ○
Sucre □
Corumbá ○
Belo Horizonte ●
Campo Grande ○
Ribeirão Prêto ○
Campos
SOUTH
PARAGUAY
Paraná
Rio de Janeiro ●
Antofagasta ○
Asunción ■
São Paulo ●
Trinidade (Braz.)
PACIFIC
Salta ○
Santos ○
Tropic of Capricorn
S.Miguel de Tucumán ○
Resistencia ○
Curitiba ○
OCEAN
Posadas ○
S.Félix (Chi.)
A
R
G
E
N
T
I
N
A
⑥
Córdoba ○
Pto Alegre ○
SOUTH
Mendoza ○
Sante Fe ○
Pelotas ○
Valparaíso ■
Rosario ○
URUGUAY
ATLANTIC
Santiago ●
Buenos Aires ■
Montevideo ■
Is Juan Fernández (Chi.)
R.de la Plata
OCEAN
Concepción ○
Mar del Plata ○
Bahía Blanca ○
Valdivia ○
⑦
Pto Montt ○
Cmd. Rivadavia ○
G.San Jorge
Falkland Is (U.K.)
Stanley ○
Rio Gallegos ○
S.Georgia (U.K.)
Punta Arenas ○
Tierra del Fuego
⑧
Ⓒ Ⓓ Ⓔ S.Shetland Is (U.K.) Ⓕ S.Orkney Is (U.K.) Ⓖ S.Sandwich Is (U.K.)
50
Ⓑ
110 100 90 80 70 60 50 40 30 20 10
⑨ Ⓐ ANTARCTICA Ⓗ

1:15M

PACIFIC

OCEAN

NICARAGUA

COSTA RICA

PANAMA

COLOMBIA

VENEZUELA

ECUADOR

PERU

BOLIVIA

CHILE

ARGENTINA

AMAZONAS

SELVAS

ACRE

RONDÔNIA

RORAIMA

LLANOS

ISLAS GALÁPAGOS
(ARCHIPIÉLAGO DO COLÓN)
(Equ.)

at the same scale

Islas Juan Fernández
(Chile)

at the same scale

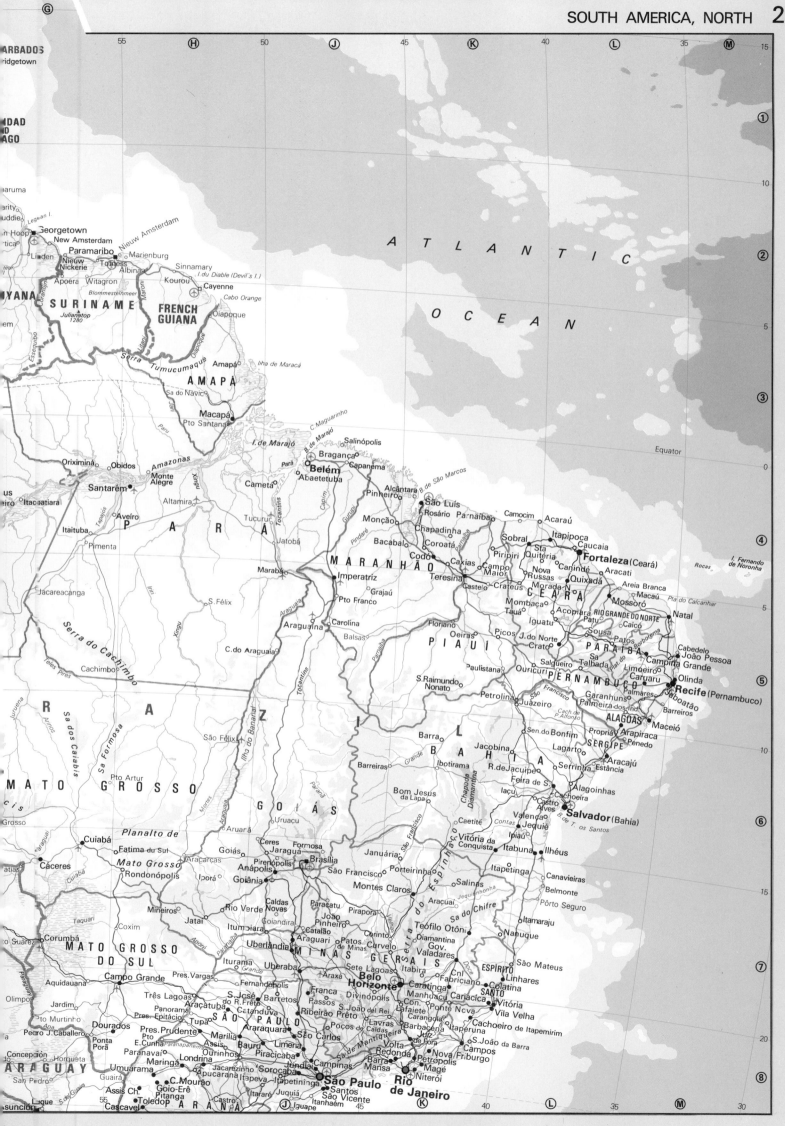

ATLANTIC

OCEAN

G

55 H 50 J 45 K 40 L 35 M 15

RBADOS
ridgetown
①

DAD
AGO

aruma
arity
uddie
tica
⑦

Georgetown
New Amsterdam
Paramaribo   Marienburg
Nieuw   Nieuw Amsterdam
Nickerie   Totness Albina
Apoera Witagron   Sinnamary
SURINAME   Kourou I.du Diable (Devil's I.)
Julianatop   FRENCH   Cayenne
1280   GUIANA
②

NYANA

em

Legean I.
Essequibo
us
eiro   Itacoatiara
us
Grosso

Blommesteinmeer

Maroni
Oiapoque
Cabo Orange

Serra Tumucumaque   AMAPÁ   Equator

Sa do Navio   Ilha de Maracá   ③

Macapá
Pto Santana

Oriximiná Obidos   Amazonas   I. de Marajó C. Maguarinho Salinópolis
Monte   de Marajó Bragança Capanema
Santarém   Alegre   Pará Belém   0
Altamira   Cametá   Abaetetuba   Pinheiro Alcântara B. de São Marcos
PARÁ   Capim   São Luís
Aveiro   Tucuruí   Guajurú Monção Chapadinha Rosário Parnaíba Camocim Acaraú   ④
Itaituba   Jatobá Tocantins Bacabal Coroatá Codó Caxias Campo Sobral Itapipoca Caucaia
Pimenta   Marabá   MARANHÃO   Teresina Maior Crateús Nova Canindé Fortaleza(Ceará)   I. Fernando
Jacareacanga   Imperatriz Pto Franco   Mombaça Russas Morada-N. Aracati   de Noronha
S. Félix Grajaú   Floriano Castelo Tauá Acopiara Quixadá   Rocas
Carolina   Oeiras Picos Iguatu Patu RIO GRANDE DO NORTE Areia Branca
Serra do Cachimbo Araguaína Balsas   J. do Norte Sousa Caicó Macaú Natal   5
Cachimbo   C. do Araguaia   PIAUÍ Crato   Patos Pta do Calcanhar
Teles Pires   Paranaíba S.Raimundo Salgueiro Talhada PARAÍBA Cabedelo
R   Nonato Paulistana Ouricuri PERNAMBUCO Limoeiro João Pessoa
A   Sa dos Caiabis   Petrolina Juazeiro São Garanhuns Caruaru Campina Grande ⑤
Z   Sa Formosa   Francisco Cach. de Palmares Olinda
São Félix Ilha do Bananal   Barra   P.Alfonso Palmeira dos Ind. Jaboatão Recife(Pernambuco)
Arinos   I   Sen.do Bonfim ALAGOAS Barreiros
L   B   Jacobina   Propriá Arapiraca Maceió
Pto Artur A   Ibotirama Serrinha Lagarto SERGIPE Penedo
cis   GOIÁS H   R.de Jacuípe Estância
Grosso Aruanã   Barreiras Grande Feira de S. Aracajú   10
MATO GROSSO   I Bom Jesus   Alagoinhas
Montes   A da Lapa Chapada Iaçu Castro Salvador(Bahia)
Planalto de   Ceres Formosa   Diamantina Valença Alves
Cuiabá   Jaraguá   Caetité Contas Jequié B.de T. os Santos ⑥
Fatima du Sul Goiás   Pirenópolis Brasília Januária   Vitória da Ipiaú
Mato Grosso Afacarças   Anápolis São Francisco Porteirinha Conquista Itabuna Ilhéus
Cáceres Rondonópolis Iporá Goiânia   Montes Claros Salinas Itapetinga
Mineiros Caldas   Paracatu Piraporá Araçuaí Canavieiras   15
Rio Verde Novas   João Corinto Sa do Chifre Belmonte
Jataí Itumbiara Goiandira   Pinheiro   Diamantina Pôrto Seguro
Corumbá Coxim   Catalão Patos Curvelo Teófilo Otôni Itamaraju
MATO GROSSO   Araguari de Minas Gov. Nanuque
DO SUL Iturama Uberlândia MINAS GERAIS Valadares
Aquidauana Pres. Vargas   Sete Lagoas Itabira ESPÍRITO São Mateus   ⑦
Jardim Campo Grande   Fernandópolis Uberaba Araxá Belo Caratinga Cnl Linhares
to Murtinho Três Lagoas   Franca Horizonte Manhuaçu Fabriciano Colatina
Pecro J. Caballero Dourados S.José Barretos Divinópolis Con. Cariacica SANTO
Olimpo   do R.Prêto Passos Ponte Nova Vitória
Panorama   Catanduva Ribeirão Prêto S.João del Rei Lafaiete Vila Velha
Ponta Pres. Epitácio Tupã Assis Araraquara SÃO PAULO Lavras Barbacena Cachoeiro de Itapemirim 20
Porã Pres. Prudente Marília São Carlos Poços de Juiz S.João da Barra
Paranavaí Bauru Piracicaba Limeira Caldas de Fora Nova Campos
ARAGUAY Maringá Londrina Jacarezinho Sorocaba Campinas Volta Friburgo
San Pedro Umuarama   Assis Jundiaí Redonda Magé
Concepción   Ourinhos Itapeva Itapetininga Barra Nova Niterói
C.Mourao Pitanga Itararé Juquiá São Paulo Mansa São Vicente
Ligue Goio-Erê   Rio ⑧
Assis Ch.   Santos de Janeiro
Toledo PARANÁ   Itanhaém
sunción Cascavel 55   J 45 K 40 L 35 M 30

55   H 50   J 45   K   L   M   15
10
2
5
0
4
5
5
6
15
7
20
8

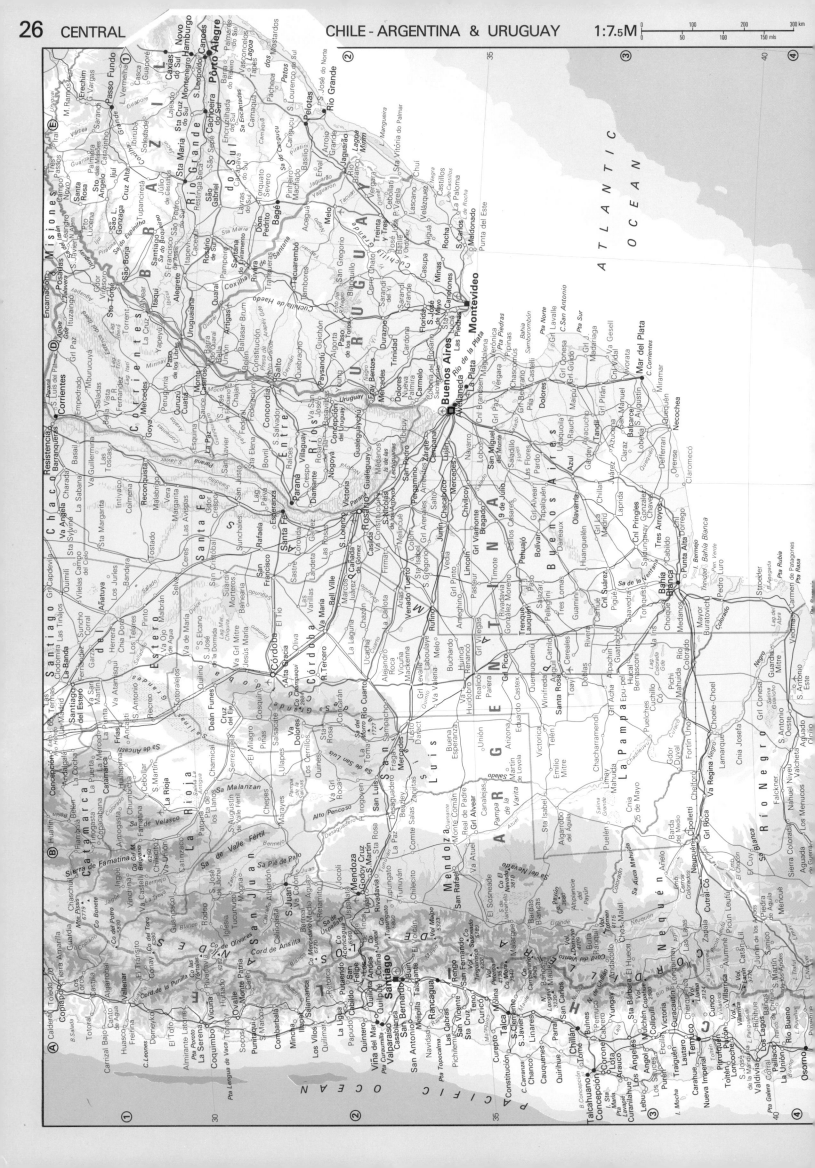

1:15M

OCEAN

O.Kolguyev

Vorkuta M

Murmánsk

Ob

③

Ukhta

Tavda

Omsk

Arkhangel'sk

Onezhskoye Oz.

FINLAND

Oulu

Kotlas

Sverdlovsk

Vaasa

ampere

Ladozhskoye Oz.

Chelyabinsk

Vyborg

Kama

Helsinki

UNION OF SOVIET SOCIALIST REPUBLICS

Leningrad

Tallinn

Yaroslavl'

Kazan'

Magnitogorsk

Volga

Gor'kiy

50

Moskva

Kuybyshev

Riga

Ural

Vilnius

Kaliningrad

Minsk

④

Saratov

wa

Aral'skoye More

D

Kiyev

Kharkov

Volgograd

kow

L'vov

Dnepr

Volga

A

Dnepropetrovsk

Astrakhan'

Rostov

Don

Shevchenko

Odessa

CASPIAN

Cluj

ROMANIA

Sevastopol

Timișoara

SEA

Galați

Bucureşti

Tbilisi

Baku

Y

Constanța

BLACK   SEA

Dunav

Varna

Yerevan

VIA

Sofiya

Samsun

Erzurum

A

BULGARIA

Tabrīz

Skopje

Plovdiv

Edirne

Firat

Tehrān

Istanbul

⑤

Thessaloniki

Ankara

GREECE

Bursa

TURKEY

IRAN

Eskişehir

Esfahan

Pátrai

Izmir

Adana

Mosul

Athínai

Antalya

Khaniá   Kriti

Kikládhes

Halab

SYRIA

Baghdād

CYPRUS

Nicosia

Hims

Kalámai

Sporádhes

LEBANON

Beirūt

IRAQ

Tigris

Basra

Abadan

H

J   Damascus

Euphrates

K

The Gulf 50

30

1:7.5M

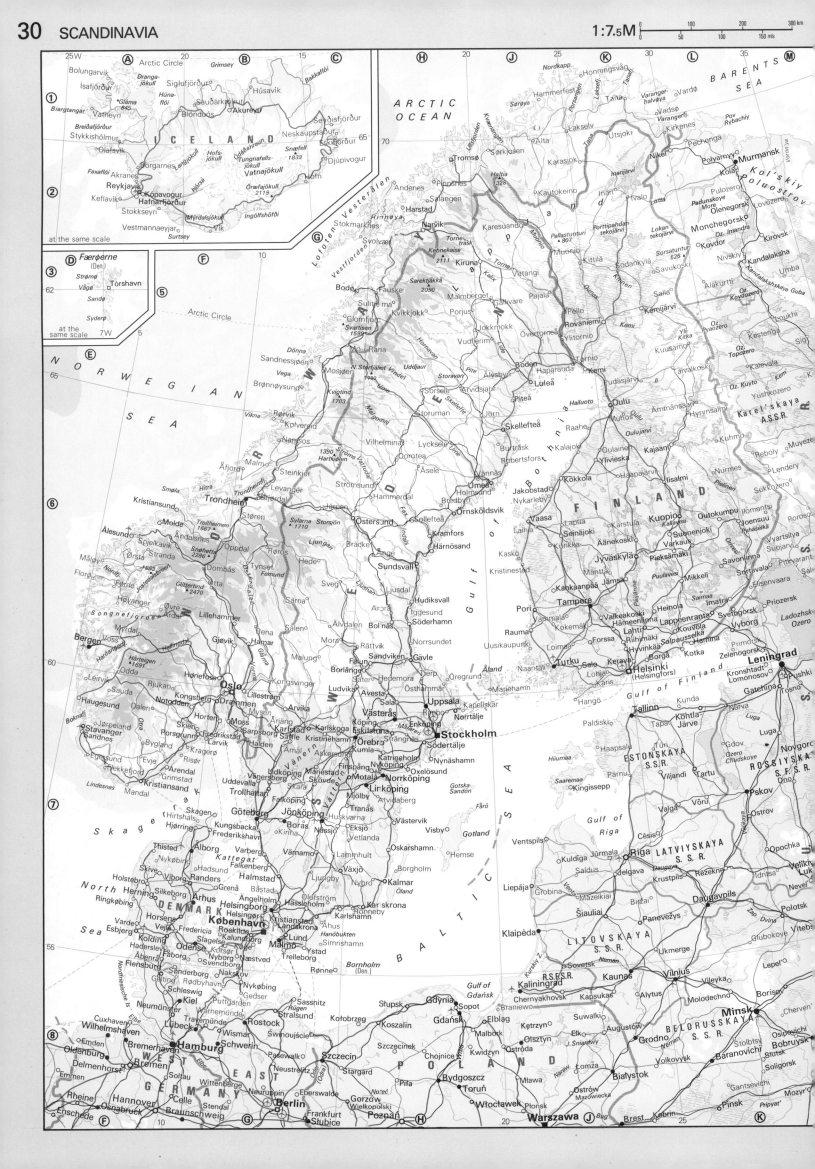

50 100 150 200 km
0
0 50 100 mls

A 10 B 5 C 0 D 5 E

NORWAY

Nordhordland
Dale
Bergen
Sotra
60
Sunnhordland Stord
Leirvik
Bømlo Haugafjorden
Skjold
Haugesund
Karmøy Boknafj.
Stavanger
Sandnes

Herma Ness
Unst
Isbister *Fetlar*
St Magnus B. *Yell* *Shetland*
Nhalsay
Foula *Lerwick*

Sumburgh Hd

Fair Isle

Westray
Rousay *Sanday*
Sule Skerry *Stronsay*
N.Rona *Stromness* *Kirkwall*
Sula Sgeir *Stack Skerry* *Hoy* *Scapa Flow* *Orkney*

Flannan Is *C. Wrath*
Thurso *Duncansby Hd*
Butt of Lewis
Stornoway *Wick*
St Kilda *Lewis* ▲Ben Hope
927 *Helmsdale*
Harris ▲Ben More *Dornoch*
N. Uist Assynt 998 *Dornoch Firth*
Ullapool *Moray Firth*
Skye *Dingwall* *Elgin* *Banff* *Fraserburgh*
S. Uist *Kyle* Lochalsh *Inverness* *Peterhead*
Barra *Fort Spey* *Buchan Ness*
Augustus ▲Ben Macdui *Aberdeen*
Mallaig 1309 *Don*
Rum *Fort William* ▲Ben Nevis *Braemar* *Dee* *Stonehaven*
SCOTLAND 1344 ▲Ben *Montrose*
Coll Lawers *Pitlochry*
Tiree 1214 ▲ *Perth* *Dundee* *Arbroath*
Oban ▲*Mull* *Stirling* *F. of Tay*
Colonsay *L. Awe* *St Andrews*
Jura *L. Lomond*
Islay *Greenock* *Kirkcaldy*
Glasgow *F. of Forth*
Paisley *Edinburgh* *St Abbs Hd*
Motherwell *Berwick-upon-Tweed*
Campbeltown *Arran* *Galashiels* *Holy I.*
Irvine *Kilmarnock* *White*
Tory I. *Ayr* Coomb *Alnwick*
Malin Hd *Moffat* ▲822 *Hawick* *Cheviots*
Rathlin I. *Girvan* ▲Merrick *Morpeth* *Blyth*
Aran I. *Coleraine* 843 *Dumfries* *Newcastle-upon-Tyne*
Londonderry *Stranraer* *Carlisle* *Gateshead* *S. Shields*
Rossan Pt *Donegal* *N. IRELAND* *Larne* *Kirkcudbright* *Durham* *Sunderland*
Donegal B. *Ballymena* *Luce B.* *Solway Firth* *Penrith* *Hartlepool*
Enniskillen *L. Neagh* *Belfast* *Scafell Pike* *Darlington* *Middlesbrough*
Sligo *Omagh* *Bangor* 977 ▲ *Yorkshire Moors* *Scarborough*
Ballina *Monaghan* *Portadown* *Douglas* *Isle of Man* *Kendal*
Castlebar *Armagh* *Barrow-* *Lancaster* *Flamborough Hd*
Boyle *Newry* in-Furness
L. Conn *Cavan* *Morecambe* *York*
L. Mask *Longford* *Dundalk* *IRISH SEA* *Blackpool* *Harrogate* *Hull*
Roscommon *Drogheda* *Preston* *Bradford* *Leeds* *Spurn Hd*
L. Corrib *L. Ree* *Athlone* *Mullingar* *Huddersfield* *Grimsby*
Galway *Liverpool* *Bolton* *Manchester* *Humber*
Galway B. *Shannon* *Dublin* *Birkenhead* *Doncaster*
Aran Is *Monasterevan* (Baile Atha Cliath) *Holyhead* *Sheffield* *Lincoln*
Nenagh *Port* *Dun Laoghaire* *Warrington*
Ennis *L. Derg* Laoise *Bray* *Anglesey* *Chester* *Stoke-* *Nottingham*
Kilrush *Carlow* *Bangor* *Crewe* on-Trent
REP. OF *Wicklow* ▲Snowdon *Derby*
Limerick *IRELAND* *Kilkenny* *Pwllheli* *Dee* 1085 *Trent*
Tralee *Tipperary* *Arklow* *Shrewsbury* *Leicester*
Clonmel *Cardigan* *King's Lynn* *Norwich* *Great Yarmouth*
▲Carrauntoohil *Waterford* *Wexford* *Bay* *Aberystwyth* *WALES* *Wolverhampton* *Coventry* *Peterborough* *Lowestoft*
1041 *Blackwater* *Rosslare* *Birmingham* *ENGLAND* *Nene* *Ouse*
Killarney *Dungarvan* *Builth* *Worcester* *Northampton* *Newmarket* *NETHERLANDS*
Cork *Youghal* *Fishguard* Wells *Wye* *Bedford* *Cambridge* *Haarlem*
Bantry *St David's* *Brecon* *Ipswich* *Leiden*
Hd *Carmarthen* *Gloucester* *Colchester* *'s-Gravenhage*
C. Clear *Old Hd* *Pembroke* *Swansea* *Newport* *Oxford* *Luton* *Felixstowe* (Den Haag)
of Kinsale *Cambrians* *Severn* *Swindon* *London* *Harwich* *Rotterdam*
Cardiff *Bath* *Reading* *Chelmsford* *Dordrecht*
Bristol *Windsor* *Thames* *Southend-* *Vlissingen*
Lundy I. *Weston-* *Maidstone* on-Sea *Zeebrugge*
super-Mare *Guildford* *Canterbury* *Oostende* *Antwerpen*
Barnstaple *Taunton* *Winchester* *Crawley* *Dover* *Brugge* *Gent* *BELGIUM* *Mechelen*
Salisbury *Southampton* *Brighton* *Hastings* *Folkestone* *Calais* *Dunkerque* *Bruxelles* *Kortrijk*
Bude *Eastbourne* *Boulogne* *St-Omer* *Tourcoing* *Roubaix* (Brüssel)
Exeter *Bournemouth* *Portsmouth* *Str.* *Bethune* *Lille* *Tournai* *Soignies* *Mons*
Dartmoor *Weymouth* *Isle of Wight* *Montreuil* *Douai* *Valenciennes* *Charleroi*
Newquay *Plymouth* *Torbay* *Arras* *Denain* *Maubeuge*
Truro *Le Tréport* *PICARDIE* *Cambrai* *Fourmies*
Penzance *Prawle Pt* *Dieppe* *Amiens* *St-Quentin*
Land's End *Falmouth* *ENGLISH CHANNEL* *Neufchâtel* *Montdidier* *Laon*
Isles of Scilly *Lizard Pt* *Beauvais* *Compiègne* *Oise* *Aisne*
C. de la Hague *Fécamp* *Bolbec* *Rouen* *Soissons* *Reims*
Pte de Barfleur *Le Havre* *Senlis* *Château-* *Epernay*
Alderney *Deauville* *Seine* *Mantes* *Cergy* Thierry
Guernsey *Cherbourg* *Bayeux* *Elbeuf* *Pontoise* *Meaux*
Sark *Valognes* *Lisieux* Louviers *Evreux* *Versailles* *Paris* *Provins*
Channel Is *Jersey* *St Helier* *St-Lô* *Caen* *Dreux* *Eure* *Sézanne*
(U.K.) *Coutances* *Argentan* *Chartres* *Étampes*
Golfe de St-Malo *Granville* *NORMANDIE* *Orne* *Domfront* *FRANCE* *Rambouillet* *Melun* *Romilly-s.-S.*
Roscoff *St-Malo* *Mont-* *Mayenne* *Alençon* *Fontainebleau* *Sens* *Troyes*
Morlaix *Dinan* St-Michel
I. d'Ouessant *Brest* *St-Brieuc* *Fougères*
Carhaix- *Dinard*
Plouguer

NORTH

SEA

5

55

5

Esbjerg
Vlieland
Texel
Den Helder *Alkmaar*
3
50
4

B C D

1:2.5M

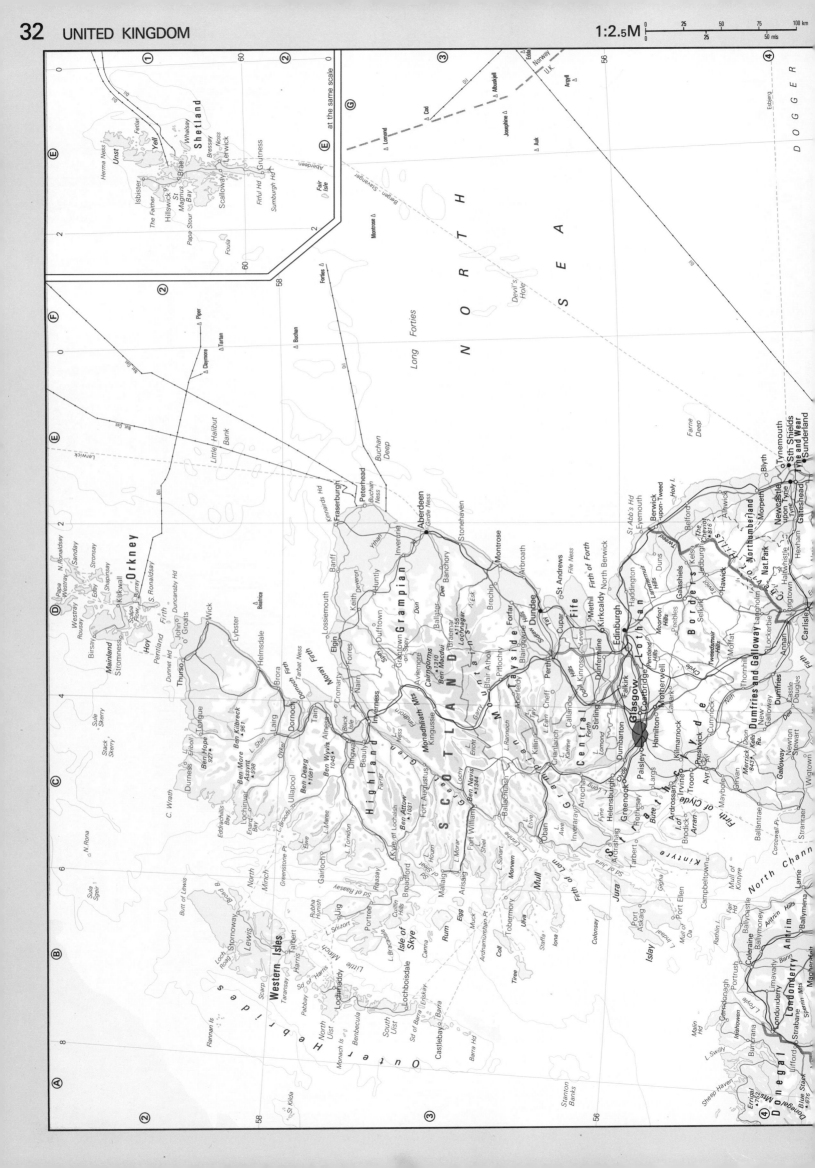

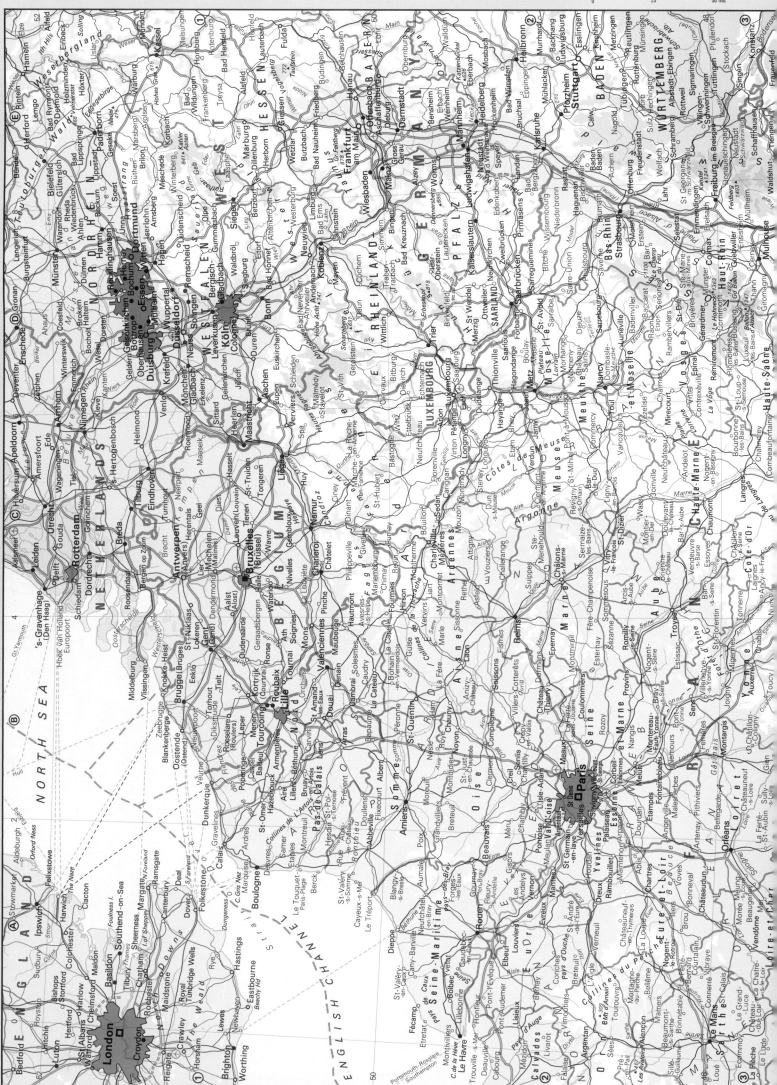

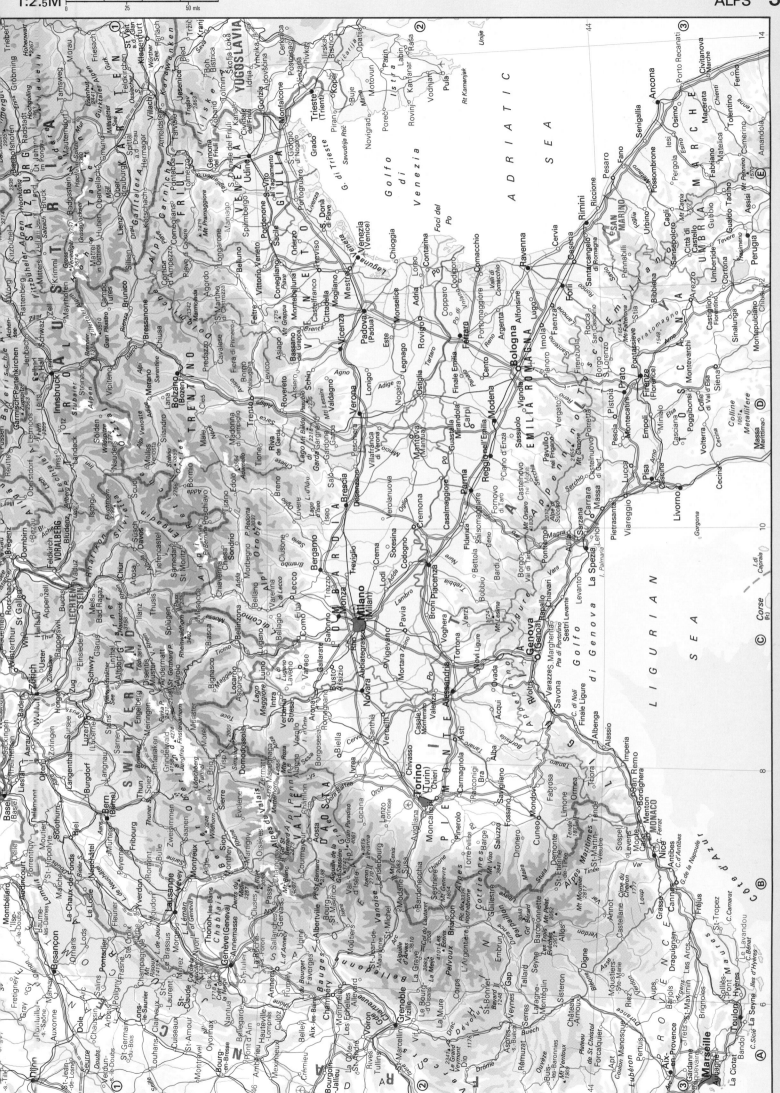

1:5M

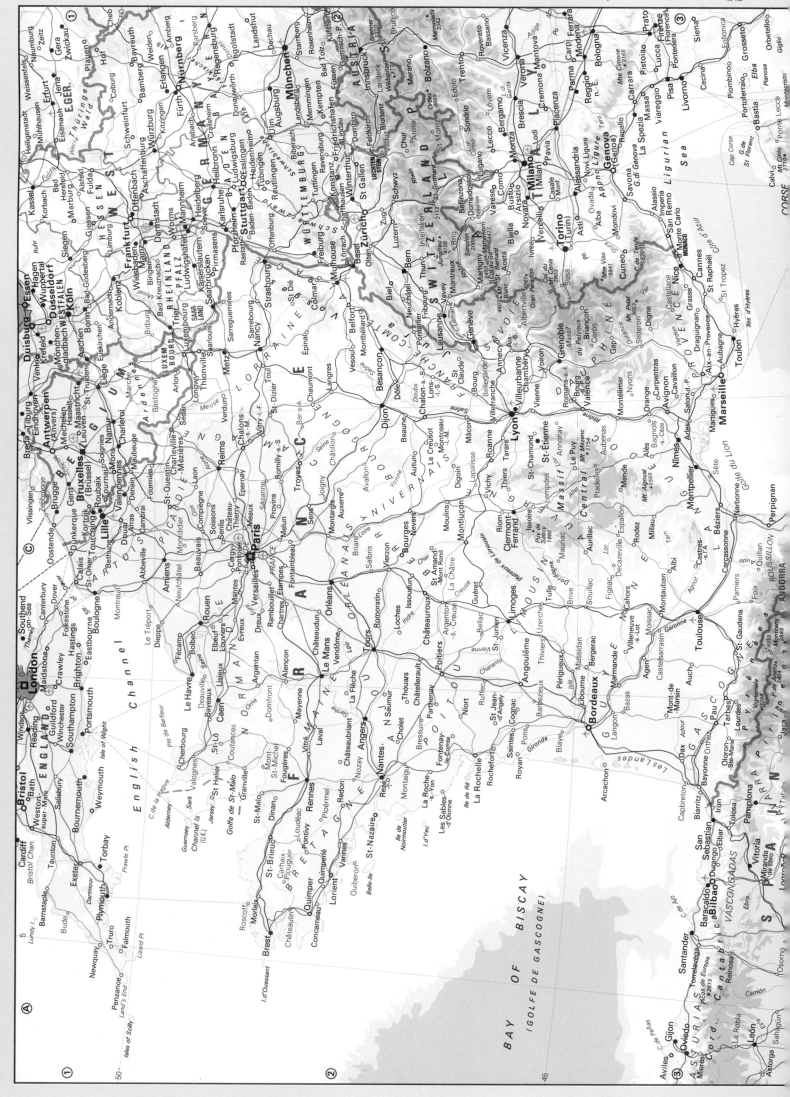

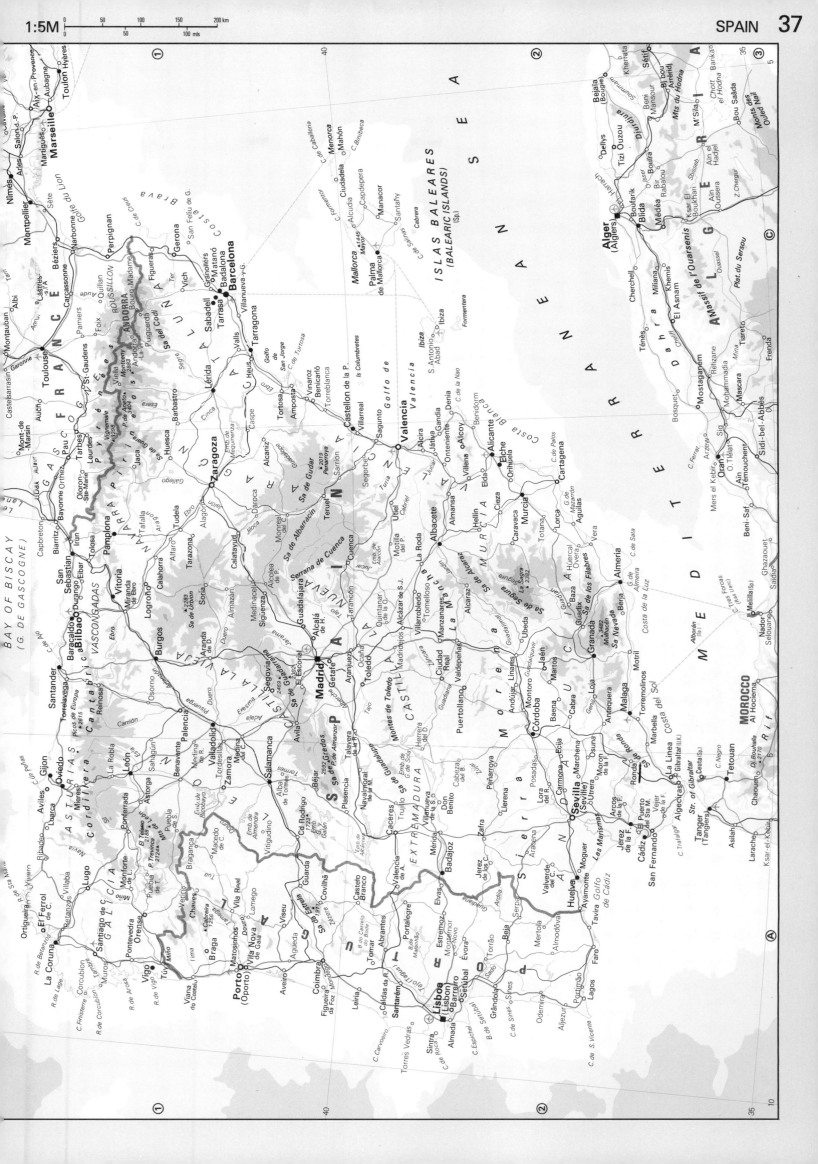

1:5M

CRESTONE, COLORADO

A Spiritual Community Takes Root

By Jeffery Paine

CRESTONE, COLO.— Seemingly in the middle of nowhere, miles from the nearest major highway, this onetime Colorado gold-mining town seems like a most unexpected locale to find a growing religious center. But Crestone today boasts a denser concentration of high Tibetan lamas than normally would be found even in Tibet, and that's just for starters. Christian Carmelites, Islamic Sufis, Jews, Hindus, Zen Buddhists, Taoists, Shintoists, and American Indians have all moved to Crestone.

There is a story behind the formation of this eclectic community. Beginning in the late 1970s, a wealthy visionary named Hanne Strong, who with her husband, Maurice, owns 200,000 acres around Crestone, has donated land with the intention of creating a sanctuary for the world's religions.

The result has been remarkable, with diverse spiritual groups living in close proximity and intermingling. At the Christmas mass at the Roman Catholic monastery, whole rows get taken by Buddhist monks in their flowing robes. Hindu nuns in saris umpire local baseball games. When American Indians held a medicine wheel ceremony this summer, the offerings to the four directions were made by a Shinto priest, a Christian nun, a Buddhist nun, and a Hindu yogi.

Mixing it up. This exotic mélange exists amid an American western landscape straight out of *Bonanza.* When the first Tibetans arrived in Crestone around 1980, the crusty old mayor was asked what he thought about it. "Better than a bunch of New Yor... he replied.

Now, a qua...

later, the area supports two distinct varieties of spiritual life—one traditional, the other free-form.

Tibetan Buddhism scholar Khenpo Tsultrim Gyamtso Rinpoche finds that having so many living masters in residence makes the area now the world's best place to practice and meditate. As one Crestone Buddhist, Erik Drew, puts it, "Why go to India and get dysentery? You would never meet there such a concentration of first-rate teachers nor have such access to them."

Sister Kaye, a Carmelite nun, finds it validating to live amid so many faiths. When she wakes before dawn to pray, she sees a fire already lit at a Hindu ashram across the hillside and thinks she is not alone: Others are devout; others have made selfless vows and aspire to the same sanctity she wishes for herself. And she begins her day ...us heartened.

...orraine Fox Davis, an ...erican Indian spokes...man, observes that peo... change when they move ...such a wintry, isolated

natural setting. First, she says, residents must become more self-reliant here to survive and, since no one can make it alone, also become part of the community. Then, free of the hassles and stresses of urban life— in Crestone, house doors are left unlocked, car keys in the ignition—people invariably "soften." And lastly, Davis says, everyone here feels a deep sense of connection to the land.

A sense of connection between inner and outer landscape. Self-reliance. Community. The softening of the heart. These have always been the goals of a religious vocation.

In Crestone, though, some experience this enhanced sense of life's interconnectedness without benefit of clergy. Surrounded by 19 major religious groups, it's the air even skeptics there breathe—this feeling of living in a larger universe.

Rabbi David Cooper, author of the bestselling *God Is a Verb,* suggests that in Crestone is occurring a strange next step in human spirituality: "postreligion," in which one can benefit from religion without being a believer/congregant. Fifty years ago, the eastern faiths that now populate the valley were all but unknown in America; today, Cooper points out, their insights about compassion and mindfulness inform even the secular vocabulary in Crestone (and elsewhere).

Crestonians tend to treat one another well, recognizing not only what the other person is but also what he or she is striving to be. And that response helps bring, for the devout and nonbelievers alike, the ideal closer to actuality. "People who move to a place they consider 'spiritual' behave differently, probably better, than they would elsewhere," current Mayor Kizzen Laki observes. "In Crestone, it becomes a self-fulfilling prophecy." ●

Annie Pace practicing yoga at the Buddhist Tashi Gomang Stupa in Crestone, Colo.

CARY JOBE—AURORA

Think Honda for the holidays.

Accord

Civic

Element

Fit

CR-V

Odyssey

Pilot

Ridgeline

During Happy Honda Days, you can get an extra sweet deal on that Honda car or truck you've been wishing for. Including the sleek and sporty Civic, the innovative five-passenger Ridgeline and spacious and responsive Odyssey. Put on your Santa hat and see your friendly neighborhood Honda dealer today.

Happy Honda Days

happ

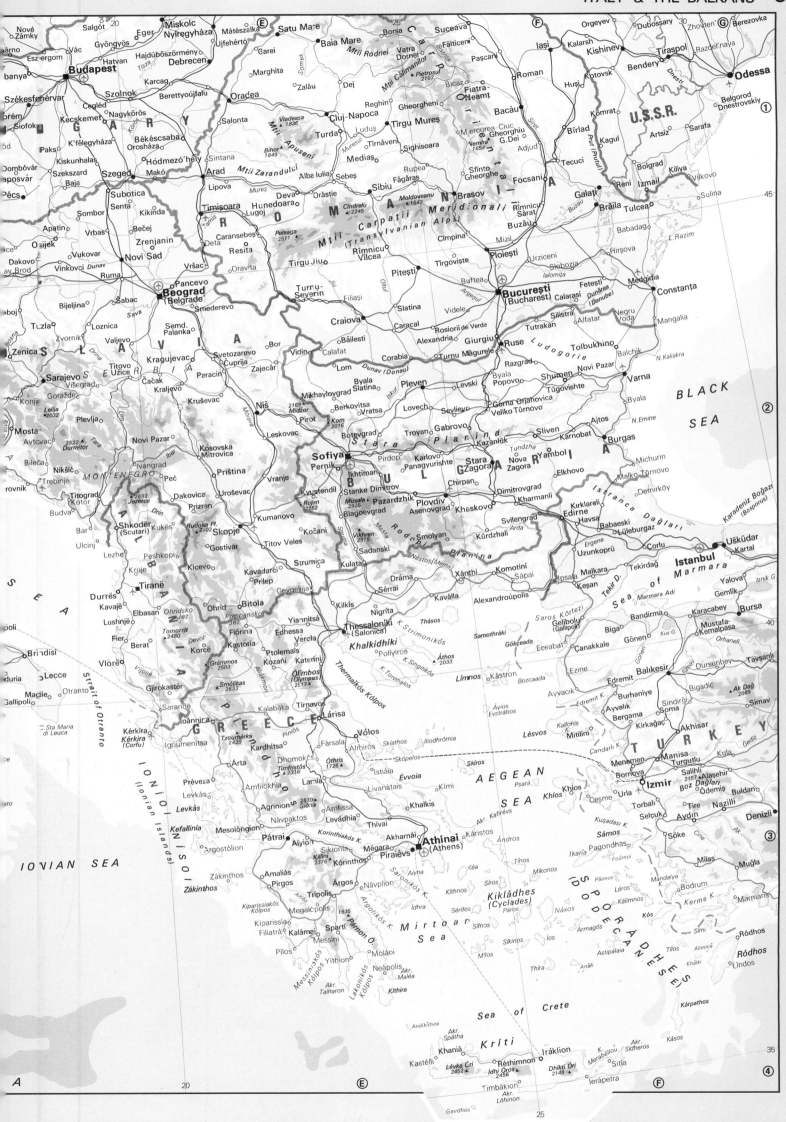

1:5M

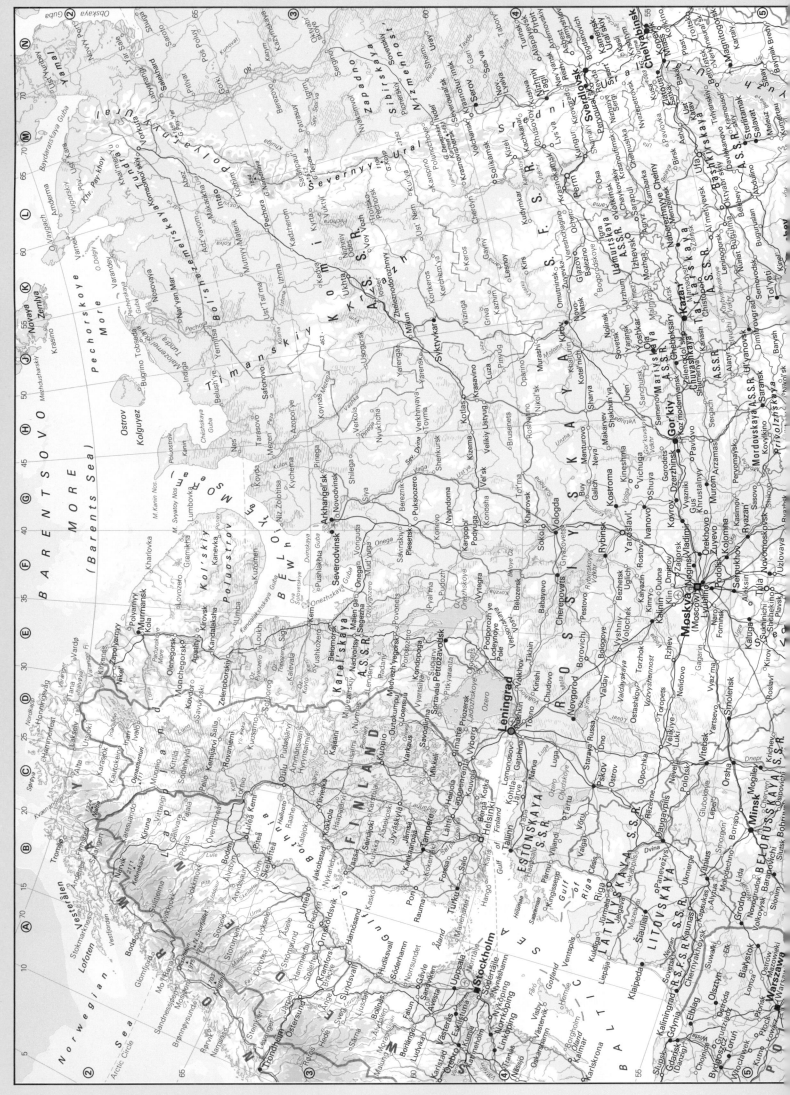

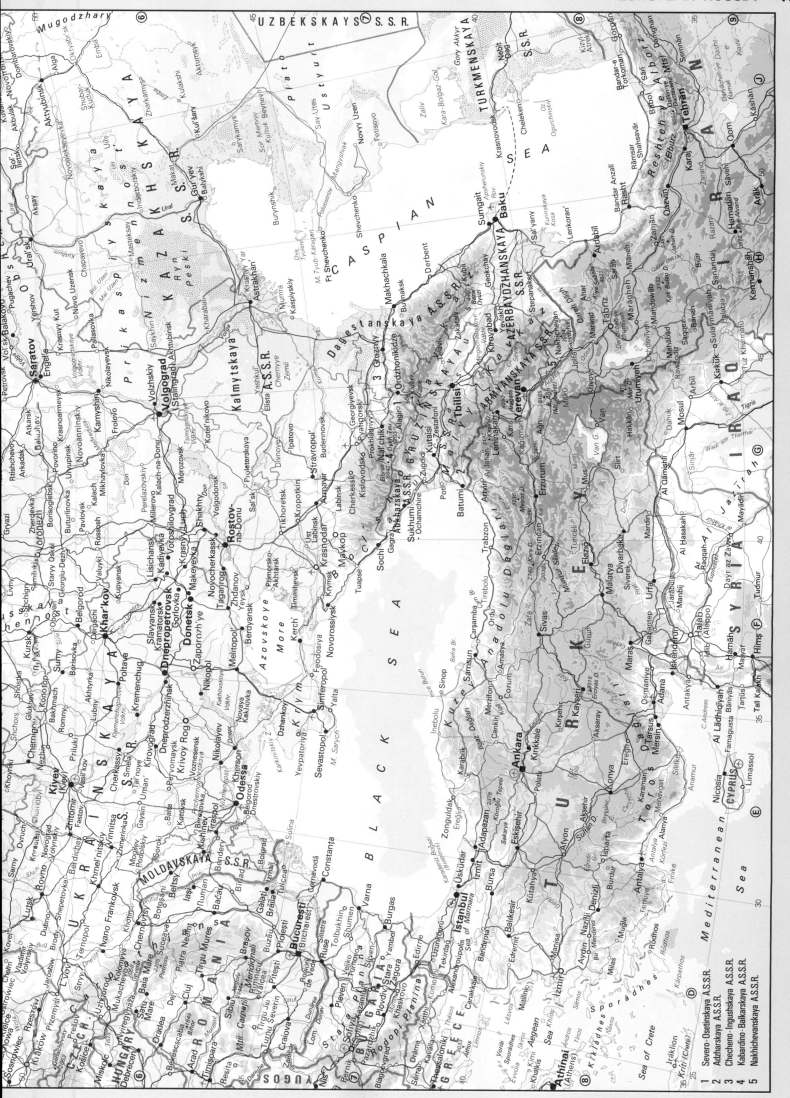

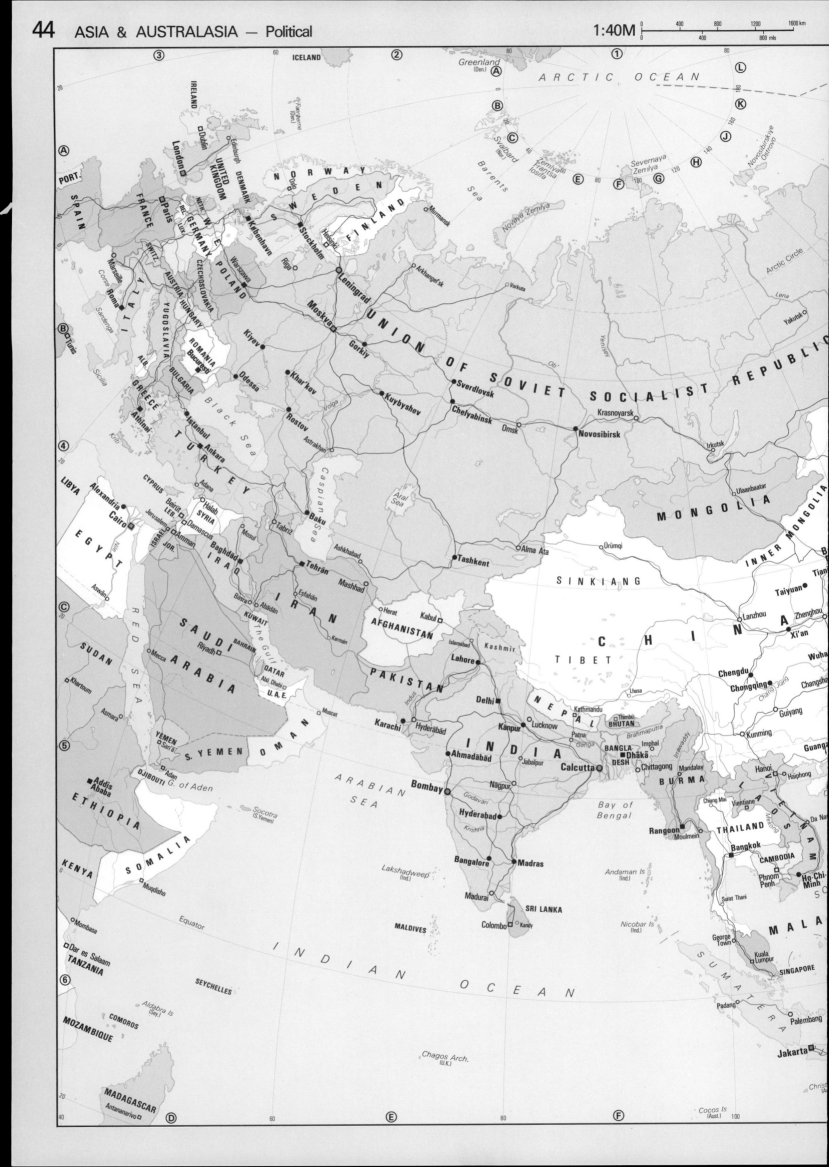

1:40M

ICELAND

③ ② ①

④ ⑤ ⑥

Ⓐ Ⓑ Ⓒ Ⓓ Ⓔ Ⓕ Ⓖ Ⓗ Ⓙ Ⓚ Ⓛ

ARCTIC OCEAN

Greenland
(Den.)

PORT.
SPAIN
FRANCE
IRELAND
Dublin
London
UNITED KINGDOM
Edinburgh
NETH.
BEL.
LUX.
GERMANY
W. E.
DENMARK
København
NORWAY
Oslo
SWEDEN
Stockholm
FINLAND
Helsinki
Riga
Murmansk
Barents Sea
Svalbard
(Nor.)
Zemlya
Franza
Iosifa
Severnaya
Zemlya
Novaya Zemlya
Arkhangel'sk
Vorkuta
Arctic Circle
Lena
Yakutsk
Novosibirskiye
Ostrova

SWITZ.
ITALY
Marseille
Corse
Roma
Sardegna
Tunis
AUSTRIA
CZECHOSLOVAKIA
POLAND
Warszawa
Leningrad
Moskva
Kiyev
Gorkiy
Sverdlovsk
UNION OF SOVIET SOCIALIST REPUBLIC
Ob'
Yenisey
Krasnoyarsk
Irkutsk

HUNGARY
YUGOSLAVIA
ROMANIA
Bucuresti
BULGARIA
ALB.
GREECE
Athinai
Kriti
Sicilia
Odessa
Khar'kov
Rostov
Volga
Kuybyshev
Astrakhan
Chelyabinsk
Omsk
Novosibirsk

TURKEY
İstanbul
Ankara
Black Sea
Adana
CYPRUS
Beirut
LEB.
Halab
SYRIA
Damascus
ISRAEL
JOR.
Amman
Baghdad
IRAQ
Mosul
Caspian Sea
Baku
Tabriz
Aral Sea
Ashkhabad
Tashkent
Alma Ata
Ürümqi
Ulaanbaatar
MONGOLIA
INNER MONGOLIA
Taiyuan

LIBYA
Alexandria
Cairo
EGYPT
Nile
Aswān
Jerusalem
KUWAIT
SAUDI ARABIA
Riyadh
BAHRAIN
QATAR
Abū Dhabi
U.A.E.
The Gulf
Basra
Abādān
IRAN
Eşfahān
Tehrān
Mashhad
Kermān
Herat
Kabul
AFGHANISTAN
Islamabad
Kashmir
Lahore
TIBET
Lhasa
CHINA
SINKIANG
Lanzhou
Zhengzhou
Xi'an
Wuhan
Chengdu
Chongqing
Chang Jiang
Changsha
Guiyang

SUDAN
Khartoum
RED SEA
Mecca
Asmara
YEMEN
San'ā
S. YEMEN
Aden
G. of Aden
DJIBOUTI
Addis Ababa
ETHIOPIA
SOMALIA
Socotra
(S.Yemen)
OMAN
Muscat
Karachi
Hyderābād
Indus
Delhi
NEPAL
Kathmandu
Kānpur
Lucknow
Patna
Ganga
BHUTAN
Thimbu
Brahmaputra
Imphal
BANGLA.
DESH
Dhāka
Chittagong
Mandalay
Kunming
Guang
INDIA
Ahmadābād
Jabalpur
Nāgpur
Bombay
Godavari
Hyderabad
Krishna
Bangalore
Madras
Irrawaddy
BURMA
Rangoon
Moulmein
Chiang Mai
THAILAND
Bangkok
LAOS
Vientiane
Mekong
Hanoi
Haiphong
Da Na

KENYA
Mombasa
SOMALIA
Muqdisho
Equator
ARABIAN SEA
Lakshadweep
(Ind.)
Calcutta
Bay of Bengal
Andaman Is
(Ind.)
Madurai
SRI LANKA
Colombo
Kandy
MALDIVES
Nicobar Is
(Ind.)
CAMBODIA
Phnom Penh
Họ-Chi-Minh
Surat Thani
George Town
Kuala Lumpur
SINGAPORE
MALA

Dar es Salaam
TANZANIA
SEYCHELLES
Aldabra Is
(Sey.)
COMOROS
MOZAMBIQUE
MADAGASCAR
Antananarivo
INDIAN OCEAN
Chagos Arch.
(U.K.)
SUMATERA
Padang
Palembang
Jakarta
Christ
Cocos Is
(Aust.)

20 60 80 80 160 140 120 100

③ ② ① 60 80

④ 60 80 100 120 140 160

⑤ ⑥ 20 0 20 40

Ⓐ Ⓑ Ⓒ Ⓓ 60 ⓔ 80 ⓕ 100

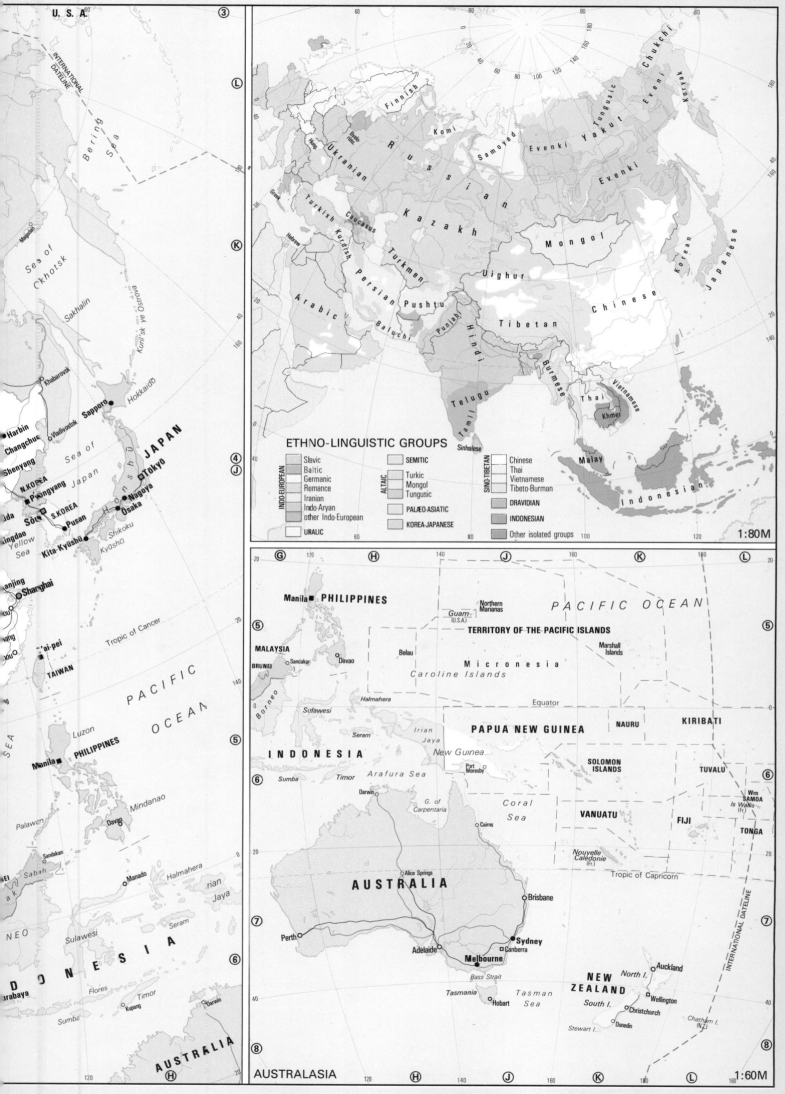

U.S.A.

③
Ⓛ

International Dateline

Bering Sea

Magadan

Ⓚ

Sea of Okhotsk

Sakhalin

Kuril'sk ye Ostrova

Khabarovsk

Harbin
Changchun
Shenyang
N.KOREA
Pyongyang
S.KOREA
Sŏul
Pusan

Vladivostok

Sapporo
Hokkaidō

Sea of Japan

Japan

Honshū

JAPAN
Tokyo
Nagoya
Osaka

④
Ⓙ

Qingdao
Yellow Sea

Kita-Kyūshū
Kyūshū
Shikoku

Nanjing
Shanghai

Tropic of Cancer

Ⓚ

T'ai-pei
TAIWAN

PACIFIC OCEAN

Luzon

PHILIPPINES
Manila

⑤

SEA

Mindanao
Davao

Palawan

Sabah
Sandakan

Manado
Halmahera

INDONESIA

Sulawesi

Surabaya
Flores
Timor
Kupang
Sumba

Irian Jaya

Seram

Darwin

AUSTRALIA

⑥

Ⓗ

ETHNO-LINGUISTIC GROUPS

Finnish
Komi
Byelo-Russ.
Ukranian
R u s s i a n
Samoyed
Evenki
Yakut
Tungusic
Eveni
Chukchi
Koryak

Greek
Turkish
Caucasus
Kurdish
Persian
Hebrew
Arabic
Baluchi
Turkmen
Pushtu
Punjabi
Hindi
Uighur
K a z a k h
Mongol
Tibetan
Chinese
Korean
Japanese

Telugu
Tamil
Sinhalese
Burmese
Thai
Khmer
Vietnamese

Malay
I n d o n e s i a

INDO-EUROPEAN
- Slavic
- Baltic
- Germanic
- Romance
- Iranian
- Indo-Aryan
- other Indo-European

URALIC

ALTAIC
- SEMITIC
- Turkic
- Mongol
- Tungusic

PALÆO-ASIATIC

KOREA-JAPANESE

SINO-TIBETAN
- Chinese
- Thai
- Vietnamese
- Tibeto-Burman

DRAVIDIAN

INDONESIAN

Other isolated groups

1:80M

Ⓖ Ⓗ Ⓙ Ⓚ Ⓛ

Manila ■ **PHILIPPINES**

Northern Marianas

PACIFIC OCEAN

Guam (U.S.A.)

TERRITORY OF THE PACIFIC ISLANDS

MALAYSIA
Sancakan
Davao

Belau

Marshall Islands

BRUNEI

Borneo

Halmahera

M i c r o n e s i a
Caroline Islands

Sulawesi

Equator

Seram

Irian Jaya

PAPUA NEW GUINEA

NAURU

KIRIBATI

INDONESIA
New Guinea

Sumba
Timor
Arafura Sea

SOLOMON ISLANDS

TUVALU

Port Moresby

Darwin
G. of Carpentaria

Coral Sea

VANUATU

FIJI

Wrn SAMOA
Is Wallis (Fr.)

TONGA

Nouvelle Calédonie (Fr.)

Tropic of Capricorn

Cairns

Alice Springs

AUSTRALIA

Brisbane

Perth

Adelaide
Melbourne
Canberra
Sydney

Bass Strait

Tasmania

NEW ZEALAND
North I.

Auckland
Wellington

Tasman Sea

Hobart

South I.

Christchurch

Dunedin

Stewart I.

Chatham I. (N.Z.)

International Dateline

AUSTRALASIA

120 Ⓗ 140 Ⓙ 160 Ⓚ 180 Ⓛ

1:60M

1:20M

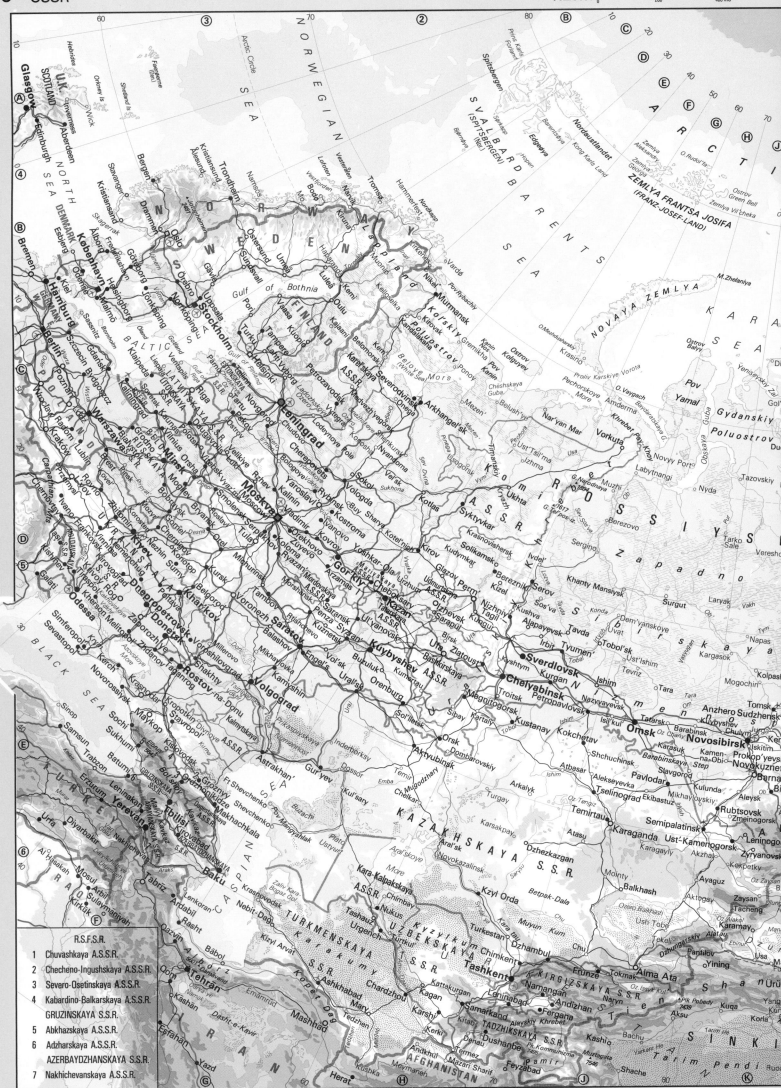

1:20M

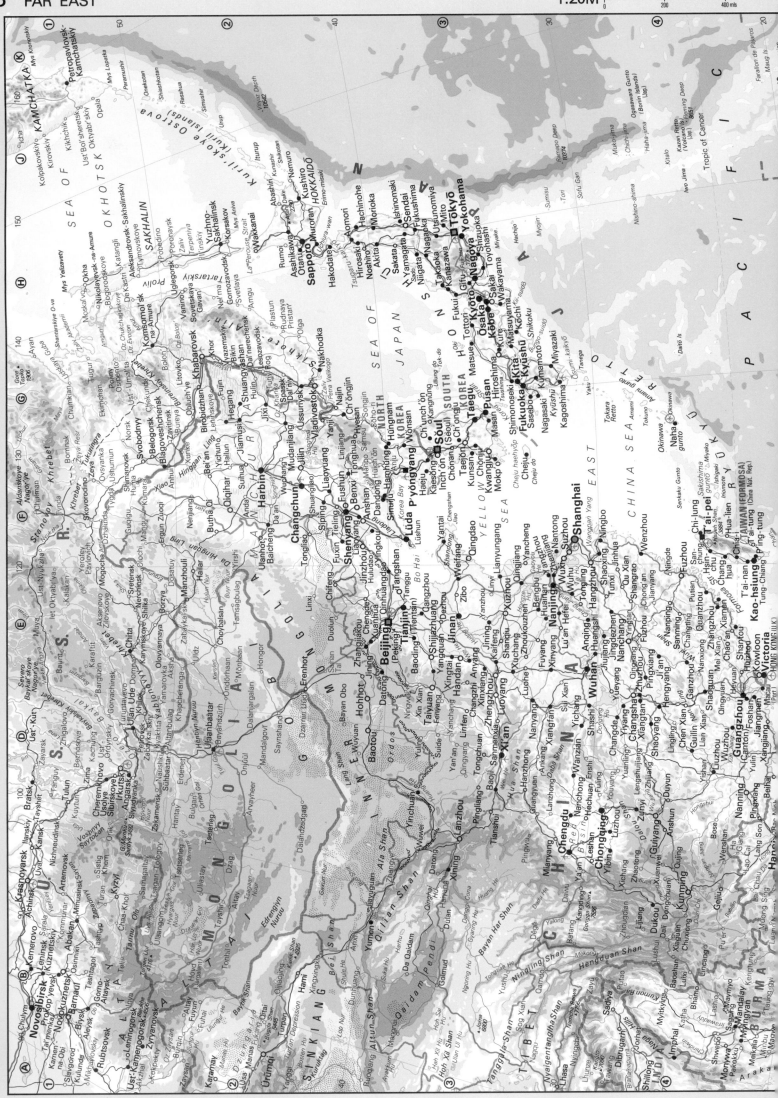

1:10M

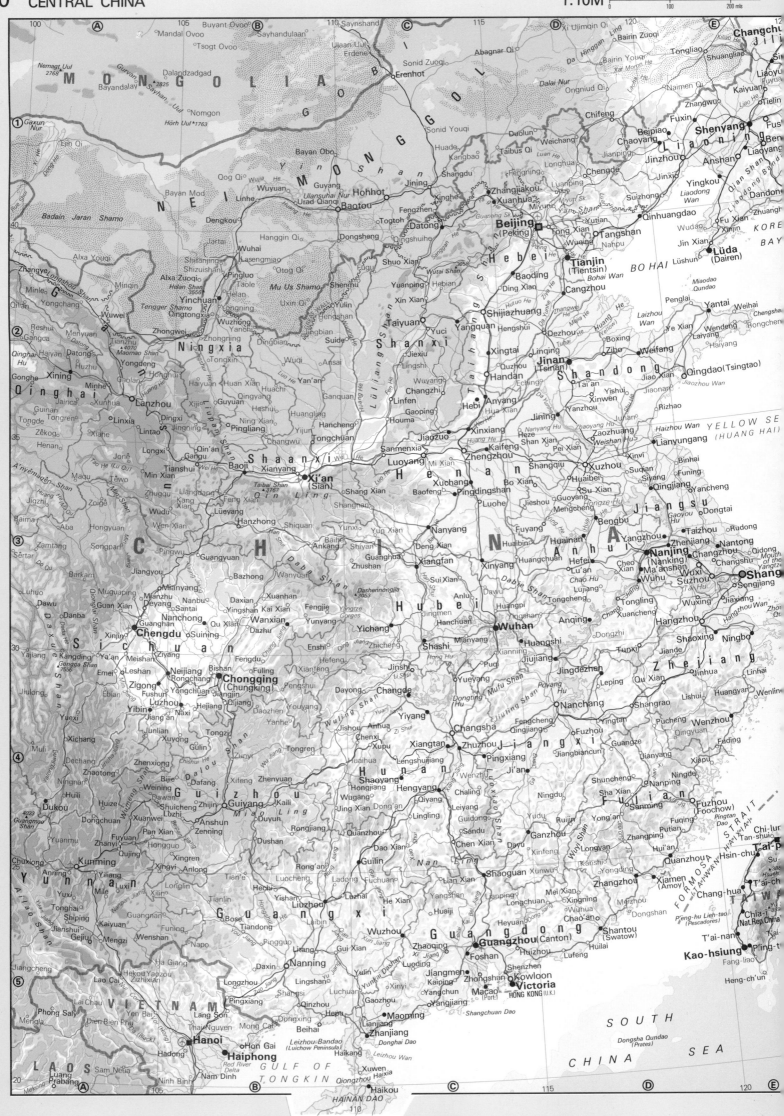

1:10M

1:5M

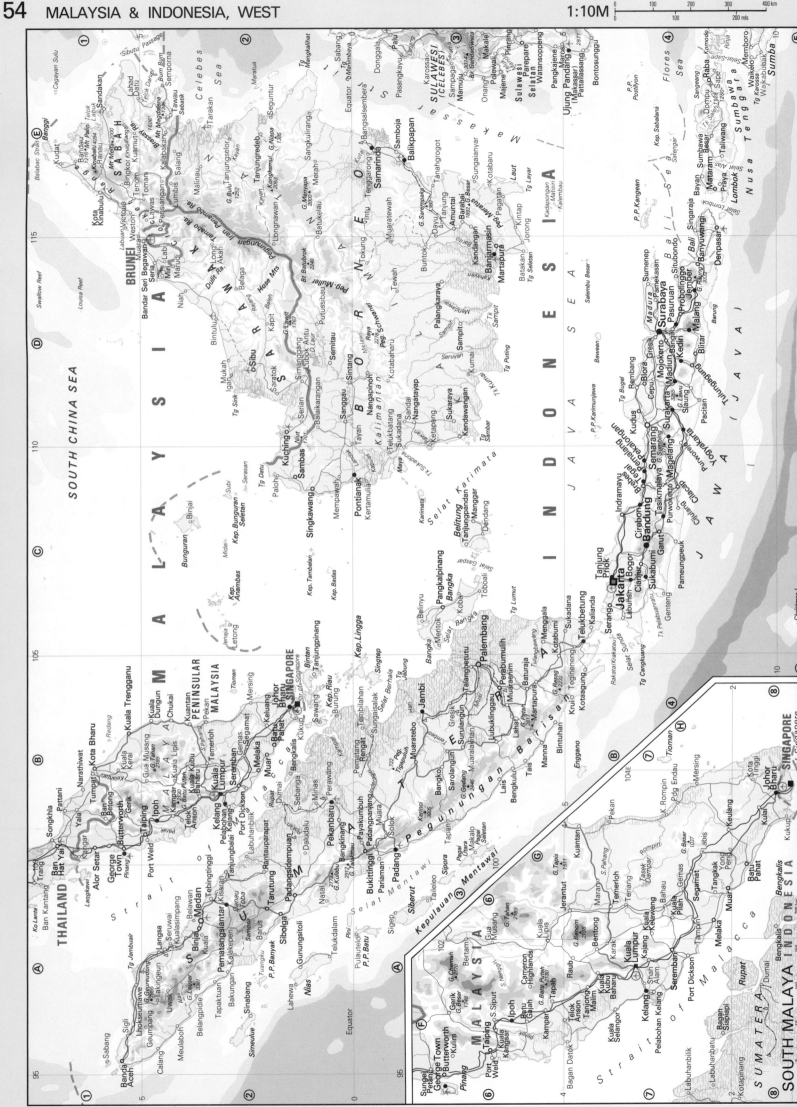

1:20M

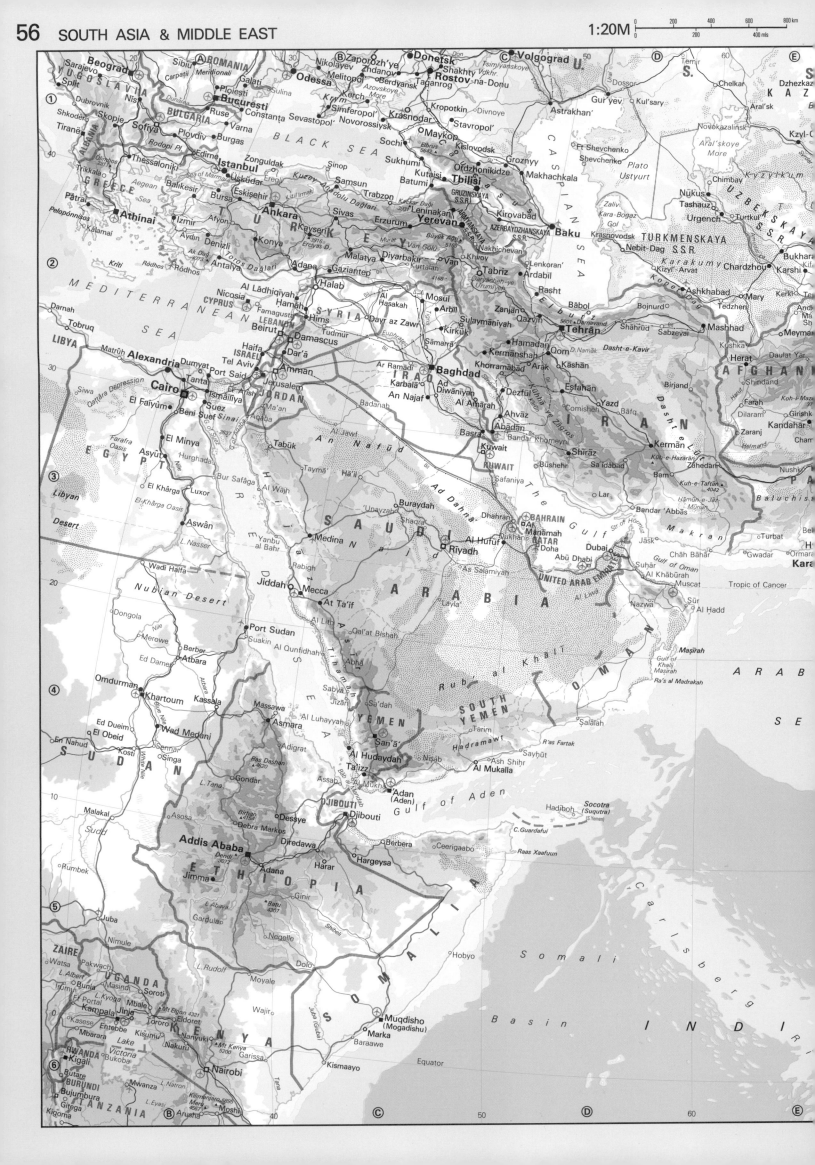

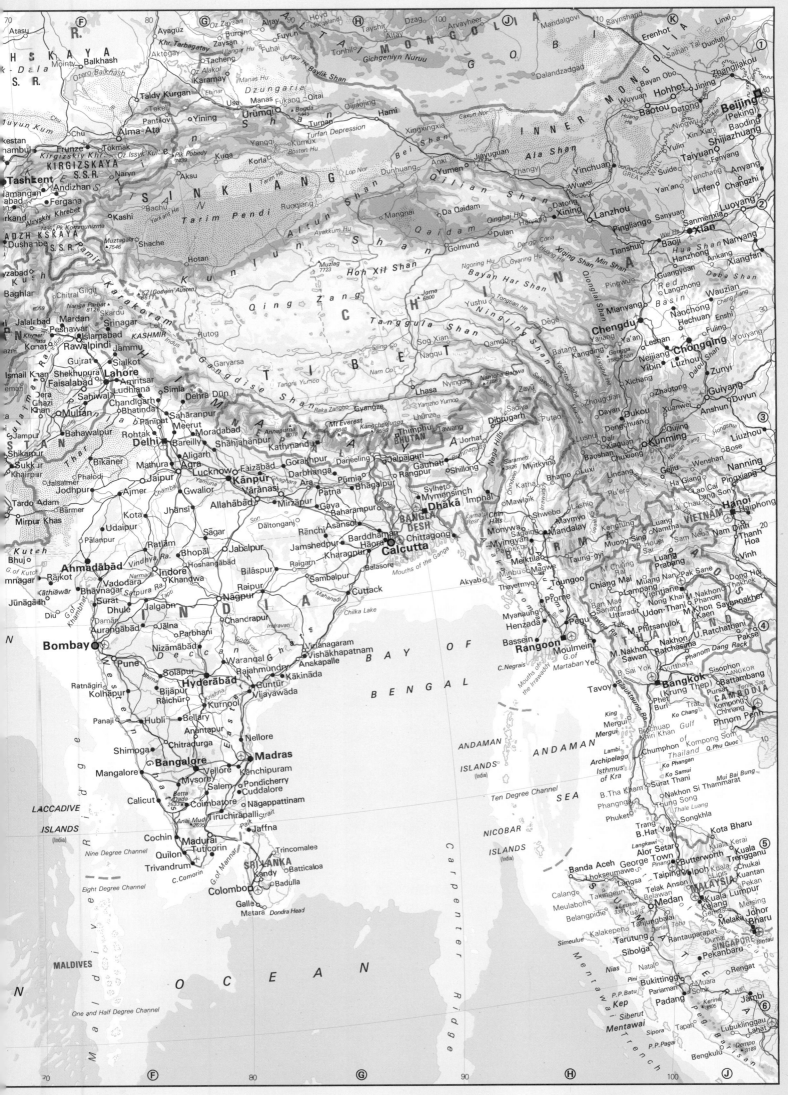

1:7.5M

1 7.5M

100   200   300 km
50   100   150 mls

1:7.5M

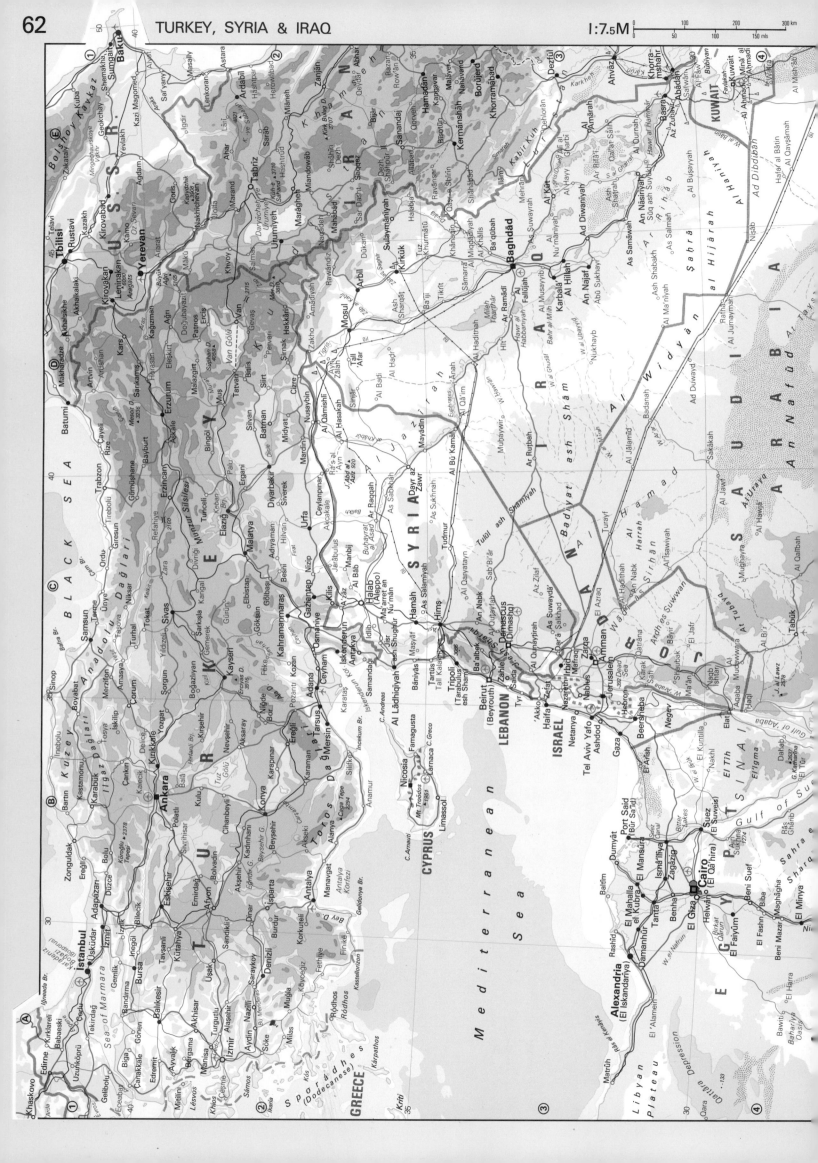

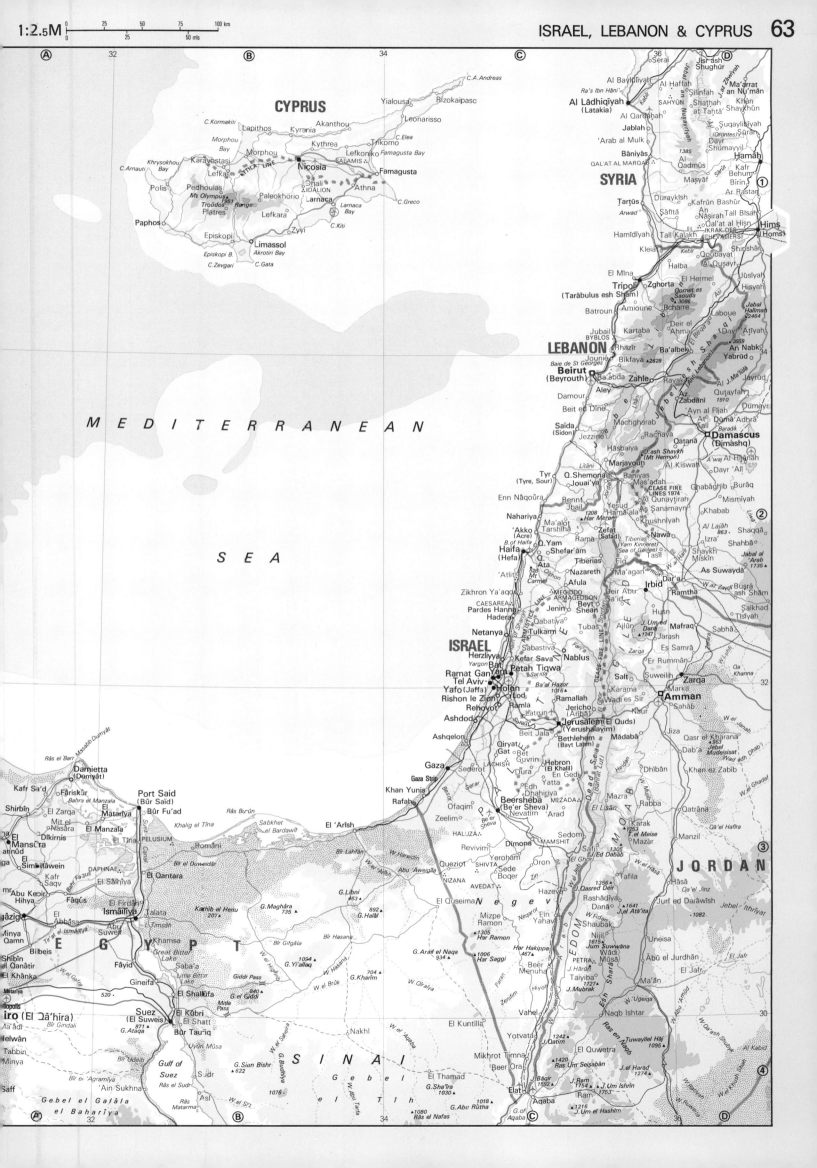

1:2.5M

CYPRUS

SYRIA

LEBANON

ISRAEL

M E D I T E R R A N E A N

S E A

Beirut
(Beyrouth)

Damascus
(Dimáshq)

Jerusalem (El Quds)
(Yerushalayim)

Amman

J O R D A N

E G Y P T

S I N A I

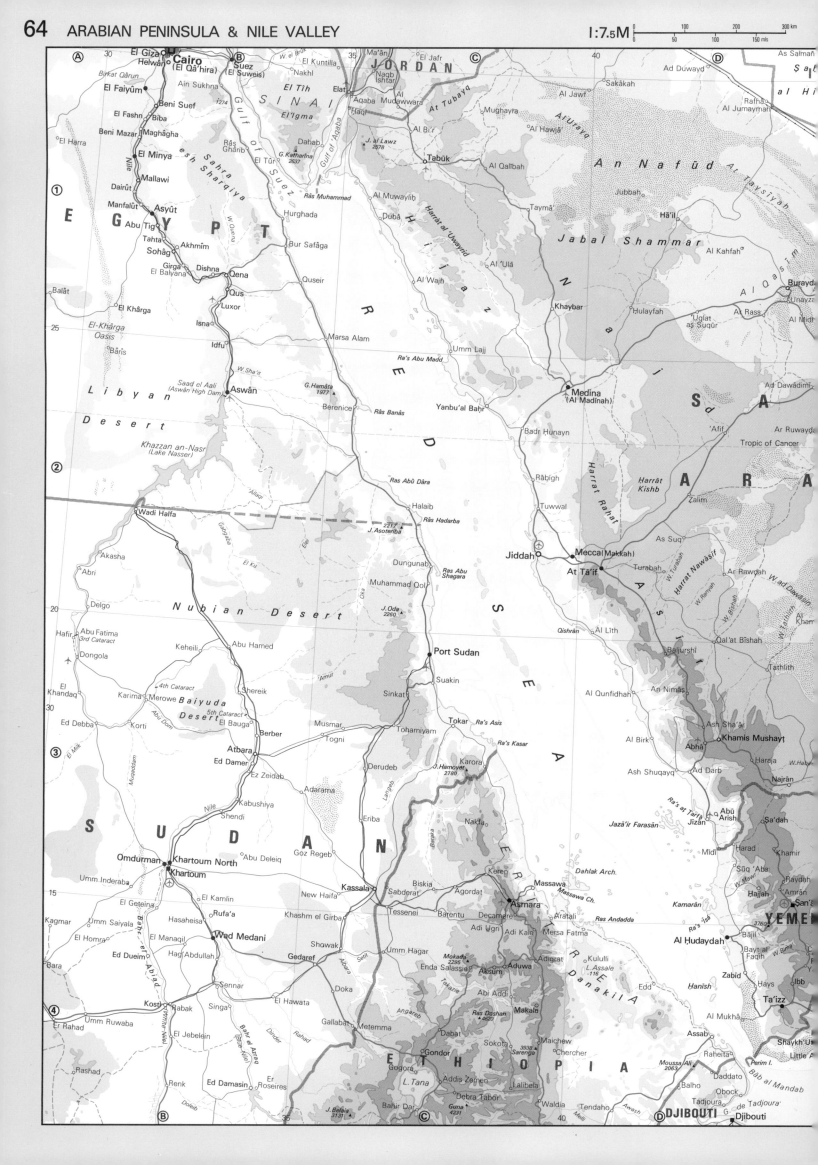

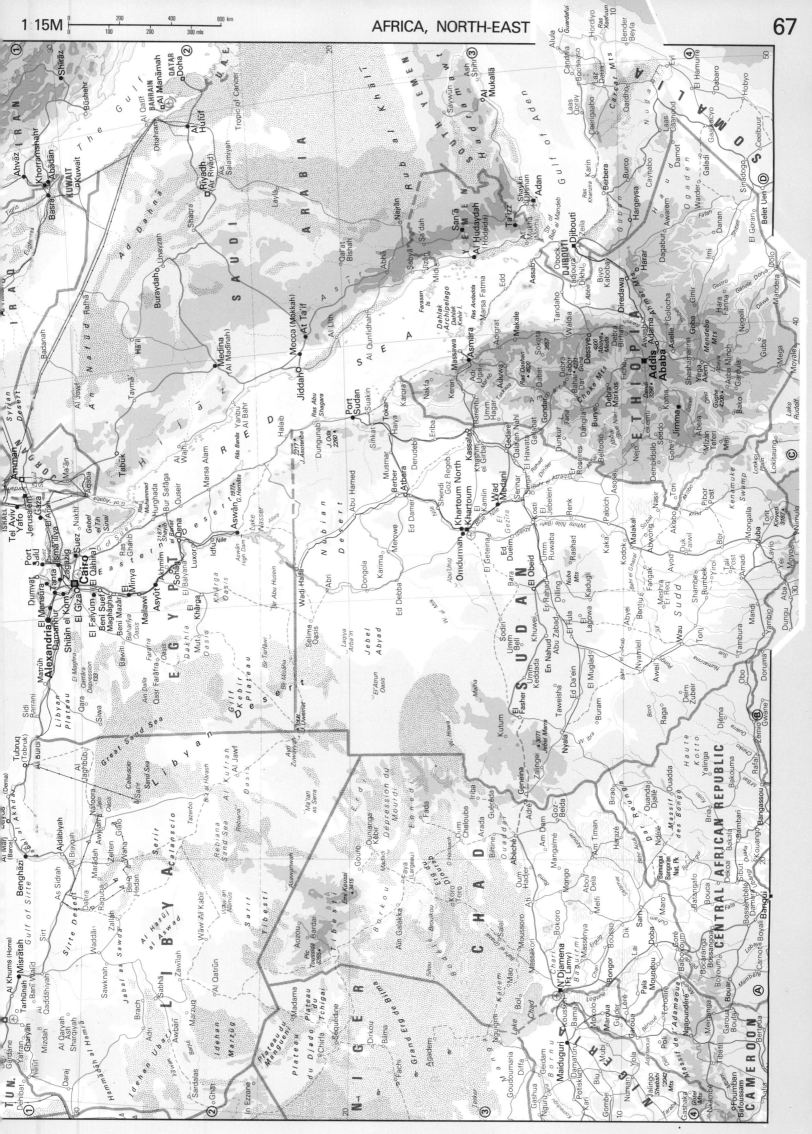

1:15M

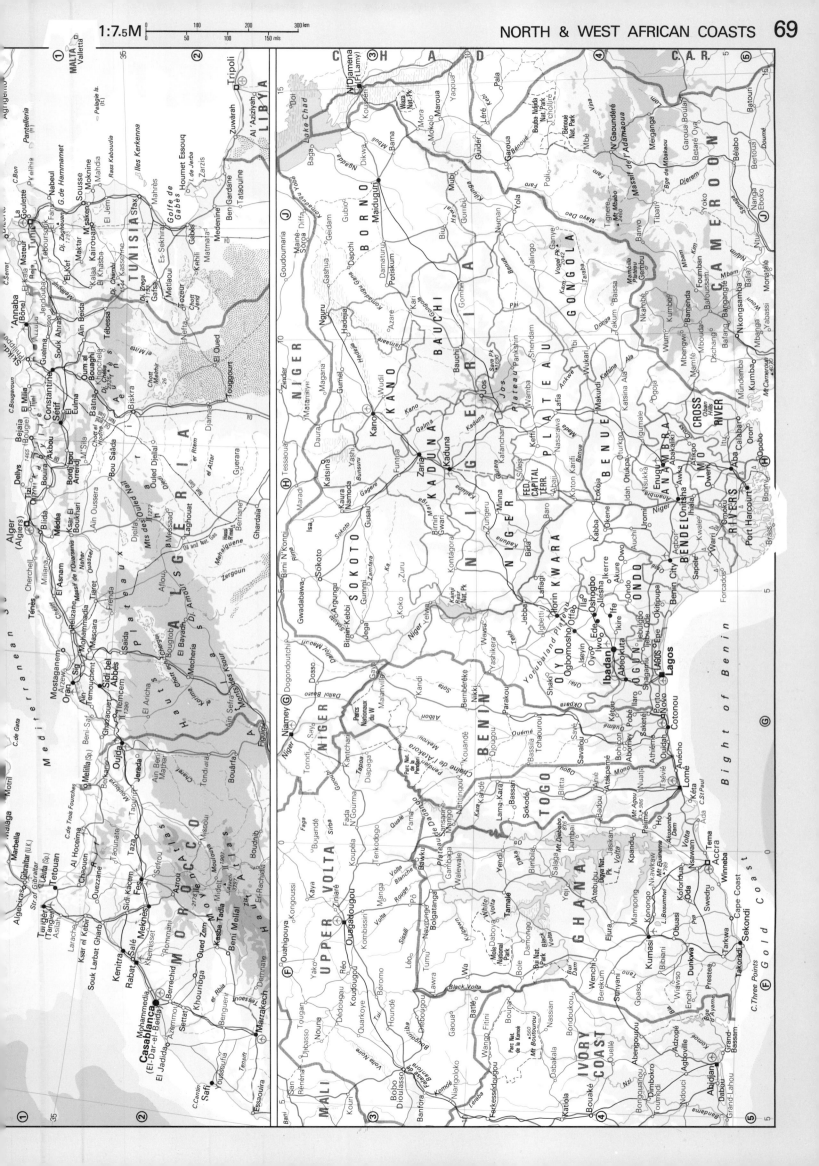

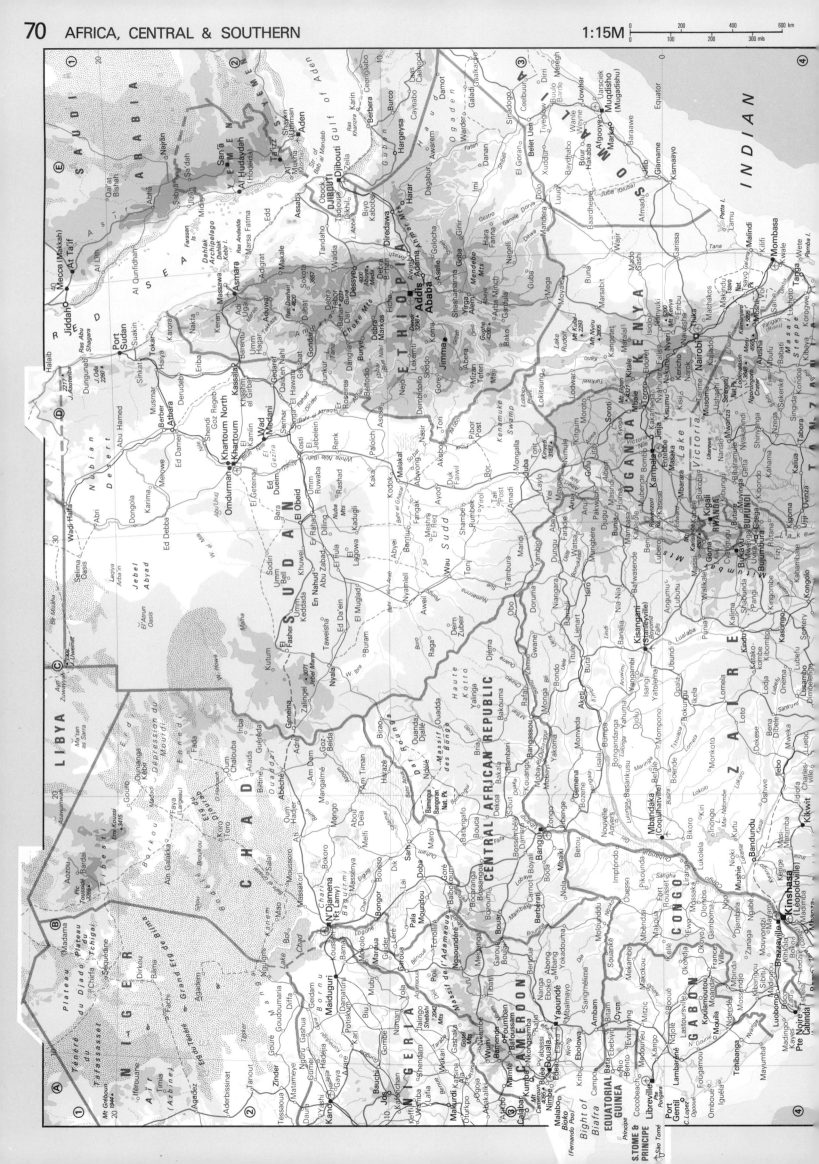

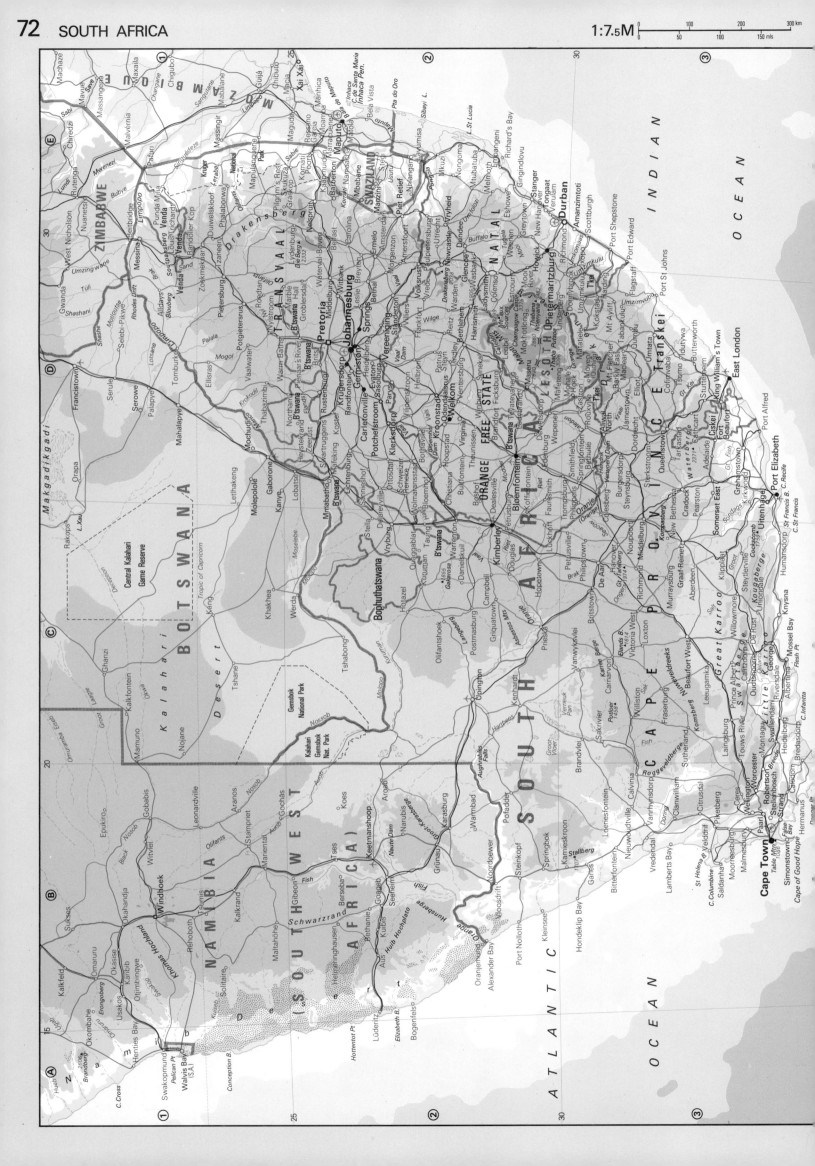

1:7.5M

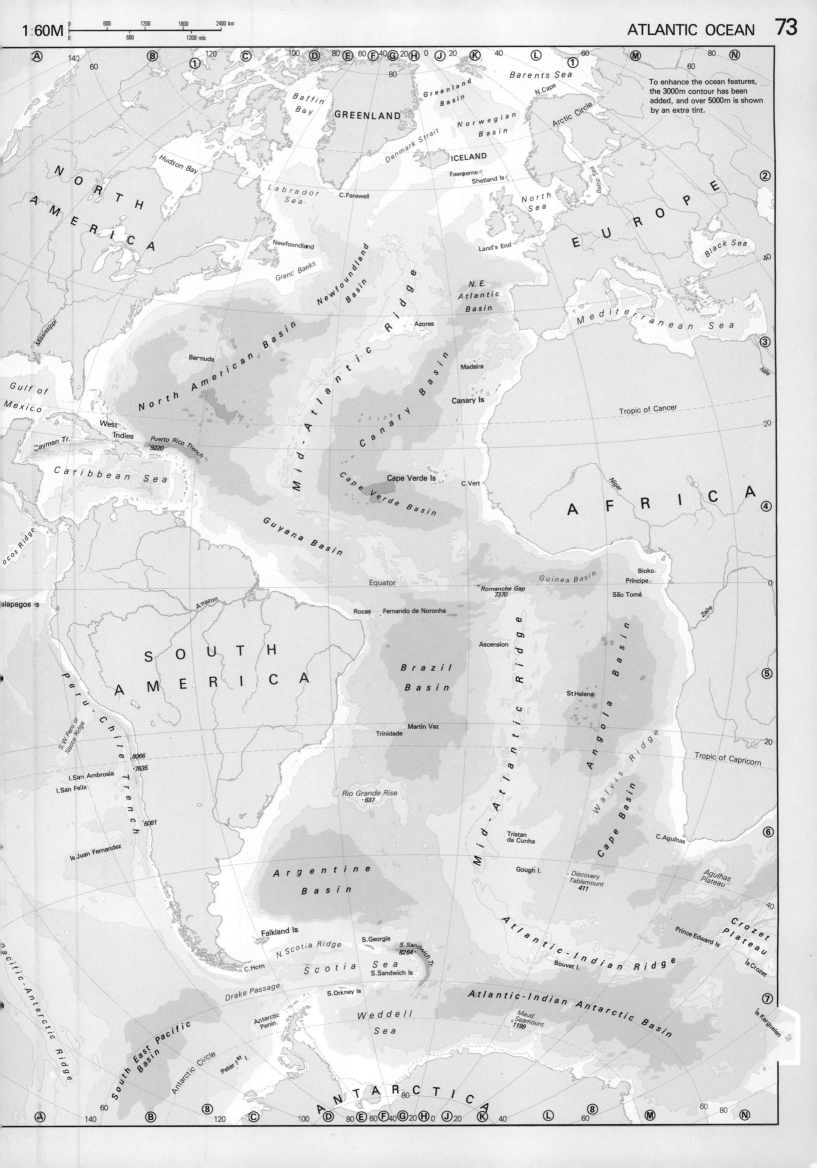

1:60M

600   1200   1800   2400 km

600   1200 mls

To enhance the ocean features,
the 3000m contour has been
added, and over 5000m is shown
by an extra tint.

NORTH AMERICA

GREENLAND

Baffin Bay

Hudson Bay

Labrador Sea

Newfoundland

Granc Banks

Baffin Basin

Greenland Basin

Denmark Strait

ICELAND

Norwegian Basin

Barents Sea

N.Cape

Arctic Circle

Faerøerne

Shetland Is

North Sea

Baltic Sea

EUROPE

Land's End

Black Sea

Mediterranean Sea

N.E. Atlantic Basin

Azores

Madeira

Newfoundland Basin

Mid-Atlantic Ridge

North American Basin

Bermuda

Canary Basin

Canary Is

Tropic of Cancer

Gulf of Mexico

West Indies

Cayman Tr.

Puerto Rico Trench 9220

Caribbean Sea

Cape Verde Basin

Cape Verde Is

C.Vert

Guyana Basin

AFRICA

Niger

ocos Ridge

Equator

Rocas

Fernando de Noronha

Romanche Gap 7370

Guinea Basin

Bioko

Príncipe

São Tomé

Zaïre

Amazon

SOUTH AMERICA

Brazil Basin

Ascension

St Helena

Angola Basin

alapagos s

Peru-Chile Trench

S.W.Paul or Nasca Ridge

I.San Ambrosia 8066

7635

I.San Felix

6081

Is Juan Fernandez

Martin Vaz

Trinidade

Rio Grande Rise 637

Mid-Atlantic Ridge

Tristan da Cunha

Walvis Ridge

Cape Basin

Tropic of Capricorn

C.Agulhas

Agulhas Plateau

Argentine Basin

Gough I.

Discovery Tablemount 411

Crozet Plateau

Prince Edward Is

Is Crozet

Falkland Is

S.Georgia

N.Scotia Ridge

S.Sandwich Tr. 8264

Atlantic-Indian Ridge

Bouvet I.

C.Horn

Scotia Sea

S.Sandwich Is

Atlantic-Indian Antarctic Basin

Maud Seamount 1199

Is Kerguelen

Drake Passage

S.Orkney Is

Weddell Sea

acific-Antarctic Ridge

South East Pacific Basin

Antarctic Circle

Peter Ist I.

Antarctic Penin.

ANTARCTICA

1:60M

0 600 1200 1800 2400 km
0 600 1200 mls

40 20 Ⓐ 0 Ⓑ 20 Ⓒ 40 Ⓓ 60 Ⓔ 80 Ⓕ 100 Ⓖ 120 Ⓗ 140 Ⓙ

Barents Sea

① Arctic Circle

*Norwegian
Basin*

ICELAND

60

*North
Sea* *Sea
of
Okhotsk*

② Sakhalin

E U R O P E A S I A

Black Sea *Caspian Sea* *Aral Sea* *Sea
of
Japan* *Vityaz D*
10542

40

③ *Mediterranean
Sea* *Huang He*

Chang Jiang

J A P A N

*Red
Sea* *The Gulf* *Ganga* TAIWAN

Arabian Sea *Bay
of
Bengal* Hainan

20 Raas Caseyr *Arabian
Basin* *Andaman Is* *Mekong* PHILIPPINES *C.Johnson
Depth
10497* Mariana Is
Guam
11022
*Challenger
Depth*

A F R I C A MALDIVES SRI
LANKA
(CEYLON) Nicobar
Is *South China Sea* Belau Caroline Is

④ *Carlsberg Ridge* *Somali
Basin* SEYCHELLES *Maldives Ridge* *Celebes
Sea* *6920*

0 *Mascarene Ridge* *Chagos Arch.* *Sumatra* Borneo Celebes

COMOROS *Mid* *Ninety-East Ridge* I N D O N E S I A New
Guinea *Planet Deep
9140*

⑤ *Mozambique Channel* *Mid-Indian Ridge* *Indian
Basin* Java *Java Trench* *7450* *Coral Sea
Basin*

MADAGASCAR *Mid-Indian Ridge* *West
Australian
Basin* Christmas I. Timor *Arafura Sea*

20 MAURITIUS *Cocos Is* *1737*

Réunion *1924*

*Madagascar
Basin* I N D I A N O C E A N Tropic of Capricorn

C.Agulhas *S.Madagascar Ridge* *W. Australian Ridge* AUSTRALIA

⑥ *Natal Basin* *2067* *7102* *South
Australia
Basin*

*Agulhas
Plateau* *South West Indian Ridge* *1198* *I.Amsterdam
I.St Paul* Tasmania

40

*Agulhas
Basin* *Crozet
Basin* *Indian-Antarctic Ridge*

⑦ Pr.Edward Is *Îs Crozet* *Îs Kerguelen* *1922*

Atlantic-Indian Ridge *Kerguelen Ridge* *Heard I.* Macquar

*Banzare Seamount
186* *Indian-Antarctic Basin*

60 *Atlantic-Indian Antarctic Basin*

⑧ A N T A R C T I C A

40 20 Ⓐ 0 Ⓑ 20 Ⓒ 40 Ⓓ 60 Ⓔ 80 Ⓕ 100 Ⓖ 120 Ⓗ 140 Ⓙ

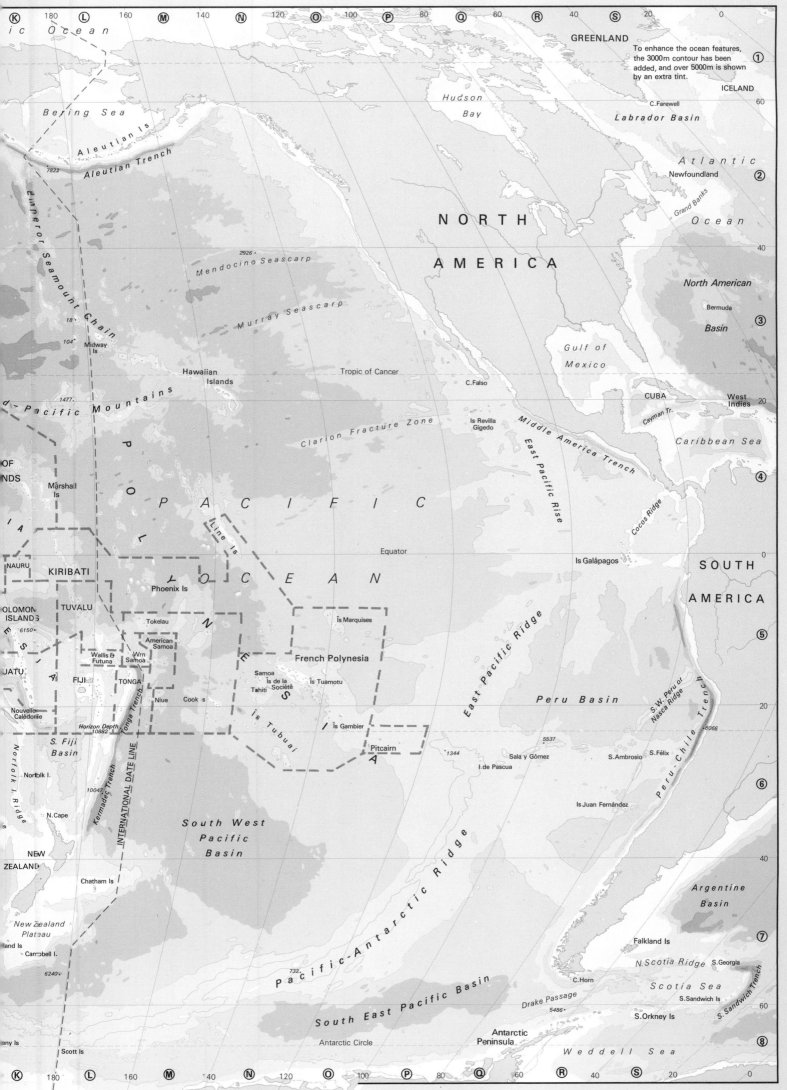

ic Ocean

(K) 180 (L) 160 (M) 140 (N) 120 (O) 100 (P) 80 (Q) 60 (R) 40 (S) 20 0

GREENLAND

To enhance the ocean features,
the 3000m contour has been
added, and over 5000m is shown
by an extra tint.

ICELAND

①

Bering Sea

Hudson
Bay

C.Farewell

60

Aleutian Is

7822

Aleutian Trench

Labrador Basin

Atlantic

Newfoundland

②

Emperor Seamount Chain

2926

Mendocino Seascarp

NORTH

AMERICA

Grand Banks

Ocean

North American

40

Murray Seascarp

18

104

Midway
Is

d-Pacific Mountains

1477

Hawaiian
Islands

Tropic of Cancer

C.Falso

Gulf of
Mexico

Bermuda

Basin

③

CUBA

West
Indies

20

Cayman Tr.

P

O

Clarion Fracture Zone

Is Revilla
Gigedo

Middle America Trench

East Pacific Rise

Caribbean Sea

④

NAURU

OF
NDS

Marshall
Is

L

PACIFIC

Equator

Is Galápagos

Cocos Ridge

0

SOUTH

AMERICA

KIRIBATI

Y

OCEAN

Line Is

Phoenix Is

SOLOMON
ISLANDS

TUVALU

E 6150

Tokelau

N

Îs Marquises

East Pacific Ridge

⑤

ESIA

Wallis &
Futuna

American
Samoa

E

French Polynesia

Peru Basin

S.W. Peru or
Nasca Ridge

8066

UATU

Wrn
Samoa

S

Samoa
Îs de la
Société

Îs Tuamotu

Peru-Chile Trench

FIJI

TONGA

Tahiti

Nouvelle
Calédonie

Niue

Cook s

1344

Sala y Gómez

S.Ambrosio

S.Félix

Îs Tubuai

Îs Gambier

20

Horizon Depth
10882

I. de Pascua

S. Fiji
Basin

Pitcairn

5537

Is Juan Fernández

⑥

Norfolk
I. Ridge

Norfolk I.

10047

INTERNATIONAL DATE LINE

Kermadec Trench

Tonga Trench

A

N.Cape

South West
Pacific
Basin

NEW
ZEALAND

40

Chatham Is

Argentine

Basin

⑦

New Zealand
Plateau

land Is

Campbell I.

6240

Pacific-Antarctic Ridge

732

South East Pacific Basin

Falkland Is

N.Scotia Ridge

S.Georgia

C.Horn

Scotia Sea

S.Sandwich Is

S.Sandwich Trench

eny Is

Scott Is

Drake Passage

5486

S.Orkney Is

60

Antarctic
Peninsula

Antarctic Circle

Weddell Sea

⑧

(K) 180 (L) 160 (M) 40 (N) 120 (O) 100 (P) 80 (Q) 60 (R) 40 (S) 20 0

0   200   400   600   800 km
0   200   400 mls

BORNEO

Tajungselor
Kavali
Tanjungredeb
Kelolokan
Samarinda
Balikpapan
Tanjung
Banjarmasin
Kintap
Tg Selatan
Laut

Manado
Minahassa Peninsula
Tolitoli
Gorontalo
Belang
Donggala
Luwuk
Palu
Poso
Toboli
Teluk Tomini
Kep. Togian
SULAWESI (CELEBES)
Palopo
Kendari
Majene
Parepare
Watampone
Butung
Bone
Mamuju
Kep. Sula
Benthain
Kabaena
Baubau
Kabia
Kep. Tukangbesi
Ujung Pandang (Makassar)

Morotai
Tubelo
Ternate
Weda
Teluk Weda
Halmahera
Waigeo
Selat Dampier
Salawatti
Misool
Obi
Ceram
Piru
Bula
Fakfak
Teluk Berau
Namlea
Buru
Ambon
Seram Sea
Kep. Banda
Kep. Kai
Dobo
Kep. Aru

MOLUCCAS
I N D O N E S I A

Kep. Asia
Kep. Ayu
P.P. Mapia

Manokwari
Biak
Numfoor
Yapen
Cendrawasih
Teluk Qendrawasih
Sarmi
IRIAN JAYA
Kaimana
Kokonau
Adi
Pegunungan Maoke
Pk. Jaya 5029
Tanahmerah
Digul
Dolak
Merauke
Tg Vals
Saibai I.

Ninigo Is
Hermit Is
Admiralty Is
Mussau
Saint Matthias Group
New Hanover
Manus
Kavieng
Schouten Is
Bismarck Archipelago
Bismarck Sea
Jayapura
Aitape
Wewak
Manam
Talasea
Sepik
Central Ra.
NEW GUINEA
PAPUA NEW GUINEA
Madang
Long
Umboi
Goroka
Mt Hagen
Mendio
Mt Wilhelm 4508
Bulolo
Lae
Morobe
New
Kikon
Gulf of Papua
Mt St Mary
Popondetta
Rokoda
Tobriand Is
D Entreca
Kupiano
Port Moresby
Kerema
Samarai
Owen Stanley Ra.
Pr. of Wales I.
Somerset
Torres Strait
C. York
C. Grenville

A r a f u r a   S e a

Morning I.
Van Diemen G.
Croker I.
Cobourg Pen.
Melville I.
Bathurst I.
Darwin
Clarence Str.
Rum Jungle
Adelaide River
Arnham Land
Wessel Is
C. Arnhem
Nhulunbuy
Groote Eylandt
Gulf of Carpentaria
Weipa
Cape York
Iron Range
Coen
Cape York Peninsula
Princess Charlotte B.
Laura
Cooktown
Mitchell River
Willis Is
Mitchell
G r e a t

T i m o r   S e a
Cartier I.
C.Londonderry
Jospen
Bonaparte Gulf
Pago Mission
Wyndham
Scott Reef
King Sound
Collier B.
C. Léveque
J a v a   T r e n c h
I N D I A N   O C E A N
Bali
Mataram
Raba
Ruteng
Ende
Lomblen
Flores
Sumbawa
Waingapu
Sumba
Sawu
Roti
Timor
Dili
Kupang
Kep. Leti
Alor
Kep. Sermata
Kep. Babar
Kep. Tanimbar
Wetar
Romang
Kep. Damar
Kep. Barat Daya
P.P. Macan
B a n d a   S e a
1440
Denpasar
Lombok
Membero
P.P. Kangean

NORTHERN TERRITORY
Adelaide River
Burrundie
Pine Creek
Katherine
Daly
Victoria
Birdum
Daly Waters
Newcastle Waters
Wave Hill
Powell Creek
Tennant Creek
Barrow Creek
Alice Springs
Mt Ziel 1510
Macdonnell Ranges
Musgrave Ra.
Mt Woodroffe 1440
Petermann Ra.
Mt Aloysius 987
Tomkinson Ra.
Roper
Limmen Bight
Sir Edward Pellew Group
Borroloola
Mornington
Wellesley Is
Burketown
Normanton
Croydon
Forsayth
Gilbert
Camooweal
Cloncurry
Mount Isa
Dajarra
Selwyn
Hughenden
Richmond
Winton
QUEENSLAND
Longreach
Barcaldine
Blackall
Clermont
Emerald
Rockhampton
Mount Morgan
Barcoo
Thomson
Diamantina
Windorah
Charleville
Quilpie
Roma
Miles
Toowoo
St George
Cunnamulla
Goond

Mt Bartle Frere 1612
Cairns
Innisfail
Ingham
Palm Is
Townsville
Charters Towers
Bowen
Proserpine
Collinsville
Mackay
Northum
Sarina
Maribo
Ravenshoe
Leichhardt
Flinders
Gregory Ra.
Great Dividing

WESTERN AUSTRALIA
Shay Gap
De Grey
Marble Bar
Nullagine
Wittenoom
Paraburdoo
Newman
Hamersley Ra.
Mt Bruce 1226
Ashburton
L. Disappointment
Gibson Desert
L. Mackay
Great Sandy Desert
Lagrange
Eighty Mile Beach
Port Hedland
Dampier
Roebourne
Fortescue
Onslow
Monte Bello Is
Barrow I.
North West C.
Carnarvon
Gascoyne
Barlee Ra.
Mt Augustus 1106
L.McLeod
Lyons
Shark B.
Dirk Hartog I.
Murchison
Meekatharra
Wiluna
L. Carnegie
L. Wells
Great Victoria Desert
Cue
Sandstone
Mt Magnet
Leonora
L. Barlee
L. Moore
Northampton
Mullewa
Geraldton
Dongara
Houtman Abrolhos
Moora
Bencubbin
Bullfinch
Merredin
Southern Cross
Kalgoorlie
Coolgardie
Norseman
Esperance
C. Pasley
Arch. of the Recherche
Norlham
Goomalling
Narrogin
Wagin
Katanning
Bunbury
Collie
Pinjarra
Busselton
Augusta
C. Naturaliste
C. Leeuwin
Manjimup
Bluff Knoll 1710
Kojonup
Albany
Perth
Fremantle
Rawlinna
Forrest
Nullarbor Plain
Eyre
Cook

SOUTH AUSTRALIA
Coober Pedy
Oodnadatta
L. Eyre
Lake Eyre Basin
Birdsville
Marree
Leigh Ck
L. Frome
Ooldea
Tarcoola
Woomera
L. Gairdner
Penong
Ceduna
Port Lincoln
Eyre Pen.
Sawler Ranges
Iron Knob
Whyalla
Port Augusta
Port Pirie
Peterborough
Quorn
St Mary Pk 1189
Marla Ra.
Simpson Desert
Eyre
Georgina
Gey Range
Milparinka
Tibooburra
NEW SOUTH WALES
Bourke
Walgett
Cobar
Wilcannia
Broken Hill
Menindee
Ivanhoe
Hay
Balranald
Griffith
Narrabri
Moree
Tamworth
Armid
Narromine
Dubbo
Orange
Bathurst
Lithgow
Sydney
Wollongong
Cootamundra
Wagga Wagga
Albury
Deniliquin
Echuca
Shepparton
Benalla
Wangaratta
Mt Kosciusko 2290
Canberra A.C.T.

Investigator Str.
Kangaroo I.
Victor Harbour
Murray Bridge
Elizabeth
Adelaide
Spencer Gulf
Gulf St Vincent
Renmark
Mildura
Swan Hill
Murray

VICTORIA
Kingston
Naracoorte
Hamilton
Mount Gambier
Portland
Port Fairy
Warrnambool
Ararat
Ballarat
Bendigo
Horsham
Colac
Geelong
Melbourne
Morwell
Sale
Bairnsdale
Orbost
Wonthaggi
Wilson's Prom.
Australian Alps
Bombala

Great Australian Bight
Flinders I.

B a s s   S t r a i t
King I.
Furneaux Group
Flinders
C. Barren
TASMANIA
C.Grim
Smithton
Burnie
Devonport
Launceston
St Mary's
Queenstown
Mt Ossa 1617
Hobart
Geeveston
South West C.
South East C.

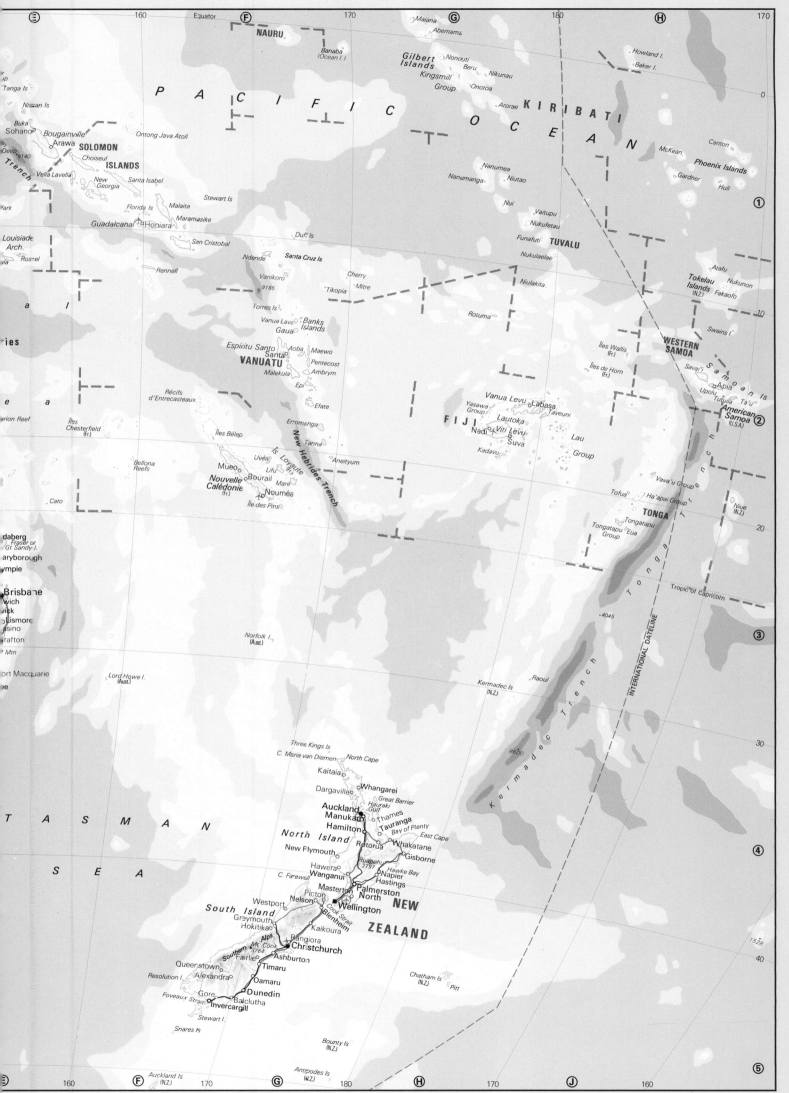

P A C I F I C   O C E A N

NAURU

Banaba
(Ocean I.)

Maiana
Abemama

Gilbert
Islands
Kingsmill
Group

Nonouti
Beru
Nikunau
Onotoa

Howland I.
Baker I.

Canton

Arorae

K I R I B A T I

McKean
Phoenix Islands
Gardner
Hull

Tanga Is

Nissan Is

Buka
Sohano
Deep 9140
Bougainville
Arawa
Choiseul
SOLOMON
ISLANDS
Vella Lavella
New
Georgia
Santa Isabel

Ontong Java Atoll

Nanumea
Niutao

Nanumanga

Nui

Vaitupu
Nukufetau

Funafuti   TUVALU

Atafu   Nukunon
Tokelau
Islands
(N.Z.)   Fakaofo

Swains I.

Trench

Louisiade
Arch.
Ros-el

Guadalcanal   Honiara

Sen Cristobal

Florida Is
Malaita
Maramasike

Stewart Is

Rennell

Duff Is

Santa Cruz Is

Ndende

Nukulaelae

Niulakita

Rotuma

WESTERN
SAMOA

Îles Wallis
(Fr.)

Îles de Horn
(Fr.)

Savai'i

Apia
Upolu   Ta'u
Tutuila
American
Samoa
(U.S.A.)

Marion Reef

Îles Chesterfield
(Fr.)

Bellona
Reefs

Cato

Vanikoro
9185

Cherry
Tikopia   Mitre

Torres Is

Vanua Lava
Gaua

Banks
Islands

Espiritu Santo
Santa
Maewo
Aoba
VANUATU
Malekula
Ambrym
Pentecost
Epi
Efate

Eromanga

Tanna

Aneityum

Îles Bélep

Récifs
d'Entrecasteaux

Mueo
Nouvelle
Calédonie
(Fr.)

Uvéa
Bourail
Lifu
Maré

Nouméa
Île des Pins

Is Loyauté

New Hebrides Trench

Vanua Levu   Labasa
Yasawa
Group
Lautoka
Taveuni

FIJI
Nadi   Viti Levu
Suva
Kadavu

Lau
Group

Vava'u Group

Tofua
Ha'apai Group

TONGA
Tongatapu
Tongatapu
Group   'Eua

Niue
(N.Z.)

Tonga Trench

daberg
Fraser or
Gt Sandy I.
aryborough
ympie

Brisbane
wich
vick
Lismore
asino
rafton
Mtn

ort Macquarie
ee

Norfolk I.
(Aust.)

Lord Howe I.
(Aust.)

4045

Tropic of Capricorn

INTERNATIONAL DATELINE

T A S M A N

S E A

Three Kings Is
C. Maria van Diemen   North Cape

Kaitaia

Dargaville
Whangarei

Auckland
Manukau
Hamilton
North Island
New Plymouth
Hawera
Wanganui
C. Farewell
Westport
Nelson
Picton
Greymouth
Hokitika
South Island
Alps
Mt Cook
3764
Southern
Fairlie
Queenstown
Resolution I.
Alexandra
Foveaux Strait
Gore
Invercargill
Stewart I.
Snares Is

Great Barrier
Hauraki
Gulf
Thames
Tauranga
Bay of Plenty
Rotorua
Whakatane
Ruapehu
2797
Napier
Hastings
Masterton
Palmerston
North
Wellington
NEW
ZEALAND
Rangiora
Christchurch
Ashburton
Timaru
Oamaru
Dunedin
Balclutha

East Cape

Gisborne

Hawke Bay

Cook Strait
Blenheim
Kaikoura

Chatham Is
(N.Z.)   Pitt

Kermadec Is
(N.Z.)

Raoul

8600

Kermadec Trench

1528

Equator

Auckland Is
(N.Z.)

Antipodes Is
(N.Z.)

Bounty Is
(N.Z.)

1:7.5M

1:5M

0 50 100 150 200 km
0 50 100 mils

1:40M

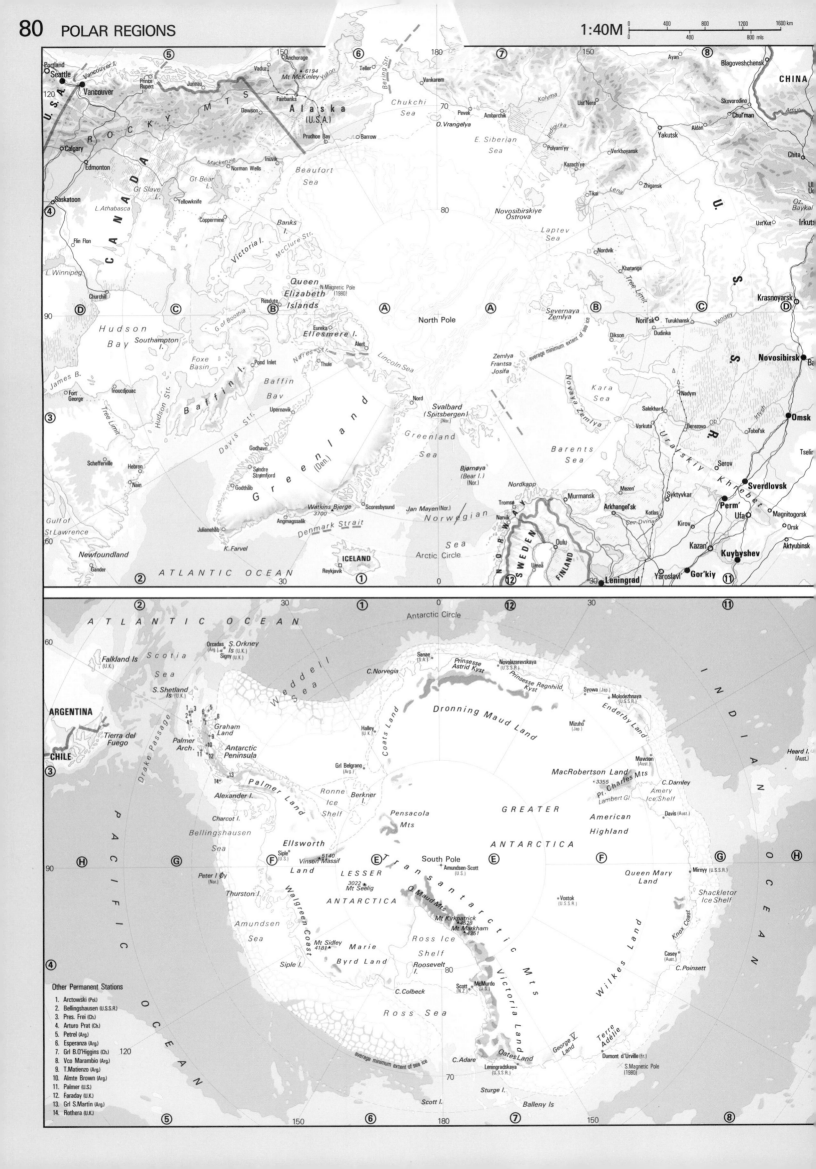

400 800 1200 1600 km
400 800 mls

Northern Polar Region

Portland
Seattle
Vancouver I.
Vancouver
Prince Rupert
Calgary
Edmonton
Saskatoon
Flin Flon
Churchill
L. Winnipeg

U.S.A.
Vaduz
Anchorage
Mt McKinley 6194
Yukon
Teller
Bering Str.
Vankarem
Fairbanks
Juneau
Dawson
Alaska (U.S.A.)
Prudhoe Bay
Barrow
Norman Wells
Inuvik
Mackenzie
Gt Bear L.
Coppermine
Yellowknife
Gt Slave L.
L. Athabasca
Saskatoon

CHINA
Blagoveshchensk
Ayan
Skovorodino
Chul'man
Amur
Chita

Chukchi Sea
Pevek
Ambarchik
O. Vrangelya
E. Siberian Sea
Polyarn'yy
Kolyma
Ust'Nera
Verkhoyansk
Indigirka
Yakutsk
Kazach'ye
Zhigansk
Tiksi
Lena
Aldan

CANADA
ROCKY MTS
Banks I.
Victoria I.
McClure Str.
Queen Elizabeth Islands
N.Magnetic Pole (1980)
Resolute
B
Eureka
Ellesmere I.
Alert
Thule
Nares Str.
Lincoln Sea
Nord
Pond Inlet
Baffin I.
Baffin Bay
Upernavik
Davis Str.
Godhavn
Sondre Stromfjord
Godthåb
Greenland (Den.)
Watkins Bjerge 3700
Scoresbysund
Angmagssalik
Julianehåb
K.Farvel

Hudson Bay
Southampton I.
Foxe Basin
G. of Boothia
Hudson Str.
James B.
Fort George
Inoucdjouac
Tree Limit
Schefferville
Hebron
Nain
Gulf of St Lawrence
Newfoundland
Gander

North Pole
80
70
Laptev Sea
Novosibirskiye Ostrova
Nordvik
Khatanga
Tree Limit
average minimum extent of sea ice
Severnaya Zemlya
Zemlya Frantsa Josifa
Dikson
Noril'sk
Turukhansk
Dudinka
Kara Sea
Novaya Zemlya
Salekhard
Vorkuta
Berezovo
Ob'
Nadym

U.S.S.R.
Ust'Kut
Irkutsk
Krasnoyarsk
Yenisey
Novosibirsk
Omsk
Tselin
Serov
Sverdlovsk
Perm'
Ufa
Magnitogorsk
Orsk
Kazan'
Kuybyshev
Aktyubinsk
Kirov
Gor'kiy
Yaroslavl'
Leningrad

Svalbard (Spitsbergen) (Nor.)
Greenland Sea
Bjornoya (Bear I.) (Nor.)
Nordkapp
Barents Sea
Murmansk
Mezen'
Arkhangel'sk
Sev. Dvina
Kotlas
Syktyvkar

Jan Mayen (Nor.)
Norwegian Sea
Tromso
Narvik
NORWAY
SWEDEN
Oulu
FINLAND
Umeå
Arctic Circle

ICELAND
Reykjavik
ATLANTIC OCEAN

Uralskiy Khrebet

Southern Polar Region

ATLANTIC OCEAN
Antarctic Circle
Falkland Is (U.K.)
Scotia Sea
Orcadas (Arg.)
S. Orkney Is (U.K.)
Signy (U.K.)
S. Shetland Is (U.K.)
ARGENTINA
Tierra del Fuego
CHILE
Drake Passage
Graham Land
Palmer Arch.
Antarctic Peninsula
Alexander I.
Palmer Land
Charcot I.
Bellingshausen Sea
Ellsworth Land
Siple (U.S.)
Vinson Massif 5140
PACIFIC OCEAN
Peter I Oy (Nor.)
Thurston I.
Walgreen Coast
Amundsen Sea
Mt Sidley 4181
Siple I.
Byrd Land

Weddell Sea
C. Norvegia
Sanae (S.A.)
Prinsesse Astrid Kyst
Novolazarevskaya (U.S.S.R.)
Prinsesse Ragnhild Kyst
Dronning Maud Land
Coats Land
Halley (U.K.)
Grl Belgrano (Arg.)
Ronne Ice Shelf
Berkner I.
Pensacola Mts
LESSER ANTARCTICA
Mt Seelig 3022
Transantarctic Mts
South Pole
Amundsen-Scott (U.S.)
ANTARCTICA
Q. Maud Mts
Mt Kirkpatrick 4528
Mt Markham 4351
Ross Ice Shelf
Roosevelt I.
Marie Byrd Land
C. Colbeck

Syowa (Jap.)
Molodezhnaya (U.S.S.R.)
Enderby Land
Mizuho (Jap.)
Mawson (Aust.)
MacRobertson Land
Pr. Charles Mts 3355
Amery Ice Shelf
C. Darnley
Lambert Gl.
Davis (Aust.)
GREATER ANTARCTICA
American Highland
Vostok (U.S.S.R.)
Queen Mary Land
Mirnyy (U.S.S.R.)
Shackleton Ice Shelf
Knox Coast
Casey (Aust.)
C. Poinsett
INDIAN OCEAN
Heard I. (Aust.)

Victoria Land
Wilkes Land
McMurdo (U.S.)
Scott (N.Z.)
Ross Sea
C. Adare
George V Land
Terre Adélie
Oates Land
Leningradskaya (U.S.S.R.)
Dumont d'Urville (Fr.)
S.Magnetic Pole (1980)
Sturge I.
Balleny Is
Scott I.

Other Permanent Stations

1. Arctowski (Pol.)
2. Bellingshausen (U.S.S.R.)
3. Pres. Frei (Ch.)
4. Arturo Prat (Ch.)
5. Petrel (Arg.)
6. Esperanza (Arg.)
7. Grl B.O'Higgins (Ch.)
8. Vco Marambio (Arg.)
9. T.Matienzo (Arg.)
10. Almte Brown (Arg.)
11. Palmer (U.S.)
12. Faraday (U.K.)
13. Grl S.Martin (Arg.)
14. Rothera (U.K.)

Abbreviations

Abbreviations used in Reference Map Section

Abbreviations	Full Form	English Form	Language
A			
a.d.	an der	on the	German
Appno	Appennino	mountain range	Italian
Aqued.	Aqueduct	aqueduct	English
Arch.	Archipelago	archipelago	English
A.S.S.R.	Autonomous Soviet Socialist Republic	Autonomous Soviet Socialist Republic	English
B			
B.	1. Baai, Bahía, Baía, Baie, Bay, Bucht, Bukhta, Bugt	bay	Dutch, Spanish, Portuguese, French, English, German, Russian, Danish
	2. Ban	village	Indo-Chinese
	3. Barrage,	dam	French
	4. Bayou	bayou	French, English
	5. Bir	well	Arabic
Bj	Bordj	fort, cliff	Arabic
Bol	Bol'sh/aya, -oy, -oye	big	Russian
Br.	1. Branch	branch	English
	2. Bridge, Brücke	bridge	English, German
	3. Burun	cape	Turkish
Brj	Baraj,-i	dam	Turkish
Bü.	Büyük	big	Turkish
C			
C.	Cabo, Cap, Cape	cape	Spanish, French, English
Car.	Canal	canal	English
Cat	Cataract, Cataratas	cataract	English, Spanish, Portuguese
Cd	Ciudad	town	Spanish
Ch.	Chott	salt lake	Arabic
Chan.	Channel	channel	English
Ck	Creek	creek	English
Cmd.	Commander, Comodoro	commander	English, Spanish
Cnia	Colonia	colony	Spanish
Cnl	Colonel, Coronel	colonel	English, Spanish
Comte	Comandante	commandant	Spanish
Cord.	Cordillera	mountain range	Spanish
Cuch.	Cuchilla	hills, ridge	Spanish
D			
D.	1. Dağ, Dāgh, Daği, Dağlari	mountain, range	Persian, Turkish
	2. Dake	mountain	Japanese
	3. Darreh	valley	Persian
	4. Daryācheh	lake	Persian
Dj.	Djebel	mountain	Arabic
E			
E.	East	east	English
Eil.	Eiland, Eilanden	island(s)	Dutch
Emb.	Embalse	reservoir	Spanish
Escarp.	Escarpment	escarpment	English
Estr.	Estrecho	strait	Spanish
F			
F.	Firth	estuary	Gaelic
Fj.	1. Fjell	mountain	Norwegian
	2. Fjord, Fjorður	fjord	Norwegian, Icelandic
Ft	Fort	fort	English
G			
G.	1. Gawa	river	Japanese
	2. Gebel	mountain	Arabic
	3. Ghedir	oasis	Arabic
	4. Göl, Gölü	lake	Turkish
	5. Golfe, Golfo, Gulf	Gulf	French, Italian, Portuguese, Spanish, English
	6. Gompa	village	Tibetan
	7. Gora, -gory	mountain, range	Russian
	8. Guba	gulf, bay	Russian
	9. Gunung	mountain	Malay, Indonesian
Gd, Gde	Grand, Grande	grand	English, French
Gdor	Gobernador	governor	Spanish
Geb.	Gebirge	mountain range	German
Gez.	Gezira	island	Arabic
Ghub.	Ghubbat	bay	Arabic
Gl.	Glacier	glacier	French, English
Gr	Grosser	greater	German
Gr	General	general	Spanish
Gt, Gtr	Great, Groot, -e, Greater	greater	English, Dutch
H			
H	1. Hawr	lake	Arabic
	2. Hoch	high	German
	3. Hora, Hory	mountain(s)	Czechoslovakian
Har.	Harbour	harbour	English
Hd	Head	head	English
Hg.	Hegy	mountain	Hungarian
Hgts	Heights	heights	English
Hwy	Highway	highway	English
I			
I.	Ile, Ilha, Insel, Isla, Island Isle, Isola, Isole	island	French, Portuguese, German Spanish, English, Italian
In.	1. Indre, Inner	inner	Norwegian, English
	2. Inlet	inlet	English
Is	Iles, Ilhas, Islands, Isles, Islas	islands	French, Portuguese, English, Spanish
Isth.	Isthmus	isthmus	English
J			
J.	1. Jabal, Jebel, Jibal	mountain	Arabic
	2. Järv, Jaure, Jazira, Jezero	lake	Finnish
	3. Jökull	glacier	Icelandic
	4. Juan	John	Spanish
Jct.	Junction	junction	English
K			
K.	1. Kaap, Kap, Kapp	cape	Dutch, German, Norwegian, Swedish
	2. Kaikyo	channel, strait	Japanese
	3. Kato	lower	Greek
	4. Karang	reef	Malay
	5. Kiarg	river	Chinese
	6. Ko	lake	Japanese
	7. Koh, Kuh, Kuhha	mountain	Persian
	8. Kolpos	gulf	Greek
	9. Kopf	peak	German
	10. Kuala	bay	Malay
	11. Kyst	coast	Danish
Kan.	Kanal	canal	German
Kep.	Kepulauan	islands	Indonesian
Kg	1. Kampong	village	Malay
	2. Kompong	riverbank	Indo-Chinese
Kh.	Khawr	wadi, river	Arabic
Khr.	Khrebet	mountain range	Russian
Kör.	Körfez. -i	gulf, bay	Turkish
L			
L.	1. Lac, Lago, Lagoa, Lake, Liman, Limni, Loch, Lough	lake	French, Italian, Spanish, Portuguese, English, Russian, Greek, Gaelic
	2. Lam	river	Thai
Lag.	Lagoon, Laguna, -e, Lagôa	lagoon	English, Spanish, French, Portuguese
Ld	Land	land	English
Lit.	Little	little	English
M			
M.	1. Meer	sea, lake	Dutch, German
	2. Mys	cape	Russian
m	metre, -s	metre(s)	English, French
Mal.	Mali, -o, -yy	small	Russian
Mf	Massif	mountain group	French
Mgna	Montagna	mountain	Italian
Mgne	Montagne(s)	mountain(s)	French
Mon.	Monasterio, Monastery	monastery	Spanish, English
Mont	Monument	monument	English
Mt	Mont, Mount	mountain	French, English
Mte	Monte	mountain	Italian, Portuguese, Spanish
Mti	Monti, Muntii	mountain, range	Italian, Romanian
Mtn	Mountain	mountain	English
Mts	Monts, Mountains, Montañas, Montes	mountains	French, English, Spanish, Italian, Portuguese
N			
N.	1. Nam	south	Korean
	2. Neu, Ny	new	German
	3. Nevado, Nudo	snow capped mtns	Spanish
	4. Noord, Nord, Norte, Nørre, North	north	Danish, French, Portuguese Spanish, Danish, English
	5. Nos	cape	Russian
Nat.	National	national	English
Nat. Pk	National Park	national park	English
Ndr	Neder, Nieder	lower	Dutch, Swedish, German
N.E.	North East	north east	English
Nizh.	Nizhne, Nizhniy	lower	Russian
Nizm.	Nizmennost	lowland	Russian
N.M.	National Monument	national monument	English

Abbreviations continued

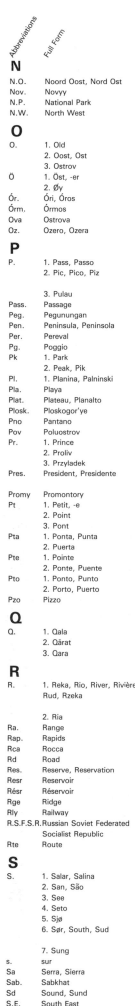

Abbreviations	Full Form	English Form	Language
N			
N.O.	Noord Oost, Nord Ost	north east	Dutch, German
Nov.	Novyy	new	Russian
N.P.	National Park	national park	English
N.W.	North West	north west	English
O			
O.	1. Old	old	English
	2. Oost, Ost	east	Dutch, German
	3. Ostrov	island	Russian
Ö	1. Öst, -er	east	Swedish
	2. Øy	island	Norwegian
Ór.	Óri, Óros	mountain(s)	Greek
Órm.	Órmos	bay	Greek
Ova	Ostrova	islands	Russian
Oz.	Ozero, Ozera	lake(s)	Russian
P			
P.	1. Pass, Passo	pass	English, German, Italian
	2. Pic, Pico, Piz	peak	French, Portuguese, Spanish, Italian
	3. Pulau	island	Malay
Pass.	Passage	passage	English
Peg.	Pegunungan	mountains	Indonesian
Pen.	Peninsula, Peninsola	peninsula	English, Italian
Per.	Pereval	pass	Russian
Pg.	Poggio	hill	Italian
Pk	1. Park	park	English
	2. Peak, Pik	peak	English, Russian
Pl.	1. Planina, Palninski	mountain range	Russian, Czechoslovakian
Pla.	Playa	beach	Spanish
Plat.	Plateau, Planalto	plateau	English, French, Portuguese
Plosk.	Ploskogor'ye	plateau	Russian
Pno	Pantano	marsh, reservoir	Spanish
Pov	Poluostrov	peninsula	Russian
Pr.	1. Prince	prince	English
	2. Proliv	strait	Russian
	3. Przyladek	cape	Polish
Pres.	President, Presidente	president	English, Spanish, Portuguese
Promy	Promontory	promontory	English
Pt	1. Petit, -e	small	French
	2. Point	point	English
	3. Pont	bridge	French
Pta	1. Ponta, Punta	point	Portuguese, Italian, Spanish
	2. Puerta	pass	Spanish
Pte	1. Pointe	point	French
	2. Ponte, Puente	bridge	Portuguese, Spanish
Pto	1. Ponto, Punto	point	Portuguese
	2. Porto, Puerto	port	Spanish
Pzo	Pizzo	peak	Italian
Q			
Q.	1. Qala	fortress, peak	Persian, Arabic
	2. Qârat	mountain	Arabic
	3. Qara	black	Persian
R			
R.	1. Reka, Rio, River, Rivière, Rud, Rzeka	river	Russian, Portuguese, Spanish English, French, Persian, Polish
	2. Ria	river mouth	English
Ra.	Range	range	English
Rap.	Rapids	rapids	English
Rca	Rocca	rock, mountain	Italian
Rd	Road	road	English
Res.	Reserve, Reservation	reserve, reservation	English
Resr	Reservoir	reservoir	English
Résr	Réservoir	reservoir	French
Rge	Ridge	ridge	English
Rly	Railway	railway	English
R.S.F.S.R.	Russian Soviet Federated Socialist Republic	Russian Soviet Federated Socialist Republic	English
Rte	Route	route	English, French
S			
S.	1. Salar, Salina	salt marsh	Spanish
	2. San, São	saint	Spanish, Portuguese
	3. See	sea, lake	German
	4. Seto	strait	Japanese
	5. Sjø	lake	Norwegian
	6. Sør, South, Sud	south	Norwegian, English, French, Italian, Spanish
	7. Sung	river	Malay
s.	sur	on	French
Sa	Serra, Sierra	mountain range	Portuguese, Spanish
Sab.	Sabkhat	salt flats	Arabic
Sd	Sound, Sund	sound	English, German, Swedish
S.E.	South East	south east	English
Seb.	Sebjet, Sebkhat, Sebkra	salt marsh, lagoon	Arabic
Sev.	Sever, Severnaya	north	Russian
Sh.	1. Sh'aib	road, ravine	Arabic

Abbreviations	Full Form	English Form	Language
	2. Shatt	river	Arabic
	3. Shima	island	Japanese
Sp.	Spitze	peak	German
Spr.	Spring,(s)	spring(s)	English
S.S.R.	Soviet Socialist Republic	Soviet Socialist Republic	English
St	Saint	saint	English
Sta	Santa	saint	Spanish
Sta.	Station	station	English
Ste	Sainte	saint	French
Sten.	Stenon, Stenos	pass, strait	Greek
Sto	Santo	saint	Portuguese, Spanish
Str.	Strait	strait	English
Sty	Staryy	old	Polish, Czechoslovakian
Sv.	Svaty, Sveti	holy	Polish, Czechoslovakian
S.W.	South West	south west	English
T			
T.	1. Tal	valley	German
	2. Tall, Tel	hill, mountain	Arabic, Hebrew
	3. Tepe, Tepesi	peak, hill	Turkish
Talsp.	Talsperre	dam	German
Tg	Tanjong, Tandjong	cape	Malay, Indonesian
Tk	Têluk, Têlok	bay	Indonesian
Tr.	Trench, Trough	trench, trough	English
Tun.	Tunnel	tunnel	English
U			
U.	Uad	wadi	Arabic
Ug	Ujung	cape	Malay
Unt.	Unter	lower	German
Upr	Upper	upper	English
V			
V.	1. Val, Valle	valley	French, Italian, Spanish
	2. Väster, Vest, Vester	west	Swedish, Danish, Norwegian
	3. Vatn	lake	Icelandic, Norwegian
	4. Ville	town	French
Va	Villa	town	Spanish
Vdkhr.	Vodokhranilishche	reservoir	Russian
Verkh.	Verkhniy	upper	Russian
Vol.	Volcán, Volcano, Vulkán	volcano	Spanish, English, Russian
Vost.	Vostochnyy	eastern	Russian
Vozv.	Vozvyshennost'	upland	Russian
W			
W.	1. Wadi	wadi	Arabic
	2. Wald	forest	German
	3. Wan	gulf, bay	Chinese, Japanese
	4. Water	water	English
	5. Well	well	English
	6. West	west	English
Y			
Yuzh.	Yuzhnaya, Yuzhno, Yuzhnyy	south	Russian
Z			
Z	1. Zahrez	intermittent lake	Arabic
	2. Zaliv	gulf, bay	Russian
Zap.	Zapadnyy,-aya,-o,-oye	western	Russian
Zem.	Zemlya	country, land	Russian

Index

Introduction to the index

In the index, the first number refers to the page, and the following letter and number to the section of the map in which the index entry can be found. For example, Paris 36C2 means that Paris can be found on page 36 where column C and row 2 meet.

Abbreviations used in the index

Afghan	Afghanistan	Hung	Hungary	Pol	Poland	Arch	Archipelago
Alb	Albania	Ird	Indonesia	Port	Portugal	B	Bay
Alg	Algeria	N Ire	Ireland	Rom	Romania	C	Cape
Ant	Antarctica	N Ire	Ireland, Northern	S Arabia	Saudi Arabia	Chan	Channel
Arg	Argentina	Leb	Lebanon	Scot	Scotland	Gl	Glacier
Aust	Australia	Lib	Liberia	Sen	Senegal	I(s)	Island(s)
Bang	Bangladesh	Liech	Liechtenstein	S Africa	South Africa	Lg	Lagoon
Belg	Belgium	Lux	Luxembourg	S Yemen	South Yemen	L	Lake
Bo	Bolivia	Madag	Madagascar	Switz	Switzerland	Mt(s)	Mountain(s)
Bulg	Bulgaria	Malay	Malaysia	Tanz	Tanzania	O	Ocean
Camb	Cambodia	Maur	Mauritania	Thai	Thailand	P	Pass
Can	Canada	Mor	Morocco	Turk	Turkey	Pass	Passage
CAR	Central African Republic	Mozam	Mozambique	USSR	Union of Soviet Socialist	Pen	Peninsula
Czech	Czechoslovakia	Neth	Netherlands		Republics	Plat	Plateau
Den	Denmark	NZ	New Zealand	USA	United States of America	Pt	Point
Dom Rep	Dominican Republic	Nic	Nicaragua	U Volta	Upper Volta	Res	Reservoir
E Germ	East Germany	Nig	Nigeria	Urug	Uruguay	R	River
El Sal	El Salvador	Nor	Norway	Ven	Venezuela	S	Sea
Eng	England	Pak	Pakistan	Viet	Vietnam	Sd	Sound
Eq Guinea	Equatorial Guinea	PNG	Papua New Guinea	W Germ	West Germany	Str	Strait
Eth	Ethiopia	Par	Paraguay	Yugos	Yugoslavia	V	Valley
Fin	Finland	Phil	Philippines	Zim	Zimbabwe		

A

Aachen W Germ	40B2
Aalst Belg	34C1
Äänekoski Fin	30K6
Aareu Switz	35C1
Aare, R Switz	35B1
Aba China	50A3
Aba Nig	69H4
Aba Zaïre	70D3
Abādān Iran	61B2
Abādeh Iran	61C2
Abadla Alg	68B1
Abaeté Brazil	27C2
Abaeté, R Brazil	27C2
Abaetetuba Brazil	25J4
Abagnar Qi China	50D1
Abaji Nig	69H4
Abajo Mts USA	17E3
Abakaliki Nig	69H4
Abakan USSR	47L4
Abala Niger	68C3
Abalessa Alg	68C2
Abancay Peru	24D6
Abarqū Iran	61C2
Abashiri Japan	51E3
Abashiri-wan, B Japan	51E3
Abasolo Mexico	20C1
Abau PNG	49H7
Abaya, L Eth	70D3
Abbai, R Eth	70D2
Abbe, L Eth	70E2
Abbeville France	36C1
Abbeville, Louisiana USA	15D4
Abbeville, S Carolina USA	13C2
Abbiategrasso Italy	35C2
Abbotsford Can	16B1
Abbotsford USA	10A2
Abbottabad Pak	58C2
Abd al-Kuri, I S Yemen	65F4
Abdulino USSR	42J5
Abéché Chad	70C2
Abengourou Ivory Coast	69F4
Åbenrå Den	30F7
Åbenra Den	40B1
Abeokuta Nig	69G4
Abera Eth	70D3
Aberaeron Wales	33C5
Aberdeen, California USA	18C2
Aberdeen, Maryland USA	11D3
Aberdeen, Mississippi USA	13B2
Aberdeen S Africa	72C3
Aberdeen Scot	32D3

Aberdeen, S Dakota USA	6D2
Aberdeen, Washington USA	6A2
Aberdeen L Can	4J3
Aberfeldy Scot	32D3
Abergavenny Wales	33D6
Aberystwyth Wales	33C5
Abez' USSR	42L2
Abhā S Arabia	64D3
Abhar Iran	61B1
Abi Addi Eth	64C4
Abidjan Ivory Coast	69F4
Abilene, Kansas USA	15C2
Abilene, Texas USA	14C3
Abingdon Eng	33E6
Abingdon USA	10C3
Abitibi, R Can	5K4
Abitibi,L Can	5L5
Abkhazskaya, Republic USSR	43G7
Ablis France	34A2
Abohar India	58C2
Abomey Benin	69G4
Abong Mbang Cam	70B3
Aborlan Phil	55B9
Abou Deïa Chad	70B2
Abqaiq S Arabia	65E1
Abrantes Port	37A2
Abri Sudan	70D1
Abrolhos, Is Aust	76A3
Absaroka Range, Mts USA	6B2
Abū al Abyad, I UAE	65F2
Abū 'Ai, I S Arabia	65E1
Abū Arish S Arabia	64D3
Abu Deleiq Sudan	64B3
Abu Dhabi UAE	65F2
'Abu Dom, Watercourse Sudan	64B3
Abū el Jurdhān Jordan	63C3
Abu Fatima Sudan	64B3
Abu Hamed Sudan	70D2
Abu Kebir Hihya Egypt	63A3
Abunã Brazil	24E5
Abuna, R Bol	24E6
Abú Sukhayr Iraq	62D3
Abu Suweir Egypt	63B3
Abut Head, C NZ	79B2
Abu Tig Egypt	64B1
Abu'Urug, Well Sudan	70D2
Abuye Meda, Mt Eth	70D2
Abu Zabad Sudan	70C2
Abwong Sudan	70D3
Åby Den	40B1
Aby 'Aweigîla, Well Egypt	63C3
Abyei Sudan	70C3

Acadia Nat Pk USA	11F2
Acambaro Mexico	19B2
Acandi Colombia	21B5
Acaponeta Mexico	19B2
Acapulco Mexico	19B3
Acaraú Brazil	25L4
Acarigua Ven	24E2
Acatlán Mexico	19C3
Acatlan Mexico	20C2
Acatzingo Mexico	20C2
Acayucan Mexico	20D2
Accra Ghana	69F4
Aceguá Urug	26E2
Achalpur India	58D4
Achao Chile	23B6
Acheng China	51B2
Achensee, L Austria	35D1
Achern W Germ	34E2
Achill, I Irish Rep	31A3
Achinsk USSR	47L4
Acireale Italy	38D3
Ackley USA	9D3
Acklins, I Caribbean	21C2
Acobamba Peru	24D6
Aconcagua, Mt Chile	23B4
Acopiara Brazil	25L5
Açores, Is Atlantic O	66B4
Acqui Italy	35C2
Acraman,L Aust	78A2
Acre = 'Akko	
Acre, State Brazil	24D5
Acton USA	18C3
Actopan Mexico	20C1
Ada Ghana	69G4
Ada USA	15C3
Adaja, R Spain	37B1
Adak, I USA	8C6
Adam Oman	65G2
Adama Eth	70D3
Adamantina Brazil	27B3
Adamaoua, Region Nig/ Cam	70B3
Adamello, Mt Italy	35D1
Adams USA	12D1
Adam's Bridge India/Sri Lanka	60B3
Adams L Can	3E3
Adams,Mt USA	6A2
Adam's Peak, Mt Sri Lanka	60C3
'Adan S Yemen	65E4
Adana Turk	43F8
Adapazari Turk	43E7
Adarama Sudan	64B3
Adare,C Ant	80F7
Adaut Indon	55D4
Adavale Aust	78B1
Adda, R Italy	35C2

Ad Dahna', Region S Arabia	65E1
Ad Damman S Arabia	65F1
Ad Darb S Arabia	64D3
Ad Dawādimi S Arabia	64D2
Ad Dibdibah, Region S Arabia	65E1
Ad Dikākah, Region S Arabia	65F3
Ad Dilam S Arabia	65E2
Ad Dir'iyah S Arabia	65E2
Addis Ababa Eth	70D3
Addis Zeman Eth	64C4
Ad Diwaniyah Iraq	62D3
Ad Dli' S Yemen	64D4
Ad Duwayd S Arabia	62D3
Adel USA	9D3
Adelaide Aust	76C4
Adelaide S Africa	72D3
Adelaide Pen Can	4J3
Adelaide River Aust	49G8
Adelanto USA	18D3
Aden = 'Adan	
Aden,G of Yemen/ Somalia	56C4
Aderbissinat Niger	68C3
Adhra Syria	63D2
Adi, I Indon	49G7
Adige, R Italy	38C1
Adigrat Eth	70D2
Adi Kale Eth	64C4
Adilābād India	58D5
Adin USA	16B2
Adirondack Mts USA	11E2
Adi Ugai Eth	70D2
Adiyaman Turk	62C2
Adjud Rom	39F1
Admiralty B USA	8G1
Admiralty I USA	4E4
Admiralty Inlet, B Can	5K2
Admiralty Is PNG	76D1
Adonara, I Indon	55B4
Adoni India	60B1
Adour, R France	36B3
Adrar, Region Maur	68A2
Adrar, Mts Alg	68C2
Adrar Soutouf, Region Mor	68A2
Adré Chad	70C2
Adri Libya	67A2
Adria Italy	35E2
Adrian, Michigan USA	10C2
Adrian, Texas USA	14B2
Adriatic S Italy/Yugos	38C2
Aduwa Eth	70D2
Adycha, R USSR	47P3
Adzopé Ivory Coast	69F4
Adz'va, R USSR	42K2

Adz'vavom USSR	42K2
Aegean, S Greece	39E3
Afghanistan, Republic Asia	56E2
Afgooye Somalia	70E3
'Afif S Arabia	64D2
Afikpo Nig	69H4
Åfjord Nor	30G6
Aflou Alg	69C2
Afmadu Somalia	70E3
Afollé, Region Maur	68A3
Afton, New York USA	12C1
Afton, Wyoming USA	16D2
Afula Israel	63C2
Afyon Turk	43E8
Aga Egypt	63A3
Agadem Niger	70B2
Agadez Niger	68C3
Agadir Mor	68B1
Agar India	58D4
Agartala India	59D3
Agassiz Can	16B1
Agattu, I USA	8A6
Agattu Str USA	8A5
Agbor Nig	69H4
Agboville Ivory Coast	69F4
Agdam USSR	62E1
Agematsu Japan	52C3
Agen France	36C3
Agha Jāri Iran	61B2
Ağin Turk	43G8
Agno, R Italy	35D2
Agordat Eth	64C3
Agordo Italy	35E1
Agou,Mt Togo	69G4
Agout, R France	36C3
Agra India	58D3
Ağri Turk	62D2
Agri, R Italy	38D2
Agrigento Italy	38C3
Agrinion Greece	39E3
Agrio, R Chile	26A3
Agropoli Italy	38C2
Agryz USSR	42J4
Agto Greenland	5N3
Agua Clara Brazil	27B3
Aguada de Guerra Arg	26B4
Aguadilla Puerto Rico	21D3
Aguado Cicilio Arg	26B4
Aguanava, R Mexico	20B1
Aguapey, R Arg	26D1
Agua Prieta Mexico	19B1
Aguaray Guazu Par	27A3
Aguascalientes Mexico	19B2
Aguascalientes, State Mexico	20B1
Aguas Formosas Brazil	27D2
Agueda Port	37A1

3

Aguelhok *Mali* 68C3
Agüenit, Well *Mor* 68A2
Aguilas *Spain* 37B2
Aguililla *Mexico* 20B2
Agulhas Basin *Indian O* 74C7
Agulhas,C *S Africa* 72C3
Agulhas Plat *Indian O* 74C6
Agusan, R *Phil* 55G9
Ahaggar = Hoggar
Ahar *Iran* 43H8
Ahipara B *NZ* 79B1
Ahlen *W Germ* 34D1
Ahmadābād *India* 58C4
Ahmadnagar *India* 60A1
Ahmar, Mts *Eth* 70E3
Ahoskie *USA* 13D1
Ahr, R *W Germ* 34D1
Ahrgebirge, Region *W Germ* 34D1
Ahuacatlán *Mexico* 20B1
Ahualulco *Mexico* 20B1
Åhus *Sweden* 30G7
Ahuvān *Iran* 61C1
Ahvāz *Iran* 61B2
Aiajuela *Costa Rica* 21A4
Aigle *Switz* 35B1
Aiguá *Urug* 26E2
Aiguille d'Arves, Mt *France* 35B2
Aiguille de la Grand Sassière, Mt *France* 35B2
Aihui *China* 51B1
Aikawa *Japan* 52C3
Aiken *USA* 13C2
Ailao Shan, Upland *China* 50A5
Aimogasta *Arg* 26B1
Aimorés *Brazil* 27D2
Ain, R *France* 35A1
Aïn Beïda *Alg* 69D1
Ain Beni Mathar *Mor* 69B2
Ain Dalla, Well *Egypt* 67B2
Aïn el Hadjel *Alg* 37C2
Aïn Galakka *Chad* 70B2
Aïn Oussera *Alg* 69C1
Aïn Sefra *Alg* 69B2
'Ain Sukhna *Egypt* 62B4
Ainsworth *USA* 9C3
Aïn Temouchent *Alg* 69B1
Aioi *Japan* 52B4
Aioun Abd el Malek, Well *Maur* 68B2
Aïoun El Atrouss *Maur* 68B3
Aiquile *Bol* 24E7
Aïr, Desert Region *Niger* 68C3
Airdrie *Can* 3F3
Aire *France* 34B1
Aire, R *Eng* 33E5
Aire, R *France* 34C2
Airforce I *Can* 5L3
Airolo *Switz* 35C1
Aishihik *Can* 4E3
Aishihik L *Can* 8L3
Aisne, Department *France* 34B2
Aisne, R *France* 36C2
Aitape *PNG* 76D1
Aiviekste, R *USSR* 41F1
Aixa Zuogi *China* 50B2
Aix-en-Provence *France* 36D3
Aix-les-Bains *France* 35A2
Aiyar Res *India* 59C3
Aíyion *Greece* 39E3
Aíyna, I *Greece* 39E3
Āīzawl *India* 59D3
Aizeb, R *Namibia* 71B6
Aizu-Wakamatsu *Japan* 51E4
Ajaccio *Corse* 38B2
Ajalpan *Mexico* 20C2
Ajdabiyah *Libya* 67B1
Ajdovščina *Yugos* 35E2
Ajigasawa *Japan* 51E3
Ajlūn *Jordan* 63C2
Ajman *UAE* 65G1
Ajmer *India* 58C3
Ajo *USA* 17D4
Ajtos *Bulg* 39F2
Ajuchitan *Mexico* 20B2
Ak, R *Turk* 39F3
Akabira *Japan* 52D2
Akaishi-sanchi, Mts *Japan* 52C3
Akalkot *India* 60B1
Akanthou *Cyprus* 63B1
Akaroa *NZ* 79B2
Akasha *Sudan* 64B2
Akashi *Japan* 52B4
Akbou *Alg* 69C1
Akbulak *USSR* 43K5
Akçakale *Turk* 62C2
Akchar, Watercourse *Maur* 68A2
Ak Dağ, Mt *Turk* 39F3
Akelamo *Indon* 55C2
Aketi *Zaïre* 70C3
Akhalkalaki *USSR* 62D1
Akhalsikhe *USSR* 62D1
Akharnái *Greece* 39E3
Akhiok *USA* 8H4
Akhisar *Turk* 62A2
Akhiste *USSR* 41F1
Akhmîm *Egypt* 67C2
Akhtubinsk *USSR* 43H6
Akhtyrka *USSR* 43E6
Aki *Japan* 52B4
Akimiski I *Can* 5K4
Akita *Japan* 51E4
Akjoujt *Maur* 68A3
'Akko *Israel* 63C2
Aklavik *Can* 8L2
Aklé Aouana, Desert Region *Maur* 68B3
Akobo *Sudan* 70D3
Akobo, R *Sudan* 70D3
Akoha *Afghan* 58B1
Akola *India* 58D4
Akosombo Dam *Ghana* 69G4
Akot *India* 58D4
Akpatok I *Can* 5M3
Ákra Kafirévs, C *Greece* 39E3
Ákra Líthinon, C *Greece* 39E4
Ákra Maléa, C *Greece* 39E3
Akranes *Iceland* 30A2
Ákra Sídheros, C *Greece* 39F3
Ákra Spátha, C *Greece* 39E3
Ákra Taínaron, C *Greece* 39E3
Akron *USA* 7E2
Akrotiri B *Cyprus* 63B1
Aksai Chin, Mts *China* 58D1
Aksaray *Turk* 43E8
Aksay *USSR* 43J5
Aksayquin Hu, L *China* 58D1
Akşehir *Turk* 62B2
Akseki *Turk* 62B2
Aksenovo Zilovskoye *USSR* 47N4
Aksha *USSR* 48E1
Aksu *China* 57G1
Aksu *USSR* 46J5
Aksum *Eth* 64C4
Aktogay *USSR* 46J5
Aktumsyk *USSR* 43K6
Aktyubinsk *USSR* 46G4
Akure *Nig* 69H4
Akureyri *Iceland* 30B1
Akutan *USA* 8E5
Akutan, I *USA* 8E5
Akutan Pass *USA* 8E5
Akzhal *USSR* 46K5
Alabama, State *USA* 7E3
Alabama, R *USA* 13B2
Alabaster *USA* 13B2
Ala Dağlari, Mts *Turk* 62C2
Alagir *USSR* 43G7
Alagna *Italy* 35B2
Alagoas, State *Brazil* 25L5
Alagoinhas *Brazil* 25L6
Alagón *Spain* 37B1
Al Ahmadi *Kuwait* 62E4
Alajuela *Costa Rica* 19D3
Alakanuk *USA* 8F3
Alakurtti *USSR* 30L5
Al Amārah *Iraq* 62E3
Alameda *USA* 17B3
Alamo *Mexico* 20C1
Alamo *USA* 17C3
Alamogordo *USA* 14A3
Alamo Heights *USA* 14C4
Alamosa *USA* 14A2
Åland, I *Fin* 30H6
Alanya *Turk* 43E8
Alapaha, R *USA* 13C2
Alapayevsk *USSR* 46H4
Alas, R *Indon* 54A2
Alaşehir *Turk* 62A2
Ala Shan, Mts *China* 48D3
Alaska, State *USA* 4C3
Alaska,G of *USA* 4D4
Alaska Mts *USA* 3B2
Alaska Pen *USA* 8G4
Alaska Range, Mts *USA* 4C3
Alassio *Italy* 38B2
Alássio, Region *Italy* 35C3
Alatna, R *USA* 8H2
Alatyr *USSR* 42H5
Alawoona *Aust* 78B2
Al'Ayn *UAE* 65G2
Alayskiy Khrebet, Mts *USSR* 57F2
Alazeya, R *USSR* 47R3
Al'Azīzīyah *Libya* 69E2
Alba *Italy* 36D3
Al Bāb *Syria* 62C2
Albacete *Spain* 37B2
Alba de Tormes *Spain* 37A1
Al Badi *Iraq* 62D2
Alba Iulia *Rom* 39E1
Albania, Republic *Europe* 39D2
Albany *Aust* 76A4
Albany, Georgia *USA* 13C2
Albany, Kentucky *USA* 10B3
Albany, New York *USA* 11E2
Albany, Oregon *USA* 6A2
Albany, R *Can* 5K4
Albara, R *Sudan* 64C4
Albardón *Arg* 26B2
Al Batinah, Region *Oman* 65G2
Albatross B *Aust* 49H8
Al Baydā *Libya* 67B1
Al Baydā' *Yemen* 65E4
Al Baylūlīyah *Syria* 63C1
Albemarle *USA* 13C1
Albemarle Sd *USA* 13D1
Albenga, Region *Italy* 35C2
Alberche, R *Spain* 37B1
Alberga *Aust* 78A1
Albert *France* 34B1
Alberta, Province *Can* 4G4
Albert Edward, Mt *PNG* 49H7
Albertinia *S Africa* 72C3
Albert,L *Uganda/Zaïre* 70D3
Albert Lea *USA* 7D2
Albert Nile, R *Uganda* 70D3
Alberton *USA* 16D1
Albertville *France* 36D2
Albi *France* 36C3
Albia *USA* 15D1
Albina *Suriname* 25H2
Albion, Michigan *USA* 10C2
Albion, Nebraska *USA* 9C3
Albion, New York *USA* 11D2
Al Bi'r *S Arabia* 62C4
Al Birk *S Arabia* 64D3
Al Biyadh, Region *S Arabia* 65E2
Alborán, I *Spain* 37B2
Ålborg *Den* 30G7
Al Brayqah *Libya* 67A1
Albstadt-Ebingen *W Germ* 34E2
Al Bū Kamāl *Syria* 62D3
Albula, R *Switz* 35C1
Albuquerque *USA* 6C3
Al Buraymi *Oman* 65G2
Al Burdī *Libya* 67B1
Albury *Aust* 76D4
Al Buşayyah *Iraq* 62E3
Albuskjell, Oilfield *N Sea* 32G3
Al Buzūn *S Yemen* 65F3
Alcalá de Henares *Spain* 37B1
Alcamo *Italy* 38C3
Alcaniz *Spain* 37B1
Alcântara *Brazil* 25K4
Alcaraz *Spain* 37B2
Alcázar de San Juan *Spain* 37B2
Alcira *Spain* 37B2
Alcobaça *Brazil* 27E2
Alcolea de Pinar *Spain* 37B1
Alcoy *Spain* 37B2
Alcudia *Spain* 37C2
Aldabra, Is *Indian O* 66J8
Aldama *Mexico* 14A4
Aldama *Mexico* 20C1
Aldan *USSR* 47O4
Aldan, R *USSR* 47P4
Aldanskoye Nagor'ye, Upland *USSR* 47O4
Aldeburgh *Eng* 33F5
Alderney, I *UK* 36B2
Aldershot *Eng* 33E6
Aleg *Maur* 68A3
Alegre, R *Brazil* 27A2
Alegrete *Brazil* 23E3
Alejandro Roca *Arg* 26C2
Aleksandrovsk Sakhalinskiy *USSR* 47Q4
Alekseyevka *USSR* 46J4
Aleksin *USSR* 42F5
Älem *Sweden* 40D1
Além Paraíba *Brazil* 27D3
Alençon *France* 36C2
Alenuihaha Chan *Hawaiian Is* 18E5
Aleppo = Ḥalab
Alert *Can* 5M1
Alès *France* 36C3
Alessandria *Italy* 38B2
Ålesund *Nor* 46B3
Aleutian Is *USA* 8B5
Aleutian Range, Mts *USA* 8G4
Aleutian Trench *Pacific O* 75L2
Alexander Arch *USA* 4E4
Alexander Bay *S Africa* 72B2
Alexander City *USA* 13B2
Alexander I *Ant* 80G3
Alexandra *NZ* 79A3
Alexandra,C *South Georgia* 23J8
Alexandra Fjord *Can* 5L2
Alexandria *Egypt* 67B1
Alexandria, Louisiana *USA* 7D3
Alexandria, Minnesota *USA* 7D2
Alexandria, Virginia *USA* 7F3
Alexandroúpolis *Greece* 39F2
Alexis Creek *Can* 3D3
Aley *Leb* 63C2
Aleysk *USSR* 46K4
Al Fallūjah *Iraq* 62D3
Al Fardah *S Yemen* 65E4
Alfaro *Spain* 37B1
Alfatar *Bulg* 39F2
Al Fāw *Iraq* 62E3
Alfeld *W Germ* 34E1
Alfensas *Brazil* 27C3
Alfiós, R *Greece* 39E3
Alfonsine *Italy* 35D2
Alfonzo Cláudio *Brazil* 27D3
Alfredo Chaves *Brazil* 27D3
Al Furūthi *S Arabia* 65E1
Alga *USSR* 43K6
Algarrobal *Chile* 26A1
Algarrobo del Águila *Arg* 26B3
Algeciras *Spain* 37A2
Alger *Alg* 69C1
Algeria, Republic *Africa* 68B2
Al Ghaydah *S Yemen* 65F3
Alghero *Sardegna* 38B2
Algiers = Alger
Algona *USA* 9D3
Algonquin Park *Can* 11D1
Algorta *Urug* 26D2
Al Hadd *Oman* 65G2
Al Hadithah *Iraq* 62D3
Al Hadithah *S Arabia* 62C3
Al Haḍr *Iraq* 62D2
Al Haffah *Syria* 63D1
Al Hajar al Gharbī, Mts *Oman* 65G2
Al Hajar ash Sharqī, Mts *Oman* 65G2
Al Hamad, Desert Region *Jordan/S Arabia* 62C3
Al Haniyah, Desert Region *Iraq* 62E4
Al Hariq *S Arabia* 65E2
Al Harrah, Desert Region *S Arabia* 62C3
Al Harūj al Aswad, Upland *Libya* 67A2
Al Hasa, Region *S Arabia* 65E1
Al Hasakah *Syria* 62D2
Al Hawjā' *S Arabia* 62C4
Al Hayy *Iraq* 62E3
Al Hibāk, Region *S Arabia* 65F2
Al Hijānah *Syria* 63D2
Al Hillah *Iraq* 62D3
Al Hillah *S Arabia* 65E2
Al Hoceima *Mor* 69B1
Al Hudaydah *Yemen* 64D4
Al Hufūf *S Arabia* 65E1
Al Humrah, Region *UAE* 65F2
Al Huwatsah *Oman* 65G2
Aliābad *Iran* 61B1
Aliabad *Iran* 61D3
Aliákmon, R *Greece* 39E2
Alī al Gharbī *Iraq* 62E3
Alībāg *India* 60A1
Alibori, R *Benin* 69B3
Alicante *Spain* 37B2
Alice *USA* 6D4
Alice Springs *Aust* 76C3
Alicudi, I *Italy* 38C3
Aligarh *India* 58D3
Aligūdarz *Iran* 61B2
Ali-Khel *Afghan* 58B2
Alimniá, I *Greece* 39F3
Alipur Duār *India* 59C2
Aliquippa *USA* 10C2
Al'Irqah *S Yemen* 65E4
Alisal *USA* 18B2
Al' Īsawiyah *S Arabia* 62C3
Aliwal North *S Africa* 72D3
Al Jaghbūb *Libya* 67B2
Al Jālamīd *S Arabia* 62D3
Al Jawf *Libya* 67B2
Al Jawf *S Arabia* 62C4
Al Jazirah *Syria* 43G8
Al Jazirah, Desert Region *Syria/Iraq* 62D2
Aljezur *Port* 37A2
Al Jubayl *S Arabia* 65E1
Al Kabid, Desert *Jordan* 63D4
Al Kahfah *S Arabia* 64D1
Al Kāmil *Oman* 65G2
Al Khābūr, R *Syria* 62D2
Al Khābūrah *Oman* 65G2
Al Khālis *Iraq* 62D3
Al Khamāsīn *S Arabia* 64D2
Al Khasab *Oman* 65G1
Al Khawr *Qatar* 65F1
Al Khums *Libya* 67A1
Al Kidan, Region *S Arabia* 65F2
Al Kiswah *Syria* 63D2
Alkmaar *Neth* 40A2
Al Kufrah Oasis *Libya* 67B2
Al Kūt *Iraq* 62E3
Al Lādhiqīyah *Syria* 62C2
Allahābād *India* 59B2
Al Lajāh, Mt *Syria* 63D2
Allakaket *USA* 8H2
Allanmyo *Burma* 53B2
'Allaqi, Watercourse *Egypt* 64B2
Allatoona L *USA* 13C2
Alldays *S Africa* 72D1
Allegheny, R *USA* 11D2
Allegheny Mts *USA* 7F3
Allegheny Res *USA* 12A2
Allendale *USA* 13C2
Allen,Mt *NZ* 79A3
Allentown *USA* 11D2
Alleppey *India* 60B3
Aller, R *France* 36C2
Allgäu, Mts *W Germ* 35D1
Alliance *USA* 9B3
Al Līth *S Arabia* 64D2
Al Liwā, Region *UAE* 65F2
Allora *Aust* 78D1
Allos *France* 35B2
Alma *Can* 11E1
Alma, Michigan *USA* 10C2
Alma, Nebraska *USA* 14C1
Alma Ata *USSR* 57F1
Almada *Port* 37A2
Al Madinah = Medina
Almagan, I *Pacific O* 49H5
Al Mahrah, Region *S Yemen* 65F3
Al Majma'ah *S Arabia* 65E1
Al Manāmah *Bahrain* 65F1
Al Ma'nīyah *Iraq* 62D3
Almanor,L *USA* 17B2
Almansa *Spain* 37B2
Alma Peak, Mt *Can* 3C2
Al Māriyyah *UAE* 65F2
Al Marj *Libya* 67B1
Almazán *Spain* 37B1
Alme, R *W Germ* 34E1
Almenara *Brazil* 27D2
Almeria *Spain* 37B2
Almes, R *Brazil* 27C2
Al'met'yevsk *USSR* 42J5
Älmhult *Sweden* 40C1
Al Midhnab *S Arabia* 64D1
Al Miqdādīyah *Iraq* 62E3
Almirante Brown, Base *Ant* 80G3
Almirante Latorre *Chile* 26A1
Almirós *Greece* 39E3
Al Mish'ab *A Arabia* 65E1
Almodôvar *Port* 37A2
Almora *India* 58D3
Al Mubarraz *S Arabia* 65E1
Al Mudawwara *Jordan* 62C4
Al Mudaybi *Oman* 65G2
Al Muharraq *Bahrain* 65F1
Al Mukallā *S Yemen* 65E4
Al Mukhā *Yemen* 64D4
Al Musayyib *Iraq* 62D3
Al Muwaylih *S Arabia* 64C1
Alness *Scot* 32C3
Al Nu'mānīyah *Iraq* 62E3
Alnwick *Eng* 32E4
Alor, I *Indon* 55B4
Alor Setar *Malay* 53C4
Alost = Aalst
Alotau *PNG* 76E2
Aloysius,Mt *Aust* 76B3
Alpachiri *Arg* 26C3
Alpe di Succiso, Mt *Italy* 35D2
Alpena *USA* 10C1
Alpes du Valais, Mts *Switz* 35B1
Alpes Maritimes, Mts *France* 35B2
Alpi Carniche, Mts *Italy* 35E1
Alpi Dolomitiche, Mts *Italy* 38C1
Alpi Graie, Mts *Italy* 35B2
Alpine, Arizona *USA* 17E4
Alpine, Texas *USA* 14B3
Alpine, Wyoming *USA* 16D2
Alpi Orobie, Mts *Italy* 35C1
Alpi Penine, Mts *Italy* 35B2
Alpi Retiche, Mts *Switz* 35C1
Alpi Venoste, Mts *Italy* 35D1
Alps, Mts *Europe* 38B1
Al Qaddāhiyah *Libya* 67A1
Al Qadmūs *Syria* 63D1
Al Qā'im *Iraq* 62D3
Al Qalībah *S Arabia* 62C4
Al Qāmishlī *Syria* 62D2
Al Qardāhah *Syria* 63D1
Al Qaryah Ash Sharqiyah *Libya* 67A1
Al Qaryatayn *Syria* 62C3
Al Qasim, Region *S Arabia* 64D1
Al Qātif *S Arabia* 65E1
Al Qatrūn *Libya* 67A2
Al Qayşāmah *S Arabia* 65E1
Al Quatayfah *Syria* 63D2
Al Qunaytirah *Syria* 62C3
Al Qunfidhah *S Arabia* 64D3
Al Qurnah *Iraq* 62E3
Al Quşayr *Syria* 63D1
Al Qutayfah *Syria* 62C3
Al Quwayīyah *S Arabia* 65E2
Als, I *Den* 40B1
Alsace, Region *France* 36D2
Alsfeld *W Germ* 40B2
Alston *Eng* 32D4
Alta *Nor* 30J5
Alta Gracia *Arg* 23D4
Altagracia de Orituco *Ven* 21D5
Altai, Mts *Mongolia* 48B2
Altamaha, R *USA* 13C2
Altamira *Brazil* 25H4
Altamira *Mexico* 20C1
Altamura *Italy* 38D2
Altanbulag *Mongolia* 48D1
Altandulag *USSR* 47M5
Altape *PNG* 49H7
Altata *Mexico* 19B2
Altay *China* 46K5

Altay *Mongolia* 47L5
Altay, Mts *USSR* 46K5
Altdorf *Switz* 35C1
Altenkirchen *W Germ* 34D1
Altiplanicie del Payún, Flat *Arg* 26B3
Altkirch *France* 35B1
Alto Araguaia *Brazil* 27B2
Alto Molócue *Mozam* 71D5
Alton *USA* 10A3
Altoona *USA* 11D2
Alto Pencoso, Mts *Arg* 26B2
Alto Sucuriú *Brazil* 27B2
Altotonga *Mexico* 20C2
Altoyac de Alvarez *Mexico* 20B2
Altun Shan, Mts *China* 57G2
Alturas *USA* 16B2
Altus *USA* 14C3
Al' Jbaylah *S Arabia* 65F2
Al' Jlā *S Arabia* 64C1
Alula *Somalia* 67E3
Aluminé *Arg* 26A3
Al Jrayq, Desert Region *S Arabia* 62C4
Al' Jruq al Mu'taridah, Region *S Arabia* 65F2
Alva *USA* 14C2
Alvarado *Mexico* 20C2
Alvarado *USA* 15C3
Älvdalen *Sweden* 30G6
Alvear *Arg* 26D1
Alvin *USA* 15C4
Alvsbyn *Sweden* 30J5
Al Wajh *S Arabia* 64C1
Alwar *India* 58D3
Al Widyān, Desert Region *Iraq/S Arabia* 62D3
Alxa Yougi *China* 50A2
Alyat *USSR* 62E2
Alytus *USSR* 30J8
Alytus *USSR* 42C5
Alzey *W Germ* 34E2
Amacuzac, R *Mexico* 20C2
Amadi *Sudan* 70D3
Amādiyah *Iraq* 62D2
Amadjuak L *Can* 5L3
Amahai *Indon* 55C3
Amakusa-shotō, I *Japan* 51B5
Åmål *Sweden* 30G7
Amalat, R *USSR* 47N4
Amaliás *Greece* 39E3
Amalner *India* 58C4
Amambai *Brazil* 27A3
Amambai, R *Brazil* 27B3
Amami, I *Japan* 48F4
Amami gunto, Arch *Japan* 48F4
Amanzimtoti *S Africa* 72E3
Amapá *Brazil* 25H3
Amapá, State *Brazil* 25H3
Amarapura *Burma* 59E3
Amarillo *USA* 14B2
Amasya *Turk* 43F7
Amatitan *Mexico* 20B1
Amaulipas *Mexico* 20C1
Amazonas = Solimões
Amazonas *Brazil* 25H4
Amazonas, State *Brazil* 24E4
Amazonas, R *Brazil* 22D4
Ambāla *India* 58D2
Ambalangoda *Sri Lanka* 60C3
Ambalavao *Madag* 71E6
Ambam *Cam* 70B3
Ambanja *Madag* 71E5
Ambarchik *USSR* 47S3
Ambato *Ecuador* 24C4
Ambato-Boeny *Madag* 71E5
Ambatolampy *Madag* 71E5
Ambatondrazaka *Madag* 71E5
Amberg *W Germ* 40C3
Ambergris Cay, I *Belize* 19D3
Ambérieu *France* 35A2
Ambikāpur *India* 59B3
Ambilobe *Madag* 71E5
Amboasary *Madag* 71E6
Ambodifototra *Madag* 71E5
Ambohimahasoa *Madag* 71E6
Ambon *Indon* 55C3
Ambon, I *Indon* 55C3
Ambositra *Madag* 71E6
Ambovombe *Madag* 71E6
Amboy *USA* 12C2
Ambriz *Angola* 71B4
Ambrym, I *Vanuatu* 77F2
Amchitka *USA* 8B6
Amchitka, I *USA* 8B6
Amchitka Pass *USA* 8C6
Am Dam *Chad* 70C2
Amderma *USSR* 46H3
Ameca *Mexico* 19B2
Ameca, R *Mexico* 20A1
Amecacameca *Mexico* 20C2
Ameghino *Arg* 26C2
Ameland, I *Neth* 40B2
Amenia *USA* 12D2
American Falls *USA* 16D2
American Falls Res *USA* 16D2
American Fork *USA* 17D2
American Highland, Upland *Ant* 80F10
American Samoa, Is *Pacific O* 75L5
Americus *USA* 13C2
Amersfoort *S Africa* 72D2
Amery *USA* 9D2
Amery Ice Shelf *Ant* 80G10
Ames *USA* 9D3
Amesbury *USA* 12E1
Amfilokhía *Greece* 39E3
Amfissa *Greece* 39E3
Amga *USSR* 47P3
Amga, R *USSR* 47P3
Amgu *USSR* 51D2
Amguema, R *USSR* 8C2
Amgun', R *USSR* 51D1
Amhara, Region *Eth* 70D2
Amherst *Can* 5M5
Amherst, Massachusetts *USA* 12D1
Amherst, Virginia *USA* 11D3
Amhur *India* 60B2
Amiens *France* 36C2
Amino *Japan* 52C3
Amioune *Leb* 63C1
Amirante Is *Indian O* 66K8
Amisk L *Can* 3H3
Amistad Res *Mexico* 14B4
Amlekhgan *Nepal* 59C2
Amlia, I *USA* 8D6
Amman *Jordan* 62C3
Ämmänsaario *Fin* 30K6
Ammersfoort *Neth* 40B2
Amnyong-dan, C *N Korea* 52A3
Amoca'ya, R *USSR* 56E1
Amol *Iran* 61C1
Amos *Can* 5L5
Amoy = Xiamen
Ampana *Indon* 55B3
Ampanihy *Madag* 71E6
Amparo *Brazil* 27C3
Amposta *Spain* 37C1
Amrān *Yemen* 64D3
Amrāvati *India* 58D4
Amreli *India* 58C4
Amritsar *India* 58C2
Amsterdam *Neth* 40A2
Amsterdam *S Africa* 72E2
Amsterdam *USA* 11E2
Am Timan *Chad* 70C2
Amu Darya, R *USSR* 66L3
Amukta, I *USA* 8D6
Amukta Pass *USA* 8D6
Amund Ringes I *Can* 5J2
Amundsen G *Can* 4F2
Amundsen S *Ant* 80F4
Amundsen-Scott, Base *Ant* 80E
Amuntai *Indon* 54E3
Amur, R *USSR* 47O4
Amur, Watercourse *Sudan* 64C3
Amurang *Indon* 55B2
Amursk *USSR* 51D1
Amurskiy Liman, Str *USSR* 51E1
Amurzet *USSR* 51C2
Anabar, R *USSR* 47N2
Anaco *Ven* 24F2
Anaconda *USA* 6B2
Anacortes *USA* 16B1
Anadarko *USA* 14C2
Anadyr' *USSR* 47T3
Anadyr', R *USSR* 47T3
Anadyrskiy Zaliv, S *USSR* 47U3
Anadyrskoye Ploskogor'ye, Plat *USSR* 47T3
Anáfi, I *Greece* 39F3
Anagé *Brazil* 27D1
'Anah *Iraq* 62D3
Anaheim *USA* 17C4
Anaimalai Hills *India* 60B2
Anakāpalle *India* 60C1
Anaktuvuk P *USA* 8J2
Analalava *Madag* 71E5
Anambra, State *Nig* 69H4
Anambra, R *Nig* 69H4
Anamosa *USA* 10A2
Anamur *Turk* 43E8
Anan *Japan* 52B4
Anantapur *India* 60B2
Anantnag *India* 58D2
Anápolis *Brazil* 25J7
Anār *Iran* 61D2
Anārak *Iran* 61C2
Anardara *Afghan* 61E2
Anatahan, I *Pacific O* 49H5
Añatuya *Arg* 23D3
Anbyŏn *N Korea* 51B4
Ancapa Is *USA* 18C4
Ancasti *Arg* 26B1
Anchorage *USA* 4D3
Ancohuma, Mt *Bol* 24E7
Ancón *Peru* 24C6
Ancona *Italy* 38C2
Ancram *USA* 12D1
Ancud *Chile* 23B6
Ancy-le-Franc *France* 34C3
Anda *China* 51B2
Andabuaylas *Peru* 24D6
Andacollo *Arg* 26A3
Andado *Aust* 78A1
Andagalá *Arg* 26B1
Andalsnes *Nor* 30F6
Andalucia, Region *Spain* 37A2
Andalusia *USA* 13B2
Andaman Is *Burma* 57H4
Andaman S *Burma* 57H4
Andamooka *Aust* 78A2
Andaraí *Brazil* 27D1
Andee *Irish Rep* 33B5
Andelot *France* 34C2
Andenes *Nor* 30H5
Andermatt *Switz* 35C1
Andernach *W Germ* 40B2
Anderson, Indiana *USA* 10B2
Anderson, Missouri *USA* 15D2
Anderson, S Carolina *USA* 13C2
Anderson, R *Can* 4F3
Andhra Pradesh, State *India* 60B1
Andikíthira, I *Greece* 39E3
Andizhan *USSR* 46J5
Andkhui *Afghan* 46H6
Andong *S Korea* 51B4
Andorra, Principality *SW Europe* 37C1
Andorra-La-Vella *Andorra* 37C1
Andover *Eng* 33E6
Andover, New Hampshire *USA* 12E1
Andover, New York *USA* 12B1
Andradina *Brazil* 27B3
Andreafsky *USA* 8F3
Andreanof Is *USA* 8C6
Andreapol' *USSR* 41G1
Andreas,C *Cyprus* 62B2
Andrews *USA* 14B3
Andria *Italy* 38D2
Andros, I *Bahamas* 7F4
Ándros, I *Greece* 39E3
Androth, I *India* 60A2
Andújar *Spain* 37B2
Andulo *Angola* 71B5
Anécho *Togo* 69G4
Anéfis *Mali* 68C3
Aneityum, I *Vanuatu* 77F3
Añelo *Arg* 26B3
Angareb, Watercourse *Eth* 64C4
Angarsk *USSR* 47M4
Ånge *Sweden* 42A3
Angel de la Guarda, I *Mexico* 19A2
Angeles *Phil* 55F7
Angelholm *Sweden* 30G7
Angellala Creek, R *Aust* 78C1
Angels Camp *USA* 18B1
Angemuk, Mt *Indon* 49G7
Angers *France* 36B2
Angerville *France* 34B2
Angkor, Hist Site *Camb* 53C3
Anglesey, I *Wales* 31C3
Angleton *USA* 15C4
Angmagssalik *Greenland* 5P3
Angoche *Mozam* 71E5
Angol *Chile* 23B5
Angola, Indiana *USA* 10C2
Angola, New York *USA* 12A1
Angola, Republic *Africa* 71B5
Angola Basin *Atlantic O* 73J5
Angoon *USA* 8M4
Angoulême *France* 36C2
Angra do Heroismo *Açores* 68A1
Angra dos Reis *Brazil* 27D3
Anguil *Arg* 26C3
Anguilla, I *Caribbean* 21E3
Anguilla Cays, Is *Caribbean* 21B2
Angul *India* 59C3
Angumu *Zaïre* 70C4
Anholt, I *Den* 40C1
Anhua *China* 50C4
Anhui, Province *China* 50D3
Anhumas *Brazil* 27B2
Anhŭng *S Korea* 52A3
Aniak *USA* 8G3
Anicuns *Brazil* 27C2
Anié *Togo* 69G4
Animas, R *USA* 14A2
Animas Peak, Mt *USA* 14A3
Anita *USA* 9D3
Anizy-le-Château *France* 34B2
Anjak *USA* 4C3
Anjou, Republic *France* 36B2
Anjouan, I *Comoros* 71E5
Anjozorobe *Madag* 71E5
Anju *N Korea* 51B4
Ankang *China* 50B3
Ankara *Turk* 43E8
Ankaratra, Mt *Madag* 71E5
Ankazoabo *Madag* 71E6
Ankazobe *Madag* 71E5
Ankeny *USA* 9D3
Anklam *E Germ* 40C2
Ankwe, R *Nig* 69H4
An Loc *Viet* 53D3
Anlong *China* 50B4
Anlu *China* 50C3
Anna *USA* 10B3
'Annaba *Alg* 69D1
An Nabk *S Arabia* 62C3
An Nabk *Syria* 62C3
Anna Creek *Aust* 78A1
An Najaf *Iraq* 62D3
Annan *Scot* 32D4
Annapolis *USA* 11D3
Annapurna, Mt *Nepal* 59B2
Ann Arbor *USA* 10C2
An Nāsirah *Syria* 63D1
An Nāsiriyah *Iraq* 62E3
Annecy *France* 35B2
Annemasse *France* 35B1
Annette I *USA* 3B2
An Nhon *Viet* 53D3
An Nimās *S Arabia* 64D3
Anning *China* 50A5
Anniston *USA* 13B2
Annonay *France* 36C2
Annot *France* 35B3
Annotto Bay *Jamaica* 21J1
Anqing *China* 50D3
Ansai *China* 50B2
Ansbach *W Germ* 40C3
Anse d'Hainault *Haiti* 21C3
Anshan *China* 50E1
Anshun *China* 50B4
Ansley *USA* 14C1
Anson *USA* 14C3
Anson B *Aust* 49F8
Ansongo *Mali* 68C3
Ansonville *Can* 10C1
Ansted *USA* 10C3
Antakya *Turk* 43F8
Antalaha *Madag* 71F5
Antalya *Turk* 43E8
Antalya Körfezi, B *Turk* 43E8
Antananarivo *Madag* 71E5
Antarctic Circle *Ant* 80G1
Antarctic Pen *Ant* 80G3
Antequera *Spain* 37B2
Anthony *USA* 14A3
Anti-Atlas, Mts *Mor* 68B1
Antibes *France* 35B3
Anticosti I *Can* 5M5
Antigo *USA* 10B1
Antigua, I *Caribbean* 21E3
Anti Lebanon = Jebel esh Sharqi
Antioch *USA* 17B3
Antipodes Is *NZ* 77G5
Antlers *USA* 15C3
Antofagasta *Chile* 23B2
Antonina *Brazil* 27C4
Antonito *USA* 14A2
Antrim, County *N Ire* 32B4
Antrim *N Ire* 32B4
Antrim *USA* 12E1
Antrim Hills *N Ire* 32B4
Antseranana *Madag* 71E5
Antsirabe *Madag* 71E5
Antsohiny *Madag* 71E5
An Tuc *Viet* 53D3
Añtuya *Arg* 26C1
Antwerpen *Belg* 34C1
An Uaimh *Irish Rep* 33B5
Anui *S Korea* 52A3
Anupgarh *India* 58C3
Anuradhapura *Sri Lanka* 60C3
Anvers = Antwerpen
Anvik *USA* 4B3
Anvil Pk, Mt *USA* 8B6
Anxi *China* 47L5
Anyang *China* 50C2
A'nyêmaqên Shan, Upland *China* 50A3
Anyuysk *USSR* 47S3
Anza, R *Italy* 35C2
Anzac *Can* 3F2
Anzhero-Sudzhensk *USSR* 46K4
Anzio *Italy* 38C2
Aoba, I *Vanuatu* 77F2
Aomori *Japan* 51E3
Aosta *Italy* 38B1
Aoukar, Desert Region *Maur* 68B3
Aoulef *Alg* 68C2
Aozou *Chad* 70B1
Apa, R *Brazil/Par* 23E2
Apalachee B *USA* 7E4
Apalachicola *USA* 13C3
Apalachicola B *USA* 13B3
Apan *Mexico* 20C2
Apaporis, R *Colombia* 24D3
Aparecida do Taboado *Brazil* 27B3
Aparri *Phil* 55F7
Apatin *Yugos* 39D1
Apatity *USSR* 42E2
Apatzingan *Mexico* 19B3
Apeldoorn *Neth* 40B2
Apia *Western Samoa* 77H2
Apiai *Brazil* 27C3
Apizolaya *Mexico* 20B1
Apoera *Suriname* 25G2
Apollo Bay *Aust* 78B3
Apo,Mt, Mt *Phil* 55G9
Apopka,L *USA* 13C3
Aporé, R *Brazil* 25H7
Apostle Is *USA* 10A1
Apostle L *USA* 7D2
Apozol *Mexico* 20B1
Appalachian Mts *USA* 7E3
Appenino Tosco-Emiliano, Mts *Italy* 35D2
Appennino Abruzzese, Mts *Italy* 38C2
Appennino Ligure, Mts *Italy* 38B2
Appennino Lucano, Mts *Italy* 38D2
Appennino Napoletano, Mts *Italy* 38D2
Appennino Tosco-Emilliano, Mts *Italy* 38C2
Appennino Umbro-Marchigiano, Mts *Italy* 38C2
Appenzell *Switz* 35C1
Appleby *Eng* 33D4
Appleton, Minnesota *USA* 9C2
Appleton, Wisconsin *USA* 10B2
Apsheronskiy Poluostrov, Pt *USSR* 43J7
Apt *France* 35A3
Apucarana *Brazil* 23F2
Apulco *Mexico* 20C1
Apure, R *Ven* 24E2
Apurimac, R *Peru* 24D6
'Aqaba *Jordan* 62C4
'Aqaba,G of *Egypt/S Arabia* 62B4
'Aqdā *Iran* 61C2
Aqidauana *Brazil* 25G8
Aqua Nueva *Mexico* 20A1
Aquidabán, R *Par* 27A3
Aquidauana *Brazil* 23E2
Aquidauana, R *Brazil* 27A2
Aquila *Mexico* 20B2
Ara *India* 59B2
Arab *USA* 13B2
'Arab al Mulk *Syria* 63C1
Arabian, S *Asia/Arabian Pen* 56E4
Arabian Basin *Indian O* 74E4
Aracajú *Brazil* 25L6
Aracanguy,Mts de *Par* 27A3
Aracati *Brazil* 25L4
Aracatu *Brazil* 27D1
Araçatuba *Brazil* 25H8
Aracena *Spain* 37A2
Araçuai *Brazil* 25K7
Arad *Israel* 63C3
Arad *Rom* 43C6
Arada *Chad* 70C2
'Arādah *UAE* 65F2
Arafura S *Indon/Aust* 76C1
Aragarças *Brazil* 25H7
Aragats, Mt *USSR* 43G7
Aragón, Region *Spain* 37B1
Aragon, R *Spain* 37B1
Araguaçu *Brazil* 27C1
Araguaia, R *Brazil* 25H6
Araguaína *Brazil* 25J5
Araguari *Brazil* 25J7
Araguari, R *Brazil* 27C2
Arai *Japan* 52C3
Arak *Alg* 68C2
Arāk *Iran* 61B2
Arakan Yoma, Mts *Burma* 53A2
Arakkonam *India* 60B2
Araks, R *USSR* 62E2
Aral S *USSR* 44D3
Aral'sk *USSR* 46H4
Aral'sk *USSR* 56E1
Aral'skoye More, S *USSR* 46G5
Aramberri *Mexico* 20C1
Aran, I *Irish Rep* 31B2
Aran, Is *Irish Rep* 31B3
Aranda de Duero *Spain* 37B1
Arandas *Mexico* 20B1
Aranjuez *Spain* 37B1
Aranos *Namibia* 72B1
Aransas Pass *USA* 15F4
Arao *Japan* 52B4
Araouane *Mali* 68B3
Arapahoe *USA* 14C1
Arapey, R *Urug* 23E4
Arapey Grande, R *Urug* 26D2
Arapiraca *Brazil* 25L6
Araporgas *Brazil* 27B3
Ararangua *Brazil* 23G3
Araraquara *Brazil* 25J8
Araras *Brazil* 27C3
Ararat *Aust* 76D4
Ararat *USSR* 62D2
Aras, R *Turk* 62D1
Aras, R *USSR* 43H8
Aratali *Eth* 64C3
Arato *Japan* 52D3
Arauca, R *Ven* 24E2
Arauco *Chile* 26A3
Arauea *Colombia* 24D2
Arāvalli Range, Mts *India* 58C3
Arawa *PNG* 77E1
Araxá *Brazil* 25J7

Araxes, R Iran 43G8
Arba Minch Eth 70D3
Arbatax Sardegna 38B3
Arbīl Iraq 43G8
Arbois France 35A1
Arbrå Sweden 30H6
Arbroath Scot 32D3
Arc, R France 35A3
Arc, R France 35B2
Arcachon France 36B3
Arcade USA 12A1
Arcadia USA 13E4
Arcata USA 16B2
Arc Dome, Mt USA 18D1
Arcelia Mexico 20B2
Archbald USA 12C2
Arches Nat Pk USA 18E3
Archipiélago de Camaguey, Arch Cuba 21B2
Archipiélago de la Reina Adelaida, Arch Chile 23B8
Archipiélago de las Chones, Arch Chile 23B6
Archipiélago de las Perlas, Arch Panama 24C2
Arcis-sur-Aube France 34C2
Arco USA 16D2
Arcos Brazil 27C3
Arcos de la Frontera Spain 37A2
Arc Senans France 35A1
Arctic Circle 80C1
Arctic Red Can 4E3
Arctic Red R Can 4E3
Arctic Village USA 4D3
Arctowski, Base Ant 80G2
Arda, R Bulg 39F2
Ardabīl Iran 43H8
Ardahan Turk 43G7
Ardar des Iforas, Upland Alg/Mali 68C2
Ardekān Iran 61C2
Ardel Nor 30F6
Ardennes, Department France 34C2
Ardennes, Region Belg 40B2
Ardestan Iran 61C2
Ardh es Suwwan, Desert Region Jordan 62C3
Ardila, R Port 37A2
Ardlethan Aust 78C2
Ardmore USA 6D3
Ardnamurchan, Pt Scot 32B3
Ardres France 33F6
Ardres France 34A1
Ardrishaig Scot 32C3
Ardrossan Scot 32C4
Arecibo Puerto Rico 21D3
Areia Branca Brazil 25L4
Arena,Pt USA 17B3
Arendal Nor 30F7
Arequipa Peru 24D7
Arezzo Italy 38C2
Argens, R France 35B3
Argenta Italy 38C2
Argentan France 36C2
Argenteuil France 34B2
Argentina, Republic S America 22D7
Argentine Basin Atlantic O 73F7
Argenton-sur-Creuse France 36C2
Argeşul, R Rom 39F2
Arghardab, R Afghan 58B2
Argolikós Kólpos, G Greece 39E3
Argonne, Region France 34C2
Árgos Greece 39E3
Argostólion Greece 39E3
Arguello,Pt USA 18B3
Argungu Nig 69G3
Argus Range, Mts USA 18D3
Argyle,L Aust 76B2
Argyll, Oilfield N Sea 32G3
Århus Den 40C1
Ariamsvlei Namibia 71C6
Arian zón, R Spain 37B1
Arias Venado Arg 26C2
Aribinda Upper Volta 68B3
Arica Chile 23B1
Arifwala Pak 58C2
Arihā = Jericho
Arikaree, R USA 14B2
Arima Trinidad 21L1
Arinos Brazil 27C2
Arinos, R Brazil 25G6
Ario de Rosales Mexico 20B2
Aripo,Mt Trinidad 21L1
Aripuana Brazil 24F5
Aripuanã, R Brazil 24F5
Arisaig Scot 32C3
Ariskere India 60B2
Arista Mexico 20B1
Arista Mexico 20D2
Aristazabal I Can 3C3
Arizona Arg 26B3
Arizona, State USA 6B3
Årjäng Sweden 30G7
Arka USSR 47Q3
Arkadak USSR 43G5
Arkadelphia USA 15D3
Arkalya USSR 46H4
Arkansas, State USA 7D3
Arkansas, R USA 7D3
Arkansas City USA 15C2
Arkhangel'sk USSR 42G3
Arkhara USSR 51C2
Arkipelag Nordenshelda, Arch USSR 47K2
Arklow Irish Rep 31B3
Arlberg P Austria 35D1
Arles France 36C3
Arlington, S Dakota USA 9C3
Arlington, Texas USA 15C3
Arlington, Virginia USA 11D3
Arlington, Washington USA 16B1
Arlington Heights USA 10B2
Arlon Belg 40B3
Armageddon = Megido
Armagh, County N Ire 33B4
Armagh N Ire 33B4
Armagós, I Greece 39F3
Armançon, R France 34B3
Armavir USSR 43G7
Armena Mexico 20B2
Armenia Colombia 24C3
Armidale Aust 76E4
Armstrong Can 3E3
Armu, R USSR 51D2
Armyanskaya SSR, Republic USSR 46F5
Arnaud, R Can 5L3
Arnauti, C Cyprus 62B2
Arnett USA 14C2
Arnhem Neth 40B2
Arnhem,C Aust 76C2
Arnhem Land Aust 76C2
Arno, R Italy 35D3
Arnold USA 18B1
Arnoldstein Austria 35E1
Arnprior Can 11D1
Arnsberg W Germ 34E1
Aroab Namibia 72B2
Arolsen W Germ 34E1
Arona Italy 35C2
Aropuk L USA 8F3
Arorae, I Kiribati 77G1
Arosa Switz 38B1
Arpajon France 34B2
Arquipélago dos Abrolhos, Arch Brazil 27E2
Arquipélago dos Bijagós, Arch Guinea-Bissau 68A3
Arraias Brazil 27C1
Ar Ramādī Iraq 62D3
Arran, I Scot 32C4
Ar Raqqah Syria 62C2
Arras France 36C1
Ar Rass S Arabia 64D1
Ar Rastan Syria 63D1
Ar Rawdah S Arabia 64D2
Arrecife Canary Is 68A2
Arrecifes Arg 26C2
Arriaga Mexico 20B1
Arriaga Mexico 20D2
Ar Rifā't Iraq 62E3
Ar Rihāb, Desert Region Iraq 62E3
Ar Riyād = Riyadh
Arrochar Scot 32C3
Arroio Grande Brazil 26E2
Arrojado, R Brazil 27C1
Arrowrock Res USA 16C2
Arrowtown NZ 79A2
Arroyo Grande USA 18B3
Arroyo Seco Mexico 20C1
Ar Ru'ays Qatar 65F1
Ar Rustaq Oman 65G2
Ar Rutbah Iraq 62D3
Ar Ruwaydah S Arabia 64D2
Arsen'yev USSR 51C3
Arsiero Italy 35D2
Arsizio Italy 36D2
Arsk USSR 42H4
Árta Greece 39E3
Arteaga Mexico 20B2
Artem USSR 51C3
Artemovsk USSR 47L4
Artemovskiy USSR 47N4
Artenay France 34A2
Artesia USA 6C3
Arthurs P NZ 79B2
Årthus Den 30G7
Artic Bay Can 5K2
Artigas Urug 23E4
Artigas Urug 26D2
Artillery L Can 4H3
Artois, Region France 36C1
Artsiz USSR 41F3
Arturo Prat, Base Ant 80G2
Artvin Turk 43G7
Aru Zaïre 70D3
Aruanā Brazil 25H6
Aruba, I Caribbean 21C4
Arun, R Nepal 59C2
Arunāchal Pradesh, Union Territory India 59D2
Arun He, R China 51A2
Arun Qi China 51A2
Aruppukkottai India 60B3
Arusha Tanz 70D4
Aruwimi, R Zaïre 70C3
Arvada USA 14A2
Arvayheer Mongolia 48D2
Arvayheer USSR 47M5
Arve, R France 35B2
Arvida Can 5L5
Arvidsjaur Sweden 30H5
Arvidsjaur Sweden 42B2
Arvika Sweden 30G7
Arvin USA 17C3
Arwad, I Syria 63C1
Arwala Indon 55C4
Arzamas USSR 42G4
Arzew Alg 69B1
Asadabad Afghan 58C2
Asahi, R Japan 52B4
Asahi dake, Mt Japan 51E3
Asahikawa Japan 51E3
Asan-man, B S Korea 52A3
Asansol India 59C3
Asawanwah, Well Libya 67A2
Asbest USSR 42L4
Asbestos Mts S Africa 72C2
Asbury Park USA 11E2
Ascension, I Atlantic O 73H5
Aschaffenburg W Germ 40B3
Aschersleben E Germ 40C2
Ascoli Piceno Italy 38C2
Ascona Switz 35C1
Asedjirad, Upland Alg 68C2
Åsele Sweden 30H6
Aselle Eth 70D3
Asenovgrad Bulg 39E2
Asfeld France 34C2
Asha USSR 42K4
Ashburn USA 13C2
Ashburton NZ 77G5
Ashburton, R Aust 76A3
Ashdod Israel 62B3
Ashdown USA 15D3
Asheboro USA 13D1
Asheville USA 7E3
Ashford Aust 78D1
Ashford Eng 33F6
Ash Fork USA 17D3
Ashibetsu Japan 52D2
Ashikaga Japan 51D4
Ashizuri-misaki, Pt Japan 52B4
Ashkhabad USSR 46G6
Ashland, Kansas USA 14C2
Ashland, Kentucky USA 7E3
Ashland, Montana USA 9A2
Ashland, Nebraska USA 15C1
Ashland, Ohio USA 10C2
Ashland, Oregon USA 6A2
Ashland, Virginia USA 11D3
Ashland, Wisconsin USA 9D2
Ashley Aust 78C1
Ashley USA 9C2
Ashokan Res USA 12C2
Ashqelon Israel 63C3
Ash Shabakh Iraq 62D3
Ash Sha'm UAE 65G1
Ash Sh'ār S Arabia 64D3
Ash Sharqāt Iraq 62D2
Ash Shatrah Iraq 62E3
Ash Shihr S Yemen 65E4
Ash Shumlul S Arabia 65E1
Ash Shuqayq S Arabia 64D3
Ashtabula USA 10C2
Ashuanipi L Can 5M4
Asi, R Syria 43F8
Asiago Italy 35D2
Asilah Mor 69A1
Asinara, I Medit S 38B2
Asino USSR 46K4
Asir, Region S Arabia 64D2
Aska India 59B4
Aşkale Turk 62D2
Askersund Sweden 30G7
Asl Egypt 63B4
Asmar Afghan 58C1
Asmara Eth 70D2
Aso Japan 52B4
Asosa Eth 70D2
Aspermont USA 14B3
Aspiring,Mt NZ 79A2
Aspres-sur-Buëch France 35A2
Assab Eth 70E2
As Sabkhah Syria 62C2
As Salamiyah S Arabia 65E2
As Salamiyah Syria 62C2
Assale,L, L Eth 64D4
As Salmān Iraq 62D3
Assam, State India 59D2
As Samāwah Iraq 62E3
As Şanām, Region S Arabia 65F2
As Sanamayn Syria 63D2
Asse, R France 35B3
Assen Neth 40B2
Assens Den 40C1
As Sidrah Libya 67A1
Assiniboia Can 4H5
Assiniboia USA 9A2
Assiniboine, R Can 9C2
Assiniboine,Mt Can 4G4
Assis Brazil 25H8
Assis Brazil 25H8
Assisi Italy 35E3
As Sukhnah Syria 62C3
As Sulayyil S Arabia 65E2
As Summan, Region S Arabia 65E2
Assumption, I Seychelles 71E4
As Suq S Arabia 64D2
As Suwaydā' Syria 62C3
As Suwayrah Iraq 62D3
Astara USSR 62E2
Asti Italy 38B2
Astipálaia, I Greece 39F3
Astorga Spain 37A1
Astoria USA 6A2
Astrakhan' USSR 43H6
Asturias, Region Spain 37A1
Asunción Par 23E3
Aswa, R Uganda 70D3
Aswân Egypt 64B2
Aswân High Dam Egypt 67C2
Asyût Egypt 67C2
As Zilaf Syria 62C3
Atafu, I Tokelau Is 77H1
Atakpamé Togo 69G4
Atambua Indon 55B5
Atangmik Greenland 5N3
Atapupu Indon 55B4
Atar Maur 68A2
Atascadero USA 18B3
Atasu USSR 46J5
Atauro, I Indon 55C4
Atbara Sudan 70D2
Atbasar USSR 46H4
Atchafalaya B USA 7D4
Atchison USA 7D3
Atco USA 12C3
Atebubu Ghana 69F4
Atenguillo Mexico 20B1
Atessa Italy 38C2
Ath Belg 34B1
Athabasca Can 3F3
Athabasca, R Can 4G4
Athabasca L Can 4H4
Athens = Athínai
Athens, Alabama USA 13B2
Athens, Georgia USA 7E3
Athens, Ohio USA 10C3
Athens, Pennsylvania USA 12B2
Athens, Tennessee USA 13C1
Athens, Texas USA 15C3
Athiémé Benin 69G4
Athínai Greece 39E3
Athlone Irish Rep 31B3
Athna Cyprus 63B1
Athol USA 12D1
Áthos, Mt Greece 39E2
Athy Irish Rep 33B5
Ati Chad 70B2
Atikoken Can 5J5
Atka USSR 47R3
Atka, I USA 8D6
Atkarsk USSR 43G5
Atkins USA 15D2
Atlacomulco Mexico 20C2
Atlanta, Georgia USA 7E3
Atlanta, Michigan USA 10C2
Atlantic USA 15C1
Atlantic City USA 7F3
Atlantic Highlands USA 12C2
Atlantic Indian Basin Atlantic O 73H8
Atlantic Indian Ridge Atlantic O 73H7
Atlas Saharien, Mts Alg 68C1
Atlin Can 4E4
Atlin L Can 4E4
Atlit Israel 63C2
Atlixco Mexico 20C2
Atmore USA 7E3
Atofinandrahana Madag 71E6
Atognak I USA 8H4
Atoka USA 15C3
Atotonilco Mexico 20B1
Atoyac, R Mexico 20C2
Atrato, R Colombia 24C2
Attaf, Region UAE 65F2
At Tā'if S Arabia 64D2
At Tall Syria 63D2
Attalla USA 13B2
Attauapiskat Can 5K4
Attauapiskat, R Can 5K4
At Taysiyah, Desert Region S Arabia 62D3
Attica, Indiana USA 10B2
Attica, New York USA 12A1
Attigny France 34C2
Attila Line Cyprus 63B1
Attleboro, Massachusetts USA 11E2
Attopeu Laos 53D3
Attu USA 8A5
Attu, I USA 8A5
At Tubayq, Upland S Arabia 62C4
Atuel, R Arg 26B3
Atvidaberg Sweden 30H7
Atwater USA 18B2
Aubagne France 36D3
Aube, Department France 34C2
Aube, R France 34C2
Aubenas France 36C3
Aubry L Can 8N2
Auburn, Alabama USA 13B2
Auburn, California USA 17B3
Auburn, Indiana USA 10B2
Auburn, Maine USA 11E2
Auburn, Nebraska USA 15C1
Auburn, New York USA 11D2
Auburn, Washington USA 16B1
Auch France 36C3
Auchi Nig 69H4
Auckland NZ 77G4
Auckland Is NZ 75K7
Aude, R France 36C3
Auden Can 5K4
Audincourt France 35B1
Audubon USA 9D3
Augathella Aust 78C1
Aughrabies Falls S Africa 72B2
Augsburg W Germ 40C3
Augusta Aust 76A4
Augusta, Georgia USA 7E3
Augusta, Kansas USA 15C2
Augusta, Maine USA 7G2
Augusta, Montana USA 16D1
Augusta, Wisconsin USA 10A2
Augustine I USA 8H4
Augustow Pol 41E2
Augustus,Mt Aust 76A3
Auk, Oilfield N Sea 32G3
Aulla Italy 35C2
Aumale France 34A2
Auob, R Namibia 72B1
Auponhia Indon 55C3
Aups France 35B3
Auraiya India 58D3
Aurangābād India 58D5
Aurès, Mts Alg 69D1
Aurillac France 36C3
Aurora, Colorado USA 6C3
Aurora, Illinois USA 10B2
Aurora, Indiana USA 10C3
Aurora, Mississippi USA 15D2
Aurora, Nebraska USA 15C1
Aus Namibia 72B2
Au Sable USA 10C2
Ausert, Well Mor 68A2
Austin, Minnesota USA 7D2
Austin, Nevada USA 17C3
Austin, Pennsylvania USA 12A2
Austin, Texas USA 6D3
Australian Alps, Mts Aust 76D4
Austria, Fed Republic Europe 28G4
Authie, R France 34A1
Autlán Mexico 19B3
Autun France 36C2
Auvergne, Region France 36C2
Auxerre France 36C2
Auxi-le-Château France 34A1
Auxonne France 35A1
Avallon France 36C2
Avalon USA 18C4
Avalon Pen Can 5N5
Avalos, R Arg 26D1
Avaré Brazil 27C3
Avaz Iran 61E2
Avedat, Hist Site Israel 63C3
Aveíro Brazil 25G4
Aveiro Port 37A1
Avellaneda Arg 23E4
Avellino Italy 38C2
Avenal USA 18B3
Avesnes-sur-Helpe France 34B1
Avesta Sweden 30H6
Avezzano Italy 38C2
Aviemore Scot 32D3
Aviemore,L NZ 79B2
Avigliana Italy 35B2
Avignon France 36C3
Avila Spain 37B1
Aviles Spain 37A1
Avisio, R Italy 35D1
Avoca, Iowa USA 9C3
Avoca, New York USA 12B1
Avoca, R Aust 78B3
Avon, County Eng 33D6
Avon USA 12B1
Avon, R, Dorset Eng 33E6
Avon, R, Warwick Eng 33E5
Avondale USA 17D4
Avonmouth Wales 33D6
Avon Park USA 13E4
Avre, R France 34B2
Avtovac Yugos 39D2
A'waj, R Syria 63D2
Awaji-shima, B Japan 51D5
Awarem Eth 70E3
Awarua Pt NZ 79A2
Awash Eth 70E3
Awash, R Eth 70E3
Awa-shima, I Japan 52C3
Awatere, R NZ 79B2
Awbārī Libya 67A2
Aweil Sudan 70C3
Awjilan Libya 67B2

Awka Nig 69H4
Awuna, R USA 8G2
Axel Can 5J1
Axminster Eng 33D6
Ayabe Japan 52C3
Ayacucho Arg 23E5
Ayacucho Colombia 21C5
Ayacucho Peru 24D6
Ayaguz USSR 46K5
Ayakkum Hu, L China 57G2
Ayamonte Spain 37A2
Ayan USSR 47P4
Ayauiri Peru 24D6
Aydin Turk 43D8
Ayios Evstrátios, I Greece 39F3
Aykhal USSR 47N3
Aylesbury Eng 33E5
Aylmer,Mt Can 3E3
'Ayn al Fijah Syria 63D2
Ayn Zālah Iraq 62D2
Ayn Zuwayyah, Well Libya 67B2
Ayod Sudan 70D3
Ayr Aust 76D2
Ayr Scot 32C4
Ayr, R Scot 32C4
Ayre,Pt of Eng 33C4
Ayutthaya Thai 53C3
Ayutla Mexico 20B1
Ayvacik Turk 39F3
Ayvalik Turk 39F3
Azamgarh India 59B2
Azaouad, Desert Region Mali 68B3
Azare Nig 69J3
A'Zaz Syria 62C2
Azbine = Aïr
Azeffal, Watercourse Maur 68A2
Azemmour Mor 69A2
Azerbaydzhanskaya SSR, Republic USSR 46F5
Azogues Ecuador 24C4
Azopol'ye USSR 42H2
Azores = Açores
Azoum, R Chad 70C2
Azovskoye More, S USSR 43F6
Azrou Mor 69A2
Aztec USA 14A2
Azucena Arg 26D3
Azuero,Pen de Panama 24B2
Azul Arg 23E5
Azzaba Alg 69D1
Az-Zabdānī Syria 63D2
Az Zāhirah, Mts Oman 65G2
Az Zilfī S Arabia 64D1
Az Zubayr Iraq 62E3

B

Baa Indon 55B5
Ba'abda Leb 63C2
Ba'albek Leb 62C3
Ba'al Hazor, Mt Israel 63C3
Baardheere Somalia 70E3
Babadag Rom 39F2
Babaeski Turk 62A1
Bab al Mandab, Str Djibouti/S Yemen 64D4
Babahoyo Ecuador 24C4
Babar, I Indon 55C4
Babati Tanz 70D4
Babayevo USSR 42F4
Babbitt USA 9D2
Barberton USA 10C2
Babine, R Can 3C2
Babine L Can 4F4
Babo Indon 76C1
Bābol Iran 61C1
Babuyan Chan Phil 55F7
Babuyan Is Phil 55F7
Bacabal Brazil 25J4
Bacan, I Indon 55C3
Bacău Rom 43D6
Bac Can Viet 53D1
Baccarat France 34D2
Bacchus Marsh Aust 78B3
Bachu China 57F2
Back, R Can 4J3
Backbone Ranges, Mts Can 8N3
Backnang W Germ 34E2
Bac Ninh Viet 53D1
Bacolod Phil 55F8
Baco,Mt Phil 55F8
Badagara India 60B2
Badain Jaran Shamo, Desert China 50A1
Badajoz Spain 37A2
Badalona Spain 37C1
Badanah S Arabia 62D3
Bad Aussee Austria 35E1
Bad Bergzabern W Germ 34E2
Bad Ems W Germ 34D1
Baden, Region W Germ 36D2
Baden Switz 35C1
Baden-Baden W Germ 40B3
Badenviller France 34D2
Baden-Württemberg, State W Germ 40B3
Badgaon Nepal 59C2
Badgastein Austria 40C3
Badger USA 18C2
Bad-Godesberg W Germ 40B2
Bad Hersfeld W Germ 40B2
Bad Honnef W Germ 34D1
Badin Pak 58B4
Bad Ischl Austria 38C1
Badiyat ash Sham, Desert Region Jordan/Iraq 62C3
Bad-Kreuznach W Germ 40B3
Badlands USA 9B2
Bad Lippspringe W Germ 34E1
Bad Nauheim W Germ 34E1
Bad Nevenahr-Ahrweiler W Germ 34D1
Badou Togo 69G4
Bad Ragaz Switz 35C1
Badr Hunayn S Arabia 64C2
Bad Ryrmont W Germ 34E1
Bad Tolz W Germ 40C3
Badulla Sri Lanka 60C3
Bad Wildungen W Germ 34E1
Bad Wimpfen W Germ 34E2
Badzhal'skiy Khrebet, Mts USSR 51C1
Baena Spain 37B2
Bafang Cam 69J4
Bafatá Guinea-Bissau 68A3
Baffin B Greenland/Can 5L2
Baffin B USA 15F4
Baffin I Can 5L2
Bafia Cam 70B3
Bafing, R Mali 68A3
Bafoulabé Mali 68A3
Bafoussam Cam 70B3
Bāfq Iran 61D2
Bafra Burun, Pt Turk 43F7
Bāft Iran 61D3
Bafwasende Zaïre 70C3
Baga Nig 69J3
Bagaha India 59B2
Bāgalkot India 60B1
Bagamoyo Tanz 71D4
Bagan Datok Malay 54F7
Bagan Siapiapi Indon 54F7
Bagdad USA 17D4
Bagé Brazil 23F4
Baggs USA 14A1
Baghdād Iraq 62D3
Bagherhat Bang 59C3
Bāghīn Iran 61D2
Baghlan Afghan 58B1
Bagley USA 9C2
Bagnoa Ivory Coast 68B4
Bagnols-sur-Cèza France 36C3
Bagoé, R Mali 68B3
Baguio Phil 55F7
Bāhādurābād India 59C2
Bahamas,The, Is Caribbean 7F4
Baharampur India 59C3
Bahar Dar Eth 70D2
Baharīya Oasis Egypt 62A4
Bahau Malay 54G7
Bahawahpur, Province Pak 58C3
Bahawalpur Pak 58C3
Bahawathagar Pak 58C3
Bahia = Salvador
Bahia, State Brazil 25K6
Bahia Anegada Arg 26C4
Bahía Blanca Arg 23D5
Bahia Blanca, B Arg 23D5
Bahia Concepción, B Chile 26A3
Bahia da Ilha Grande, B Brazil 27D3
Bahia de Banderas, B Mexico 19B2
Bahia de Campeche, B Mexico 19C2
Bahia de Corando, B Costa Rica 24B2
Bahia de la Ascension, B Mexico 19D3
Bahia de Petacalco, B Mexico 19B3
Bahia de Rio de Oro, B Mor 68A2
Bahia de Sepetiba B Brazil 27D3
Bahiá de Todos Santos, B Mexico 17C4
Bahía Grande, B Arg 23C8
Bahia Kino Mexico 6B4
Bahia Magdalena, B Mexico 19A2
Bahia Salada, B Chile 26A1
Bahia Samborombon, B Arg 26D3
Bahia Sebastia Vizcaino, B Mexico 19A2
Bahir Dar Eth 64C4
Bahrael Manzala, L Egypt 63A3
Bahraich India 59B2
Bahrain, Sheikdom Arabian Pen 56D3
Bahr al Milh, L Iraq 62D3
Bahr Aouk, R Chad/CAR 70C3
Bahrat Lut = Dead S
Bahr el Abiad = White Nile
Bahr el Abiad, R Sudan 64B4
Bahr el Arab, Watercourse Sudan 70C3
Bahr el Azraq = Blue Nile
Bahr el Azraq, R Sudan 64B4
Bahr el Ghazal, R Sudan 70D3
Bahr el Ghazal, Watercourse Chad 70B2
Bahr Fâqûs, R Egypt 63A3
Bāhū-Kalāt Iran 61E3
Bahumbelu Indon 55B3
Baia de Maputo, B Mozam 72E2
Baia de Marajó, B Brazil 25J4
Baiá de Pemba, B Mozam 71E5
Baia de São Marcos, B Brazil 25K4
Baia de Setúbal, B Port 37A2
Baia de Todos os Santos B Brazil 25L6
Baia dos Tigres Angola 71B5
Baiá Guaratuba Brazil 27C4
Baia Mare Rom 43C6
Baïbokoum Chad 70B3
Baicheng China 51A2
Baie Antongila, B Madag 71F5
Baie-Comeau Can 5M5
Baie de Bombetoka, B Madag 71E5
Baie de Mahajamba, B Madag 71E5
Baie de St Augustin, B Madag 71E6
Baie de St Georges, B Leb 63C2
Baie des Chaleurs, B Can 7G2
Baie-du-Poste Can 5L4
Baie St Paul Can 11E1
Baihe China 50B3
Bai He, R China 50C3
Ba'ījī Iraq 62D3
Baikunthpur India 59B3
Baile Atha Cliath = Dublin
Băilesti Rom 39E2
Bailleul France 34B1
Baillie Is Can 8N1
Baima China 50A3
Bainbridge USA 13C2
Baing Indon 55B5
Baiquan China 51B2
Baird Inlet USA 8F3
Baird Mts USA 4B3
Bairin Youqi China 50D1
Bairin Zuoqi China 50D1
Bairnsdale Aust 76D4
Bais Phil 55F9
Baissa Nig 69J4
Baitadi Nepal 59B2
Baiyuda, Desert Sudan 64B3
Baja Hung 39D1
Baja California, State Mexico 6B3
Baja California, Pen Mexico 19A1
Baja California Norte Mexico 17C4
Bajawi Indon 55B4
Bājil Yemen 64D4
Bajo Indon 55B2
Bakal USSR 42K4
Bakala CAR 70C3
Bakel Sen 68A3
Baker, California USA 17C3
Baker, Montana USA 6C2
Baker, Oregon USA 6B2
Baker USA 4G5
Baker Foreland, Pt Can 5J3
Baker L Can 4J3
Baker Lake Can 4J3
Baker,Mt USA 6A2
Bakersfield USA 6B3
Bakharden USSR 61D1
Bakhardok USSR 61D1
Bakhmach USSR 43E5
Bakkaflói, B Iceland 30C1
Bako Eth 70D3
Bakouma CAR 70C3
Baku USSR 43H7
Bakudek, I Indon 55B3
Bakungan Indon 54A2
Balâ Turk 62B2
Balabac, I Phil 55E9
Balabac, Str Malay 54E1
Bālaghāt India 59B3
Balaikarangan Indon 54D2
Balaklava Aust 78A2
Balakovo USSR 43H5
Bala Murghab Afghan 61E1
Balāngir India 59B3
Balashov USSR 43G5
Balasore India 59C3
Balât Egypt 64A1
Balaton, L Hung 39D1
Balbriggan Irish Rep 33B5
Balcarce Arg 23E5
Balchik Bulg 39F2
Balclutha NZ 77F5
Bald Knob USA 15D2
Baldwin USA 13C2
Baldy Mt USA 16E1
Baldy Peak, Mt USA 6C3
Balearic Is = Islas Baleares
Baleh, R Malay 54D2
Baler Phil 55F7
Balezino USSR 42J4
Balhāf S Yemen 65E4
Balho Djibouti 64D4
Bali, I Indon 76A1
Balıkesir Turk 62A2
Balikh, R Syria 62C2
Balikpapan Indon 54E3
Balintang Chan Phil 55F7
Bali S Indon 54D4
Baliza Brazil 27B2
Baljurshī S Arabia 64D3
Balkh Afghan 58B1
Balkhash USSR 46J5
Ballachulish Scot 32C3
Ballantrae Scot 32C4
Ballantyne Str Can 4G2
Ballapur India 60B2
Ballarat Aust 76D4
Ballater Scot 32D3
Balleny Is Ant 80F7
Ballia India 59B2
Ballina Aust 78D1
Ballina Irish Rep 31B3
Ballinger USA 14C3
Ballon d'Alsace, Mt France 34D3
Ballston Spa USA 12D1
Ballycastle N Ire 32B4
Ballymena N Ire 32B4
Ballymoney N Ire 32B4
Ballyshannon Irish Rep 33A4
Balmoral Aust 78B3
Balmorhea USA 14B3
Balnearia Arg 26C2
Balombo Angola 71B5
Balonn, R Aust 78C1
Balotra India 58C3
Balrāmpur India 59B2
Balranald Aust 76D4
Balsas Brazil 25J5
Balsas Mexico 20C2
Balsas, R Mexico 19B3
Balta USSR 43D6
Baltasar Brum Urug 26D2
Baltic S N Europe 30H7
Baltîm Egypt 62B3
Baltimore USA 7F3
Baluchistan, Region Pak 58B3
Bālurghāt India 59C2
Balykshi USSR 43J6
Bam Iran 61D3
Bama Nig 70B2
Bamako Mali 68B3
Bambari CAR 70C3
Bamberg USA 13C2
Bamberg W Germ 40C3
Bambili Zaïre 70C3
Bambui Brazil 27C3
Bamenda Cam 70B3
Bamfield Can 3D4
Bamingui, R CAR 70B3
Bamingui Bangoran, National Park CAR 70B3
Bamiyan Afghan 58B2
Bampur Iran 61E3
Bampur, R Iran 61E3
Banaba, I Kiribati
Banalia Zaïre 70C3
Banamba Mali 68B3
Bananga Nicobar Is 60E3
Ban Aranyaprathet Thai 53C3
Ban Ban Laos 53C2
Ban Betong Thai 53C4
Banbridge N Ire 33B4
Banbury Eng 33E5
Banchory Scot 32D3
Banco Chinchorro, Is Mexico 19D3
Bancroft Can 11D1
Bānda India 59B2
Banda Aceh Indon 54A1
Bandama, R Ivory Coast 68B4
Bandar Abbās Iran 61D3
Bandar Anzalī Iran 43H8
Bandar-e Daylam Iran 61C3
Bandar-e Lengheh Iran 61C3
Bandar-e Māqām Iran 61C3
Bandar-e Rig Iran 61C3
Bandar-e Torkoman Iran 43J8
Bandar Khomeynī Iran 61B2
Bandar Seri Begawan Brunei 54D2
Banda S Indon 49F7
Bandau Malay 54E1
Band Bont Iran 61D3
Bandeira, Mt Brazil 27D3
Bandera Arg 26C1
Banderantes Brazil 27B1
Bandiagara Mali 68B3
Band-i-Baba, Upland Afghan 61E2
Bandirma Turk 43D7
Band-i-Turkestan, Mts Afghan 61E1
Bandol France 35A3
Bandolier Kop S Africa 72D1
Bandundu Zaïre 70B4
Bandung Indon 54C4
Baneh Iran 43H8
Banermo Indon 55C2
Banes Cuba 19E2
Banff Can 3E3
Banff Scot 32D3
Banff, R Can 4G4
Banff Nat Pk Can 3E3
Banfora U Volta 69F3
Bangalore India 60B2
Bangangté Cam 69J4
Bangassou CAR 70C3
Banggi, I Malay 54E1
Bang Hieng, R Laos 53D2
Bangka, I Indon 54C3
Bangkinang Indon 54B2
Bangko Indon 54B3
Bangkok Thai 53C3
Bangladesh, Republic Asia 57H3
Bangong Co, L China 58D2
Bangor, Maine USA 7G2
Bangor N Ire 32B4
Bangor, Pennsylvania USA 12C2
Bangor Wales 33C5
Bangsalsembera Indon 54E3
Bang Saphan Yai Thai 53B3
Bangued Phil 55F7
Bangui CAR 70B3
Bangweulu, L Zambia 71D5
Ban Hat Yai Thai 53C4
Ban Hin Heup Laos 53C2
Ban Houei Sai Laos 53C1
Ban Hua Hin Thai 53B3
Bani, R Mali 68B3
Bani Bangou Niger 68C3
Banī Ma'arid, Region S Arabia 65E3
Banī Walīd Libya 67A1
Bāniyās Syria 62C2
Baniyas Syria 63C2
Banja Luka Yugos 38D2
Banjarmasin Indon 54D3
Banjul The Gambia 68A3
Ban Kantang Thai 53B4
Ban Khemmarat Laos 53D2
Ban Khok Kloi Thai 53B4
Banks, Is Vanuatu 77F2
Banks I Aust 49H8
Banks I, British Columbia Can 4E4
Banks I, Northwest Territories Can 4F2
Banks L USA 16C1
Banks Pen NZ 79B2
Banks Str Aust 78E3
Bankura India 59C3
Ban Mae Sariang Thai 53B2
Ban Mae Sot Thai 53B2
Banmauk Burma 59E3
Ban Me Thuot Viet 53D3
Bann, R N Ire 32B4
Ban Na San Thai 53B4
Bannu Pak 58C2
Baños de Chihuio Chile 26A4
Baños Maule Chile 26A3
Ban Pak Neun Laos 53C2
Ban Pak Phanang Thai 53C4
Ban Ru Kroy Camb 53D3
Ban Sai Yok Thai 53B3
Ban Sattahip Thai 53C3
Banská Bystrica Czech 41D3
Bānswāra India 58C4
Bantaeng Indon 55B4
Ban Tha Kham Thai 53B4
Ban Thateng Laos 53D2
Ban Tha Tum Thai 53C2
Bantry Irish Rep 31B3
Bantry, B Irish Rep 31A3
Ban Ya Soup Viet 53D3
Banyo Cam 69J4
Banyuwangi Indon 54D4
Banzare Seamount Indian O 74E7
Baofeng China 50C3
Bao Ha Viet 53C1
Baoji China 50B3
Bao Loc Viet 53D3
Baoqing China 51C2
Baoshan China 48C4
Baotou China 50C1
Bāpatla India 60C1
Bapaume France 34B1
Ba'Qūbah Iraq 62D3
Bar Yugos 39D2
Bara Indon 55C3
Bara Sudan 70D2
Baraawe Somalia 70E3
Barabai Indon 54E3

Bāra Banki *India* 59B2
Barabinsk *USSR* 46J4
Barabinskaya Step, Steppe *USSR* 46J4
Baracaldo *Spain* 37B1
Baracoa *Cuba* 21C2
Baradá, R *Syria* 63D2
Baradine *Aust* 78C2
Baraka, Watercourse *Eth* 64C3
Bārāmati *India* 60A1
Baramula *Pak* 58C2
Bārān *India* 58D3
Barangas *Phil* 55F8
Baranof I *USA* 4E4
Baranovichi *USSR* 42D5
Baratta *Aust* 78A2
Barauni *India* 59C2
Barbacena *Brazil* 25K8
Barbados, I *Caribbean* 21F4
Barbastro *Spain* 37C1
Barberton *S Africa* 72E2
Barbezieux *France* 36B2
Barbòsa *Colombia* 24D2
Barbuda, I *Caribbean* 21E3
Barcaldine *Aust* 76D3
Barce = Al Marj
Barcellona *Italy* 38D3
Barcelona *Spain* 37C1
Barcelona *Ven* 24F1
Barcelonnette *France* 35B2
Barcoo, R *Aust* 76D3
Barda del Medio *Arg* 26B3
Bardai *Chad* 70B1
Bardas Blancas *Arg* 23C5
Barddhamān *India* 59C3
Bardejov *Czech* 41E3
Bardi *Italy* 35C2
Bardonecchia *Italy* 35B2
Bardsey, I *Wales* 33C5
Bardstown *USA* 10B3
Bareeda *Somalia* 65F4
Bareilly *India* 58D3
Barentsovo More, S *USSR* 42F1
Barentsøya, I *Barents S* 46D2
Barents S = Barentsovo More
Barentu *Eth* 70D2
Bargarh *India* 59B3
Barge *Italy* 35B2
Barguzin *USSR* 47N4
Barguzin, R *USSR* 47N4
Bar Harbour *USA* 11F2
Barhi *India* 59C3
Bari *Italy* 38D2
Barika *Alg* 37D2
Barinas *Ven* 24D2
Baripāda *India* 59C3
Bârîs *Egypt* 64B2
Bari Sādri *India* 58C4
Barisal *Bang* 59D3
Barito, R *Indon* 54D3
Barjols *France* 35B3
Barjuj, Watercourse *Libya* 67A2
Barkam *China* 50A3
Barkley,L *USA* 10B3
Barkley,L *USA* 15E2
Barkley Sd *Can* 3C4
Barkly East *S Africa* 72D3
Barkly Tableland, Mts *Aust* 76C2
Bar-le-Duc *France* 34C2
Barlee,L *Aust* 76A3
Barlee Range, Mts *Aust* 76A3
Barletta *Italy* 38D2
Barmer *India* 58C3
Barmera *Aust* 78B2
Barmouth *Wales* 33C5
Barnard Castle *Eng* 33E4
Barnaul *USSR* 46K4
Barnegat *USA* 12C3
Barnegat B *USA* 12C3
Barnesboro *USA* 12A2
Barnes Icecap *Can* 5L2
Barnesville, Georgia *USA* 13C2
Barnesville, Ohio *USA* 10C3
Barnhart *USA* 14B3
Barnsley *Eng* 33E5
Barnstaple *Eng* 33C6
Baro *Nig* 69H4
Barpeta *India* 59D2
Barquisimeto *Ven* 24E1
Barr *France* 34D2
Barra *Brazil* 25K6
Barra, I *Scot* 32B3
Barraba *Aust* 78D2
Barra da Estiva *Brazil* 27D1
Barra de Navidad *Mexico* 20B2
Barra de Piraí *Brazil* 27D3
Barra de Tonalá *Mexico* 20D2
Barra do Bugres *Brazil* 27A2
Barra do Garças *Brazil* 27B2
Barra do Quarai *Brazil* 26D2
Barra do Ribeiro *Brazil* 26E2
Barrage d'Ayama *Ivory Coast* 69F4
Barrage de Mbakaou, Dam *Cam* 69J4
Barragem do Castelo do Bode, Res *Port* 37A2
Barragem do Maranhão *Port* 37A2
Barra Head, Pt *Scot* 32B3
Barra Mansa *Brazil* 25K8
Barranca *Peru* 24C6
Barrancabermeja *Colombia* 24D2
Barrancas *Ven* 24F2
Barranqueras *Arg* 85E3
Barranquilla *Colombia* 24D1
Barra,Sound of, Chan *Scot* 32B3
Barre *USA* 12D1
Barreal *Arg* 26B2
Barreiras *Brazil* 25K6
Barreiro *Port* 37A2
Barreiros *Brazil* 25L5
Barren,C *Aust* 76D5
Barren Is *USA* 8H4
Barretos *Brazil* 25J8
Barrhead *Can* 3F3
Barrie *Can* 11D2
Barrière *Can* 3D3
Barrier Range, Mts *Aust* 78B2
Barrington L *Can* 3H2
Barrington,Mt *Aust* 76E4
Barro Alto *Brazil* 27C2
Barroloola *Aust* 49G8
Barron *USA* 10A1
Barrouaillie *St Vincent* 21N2
Barrow *USA* 4C2
Barrow, R *Irish Rep* 31B3
Barrow, R *Irish Rep* 33B5
Barrow Creek *Aust* 76C3
Barrow I *Aust* 76A3
Barrow-in-Furness *Eng* 33D4
Barrow,Pt *USA* 4C2
Barrow Str *Can* 5J2
Barry's Bay *Can* 11D1
Barryville *USA* 12C2
Barsi *India* 60B1
Barstow *USA* 6B3
Bar-sur-Aube *France* 36C2
Bar-sur-Seine *France* 34C2
Bartica *Guyana* 25G2
Bartın *Turk* 62B1
Bartle Frere,Mt *Aust* 76D2
Bartlesville *USA* 6D3
Bartlett *USA* 9C3
Bartolomeu Dias *Mozam* 71D6
Bartoszyce *Pol* 41E2
Barung, I *Indon* 54D4
Barus *Indon* 54A2
Barwāh *India* 58D4
Barwāni *India* 58C4
Barwon, R *Aust* 78C1
Barysh *USSR* 42H5
Basail *Arg* 26D1
Basalt *USA* 18C1
Basankusu *Zaïre* 70B3
Basavilbas *Arg* 26D2
Basco *Phil* 55F6
Basel *Switz* 34D3
Basel *Switz* 38B1
Basento, R *Italy* 38D2
Bashaw *Can* 3F3
Bashi Chan *Phil* 55F6
Bashkirskaya ASSR, Republic *USSR* 42J5
Basiano *Indon* 55B3
Basilan, I *Phil* 55F9
Basildon *Eng* 33F6
Basilio *Brazil* 26E2
Basin *USA* 16E2
Basingstoke *Eng* 33E6
Basin Region *USA* 6B2
Basra *Iraq* 62E3
Bas-Rhin, Department *France* 34D2
Bassac, R *Camb* 53D3
Bassano *Can* 3F3
Bassano *Italy* 38C1
Bassano del Grappa *Italy* 35D2
Bassari *Togo* 69G4
Bassas da India, I *Mozam Chan* 71D6
Bassein *Burma* 53A2
Basse Terre *Guadeloupe* 21E3
Bassett *USA* 9C3
Bassila *Benin* 69G4
Bass Lake *USA* 18C2
Bass Str *Aust* 76D5
Båstad *Sweden* 30G7
Bastak *Iran* 61C3
Basti *India* 59B2
Bastia *Corse* 38B2
Bastogne *Belg* 40B3
Bastrop, Louisiana *USA* 15D3
Bastrop, Texas *USA* 15C3
Bata *Eq Guinea* 70A3
Batakan *Indon* 54D3
Batala *India* 58D2
Batang *China* 48C3
Batangafo *CAR* 70B3
Batan Is *Phil* 55F6
Batanta, I *Indon* 55D3
Batatais *Brazil* 27C3
Batavia *USA* 11D2
Batemans Bay *Aust* 78D3
Batesburg *USA* 13C2
Batesville, Arkansas *USA* 15D2
Batesville, Mississippi *USA* 15E3
Bath *Can* 11F1
Bath *Eng* 33D6
Bath, Maine *USA* 11F2
Bath, New York *USA* 11D2
Batha, R *Chad* 70B2
Bathawana Mt *Can* 10C1
Bathurst *Aust* 76D4
Bathurst *Can* 5M5
Bathurst,C *Can* 4F2
Bathurst I *Aust* 76C2
Bathurst I *Can* 4H2
Bathurst Inlet, B *Can* 4H3
Batié *U Volta* 69F4
Bātlāq-e-Gavkhūnī, Salt Flat *Iran* 61C2
Batlow *Aust* 78C3
Batman *Turk* 62D2
Batna *Alg* 69D1
Baton Rouge *USA* 7D3
Batroun *Leb* 63C1
Battambang *Camb* 53C3
Batticaloa *Sri Lanka* 60C3
Batti Malv, I *Indian O* 60E3
Battle, R *Can* 3G3
Battle Creek *USA* 7E2
Battle Harbour *Can* 5N4
Battle Mountain *USA* 16C2
Batu Gajah *Malay* 54F6
Batukelau *Indon* 54E2
Batumi *USSR* 43G7
Batu Pahat *Malay* 53C5
Baturaja *Indon* 54B3
Bat Yam *Israel* 63C2
Baubau *Indon* 76B1
Bauchi *Nig* 69H3
Bauchi, State *Nig* 69H3
Baudette *USA* 9D2
Bauges, Mts *France* 35B2
Bauld,C *Can* 5N4
Baumes-les-Dames *France* 35B1
Baunt *USSR* 47N4
Bauru *Brazil* 25J8
Baus *Brazil* 27B2
Bautzen *E Germ* 40C2
Baween, I *Indon* 54D4
Bawîti *Egypt* 67B2
Bawku *Ghana* 69F3
Bawlake *Burma* 53B2
Bawlen *Aust* 78A2
Baxley *USA* 13C2
Baxoi *China* 59E1
Bayamo *Cuba* 19E2
Bayan *China* 51B2
Bayan *Indon* 54E4
Bayandalay *Mongolia* 50A1
Bayandzürh *Mongolia* 48D2
Bayandzürh *USSR* 47M5
Bayan Har Shan, Mts *China* 48C3
Bayan Mod *China* 50A1
Bayan Obo *China* 50B1
Bayard, Nebraska *USA* 9B3
Bayard, New Mexico *USA* 14A3
Bayard, P *France* 35B2
Bayard,Mt *Can* 8N4
Baybay *Phil* 55F8
Bayburt *Turk* 62D1
Bay City, Michigan *USA* 7E2
Bay City, Texas *USA* 15C4
Bay Dağlari *Turk* 62B2
Baydaratskaya Guba, B *USSR* 46H3
Baydhabo *Somalia* 70E3
Bayeaux *France* 36B2
Bayerische Alpen, Mts *W Germ* 35D1
Bayern, State *W Germ* 40C3
Bayfield *USA* 10A1
Bayhan al Qisāb *S Yemen* 65E4
Bāyir *Jordan* 62C3
Baykalskiy Khrebet, Mts *USSR* 48D1
Baykit *USSR* 47L3
Baylik Shan, Mts *China/ Mongolia* 47L5
Baymak *USSR* 42K5
Bay Minette *USA* 13B2
Bayombang *Phil* 55F7
Bayonne *France* 36B3
Bayram Ali *USSR* 61E1
Bayreuth *W Germ* 40C3
Bay St Louis *USA* 15E3
Bay Shore *USA* 11E2
Bays,L of *Can* 11D1
Bayt al Faqīh *Yemen* 64D4
Baytik Shan, Mts *China* 48B2
Bayt Lahm = Bethlehem
Baytown *USA* 15D4
Baza *Spain* 37B2
Bazaliya *USSR* 41F3
Bazar-Dyuzi *USSR* 43H7
Bazas *France* 36B3
Bazhong *China* 50B3
Bazmān *Iran* 61E3
Bcharre *Leb* 63D1
Beach *USA* 9B2
Beach Haven *USA* 12C3
Beachy Head *Eng* 33F6
Beacon *USA* 12D2
Bealanana *Madag* 71E5
Bear, R *USA* 16D2
Beardstown *USA* 10A2
Bear I = Bjørnøya
Bear L *USA* 16D2
Bear Valley *USA* 18B1
Beatrice *USA* 6D2
Beatrice, Oilfield *N Sea* 32D2
Beatton, R *Can* 3D2
Beatton River *Can* 4F4
Beatty *USA* 6B3
Beattyville *Can* 11D1
Beauce, Region *France* 34A2
Beauchene Is *Falkland Is* 23E8
Beaudesert *Aust* 78D1
Beaufort S *Can* 80B5
Beaufort West *S Africa* 72C3
Beaugeney *France* 34A3
Beauharnois *Can* 11E1
Beauly *Scot* 32C3
Beaumont, California *USA* 17C4
Beaumont, Texas *USA* 7D3
Beaumont-sur-Sarthe *France* 34A2
Beaune *France* 36C2
Beausejour *Can* 9C2
Beauvais *France* 36C2
Beauval *Can* 3G2
Beaver, Alaska *USA* 8J2
Beaver, Utah *USA* 17D3
Beaver, R, Saskatchewan *Can* 3G3
Beaver, R, Yukon *Can* 3C1
Beaver Creek *Can* 4D3
Beaver Creek *USA* 8J2
Beaver Dam, Kentucky *USA* 10B3
Beaver Dam, Wisconsin *USA* 10B2
Beaverhead Mts *USA* 16D1
Beaverhill L *Can* 3F3
Beaver I *USA* 10B1
Beaver L *USA* 15D2
Beaverlodge *Can* 3E2
Beawar *India* 58C3
Beazley *Arg* 26B2
Bebedouro *Brazil* 27C3
Beccles *Eng* 33F5
Bečej *Yugos* 39E1
Béchar *Alg* 68B1
Becharof L *USA* 8G4
Bechevin B *USA* 8F4
Beckley *USA* 7E3
Beckum *W Germ* 34E1
Bedford, County *Eng* 33E5
Bedford *Eng* 33E5
Bedford, Indiana *USA* 10B3
Bedford, Pennsylvania *USA* 12A3
Bedford Pt *Grenada* 21M2
Beech Creek *USA* 12B2
Beechey, Pt *USA* 4D2
Beechworth *Aust* 78C3
Beenleigh *Aust* 78D1
Beer Menuha *Israel* 63C3
Beer Ora *Israel* 63C4
Beersheba *Israel* 62B3
Beèr Sheva = Beersheba
Beér Sheva, R *Israel* 63C3
Beeville *USA* 6D4
Befale *Zaïre* 70C3
Befandriana *Madag* 71E5
Bega *Aust* 78C3
Behbehān *Iran* 61C2
Behm Canal, Sd *USA* 8M4
Behshahr *Iran* 61C1
Behsud *Afghan* 58B2
Bei'an *China* 51B2
Beihai *China* 50B5
Beihai *China* 53D1
Beijing *China* 50D2
Beiliu *China* 53E1
Beipan Jiang, R *China* 50B4
Beipiao *China* 50E1
Beira = Sofala
Beirut *Leb* 62C3
Bei Shan, Mts *China* 48C2
Beitbridge *Zim* 72E1
Beit ed Dine *Leb* 63C2
Beit Jala *Israel* 63C3
Beja *Port* 37A2
Beja *Tunisia* 69D1
Bejaïa *Alg* 69D1
Béjar *Spain* 37A1
Bejestān *Iran* 61D2
Békéscsaba *Hung* 41E3
Bekily *Madag* 71E6
Bela *India* 59B2
Bela *Pak* 58B3
Belaga *Malay* 54D2
Bel Air *USA* 12B3
Belamoalli *India* 60B1
Belang *Indon* 55B2
Belangpidie *Indon* 54A2
Belau, Republic *Pacific O* 49G6
Belau, I *Pacific O* 74H4
Bela Vista *Mozam* 72E2
Béla Vista *Par/Brazil* 27A3
Belawan *Indon* 54A2
Belaya, R *USSR* 42K4
Belaya Tserkov *USSR* 41G3
Belcher Chan *Can* 5J2
Belcher Is *Can* 5L4
Belchiragh *Afghan* 58B1
Belebey *USSR* 42J5
Belém *Brazil* 25J4
Belén *Arg* 26B1
Belén *Colombia* 24C3
Belén *Par* 27A3
Belén *Urug* 26D2
Belen *USA* 6C3
Belén, R *Arg* 26B1
Belet Uen *Somalia* 70E3
Belfast *N Ire* 32B4
Belfast *S Africa* 72E2
Belfast Lough, Estuary *N Ire* 32B4
Belfield *USA* 9B2
Belfodio *Eth* 70D2
Belford *Eng* 32E4
Belfort *France* 36D2
Belgaum *India* 60A1
Belgium, Kingdom *N W Europe* 40A2
Belgorod *USSR* 43F5
Belgorod Dnestrovskiy *USSR* 43E6
Belgrade = Beograd
Belgrade *USA* 16D1
Bel Hedan *Libya* 67A2
Belinyu *Indon* 54C3
Belitung, I *Indon* 54C3
Belize *Belize* 19D3
Belize, Republic *C America* 19D3
Bellac *France* 36C2
Bella Coola *Can* 4F4
Bellagio *Italy* 35C2
Bellaire *USA* 15C4
Bellano *Italy* 35C1
Bellary *India* 60B1
Bellata *Aust* 78C1
Bella Union *Urug* 26D2
Bella Vista *Arg* 26D1
Belledonne, Mts *France* 35B2
Bellefonte *USA* 12B2
Belle Fourche *USA* 6C2
Belle Fourche, R *USA* 9B3
Bellegarde *France* 36D2
Belle Glade *USA* 13E4
Belle I *Can* 5N4
Belle-Ile, I *France* 36B2
Belle Isle,Str of *Can* 5N4
Bellême *France* 34A2
Belleville *Can* 5L5
Belleville, Illinois *USA* 10B3
Belleville, Kansas *USA* 15C2
Bellevue, Idaho *USA* 16D2
Bellevue, Iowa *USA* 10A2
Bellevue, Washington *USA* 16B1
Belley *France* 35A2
Bellin *Can* 5L3
Bellingen *Aust* 78D2
Bellingham *USA* 6A2
Bellingshausen, Base *Ant* 80G2
Bellingshausen S *Ant* 80G3
Bellinzona *Switz* 38B1
Bello *Colombia* 24C2
Bellona Reefs *Nouvelle Calédonie* 77E3
Bellota *USA* 18B1
Bellows Falls *USA* 11E2
Bell Pen *Can* 5K3
Belluno *Italy* 38C1
Bell Ville *Arg* 23D4
Belmont *USA* 12B1
Belmonte *Brazil* 25L7
Belmopan *Belize* 19D3
Belogorsk *USSR* 51B1
Beloha *Madag* 71E6
Belo Horizonte *Brazil* 25K7
Beloit, Kansas *USA* 14C2
Beloit, Wisconsin *USA* 7E2
Belomorsk *USSR* 46E3
Beloretsk *USSR* 42K5
Belorusskaya SSR, Republic *USSR* 42D5
Belo-Tsiribihina *Madag* 71E5
Beloye More, S *USSR* 46E3
Beloye Ozero, L *USSR* 42F3
Belozersk *USSR* 42F3
Belpre *USA* 10C3
Beltana *Aust* 78A2
Belton *USA* 15C3
Bel'tsy *USSR* 41F3
Belukha, Mt *USSR* 46K5
Belush'ye *USSR* 42H2
Belvidere, Illinois *USA* 10B2
Belvidere, New Jersey *USA* 12C2
Bembe *Angola* 71B4
Bembéréke *Benin* 69G3
Bemidji *USA* 7D2

Bemis USA 13B1
Bena Nor 30G6
Bena Dibele Zaïre 70C4
Benalla Aust 78C3
Ben Attow, Mt Scot 32C2
Benavente Spain 37A1
Benbecula, I Scot 32B3
Bencubbin Aust 76A4
Bend USA 6A2
Ben Dearg, Mt Scot 32C3
Bendel, State Nig 69H4
Bender Beyla Somalia 67E3
Bendery USSR 43D6
Bendigo Aust 76D4
Benedery USSR 41F3
Bénéna Mali 69F3
Benešov Czech 40C3
Benevento Italy 38C2
Bengal,B of Asia 57G4
Ben Gardane Libya 67A1
Ben Gardane Tunisia 69E2
Bengbu China 50D3
Benggai, I Indon 55B3
Benghāzi Libya 67B1
Bengkalis Indon 54B2
Bengkulu Indon 54B3
Benguela Angola 71B5
Benguerir Mor 69A2
Benha Egypt 62B3
Ben Hope, Mt Scot 32C2
Beni Zaïre 70C3
Béni, R Bol 24E6
Beni Abbes Alg 68B1
Benicarló Spain 37C1
Benidji USA 5J5
Benidorm Spain 37B2
Beni Manscur Alg 37C2
Beni Mazar Egypt 67C2
Beni Mellal Mor 69A2
Benin, Republic Africa 68C4
Benin City Nig 69H4
Beni-Saf Alg 69B1
Beni Suef Egypt 67C2
Benkelman USA 14B2
Ben Kilbreck, Mt Scot 32C2
Ben Lawers, Mt Scot 31C2
Ben Lomond, Mt Aust 78E3
Ben Macdui, Mt Scot 32D3
Ben More Assynt, Mt Scot 32C2
Benmore,L NZ 79B2
Ben Nevis, Mt Scot 32C3
Bennington USA 11E2
Bennt Jbail Leb 63C2
Bénoué, R Cam 70B3
Bénoué Nat Pk Cam 69J4
Bensheim W Germ 34E2
Benson, Arizona USA 6B3
Benson, Minnesota USA 9C2
Bentiu Sudan 70C3
Bento Gomes, R Brazil 27A2
Benton, Arkansas USA 15D3
Benton, California USA 18C2
Benton, Kentucky USA 10B3
Benton Harbor USA 10B2
Benue, State Nig 69H4
Benue, R Nig 69H4
Ben Wyvis, Mt Scot 32C3
Benxi China 50E1
Beo Indon 55C2
Beograd Yugos 39E2
Beohāri India 59B3
Beppu Japan 51C5
Berat Alb 39D2
Berber Sudan 70D2
Berbera Somalia 70E2
Berbérati CAR 70B3
Berck France 34A1
Berdichev USSR 41F3
Berdichev USSR 43D6
Berdyansk USSR 43F6
Berea USA 10C3
Berebere Indon 55C2
Berekum Ghana 69F4
Berenda USA 18B2
Berenice Egypt 64C2
Berens, R Can 4J4
Berens River Can 4J4
Beresford Aust 78A1
Beresford USA 9C3
Berettyoújfalu Hung 41E3
Bereza USSR 41F2
Berezhany USSR 41E3
Berezina, R USSR 41F2
Bereznik USSR 42G3
Berezniki USSR 46G4
Berezovka USSR 43E6
Berezovo USSR 46H3
Berezovyy USSR 51D1
Bergama Turk 62A2
Bergamo Italy 38B1
Bergen Nor 30F6
Bergen USA 12B1
Bergen op Zoom Neth 34C1
Bergerac France 36C3
Bergisch-Gladbach W Germ 34D1
Berhampur India 60C1
Bering Gl USA 8K3
Beringovskiy USSR 47U3
Bering S USSR/USA 75K2
Bering Str USSR/USA 80C6
Berizak Iran 61D3
Berja Spain 37B2
Berkane Mor 69B2
Berkeley USA 6A3
Berkeley Spring USA 12A3
Berkner I Ant 80F2
Berkovitsa Bulg 39E2
Berkshire, County Eng 33E6
Berkshire Hills USA 12D1
Berland, R Can 3E3
Berlin E Germ 40C2
Berlin, New Hampshire USA 11E2
Berlin, Pennsylvania USA 12A3
Bermejo Bol 24F8
Bermejo, R Arg 23E3
Bermuda, I Atlantic O 2M5
Bern Switz 38B1
Bernalillo USA 14A2
Bernardo de Irigoyen Arg 27B4
Bernardsville USA 12C2
Bernasconi Arg 26C3
Bernay France 34A2
Bernburg E Germ 40C2
Berner Orberland, Mts Switz 35B1
Bernier B Can 5K2
Berounka, R Czech 40C3
Berrechid Mor 69A2
Berri Aust 78B2
Berriane Alg 69C2
Berry, Region France 36C2
Berryessa,L USA 18A1
Berry Is Bahamas 7F4
Berryville USA 12B3
Berseba Namibia 72B2
Bertam Malay 54F6
Berthoud P USA 14A2
Bertoua Cam 70B3
Beru, I Kiribati 77G1
Berwick USA 11D2
Berwick-upon-Tweed Eng 32D4
Berwyn, Mts Wales 33D5
Besalampy Madag 71E5
Besançon France 36D2
Beskidy Zachodnie, Mts Pol 41E3
Besnard L Can 3G2
Besni Turk 62C2
Besor, R Israel 63C3
Bessemer, Alabama USA 13B2
Bessemer, Michigan USA 10B1
Betafo Madag 71E5
Betanzos Spain 37A1
Betaré Oya Cam 69J4
Bet Guvrin Israel 63C3
Bethal S Africa 72D2
Bethanie Namibia 72B2
Bethany, Missouri USA 15D1
Bethany, Oklahoma USA 15C2
Bethel, Alaska USA 4B3
Bethel, Connecticut USA 12D2
Bethel Park USA 10C2
Bethesda USA 11D3
Bethlehem Israel 63C3
Bethlehem S Africa 72D2
Bethlehem USA 11D2
Bethulie S Africa 72D3
Bethune France 36C1
Béthune, R France 34A2
Betioky Madag 71E6
Betoota Aust 78B1
Betou Congo 70B3
Betpak Dala, Steppe USSR 57E1
Betroka Madag 71E6
Betsiamites Can 5M5
Bettendorf USA 10A2
Bettiah India 59B2
Bettles USA 8H2
Béttola Italy 35C2
Betul India 58D4
Betuwe, Province Neth 34C1
Betwa, R India 58D3
Betzdorf W Germ 34D1
Beverley,L USA 8G4
Beverly USA 12E1
Beverly Hills USA 17C4
Beyla Guinea 68B4
Beypore India 60B2
Beyrouth = Beirut
Beyşehir Turk 62B2
Beysehir Gölü, L Turk 43E8
Beyt Shean Israel 63C2
Bezan Austria 35C1
Bezhetsk USSR 42F4
Béziers France 36C3
Bezmein USSR 61D1
Beznosova USSR 48D1
Bhadrāchalam India 60C1
Bhadrakh India 59C3
Bhadra Res India 60B2
Bhadrāvati India 60B2
Bhag Pak 58B3
Bhāgalpur India 59C2
Bhakkar Pak 58C2
Bhamo Burma 59E3
Bhandāra India 58D4
Bharatpur India 58D3
Bharūch India 58C4
Bhātiāpāra Ghat Bang 59C3
Bhatinda India 58C2
Bhatkal India 60A2
Bhātpāra India 59C3
Bhāvnagar India 58C4
Bhawānipatna India 59B4
Bhera Pak 58C2
Bheri, R Nepal 59B2
Bhilai India 59B3
Bhilwāra India 58C3
Bhimavaram India 60C1
Bhind India 58D3
Bhiwāni India 58D3
Bhongir India 60B1
Bhopāl India 58D4
Bhubaneshwar India 59C3
Bhuj India 58B4
Bhusāwal India 58D4
Bhutan, Kingdom Asia 57H3
Bia, R Ghana 69F4
Biak, I Indon 49G7
Biala Podlaska Pol 41E2
Bialograd Pol 40D2
Bialystok Pol 41E2
Biargtangar, C Iceland 30A1
Biarjmand Iran 61D1
Biaro, I Indon 55C2
Biarritz France 36B3
Biasca Switz 35C1
Biba Egypt 62B4
Bibai Japan 51E3
Bibala Angola 71B5
Bibbiena Italy 35D3
Biberach W Germ 40B3
Bibiani Ghana 69F4
Bicaz Rom 39F1
Bichi, R USSR 51D1
Bicknell USA 17D3
Bida Nig 69H4
Bidar India 60B1
Bidbid Oman 65G2
Biddeford USA 11E2
Bideford Eng 33C6
Bideford B Eng 33C6
Bidon 5 Alg 68C2
Bié Angola 71B5
Biebrza Pol 41E2
Biel Switz 38B1
Bielawa Pol 40D2
Bielefeld W Germ 40B2
Bieler See, L Switz 35B1
Biella Italy 38B1
Bielsk Podlaski Pol 41E2
Bien Hoa Viet 53D3
Biferno, R Italy 38C2
Biga Turk 62A1
Bigadiç Turk 39F3
Big Band Nat Pk USA 14B4
Big Belt Mts USA 16D1
Big Black, R USA 15E3
Big Blue, R USA 15C1
Big Cypress Swamp USA 13E4
Big Delta USA 4D3
Bigent W Germ 36D2
Biggar Can 3G3
Biggar Kindersley Can 4H4
Biggenden Aust 78D1
Bigger,Mt Can 8L4
Big Hole, R USA 16D1
Bighorn, R USA 9A2
Bighorn L USA 9A2
Bighorn Mts USA 9A3
Bight of Bangkok, B Thai 53C3
Bight of Benin, B W Africa 68C4
Bight of Biafra, B Cam 68C4
Big I Can 5L3
Big Koniuji, I USA 8G4
Big Lake USA 14B3
Bignasco Switz 35C1
Bignona Sen 68A3
Big Pine USA 17C3
Big Pine Key USA 13E4
Big Pine Mt USA 18C3
Big Rapids USA 10B2
Big River Can 4H4
Big Sandy USA 16D1
Big Sandy L Can 3H3
Big Sioux, R USA 9C3
Big Smokey V USA 18D1
Big Spring USA 6C3
Big Springs USA 14B1
Big Stone City USA 9C2
Big Stone Gap USA 10C3
Big Sur USA 18B2
Big Timber USA 16E1
Big Trout L Can 5J4
Big Trout Lake Can 5K4
Bihać Yugos 38D2
Bihār India 59C2
Bihar, State India 59C3
Biharamulo Tanz 70D4
Bihor, Mt Rom 43C6
Bijāpur India 60B1
Bijāpur India 60C1
Bijār Iran 61B1
Bijauri Nepal 59B2
Bijeljina Yugos 39D2
Bijie China 50B4
Bijnor India 58D3
Bijnot Pak 58C3
Bikāner India 58C3
Bikfaya Leb 63C2
Bikin USSR 51C2
Bikin, R USSR 51D2
Bikoro Zaïre 70B4
Bila He, R China 51A2
Bilara India 58C3
Bilaspur India 58D2
Bilāspur India 59B3
Bilauktaung Range, Mts Thai 53B3
Bilbao Spain 37B1
Bilbeis Egypt 63A3
Bílé, R Czech 40D3
Bileća Yugos 39D2
Bilecik Turk 62B1
Bili, R Zaïre 70C3
Bilibino USSR 47S3
Biliran, I Phil 55F8
Billings USA 6C2
Bilma Niger 70B2
Biloxi USA 7E3
Biltine Chad 70C2
Bimbita Ghana 69F4
Bina-Etawa India 58D4
Binalbagan Phil 55F8
Bindura Zim 71D5
Binga Zim 71C5
Binga, Mt Zim 71D5
Bingara Aust 78D1
Bingen W Germ 40B3
Bingham USA 11F1
Binghamton USA 7F2
Bingkor Malay 54E1
Bingöl Turk 62D2
Binhai China 50D3
Binjai Indon 54A2
Binjai Indon 54C2
Binongko, I Indon 55B4
Bintan, I Indon 54B2
Bintuhan Indon 54B3
Bintulu Malay 54D2
Bió Bió, R Chile 23B5
Bioko, I Atlantic O 73J4
Bir India 60B1
Bira USSR 51C2
Bîr Abu Husein, Well Egypt 67B2
Bi'r al Harash, Well Libya 67B2
Birao CAR 70C2
Biratnagar Nepal 59C2
Birch, R Can 3F2
Birch Creek USA 8J2
Birchip Aust 78B3
Birch L USA 9D2
Birch Mts Can 4G4
Bird Can 5J4
Birdsville Aust 76C3
Birdum Aust 76C2
Bîr el 'Agramîya, Well Egypt 63A4
Bir el Duweidâr, Well Egypt 63B3
Birganj Nepal 59B2
Bîr Gifgâfa, Well Egypt 63B3
Bîr Gindali, Well Egypt 63A4
Bîr Hasana, Well Egypt 63B3
Birigui Brazil 27B3
Birin Syria 63D1
Birjand Iran 61D2
Birkat Qarun, L Egypt 62B4
Birkenfeld W Germ 34D2
Birkenhead Eng 33D5
Bîrlad Rom 43D6
Bir Lahfân, Well Egypt 63B3
Birmingham Eng 33D5
Birmingham USA 7E3
Bîr Misâha, Well Egypt 67B2
Bir Moghrein Maur 68A2
Birnin Gwari Nig 69H3
Birnin Kebbi Nig 69G3
Birni N'Konni Nig 69H3
Birobidzhan USSR 51C2
Birr Irish Rep 33B5
Bir Rabalou Alg 37C2
Birrie, R Aust 78C1
Birsay Scot 32D2
Birsk USSR 42K4
Bîr Tarfâwi, Well Egypt 67B2
Birtle Can 9B1
Bîr Udelb, Well Egypt 63B4
Biryusa USSR 47L4
Birzai USSR 30J7
Bir Zreigat, Well Maur 68B2
Bisa, I Indon 55C3
Bisbee USA 17E4
Biscay,B of Spain/France 36A2
Biscayne B USA 13E4
Bischofshofen Austria 35E1
Bischwiller France 34D2
Biscotasi L Can 10C1
Bishan China 50B4
Bishop USA 6B3
Bishop Auckland Eng 33E4
Bishop's Stortford Eng 33F6
Bishrāmpur India 59B3
Bishui China 51A1
Biskia Eth 64C3
Biskra Alg 69D2
Bislig Phil 55G9
Bismarck USA 6C2
Bismarck Arch PNG 76D1
Bismarck Range, Mts PNG 76D1
Bismarck S PNG 76D1
Bisotūn Iran 61B2
Bissau Guinea-Bissau 68A3
Bissett Can 7D1
Bistcho L Can 4G4
Bistrita, R Rom 39F1
Bitam Gabon 70B3
Bitau L Can 3G1
Bitburg W Germ 40B3
Bitche France 34D2
Bitlis Turk 62D2
Bitola Yugos 39E2
Bitterfeld E Germ 40C2
Bitterfontein S Africa 72B3
Bitter Lakes Egypt 62B3
Bitteroot Range, Mts USA 6B2
Bitung Indon 55C2
Biu Nig 69J3
Biwa-ko, L Japan 51D4
Biyo Kaboba Eth 70E2
Biysk USSR 46K4
Bizerte Tunisia 69D1
Bj bou Arréridj Alg 37C2
Bjelovar Yugos 38D1
Bj Flye Ste Marie Alg 68B2
Bjørnøya, I Barents S 46C2
Black, R USA 8K2
Black, R USA 15D2
Blackall Aust 76D3
Black B Can 10B1
Black Birch L Can 3G2
Blackburn Eng 33D5
Blackburn,Mt USA 4D3
Black Canyon City USA 17D4
Black Diamond Can 3F3
Blackduck USA 9D2
Black Eagle USA 16D1
Blackfoot USA 16D2
Blackfoot, R USA 16D1
Black Hills USA 4H5
Black Isle, Pen Scot 32C3
Black L Can 3H2
Black Lake Can 3G2
Blackman's Barbados 21Q2
Black Mts USA 17D3
Black Mts Wales 33D6
Black Nossob, R Namibia 72B1
Blackpool Eng 33D5
Black River Jamaica 21H1
Black River Falls USA 10A2
Black Rock Desert USA 6B2
Black S USSR/Europe 46E5
Blacksburg USA 10C3
Black Sugarloaf, Mt Aust 78D2
Black Volta, R Ghana 69F4
Black Warrior, R USA 13B2
Blackwater, R Irish Rep 31B3
Blackwater L Can 8O3
Blackwell USA 15C2
Blagoevgrad Bulg 39E2
Blagoveshchensk USSR 47O4
Blaikiston,Mt Can 16D1
Blaine USA 16B1
Blair USA 9C3
Blair Atholl Scot 32D3
Blairgowrie Scot 32D3
Blakely USA 13C2
Blanca Peak, Mt USA 14A2
Blanche,L Aust 78A1
Blanco, R Arg 26A2
Blanco, R Arg 26B1
Blanco, R Mexico 20C1
Blanco,C USA 6A2
Blanc Sablon Can 5N4
Blandford Forum Eng 33D6
Blanding USA 17E3
Blangy-sur-Bresle France 34A2
Blankenberge Belg 34B1
Blanquillo Urug 26D2
Blantyre Malawi 71D5
Blaye France 36B2
Blayney Aust 78C2
Blenheim NZ 77G5
Bléone, R France 35B2
Blida Alg 69C1
Blind River Can 10C1
Blinman Aust 78A2
Blitar Indon 54D4
Blitta Togo 69G4
Block I USA 11E2
Block Island Sd USA 12E2
Bloemfontein S Africa 72D2
Bloemhof S Africa 72D2
Bloemhof Dam, Res S Africa 72D2
Blois France 34A3
Blommesteinmeer, L Suriname 25G3
Blonduós Iceland 30A1
Bloomfield, Indiana USA 10B3
Bloomfield, Iowa USA 15D1

Bloomfield, Nebraska USA 9C3
Bloomfield, New Mexico USA 14A2
Bloomington, Illinois USA 10B2
Bloomington, Indiana USA 10B3
Bloomington, Minnesota USA 9D3
Bloomsburg USA 12B2
Blora Indon 54D4
Blossburg USA 12B2
Blosseville Kyst, Mts Greenland 5Q3
Blouberg, Mt S Africa 72D1
Bludenz Austria 40B3
Bluefield USA 7E3
Bluefields Nic 24B1
Blue Hill USA 14C1
Blue Knob, Mt USA 12A2
Blue Mountain Peak, Mt Jamaica 21B3
Blue Mt USA 12B2
Blue Mts Aust 78D2
Blue Mts Jamaica 21J1
Blue Mts USA 6A2
Blue Nile = Bahr el Azraq
Blue Nile = Abbai
Blue Nile, R Sudan 70D2
Bluenose L Can 4G3
Blue Ridge USA 13C2
Blue Ridge Mts USA 7E3
Blue River Can 3E3
Blue Stack, Mt Irish Rep 32A4
Bluff NZ 79A3
Bluff USA 17E3
Bluff Knoll, Mt Aust 76A4
Blumenau Brazil 23G3
Blundez Austria 36D2
Blunt USA 9C3
Bly USA 16B2
Blying Sd USA 8J4
Blyth Eng 32E4
Blythe USA 6B3
Blytheville USA 7E3
Bo Sierra Leone 68A4
Boac Phil 55F8
Boading China 50D2
Boano, I Indon 55C3
Boa Nova Brazil 27D1
Boardman USA 10C2
Boatou China 47M5
Boa Vista Brazil 24F3
Boa Vista, I Cape Verde 68A4
Bobai China 53E1
Bobbili India 60C1
Bóbbio Italy 35C2
Bobo Dioulasso U Volta 69F3
Bobrovica USSR 41G2
Bobruysk USSR 42D5
Boca Chica Key, I USA 13E4
Bôca do Acre Brazil 24E4
Bocaiúva Brazil 27D2
Boca Jesús Maria Mexico 20C1
Bocaranga CAR 70B3
Boca Raton USA 13E4
Bochnia Pol 41E3
Bocholt W Germ 40B2
Bochum W Germ 34D1
Bocoio Angola 71B5
Boda CAR 70B3
Bodaybo USSR 47N4
Bodega Head, Pt USA 17B3
Bodélé, Desert Region Chad 70B2
Boden Sweden 30J5
Bodensee, L Switz/W Germ 35C1
Bodhan India 60B1
Bodināyakkanūr India 60B2
Bodmin Eng 33C6
Bodmin Moor, Upland Eng 33C6
Bodø Nor 30G5
Bodorodskoye USSR 47Q4
Bodrum Turk 39F3
Boende Zaïre 70C4
Boffa Guinea 68A3
Bogale Burma 53B2
Bogalusa USA 15E3
Bogan, R Aust 78C2
Bogandé U Volta 69F3
Bogarnes Iceland 5Q3
Boğazlıyan Turk 62C2
Bogdanovich USSR 42L4
Bogda Shan, Mt China 48B2
Bogenfels Namibia 72B2
Boggabilla Aust 78D1
Boggabri Aust 78C2
Bogo Phil 55F8
Bogong,Mt Aust 78C3
Bogor Indon 54C4
Bogorodskoye USSR 42J4
Bogotá Colombia 24D3
Bogotol USSR 47K4
Bogra Bang 59C3
Bo Hai, B China 50D2
Bohain-en-Vermandois France 34B2
Bohai Wan, B China 50D2
Boh Bistrica Yugos 35E1
Bohicon Benin 69G4
Bohmer-wald, Upland W Germ 40C3
Bohol, I Phil 55F9
Bohol S Phil 55F9
Bois, R Brazil 27B2
Bois Blanc I USA 10C1
Boise USA 6B2
Boise City USA 14B2
Boissevain Can 9B2
Bojador,C Mor 68A2
Bojeador,C Phil 55F7
Bojnürd Iran 61D1
Boké Guinea 68A3
Bokhara, R Aust 78C1
Boknafjord, Inlet Nor 30F7
Boko Congo 70B4
Bokor Camb 53C3
Bokoro Chad 70B2
Bokungu Zaïre 70C4
Bol Chad 70B2
Bolaãnos Mexico 20B1
Bolama Guinea-Bissau 68A3
Bolanos, R Mexico 20B1
Bolbec France 36C2
Bole Ghana 69F4
Bolen USSR 51D1
Boleslawiec Pol 40D2
Bolgatanga Ghana 69F3
Bolgrad USSR 43D6
Boli China 51C2
Bolívar Arg 26C3
Bolivar, Missouri USA 15D2
Bolivar, Tennessee USA 15E2
Bolivia, Republic S America 24E7
Bollnas Sweden 30H6
Bollon Aust 78C1
Bollvar, Mt Ven 24D2
Bologna Italy 38C2
Bologoye USSR 42E4
Bolon USSR 51D2
Bol'shezemel'skaya Tundra, Plain USSR 42J2
Bol'shoy Anyuy, R USSR 47S3
Bol'shoy Irgiz, R USSR 43H5
Bol'shoy Kamen USSR 51C3
Bolshoykavka, Mts USSR 43G7
Bol'shoy Kavkaz, Mts USSR 46F5
Bol'shoy Uzen, R USSR 43H6
Bolson de Mapimi, Desert Mexico 6C4
Bolton Eng 33D5
Bolu Turk 62B1
Bolugarvik Iceland 30A1
Bolvadin Turk 62B2
Bolzano Italy 38C1
Boma Zaïre 70B4
Bombala Aust 76D4
Bombay India 60A1
Bombo Uganda 70D3
Bomdila India 59D2
Bomi China 59E2
Bomi Hills Lib 68A4
Bom Jesus da Lapa Brazil 25K6
Bomnak USSR 47O4
Bomokandi, R Zaïre 70C3
Bomu, R CAR/Zaïre 70C3
Bon Air USA 11D3
Bonaire, I Caribbean 21D4
Bona,Mt USA 8K3
Bonanza Nic 19D3
Bonavista Can 5N5
Bon Bon Aust 78A2
Bon Despacho Brazil 27C2
Bondo Zaïre 70C3
Bondoukou Ivory Coast 69F4
Bône = 'Annaba
Bone Indon 55B4
Bonelipu Indon 55B3
Bonesteel USA 9C3
Bonfim Guyana 25G3
Bongandanga Zaïre 70C3
Bongka, R Indon 55B3
Bongor Chad 70B2
Bongouanou Ivory Coast 69F4
Bonham USA 15C3
Bonifacio Corse 38B2
Bonifacio,Str of, Chan Medit S 38B2
Bonin Is = Ogasawara Gunto
Bonita Springs USA 13E4
Bonito Brazil 27A3
Bonn W Germ 40B2
Bonners Ferry USA 16C1
Bonnétable France 34A2
Bonnet Plume, R Can 8M2
Bonneval France 34A2
Bonnyville Can 3F3
Bonthain Indon 76A1
Bonthe Sierra Leone 68A4
Bontosunggu Indon 55A4
Booaaso Somalia 67D3
Booligal Aust 78B2
Boonah Aust 78D1
Boone, Colorado USA 14B2
Boone, Iowa USA 9D3
Boone, North Carolina USA 13C1
Boonville USA 11D2
Boorowa Aust 78C2
Boothia,G of Can 5J2
Boothia Pen Can 5J2
Booué Gabon 70B4
Bopeechee Aust 78A1
Bophuthatswana, Self governing homeland S Africa 72C2
Boquillas Mexico 14B4
Bor Sudan 70D3
Bor Turk 62B2
Bor Yugos 39E2
Borah Peak, Mt USA 6B2
Borås Sweden 30G7
Borāzjān Iran 61C3
Borda,C Aust 78A3
Bordeaux France 36B3
Borden I Can 4G2
Borden Pen Can 5K2
Bordentown USA 12C2
Borders, Region Scot 32D4
Bordertown Aust 78B3
Bordighera Italy 35B3
Bordi Omar Dris Alg 68C2
Bordj bou Arreridj Alg 69C1
Borens River Can 6D1
Borgå Fin 30K6
Borgarnes Iceland 30A2
Borger USA 6C3
Borgholm Sweden 30H7
Borgo San Lorenzo Italy 35D3
Borgosia Italy 35C2
Borgo Val di Taro Italy 35C2
Borgo Valsugana Italy 35D1
Borislav USSR 41E3
Borisoglebsk USSR 43G5
Borisov USSR 42D5
Borisovka USSR 43F5
Borja Par 27A4
Borkou, Desert Region Chad 70B2
Borlänge Sweden 30H6
Bormida Italy 35C2
Bormio Italy 35D1
Borneo, I Malaysia/Indon 45G5
Bornholm, I Den 30H7
Borno, State Nig 69J3
Bornova Turk 39F3
Boro, R Sudan 70C3
Borogontsy USSR 47P3
Boromo U Volta 69F3
Boron USA 18D3
Borovichi USSR 42E4
Borroloola Aust 76C2
Borsa Rom 39E1
Borūjed Iran 61B2
Borūjen Iran 61C2
Bory Tucholskie, Region Pol 40D2
Borzna USSR 41G2
Borzya USSR 47N4
Bose China 50B5
Boshnyakovo USSR 51E2
Boshof S Africa 72D2
Bosna, R Yugos 39D2
Bōsō-hantō, B Japan 52D3
Bosporus = Karadeniz Boğazi
Bosquet Alg 37C2
Bossangoa CAR 70B3
Bossèmbélé CAR 70B3
Bossier City USA 15D3
Bosten Hu, L China 46K5
Boston Eng 33E5
Boston USA 7F2
Boston Mts USA 7D3
Bosumtwi,L Ghana 69F4
Botād India 58C4
Botevgrad Bulg 39E2
Bothaville S Africa 72D2
Bothnia,G of Sweden/Fin 42B3
Botletli, R Botswana 71C6
Botosani Rom 43D6
Botswana, Republic Africa 71C6
Botte Donato, Mt Italy 38D3
Bottineau USA 9B2
Bottrop W Germ 34D1
Botucatu Brazil 27C3
Botupora Brazil 27D1
Botwood Can 5N5
Bouaflé Ivory Coast 68B4
Bouaké Ivory Coast 66D7
Bouar CAR 70B3
Bouârfa Mor 69B2
Bouba Ndija Nat Pk Cam 69J4
Bouca CAR 70B3
Boudnib Mor 69B2
Boufarik Alg 37C2
Bougainville, I PNG 77E1
Bougie = Bejaïa
Bougouni Mali 68B3
Bougouriba, R U Volta 69F3
Bougtob Alg 69C2
Bouillon France 34C2
Bouira Alg 69C1
Bou Izakarn Mor 68B2
Boulay-Moselle France 34D2
Boulder, Colorado USA 6C2
Boulder, Montana USA 16D1
Boulder City USA 6B3
Boulder Creek USA 18A2
Boulogne France 36C1
Boumba, R CAR 70B3
Bouna Ivory Coast 69F4
Boundary Peak, Mt USA 6B3
Boundiali Ivory Coast 68B4
Bountiful USA 16D2
Bounty Is NZ 77G5
Bourail Nouvelle Calédonie 77F3
Bourbonne-les-Bains France 34C3
Bourem Mali 68B3
Bourg France 36D2
Bourg de Péage France 36D2
Bourg-en-Bresse France 35A1
Bourges France 36C2
Bourg-Madame France 36C3
Bourgogne, Region France 36C2
Bourgoin-Jallieu France 35A2
Bourg-St-Maurice France 35B2
Bourke Aust 78C2
Bournemouth Eng 33E6
Bou Saâda Alg 69C1
Bousso Chad 70B2
Boutilmit Maur 68A3
Boutourou,Mt Ivory Coast 69F4
Bouvet I Atlantic O 73J7
Bovril Arg 26D2
Bow, R Can 3F3
Bowbells USA 9B2
Bowen Aust 76D2
Bowie, Arizona USA 17E4
Bowie, Texas USA 15C3
Bow Island Can 3F3
Bowling Green, Kentucky USA 7E3
Bowling Green, Missouri USA 15D2
Bowling Green, Ohio USA 10C2
Bowling Green, Virginia USA 11D3
Bowman USA 9B2
Bowmanville Can 11D2
Bowral Aust 78D2
Bowron, R Can 3D3
Bo Xian China 50D3
Boxing China 50D2
Boyabat Turk 62B1
Boyali CAR 70B3
Boyarka USSR 41G2
Boyd Can 4J4
Boyertown USA 12C2
Boyle Can 3F3
Boyle Irish Rep 31B3
Boyne, R Irish Rep 33B5
Boynoton Beach USA 13E4
Boyoma Falls Zaïre 70C3
Boysen Res USA 16E2
Bozcaada, I Turk 39F3
Boz Dağlari, Mts Turk 39F3
Bozeman USA 6B2
Bozen = Bolzano
Bozene Zaïre 70B3
Bozoum CAR 70B3
Bra Italy 35B2
Brač, I Yugos 38D2
Bracebridge Can 11D1
Brach Libya 67A2
Bräcke Sweden 30H6
Brackettville USA 14B4
Bradenton USA 13E4
Bradford Eng 33E5
Bradford USA 12A2
Bradley USA 18B3
Brady USA 14C3
Brae Scot 32E1
Braemar Scot 32D3
Braga Port 37A1
Bragado Arg 26C3
Bragana Port 37A1
Bragança Brazil 25J4
Bragança Paulista Brazil 27C3
Brahman-Baria Bang 59D3
Brāhmani, R India 59C3
Brahmaputra, R India 59D2
Braie Verte Can 5N5
Brăila Rom 43D6
Brainerd USA 7D2
Brak, R S Africa 72C3
Brak, R S Africa 72D1
Brakna, Region Maur 68A3
Bralorne Can 4F4
Brampton Can 11D2
Branco, R Brazil 24F3
Brandberg, Mt Namibia 71B6
Brandenburg E Germ 40C2
Brandfort S Africa 72D2
Brandon Can 6D2
Brandon USA 9C3
Brandvlei S Africa 72C3
Brandys nad Lebem Czech 40C2
Braniewo Pol 41D2
Brantford Can 7E2
Branxholme Aust 78B3
Bras D'Or L Can 5M5
Brasíla de Minas Brazil 27D2
Brasiléia Brazil 24E6
Brasilia Brazil 25J7
Brasov Rom 39F1
Brassay Range, Mts Malay 54E2
Bratislava Czech 40D3
Bratsk USSR 47M4
Bratslav USSR 41F3
Brattleboro USA 11E2
Braunschweig W Germ 40C2
Brava, I Cape Verde 68A4
Brawley USA 6B3
Bray Irish Rep 33B5
Bray I Can 5L3
Bray-sur-Seine France 34B2
Brazeau, R Can 3E3
Brazeau,Mt Can 3E3
Brazil, Republic S America 22E5
Brazil Basin Atlantic O 73G5
Brazos, R USA 6D3
Brazzaville Congo 70B4
Brdy, Upland Czech 40C3
Breaksea Sd NZ 79A3
Bream B NZ 79B1
Brebes Indon 54C4
Brechin Scot 32D3
Brecht Belg 34C1
Breckenridge, Minnesota USA 9C2
Breckenridge, Texas USA 14C3
Břeclav Czech 40D3
Brecon Wales 33D6
Brecon Beacons, Mts Wales 33D6
Brecon Beacons Nat Pk Wales 33C5
Breda Neth 40A2
Bredasdorp S Africa 72C3
Bredby Sweden 30H6
Bredbyn Sweden 42B3
Bredy USSR 42K5
Breede, R S Africa 72B3
Breezewood USA 11D2
Bregenz Austria 35C1
Bregenzer Ache, R Austria 35C1
Breiðafjörður, B Iceland 30A1
Breisach W Germ 34D2
Brembo Italy 35C2
Brembo, R Italy 35C2
Bremen USA 13B2
Bremen W Germ 40B2
Bremerhaven W Germ 40B2
Bremerton USA 16B1
Brendel USA 17E3
Brenham USA 15C3
Brenner, Mt Austria 36E2
Brenner, P Austria/Italy 40C3
Breno Italy 35D2
Brenta, R Italy 35D2
Brentwood USA 18B2
Brescia Italy 38C1
Breslau = Wrocław
Bressanone Italy 35D1
Bressay, I Scot 32E1
Bressuire France 36B2
Brest France 36B2
Brest USSR 41E2
Bretagne, Region France 36B2
Breteuil France 34B2
Bretevil France 34A2
Breton Sd USA 13B3
Breton Woods USA 12C2
Brett,C NZ 79B1
Brevard USA 13C1
Brewarrina Aust 78C1
Brewer USA 11F2
Brewster, New York USA 12D2
Brewster, Washington USA 16C1
Brewton USA 13B2
Breyten S Africa 72D2
Brežice Yugos 38D1
Bria CAR 70C3
Briancon France 36D3
Briare France 36C2
Bridgeport, Alabama USA 13B2
Bridgeport, California USA 17C3
Bridgeport, Connecticut USA 11E2
Bridgeport, Nebraska USA 9B3
Bridgeport, Texas USA 15C3
Bridgeport Res USA 18C1
Bridger USA 16E1
Bridger Peak USA 14A1
Bridgeton USA 12C3
Bridgetown Barbados 21F4
Bridgewater Can 5M5

Bridgewater *USA* 12E2
Bridgwater *Eng* 33D6
Bridgwater B *Eng* 33D6
Bridlington *Eng* 33E4
Bridport *Aust* 78E3
Brienne-le-Château *France* 34C2
Brienzer See, L *Switz* 35B1
Briey *France* 34C2
Brig *Switz* 38B1
Brigham City *USA* 6B2
Bright *Aust* 78C3
Brighton *Eng* 33E6
Brignoles *France* 35B3
Brilhante, R *Brazil* 27A3
Brilon *W Germ* 34E1
Brindisi *Italy* 39D2
Brinkley *USA* 15D3
Brisbane *Aust* 77E3
Bristol, Connecticut *USA* 11E2
Bristol *Eng* 33D6
Bristol, Pennsylvania *USA* 11E2
Bristol, Rhode Island *USA* 12E2
Bristol, Tennessee *USA* 7E3
Bristol B *USA* 8F4
Bristol Chan *Eng/Wales* 33C6
British Columbia, Province *Can* 4F4
British Empire Range, Mts *Can* 5K1
British Mts *USA/Can* 8K2
Brits *S Africa* 72D2
Britstown *S Africa* 72C3
Britton *USA* 9C2
Brive *France* 36C2
Brno *Czech* 40D3
Broad, R *USA* 13C2
Broadalbin *USA* 12C1
Broadback, R *Can* 5L4
Broad Bay, Inlet *Scot* 32B2
Broadford *Scot* 32C3
Broadus *USA* 9A2
Broadview *Can* 9B1
Broadwater *USA* 9B3
Brochet *Can* 4H4
Brock I *Can* 4G2
Brockport *USA* 11D2
Brockton *USA* 12E1
Brockville *Can* 11D2
Brockway *USA* 12A2
Brodeur Pen *Can* 5K2
Brodick *Scot* 32C4
Brodnica *Pol* 41D2
Brody *USSR* 43D5
Brokem Haltern *W Germ* 34D1
Broken Bow, Nebraska *USA* 14C1
Broken Bow, Oklahoma *USA* 15D3
Broken Bow L *USA* 15D3
Broken Hill *Aust* 76D4
Broni *Italy* 35C2
Brønnøysund *Nor* 30G5
Bronx, Borough, New York *USA* 12D2
Brooke's Point *Phil* 55E9
Brookfield, Missouri *USA* 15D2
Brookfield, Wisconsin *USA* 10B2
Brookhaven *USA* 7D3
Brookings, Oregon *USA* 16B2
Brookings, South Dakota *USA* 6D2
Brookline *USA* 12E1
Brooklyn *USA* 9D3
Brooklyn, Borough, New York *USA* 12D2
Brooklyn Center *USA* 9D2
Brooks *Can* 4G4
Brooks,L *USA* 8G4
Brooks Mt *USA* 8E2
Brooks Range, Mts *USA* 4C3
Brooksville *USA* 13C3
Brookton *USA* 11E2
Brooloo *Aust* 78D1
Broome *Aust* 76B2
Brora *Scot* 32D2
Brothers *USA* 16B2
Brothers,The, Is *S Yemen* 65F4
Brou *France* 34A2
Broulkou, Well *Chad* 70B2
Brovary *USSR* 41G2
Browerville *USA* 9D2
Brownfield *USA* 14B3
Browning *USA* 3F4
Brownsville *USA* 6D4
Brownwood *USA* 6D3
Browse, I *Aust* 49F8
Bruay-en-Artois *France* 34B1
Bruce,Mt *Aust* 76A3
Bruce Pen *Can* 10C1
Bruchsal *W Germ* 34E2
Bruck *Austria* 35E1
Bruck an der Mur *Austria* 40D3
Bruges = Brugge
Brugge *Belg* 34B1
Brühl *W Germ* 34D1
Brumado *Brazil* 27D1
Brumath *France* 34D2
Bruneau *USA* 16C2
Bruneau, R *USA* 16C2
Brunei, Sultanate *S E Asia* 54D2
Brunico *Italy* 38C1
Brunner,L *NZ* 79B2
Brunswick, Georgia *USA* 7E3
Brunswick, Maine *USA* 11F2
Brunswick, Mississippi *USA* 15D2
Brunswick,Pen de *Chile* 23B8
Bruny I *Aust* 78E3
Brusenets *USSR* 42G3
Brush *USA* 14B1
Brus Laguna *Honduras* 21A3
Brüssel = Bruxelles
Bruxelles *Belg* 40A2
Bruyères *France* 34D2
Bryan *USA* 6D3
Bryan,Mt *Aust* 78A2
Bryansk *USSR* 42E5
Bryant *USA* 15D3
Bryce Canyon Nat Pk *USA* 18D3
Brzeg *Pol* 40D2
Bubīyan, I *Kuwait/Iraq* 62E4
Bubu, R *Tanz* 70D4
Bubve, R *Zim* 72E1
Bucaramanga *Colombia* 24D2
Buchan, Oilfield *N Sea* 32E3
Buchanan *Lib* 68A4
Buchanan,L *USA* 14C3
Buchan Deep *N Sea* 32E3
Buchan G *Can* 5L2
Buchan Ness, Pen *Scot* 31C2
Buchans *Can* 5N5
Buchardo *Arg* 26C2
Bucharest = Bucureşti
Buchon,Pt *USA* 18B3
Buchs *Switz* 35C1
Buckeye *USA* 17D4
Buckingham *Eng* 33E5
Buckland *USA* 8F2
Buckland, R *USA* 8F2
Buckleboo *Aust* 78A2
Bucksport *USA* 11F2
Buco Zau *Congo* 70B4
Bucureşti *Rom* 39F2
Budapest *Hung* 41D3
Budaun *India* 58D3
Bude *Eng* 33C6
Bude *USA* 15D3
Budennovsk *USSR* 43G7
Büdingen *W Germ* 34E1
Budva *Yugos* 39D2
Buéa *Cam* 70A3
Buech, R *France* 35A2
Buellton *USA* 18B3
Buena Esperanza *Arg* 26B2
Buenaventura *Colombia* 24C3
Buenaventura *Mexico* 14A4
Buena Vista, Colorado *USA* 14A2
Buenavista *Mexico* 20B2
Buena Vista, Virginia *USA* 11D3
Buena Vista L *USA* 18C3
Bueno, R *Chile* 26A4
Buenos Aires *Arg* 23E4
Buenos Aires, State *Arg* 23E5
Buffalo, Mississippi *USA* 15D2
Buffalo, New York *USA* 7F2
Buffalo, South Dakota *USA* 9B2
Buffalo, Texas *USA* 15C3
Buffalo, Wyoming *USA* 6C2
Buffalo, R *S Africa* 72E2
Buffalo Head Hills, Mts *Can* 3E2
Buffalo Hump *USA* 16C1
Buffalo L, Alberta *Can* 3F3
Buffalo L, Northwest Territories *Can* 3E1
Buffalo Narrows *Can* 4H4
Buford *USA* 13C2
Buftea *Rom* 39F2
Bug, R *USSR/Pol* 41E2
Buga *Colombia* 24C3
Bugdayli *USSR* 61C1
Bugt *China* 51A2
Bugulma *USSR* 42J5
Buguruslan *USSR* 42J5
Buhayrat al Asad, Res *Syria* 62C2
Buhl, Idaho *USA* 16D2
Buhl, Minnesota *USA* 9D2
Bui Dam *Ghana* 69F4
Builth Wells *Wales* 31C3
Buin *Chile* 26A2
Buis-les-Baronnies *France* 35A2
Buith Wells *Wales* 33D5
Buje *Yugos* 35E2
Bujumbura *Burundi* 70C4
Buka, I *PNG* 77E1
Bukama *Zaïre* 71C4
Bukavu *Zaïre* 70C4
Bukhara *USSR* 56E2
Bukit Batubrok, Mt *Indon* 54D2
Bukittinggi *Indon* 54B3
Bukoba *Tanz* 70D4
Buku Gandadiwata, Mt *Indon* 55B3
Buku Saolat, Mt *Indon* 55C2
Bula *Indon* 49G7
Bulan *Phil* 55F8
Bulandshahr *India* 58D3
Bulawayo *Zim* 71C6
Buldan *Turk* 39F3
Buldāna *India* 58D4
Buldir I *USA* 8B6
Bulgan *Mongolia* 48D2
Bulgaria, Republic *Europe* 39E2
Buli *Indon* 55C2
Bulle *Switz* 35B1
Buller, R *NZ* 79B2
Buller,Mt *Aust* 78C3
Bullfinch *Aust* 76A4
Bulloo, R *Aust* 78B1
Bulloo Downs *Aust* 78B1
Bulloo L *Aust* 78B1
Bull Shoals Res *USA* 15D2
Bulnes *Chile* 26A3
Bulolo *PNG* 76D1
Bultfontein *S Africa* 72D2
Bulukumba *Indon* 55B4
Bum Bum, I *Malay* 54E2
Bu Menderes, R *Turk* 43D8
Bumpa *Zaïre* 70C3
Bumphal Dam *Thai* 53B2
Buna *Kenya* 70D3
Bunbury *Aust* 76A4
Buncrana *Irish Rep* 32B4
Bundaberg *Aust* 77E3
Bundarra *Aust* 78D2
Bündi *India* 58D3
Bungil, R *Aust* 78C1
Bungo *Angola* 71B4
Bungo-suidō, Str *Japan* 52B4
Bunguran, I *Indon* 54C2
Bunia *Zaïre* 70D3
Bunker *USA* 15D2
Bunkie *USA* 15D3
Bunnell *USA* 13C3
Bunsuru, R *Nig* 69H3
Buntok *Indon* 54D3
Buol *Indon* 55B2
Burāq *Syria* 63D2
Buram *Sudan* 70C2
Burang *China* 59B1
Burauen *Phil* 55G8
Buraydah *S Arabia* 64D1
Burbank *USA* 17C4
Burcher *Aust* 78C2
Burco *Somalia* 70E3
Burdalyk *USSR* 61E1
Burdur *Turk* 43E8
Bureinskiy Khrebet, Mts *USSR* 51C1
Bureya, R *USSR* 51C1
Bûr Fu'ad *Egypt* 63B3
Burg *E Germ* 40C2
Burgas *Bulg* 39F2
Burgaw *USA* 13D2
Burgdorf *Switz* 35B1
Burgersdorp *S Africa* 72D3
Burgin *USSR* 46K5
Burgos *Mexico* 20C1
Burgos *Spain* 37B1
Burgrino *USSR* 42H2
Burgsvik *Sweden* 41D1
Burgut *USSR* 46J3
Burhaniye *Turk* 39F3
Burhānpur *India* 58D4
Burias, I *Phil* 55F8
Buriram *Thai* 53C2
Buritis *Brazil* 27C2
Burke Chan *Can* 3C3
Burketown *Aust* 76C2
Burks Falls *Can* 11D1
Burley *USA* 6B2
Burlington, Colorado *USA* 14B2
Burlington, Iowa *USA* 7D2
Burlington, New Jersey *USA* 12C2
Burlington, North Carolina *USA* 13D1
Burlington, Vermont *USA* 7F2
Burlington, Washington *USA* 16B1
Burma, Republic *Asia* 57H3
Burnet *USA* 14C3
Burney *USA* 16B2
Burnham *USA* 12B2
Burnie *Aust* 76D5
Burnley *Eng* 33D5
Burns *USA* 16C2
Burns Lake *Can* 4F4
Burqin *China* 57G1
Burra *Aust* 78A2
Burragorang,L *Aust* 78D2
Burray, I *Scot* 32D2
Burren Junction *Aust* 78C2
Burrinjuck Res *Aust* 78C2
Burrundie *Aust* 49G8
Bursa *Turk* 43D7
Bur Safâga *Egypt* 64B1
Bûr Sa'îd = Port Said
Bûr Taufiq *Egypt* 63B4
Burton *USA* 10C2
Burton upon Trent *Eng* 33E5
Burtrask *Sweden* 30J6
Burtundy *Aust* 78B2
Buru *Indon* 55C3
Burundi, Republic *Africa* 70C4
Burung *Indon* 54B2
Burwell *USA* 9C3
Buryatskaya ASSR, Republic *USSR* 47N4
Burye *Eth* 70D2
Burynshik *USSR* 43J6
Bury St Edmunds *Eng* 33F5
Būshehr *Iran* 61C3
Busira, R *Zaïre* 70B4
Buskozdroj *Pol* 41E2
Busrā ash Shām *Syria* 63D2
Bussang *France* 34D3
Busselton *Aust* 76A4
Busto *Italy* 36D2
Busto Arsizio *Italy* 38B1
Bustol *USA* 10C3
Busuanga, I *Phil* 55E8
Buta *Zaïre* 70C3
Buta Ranquil *Arg* 26B3
Butare *Rwanda* 70C4
Bute, I *Scot* 32C4
Butha Qi *China* 51A2
Butler *USA* 11D2
Butte *USA* 6B2
Butterworth *Malay* 53C4
Butterworth *S Africa* 72D3
Butt of Lewis, C *Scot* 31B2
Button Is *Can* 5M3
Buttonwillow *USA* 18C3
Butuan *Phil* 55G9
Butung, I *Indon* 55B4
Butung, I *Indon* 76B1
Buturlinovka *USSR* 43G5
Butwal *Nepal* 59B2
Butzbach *W Germ* 34E1
Buulo Barde *Somalia* 70E3
Buur Hakaba *Somalia* 70E3
Buy *USSR* 42G4
Buyant Ovvo *Mongolia* 50B1
Buynaksk *USSR* 43H7
Buyr Nuur, L *Mongolia* 47N5
Büyük Ağri Daği, Mt *Turk* 43G8
Buyukly *USSR* 51E2
Büyük Menderes, R *Turk* 62A2
Buzău *Rom* 39F1
Buzau, R *Rom* 39F1
Buzuluk *USSR* 42J5
Buzzards B *USA* 12E2
Byala *Bulg* 39F2
Byala Slatina *Bulg* 39E2
Byam Martin, Chan *Can* 4H2
Byam Martin I *Can* 4H2
Byblos
Bydgoszcz *Pol* 41D2
Byers *USA* 14B2
Bygland *Nor* 30F7
Bykov *USSR* 51E2
Bylot I *Can* 5L2
Byrhov *USSR* 41G2
Byrock *Aust* 78C2
Byron *USA* 18B2
Byron,C *Aust* 78D1
Bytantay, R *USSR* 47P3
Bytom *Pol* 41D2

C

Caacupé *Par* 23E3
Caaguazú *Par* 27A4
Caála *Angola* 71B5
Caamano Sd *Can* 3C3
Caapucú *Par* 27A4
Caarapó *Brazil* 27B3
Caazapá *Par* 23E3
Caballo Res *USA* 14A3
Cabanatuan *Phil* 55F7
Cabano *Can* 11F1
Cabedelo *Brazil* 25M5
Cabeza del Buey *Spain* 37A2
Cabildo *Arg* 26C3
Cabildo *Chile* 26A2
Cabimas *Ven* 24D1
Cabinda *Angola* 70B4
Cabinda, Province *Angola* 70B4
Cabinet Mts *USA* 16C1
Cabo Beata *Dom Rep* 21C3
Cabo Binibeca, C *Spain* 37C2
Cabo Cantin, C *Mor* 69A2
Cabo Carbonara, C *Sardegna* 38B3
Cabo Carranza, C *Chile* 26A3
Cabo Carvoeiro, C *Port* 37A2
Cabo Colnett, C *Mexico* 6B3
Cabo Corrientes, C *Arg* 26D3
Cabo Corrientes, C *Colombia* 24C2
Cabo Corrientes, C *Mexico* 19B2
Cabo Cruz, C *Cuba* 21B3
Cabo de Ajo, C *Spain* 37B1
Cabo de Caballeria, C *Spain* 37C1
Cabo de Creus, C *Spain* 37C1
Cabo de Hornos, C *Chile* 23C9
Cabo de la Nao, C *Spain* 37C2
Cabo de Peñas, C *Spain* 37A1
Cabo de Roca, C *Port* 37A2
Cabo de Salinas, C *Spain* 37C2
Cabo de Santa Maria, C *Mozam* 72E2
Cabo de São Tomé, C *Brazil* 27D3
Cabo de São Vicente, C *Port* 37A2
Cabo de Sata, C *Spain* 37B2
Cabo de Sines, C *Port* 37A2
Cabo de Tortosa, C *Spain* 37C1
Cabo Dos Bahias, C *Arg* 23C6
Cabo Espichel, C *Port* 37A2
Cabo Falso, C *Mexico* 6B4
Cabo Ferrat, C *Alg* 37B2
Cabo Finisterre, C *Spain* 37A1
Cabo Formentor, C *Spain* 37C1
Cabo Frio *Brazil* 27D3
Cabo Frio, C *Brazil* 27D3
Cabo Gracias à Dios *Honduras* 21A4
Cabo Leones, C *Chile* 26A1
Cabo Maguarinho, C *Brazil* 25J4
Cabo Negro, C *Mor* 37A2
Caboolture *Aust* 78D1
Cabo Orange, C *Brazil* 25H3
Cabo Punta Banda, C *Mexico* 17C4
Cabora Bassa Dam *Mozam* 71D5
Caborca *Mexico* 19A1
Cabo Rojo, C *Mexico* 19C2
Cabos *Mexico* 20C1
Cabo San Antonio, C *Arg* 26D3
Cabo San Antonio, C *Cuba* 21A2
Cabo San Diego, C *Arg* 23C8
Cabo San Lorenzo, C *Ecuador* 24B4
Cabo Teulada, C *Sardegna* 38B3
Cabo Trafalgar, C *Spain* 37A2
Cabo Tres Forcas, C *Mor* 37B2
Cabo Tres Puntas, C *Arg* 23C7
Cabot Str *Can* 5M5
Cabra *Spain* 37B2
Cabreira, Mt *Port* 37A1
Cabrera, I *Spain* 37C2
Cabrero *Chile* 26A3
Cabriel, R *Spain* 37B2
Cacahuamilpa *Mexico* 20C2
Čačak *Yugos* 39E2
Cacapava do Sul *Brazil* 26E2
Cacapon, R *USA* 12A3
C A Carillo *Mexico* 20C2
Caceoul *Brazil* 26E1
Cáceres *Brazil* 25G7
Caceres *Spain* 37A2
Cache, R *USA* 15D2
Cache Creek *Can* 3D3
Cache Creek, R *USA* 18A1
Cache Peak, Mt *USA* 16D2
Cachi *Arg* 23C3
Cachimbo *Brazil* 25G5
Cachoeira *Brazil* 25L6
Cachoeira Alta *Brazil* 27B2
Cachoeira de Paulo Afonso, Waterfall *Brazil* 25L5
Cachoeira do Sul *Brazil* 23F4
Cachoeiro de Itapemirim *Brazil* 25K8
Cachuma,L *USA* 18C3
Cacolo *Angola* 71B5
Caconda *Angola* 71B5
Cactus *USA* 14B2
Caçu *Brazil* 27B2
Caculé *Brazil* 27D1
Caculuvar, R *Angola* 71B5
Čadca *Czech* 41D3
Cader Idris, Mts *Wales* 33D5
Cadillac *Can* 9A2
Cadillac *USA* 7E2
Cadiz *Phil* 55F8
Cadiz *Spain* 37A2
Caetié *Brazil* 25K6
Caen *France* 36B2
Caernarfon *Wales* 33C5
Caernarfon B *Wales* 33C5
Caesarea, Hist Site *Israel* 63C2
Caetité *Brazil* 27D1
Cafayate *Arg* 23C3
Caga Tepe *Turk* 62B2
Cagayan, R *Phil* 55F7
Cagayan de Oro *Phil* 55F9
Cagayan Is *Phil* 55F9
Cagayan Sulu, I *Phil* 55E9
Cagli *Italy* 35E3
Cagliari *Sardegna* 38B3

Caguas Puerto Rico 21D3
Cahaba, R USA 13B2
Cahir Irish Rep 33B5
Cahone Pt Irish Rep 33B5
Cahors France 36C3
Caia Mozam 71D5
Caianda Angola 71C5
Caiapó, R Brazil 27B2
Caiapônia Brazil 27B2
Caicó Brazil 25L5
Caicos Is Caribbean 21C2
Caicos Pass Bahamas 7F4
Cairn Mt USA 8G3
Cairngorms, Mts, Scot 32D3
Cairns Aust 76D2
Cairo Egypt 62B3
Cairo USA 7E3
Caiwarro Aust 78B1
Cajabamba Peru 24C5
Cajamarca Peru 24C5
Calabozo Ven 21D5
Calafat Rom 39E2
Calafate Arg 23B8
Calagua Is Phil 55F8
Calahorra Spain 37B1
Calais France 36C1
Calais USA 11F1
Calama Chile 23C2
Calamar Colombia 24D3
Calamian Group, Is Phil 55E8
Calang Indon 54A2
Calanscio Sand Sea Libya 67B2
Calapan Phil 55F8
Calarasi Rom 39F2
Calatayud Spain 37B1
Calaveras Res USA 18B2
Calbayog Phil 55F8
Calcasieu L USA 15D4
Calcutta India 59C3
Caldas da Rainha Port 37A2
Caldas Novas Brazil 25J7
Caldera Chile 23B3
Caldwell USA 6B2
Caledon S Africa 72B3
Caledon, R S Africa 72D3
Caledonia, Minnesota USA 10A2
Caledonia, New York USA 12B1
Calera Mexico 20B1
Caleta Olivia Arg 23C7
Calexico USA 6B3
Calgary Can 4G4
Calhoun USA 13C2
Calhoun Falls USA 13C2
Cali Colombia 24C3
Calicut India 60B2
Caliente, California USA 18C3
Caliente, Nevada USA 6B3
Caliente, New Mexico USA 14A2
California, State USA 6A3
California Aqueduct USA 18C3
Calimera,Pt India 60B2
Calingasta Arg 26B2
Calipatria USA 17C4
Calistoga USA 18A1
Calitzdorp S Africa 72C3
Callabonna, R Aust 78B1
Callabonna,L Aust 78A1
Callander Can 11D1
Callander Scot 32C3
Callanna Aust 78A1
Callao Peru 24C6
Calles Mèxico 20C1
Callicoon USA 12C2
Calling L Can 3F2
Calnali Mexico 20C1
Caloosahatchee, R USA 13E4
Caloundra Aust 78D1
Calpulalpan Mexico 20C2
Caltanissetta Italy 38C3
Caluango Angola 71B4
Calulo Angola 71B5
Caluquembe Angola 71B5
Caluula Somalia 65F4
Calvert I Can 3C3
Calvi Corse 38B2
Calvillo Mexico 20B1
Calvinia S Africa 72B3
Calw W Germ 34E2
Camacari Brazil 27E1
Camacho Mexico 20B1
Camaguã Brazil 26E2
Camaguã, R Brazil 26E2
Camagüey Cuba 19E2
Camagüey,Arch de, Is Cuba 19E2
Camamu Brazil 27E1
Camaná Peru 24D7
Camania, I Can 8N5
Camapuã Brazil 27B2
Camargo Bol 24E8
Camarillo USA 18C3
Camarones Arg 23C6
Camas USA 16B1
Camaxilo Angola 71B4
Cambatela Angola 71B4
Cambodia, Republic S E Asia 53C3
Camborne Eng 33C6
Cambrai France 36C1
Cambria USA 18B3
Cambrian Mts Wales 33D5
Cambridge Can 10C2
Cambridge, County Eng 33E5
Cambridge Eng 33F5
Cambridge Jamaica 21H1
Cambridge, Maryland USA 11D3
Cambridge, Massachussets USA 11E2
Cambridge, Minnesota USA 9D2
Cambridge NZ 79C1
Cambridge, Ohio USA 10C2
Cambridge Bay Can 4H3
Cambridge G Aust 49F8
Cam Burun, Pt Turk 43F7
Camden, Arkansas USA 7D3
Camden Aust 78D2
Camden, New Jersey USA 11E3
Camden, New York USA 12C1
Camden, South Carolina USA 13C2
Camden B USA 8J1
Camerino Italy 35E3
Cameron, Missouri USA 15D2
Cameron, Texas USA 15C3
Cameron Highlands Malay 54F6
Cameron I Can 4H2
Cameron Mts NZ 79A3
Cameroon, Federal Republic Africa 70B3
Cameroun, Mt Cam 70A3
Cametá Brazil 25J4
Camiguin, I Phil 55F9
Camiling Phil 55F7
Camilla USA 13C2
Camino USA 18B1
Camiri Bol 24F8
Camocim Brazil 25K4
Camooweal Aust 76C2
Camorta, I Indian O 60E3
Campana Arg 26D2
Campana, I Chile 23A7
Campania I Can 3C3
Campbell S Africa 72C2
Campbell,C NZ 79B2
Campbell I Can 3C3
Campbell I NZ 75N7
Campbell L Can 8M2
Campbell,Mt Can 4E3
Campbellpore Pak 58C2
Campbell River Can 4F5
Campbellsville USA 10B3
Campbellton Can 5M5
Campbelltown Aust 78D2
Campbeltown Scot 32C4
Campeche Mexico 19C3
Camperdown Aust 78B3
Campina Grande Brazil 25L5
Campinas Brazil 25J8
Campina Verde Brazil 27C2
Camplong Indon 55B5
Camp Nelson USA 18C2
Campo Cam 70A3
Campobasso Italy 38C2
Campo Belo Brazil 27C3
Campo del Cielo Arg 26C1
Campo Florido Brazil 27C2
Campo Gallo Arg 23D3
Campo Grande Brazil 23F2
Campo Maior Brazil 25K4
Campo Mourão Brazil 23F2
Campo Novo Brazil 26E1
Campos Brazil 27D3
Campos Altos Brazil 27C2
Campo Tures Italy 35D1
Camp Verde USA 17D4
Cam Ranh Viet 53D3
Camrose Can 4G4
Camucuio Angola 71B5
Canaan Tobago 21K1
Canaan USA 12D1
Canacupa Angola 71B5
Canada, Dominion N America 2F3
Cañada de Gomez Arg 23D4
Canadensis USA 12C2
Canadian USA 14B2
Canadian, R USA 6C3
Canakkale Turk 43D7
Canalejas Arg 26B3
Canal Flats Can 3E3
Canandaigua USA 12B1
Canandaigua L USA 12B1
Cananea Mexico 19A1
Cananeia Brazil 27C4
Canary Basin Atlantic O 73G3
Canary Is = Islas Canarias
Canas Mexico 20B2
Canatlán Mexico 19B2
Canaveral,C USA 7E4
Canavieriras Brazil 25L7
Canberra Aust 76D4
Canby, California USA 16B2
Canby, Minnesota USA 9C3
Candala Somalia 67E3
Çandarli Körfezi, B Turk 39F3
Candle L Can 3G3
Candlewood,L USA 12D2
Cando USA 9C2
Candor USA 12B1
Candroz, Mts Belg 34C1
Canelones Urug 23E4
Caney USA 15C2
Cangamba Angola 71C5
Cangombe Angola 71C5
Cangucu Brazil 26E2
Cangzhou China 50D2
Caniapiscau, R Can 5M4
Caniapiscau,L Can 5M4
Canicatti Italy 38C3
Canindé Brazil 25L4
Canisteo USA 12B1
Canisteo, R USA 12B1
Canitas de Felipe Pescador Mexico 20B1
Canjilon USA 14A2
Çankırı Turk 62B1
Canmore Can 3E3
Canna, I Scot 32B3
Cannanore India 60B2
Cannes France 36D3
Cannonball, R USA 9B2
Cann River Aust 78C3
Canôas Brazil 23F3
Canoe L Can 3G2
Canoinhas Brazil 27B4
Canon City USA 14A2
Canopus Aust 78B2
Canora Can 4H4
Canowindra Aust 78C2
Cansore Pt Irish Rep 33B5
Canterbury Eng 33F6
Canterbury Bight, B NZ 79B2
Canterbury Plains NZ 79B2
Can Tho Viet 53D4
Cantil USA 18D3
Canto de Augua Chile 26A1
Canton = Guangzhou
Canton, Mississippi USA 15E3
Canton, Missouri USA 10A2
Canton, Ohio USA 7E2
Canton, Pensylvania USA 12B2
Canton, S Dakota USA 9C3
Canton, I Phoeniz Is 77H1
Cantwell USA 8J3
Cany-Barville France 34A2
Canyon USA 14B3
Canyon City USA 16C2
Canyon Ferry L USA 16D1
Canyonlands Nat Pk USA 18E3
Canyon Range, Mts Can 8N3
Canyonville USA 16B2
Canzar Angola 71C4
Cao Bang Viet 53D1
Capanema Brazil 25J4
Capão Bonito Brazil 27C3
Cap Bénat, C France 35B3
Cap Blanc, C Tunisia 69D1
Cap Bon, C Tunisia 69E1
Cap Bougaron, C Alg 69D1
Capbreton France 36B3
Cap Camarat, C France 35B3
Cap Corrientes, C Mexico 20A1
Cap Corse, C Corse 38B2
Cap d'Ambre, C Madag 71E5
Cap d'Antibes, C France 35B3
Cap de la Hague, C France 36B2
Cap-de-la-Madeleine Can 11E1
Cap de Nouvelle-France, C Can 5L3
Capdepera Spain 37C2
Cap de Tancitiario, C Mexico 20B2
Cap de Trois Fourches, C Mor 69B1
Cape Barren I Aust 78E3
Cape Basin Atlantic O 73J6
Cape Breton I Can 5N5
Cape Coast Ghana 69F4
Cape Cod B USA 11E2
Cape Dorset Can 5L3
Cape Fear, R USA 13D2
Cape Girardeau USA 15E2
Cape Henrietta Maria Can 5K3
Cape Horn = Cabo de Hornos
Cape Johnston Depth Pacific O 74H4
Capelinha Brazil 27D2
Cape Lisburne USA 8E2
Capelongo Angola 71B5
Cape May USA 11E3
Cape Mendocino USA 4F5
Capenda Camulemba Angola 71B4
Cape Perry Can 4F2
Cape Province S Africa 72C3
Cape Tatnam Can 5J4
Cape Town S Africa 72B3
Cape Verde, Is Atlantic O 73G4
Cape Verde Basin Atlantic O 73G4
Cape Yakataga USA 8K4
Cape York Pen Aust 76D2
Cap Ferrat, C France 35B3
Cap Gris Nez, C France 34A1
Cap-Haitien Haiti 21C3
Capim, R Brazil 25J4
Capitán Bado Par 27A3
Capitol Reef Nat Pk USA 18D3
Capivari, R Brazil 27A2
Cap Moule à Chique, C St Lucia 21P2
Capo di Noli, C Italy 35C2
Capo Isola de Correnti, C Italy 38D3
Capo Rizzuto, C Italy 38D3
Capo Santa Maria di Leuca, C Italy 39D3
Capo San Vito Italy 38C3
Capo Spartivento, C Italy 38D3
Cap Pt St Lucia 21P2
Capri, I Italy 38C2
Caprivi Strip, Region Namibia 71C5
Cap Rosso, C Corse 38B2
Cap Serrat, C Tunisia 69D1
Cap Sicié, C France 35A3
Cap Vert, C Sen 68A3
Caquetá, R Colombia 24D4
Caracal Rom 39E2
Caracaraí Brazil 24F3
Caracas Ven 24E1
Caracol Brazil 27A3
Caraguatatuba Brazil 27C3
Carahue Chile 23B5
Caraí Brazil 27D2
Carandaí Brazil 27D3
Carandazal Brazil 27A2
Carangola Brazil 25K8
Caransebeş Rom 39E1
Carappee Hill, Mt Aust 78A2
Caratasca Honduras 21A3
Caratinga Brazil 27D2
Caravaca Spain 37B2
Caravelas Brazil 27E2
Carazinho Brazil 26E1
Carbondale, Illinois USA 10B3
Carbondale, Pennsylvania USA 12C2
Carbonia Sardegna 38B3
Carborear Can 5N5
Carcaion Can 4G4
Carcar Mts Somalia 67D3
Carcassonne France 36C3
Carcross Can 4E3
Cardel Mexico 20C2
Cardenas Cuba 19D2
Cárdenas Mexico 20C1
Cárdenas Mexico 20D2
Cardiff Wales 33D6
Cardigan Wales 33C5
Cardigan B Wales 33C5
Cardôna Urug 26D2
Cardston Can 3F3
Careen L Can 3G2
Carei Rom 39E1
Careiro Brazil 25G4
Carén Chile 26A2
Carey USA 10C2
Carhaix-Plouguer France 36B2
Carhué Arg 23D5
Cariacica Brazil 25K8
Caribbean S C America 22C2
Caribou Can 4J4
Caribou USA 11F1
Caribou, R Can 8N3
Caribou Mts, Alberta Can 4G4
Caribou Mts, British Columbia Can 4F4
Carigara Phil 55F8
Carignan France 34C2
Carin France 34B1
Carinhanha Brazil 27D1
Carinhanha, R Brazil 27D1
Caripito Ven 24F1
Carleton Place Can 11D1
Carletonville S Africa 72D2
Carlin USA 16C2
Carlinville USA 10B3
Carlisle Eng 32D4
Carlisle USA 11D2
Carlisle, I USA 8D5
Carlos Arg 26C3
Carlos Chagas Brazil 27D2
Carlow, County Irish Rep 33B5
Carlow Irish Rep 33B5
Carlsbad, California USA 17C4
Carlsbad, New Mexico USA 6C3
Carlsbad Caverns Nat Pk USA 14B3
Carlsberg Ridge Indian O 74E4
Carlyle Can 4H5
Carmacks Can 8L3
Carmagnola Italy 35B2
Carmarthen Wales 33C6
Carmarthen B Wales 33C6
Carmel, California USA 18B2
Carmel, New York USA 12D2
Carmel,Mt Israel 63C2
Carmelo Urug 26D2
Carmel Valley USA 18B2
Carmen, I Mexico 6B4
Carmen de Patagones Arg 23D6
Carmi USA 10B3
Carmichael USA 17B3
Carmo do Paranaiba Brazil 27C2
Carmona Spain 37A2
Carnarvon Aust 76A3
Carnarvon S Africa 72C3
Carncacá Brazil 27E2
Carndonagh Irish Rep 32B4
Carnegi,L Aust 76B3
Car Nicobar, I Indian O 60E3
Carnot CAR 70B3
Carnot,C Aust 78A2
Carnwath, R Can 8N2
Carol City USA 13E4
Carolina Brazil 25J5
Carolina S Africa 72E2
Carolina Beach USA 13D2
Caroline Is Pacific O 74J4
Carpathians, Mts E Europe 43C6
Carpatii Orientali, Mts Rom 41F3
Carpentaria,G of Aust 76C2
Carpenter Ridge Indian O 57H5
Carpentras France 36D3
Carpi Italy 38C2
Carpinteria USA 18C3
Carrabelle USA 13C3
Carrara Italy 38C2
Carrauntoohill, Mt Irish Rep 31B3
Carrickmacross Irish Rep 33B5
Carrick-on-Suir Irish Rep 33B5
Carrieton Aust 78A2
Carrington USA 4J5
Carrington USA 6D2
Carrión, R Spain 37B1
Carrizal Bajo Chile 26A1
Carrizo Spring USA 15F4
Carrizozo USA 14A3
Carroll USA 7D2
Carrollton, Georgia USA 13B2
Carrollton, Kentucky USA 10B3
Carrollton, Missouri USA 15D2
Carrot, R Can 3H3
Carruthersville USA 15E2
Carsamba Turk 43F7
Carsamba, R Turk 43E8
Carson City USA 6B3
Carsonville USA 10C2
Cartagena Colombia 21B4
Cartagena Spain 37B2
Cartago Colombia 24C3
Cartago Costa Rica 19D4
Cartago USA 18C2
Cartegena Colombia 24D1
Carterton NZ 79C2
Carthage, Missouri USA 15D2
Carthage, New York USA 11D2
Carthage, Texas USA 15D3
Cartier I Timor S 76B2
Cartwright Can 5N4
Caruaru Brazil 25L5
Carúpano Ven 24F1
Cary USA 13D1
Casablanca Chile 26A2
Casablanca Mor 69A2
Casa Branca Brazil 27C3
Casa Grande USA 6B3
Casale Monferrato Italy 38B1
Casalmaggiore Italy 35D2
Casares Arg 26C3
Casas Mexico 20C1
Casca Brazil 26E1
Cascade USA 16D1
Cascade Mts Can/USA 3D4
Cascade Pt NZ 79A2
Cascade Range, Mts USA 6A2
Cascade Res USA 16C2
Cascavel Brazil 23F2
Casciana Italy 35D3
Cascina Italy 35D3
Caserta Italy 38C2
Casey, Base Ant 80G9
Cashel Irish Rep 33B5
Casilda Arg 26C2
Casino Aust 77E3
Casma Peru 24C5
Casmalia USA 18B3
Caspe Spain 37C1
Casper USA 6C2
Caspian S USSR 46G5
Cass USA 11D3
Cassamba Angola 71C5
Cassel France 34B1
Casselton USA 9C2
Cassiar Can 3C2

Cassiar Mts *Can* **4E3**
Cassilândia *Brazil* **27B2**
Cassino *Italy* **38C2**
Cass Lake *USA* **9D2**
Castaic *USA* **18C3**
Castaño, R *Arg* **26B2**
Castelfranco *Italy* **35D2**
Castellane *France* **36D3**
Castelli *Arg* **26D3**
Castellon de la Plana *Spain* **37C1**
Castelnovo ne'Monti *Italy* **35D2**
Castelnuovo di Garfagnana *Italy* **35D2**
Castelo *Brazil* **25K5**
Castelo Branco *Port* **37A2**
Castelsarrasin *France* **36C3**
Castelvetrano *Italy* **38C3**
Casterton *Aust* **78B3**
Castiglion Fiorentino *Italy* **35D3**
Castilla *Chile* **26A1**
Castilla La Nueva, Region *Spain* **37B2**
Castilla La Vieja, Region *Spain* **37B1**
Castillos *Urug* **26E2**
Castlebar *Irish Rep* **31B3**
Castlebay *Scot* **32B3**
Castle Dale *USA* **17D3**
Castle Douglas *Scot* **32D4**
Castlegar *Can* **16C1**
Castlemain *Aust* **78B3**
Castle,Mt *USA* **18B3**
Castle Peak *USA* **16D2**
Castlereagh *Aust* **78C2**
Castle Rock *USA* **14B2**
Castres-sur-l'Agout *France* **36C3**
Castries *St Lucia* **21E4**
Castro *Arg* **23B6**
Castro *Brazil* **23F2**
Castro Alves *Brazil* **25L6**
Castrovillari *Italy* **38D3**
Castroville *USA* **18B2**
Casupa *Urug* **26D2**
Caswell Sd *NZ* **79A2**
Cat, I *Bahamas* **19E2**
Catabalogan *Phil* **55F8**
Catacaos *Peru* **24B5**
Cataguases *Brazil* **27D3**
Catahoula L *USA* **15D3**
Catalão *Brazil* **27C2**
Cataluña, Region *Spain* **37C1**
Catamarca *Arg* **23C3**
Catamarca, State *Arg* **23C3**
Catandica *Mozam* **71D5**
Catanduanes, I *Phil* **55F8**
Catanduva *Brazil* **23G2**
Catanduvas *Brazil* **27B4**
Catania *Italy* **38D3**
Catan-Lil *Arg* **26A3**
Catanzaro *Italy* **38D3**
Catarina *USA* **15F4**
Catarman *Phil* **55F8**
Catastrophe,C *Aust* **78A2**
Catatumbo, R *Ven* **21C5**
Catawissa *USA* **12B2**
Catemaco *Mexico* **20C2**
Cater *Corse* **36D3**
Cateraggio *Corse* **38B2**
Catete *Angola* **71B4**
Cathcart *S Africa* **72D3**
Catinzaco *Arg* **26B1**
Catio *Guinea-Bissau* **68A3**
Cat Lake *Can* **5J4**
Catlegar *Can* **3E4**
Cato, I *Aust* **77E3**
Catoche,C *Mexico* **19D2**
Catoctin Mt *USA* **12B3**
Catonsville *USA* **11D3**
Catrilo *Arg* **26C3**
Catskill *USA* **11E2**
Catskill Mts *USA* **11E2**
Cauca, R *Colombia* **24D2**
Caucaia *Brazil* **25L4**
Caucasia *Colombia* **24C2**
Caucasus, Mts *USSR* **43G7**
Caudebec-en-Caux *France* **34A2**
Caudry *France* **34B1**
Caungula *Angola* **71B4**
Cauquenes *Chile* **23B5**
Causapscal *Can* **11F1**
Cauvery, R *India* **60B2**
Cavaillon *France* **36D3**
Cavalcanta *Brazil* **27C1**
Cavalese *Italy* **35D1**
Cavalier *USA* **9C2**
Cavally, R *Lib* **68B4**
Cavan, County *Irish Rep* **33B5**
Cavan *Irish Rep* **33B5**
Cavite *Phil* **55F8**
Caxias *Brazil* **24D4**
Caxias *Brazil* **25K4**
Caxias do Sul *Brazil* **23F3**
Caxito *Angola* **71B4**
Cayce *USA* **13C2**
Çayeli *Turk* **62D1**
Cayenne *French Guiana* **25H3**
Cayeux-sur-Mer *France* **34A1**
Cayman Brac, I *Caribbean* **19E3**
Cayman Is *Caribbean* **21A3**
Cayman Trench *Caribbean* **21A3**
Caynabo *Somalia* **70E3**
Cayucos *USA* **18B3**
Cayo Romana, I *Cuba* **19E2**
Cayos Mistikos, Is *Nic* **19D3**
Cay Sal, I *Caribbean* **21A2**
Cayuga L *USA* **12B1**
Cazenova *USA* **12C1**
Cazombo *Angola* **71C5**
Ceará = Fortaleza
Ceara, State *Brazil* **25K5**
Cebollar *Arg* **26B1**
Cebollati *Urug* **26E2**
Cebu *Phil* **55F8**
Cebu, I *Phil* **55F8**
Cecilton *USA* **12C3**
Cecina *Italy* **38C2**
Cecina, R *Italy* **35D3**
Cedar, R *USA* **9D3**
Cedar City *USA* **6B3**
Cedar Creek Res *USA* **15C3**
Cedar Falls *USA* **9D3**
Cedar L *Can* **4J4**
Cedar Mts *USA* **18D1**
Cedar Rapids *USA* **7D2**
Cedartown *USA* **13B2**
Cedral *Mexico* **20B1**
Cedros, I *Mexico* **19A2**
Ceduna *Aust* **76C4**
Ceelbuur *Somalia* **70E3**
Ceerigaabo *Somalia* **67D3**
Cefalù *Italy* **38C3**
Cegléd *Hung* **41D3**
Cela *Angola* **71B5**
Celaya *Mexico* **19B2**
Celebes = Sulawesi
Celebes S *S E Asia* **49F6**
Celina *USA* **10C2**
Celje *Yugos* **38D1**
Celle *W Germ* **40C2**
Celtic S *UK* **33B6**
Cendrawasih, Pen *Indon* **49G7**
Ceno, R *Italy* **35C2**
Center *USA* **15D3**
Center Hill L *USA* **13B1**
Center Moriches *USA* **12D2**
Cento *Italy* **35D2**
Central, Region *Scot* **32C3**
Central *USA* **14A3**
Central African Republic *Africa* **70B3**
Central City, Nebraska *USA* **15C1**
Central City, Pennsylvania *USA* **12A2**
Centralia, Illinois *USA* **10B3**
Centralia, Washington *USA* **6A2**
Central Kalahari Game Res *Botswana* **72C1**
Central Makran Range, Mts *Pak* **61E3**
Central Point *USA* **16B2**
Central Range, Mts *PNG* **49H7**
Central Square *USA* **12B1**
Centre Point *USA* **13B2**
Centreville, Alabama *USA* **13B2**
Centreville, Maryland *USA* **12B3**
Cepu *Indon* **54D4**
Ceram = Seram
Ceram Sea *Indonesia* **49F7**
Cereales *Arg* **26C3**
Ceres *Arg* **26C1**
Ceres *Brazil* **25J7**
Ceres *S Africa* **72B3**
Ceres *USA* **18B2**
Cergy-Pontoise *France* **36C2**
Cerignola *Italy* **38D2**
Cernavodă *Rom* **43D7**
Cernay *France* **34D3**
Cerralvo, I *Mexico* **6C4**
Cerritos *Mexico* **20B1**
Cerro Aconcagua, Mt *Arg* **26B2**
Cerro Azul *Mexico* **20C1**
Cerro Boneta, Mt *Arg* **26B1**
Cerro Campanario, Mt *Chile* **26A3**
Cerro Champaqui, Mt *Arg* **26C2**
Cerro Chatto *Urug* **26D2**
Cerro Cuachaia, Mt *Mexico* **20B2**
Cerro de Astillero *Mexico* **20C1**
Cerro del Potro, Mt *Chile/Arg* **26B1**
Cerro del Tigre, Mt *Mexico* **20C1**
Cerro del Toro, Mt *Chile/Arg* **26B1**
Cerro de Olivares, Mt *Arg* **26B2**
Cerro de Pasco *Peru* **24C6**
Cerro de Punta, Mt *Puerto Rico* **21D3**
Cerro El Cantado, Mt *Mexico* **20B2**
Cerro El Nevado *Arg* **26B3**
Cerro General M Belgrano, Mt *Arg* **26B1**
Cerro Grande, Mts *Mexico* **20B2**
Cerro Huehueto, Mt *Mexico* **20A1**
Cerro Juncal, Mt *Arg/Chile* **26A2**
Cerro la Ardilla, Mts *Mexico* **20B1**
Cerro las Tortolas, Mt *Chile* **26A1**
Cerro Laurel, Mt *Mexico* **20B2**
Cerro Mercedario, Mt *Arg* **26A2**
Cerro Mora, Mt *Chile* **26A3**
Cerron, Mt *Ven* **21C4**
Cerro Payún, Mt *Arg* **26B3**
Cerro Peña Nevada, Mt *Mexico* **20C1**
Cerro Penón del Rosario, Mt *Mexico* **20C2**
Cerro Sosneado, Mt *Arg* **26B2**
Cerro Teotepec, Mt *Mexico* **20B2**
Cerro Tupungato, Mt *Arg* **26B2**
Cerro Yucuyacau, Mt *Mexico* **20C2**
Cervia *Italy* **35E2**
Cervo, R *Italy* **35C2**
Cesena *Italy* **38C2**
Cēsis *USSR* **42C4**
České Budějovice *Czech* **40C3**
České Zemé, Region *Czech* **40C3**
Českomoravská Vysočina U *Czech* **40D3**
Çeşme *Turk* **39F3**
Cessnock *Aust* **76E4**
Cetina, R *Yugos* **38D2**
Ceuta *N W Africa* **69A1**
Ceyham *Turk* **62C2**
Ceyhan, R *Turk* **62C2**
Ceylanpınar *Turk* **62C2**
Ceylon = Sri Lanka
Chaa-Khol *USSR* **47L4**
Chaâteaudun *France* **36C2**
Chablais, Region *France* **35B1**
Chablis *France* **34B3**
Chacabuco *Arg* **26C2**
Chachapoyas *Peru* **24C5**
Chacharramendi *Arg* **26B3**
Chachran *Pak* **58C3**
Chaco, State *Arg* **23D3**
Chad, Republic *Africa* **70B2**
Chad, L *C Africa* **70B2**
Chadileuvu, R *Arg* **26B3**
Chadron *USA* **6C2**
Chaffee *USA* **15E2**
Chagai *Pak* **58A3**
Chagai Hills *Pak* **61E3**
Chagda *USSR* **47P4**
Chaghcharan *Afghan* **58B2**
Chagos Arch *Indian O* **74E5**
Chaguanas *Trinidad* **21L1**
Chahah Burjak *Afghan* **61E2**
Chāh Bahār *Iran* **61E3**
Ch'aho *N Korea* **52A2**
Chai Badan *Thai* **53C2**
Chaîne de l'Atakor, Mts *Benin* **69G3**
Chaine des Cardamomes Mts *Camb* **53C3**
Chaine des Mitumba, Mts *Zaïre* **71C4**
Chaiyaphum *Thai* **53C2**
Chajari *Arg* **26D2**
Chakhansur *Afghan* **61E2**
Chakwal *Pak* **58C2**
Chala *Peru* **24D7**
Chalabesa *Zambia* **71D5**
Chalap Dalam, Mts *Afghan* **58A2**
Chalindrey *France* **34C3**
Chaling *China* **50C4**
Chālisgaon *India* **58D4**
Chalkyitsik *USA* **8K2**
Challerange *France* **34C2**
Challis *USA* **16D2**
Châlons sur Marne *France* **34C2**
Chalon sur Saône *France* **36C2**
Cham *W Germ* **40C3**
Chama *USA* **14A2**
Chaman *Pak* **58B2**
Chamba *India* **58D2**
Chambal, R *India* **58D3**
Chamberlain *USA* **9C3**
Chamberlin,Mt *USA* **8J2**
Chambersburg *USA* **11D3**
Chambéry *France* **36D2**
Chambly *France* **34B2**
Chambord *Can* **11E1**
Chambor Kalat *Pak* **58A3**
Chamela *Mexico* **20A2**
Chamgordan *Iran* **61C2**
Chamical *Arg* **26B2**
Chamonix *France* **35B2**
Champa *India* **59B3**
Champagne, Region *France* **36C2**
Champagne Castle, Mt *Lesotho* **72D2**
Champagnole *France* **35A1**
Champaign *USA* **7E2**
Champassak *Laos* **53D3**
Champlain,L *USA* **7F2**
Champlitte *France* **35A1**
Chāmrājnagar *India* **60B2**
Chañaral *Chile* **23B3**
Chanco *Chile* **26A3**
Chandalar *USA* **4D3**
Chandalar, R *USA* **4D3**
Chandeleur Is *USA* **13B3**
Chandigarh *India* **58D2**
Chandler *USA* **17D4**
Chandpur *Bang* **59D3**
Chandrapur *India* **58D5**
Chānf *Iran* **61E3**
Changane, R *Mozam* **72E1**
Changara *Mozam* **71D5**
Changbai *China* **51B3**
Changchun *China* **51B3**
Changde *China* **50C4**
Changdo *N Korea* **52A3**
Changhang *S Korea* **52A3**
Changhowan *S Korea* **52A3**
Chang-hua *Taiwan* **48E4**
Changhung *S Korea* **52A4**
Changjiang *China* **53D2**
Chang Jiang, R *China* **50D3**
Changjin *N Korea* **51B3**
Changjin, R *N Korea* **52A2**
Changjin Res *N Korea* **52A2**
Changling *China* **51A3**
Changsha *China* **50C4**
Changshu *China* **50E3**
Changtu *China* **51A3**
Changwu *China* **50B2**
Changyŏn *N Korea* **51B4**
Changzhi *China* **50C2**
Changzhou *China* **50E3**
Channel Is *UK* **36B2**
Channel Is *USA* **6B3**
Channel Port-aux-Basques *Can* **5N5**
Chanthaburi *Thai* **53C3**
Chantilly *France* **34B2**
Chanute *USA* **15C2**
Chaoàn *China* **50D5**
Chao'an *China* **50D5**
Chao Hu, L *China* **50D3**
Chao Phraya, R *Thai* **53C3**
Chaor He, R *China* **51A2**
Chaouen *Mor* **69A1**
Chaoyang *China* **50E1**
Chaozhong *China* **51A1**
Chapada Diamantina, Mts *Brazil* **25K6**
Chapadinha *Brazil* **25K4**
Chapala *Mexico* **20B1**
Chapala,Lac de, L *Mexico* **20B1**
Chapayevo *USSR* **43J5**
Chapecó *Brazil* **23F3**
Chapel Hill *USA* **13D1**
Chapeltown *Jamaica* **21H1**
Chapleau *Can* **5K5**
Chaplygin *USSR* **42G5**
Chappell *USA* **14B1**
Charada *Arg* **26D1**
Charcot I *Ant* **80G3**
Chardzhou *USSR* **56E2**
Charef *Mor* **69B2**
Charente, R *France* **36C2**
Chari, R *Chad* **70B2**
Chari Baguirmi, Region *Chad* **70B2**
Charikar *Afghan* **58B1**
Chariton, R *USA* **15D1**
Charity *Guyana* **25G2**
Charkhāri *India* **58D3**
Charleroi *Belg* **34C1**
Charles,C *USA* **7F3**
Charleston, Illinois *USA* **10B3**
Charleston, Missouri *USA* **15E2**
Charleston, S Carolina *USA* **7F3**
Charleston, W Virginia *USA* **7E3**
Charleston Peak, Mt *USA* **17C3**
Charles Town *USA* **12B3**
Charlestown *USA* **12D1**
Charlesville *Zaïre* **70C4**
Charleville *Aust* **76D3**
Charleville-Mézières *France* **36C2**
Charlevoix *USA* **10B1**
Charlotte, Michigan *USA* **10C2**
Charlotte, N Carolina *USA* **7E3**
Charlotte Harbour, B *USA* **13E4**
Charlottesville *USA* **7F3**
Charlottetown *Can* **5M5**
Charlotteville *Tobago* **21K1**
Charlton *Aust* **78B3**
Charlton I *Can* **7F1**
Charmes *France* **34D2**
Charsadda *Pak* **58C2**
Charters Towers *Aust* **76D3**
Chartres *France* **36C2**
Chaschuil *Arg* **26B1**
Chascomús *Arg* **23E5**
Chase *Can* **3E3**
Chasong *N Korea* **52A2**
Château-Arnoux *France* **35A2**
Châteaubriant *France* **36B2**
Château-du-Loir *France* **34A3**
Châteaudun *France* **34A2**
Châteaulin *France* **36B2**
Châteauneuf-en Thymerais *France* **34A2**
Châteauneuf-sur-Loire *France* **34B3**
Château Renault *France* **34A3**
Châteauroux *France* **36C2**
Chäteau-Salins *France* **34D2**
Cháteau-Thierry *France* **36C2**
Chateh *Can* **3E2**
Châtelet *Belg* **34C1**
Châtellerault *France* **36C2**
Chatfield *USA* **9D3**
Chatham *Eng* **33F6**
Chatham, Massachusets *USA* **12E2**
Chatham, New Brunswick *Can* **5M5**
Chatham, New York *USA* **12D1**
Chatham, Ontario *Can* **10C2**
Chatham, Virginia *USA* **11D3**
Chatham Is *NZ* **77H5**
Chatham Sd *Can* **3B3**
Chatham Str *USA* **8M4**
Châtillon *France* **36C2**
Châtillon-Coligny *France* **34B3**
Châtillon-sur-Siene *France* **34C3**
Chatrapur *India* **59B4**
Chatsworth *USA* **12C3**
Chattahoochee *USA* **13C2**
Chattahoochee, R *USA* **13B2**
Chattanooga *USA* **7E3**
Chåttilon *Italy* **35B2**
Chauk *Burma* **53A1**
Chaumont *France* **36D2**
Chauny *France* **34B2**
Chau Phu *Viet* **53D3**
Chaura, I *Indian O* **60E3**
Chaussin *France* **35A1**
Chaves *Port* **37A1**
Chazaouet *Alg* **37B2**
Chazón *Arg* **26C2**
Chcontá *Colombia* **24D2**
Cheb *Czech* **40C2**
Cheboksary *USSR* **46F4**
Cheboygan *USA* **7E2**
Chechersk *USSR* **41G2**
Chech'on *S Korea* **51B4**
Chechro *Pak* **58C3**
Checotah *USA* **15C2**
Cheduba, I *Burma* **53A2**
Cheepie *Aust* **78B1**
Chegdomyn *USSR* **51C1**
Chegga *Maur* **68B2**
Chegutu *Zim* **71D5**
Chegytun' *USSR* **8D2**
Chehalis *USA* **16B1**
Cheju *S Korea* **51B5**
Cheju do, I *S Korea* **51B5**
Cheju-haehyŏp, Str *S Korea* **51B5**
Chekhov *USSR* **51E2**
Chekunda *USSR* **47P4**
Chelan *USA* **3D4**
Chelan,L *USA* **16B1**
Cheleken *USSR* **43J8**
Chelforo *Arg* **26B3**
Chéliff, R *Alg* **69C1**
Chelkar *USSR* **56D1**
Chelm *Pol* **41E2**
Chelmno *Pol* **41D2**
Chelmsford *Eng* **33F6**
Cheltenham *Eng* **33D6**
Chelyabinsk *USSR* **46H4**
Chemba *Mozam* **71D5**
Chemung *USA* **12B1**
Chenab, R *India/Pak* **58D2**
Chenachen *Alg* **68B2**
Chenango, R *USA* **12C1**
Cheney *USA* **16C1**
Cheney Res *USA* **15C2**
Chengda *China* **50D1**
Chengdu *China* **50A3**
Chengshan Jiao, Pt *China* **50E2**
Chenxi *China* **50C4**
Chen Xian *China* **50C4**
Cheo Xian *China* **50D3**
Chepén *Peru* **24C5**
Chepes *Arg* **26B2**
Chequamegon B *USA* **10A1**
Cher, R *France* **36C2**
Cheran *Mexico* **20B2**

Cheraw USA	13D2	Chihuahua, State Mexico	14A4	Chivilcoy Arg	23D4	Churáchándpur India	59D3
Cherbourg France	36B2	Chik Ballápur India	60B2	Chivu Zim	71D5	Churapcha USSR	47P3
Chercas Mexico	20B1	Chikmagalūr India	60B2	Chizu Japan	52B3	Churchill Can	5J4
Cherchell Alg	69C1	Chikuminuk L USA	8G3	Choch'iwŏn S Korea	52A3	Churchill, R, Labrador	
Chercher Eth	64C4	Chikwawa Malawi	71D5	Ch'o-do, I S Korea	52A4	Can	5M4
Cherdyn USSR	42K3	Chilakalūrupet India	60C1	Choele Choel Arg	23C5	Churchill, R, Manitoba	
Cheremkhovo USSR	47M4	Chilapa Mexico	20C2	Choique Arg	26C3	Can	5J4
Cherepovets USSR	42F4	Chilaw Sri Lanka	60B3	Choiseul, I Solomon Is	77E1	Churchill,C Can	5J4
Cherkassy USSR	43E6	Childers Aust	78D1	Choix Mexico	19B2	Churchill Falls Can	5M4
Cherkessk USSR	43G7	Childress USA	14B3	Chojnice Pol	41D2	Churchill L Can	4H4
Chernigov USSR	43E5	Chile, Republic	22C6	Chokai-san, Mt Japan	52D3	Chūru India	58C3
Chernobyl USSR	41G2	Chilecito, La Rioja Arg	26B1	Choke, Mts Eth	70D2	Churumuco Mexico	20B2
Chernovtsy USSR	43D6	Chilecito, Mendoza Arg	26B2	Chokurdakh USSR	47Q2	Chusovoy USSR	42K4
Chernushka USSR	42K4	Chililabombwe Zambia	71C5	Cholame USA	18B3	Chuvashskaya ASSR,	
Chernyakhovsk USSR	42C5	Chilka, L India	59C3	Cholame Creek, R USA	18B3	Republic USSR	42H4
Chernyye Zemli, Region		Chilko, R Can	3D3	Cholet France	36B2	Chuxiong China	48C4
USSR	43H6	Chilko L Can	4F4	Cholula Mexico	20C2	Chu Yang Sin, Mt Viet	53D3
Cherokee, Iowa USA	9C3	Chilkotin, R Can	3D3	Choluteca Honduras	24A1	Cianjur Indon	54C4
Cherokee, Oklahoma		Chillán Chile	26A3	Choma Zambia	71C5	Ciano d'Enza Italy	35D2
USA	14C2	Chillar Arg	26C3	Chŏmch'ŏn S Korea	52A3	Cianorte Brazil	27B3
Cherokees,L o'the USA	15C2	Chillicothe, Missouri		Chomo Yummo, Mt		Ciechanow Pol	41E2
Cherquenco Chile	26A3	USA	15D2	China/India	59C2	Ciedad Altamirano	
Cherrapunji India	59D2	Chillicothe, Ohio USA	10C3	Chomutov Czech	40C2	Mexico	20B2
Cherry, I Solomon Is	77F2	Chilliwack Can	3D4	Chona, R USSR	47M3	Ciedad Ojeda Ven	24D1
Cherskiy USSR	47S3	Chilmari India	59C2	Ch'ŏnan S Korea	51B4	Ciego de Avila Cuba	19E2
Cherven' USSR	42D5	Chilmborazo, Mt		Chŏn Buri Thai	53C3	Ciénaga Colombia	24D1
Chervonograd USSR	41E2	Ecuador	24C4	Chonchon N Korea	52A2	Cienfuegos Cuba	19D2
Chesapeake USA	11D3	Chilongozi Zambia	71D5	Chondo S Korea	52A3	Cieszyn Pol	41D3
Chesapeake B USA	11D3	Chiloquin USA	16B2	Chone Ecuador	24C4	Cieza Spain	37B2
Cheshire, County Eng	33D5	Chilpancingo Mexico	19C3	Chongdo S Korea	52A3	Cihanbeyli Turk	62B2
Cheshire USA	12D1	Chiltern Hills, Upland		Ch'ŏngjin N Korea	51B3	Cihuatlán Mexico	20B2
Chëshskaya Guba, B		Eng	33E6	Chongju S Korea	51B4	Cijulang Indon	54C4
USSR	42H2	Chilton USA	10B2	Ch'ŏngju S Korea	51B4	Cilacap Indon	54C4
Chester, California USA	17B2	Chilumba Malawi	71D5	Chongoroi Angola	71B5	Cimarron USA	14B2
Chester Eng	33D5	Chi-lung Taiwan	48F4	Chongpyong N Korea	52A3	Cimarron, R USA	14C2
Chester, Illinois USA	10B3	Chilwa, L Malawi	71D5	Chongqing China	50B4	Cime du Cheiron, Mt	
Chester, Massachusets		Chimay Belg	34C1	Chŏngsŏn S Korea	52A3	France	35B3
USA	12D1	Chimbay USSR	46G5	Chŏngŭp S Korea	51B4	Cîmpina Rom	39F1
Chester, Montana USA	16D1	Chimbote Peru	24C5	Chŏnju S Korea	51B4	Cinca, R Spain	37C1
Chester, Pennsylvania		Chimkent USSR	46H5	Chooyu, Mt China/Nepal	59C2	Činčer, Mt Yugos	38D2
USA	11D3	Chimoio Mozam	71D5	Chopim, R Brazil	27B4	Cincinnati USA	10C3
Chester, S Carolina USA	13C2	China, Republic Asia	44F4	Chortkov USSR	41F3	Cindad Obregon Mexico	19B2
Chester, Vermont USA	12D1	Chinacates Mexico	20A1	Ch'ŏrwŏn N Korea	51B4	Cindrelu, Mt Rom	39E1
Chester, R USA	12B3	China L USA	18D3	Chorzow Pol	41D2	Cine, R Turk	39F3
Chesterfield Eng	33E5	China Lake USA	18D3	Chosan N Korea	52A2	Ciney Belg	34C1
Chesterfield Inlet Can	5J3	China National Republic		Choshi Japan	51E4	Cintalapa Mexico	20D2
Chestertown USA	12B3	= Taiwan		Chos-Malal Arg	26A3	Cipolletti Arg	26B3
Chesuncook L USA	11F1	Chinandega Nic	19D3	Choszczno Pol	40D2	Circle, Alaska USA	4D3
Chetumal Mexico	19D3	Chinati Peak, Mt USA	14B4	Chotanágpur, Region		Circle, Montana USA	9A2
Chetwynd Can	3D2	Chincha Alta Peru	24C6	India	59B3	Circleville USA	10C3
Chevak USA	8E3	Chinchaga, R Can	3E2	Choteau USA	16D1	Cirebon Indon	54C4
Cheviot NZ	79B2	Chinchilla Aust	78D1	Chott ech Chergui Alg	69B2	Cirencester Eng	33E6
Cheviots, Hills Eng/Scot	31C2	Chinde Mozam	71D5	Chott el Hodna Alg	69D1	Cisco USA	14C3
Chewelah USA	3E4	Chindo S Korea	52A4	Chott Jerid Tunisia	69D2	Citadella Italy	35D2
Cheyenne USA	14B1	Chindwin, R Burma	59D3	Chott Melrhir Alg	69D2	Citlaltepetl, Mt Mexico	19C3
Cheyenne, R USA	9B3	Chingola Zambia	71C5	Chowchilla USA	18B2	Citrusdal S Africa	72B3
Cheyenne Wells USA	14B2	Chinguar Angola	71B5	Choybalsan Mongolia	47N5	Citta del Vaticano Italy	38C2
Chhapra India	59B2	Chinguetti Maur	68A2	Chranberry Inlet, B Can	5J3	Citta di Castello Italy	38C2
Chhātak Bang	59D2	Chinhae S Korea	51B4	Chraykovskiy USSR	42J4	Ciudad Acuña Mexico	19B2
Chhatarpur India	58D4	Chinhoyi Zim	71D5	Christchurch NZ	79B2	Ciudad Bolivar Ven	24F2
Chhindwāra India	58D4	Chiniak,C USA	8H4	Christiana S Africa	72D2	Ciudad Camargo Mexico	19B2
Chhuka Bhutan	59C2	Chiniot Pak	58C2	Christian,C Can	5M2	Ciudad del Carmen	
Chia'I Taiwan	50E5	Chinju S Korea	51B4	Christian Sd USA	8M4	Mexico	19C3
Chiange Angola	71B5	Chinko, R CAR	70C3	Christianshab Greenland	5N3	Ciudadela Spain	37C2
Chiang Kham Thai	53C2	Chino Japan	52C3	Christmas I Indian O	74G5	Ciudad Guayana Ven	24F2
Chiang Mai Thai	53B2	Chinsali Zambia	71D5	Christopol USSR	42H4	Ciudad Guzman Mexico	19B3
Chiapa, R Mexico	20D2	Chioggia Italy	38C1	Chu USSR	46J5	Ciudad Hidalgo Mexico	20B2
Chiavari Italy	35C2	Chipata Zambia	71D5	Chu, R USSR	46J5	Ciudad Juárez Mexico	19B1
Chiavenna Italy	35C1	Chipinge Zim	71D6	Chubbuck USA	16D2	Ciudad Lerdo Mexico	6C4
Chiba Japan	51E4	Chiplūn India	60A1	Chubut, State Arg	23C6	Ciudad Madero Mexico	19C2
Chibāsa India	59C3	Chipman, R Can	3H2	Chubut, R Arg	23C6	Ciudad Mendoza Mexico	20C2
Chibia Angola	71B5	Chippenham Eng	33D6	Chudovo USSR	42E4	Ciudad Obregon Mexico	19B2
Chibougamou Can	5L4	Chippewa, R USA	10A1	Chudskoye Ozer, L USSR	46D4	Ciudad Ojeda Ven	21C4
Chiburi-jima, I Japan	52B3	Chippewa Falls USA	7D2	Chugach Mts USA	4D3	Ciudad Piar Ven	24F2
Chibuto Mozam	72E1	Chippewa,L USA	10A1	Chugiak USA	8J3	Ciudad Real Spain	37B2
Chicago USA	7E2	Chipuriro Zim	71D5	Chuginadak, I USA	8E5	Ciudad Rodrigo Spain	37A1
Chicago Heights USA	10B2	Chira, R Peru	24B4	Chūgoku-sanchi, Mts		Ciudad Valles Mexico	19C2
Chichagof I USA	8L4	Chirāla India	60C1	Japan	52B3	Ciudad Victoria Mexico	19C2
Chichester Eng	33E6	Chiredzi Zim	71D6	Chugwater USA	9B3	Cividale del Friuli Italy	35E1
Chichibu Japan	52C3	Chirfa Niger	70B1	Chuí Brazil	26E2	Civitanova Marche Italy	35E3
Chichi-jima, I Japan	48H4	Chiricahua Peak, Mt		Chuillán Chile	23B5	Civitavecchia Italy	38C2
Chickamauga L USA	7E3	USA	17E4	Chukai Malay	53C5	Cizre Turk	62D2
Chickasawhay, R USA	15E3	Chirikof I USA	8G4	Chukchi S USSR/USA	8E2	Clacton-on-Sea Eng	33F6
Chickasha USA	6D3	Chiriqui, Mt Panama	24B2	Chukotskiy Khrebet, Mts		Claire,L Can	4G4
Chicken USA	8K3	Chirpan Bulg	39F2	USSR	47T3	Clairton USA	11D2
Chiclayo Peru	24B5	Chirrípo Grande, Mt		Chukotskiy Poluostrov,		Clairvaux France	35A1
Chico USA	6A3	Costa Rica	24B2	Pen USSR	47U3	Clanton USA	13B2
Chico, R Arg	23C6	Chirstchurch NZ	77G5	Chu Lai Viet	53D2	Clanwilliam S Africa	72B3
Chicoa Mozam	71D5	Chirundu Zim	71C5	Chula Vista USA	17C4	Clara Irish Rep	33B5
Chicopee USA	11E2	Chisamba Zambia	71C5	Chulitna USA	8J3	Claraz Arg	26D3
Chicoutimi Can	5L5	Chisholm USA	9D2	Chulman USSR	48F1	Clare USA	10C2
Chicualacuala Mozam	71D6	Chishui He, R China	50B4	Chulucanas Peru	24B5	Claremont USA	11E2
Chidambaram India	60B2	Chisimaio Somalia	66J8	Chulumani Bol	24E7	Claremore USA	15C2
Chidley,C Can	5M3	Chisone Italy	35B2	Chulym USSR	50B4	Clarence, R Aust	78D1
Chief, R Can	3D2	Chita USSR	48E1	Chulym, R USSR	46K4	Clarence, R NZ	79B2
Chiefland USA	13C3	Chitado Angola	71B5	Chulyma, R USSR	47K4	Clarence Str Aust	76C2
Chiehn Lib	68B4	Chitembo Angola	71B5	Chumar India	58D2	Clarence Str USA	8M4
Chiengi Zambia	71C4	Chitina USA	8K3	Chumbicha Arg	26B1	Clarendon USA	15D3
Chienti, R Italy	35E3	Chitina, R USA	8K3	Chumikan USSR	47P4	Clarenville Can	5N5
Chieri Italy	35B2	Chitose Japan	52D2	Chumphon Thai	53B3	Claresholm Can	4G4
Chiesa, R France	34C2	Chitradurga India	60B2	Ch'unch'ŏn S Korea	51B4	Clarinda USA	15C1
Chiesa Italy	35C1	Chitral Pak	58C1	Chunchura India	59C3	Clarion, Iowa USA	9D3
Chiese, R Italy	35D2	Chitré Panama	24B2	Ch'ungju S Korea	51B4	Clarion, Pennsylvania	
Chieti Italy	38C2	Chittagong Bang	59D3	Chungking = Chongqing		USA	11D2
Chifeng China	50D1	Chittaurgarh India	58C4	Ch'ungmu S Korea	52A4	Clarion, R USA	11D2
Chiginak,Mt USA	8G4	Chittoor India	60B2	Chungwa N Korea	52A3	Clarión, I Mexico	19A3
Chigmit Mts USA	4C2	Chiume Angola	71C5	Chunya Tanz	71D4	Clarion Fracture Zone	
Chignahuapán Mexico	20C2	Chiusa L Italy	35D1	Chunya, R USSR	47M3	Pacific O	75M4
Chignik USA	8G4	Chiusi Italy	35D3	Ch'unyang S Korea	52A3	Clark Hill Res USA	7E3
Chigubo Mozam	72E1	Chivasso Italy	35B2	Chupara Pt Trinidad	21L1	Clark,Mt Can	8O3
Chihuahua Mexico	19B2			Chuquicamata Chile	23C2	Clark Mt USA	17C3
				Chur Switz	38B1		

Clark,Pt Can	10C2
Clarksburg USA	10C3
Clarksdale USA	7D3
Clarks Point USA	8G4
Clarkston USA	16C1
Clarksville, Arkansas	
USA	15D2
Clarksville, Tennessee	
USA	13B1
Claro, R Brazil	27B2
Claromecó Arg	23E5
Clay Center USA	15C2
Claymore, Oilfield N Sea	32E2
Clayoquot Sd Can	3C4
Clayton, New Mexico	
USA	6C3
Clayton, New York USA	11D2
Clear, C Irish Rep	31B3
Cleare,C USA	8J4
Clearfield, Pennsylvania	
USA	12A2
Clearfield, Utah USA	16D2
Clear Hills, Mts Can	3E2
Clear L USA	17B3
Clear Lake USA	9D3
Clear Lake Res USA	16B2
Clearmont USA	9A3
Clearwater Can	3E3
Clearwater USA	7E4
Clearwater, R Can	3F2
Clearwater L Can	3D3
Clearwater Mts USA	16C1
Cleburne USA	6D3
Clements USA	18B1
Cleopatra Needle, Mt	
Phil	55E8
Clermont Aust	76D3
Clermont France	34B2
Clermont-en-Argonne	
France	34C2
Clermont-Ferrand France	36C2
Clervaux W Germ	34D1
Cles Italy	35D1
Cleve Aust	78A2
Cleveland, County Eng	33E4
Cleveland, Mississippi	
USA	15D3
Cleveland, Ohio USA	7E2
Cleveland, Tennessee	
USA	13C1
Cleveland, Texas USA	15C3
Clevelândia Brazil	27B4
Cleveland,Mt USA	16D1
Clew, B Irish Rep	31B3
Clifton, Arizona USA	17E4
Clifton Aust	78D1
Clifton, New Jersey USA	12C2
Clifton Hills Aust	78A1
Clifton L Can	3J2
Climax Can	3G4
Clinch, R USA	13C1
Clinch Mts USA	13C1
Clinton, Arkansas USA	15D2
Clinton Can	4F4
Clinton, Connecticut	
USA	12D2
Clinton, Iowa USA	10A2
Clinton, Massachusetts	
USA	12E1
Clinton, Mississippi USA	15D3
Clinton, Missouri USA	15D2
Clinton, N Carolina USA	13D2
Clinton, New Jersey	
USA	12C2
Clinton, Oklahoma USA	14C2
Clinton-Colden L Can	4H3
Clipperton I Pacific O	19B3
Cliza Bol	24E7
Clodomira Arg	26C1
Cloncurry Aust	76D3
Clones Irish Rep	33B4
Clonmel Irish Rep	33B5
Cloquet USA	7D2
Clorinda Arg	27A4
Cloud Peak, Mt USA	9A3
Cloudy Mt USA	8G3
Cloverdale USA	18A1
Clovis, California USA	18C2
Clovis, New Mexico	
USA	6C3
Cluj Rom	43C6
Cluj-Napoca Rom	39E1
Cluses France	35B1
Clusone Italy	35C2
Clutha, R NZ	79A3
Clwyd, County Wales	33D5
Clyde Can	5M2
Clyde NZ	79A3
Clyde USA	12B1
Clyde, R Scot	32C4
Coachella USA	17C4
Coahuayana Mexico	20B2
Coahuila, State Mexico	14B4
Coal, R Can	8N3
Coalcomán Mexico	20B2
Coaldale USA	3F3
Coaldale USA	17C3
Coalinga USA	17B3
Coalville USA	16D2
Coaraci Brazil	27E1
Coari, R Brazil	24F5

Coastal Plain USA 13B2
Coast Mts Can 4E4
Coast Ranges, Mts USA 6A2
Coatbridge Scot 32C4
Coatepec Mexico 20C2
Coatesville USA 12C3
Coaticook Can 11E1
Coats I Can 5K3
Coats Land, Region Ant 80F1
Coatzacoalcos Mexico 19C3
Coatzacoalcos, R Mexico 20D2
Cobalt Can 5L5
Cobán Guatemala 19C3
Cobar Aust 76D4
Cobargo Aust 78C3
Cobija Bol 24E6
Cobleskill USA 12C1
Cobo de Palos, C Spain 37B2
Cobourg Can 5L5
Cobourg Pen Aust 76C2
Coburg W Germ 40C2
Coca Ecuador 24C4
Coca Chile 13C3
Cocalinho Brazil 27B1
Cochabamba Bol 24E7
Cochem W Germ 34D1
Cochin India 60B3
Cochrane, Alberta Can 3F3
Cochrane, Ontario Can 5K5
Cochrane, R Can 3H2
Cockburn Aust 78B2
Cockeysville USA 12B3
Cockpit Country, The Jamaica 21H1
Cockscomb, Mt S Africa 72C3
Coco, R Honduras/Nic 19D3
Cocobeach Gabon 70A3
Coco Channel Andaman Is 60E2
Cocos Brazil 27D1
Cocos B Trinidad 21L1
Cocos Is Indian O 74F5
Cocos Ridge Pacific O 75P4
Cocula Mexico 20B1
Cod, Oilfield N Sea 32G3
Cod, C USA 7F2
Codfish I NZ 79A3
Cod I Can 5M4
Codigoro Italy 35E2
Codó Brazil 25K4
Codogno Italy 35C2
Cody USA 6C2
Coen Aust 49H8
Coesfeld W Germ 40B2
Coeur d'Alene USA 6B2
Coffeyville USA 6D3
Coffin B Aust 78A2
Coff's Harbour Aust 78D2
Cofimvaba S Africa 72D3
Cofre de Perote, Mt Mexico 20C2
Cognac France 36B2
Cohocton USA 12B1
Cohocton, R USA 12B1
Cohoes USA 11E2
Coiguna Aust 78B3
Coihaique Chile 23B7
Coimbatore India 60B2
Coimbra Port 37A1
Cojimies Ecuador 24B3
Cokeville USA 16D2
Colac Aust 76D4
Colatina Brazil 25K7
Colbeck, C Ant 80F6
Colby USA 14B2
Colchester Eng 33F6
Colchester USA 12D2
Co de la Faucille France 35B1
Cod L Can 3F3
Co du Grand St Bernard P Switz/Italy 38B1
Co du Lautaret, P France 35B2
Col du Mont Cenis, P Italy/France 38B1
Col du Mt Cenis, P Italy 36D2
Coldwater USA 10C2
Coleen, R USA 8K2
Coleman Can 16D1
Coleman, Michigan USA 10C2
Coleman, Texas USA 14C3
Colenso S Africa 72D2
Coleraine N Ire 32B4
Coleridge, L NZ 79B2
Colesberg S Africa 72D3
Coleville USA 18C1
Colfax, California USA 17B3
Colfax, Louisiana USA 15D3
Colfax, Washington USA 16C1
Colima Mexico 19B3
Colima, State Mexico 20B2
Colina Chile 26A2
Coll I Scot 32B3
Collarenebri Aust 78C1
Colle de Tende, P Italy/France 38B2
Colle di Val d'Elsa Italy 35D3
College USA 8J3
College Park, Georgia USA 13C2

College Park, Washington USA 12B3
College Station USA 15C3
Collie Aust 76A4
Collier B Aust 76B2
Colline Metallifere, Mts Italy 35D3
Collines de L'Artois, Mts France 34A1
Collines De Thiérache France 34B2
Collines du Perche, Mts France 34A2
Collingwood Can 10C2
Collingwood NZ 79B2
Collins, Mississippi USA 15E3
Collins, New York USA 12A1
Collinson Pen Can 4H2
Collinsville Aust 76D3
Collinsville, Illinois USA 10B3
Collinsville, Oklahoma USA 15C2
Collipulli Chile 26A3
Colmar France 36D2
Colmena Arg 26C1
Colne, R Eng 34A1
Cologne = Köln
Colômbia Brazil 27C3
Colombia, Republic S America 24D3
Colombia USA 11D3
Colombo Sri Lanka 60B3
Colón Arg 23E4
Colon Cuba 19D2
Colón Panama 24C2
Colonia Arg 23E4
Colonia del Sacramento Urug 26D2
Colonia 25 de Mayo Arg 25B3
Colonia Dora Arg 26C1
Colonia Josefa Arg 25B3
Colonia Las Heras Arg 23C7
Colonial Heights USA 11D3
Colonsay, I Scot 32B3
Coloradito Ven 21E5
Colorado, State USA 6C3
Colorado, R, Arizona USA 6B3
Colorado, R, Buenos Aires Arg 23D5
Colorado, R, La Rioja Arg 26B1
Colorado, R, Texas USA 6D3
Colorado City USA 14B3
Colorado Plat USA 6B3
Colorado Springs USA 6C3
Colptán Mexico 20B1
Colton USA 18D3
Columbia, Maryland USA 12B3
Columbia, Mississippi USA 15E3
Columbia, Missouri USA 7D3
Columbia, Pennsylvania USA 11D2
Columbia, S Carolina USA 7E3
Columbia, Tennessee USA 7E3
Columbia, R Can 3E3
Columbia, R USA 6A2
Columbia Falls USA 16D1
Columbia,Mt Can 4G4
Columbia Plat USA 16C1
Columbine, C S Africa 72B3
Columbus, Georgia USA 7E3
Columbus, Indiana USA 10B3
Columbus, Mississippi USA 7E3
Columbus, Montana USA 16E1
Columbus, Nebraska USA 6D2
Columbus, New Mexico USA 14A3
Columbus, Ohio USA 7E2
Columbus, Texas USA 15C4
Columbus, Wisconsin USA 10B2
Colville USA 16C1
Colville, R USA 4C3
Colville,C NZ 79C1
Colville L Can 4F3
Colwyn Bay Wales 33D5
Comacchio Italy 35E2
Comalcalco Mexico 20D2
Comarche USA 14C3
Comarche Res USA 18B1
Comayagua Honduras 19D3
Comber N Ire 33C4
Combermere B Burma 59D4
Combeufontaine France 34C3
Comeclians Italy 35E1
Comeragh, Mts Irish Rep 33B5
Comfort USA 14C3
Comilla Bang 59D3
Comitán Mexico 19C3
Commercy France 34C2
Committees B Can 5K3
Como Italy 38B1
Comodoro Rivadavia Arg 23C7

Comonfort Mexico 20B1
Comorin,C India 60B3
Comoros, Is Indian O 71E5
Compiègne France 36C2
Compostela Mexico 20B1
Comte Salas Arg 26B2
Cona China 59D2
Conakry Guinea 68A4
Conay Chile 26A1
Concarán Arg 26B2
Concarneau France 36B2
Conceição da Barra Brazil 27E2
Conceição do Araguaia Brazil 25JE
Conceiçao do Mato Dentro Brazil 27D2
Concepción Arg 26B1
Concepción Brazil/Par 27A3
Concepción Chile 23B5
Concepción Par 23E2
Concepción, R Arg 23E4
Concepcion del Oro Mexico 19B2
Concepcion del Uruguay Arg 26D2
Conception B Namibia 72A1
Conception,Pt USA 6A3
Conchas Brazil 27C3
Conchas, L USA 14B2
Conches France 34A2
Conchos, R Mexico 6C4
Concord, California USA 17B3
Concord, New Hampshire USA 7F2
Concord, North Carolina USA 13C1
Concordia Arg 23E4
Concordia Mexico 20A1
Concordia USA 6D3
Concrete USA 16B1
Condamine Aust 78D1
Condeuba Brazil 27D1
Condobolin Aust 76D4
Condon USA 16B1
Condrina Brazil 25H8
Conecuh, R USA 13B2
Conegliano Italy 35E2
Conesus L USA 12B1
Confuso, R Par 27A3
Congo, Republic Africa 66F8
Congo, R Congo 66F8
Congo,R = Zaire
Coniston Can 10C1
Conneaut USA 10C2
Connecticut, State USA 7F2
Connecticut, R USA 11E2
Connellsville USA 11D2
Connerré France 34A2
Connersville USA 10B3
Conoble Aust 78B2
Conrad USA 16D1
Conroe USA 15C3
Conselheiro Lafaiete Brazil 27D3
Con Son, Is Viet 53D4
Constance,L = Bodensee
Constanta Rom 43D7
Constantine Alg 69D1
Constantine,C USA 8G4
Constitución Chile 23B5
Constitución Urug 26D2
Consul Can 3G4
Contact USA 16D2
Contarina Italy 35E2
Contas, R Brazil 25K6
Contreras Mexico 20C2
Contrexéville France 34C2
Contuoyto L Can 4H3
Conway, Arkansas USA 7D3
Conway, New Hampshire USA 11E2
Conway, South Carolina USA 13D2
Conway,L Aust 78A1
Conwy Wales 33D5
Coober Pedy Aust 76C3
Cook,C Can 3C3
Cookeville USA 13B1
Cook Inlet, B USA 4C3
Cook Is Pacific O 75L5
Cook,Mt NZ 79B2
Cook Str NZ 77G5
Cooktown Aust 76D2
Coolabah Aust 78C2
Cooladdi Aust 78C1
Coolah Aust 78C2
Coolamon Aust 78C2
Coolgardie Aust 76B4
Coolidge USA 17D4
Cooma Aust 78C3
Coonabarabran Aust 78C2
Coonamble Aust 78C2
Coonbah Aust 78B2
Coondambo Aust 78A2
Coondapoor India 60A2
Coongoola Aust 78C1
Coonoor India 60B2
Cooper Basin Aust 78B1
Cooper Creek Aust 76C3

Cooper Creek, R Aust 78B1
Cooperstown, New York USA 12C1
Cooperstown, North Dakota USA 9C2
Coorong,The Aust 78A3
Cooroy Aust 78D1
Coos B USA 16B2
Coos Bay USA 16B2
Cootamundra Aust 76D4
Cootehill Irish Rep 33B4
Copacabana Arg 26B1
Copala Mexico 20C2
Copalillo Mexico 20C2
Cope USA 14B2
Copenhagen = København
Copiapó Chile 23B3
Copiapó, R Chile 26B1
Copparo Italy 35D2
Copper, R USA 8K3
Copper Centre USA 4D3
Copper Cliff Can 10C1
Copper Harbour USA 10B1
Coppermine Can 4G3
Coppermine, R Can 4G3
Coppermine Pt Can 10C1
Co Prieto, Mt Mexico 20A1
Coquilhatville = Mbandaka
Coquimbo Chile 23B3
Corabia Rom 39E2
Coral Gables USA 13E4
Coral Harbour Can 5K3
Coral S Aust/PNG 76E2
Coral Sea Basin Pacific O 74J5
Coral Sea Island Territories Aust 76E2
Corangamite,L Aust 78B3
Corantijn, R Suriname/Guyana 25G3
Corbeil-Essonnes France 34B2
Corbin USA 10C3
Corcoran USA 18C2
Corcubíon Spain 37A1
Cord Cantabrica, Mts Spain 36A3
Cordele USA 7E3
Cordillera Cantabrica, Mts Spain 37A1
Cordillera Central, Mts Dom Rep 21C3
Cordillera Central, Mts Phil 55F7
Cordillera de Ansita, Mts Arg 26B2
Cordillera de Caaguazú Par 27A4
Cordillera de la Punilla, Mts Chile 26A1
Cordillera de los Andes, Mts Peru 24C5
Cordillera del Toro, Mt Arg 23C3
Cordillera de Mérida Ven 24D2
Cordillera de Viento, Mts Arg 26A3
Cordillera Isabelia, Mts Nicaragua 19D3
Cordillera Occidental, Mts Colombia 24C2
Cordillera Oriental, Mts Colombia 24C3
Cordillo Downs Aust 78B1
Córdoba Arg 23D4
Córdoba Mexico 19C3
Córdoba Spain 37B2
Córdoba, State Arg 23D4
Cordova USA 4D3
Cordova B USA 8M5
Corfu = Kérkira
Coribe Brazil 27D1
Coricudgy,Mt Aust 78D2
Corigliano Calabro Italy 38D3
Corinth, Mississippi USA 7E3
Corinth, New York USA 12D1
Corinto Brazil 25K7
Cork Irish Rep 31B3
Çorlu Turk 62A1
Cormorant L Can 3H3
Cornel Fabriciano Brazil 25K7
Cornelio Procópio Brazil 27B3
Corner Brook Can 5N5
Corner Inlet, B Aust 78C3
Cornimont France 34D3
Corning USA 11D2
Cornwall Can 5L5
Cornwall, County Eng 33C6
Cornwall,C Eng 33C6
Cornwall I Can 4H2
Cornwallis I Can 5J2
Coro Ven 24D1
Coroatá Brazil 25K4
Coroico Bol 24E7
Coromandel Brazil 27C2
Coromandel Coast India 60C2
Coromandel Pen NZ 79C1
Coromandel Range, Mts NZ 79C1

Corona, California USA 18D4
Corona, New Mexico USA 14A3
Coronation Can 3F3
Coronation G Can 4G3
Coronda Arg 26C2
Coronel Chile 23B5
Coronel Brandsen Arg 26D3
Coronel Dorrego Arg 26C3
Coronel Fabriciano Brazil 27D2
Coronel Oviedo Par 23E3
Coronel Pringles Arg 23D5
Coronel Suárez Arg 26C3
Coronel Vidal Arg 26D3
Coropuna, Mt Peru 24D7
Corowa Aust 78C3
Corps France 36D3
Corpus Christi USA 6D4
Corpus Christi,L USA 15F4
Corral Chile 26A3
Corregidor, I Phil 55F8
Corrente, R, Bahia Brazil 27D1
Corrente, R, Goias Brazil 27C1
Corrente, R, Mato Grosso Brazil 27B2
Correntina Brazil 27D1
Corrientes Arg 23E3
Corrientes, State Arg 23E3
Corrientes, R Arg 26D1
Corrigan USA 15D3
Corrigin Aust 76A4
Corringe Is Aust 76E2
Corryong Aust 78C3
Corse, I Medit S 38B2
Corse = Corse
Corsewall, Pt Scot 32C4
Corsica = Corse
Corsicana USA 6D3
Corte Corse 38B2
Cortez USA 6C3
Cortina d'Ampezzo Italy 38C1
Cortland USA 11D2
Cortona Italy 35D3
Coruca de Catalan Mexico 20B2
Çoruh, R Turk 43G7
Corum Turk 43F7
Corumbá Brazil 25G7
Corumba, R Brazil 27C2
Corumbaiba Brazil 27C2
Corvallis USA 16B2
Corvo, I Açores 68A1
Corwen Wales 33D5
Corwin,C USA 8E4
Cosala Mexico 20A1
Coscomatepec Mexico 20C2
Cosenza Italy 38D3
Cosmoledo, Is Seychelles 71E5
Coso Junction USA 18D2
Cosquín Arg 26C2
Costa Blanca, Region Spain 37B2
Costa Brava, Region Spain 37C1
Costa de la Luz, Region Spain 37B2
Costa del Sol, Region Spain 37B2
Costa Mesa USA 18D4
Costa Rica, Republic C America 19D3
Cotabato Phil 55F9
Cotagaita Bol 24E8
Coteau,The, Region Can 3G3
Côte d'Azur, Region France 36D3
Côte-d'Or, Department France 34C3
Côtes de Meuse, Mts France 34C2
Cotonou Benin 69G4
Cotopaxi, Mt Ecuador 24C4
Cotswold Hills, Upland Eng 33D6
Cottage Grove USA 16B2
Cottbus E Germ 40C2
Cottonwood USA 17D4
Cotulla USA 15F4
Coudersport USA 12A2
Couedic,C du Aust 78A3
Couer d'Alene USA 3E4
Couer d'Alene L USA 16C1
Coulommiers France 34B2
Coulon, R France 35A3
Coulonge, R Can 11D1
Coulterville USA 18B2
Council USA 4B3
Council Bluffs USA 6D2
Courmayeur Italy 35B2
Courtalain France 34A2
Courtenay Can 3C4
Courtrai = Kortrijk
Coutances France 36B2
Coventry Eng 33E5
Covilhã Spain 37A1
Covington, Georgia USA 13C2
Covington, Kentucky USA 10C3
Covington, Louisiana USA 15D3
Covington, Virginia USA 11D3

Cowal,L *Aust* 78C2
Cowangie *Aust* 78B3
Cowansville *Can* 11E1
Coward Springs *Aust* 78A1
Cowell *Aust* 78A2
Cowes *Aust* 78C3
Cowichan L *Can* 16B1
Cowiltz, R *USA* 16B1
Cowra *Aust* 78C2
Coxilha de Santana, Mts *Brazil/Urug* 26D2
Coxilha Grande, Mts *Brazil* 26E1
Coxim *Brazil* 25H7
Coxim, R *Brazil* 27B2
Coxsackie *USA* 12D1
Cox's Bazar *Bang* 59D3
Coyobitan *Mexico* 20A1
Coyote *USA* 18B2
Coyuca de Benitez *Mexico* 20B2
Cozad *USA* 14C1
Cracow *Aust* 78D1
Cradock *S Africa* 72D3
Craig *USA* 6C2
Crailsheim *W Germ* 40C3
Craiova *Rom* 39E2
Cranberry L *USA* 11E2
Cranbrook *Can* 4G5
Crane, Oregon *USA* 16C2
Crane, Texas *USA* 14B3
Cranston *USA* 12E2
Crater L *USA* 16B2
Crater Lake Nat Pk *USA* 16B2
Crateus *Brazil* 25K5
Crato *Brazil* 25L5
Crawford *USA* 9B3
Crawfordsville *USA* 10B2
Crawfordville *USA* 13C2
Crawley *Eng* 33E6
Crazy Mts *USA* 16D1
Crean L *Can* 3G3
Cree, R *Can* 3G2
Cree L *Can* 4H4
Creil *France* 34B2
Crema *Italy* 35C2
Crémieu *France* 35A2
Cremona *Italy* 38C1
Crentral Falls *USA* 12E2
Crépy-en-Valois *France* 34B2
Cres, I *Yugos* 38C2
Crescent *USA* 16B2
Crescent City *USA* 6A2
Cresco *USA* 9D3
Crespo *Arg* 26C2
Creston *Can* 3E4
Creston *USA* 15D1
Crestview *USA* 13B2
Creswick *Aust* 78B3
Crêt de la Neige, Mt *France* 35A1
Crete = Kríti
Crete *USA* 15C1
Crete,S of *Greece* 39E3
Creuse, R *France* 36C2
Crewe *Eng* 33D5
Crianlarich *Scot* 32C3
Criciuma *Brazil* 23G3
Crieff *Scot* 32D3
Crillon,Mt *USA* 8L4
Cristalina *Brazil* 27C2
Cristalina, R *Brazil* 27B1
Crixás *Brazil* 27C1
Crixás Acu, R *Brazil* 27C1
Crixás Mirim, R *Brazil* 27B1
Croatia, Region *Yugos* 38D1
Crocker Range, Mts *Malay* 54E1
Crockett *USA* 15C3
Crofton *USA* 9C3
Croker I *Aust* 76C2
Cromarty *Scot* 32D3
Cromer *Eng* 33F5
Cromwell *NZ* 79A3
Crooked, I *Bahamas* 7F4
Crooked, R *Can* 3D3
Crookston *USA* 9C2
Crookwell *Aust* 78C2
Croppa Creek *Aust* 78D1
Crosby *USA* 9D2
Cross, R *Nig* 69H4
Cross,C, C *Namibia* 72A1
Crossett *USA* 7D3
Cross River, State *Nig* 69H4
Cross Sd *USA* 8L4
Crossville *USA* 13B1
Crotone *Italy* 38D3
Crowley *USA* 15D3
Crowley,L *USA* 18C2
Crown Pt *Tobago* 21K1
Crows Nest *Aust* 78D1
Croydon *Aust* 76D2
Croydon *Eng* 33E6
Crozet Basin *Indian O* 74E6
Crozier Chan *Can* 4F2
Cruillas *Mexico* 20C1
Cruz Alta *Brazil* 23F3
Cruz,C *Cuba* 19E3
Cruz del Eje *Arg* 23D4
Cruzeiro *Brazil* 27D3
Cruzeiro do Sul *Brazil* 24D5
Crysdale,Mt *Can* 3D2
Crystal Brook *Aust* 78A2
Crystal City, Missouri *USA* 15D2
Crystal City, Texas *USA* 15F4
Crystal Falls *USA* 10B1
Cuamba *Mozam* 71D5
Cuando, R *Angola* 71C5
Cuangar *Angola* 71B5
Cuango,R = Kwango,R
Cuarto, R *Arg* 26C2
Cuauhtémoc *Mexico* 19B2
Cuautla *Mexico* 20C2
Cuba, Republic *Caribbean* 19D2
Cuba *USA* 12A1
Cubango, R *Angola* 71B5
Cuchi *Angola* 71B5
Cuchi, R *Angola* 71B5
Cuchilla de Haedo, Mts *Urug* 26D2
Cuchilla Grande, Mts *Urug* 26D2
Cuchillo Có *Arg* 26C3
Cucui *Brazil* 24E3
Cúcuta *Colombia* 24D2
Cuddalore *India* 60B2
Cuddapah *India* 60B2
Cuddeback L *USA* 18D3
Cue *Aust* 76A3
Cuenca *Ecuador* 24C4
Cuenca *Spain* 37B1
Cuencame *Mexico* 20B1
Cuernavaca *Mexico* 19C3
Cuero *USA* 15C4
Cuiabá *Brazil* 25G7
Cuiabá, R *Brazil* 27A1
Cuicatlan *Mexico* 20C2
Cuieté, R *Brazil* 27D2
Cuillin Hills, Mts *Scot* 32B3
Cuilo, R *Angola* 71B4
Cuiseaux *France* 35A1
Cuito, R *Angola* 71B5
Cuito Cunavale *Angola* 71B5
Cuitzeo *Mexico* 20B2
Cu Lao Hon, I *Viet* 53D3
Culbertson, Montana *USA* 9B2
Culbertson, Nebraska *USA* 14B1
Culcairn *Aust* 78C3
Culgoa, R *Aust* 78C1
Culiacán *Mexico* 19B2
Culion, I *Phil* 55E8
Cullman *USA* 13B2
Culoz *France* 35A2
Culpeper *USA* 11D3
Culter Ridge *USA* 13E4
Culuene, R *Brazil* 27B1
Culverden *NZ* 79B2
Cumaná *Ven* 24F1
Cumberland, Maryland *USA* 7F3
Cumberland, Wisconsin *USA* 10A1
Cumberland, R *USA* 7E3
Cumberland L *Can* 3H3
Cumberland Pen *Can* 5M3
Cumberland Plat *USA* 10C3
Cumbernauld Sd *Can* 5M3
Cumbria *Eng* 33D4
Cummings *USA* 17B3
Cummins *Aust* 78A2
Cumnock *Scot* 32C4
Cunco *Chile* 26A3
Cunene, R *Angola/Namibia* 71B5
Cuneo *Italy* 38B2
Cunnamulla *Aust* 76D3
Cupar *Scot* 32D3
Čuprija *Yugos* 39E2
Curaçao, I *Caribbean* 21D4
Curacautin *Chile* 26A3
Curaco, R *Arg* 26B3
Curanilahue *Chile* 26A3
Curepto *Chile* 26A3
Curicó *Chile* 23B4
Curisevo, R *Brazil* 27B1
Curitiba *Brazil* 23G3
Curnamona *Aust* 78A2
Curoca, R *Angola* 71B5
Curuzú Cuatiá *Arg* 26D1
Curvelo *Brazil* 25K7
Curwensville *USA* 12A2
Cushing *USA* 15C2
Custer, Montana *USA* 16E1
Custer, S Dakota *USA* 9B3
Cut Bank *USA* 16D1
Cutbank, R *Can* 3E3
Cuthbert *USA* 13C2
Cutral-Có *Arg* 26B3
Cuttack *India* 59C3
Cuvelai *Angola* 71B5
Cuxhaven *W Germ* 40B2
Cuyahoga Falls *USA* 10C2
Cuyama, R *USA* 18C3
Cuyo Is *Phil* 55F8
Cuzco *Peru* 24D6
Cyangugu *Zaïre* 70C4
Cyclades = Kikládhes
Cypress Hills, Mts *Can* 3G4
Cyprus, Republic *Medit S* 62B3
Cyrus Field B *Can* 5M3
Czechoslovakia, Republic *Europe* 41D3
Częstochowa *Pol* 41D2

D

Da, R *Viet* 53C1
Da'an *China* 51A2
Dab'a *Jordan* 63D3
Dabajuro *Ven* 21C4
Dabaro *Somalia* 67D4
Daba Shan, Mts *China* 50B3
Dabat *Eth* 70D2
Dabhoi *India* 58C4
Dabie Shan, U *China* 50C3
Dabola *Guinea* 68A3
Dabou *Ivory Coast* 68B4
Daboya *Ghana* 69F4
Dabrowa Gorn *Pol* 41D2
Dachau *W Germ* 40C3
Dachstein, Mt *Austria* 38C1
Dada He, R *China* 50A3
Daddato *Djibouti* 64D4
Dade City *USA* 13C3
Dadhar *Pak* 58B3
Dadu *Pak* 58B3
Dadu He, R *China* 48D3
Daet *Phil* 55F8
Dafang *China* 50B4
Daga, R *Burma* 53B2
Dagabur *Eth* 70E3
Dagana *Sen* 68A3
Dagestanskaya ASSR, Republic *USSR* 46F5
Dagupan *Phil* 55F7
Dagzê *China* 59D2
Dahab *Egypt* 62B4
Da Hinggan Line, Mts *China* 47O5
Dahlak Arch *Eth* 64D3
Dahlonega *USA* 13C2
Dāhod *India* 58C4
Dahra *Libya* 67A2
Dahra, Region *Alg* 37C2
Dailekh *Nepal* 59B2
Daireaux *Arg* 26C3
Dairen = Lüda
Dairût *Egypt* 64B1
Daitō, Is *Pacific Oc* 48G4
Dajarra *Aust* 76C3
Daka, R *Ghana* 69F4
Dakar *Sen* 68A3
Dakhla *Mor* 68A2
Dakhla Oasis *Egypt* 67B2
Dakoro *Niger* 68C3
Dakota City *USA* 9C3
Dakovica *Yugos* 39E2
Dakovo *Yugos* 39D1
Dala *Angola* 71C5
Dalaba *Guinea* 68A3
Dalai Nur, L *China* 50D1
Dalälven, R *Sweden* 42B3
Dalandzadgad *Mongolia* 48D2
Dalanganem Is *Phil* 55F8
Dalanjargalan *Mongolia* 48D2
Da Lat *Viet* 53D3
Dalbandin *Pak* 61E3
Dalby *Aust* 76E3
Dale Hollow L *USA* 13B1
Dalen *Nor* 30F7
Dales,The, Upland *Eng* 33D4
Daleville *USA* 13B2
Dalhart *USA* 6C3
Dalhousie *Can* 11F1
Dalhousie,C *Can* 4E2
Dalion, Hist Site *Cyprus* 63B1
Dallas *USA* 6D3
Dalles,The *USA* 16B1
Dall I *USA* 8M5
Dalli Rajhara *India* 59B3
Dallol, R *Niger* 68C3
Dallol Bosso, R *Niger* 69G3
Dallol Maouri, R *Niger* 69G3
Dalmatia, Region *Yugos* 38D2
Dal'negorsk *USSR* 51D3
Dal'nerechensk *USSR* 51C2
Daloa *Ivory Coast* 68B4
Dalou Shan, Mts *China* 50B4
Dāltenganj *India* 59B3
Dalton, Georgia *USA* 13C2
Dalton, Massachusetts *USA* 12D1
Daludalu *Indon* 54B2
Daly, R *Aust* 76C2
Daly City *USA* 17B3
Daly Waters *Aust* 76C2
Damaguete *Phil* 55F9
Damān *India* 58C4
Damanhûr *Egypt* 62B3
Damar, I *Indon* 76B1
Damara *CAR* 70B3
Damascus *Syria* 62C3
Damascus *USA* 12B3
Damaturu *Nig* 69J3
Damavand *Iran* 61C1
Damba *Angola* 71B4
Dambulla *Sri Lanka* 60C3
Damghan *Iran* 61C1
Damietta *Egypt* 63A3
Damoh *India* 58D4
Damongo *Ghana* 69F4
Damot *Eth* 70E3
Damour *Leb* 63C2
Dampier *Aust* 76A3
Damqawt *S Yemen* 65F3
Danā *Jordan* 63C3
Danakil, Region *Eth* 64D4
Dana,Mt *USA* 18C2
Danané *Lib* 68B4
Da Nang *Viet* 53D2
Danao *Phil* 55F8
Danau Poso, Mt *Indon* 55B3
Danau Tobu, L *Indon* 54A2
Danau Tuwuti, L *Indon* 55B3
Danbu *China* 50A3
Danbury *USA* 11E2
Danby *USA* 12D1
Dandeldhura *Nepal* 59B2
Dandeli *India* 60A1
Dandenong *Aust* 78C3
Dandong *China* 51A3
Danger Pt *S Africa* 72B3
Dangila *Eth* 70D2
Danguard Jenson Land, Region *Can* 5M1
Daniel *USA* 16D2
Daniels Harbour *Can* 5N4
Danielskuil *S Africa* 72C2
Dannebrogs Øy, I *Greenland* 5P3
Dannevirke *NZ* 79C2
Dansville *USA* 12B1
Dantewāra *India* 60C1
Danube = Dunărea
Danube = Donau
Danuk *Iraq* 43G8
Danville, Illinois *USA* 7E2
Danville, Kentucky *USA* 7E3
Danville, Pennsylvania *USA* 12B2
Danville, Virginia *USA* 7F3
Danzig = Gdańsk
Dao Xian *China* 50C4
Daozhen *China* 50B4
Dapchi *Nig* 69J3
Dapha Bum, Mt *India* 59E2
Daphnae, Hist Site *Egypt* 63B3
Dapiak,Mt *Phil* 55F9
Dapitan *Phil* 55F9
Da Qaidam *China* 48C3
Dar'a *Syria* 63D2
Dārāb *Iran* 61C3
Daraj *Libya* 67A1
Dārān *Iran* 61C2
Dar'ā Salkhad *Syria* 62C3
Darbhanga *India* 59C2
Dardanelle *USA* 18C1
Dardanelle,L *USA* 15D2
Dar Es Salaam *Tanz* 71D4
Dargaville *NZ* 79B1
Darien *USA* 13C2
Darjeeling = Dārjiling
Dārjiling *India* 59C2
Darling, R *Aust* 76D4
Darling Downs *Aust* 78C1
Darling Pen *Can* 5L1
Darlington *Aust* 78B2
Darlington *Eng* 33E4
Darlington *USA* 13D2
Darmstadt *W Germ* 40B3
Darnah *Libya* 67B1
Darnick *Aust* 78B2
Darnley B *Can* 4F3
Darnley,C *Ant* 80G10
Daroca *Spain* 37B1
Dar Rounga, Region *CAR* 70C3
Darsa, I *S Yemen* 65F4
Dart, R *Eng* 33D6
Dartmoor, Moorland *Eng* 31C3
Dartmoor Nat Pk *Eng* 33D6
Dartmouth *Can* 5M5
Dartmouth *Eng* 33D6
Daru *PNG* 76D1
Daruvar *Yugos* 38D1
Darweshan *Afghan* 61E2
Darwin *Aust* 76C2
Daryacheh-ye Bakhtegan, L *Iran* 61C3
Daryacheh-ye Mahārlū, L *Iran* 61C3
Daryācheh-ye Namak, Salt Flat *Iran* 61C2
Daryacheh-ye-Sistan, Salt Lake *Iran/Afghan* 61E2
Daryacheh-ye Tashk, L *Iran* 61C3
Daryācheh-ye Urumīyeh, L *Iran* 43H8
Dārzīn *Iran* 61D3
Das, I *UAE* 65F1
Dashennonglia, Mt *China* 50C3
Dasht *Iran* 61D1
Dasht, R *Pak* 61E3
Dasht-e-Kavir, Salt Desert *Iran* 61C2
Dasht-e Lut, Salt Desert *Iran* 61D2
Dasht-e Naomid, Desert Region *Iran* 61E2
Dasht-i-Margo, Desert *Afghan* 61E2
Date *Japan* 52D2
Datia *India* 58D3
Datong *China* 50A2
Datong *China* 50C1
Datong He, R *China* 50A2
Datu Piang *Phil* 55F9
Daugava, R *USSR* 30K7
Daugavpils *USSR* 42D4
Daughiné, Region *France* 36D2
Dauguard Jensen Land *Greenland* 5M1
Daulatabad *Afghan* 58A1
Daulpur *India* 58D3
Daun *W Germ* 34D1
Daund *India* 60A1
Dauphin *Can* 4H4
Dauphin *USA* 12B2
Dauphin I *USA* 13B2
Daura *Nig* 68C3
Dausa *India* 58D3
Dāvah Panāh *Iran* 61E3
Dāvangere *India* 60B2
Davao *Phil* 55G9
Davao G *Phil* 55G9
Davenport, California *USA* 18A2
Davenport, Iowa *USA* 7D2
David *Panama* 24B2
Davidson *Can* 3G3
Davidson Mts *USA* 4D3
Davin L *Can* 3H2
Davis *USA* 17B3
Davis, Base *Ant* 80G10
Davis Inlet *Can* 5M4
Davis Str *Greenland/Can* 5N3
Davlekanovo *USSR* 42K5
Davos *Switz* 35C1
Davy L *Can* 3G2
Dawa, R *Eth* 70E3
Dawan *China* 50A4
Dawat Yar *Afghan* 58B2
Dawḩat Salwah, B *Qatar/S Arabia* 65F1
Dawkah *Oman* 65F3
Dawna Range, Mts *Burma* 53B2
Dawson *Can* 4E3
Dawson, Georgia *USA* 13C2
Dawson, N Dakota *USA* 9C2
Dawson, R *Aust* 76D3
Dawson Creek *Can* 4F4
Dawson Landing *Can* 3F1
Dawson,Mt *Can* 3E3
Dawson Range, Mts *Can* 8L3
Dawu *China* 50A3
Dawu *China* 50C3
Dax *France* 36B3
Daxian *China* 50B3
Daxin *China* 50B5
Daxue Shan, Mts *China* 50A3
Dayman, R *Urug* 26D2
Dayong *China* 50C4
Dayr'Ali *Syria* 63D2
Dayr'Atiyah *Syria* 63D1
Dayr az Zawr *Syria* 62D2
Dayr Shumayyil *Syria* 63D1
Dayton, Ohio *USA* 7E3
Dayton, Tennessee *USA* 13B1
Dayton, Texas *USA* 15D4
Dayton, Washington *USA* 16C1
Daytona Beach *USA* 7E4
Dayu *China* 50C4
Dayu *Indon* 54E3
Da Yunhe *China* 50D2
Da Yunhe, R *China* 50D2
Dayville *USA* 16C2
Dazhu *China* 50B3
De Aar *S Africa* 72C3
Deadman's Cay *Bahamas* 21C2
Dead S *Israel/Jordan* 62C3
Deadwood *USA* 9B3
Deal *Eng* 34A1
Dealesville *S Africa* 72D2
Dean, R *Can* 3C3
Dean Chan *Can* 3C3
Deán Funes *Arg* 26C2
Dearborn *USA* 10C2
Dease *Can* 3C2
Dease, R *Can* 3C2
Dease Arm, B *Can* 4F3
Dease Lake *Can* 4E4
Death V *USA* 6B3
Death Valley Nat Mon *USA* 18D2
Deauville *France* 36C2
Debakala *Ivory Coast* 69F4
Debauch Mt *USA* 8F3
Debden *Can* 3G3
Débé *Trinidad* 21L1
Debica *Pol* 41E2
Deblin *Pol* 41E2
Débo,L *Mali* 68B3
Debra Birhan *Eth* 70D3
Debra Markos *Eth* 70D2
Debra Tabor *Eth* 70D2

Debrecen Hung 41E3
Decamere Eth 64C3
Decatur, Alabama USA 7E3
Decatur, Georgia USA 13C2
Decatur, Illinois USA 7E3
Decatur, Indiana USA 10C2
Decazeville France 36C3
Deception, R Botswana 72C1
Dechang China 50A4
Decorah USA 9D3
Dedougou U Volta 69F3
Dedu China 51B2
Dedza Malawi 71D5
Dee, R, Dumfries and Galloway Scot 32C4
Dee, R Eng/Wales 33D5
Dee, R, Grampian Scot 32D3
Deep River Can 11D1
Deep River USA 12D2
Deep Springs USA 18D2
Deepwater Aust 78D1
Deer I USA 8F5
Deer Lake Can 5N5
Deer Lodge USA 6B2
Deésaguadero, R Bol 24E7
Deeth USA 16C2
Defferrari Arg 26D3
De Funiak Springs USA 13B2
Dêgê China 48C3
De Grey, R Aust 76A3
Deh Bid Iran 61C2
Dehi Afghan 58B1
Dehibat Tunisia 68D1
Dehiwala-Mt Lavinia Sri Lanka 60B3
Dehlorān Iran 61B2
Dehra Dūn India 58D2
Dehri India 59B3
Dehui China 51B3
Deim Zubeir Sudan 70C3
Deir Abu Sa'id Jordan 63C2
Deir el Ahmar Leb 63D1
Dej Rom 43C6
De Kalb, Illinois USA 10B2
De Kalb, Texas USA 15D3
De Kastri USSR 47Q4
Dekese Zaïre 70C4
Dekoa CAR 70B3
Delano USA 6B3
Delano Peal, Mt USA 17D3
Delareyville S Africa 72D2
Delarof Is USA 8C6
Delaware, State USA 7F3
Delaware USA 10C2
Delaware, R USA 11D2
Delaware B USA 7F3
Delegate Aust 78C3
Delemont Switz 35B1
Delgado, C Mozam 71E5
Delgo Sudan 64B2
Delhi, Colorado USA 14B2
Delhi India 58D3
Delhi, New York USA 11E2
Delice Turk 62B1
Delicias Mexico 19B2
Delījān Iran 61C2
Delle France 35B1
Dell Rapids USA 9C3
Dellys Alg 69C1
Del Mar USA 18D4
Delmenhorst W Germ 30F8
De Long Mts USA 8F2
Deloraine Aust 78E3
Deloraine Can 4H5
Delray Beach USA 13E4
Del Rio USA 6C4
Delta USA 6B3
Delta, R USA 8J3
Delta Junction USA 8J3
Delta Res USA 12C1
Dembidollo Eth 70D3
Demer, R Belg 34C1
Demidov USSR 41G1
Deming USA 14A3
Demirköy Turk 39F2
Demnate Mor 69A2
Demonte Italy 35B2
Demopolis USA 13B2
Denain France 36C1
Denau USSR 57E2
Denbigh Wales 33D5
Denbigh,C USA 8F3
Dendang Indon 54C3
Dendermond Belg 34C1
Dendi, Mt Eth 70D3
Dendre, R Belg 34B1
Dengkou China 50B1
Deng Xian China 50C3
Den Haag = 's-Gravenhage
Denham,Mt Jamaica 21H1
Den Helder Neth 40A2
Denia Spain 37C2
Deniliquin Aust 76D4
Denio USA 16C2
Denison, Iowa USA 9C3
Denison, Texas USA 6D3
Denison,Mt USA 8H4
Denizli Turk 43D8
Denmark, Kingdom Europe 30F7
Denmark Str Greenland/Iceland 80C1
Dennery St Lucia 21P2
Denpasar Indon 54E4
Denton, Maryland USA 12C3
Denton, Texas USA 6D3
D'Entrecasteaux Is PNG 76E1
Dents du Midi, Mt Switz 35B1
Denver USA 6C3
Déo, R Cam 70B3
Deoghar India 59C3
Deolāli India 58C5
Deosai Plain India 58D1
Depew USA 12A1
Deposit USA 12C1
Dépression du Mourdi, Desert Region Chad 70C2
Deputatskiy USSR 47Q3
De Queen USA 15D3
Dera Pak 58C3
Dera Bugti Pak 58B3
Dera Ismail Khan Pak 58B2
Derbent USSR 43H7
Derby Aust 76B2
Derby, Connecticut USA 12D2
Derby, County Eng 33E5
Derby Eng 33E5
Derby, Kansas USA 15C2
Dergachi USSR 43F5
De Ridder USA 15D3
Derna Libya 67B1
Derry USA 12E1
Derudeb Sudan 70D2
De Rust S Africa 72C3
De Ruyter USA 12C1
Derwent Bridge Aust 78E3
Desaguadero Arg 26B2
Desaguadero, R Arg 26B2
Descanso Mexico 17C4
Deschambault L Can 3H3
Deschutes, R USA 16B2
Deseado Arg 23C7
Deseado, R Arg 23C7
Desenzano Italy 35D2
Deserta Grande, I Medeira 68A1
Desert Centre USA 17C4
Desert Peak, Mt USA 17D2
Deshu Afghan 61E2
Desierto de Atacama, Desert Chile 23C2
Desloge USA 15D2
Des Moines, Iowa USA 7D2
Des Moines, New Mexico USA 14B2
Des Moines, R USA 9D3
Desna, R USSR 43E5
Desolación, I Chile 23B8
Des Plaines USA 10B2
Dessau E Germ 40C2
Dessye Eth 70D2
Destruction Bay Can 8L3
Desvres France 34A1
Deta Rom 39E1
Dete Zim 71C5
Detmold W Germ 34E1
Detroit USA 7E2
Detroit Lakes USA 9C2
Det Udom Thai 53D3
Deva Rom 39E1
Deventer Neth 40B2
Deveron, R Scot 32D3
Devikot India 58C3
Devil Postpile Nat Mon USA 18C2
Devils Den USA 18C3
Devils Gate, P USA 18C1
Devil's Hole, Region N Sea 32F3
Devil's Island = Isla du Diable
Devils L, N Dakota USA 9C2
Devils L, Texas USA 14B4
Devils Lake USA 6D2
Devils Paw, Mt Can 8M4
Devizes Eng 33E6
Devli India 58D3
Devoll, R Alb 39E2
Dévoluy, Mts France 35A2
Devon, County Eng 33C6
Devon I Can 5J2
Devonport Aust 76D5
Dewangiri Bhutan 59D2
Dewās India 58D4
Dewetsdorp S Africa 72D2
Dewey Res USA 7E3
De Witt USA 15D3
Dexter, Missouri USA 15E2
Dexter, New Mexico USA 14B3
Deyang China 50A3
Deyhuk Iran 61D2
Dezfūl Iran 61B2
Dezhou China 50D2
Dezh Shāhpūr Iran 61B1
Dhahran S Arabia 65F1
Dhākā Bang 59D3
Dhali Cyprus 63B1
Dhamār Yemen 64D4
Dhamavaram India 60B2
Dhamtari India 59B3
Dhanbād India 59C3
Dhangarhi Nepal 59B2
Dhankuta Nepal 59C2
Dhār India 58D4
Dharmapuri India 60B2
Dharmsāla India 58D2
Dhar Oualata, Desert Region Maur 68B3
Dhaulagiri, Mt Nepal 59B2
Dhenkānāl India 59C3
Dhibah Jordan 63C3
Dhíkti Óri, Mt Greece 39F3
Dhofar, Region Oman 65F3
Dhomokós Greece 39E3
Dhone India 60B1
Dhoraji India 58C4
Dhrāngadhra India 58C4
Dhuburi India 59C2
Dhule India 58C4
Diablo,Mt USA 18B2
Diablo Range, Mts USA 17B3
Diamante Arg 26C2
Diamante, R Arg 26B2
Diamantina Brazil 25K7
Diamantina, R Aust 76D3
Diamantino Brazil 27A1
Diamond Harbours India 59C3
Diamond Springs USA 18B1
Diamondville USA 16D2
Diapaga U Volta 69G3
Dibā UAE 65G1
Dibaya Zaïre 71C4
Dibrugarh India 59D2
Dickens USA 14B3
Dickinson USA 6C2
Dickson USA 13B1
Dickson City USA 11D2
Dicle, R Turk 43G8
Didsbury Can 3F3
Didwāna India 58C3
Die France 35A2
Die Berg, Mt S Africa 72E2
Diebougou U Volta 69F3
Dieburg W Germ 34E2
Diefenbaker,L Can 3G3
Diekirch Lux 34D2
Diéma Mali 68B3
Dien Bien Phu Viet 53C1
Diepholz W Germ 40B2
Dieppe France 36C2
Dier Songhua Jiang, R China 51B3
Diest Belg 34C1
Dieuze France 34D2
Diffa Niger 69J3
Digboi India 59E2
Digby Can 5M5
Digne France 36D3
Digoin France 36C2
Digos Phil 55G9
Digul, R Indon 76C1
Digya Nat Pk Ghana 69F4
Dihang, R India 59D2
Dijlah = Tigris
Dijon France 35A1
Dik Chad 70B3
Dikhil Djibouti 70E2
Dīkirnis Egypt 63A3
Diksmuide Belg 34B1
Dikson USSR 46K2
Dikwa Nig 69J3
Dilaram Afghan 61E2
Dili Indon 76B1
Di Linh Viet 53D3
Dillenburg W Germ 34E1
Dilley USA 15F4
Dilling Sudan 70C2
Dillingham USA 8G4
Dillon USA 6B2
Dillsburg USA 12B2
Dilolo Zaïre 71C5
Dimas Mexico 20A1
Dimashq = Damascus
Dimbelenge Zaïre 70C4
Dimbokro Ivory Coast 69F4
Dimitrovgrad Bulg 39F2
Dimitrovgrad USSR 42H5
Dimona Israel 63C3
Dimpāpur India 59D2
Dinagat, I Phil 55G8
Dinajpur India 59C2
Dinan France 36B2
Dinant Belg 34C1
Dinar Turk 62B2
Dinder, R Sudan 70D2
Dindigul India 60B2
Dingbian China 50B2
Dinggyê China 59C2
Dingle Irish Rep 31A3
Dingle, B Irish Rep 31A3
Dinguiraye Guinea 68A3
Dingwall Scot 32C3
Dingxi China 50A2
Ding Xian China 50D2
Dinh Lap Viet 53D1
Dinorwic L Can 9D2
Dinosaur USA 14A1
Dinuba USA 18C2
Diomede Is USSR/USA 8E2
Diouloulou Sen 68A3
Diphu India 59D2
Diredawa Eth 70E3
Dirk Hartog, I Aust 76A3
Dirkou Niger 70B2
Dirranbandi Aust 78C1
Dirri Somalia 70E3
Disappointment,C South Georgia 23J8
Disappointment,C USA 16B1
Disappointment,L Aust 76B3
Discovery B Aust 78B3
Discovery Tablemount Atlantic O 73J6
Disentis Muster Switz 35C1
Dishna Egypt 64B1
Disko Greenland 5N3
Disko Bugt, B Greenland 5N3
Diskorjord Greenland 5N3
Dismal Swamp USA 11D3
Disna, R USSR 41F1
Distrito Federal, Federal District Brazil 27C2
Diu India 58C4
Diuat Mts Phil 55G9
Dives, R France 34A2
Divinópolis Brazil 25K8
Divnoye USSR 43G6
Divriği Turk 62C2
Dixon, California USA 18B1
Dixon, Illinois USA 10B2
Dixon, Montana USA 16D1
Dixon Entrance, Sd Can/USA 4E4
Dixonville Can 3E2
Diyālā, R Iraq 62E3
Diyarbakir Turk 43G8
Diz Pak 61E3
Diz, R Iran 61B2
Dja, R Cam 70B3
Djadi, R Alg 69C2
Djado,Plat du Niger 70B1
Djamaa Alg 69D2
Djambala Congo 70B4
Djanet Alg 68C2
Djebel Amour, Mts Alg 69C2
Djebel Bouhalla, Mt Mor 37A2
Djebel Chambi, Mt Tunisia 69D1
Djebel Chélia, Mts Alg 69D1
Djebel Zaghouan, Mt Tunisia 69E1
Djebel Zrega, Mt Tunisia 69D2
Djebobo, Mt Ghana 69G4
Djelfa Alg 69C2
Djéma CAR 70C3
Djenné Mali 68B3
Djerem, R Cam 69J4
Djibasso U Volta 69F3
Djibo Upper Volta 68B3
Djibouti Djibouti 70E2
Djibouti, Republic E Africa 70E2
Djolu Zaïre 70C3
Djougou Benin 69G4
Djugu Zaïre 70D3
Djúpivogur Iceland 30C2
Djurdjura, Mts Alg 37C2
Dmitrov USSR 42F4
Dnepr, R USSR 43E6
Dneprodzerzhinsk USSR 43E6
Dnepropetrovsk USSR 43F6
Dneprovskaya Nizmennost', Region USSR 42D5
Dnestr, R USSR 43C6
Dno USSR 42E4
Doba Chad 70B3
Dobele USSR 41E1
Doblas Arg 26C3
Dobo Indon 76C1
Doboj Yugos 39D2
Dobrush USSR 43E5
Doce, R Brazil 25K7
Doctor R P Peña Arg 23D2
Dod India 60B2
Doda Betta, Mt India 60B2
Dodecanese = Sporádhes
Dodge City USA 6C3
Dodge L Can 3G2
Dodgeville USA 10A2
Dodoma Tanz 70D4
Dogger Bank, Sand-bank N Sea 32G4
Dog L Can 10B1
Dog L Can 10C1
Dōgo, I Japan 52B3
Dogondoutchi Niger 68C3
Doğubayazit Turk 62D2
Doha Qatar 65F1
Doilungdêqên China 59D2
Doka Sudan 64C4
Dolak, I Indon 76C1
Doland USA 9C3
Dolbeau Can 5L5
Dôle France 36D2
Doleib, Watercourse Sudan 64B4
Dolgellau Wales 33D5
Dolgeville USA 12C1
Dolinsk USSR 51E2
Dolo Eth 70E3
Dolomitche, Mts Italy 35D1
Dolores Arg 23E5
Dolores Urug 26D2
Dolores, R USA 14A2
Dolores Hidalgo Mexico 20B1
Dolphin and Union Str Can 4G3
Dolphin,C Falkland Is 23E8
Dom, Mt Indon 49G7
Dombarovskiy USSR 46G4
Dombas Nor 30F6
Dombasle-sur-Meurthe France 34D2
Dombóvár Hung 39D1
Domeyko Chile 26A1
Domfront France 36B2
Dominica, I Caribbean 21E3
Dominican Republic Caribbean 21C3
Dominion,C Can 5L3
Domino Can 5N4
Domna USSR 48E1
Domodossola Italy 38B1
Dom Pedrito Brazil 26E2
Dompu Indon 54E4
Domuyo, Mt Arg 23B5
Domville,Mt Aust 78D1
Dom-yanskoya USSR 46H4
Don, R Scot 32D3
Don, R USSR 43G6
Donaghadee N Ire 32B4
Donato Guerta Mexico 20B1
Donau = Dunav
Donau, R Austria 40C3
Donau, R W Germ 40C3
Donaueschingen W Germ 34E3
Donauwörth W Germ 40C3
Don Benito Spain 37A2
Doncaster Eng 33E5
Dondo Angola 71B4
Dondo Mozam 71D5
Dondra Head, C Sri Lanka 60C3
Donegal, County Irish Rep 32B4
Donegal Irish Rep 31B3
Donegal, B Irish Rep 31B3
Donegal, Mts Irish Rep 32A4
Donetsk USSR 43F6
Donga, R Nig 69J4
Dong'an China 50C4
Dongara Aust 76A3
Dongchuan China 50A4
Dongfang China 53D2
Dongfeng China 51B3
Donggala Indon 76A1
Donggi Cona, L China 48C3
Donggou China 51A4
Donghai Dao, I China 50C5
Dong He, R China 50A1
Dong Hoi Viet 53D2
Dong Jiang, R China 50C5
Donglanghong China 51C2
Dongning China 51C3
Dongola Sudan 70D2
Dongshan China 50D5
Dongsha Qundao, I China 48E4
Dongsheng China 50C2
Dongtai China 50E3
Dongting Hu, L China 50C4
Dongxing China 50B5
Dongzhi China 50D3
Doniphan USA 15D2
Donji Vakuf Yugos 38D2
Dönna, I Nor 30G5
Donner, P USA 17B3
Donnersberg, Mt W Germ 34D2
Donnybrook S Africa 72D2
Don Pedro Res USA 18B2
Doonerak,Mt USA 8H2
Dopolong Phil 55F9
Do Qu, R China 50A3
Dora Baltea, R Italy 35B2
Dorbirn Austria 36D2
Dorbod China 51A2
Dorchester Eng 33D6
Dorchester,C Can 5L3
Dordogne, R France 36C2
Dordrecht Neth 40A2
Dordrecht S Africa 72D3
Doré, L Can 3G3
Doré Lake Can 3G3
Dorest Peak, Mt USA 12D1
Dori Upper Volta 68B3
Doring, R S Africa 72B3
Dormans France 34B2
Dornbirn Austria 40B3
Dornoch Scot 32C3
Dornoch Firth, Estuary Scot 32C3
Dorotea Sweden 30H6
D'Or Prairie Can 3E2
Dorrigo Aust 78D2
Dorris USA 16B2
Dorset, County Eng 33D6
Dorsten W Germ 34D1
Dortmund W Germ 40B2
Doruma Zaïre 70C3

Dosatuy *USSR* 47N4
Doshi *Afghan* 58B1
Dos Palos *USA* 18B2
Dosso *Niger* 69G3
Dossor *USSR* 46G5
Dothan *USA* 7E3
Douai *France* 36C1
Douala *Cam* 70A3
Double Island Pt *Aust* 78D1
Double Mountain Fork, R *USA* 14B3
Double Mt *USA* 18C3
Doubs, R *France* 36D2
Doubtful Sd *NZ* 79A3
Douentza *Mali* 68B3
Douglas, Alaska *USA* 3B2
Douglas, Arizona *USA* 6C3
Douglas *Eng* 33C4
Douglas, Georgia *USA* 13C2
Douglas *S Africa* 72C2
Douglas, Wyoming *USA* 6C2
Douglas,C *USA* 8E2
Douglas Chan *Can* 3C3
Douglas L *USA* 13C1
Douglas,Mt *USA* 8H4
Doulevant-le-Château *France* 34C2
Doullens *France* 34B1
Doun, County *N Ire* 33B4
Dourados *Brazil* 25H8
Dourados, R *Brazil* 27B3
Dourdan *France* 34B2
Douro, R *Port* 37A1
Dove Creek *USA* 14A2
Dover, Delaware *USA* 11D3
Dover *Eng* 33F6
Dover, New Hampshire *USA* 11E2
Dover, New Jersey *USA* 12C2
Dover, Ohio *USA* 10C2
Dover, R *Eng* 33E5
Dover,Str of *Eng/France* 33F6
Dovsk *USSR* 41G2
Downington *USA* 12C3
Downpatrick *N Ire* 33C4
Downsville *USA* 12C1
Downton,Mt *Can* 3D3
Doylestown *USA* 12C2
Dōzen, I *Japan* 52B3
Dr'aa, R *Mor* 68A2
Drac, R *France* 35A2
Dracena *Brazil* 27B3
Dracut *USA* 12E1
Draguignan *France* 36D3
Drake *USA* 9B2
Drakensberg, Mts *S Africa* 71D6
Drakensberg, Mt *S Africa* 72D2
Drake Pass *Pacific/ Atlantic O* 73E7
Dráma *Greece* 39E2
Drammen *Nor* 30G6
Drangajökull *Iceland* 30A1
Dr Arroyo *Mexico* 20B1
Drau, R *Austria* 35E1
Drava, R *Yugos* 38D1
Drayton Valley *Can* 3E3
Dreaux *France* 36C2
Dresden *E Germ* 40C2
Dreux *France* 34A2
Drewsey *USA* 16C2
Driftwood *USA* 12A2
Drin, R *Alb* 39E2
Drina, R *Yugos* 39D2
Drissa, R *USSR* 41F1
Drogheda *Irish Rep* 33B5
Drogobych *USSR* 41E3
Drôme, R *France* 35A2
Dronera *Italy* 35B2
Dronning Maud Land, Region *Ant* 80F12
Dr P.P. Pená *Par* 24F8
Drumheller *Can* 4G4
Drummond *USA* 16D1
Drummond I *USA* 10C1
Drummondville *Can* 11E1
Druskininksi *USSR* 41E2
Druzhina *USSR* 47Q3
Dry B *USA* 8L4
Dryberry L *Can* 9D2
Dryden *Can* 5J5
Dryden *USA* 12B1
Dry Harbour Mts *Jamaica* 21H1
Dschang *Cam* 69J4
Duang, I *Burma* 53B3
Dubâ *S Arabia* 64C1
Dubai *UAE* 65G1
Dubawnt, R *Can* 4H3
Dubawnt L *Can* 4H3
Dubbo *Aust* 76D4
Dublin, County *Irish Rep* 33B5
Dublin *Irish Rep* 33B5
Dublin *USA* 13C2
Dubna *USSR* 42F4
Dubno *USSR* 43D5
Dubois, Idaho *USA* 16D2
Du Bois *USA* 11D2
Dubois, Wyoming *USA* 16E2
Dubose,Mt *Can* 3C3
Dubossary *USSR* 41F3
Dubrovica *USSR* 41F2
Dubrovnik *Yugos* 39D2
Dubuque *USA* 7D2
Duchesne *USA* 17D2
Duck, R *USA* 13B1
Duck Mts *Can* 3H3
Ducor *USA* 18C3
Dudelange *Lux* 34D2
Dudinka *USSR* 46K3
Dudley *Eng* 33D5
Dudypta, R *USSR* 47L2
Duekoué *Ivory Coast* 68B4
Duero, R *Spain* 37B1
Duff Is *Solomon Is* 77F1
Dufftown *Scot* 32D3
Dugi Otok, I *Yugos* 38C2
Duisburg *W Germ* 40B2
Duiwelskloof *S Africa* 72E1
Dūkan *Iraq* 62E3
Duke I *USA* 8M5
Duk Faiwil *Sudan* 70D3
Dukhān *Qatar* 65F1
Dukou *China* 50A4
Dulan *China* 48C3
Dulce, R *Arg* 26C2
Dulit Range, Mts *Malay* 54D2
Dullabchara *India* 59D3
Dülmen *W Germ* 34D1
Duluth *USA* 7D2
Dūmā *Syria* 63D2
Dumai *Indon* 54B2
Dumaran, I *Phil* 55E8
Dumas *USA* 6C3
Dumayr *Syria* 63D2
Dumbai *Ghana* 69G4
Dumbarton *Scot* 32C4
Dumfries *Scot* 32D4
Dumfries and Galloway, Region *Scot* 32C4
Dumka *India* 59C3
Dumoga Kecil *Indon* 55B2
Dumoine,L *Can* 11D1
Dumont d'Urville, Base *Ant* 80G8
Dumyât = Damietta
Dumyat *Egypt* 67C1
Dunărea, R *Rom* 39F2
Dunary Head, Pt *Irish Rep* 33B5
Dunav, R *Bulg* 39E2
Dunav, R *Yugos* 39D1
Dunayevtsy *USSR* 41F3
Duncan *Can* 3D4
Duncan *USA* 15C3
Duncannon *USA* 12B2
Duncan Pass *Andaman Is* 60E2
Duncansby Head, Pt *Scot* 32D2
Dundalk *Irish Rep* 33B4
Dundalk *USA* 12B3
Dundalk B *Irish Rep* 33B5
Dundas *Greenland* 5M2
Dundas I *Can* 8M5
Dundas Pen *Can* 4G2
Dundas Str *Aust* 49G8
Dundee *S Africa* 72E2
Dundee *Scot* 32D3
Dundee *USA* 12B1
Dundoo *Aust* 78B1
Dundrum, B *N Ire* 33C4
Dunedin *NZ* 77G5
Dunedin *USA* 13C3
Dunedoo *Aust* 78C2
Dunfermline *Scot* 32D3
Dungarpur *India* 58C4
Dungarvan *Irish Rep* 33B5
Dungeness *Eng* 33F6
Dungog *Aust* 78D2
Dungu *Zaïre* 70C3
Dungunab *Sudan* 70D1
Dunhua *China* 51B3
Dunhuang *China* 48C2
Dunkerque *France* 34B1
Dunkirk *USA* 7F2
Dunkur *Eth* 70D2
Dunkwa *Ghana* 69F4
Dun Laoghaire *Irish Rep* 31B3
Dunmore *USA* 12C2
Dunmore Town *Bahamas* 21B1
Dunn *USA* 13D1
Dunnet Head, Pt *Scot* 32D2
Dunning *USA* 9B3
Duns *Scot* 32D4
Dunseith *USA* 9B2
Dunsmuir *USA* 16B2
Dunstan Mts *NZ* 79A2
Dun-sur-Meuse *France* 34C2
Duolun *China* 50D1
Dupree *USA* 9B2
Duque de Braganca *Angola* 71B4
Du Quoin *USA* 10B3
Dura *Israel* 63C3
Durance, R *France* 36D3
Durand *USA* 10A2
Durango *Mexico* 19B2
Durango *Spain* 37B1
Durango, State *Mexico* 20A1
Durango *USA* 6C3
Durant *USA* 6D3
Duraykish *Syria* 63D1
Durazho *Urug* 23E4
Durban *S Africa* 72E2
Duren *W Germ* 34D1
Durg *India* 59B3
Durgapur *India* 59C3
Durham, County *Eng* 32E4
Durham *Eng* 32E4
Durham, N Carolina *USA* 7F3
Durham, New Hampshire *USA* 12E1
Durham Downs *Aust* 78B1
Durmitor, Mt *Yugos* 39D2
Durness *Scot* 32C2
Durrës *Alb* 39D2
Durrie *Aust* 78B1
Dursunbey *Turk* 39F3
D'Urville I *NZ* 79B2
Dushak *USSR* 61E1
Dushan *China* 50B4
Dushanbe *USSR* 57E2
Dushore *USA* 12B2
Dusky Sd *NZ* 79A3
Düsseldorf *W Germ* 40B2
Dutch Harbour *USA* 8E5
Dutton,Mt *USA* 17D3
Duyun *China* 50B4
Düzce *Turk* 62B1
Dvina, R *USSR* 42D4
Dvinskaya Guba, B *USSR* 42F2
Dwārka *India* 58B4
Dworshak Res *USA* 16C1
Dyer,C *Can* 5M3
Dyersburg *USA* 7E3
Dyfed, County *Wales* 33C5
Dykh Tau Dağlari, Mt *USSR* 43G7
Dynevor Downs *Aust* 78B1
Dzag *Mongolia* 48C2
Dzamin Üüd *USSR* 47M5
Dzaoudzi *Mayotte* 71E5
Dzarnïn Üüd *Mongolia* 48D2
Dzavhan Gol, R *Mongolia* 48C2
Dzehezkazgan *USSR* 56E1
Dzerzhinsk *USSR* 42G4
Dzhalinda *USSR* 47O4
Dzhambul *USSR* 46J5
Dzhankoy *USSR* 43E6
Dzhezkazgan *USSR* 46H4
Dzhilikul' *USSR* 58B1
Dzhungarskiy Alatau, Mts *USSR* 46J5
Dzierzoniow *Pol* 40D2
Dzungaria, Basin *China* 57G1

E

Eabamet L *Can* 5K4
Eagle, Alaska *USA* 8K3
Eagle, Colorado *USA* 14A2
Eagle Butte *USA* 9B2
Eagle L, California *USA* 16B2
Eagle L *Can* 9D2
Eagle L, Maine *USA* 11F1
Eagle Lake *USA* 11F1
Eagle Mountain L *USA* 15C3
Eagle Pass *USA* 6C4
Eagle Peak, Mt *USA* 14A3
Eagle Plain *Can* 4E3
Eagle River *USA* 8J3
Ear Falls *Can* 9D1
Earlimart *USA* 17C3
Earp *USA* 17D4
Earth *USA* 14B3
Easley *USA* 13C2
East Aurora *USA* 11D2
East B *USA* 13B3
Eastbourne *Eng* 33F6
East Branch Delaware, R *USA* 12C1
East,C *NZ* 77G4
East C *USA* 8B6
East Chicago *USA* 10B2
East China Sea *China/ Japan* 48F3
Eastern Ghats, Mts *India* 59B4
East Falkland, I *Falkland Is* 23E8
East Fork, R *USA* 8J2
Eastgate *USA* 17C3
East Germany, Republic *Europe* 40C2
East Grand Forks *USA* 9C2
Easthampton *USA* 12D1
East Hampton *USA* 12D2
East Lake *USA* 10B2
East Liverpool *USA* 10C2
East London *S Africa* 72D3
Eastmain *Can* 5L4
Eastmain, R *Can* 5L4
Eastman *USA* 13C2
East Moline *USA* 10A2
Easton, Maryland *USA* 11D3
Easton, Pennsylvania *USA* 11D2
East Orange *USA* 12C2
East Pacific Ridge *Pacific O* 75O5
East Pacific Rise *Pacific O* 75O4
East Point *USA* 13C2
Eastport *USA* 11F2
East Retford *Eng* 33E5
East Ridge *USA* 13B1
East St Louis *USA* 7D3
East Siberian S *USSR* 47R2
East Sussex, County *Eng* 33F6
Eastville *USA* 11D3
East Walker *USA* 18C1
Eatonton *USA* 13C2
Eau Claire *USA* 9D3
Eauripik, I *Pacific O* 49H6
Ebano *Mexico* 20C1
Ebebiyin *Eq Guinea* 70B3
Eberbach *W Germ* 34E2
Eberswalde *E Germ* 40C2
Ebetsu *Japan* 52D2
Ebian *China* 50A4
Ebinur, L *China* 46K5
Eboli *Italy* 38D2
Ebolowa *Cam* 70B3
Ebro, R *Spain* 37B1
Eceabat *Turk* 62A1
Eching *China* 50D2
Echo *USA* 16C1
Echo Bay = Port Radium
Echo Bay *Can* 4G3
Echternach *Lux* 34D2
Echuca *Aust* 78B3
Ecija *Spain* 37A2
Eclipse Sd *Can* 5K2
Ecommoy *France* 34A3
Ecuador, Republic *S America* 24C4
Eday, I *Scot* 32D2
Edd *Eth* 70E2
Edda, Oilfield *N Sea* 32G3
Ed Da'ein *Sudan* 70C2
Ed Damasin *Sudan* 64B4
Ed Damer *Sudan* 70D2
Ed Debba *Sudan* 70D2
Eddrachillis, B *Scot* 32C2
Ed Dueim *Sudan* 70D2
Eddystone Pt *Aust* 78E3
Ede *Nig* 69G4
Edea *Cam* 70A3
Eden *Aust* 78C3
Eden, Texas *USA* 14C3
Eden, Wyoming *USA* 16E2
Eden, R *Eng* 32D4
Edenburg *S Africa* 72D2
Edendale *NZ* 79A3
Edenkoben *W Germ* 34D2
Edensburg *USA* 12A2
Eder, R *W Germ* 34E1
Edgeley *USA* 9C2
Edgell I *Can* 5M3
Edgemont *USA* 9B3
Edgeøya, I *Barents S* 46D2
Edgewood *USA* 12B3
Edh Dhahiriya *Israel* 63C3
Edhessa *Greece* 39E2
Edinburg *USA* 15F4
Edinburgh *Scot* 32D3
Edirne *Turk* 43D7
Edison *USA* 18C3
Edisto, R *USA* 13C2
Edith Cavell,Mt *Can* 3E3
Edmonds *USA* 16B1
Edmonton *Can* 4G4
Edmore *USA* 9C2
Edmundston *Can* 5M5
Edna *USA* 15C4
Edna Bay *USA* 8M4
Edolo *Italy* 38C1
Edom, Region *Jordan* 63C3
Edremit *Turk* 43D8
Edremit Körfezi, B *Turk* 39F3
Edrengiyn Nuruu, Mts *Mongolia* 48C2
Edson *Can* 4G4
Eduardo Castex *Arg* 26C3
Eduni,Mt *Can* 8N3
Edward, R *Aust* 78B3
Edward,L *Zaïre/Uganda* 70C4
Edwards *USA* 18D3
Edwards Creek *Aust* 78A1
Edwards Plat *USA* 6C3
Edwardsville *USA* 10B3
Edziza,Mt *Can* 3B2
Eek *USA* 8F3
Eeklo *Belg* 34B1
Efate, I *Vanuatu* 77F2
Effingham *USA* 7E3
Egan Range, Mts *USA* 17D3
Egedesminde *Greenland* 5N3
Egegik *USA* 8G4
Egenolf L *Can* 3J2
Eger *Hung* 41E3
Egersund *Nor* 30F7
Eggegebirge, Region *W Germ* 34E1
Egg Harbor City *USA* 12C3
Eglinton I *Can* 4G2
Egmont,C *NZ* 79B1
Egmont,Mt *NZ* 79B1
Eğridir Gölü, L *Turk* 62B2
Eguas, R *Brazil* 27C1
Egvekinot *USSR* 47T3
Egypt, Republic *Africa* 67B2
Ehsenvaara *Fin* 30K6
Eibar *Spain* 37B1
Eibeuf *France* 36C2
Eidsvolo *Aust* 78D1
Eifel, Region *W Germ* 34D1
Eigg, I *Scot* 32B3
Eight Degree Chan *Indian O* 57F5
Eighty Mile Beach *Aust* 76B2
Eildon,L *Aust* 78C3
Einbeck *W Germ* 34E1
Eindhoven *Neth* 40B2
Einsiedeln *Switz* 35C1
Ein Yahav *Israel* 63C3
Eisenach *E Germ* 40C2
Eisenerz *Austria* 40C3
Eisenhut, Mt *Austria* 35E1
Eitorf *W Germ* 34D1
Ejin qi *China* 50A1
Ejuanema,Mt *Ghana* 69F4
Ejura *Ghana* 69F4
Ejutla *Mexico* 20C2
Ekalaka *USA* 9B2
Eketahuna *NZ* 79C2
Ekibastuz *USSR* 46J4
Ekimchan *USSR* 47P4
Ek Mahalla el Kubra *Egypt* 62B3
Eksjo *Sweden* 30H7
Ekwen, R *Can* 7E1
El Abbâsa *Egypt* 63A3
El'Alamein *Egypt* 62A3
Elands, R *S Africa* 72D2
Elands Berg *S Africa* 72C3
El Arenal *Mexico* 20B1
El Aricha *Alg* 69B2
El'Arîsh *Egypt* 62B3
El Asnam *Alg* 69C1
Elat *Israel* 62B4
El' Atrun Oasis *Sudan* 70C2
el Attar, R *Alg* 69C2
Elazig *Turk* 43F8
El Azraq *Jordan* 62C3
Elba, I *Italy* 38C2
El Balyana *Egypt* 67C2
El'ban *USSR* 51D1
El Banco *Colombia* 24D2
Elbasan *Alb* 39E2
El Bauga *Sudan* 64B3
El Baúl *Ven* 21D5
El Bayadh *Alg* 69C2
Elbe, R *E Germ/W Germ* 40C2
El Bega'a, R *Leb* 63D1
Elberta *USA* 10B2
Elbert,Mt *USA* 6C3
Elberton *USA* 13C2
Elbeuf *France* 34A2
Elbistan *Turk* 62C2
Elblag *Pol* 41D2
El Bolson *Arg* 23B6
Elbow Lake *USA* 9C2
El Bozal *Mexico* 20B1
Elbrus, Mt *USSR* 43G7
Elburz Mts = Reshteh-ye Alborz
El Cajon *USA* 17C4
El Campo *USA* 15C4
El Centro *USA* 17C4
Elche *Spain* 37B2
El Cuy *Arg* 26B3
Elda *Spain* 37B2
El'dikan *USSR* 47P3
El Diviso *Colombia* 24C3
El Djouf, Desert Region *Maur* 68B2
Eldon *USA* 15D2
Eldorado *Arg* 27B4
El Dorado, Arkansas *USA* 7D3
Eldorado *Brazil* 27C3
Eldorado *Can* 3G2
El Dorado, Kansas *USA* 6D3
El Dorado *Mexico* 19B2
Eldorado, Texas *USA* 14B3
El Dorado *Ven* 24F2
Eldoret *Kenya* 70D3
Eldred *USA* 12A2
Elea,C *Cyprus* 63C1
Eleanor,L *USA* 18C1
Electric Peak, Mt *USA* 16D2
El Eglab, Region *Alg* 68B2
Elel, Watercourse *Egypt* 64B2
Elephant Butte Res *USA* 14A3
El Escorial *Spain* 37B1
Eleşkirt *Turk* 62D2
El Eulma *Alg* 69D1
Eleuthera, I *Bahamas* 7F4
El Fahs *Tunisia* 69D1
El Faiyûm *Egypt* 62B4
El Farsia, Well *Mor* 68B2
El Fasher *Sudan* 70C2
El Fashn *Egypt* 62B4
El Ferrol del Caudillo *Spain* 37A1
El Firdân *Egypt* 63B3
El Fula *Sudan* 70C2
El Gassi *Alg* 68C1
El Geteina *Sudan* 70D2
El Gezīra, Region *Sudan* 70D2

El Ghor, V *Israel/Jordan*	63C3
Elgin, Illinois *USA*	7E2
Elgin, N Dakota *USA*	9B2
Elgin *Scot*	32D3
El Gîza *Egypt*	62B3
El Golea *Alg*	68C1
El Golfo de Santa Clara *Mexico*	17D4
Elgon,Mt *Uganda/Kenya*	70D3
El Goran *Eth*	70E3
El Grullo *Mexico*	20B2
El Guettara, Well *Mali*	68B2
El Hamurre *Somalia*	67D4
El Haricha, Desert Region *Mali*	68B2
El Harra *Egypt*	62A4
El Harrach *Alg*	37C2
El Hawata *Sudan*	64B4
El Hig *Mexico*	20C1
El Homra *Sudan*	64B4
El Huecu *Arg*	26A3
El Igma, Desert Region *Egypt*	62B4
Elim *USA*	8F3
Elira,C *Can*	4H2
Elisabethville = Lubumbashi	
El Iskandarîya = Alexandria	
Elista *USSR*	43G6
Elizabeth *Aust*	76C4
Elizabeth *USA*	11E2
Elizabeth B *Namibia*	72B2
Elizabeth City *USA*	7F3
Elizabeth Is *USA*	12E2
Elizabethton, Tennessee *USA*	13C1
Elizabethtown, Kentucky *USA*	10B3
Elizabethtown, N Carolina *USA*	13D2
Elizabethtown, Pennsylvania *USA*	12B2
El Jadida *Mor*	69A2
El Jafr *Jordan*	62C3
El Jafr, L *Jordan*	63D3
El Jebelein *Sudan*	70D2
El Jem *Tunisia*	69E1
Elk *Pol*	41E2
Elk, R, Maryland *USA*	12C3
Elk, R, W Virginia *USA*	10C3
Elkader *USA*	9D3
El Kala *Alg*	69D1
El Kamlin *Sudan*	70D2
El Kef *Tunisia*	69D1
Elk Grove *USA*	18B1
El Khalil = Hebron	
El Khandaq *Sudan*	64B3
El Khânka *Egypt*	63A3
El Khârga *Egypt*	64B1
El-Khârga Oasis *Egypt*	64B1
Elkhart *USA*	10B2
El Khenachich, Desert Region *Mali*	68B2
Elkhorn, R *USA*	9C3
Elkhovo *Bulg*	39F2
Elkins *USA*	11D3
Elkland *USA*	12B2
Elk Mt *USA*	9A3
Elko *Can*	16C1
Elko *USA*	6B2
el Korima, R *Alg*	69B2
Elkton *USA*	12C3
El Ku, Watercourse *Egypt*	64B2
El Kûbri *Egypt*	63B3
El Kuntilla *Egypt*	62B3
El Lagowa *Sudan*	70C2
Ellef Ringnes I *Can*	4H2
Ellendale *USA*	9C2
Ellen,Mt *USA*	17D3
Ellensburg *USA*	6A2
Ellenville *USA*	12C2
Ellesmere I *Can*	5K2
Ellesmere,L *NZ*	79B2
Ellicott City *USA*	12B3
Elliot *S Africa*	72D3
Elliot Lake *Can*	5K5
Ellis *USA*	16D2
El Lisan, Pen *Jordan*	63C3
Ellisras *S Africa*	72D1
Ellsworth *USA*	11F2
Ellsworth Land, Region *Ant*	80F3
El Ma'âdi *Egypt*	63A4
El Maghra, L *Egypt*	67B1
El Manaqil *Sudan*	64B4
El Mansûra *Egypt*	62B3
El Manzala *Egypt*	63A3
El Matariya *Egypt*	63A3
El Matarîya *Egypt*	63B3
Elmer *USA*	12C3
El Merelé, Desert Region *Maur*	68B3
El Milagro *Arg*	26B2
El Milia *Alg*	69D1
El Milk, Watercourse *Sudan*	64B3
El Mîna *Leb*	63C1
El Minya *Egypt*	62B4
Elmira, California *USA*	18B1
Elmira, New York *USA*	7F2
El Mirage *USA*	17D4
el Mitta, R *Alg*	69D2
El Moral *Mexico*	15F4
El Mreitl, Well *Maur*	68B2
Elmshorn *W Germ*	40B2
El Muglad *Sudan*	70C2
El Mzereb, Well *Mali*	68B2
El Nido *Phil*	55E8
El Obeid *Sudan*	70D2
El Oro *Mexico*	20B2
Elota *Mexico*	20A1
El Oued *Alg*	69D2
Eloy *USA*	17D4
El Paso *USA*	6C3
El Porta *USA*	17B3
El Portal *USA*	18C2
El Porvenir *Mexico*	14A3
El Potosí *Mexico*	20B1
El Puerto del Sta Maria *Spain*	37A2
El Qâhira = Cairo	
El Qantara *Egypt*	63B3
El Quds = Jerusalem	
El Quelite *Mexico*	20A1
El Quseima *Egypt*	63C3
El Quwetra *Jordan*	63C4
El Reno *USA*	6D3
Elsa *Can*	4E3
Elsa, R *Italy*	35D3
El Saff *Egypt*	63A4
El Sâlhîya *Egypt*	63B3
El Salto *Mexico*	20A1
El Salvador, Republic *C America*	19D3
El Sauzal *Mexico*	17C4
El Shallûfa *Egypt*	63B3
El Shatt *Egypt*	63B4
El Simbillâwein *Egypt*	63A3
Elsinore L *USA*	18D4
El Sosneade *Arg*	26B3
Elsterwerde *E Germ*	40C2
El Sueco *Mexico*	14A4
El Suweis = Suez	
El Tabbin *Egypt*	63A4
El Teleno, Mt *Spain*	37A1
Eltham *NZ*	79B1
El Thamad *Egypt*	63C4
El Tigre *Ven*	24F2
El Tîh, Desert Region *Egypt*	62B4
El Tîna *Egypt*	63B3
El Tío *Arg*	26C2
Eltopia *USA*	16C1
El Toro *Chile*	26A1
El Transito *Chile*	26A1
El Tuito *Mexico*	20A1
El Tûr *Egypt*	62B4
Elûru *India*	60C1
Elvas *Port*	37A2
Elvira *Brazil*	24D5
El Volcán *Chile*	26A2
Elwood *USA*	10B2
Ely *Eng*	33F5
Ely, Minnesota *USA*	7D2
Ely, Nevada *USA*	6B3
Elyria *USA*	10C2
El Zarqa *Egypt*	63A3
Emāmrūd *Iran*	61D1
Emām Sāheb *Afghan*	58B1
Eman, R *Sweden*	40D1
Emba *USSR*	43K6
Emba, R *USSR*	43K6
Embalse Cerros Colorados, L *Arg*	23C5
Embalse de Alarcón, Res *Spain*	37B2
Embalse de Alcántarà, Res *Spain*	37A2
Embalse de Almendra, Res *Spain*	37A1
Embalse de Garcia de Sola, Res *Spain*	37A2
Embalse de Gur., L *Ven*	24F2
Embalse de Mequinenza, Res *Spain*	37B1
Embalse de Ricobayo, Res *Spain*	37A1
Embalse de Rio Negro, Res *Urug*	23E4
Embalse El Chocón, Res *Arg*	26B3
Embalse Ezequil Ramos Mexia, L *Arg*	23C5
Embalse Florentine Ameghino, L *Arg*	23C6
Embalse Gabriel y Galan, Res *Spain*	37A1
Embalse Rio Hondo, Res *Arg*	26B1
Embarcación *Arg*	23D2
Embarras Portage *Can*	4G4
Embrun *France*	35B2
Embu *Kenya*	70D4
Emden *W Germ*	40B2
Emei *China*	50A4
Emerald *Aust*	76D3
Emeri *Can*	5M4
Emerson *Can*	4J5
Emigrant P *USA*	16C2
Emi Koussi, Mt *Chad*	70B1
Emilo Mitre *Arg*	26B3
Emirdağ *Turk*	62B2
Emmaus *USA*	12C2
Emmen *Neth*	40B2
Emmendingen *W Germ*	34D2
Emmerich *W Germ*	34D1
Emmett *USA*	16C2
Emmitsburg *USA*	12B3
Emmonak *USA*	8F3
Emory Peak, Mt *USA*	6C4
Empalme *Mexico*	19A2
Empangeni *S Africa*	72E2
Empedrado *Arg*	23E3
Emperor Seamount Chain *Pacific O*	75K2
Empoli *Italy*	35D3
Emporia, Kansas *USA*	15C2
Emporia, Virginia *USA*	11D3
Emporium *USA*	12A2
Ems, R *W Germ*	40B2
Enard, B *Scot*	32C2
Encarnacion *Mexico*	20B1
Encarnación *Par*	23E3
Enchi *Ghana*	69F4
Encinal *USA*	15F4
Encinitas *USA*	18D4
Encruzilhada *Brazil*	27D2
Encruzilhada do Sul *Brazil*	26E2
Enda Salassie *Eth*	64C4
Ende *Indon*	76B1
Enderby *Can*	3E3
Enderby Land, Region *Ant*	80G11
Enderlin *USA*	9C2
Endicott *USA*	11D2
Endicott Mts *USA*	8H2
Enfield *USA*	13D1
Engadin, Mts *Switz*	35D1
Engaño,C *Phil*	55F7
Engaru *Japan*	52D2
En Gedi *Israel*	63C3
Engelberg *Switz*	35C1
Engel's *USSR*	43H5
Enggano, I *Indon*	54B4
England, Country *UK*	31C3
Englee *Can*	5N4
Englehard *USA*	13D1
Englehart *Can*	11D1
Englewood *USA*	14B2
English, R *Can*	9D1
English Channel *Eng/France*	31C3
Enid *USA*	15C2
Eniwa *Japan*	52D2
Enji, Well *Maur*	68B3
Enkoping *Sweden*	30H7
Enna *Italy*	38C3
En Nahud *Sudan*	70C2
Ennedi, Desert Region *Chad*	70C2
Ennelen *USSR*	8C2
Enngonia *Aust*	78C1
Enning *USA*	9B3
Ennis *Irish Rep*	31B3
Ennis, Montana *USA*	16D1
Ennis, Texas *USA*	15C3
Enniscorthy *Irish Rep*	33B5
Enniskillen *N Ire*	33B4
Enn Nâqoûra *Leb*	63C2
Enns, R *Austria*	40C3
Enrekang *Indon*	55A3
Enschede *Neth*	30F8
Ensenada *Mexico*	19A1
Enshi *China*	50B3
Ensisheim *France*	34D3
Entebbe *Uganda*	70D4
Enterprise, Alabama *USA*	13B2
Enterprise *Can*	3E1
Enterprise, Oregon *USA*	16C1
Enugu *Nig*	69H4
Enurmino *USSR*	8D2
Enz, R *w Germ*	34E2
Enzan *Japan*	52C3
Epe *Nig*	69G4
Epernay *France*	36C2
Ephraim *USA*	17D3
Ephrata, Pennsylvania *USA*	12B2
Ephrata, Washington *USA*	16C1
Epi, I *Vanuatu*	77F2
Épinal *France*	36D2
Episkopi *Cyprus*	63B1
Episkopi B *Cyprus*	63B1
Eppingen *W Germ*	34E2
Epte, R *France*	34A2
Epukiro *Namibia*	72B1
Epu pel *Arg*	26C3
Eqlid *Iran*	61C2
Equator	66D7
Equatorial Guinea, Republic *Africa*	70A3
Equinox Mt *USA*	12D1
Equinunk *USA*	12C2
Erba *Italy*	35C2
Erbach *W Germ*	34E2
Erbeskopf, Mt *W Germ*	34D2
Ercilla *Chile*	26A3
Erciş *Turk*	62D2
Erciyas Daglari, Mt *Turk*	43F8
Erdaobaihe *China*	51B3
Erdene *Mongolia*	50C1
Erdenet *Mongolia*	48D2
Erdi, Desert Region *Chad*	70C2
Erechim *Brazil*	23F3
Ereğli *Turk*	62B1
Ereğli *Turk*	62B2
Erenhot *China*	48E2
Eresma, R *Spain*	37B1
Erft, R *W Germ*	34D1
Erfurt *E Germ*	40C2
Ergani *Turk*	62C2
Erg Chech, Desert Region *Alg*	68B2
Erg du Djourab, Desert Region *Chad*	70B2
Erg Du Ténéré, Desert Region *Niger*	68D3
Ergene, R *Turk*	62A1
Erg Iguidi, Region *Alg*	68B2
Ergli *USSR*	41F1
Erguig, R *Chad*	70B2
Ergun' *USSR*	47N4
Ergun, R *USSR*	48E1
Ergun Zuoqi *China*	47O4
Erguveyem, R *USSR*	8C2
Eriba *Sudan*	70D2
Erie *USA*	7F2
Erie,L *USA/Can*	7E2
Erimo-misaki, C *Japan*	52D2
Erin Port *Eng*	33C4
Eriskay, I *Scot*	32B3
Eritrea, Region *Eth*	64C3
Erkelenz *W Germ*	34D1
Erlangen *W Germ*	40C3
Erling,L *USA*	15D3
Ermelo *S Africa*	72D2
Ernākulam *India*	60B3
Erode *India*	60B2
Eromanga *Aust*	78B1
Erongoberg, Mt *Namibia*	72B1
Er Rachidia *Mor*	69B2
Er Rahad *Sudan*	70D2
Errego *Mozam*	71D5
Errigal, Mt *Irish Rep*	31B2
Erris Head, Pt *Irish Rep*	31A3
Erromanga, I *Vanuatu*	77F2
Er Roseires *Sudan*	70D2
er Rtem, R *Alg*	69C2
Er Rummān *Jordan*	63C2
Erskine *USA*	9C2
Erstein *France*	34D2
Erval *Brazil*	26E2
Erzgebirge, Upland *E Germ*	40C2
Erzincan *Turk*	43F8
Erzurum *Turk*	43G8
Esan-misaki, C *Japan*	52D2
Esara, R *Spain*	36C3
Esashi *Japan*	52D2
Esbjerg *Den*	40B1
Escalante *USA*	17D3
Escalón *Mexico*	6C4
Escanaba *USA*	7E2
Escárcega *Mexico*	19C3
Esch *Luxembourg*	34C2
Escondido *USA*	17C4
Escuinapa *Mexico*	19B2
Escuintla *Guatemala*	19C3
Eséka *Cam*	70B3
Esera, R *Spain*	37C1
Eşfahān *Iran*	61C2
Eshowe *S Africa*	72E2
Esh Sharā, Upland *Jordan*	63C3
Esino *Italy*	35E3
Eskdale *NZ*	79C1
Eskifjörður *Iceland*	30C1
Eskilstuna *Sweden*	30H7
Eskimo L *Can*	4E3
Eskimo Point *Can*	5J3
Eskisehir *Turk*	43E8
Esla, R *Spain*	37A1
Esmeraldas *Ecuador*	24C3
Esmerelda *Cuba*	21B2
Esmerelda, I *Chile*	23A7
Espalion *France*	36C3
Espanola *Can*	10C1
Espanola *USA*	14A2
Esperance *Aust*	76B4
Esperanza *Arg*	26C2
Esperanza, Base *Ant*	80G2
Espírito Santo, State *Brazil*	27D2
Espiritu Santo, I *Vanuatu*	77F2
Espungabera *Mozam*	71D6
Esquel *Arg*	23B6
Esquimalt *Can*	16B1
Esquina *Arg*	26D2
Es Samra *Jordan*	63D2
Essaourira *Mor*	69A2
Es-Sekhira *Tunisia*	69E2
Essen *W Germ*	40B2
Essequibo *Guyana*	25G3
Essex, County *Eng*	33F6
Essexville *USA*	10C2
Esslingen *W Germ*	40B3
Essonne *France*	34B2
Essoyes *France*	34C2
Estância *Brazil*	25L6
Estcourt *S Africa*	72D2
Este *Italy*	35D2
Esteli *Nic*	24A1
Esternay *France*	34B2
Estero B *USA*	18B3
Esteros *Mexico*	20C1
Esteros *Par*	23D2
Esteros del Iberá, Swamp *Arg*	26D1
Estes Park *USA*	14A1
Estevan *Can*	4H5
Estherville *USA*	9D3
Estill *USA*	13C2
Estissac *France*	34B2
Estonskaya SSR, Republic *USSR*	42C4
Estrecho de Magallanes, Str *Chile*	23B8
Estrella, R *USA*	18B3
Estremoz *Port*	37A2
Esztergom *Hung*	41D3
Etadunna *Aust*	78A1
Etam *France*	34C2
Etampes *France*	36C2
Etamunbanie,L *Aust*	78A1
Etaples *France*	34A1
Etāwah *India*	58D3
Ethiopia, Republic *Africa*	70D3
Etla *Mexico*	20C2
Etna, Mt *Italy*	38C3
Etolin I *USA*	8M4
Etolin Str *USA*	8E3
Eton *Can*	5L2
Etosha Nat Pk *Namibia*	71B5
Etosha Pan, Salt L *Namibia*	71B5
Etowah, R *USA*	13C2
Etretat *France*	34A2
Etsha, Plat *Can*	3D2
Ettelbruck *Lux*	34C2
Eua, I *Tonga*	77H3
Euabalong *Aust*	78C2
Euclid *USA*	10C2
Eucumbene,L *Aust*	78C3
Eudunda *Aust*	78A2
Eufala L *USA*	15C2
Eufaula *USA*	13B2
Eugene *USA*	6A2
Eulo *Aust*	78C1
Eunice, Louisiana *USA*	15D3
Eunice, New Mexico *USA*	14B3
Eupen *W Germ*	34D1
Euphrates, R *Iraq*	62D3
Eupora *USA*	15E3
Eure, Department *France*	34A2
Eure, R *France*	36C2
Eure-et-Loir, Department *France*	34A2
Eureka, California *USA*	16B2
Eureka *Can*	5K1
Eureka, Montana *USA*	16C1
Eureka, Nevada *USA*	6B3
Eureka, S Dakota *USA*	9C2
Eureka, Utah *USA*	17D3
Eureka, Sd *Can*	5K2
Eureka V *USA*	18D2
Euroa *Aust*	78C3
Eurombah, R *Aust*	78C1
Europa, I *Mozam Chan*	71E6
Europort *Neth*	34C1
Euskirchen *W Germ*	40B2
Eutaw *USA*	13B2
Eutsuk L *Can*	3C3
Evansburg *Can*	3E3
Evans,C *Can*	5K1
Evans,L *Can*	5L4
Evans,Mt, Colorado *USA*	14A2
Evans,Mt, Montana *USA*	16D1
Evans Str *Can*	5K3
Evanston, Illinois *USA*	10B2
Evanston, Wyoming *USA*	6B2
Evansville, Indiana *USA*	7E3
Evansville, Wyoming *USA*	9A3
Evaton *S Africa*	72D2
Everard,L *Aust*	76C4
Everest,Mt *Nepal/China*	57G3
Everett, Pennsylvania *USA*	12A2
Everett, Washington *USA*	6A2
Everett,Mt *USA*	12D1
Everglades,The, Swamp *USA*	7E4
Evergreen *USA*	13B2
Evesham *Eng*	33E5
Evinayong *Eq Guinea*	70B3
Evje *Nor*	30F7
Evolène *Switz*	35B1
Évora *Port*	37A2
Evreux *France*	36C2
Évvoia, I *Greece*	39E3
Ewo *Congo*	70B4
Excelisor Mt *USA*	18C1
Excelisor Mts *USA*	18C1
Excelsior Springs *USA*	15D2
Exeter, California *USA*	17C3
Exeter *Eng*	33D6

Exeter, New Hampshire *USA* 11E2
Exmoor Nat Pk *Eng* 33D6
Exmouth *Eng* 33D6
Extremadura, Region *Spain* 37A2
Exuma Sd *Bahamas* 19E2
Eyasi, L *Tanz* 70D4
Eyemouth *Scot* 32D4
Eyl *Somalia* 67D4
Eyre *Aust* 76B4
Eyre Creek, R *Aust* 76C3
Eyre,L *Aust* 76C3
Eyre Pen *Aust* 76C4
Eyrie L *Can* 3H2
Eyte, I *Phil* 55F8
Ezatlan *Mexico* 20B1
Ezine *Turk* 39F3
Ez Zeidab *Sudan* 64B3

F

Faber L *Can* 4G3
Fåborg *Den* 30F7
Fabriano *Italy* 38C2
Fabrosa *Italy* 35B2
Fachi *Niger* 70B2
Fada *Chad* 70C2
Fada N'Gourma *U Volta* 69G3
Faenza *Italy* 38C2
Faeringehavn *Greenland* 5N3
Faeroerne, Is *N Atlantic* 28E2
Fafa, R *CAR* 70B3
Fafan, R *Eth* 70E3
Faga, R *U Volta* 69G3
Făgăras *Rom* 39E1
Fagnes, Region *Belg* 34C1
Faguibine,L, L *Mali* 68B3
Fahud *Oman* 65G2
Faiol, I *Açores* 68A1
Fairacres *USA* 14A3
Fairbanks *USA* 4D3
Fairbault *USA* 5J5
Fairborn *USA* 10C3
Fairbury *USA* 6D2
Fairfax *USA* 12B3
Fairfield, California *USA* 17B3
Fairfield, Connecticut *USA* 12D2
Fairfield, Idaho *USA* 16D2
Fairfield, Montana *USA* 16D1
Fairfield, Ohio *USA* 10C3
Fair Head, Pt *N Ire* 32B4
Fair Isle, I *Scot* 31C2
Fairlie *NZ* 79B2
Fairmont, Minnesota *USA* 9D3
Fairmont, W Virginia *USA* 10C3
Fairport *USA* 12B1
Fairview *Can* 3E2
Fairview *USA* 14C2
Fairweather,Mt *USA* 4E4
Fais, I *Pacific O* 49H6
Faisalabad *Pak* 58C2
Faith *USA* 9B2
Faither,The, Pen *Scot* 32E1
Faizabad *Afghan* 58C1
Faizābād *India* 59B2
Fakaofo, I *Tokeau Is* 77H1
Fakenham *Eng* 33F5
Fakfak *Indon* 76C1
Faköping *Sweden* 30G7
Falaise de Banfora *U Volta* 69F3
Falam *Burma* 59D3
Falckner *Arg* 26B4
Falcon Res *USA/Mexico* 19C2
Falémé, R *Mali/Sen* 68A3
Falfurrias *USA* 15F4
Falkenberg *Sweden* 30G7
Falkirk *Scot* 32D4
Falkland Is, Dependency *S Atlantic* 23D8
Falkland Sd *Falkland Is* 23E8
Fallbrook *USA* 18D4
Fallon *USA* 6B3
Fall River *USA* 11E2
Fall River P *USA* 14A1
Falls City *USA* 15C1
Falmouth *Eng* 33C6
Falmouth *Jamaica* 21H1
Falmouth, Maine *USA* 11E2
Falmouth, Massachusetts *USA* 12E2
False B *S Africa* 72B3
Falso,C *Mexico* 19A2
Falster, I *Den* 40C2
Fălticeni *Rom* 39F1
Falun *Sweden* 30H6
Famagusta *Cyprus* 62B2
Famagusta B *Cyprus* 63B1
Famatina *Arg* 26B1
Famenne, Region *Belg* 34C1
Famoso *USA* 18C3
Fang *Thai* 53B2
Fangak *Sudan* 70D3
Fang liao *Taiwan* 50E5
Fangzheng *China* 51B2
Fano *Italy* 38C2
Fâqûs *Egypt* 63A3
Faraday, Base *Ant* 80G3
Faradje *Zaïre* 70C3
Farafangana *Madag* 71E6
Farafra Oasis *Egypt* 67B2
Farah *Afghan* 61E2
Farah, R *Afghan* 61E2
Farallon de Medinilla, I *Pacific O* 49H5
Faranah *Guinea* 68A3
Faraulep, I *Pacific O* 49H6
Fareham *Eng* 33E6
Farewell,C = Kap Farvel
Farewell,C *NZ* 77G5
Farewell Spit, Pt *NZ* 79B2
Fargo *USA* 6D2
Fari'a, R *Israel* 63C2
Faribault *USA* 7D2
Faridpur *Bang* 59C3
Farīmān *Iran* 61D1
Fâriskûr *Egypt* 63A3
Farmington, Maine *USA* 11E2
Farmington, Missouri *USA* 15D2
Farmington, New Hampshire *USA* 12E1
Farmington, New Mexico *USA* 6C3
Farmington, Utah *USA* 16D2
Farmington Res *USA* 18B2
Farne Deep *N Sea* 32E4
Farnham,Mt *Can* 3E3
Faro *Can* 8M3
Faro *Port* 37A2
Fåro, I *Sweden* 30H7
Faro, R *Cam* 69J4
Farquhar, Is *Indian O* 66K8
Farrar, R *Scot* 32C3
Farrell *USA* 10C2
Fársala *Greece* 39E3
Farsi *Afghan* 61E2
Farwell *USA* 14B3
Fasā *Iran* 61C3
Fastov *USSR* 43D5
Fatehpur *India* 59B2
Father *Can* 3E2
Fatima du Sul *Brazil* 25H7
Fauquier *Can* 16C1
Fauresmith *S Africa* 72D2
Faverges *France* 35B2
Fawn, R *Can* 5K4
Fax, R *Sweden* 30H6
Faxaflóri, B *Iceland* 30A2
Faya *Chad* 70B2
Fayette *USA* 13B2
Fayetteville, Arkansas *USA* 7D3
Fayetteville, N Carolina *USA* 7F3
Fayetteville, Tennessee *USA* 13B1
Fâyid *Egypt* 63B3
Faylakah, I *Kuwait* 62E4
Fāzilka *India* 58C2
Fdérik *Maur* 68A2
Fear,C *USA* 7F3
Feather Middle Fork, R *USA* 17B3
Feather Middle Fork, R *USA* 18B1
Fécamp *France* 34A2
Federación *Arg* 26D2
Federal *Arg* 26D2
Federal Capital Territory *Nig* 69H4
Federated States of Micronesia, Is *Pacific O* 49H6
Fehmarn, I *W Germ* 40C2
Feijó *Brazil* 24D5
Feilai Xai Bei Jiang, R *China* 50C5
Feilding *NZ* 79C2
Feira *Zambia* 71D5
Feira de Santan *Brazil* 25L6
Feke *Turk* 62C2
Feldberg, Mt *W Germ* 34D3
Feldkirch *Austria* 40B3
Feliciano, R *Arg* 26D2
Felixstowe *Eng* 31D3
Feltre *Italy* 35D1
Femund, L *Nor* 30G6
Fengcheng *China* 51A3
Fengdu *China* 50B4
Fenging *China* 50D1
Fengjie *China* 50B3
Fengshui Shan, Mt *China* 51A1
Feng Xian *China* 50B3
Fengzhen *China* 50C1
Fen He, R *China* 50C2
Fenimore Pass *USA* 8C6
Fenoarivo Atsinanana *Madag* 71E5
Feodosiya *USSR* 43F7
Ferdow *Iran* 61D2
Fère *France* 34B2
Fère-Champenoise *France* 34B2
Fergana *USSR* 57F2
Fergus, R *Can* 3J2
Fermanagh, County *N Ire* 33B4
Fermo *Italy* 35E3
Fern, Mt *Austria* 35D1
Fernandez *Arg* 26C1
Fernandina Beach *USA* 13C2
Fernando de Noronha, I *Atlantic O* 73G5
Fernandópolis *Brazil* 27B3
Fernando Poo, I *Eq Guinea* 68C4
Ferndale *USA* 16B1
Fernie *Can* 16C1
Fernley *USA* 17C3
Ferrara *Italy* 38C2
Ferreñafe *Peru* 24C5
Ferriday *USA* 15D3
Ferriéres *France* 34B2
Fès *Mor* 69A2
Festus *USA* 15D2
Feteşti *Rom* 39F2
Fethiye *Turk* 62A2
Fetisovo *USSR* 43J7
Fetlar, I *Scot* 32E1
Fevral'skoye *USSR* 51C1
Feyzabad *Afghan* 46J6
Fiambalá *Arg* 26B1
Fianarantsoa *Madag* 71E6
Fiche *Eth* 70D3
Ficksburg *S Africa* 72D2
Fidenza *Italy* 35D2
Fier *Alb* 39D2
Fiera Di Primeiro *Italy* 35D1
Fife, Region *Scot* 32D3
Fife Ness, Pen *Scot* 32D3
Figeac *France* 36C3
Figueira da Foz *Port* 37A1
Figueras *Spain* 37C1
Figuig *Mor* 69B2
Fiji, Is *Pacific O* 77G2
Filadelpia *Par* 25G8
Filiaşi *Rom* 39E2
Filiatrá *Greece* 39E3
Filicudi, I *Italy* 38C3
Fillmore, California *USA* 17C4
Fillmore, Utah *USA* 17D3
Finale Ligure *Italy* 35C2
Findhorn, R *Scot* 32C3
Findlay *USA* 7E2
Findlay,Mt *Can* 3E3
Finger Lakes *USA* 11D2
Fingoè *Mozam* 71D5
Finike *Turk* 43E8
Finke, R *Aust* 76C3
Finke Flood Flats *Aust* 78A1
Finland, Republic *N Europe* 42C3
Finland,G of *N Europe* 30J7
Finlay, R *Can* 4F4
Finlay Forks *Can* 4F4
Finley *Aust* 78C3
Finnsnes *Nor* 30H5
Finschhafen *PNG* 49H7
Finsteraarhorn, Mt *Switz* 35C1
Finsterwalde *E Germ* 40C2
Fintona *N Ire* 33B4
Fiordland Nat Pk *NZ* 79A3
Fiq *Syria* 63C2
Firat, R *Turk* 43F8
Firebag, R *Can* 3F2
Firebaugh *USA* 18B2
Firenze *Italy* 38C2
Firenzuola *Italy* 35D2
Fireside *Can* 3C2
Firmat *Arg* 26C2
Firozābād *India* 58D3
Firozpur *India* 58C2
Firspång *Sweden* 30H7
Firth of Clyde, Estuary *Scot* 32C4
Firth of Forth, Estuary *Scot* 32D3
Firth of Lorn, Estuary *Scot* 32B3
Firth of Tay, Estuary *Scot* 31C2
Firūzābād *Iran* 61C3
Fish, R *Namibia* 72B2
Fish, R *S Africa* 72C3
Fish Camp *USA* 18C2
Fishers I *USA* 12D2
Fisher Str *Can* 5K3
Fishguard *Wales* 33C6
Fish L *Can* 8O3
Fiskenaesset *Greenland* 5N3
Fismes *France* 34B2
Fitchburg *USA* 11E2
Fitful Head, Pt *Scot* 32E2
Fitzgerald *Can* 3F2
Fitzgerald *USA* 13C2
Fitzroy, R *Aust* 76B2
Fitzroy Crossing *Aust* 76B2
Fitzwilliam I *Can* 10C1
Fiume = Rijeka
Fizi *Zaïre* 70C4
Flagstaff *S Africa* 72D3
Flagstaff *USA* 6B3
Flagstaff L *USA* 11E1
Flamborough Head, C *Eng* 33E4
Flaming Gorge Res *USA* 6C2
Flannan Isles, Is *Scot* 32B2
Flat, R *Can* 8N3
Flathead, R *USA* 3F4
Flathead L *USA* 6B2
Flat River *USA* 15D2
Flattery,C *Aust* 49H8
Flattery,C *USA* 6A2
Fleetwood *Eng* 33D5
Flekkefjord, Inlet *Nor* 30F7
Fleming Deep *Pacific Oc* 48H4
Flemington *USA* 12C2
Flensburg *W Germ* 40B2
Fleurier *Switz* 35B1
Fleury-sur-Andelle *France* 34A2
Flinders, I *Aust* 76C4
Flinders, I *Aust* 76D5
Flinders, R *Aust* 76D2
Flinders Range, Mts *Aust* 76C4
Flin Flon·*Can* 4H4
Flint *USA* 7E2
Flint *Wales* 33D5
Flint, R *USA* 7E3
Flixecourt *France* 34B1
Floodwood *USA* 10A1
Florala *USA* 13B2
Florence = Firenze
Florence, Alabama *USA* 7E3
Florence, Arizona *USA* 17D4
Florence, Colorado *USA* 14A2
Florence, Kansas *USA* 15C2
Florence, Oregon *USA* 16B2
Florence, S Carolina *USA* 7F3
Florence L *USA* 18C2
Florencia *Colombia* 24C3
Florenville *Belg* 34C2
Flores *Guatemala* 19D3
Flores, I *Açores* 68A1
Flores, I *Indon* 76B1
Flores, R *Arg* 26D3
Flores S *Indon* 49E7
Floriano *Brazil* 25K5
Florianópolis *Brazil* 23G3
Florida, State *USA* 19D2
Florida *Urug* 23E4
Florida B *USA* 13E4
Florida City *USA* 13E4
Florida Is *Solomon Is* 77E1
Florida Keys, Is *USA* 7E4
Florida,Strs of *USA* 7E4
Flórina *Greece* 39E2
Florø *Nor* 30F6
Floydada *USA* 14B3
Fluchthorn, Mt *Austria* 35D1
Fluk *Indon* 55C3
Fly, R *PNG* 76D1
Foci del Po, Delta *Italy* 35E2
Focsani *Rom* 39F1
Foggia *Italy* 38D2
Foglia, R *Italy* 35E3
Fogo, I *Cape Verde* 68A4
Foix *France* 36C3
Foleyet *Can* 10C1
Foley I *Can* 5L3
Foligno *Italy* 38C2
Folkestone *Eng* 33F6
Folkston *USA* 13C2
Follonica *Italy* 38C2
Folsom *USA* 18B1
Folsom L, L *USA* 18B1
Fonda *USA* 12C1
Fond-du-Lac *Can* 4H4
Fond du Lac *USA* 7E2
Fontainbleau *France* 36C2
Fontas, R *Can* 3D2
Fontenac *USA* 15D2
Fontenay-le-Comte *France* 36B2
Fonyód *Hung* 39D1
Foochow = Fuzhou
Foraker,Mt *USA* 8H3
Forbach *France* 34D2
Forbes *Aust* 78C2
Forcados *Nig* 69H4
Forcalquier *France* 35A3
Ford City *USA* 18C3
Forde *Nor* 30F6
Fords Bridge *Aust* 78C1
Fordyce *USA* 15D3
Forécarian *Guinea* 68A4
Forel,Mt *Greenland* 5P3
Foremost *Can* 16D1
Forest *Can* 10C2
Forest *USA* 13B2
Forest City, Iowa *USA* 9D3
Forest City, Pennsylvania *USA* 12C2
Forest Park *USA* 13C2
Forestville *USA* 18A1
Forêt d'Othe *France* 34B2
Forfar *Scot* 32D3
Forgan *USA* 14B2
Forges-les-Eaux *France* 34A2
Forks *USA* 16B1
Forlì *Italy* 38C2
Formentera, I *Spain* 37C2
Formia *Italy* 38C2
Formigas, I *Açores* 68A1
Formosa = Taiwan
Formosa *Arg* 23E3
Formosa *Brazil* 25J7
Formosa, State *Arg* 23D2
Formosa Str *Taiwan/China* 50D5
Formoso *Brazil* 27C1
Formoso, R *Brazil* 27C1
Fornovo di Taro *Italy* 35D2
Forres *Scot* 32D3
Forrest *Aust* 76B4
Forrest City *USA* 7D3
Forrest L *Can* 3G2
Forsayth *Aust* 76D2
Forssa *Fin* 30J6
Forster *Aust* 78D2
Forsyth, Missouri *USA* 15D2
Forsyth, Montana *USA* 9A2
Fort Abbas *Pak* 58C3
Fort Albany *Can* 5K4
Fortaleza *Brazil* 25L4
Fort Augustus *Scot* 32C3
Fort Beaufort *S Africa* 72D3
Fort Benton *USA* 16D1
Fort Bragg *USA* 17B3
Fort Chimo *Can* 5M4
Fort Chipewyan *Can* 3F2
Fort Cobb Res *USA* 14C2
Fort Collins *USA* 6C2
Fort Coulogne *Can* 11D1
Fort Davis *USA* 14B3
Fort de France *Martinique* 21E4
Fort Deposit *USA* 13B2
Fort Dodge *USA* 7D2
Fortescue, R *Aust* 76A3
Fort Frances *Can* 5J5
Fort Franklin *Can* 4F3
Fort George *Can* 5L4
Fort Good Hope *Can* 4F3
Fort Grey *Aust* 78B1
Forth, R *Scot* 32C3
Fort Hancock *USA* 14A3
Fort Hope *Can* 5K4
Forties, Oilfield *N Sea* 32F3
Fortin Uno *Arg* 26B3
Fort Kent *USA* 11F1
Fort Laird *Can* 4F3
Fort Lallemand *Alg* 68C1
Fort Lamy = N'Djamena
Fort Laramie *USA* 9B3
Fort Lauderdale *USA* 7E4
Fort Liard *Can* 3D1
Fort Mackay *Can* 4G4
Fort Macleod *Can* 4G5
Fort McMurray *Can* 4G4
Fort McPherson *Can* 4E3
Fort Madison *USA* 10A2
Fort Morgan *USA* 6C2
Fort Myers *USA* 7E4
Fort Nelson *Can* 4F4
Fort Nelson, R *Can* 3D2
Fort Norman *Can* 4F3
Fort Payne *USA* 13B2
Fort Peck *USA* 9A2
Fort Peck Res *USA* 6C2
Fort Pierce *USA* 7E4
Fort Pierre *USA* 9B3
Fort Plain *USA* 12C1
Fort Providence *Can* 4G3
Fort Qu'Appelle *Can* 3G3
Fort Randall *USA* 8F4
Fort Resolution *Can* 4G3
Fort Rousset *Congo* 70B4
Fort Rupert *Can* 5L4
Fort St James *Can* 4F4
Fort St John *Can* 3D2
Fort Saskatchewan *Can* 3F3
Fort Scott *USA* 15D2
Fort Selkirk *Can* 4E3
Fort Severn *Can* 5K4
Fort Shevchenko *USSR* 43J7
Fort Simpson *Can* 4F3
Fort Smith *Can* 4G3
Fort Smith *USA* 7D3
Fort Stockton *USA* 6C3
Fort Sumner *USA* 14B3
Fort Supply *USA* 14C2
Fortuna, California *USA* 16B2
Fortuna, N Dakota *USA* 9B2
Fort Vermillion *Can* 4G4
Fort Walton Beach *USA* 13B2
Fort Wayne *USA* 7E2
Fort William *Scot* 32C3
Fort Wingate *USA* 14A2
Fort Worth *USA* 6D3
Fortymile, R *USA* 8K3
Fort Yukon *USA* 8J2
Foshan *China* 50C5
Fossano *Italy* 35B2
Fossombrone *Italy* 35E3
Fosston *USA* 9C2
Foster L *Can* 3G2
Foster,Mt *USA* 8L4
Fougamou *Gabon* 70B4
Fougères *France* 36B2
Foula, I *Scot* 32D1
Foulness I *Eng* 33F6
Foulwind,C *NZ* 79B2
Foumban *Cam* 70B3
Fourmies *France* 36C1
Four Mountains,Is of *USA* 8E5
Foúrnoi, I *Greece* 39F3

Fouta Djallon, Mts *Guinea* 68A3
Foveaux Str *NZ* 77F5
Fowey *Eng* 33C6
Fowler *USA* 14B2
Fox, R *Can* 3C2
Fox, R *USA* 10B2
Fox Creek *Can* 3E3
Foxe Basin, G *Can* 5K3
Foxe Chan *Can* 5K3
Foxe Pen *Can* 5L3
Fox Is *USA* 8E5
Fox Lake *Can* 3F2
Foxpark *USA* 14A1
Foxton *NZ* 79C2
Fox Valley *Can* 3G3
Foz do Cuene *Angola* 71B5
Foz do Iquaçu *Brazil* 23F3
Francisco I Madero *Mexico* 20B1
Frackville *USA* 12B2
Fraga *Arg* 26B2
Framingham *USA* 12E1
Franca *Brazil* 25J8
France, Republic *Europe* 36C2
Frances *Can* 7D2
Frances, R *Can* 8N3
France Ville *Gabon* 70B4
Franche Comté, Region *France* 36D2
Francistown *Botswana* 72D1
Francois L *Can* 3C3
Francs Peak, Mt *USA* 16E2
Frankenberg *W Germ* 34E1
Frankfort, Indiana *USA* 10B2
Frankfort, Kentucky *USA* 7E3
Frankfort, New York *USA* 12C1
Frankfort *S Africa* 72D2
Frankfurt *W Germ* 40B2
Frankfurt am Main *W Germ* 34E1
Frankfurt-an-der-Oder *E Germ* 40C2
Fränkischer Alb, Upland *W Germ* 40C3
Franklin, Idaho *USA* 16D2
Franklin, Indiana *USA* 10B3
Franklin, Louisiana *USA* 15D4
Franklin, Massachusetts *USA* 12E1
Franklin, N Carolina *USA* 13C1
Franklin, New Hampshire *USA* 12E1
Franklin, New Jersey *USA* 12C2
Franklin, Pennsylvania *USA* 11D2
Franklin, Tennessee *USA* 13B1
Franklin, Virginia *USA* 11D3
Franklin, Region *Can* 4G2
Franklin B *Can* 4F2
Franklin D Roosevelt, L *USA* 16C1
Franklin Mts *Can* 4F3
Franklin,Pt *USA* 8G1
Franklin Str *Can* 4J2
Franklinville *USA* 12A1
Frankovsk *USSR* 46D5
Franz Josef Glacier *NZ* 79B2
Franz-Joseph-Land = Zemlya Franza Josifa
Fraser, R *Can* 4F5
Fraserburg *S Africa* 72C3
Fraserburgh *Scot* 32D3
Fraser I *Aust* 78D1
Fraser L *Can* 3C3
Frasne *France* 35B1
Frauenfeld *Switz* 35C1
Fray Bentos *Urug* 26D2
Frazerburgh *Scot* 31C2
Frederica *USA* 12C3
Fredericia *Den* 40B1
Frederick, Maryland *USA* 11D3
Frederick, Oklahoma *USA* 14C3
Fredericksburg, Texas *USA* 14C3
Fredericksburg, Virginia *USA* 11D3
Frederick Sd *USA* 8M4
Frederickstown *USA* 10A3
Fredericktown *USA* 15D2
Fredericton *Can* 5M5
Frederikshap *Greenland* 5N3
Frederikshavn *Den* 30G7
Fredonia *USA* 11D2
Fredrikstad *Nor* 30G7
Freehold *USA* 12C2
Freel Peak, Mt *USA* 18C1
Freeman *USA* 9C3
Freeport *Bahamas* 21B1
Freeport, Illinois *USA* 10B2
Freeport, Texas *USA* 15C4
Freer *USA* 15F4
Freetown *Sierra Leone* 68A4
Freiburg *W Germ* 40B3
Freiburg im Breisgau *W Germ* 34D2
Freirina *Chile* 26A1
Freistadt *Austria* 40C3
Fréjus *France* 35B3
Fremantle *Aust* 76A4
Fremont, California *USA* 18B2
Fremont, Nebraska *USA* 15C1
Fremont, Ohio *USA* 10C2
French Guiana, Dependency *S America* 25H3
Frenchman, R *USA* 9A2
Frenchmans Cap, Mt *Aust* 78E3
French Polynesia, Is *Pacific O* 75M5
Frenda *Alg* 69C1
Fresnillo *Mexico* 19B2
Fresno *USA* 6B3
Fresno, R *USA* 18C2
Fresno Res *USA* 16D1
Fretigney *France* 35A1
Freudenstadt *W Germ* 34E2
Frévent *France* 34B1
Freycinet Pen *Aust* 78E3
Fria *Guinea* 68A3
Friant *USA* 18C2
Friant Dam *USA* 18C2
Frías *Arg* 26B1
Fribourg *Switz* 38B1
Friedberg *W Germ* 34E1
Friedrichshafen *W Germ* 40B3
Frio, R *USA* 14C4
Friona *USA* 14B3
Friuli, Region *Italy* 35E1
Frobisher B *Can* 5M3
Frobisher Bay *Can* 5M3
Frobisher L *Can* 4H4
Frolovo *USSR* 43G6
Frome *Eng* 33D6
Frome, R *Aust* 78A1
Frome, R *Eng* 33D6
Frome,L *Aust* 76C4
Frontera *Mexico* 19C3
Front Royal *USA* 11D3
Frosinone *Italy* 38C2
Frostburg *USA* 12A3
Fruita *USA* 14A2
Frunze *USSR* 57F1
Fuchuan *China* 50C5
Fuding *China* 50E4
Fuerte, R *Mexico* 19B2
Fuerte Olimpo *Brazil* 27A3
Fuerte Olimpo *Par* 23E2
Fuerteventura, I *Canary Is* 68A2
Fugu *China* 50C2
Fuhai *China* 48B2
Fujairah *UAE* 65G1
Fuji *Japan* 52C3
Fujian Province *China* 50D4
Fujin *China* 51C2
Fujinomiya *Japan* 52C3
Fuji-san, Mt *Japan* 51D4
Fujisawa *Japan* 52C3
Fuji-Yoshida *Japan* 52C3
Fukagawa *Japan* 52D2
Fukang *China* 46K5
Fukuchiyima *Japan* 51C4
Fukue *Japan* 52A4
Fukue, I *Japan* 52A4
Fukui *Japan* 51D4
Fukuoka *Japan* 51C5
Fukushima *Japan* 51E4
Fukuyama *Japan* 51C5
Fulda *USA* 9C3
Fulda *W Germ* 40B2
Fulda, R *W Germ* 40B2
Fuling *China* 50B4
Fullarton *Trinidad* 21L1
Fullerton *USA* 18D4
Fulton, Illinois *USA* 10A2
Fulton, Kentucky *USA* 10B3
Fulton, New York *USA* 11D2
Fumay *France* 34C1
Funabashi *Japan* 52D3
Funafuti, I *Tuvalu* 77G1
Funchal *Medeira* 68A1
Fundão *Brazil* 27D2
Fundy,B of *Can* 5M5
Funhalouro *Mozam* 71D6
Funing *China* 50B5
Funing *China* 50D3
Funtua *Nig* 69H3
Fuqing *China* 50D4
Furancungo *Mozam* 71D5
Furano *Japan* 52D2
Fürg *Iran* 61D3
Furka, P *Switz* 35C1
Furneaux Group, Is *Aust* 76D5
Fürstenwalde *E Germ* 40C2
Fürth *W Germ* 40C3
Furubira *Japan* 52D2
Furukawa *Japan* 51D4
Fury and Hecla St *Can* 5K3
Fushun, Liaoning *China* 51A3
Fushun, Sichuan *China* 50A4
Fusong *China* 51B3
Füssen *W Germ* 40C3
Fu Xian *China* 50E2
Fuxin *China* 50E1
Fuyang *China* 50D3
Fuyu *China* 51A2
Fuyuan, Heilongjiang *China* 51C2
Fuyuan, Liaoning *China* 50E1
Fuyuan, Yunnan *China* 50A4
Fuyun *China* 48B2
Fuzhou *China* 50D4
Fyn, I *Den* 40C1

G

Gaalkacyo *Somalia* 70E3
Gabbs *USA* 17C3
Gabbs Valley Range, Mts *USA* 18C1
Gabela *Angola* 71B5
Gabe's *Tunisia* 69E2
Gabgaba, Watercourse *Egypt* 64B2
Gabilan Range, Mts *USA* 18B2
Gabon, Republic *Africa* 70B4
Gaborone *Botswana* 72D1
Gabrovo *Bulg* 39F2
Gach Sārān *Iran* 61C2
Gadsden, Alabama *USA* 13B2
Gadsden, Arizona *USA* 17D4
Gads L *Can* 7D1
Gaeta *Italy* 38C2
Gaferut, I *Pacific O* 49H6
Gaffney *USA* 13C1
Gafsa *Tunisia* 69D2
Gafsa *Tunisia* 69D2
Gagarin *USSR* 42E4
Gagere, R *Nig* 69H3
Gagnon *Can* 5M4
Gagra *USSR* 43G7
Gaibanda *India* 59C2
Gailtaler Alpen, Mts *Austria* 35E1
Gaimán *Arg* 23C6
Gainesville, Florida *USA* 13C3
Gainesville, Georgia *USA* 13C2
Gainesville, Texas *USA* 15C3
Gainsborough *Eng* 33E5
Gairdner,L *Aust* 78A2
Gairloch *Scot* 32C3
Gaithersburg *USA* 12B3
Gajendragarh *India* 60B1
Ga Jiang, R *China* 50D4
Gakarosa, Mt *S Africa* 72C2
Galadi *Eth* 70E3
Galana, R *Kenya* 70D4
Galapagos Is *Pacific O* 73D4
Galashiels *Scot* 32D4
Galaţi *Rom* 39F1
Galax *USA* 10C3
Galeana *Mexico* 14A3
Galela *Indon* 55C2
Galena, Alaska *USA* 4C3
Galena, Illinois *USA* 10A2
Galena, Kansas *USA* 15D2
Galeota Pt *Trinidad* 21L1
Galera Pt *Trinidad* 21L1
Galesburg *USA* 10A2
Galeton *USA* 12B2
Galich *USSR* 42G4
Galicia, Region *Spain* 37A1
Galilee,S of = Tiberias,L
Galina Pt *Jamaica* 21J1
Gallabat *Sudan* 64C4
Gallarate *Italy* 35C2
Gallatin *USA* 13B1
Gallatin, R *USA* 16D1
Galle *Sri Lanka* 60C3
Gallego *Mexico* 14A4
Gállego, R *Spain* 37B1
Gallipoli = Gelibolu
Gallipoli *Italy* 39D2
Gällivare *Sweden* 42C2
Galloway, District 32C4
Galloway,Mull of, C *Scot* 33C4
Gallup *USA* 14A2
Galma, R *Nig* 69H3
Galt *USA* 18B1
Galveston *USA* 19C2
Galveston B *USA* 7D4
Galvez *Arg* 26C2
Galvi *Corse* 36D3
Galway *Irish Rep* 31B3
Galway, B *Irish Rep* 31B3
Gam, I *Indon* 55D3
Gamba *China* 59C2
Gambaga *Ghana* 69F3
Gambell *USA* 8D3
Gambia, R *The Gambia/Sen* 68A3
Gambia,The, Republic *Africa* 68A3
Gambia,The, Republic *W Africa* 66C6
Gamboma *Congo* 70B4
Gambos *Angola* 71B5
Gampola *Sri Lanka* 60C3
Ganado *USA* 17E3
Ganale Dorya, R *Eth* 70E3
Gananoque *Can* 11D2
Gand = Gent
Ganda *Angola* 71B5
Gandajika *Zaïre* 71C4
Gandava *Pak* 58B3
Gander *Can* 5N5
Gāndhīdhām *India* 58B4
Gāndhīnagar *India* 58C4
Gāndhi Sāgar, L *India* 58D4
Gandia *Spain* 37B2
Gandu *Brazil* 27E1
Ganga, R *India* 44F4
Ganga, R *India* 59C3
Ganganar *India* 58C3
Gangaw *Burma* 59D3
Gangaw Range, Mts *Burma* 59E3
Gangca *China* 50A2
Gangdise Shan, Mts *China* 57G2
Ganges = Ganga
Gangtok *India* 59C2
Gangu *China* 50B3
Gan He, R *China* 51A1
Gani *Indon* 55C3
Gannan *China* 51A2
Gannett Peak, Mt *USA* 16E2
Ganquan *China* 50B2
Gantheaume, C *Aust* 78A3
Gantseviohi *USSR* 30K8
Ganye *Nig* 69J4
Ganzhou *China* 50D4
Gao *Mali* 68C3
Gaolan *China* 50A2
Gaoping *China* 50C2
Gaoua *U Volta* 69F3
Gaoual *Guinea* 68A3
Gaoyou Hu, L *China* 50D3
Gaozhou *China* 50C5
Gap *France* 36D3
Gapan *Phil* 55F7
Gar *China* 58D2
Garah *Aust* 78C1
Garanhuns *Brazil* 25L5
Garberville *USA* 17B2
Garça *Brazil* 27C3
Garcias *Brazil* 27B3
Garda *Italy* 35D2
Gardanne *France* 35A3
Garden City *USA* 14B2
Garden Pen *USA* 10B1
Gardey *Arg* 26D3
Gardez *Afghan* 58B2
Gardiner *USA* 16D1
Gardiners I *USA* 12D2
Gardner *USA* 12E1
Gardner, I *Phoenix Is* 77H1
Gardnerville *USA* 18C1
Gardone *Italy* 35D2
Gardula *Eth* 70D3
Gareloi, I *USA* 8C6
Gargano *Italy* 35D2
Garhākota *India* 58D4
Gari *USSR* 42L4
Garies *S Africa* 72B3
Garissa *Kenya* 70D4
Garland *USA* 15C3
Garmisch-Partenkirchen *W Germ* 40C3
Garmsar *Iran* 61C1
Garnett *USA* 15C2
Garnett Peak, Mt *USA* 6B2
Garonne, R *France* 36C3
Garoua *Cam* 69J4
Garoua Boulai *Cam* 69J4
Garrison *USA* 9B2
Garry, R *Scot* 32C3
Garut *Indon* 54C4
Garwa *India* 59B3
Gary *USA* 10B2
Garyarsa *China* 57G2
Gary L *Can* 4H3
Garza *Arg* 26C1
Garza-Little Elm, Res *USA* 15C3
Gasan Kuli *USSR* 61C1
Gascogne, Region *France* 36B3
Gasconade, R *USA* 15D2
Gascoyne, R *Aust* 76A3
Gashaka *Nig* 70B3
Gasht *Iran* 61E3
Gashua *Nig* 69J3
Gaspé *Can* 7G2
Gaspé,C *Can* 7G2
Gaspé Pen *Can* 7G2
Gastonia *USA* 13C1
Gaston,L *USA* 13D1
Gata,C *Cyprus* 63B1
Gatchina *USSR* 42D4
Gateshead *Eng* 32D4
Gatesville *USA* 15C3
Gâtinais, Region *France* 34B2
Gatineau *Can* 11D1
Gatineau, R *Can* 11D1
Gatlinburg *USA* 13C1
Gatton *Aust* 78D1
Gaua, I *Vanuatu* 77F2
Gaud-i-Zirreh, Salt Desert *Afghan* 61E2
Gauhāti *India* 59D2
Gauja, R *USSR* 41E1
Gaurdak *USSR* 61F1
Gauri Phanta *India* 59B2
Gavdhos, I *Greece* 39E4
Gavião, R *Brazil* 27D1
Gaviota *USA* 18B3
Gävle *Sweden* 30H6
Gawler Ranges, Mts *Aust* 78A2
Gaxun Nur, L *China* 50A1
Gaya *India* 59B3
Gaya *Niger* 69G3
Gaya, R *China* 51B3
Gaylord *USA* 10C1
Gayndah *Aust* 78D1
Gayny *USSR* 42J3
Gaysin *USSR* 41F3
Gaza *Israel* 62B3
Gaziantep *Turk* 62C2
Gbaringa *Lib* 68B4
Gdańsk *Pol* 41D2
Gdansk *Sweden* 66F2
Gdańsk,G of *Pol* 41D2
Gdov *USSR* 30K7
Gdynia *Pol* 41D2
Gebe, I *Indon* 55C3
Gebel Abu Rûtha, Mt *Egypt* 63C4
Gebel Araif el Naqa, Mt *Egypt* 63C3
Gebel Ataqa, Mt *Egypt* 63B4
Gebel Budhiya *Egypt* 63B4
Gebel el Galâla Baharîya, Desert *Egypt* 63A4
Gebel El Giddi, Mt *Egypt* 63B3
Gebel El Tîh, Upland *Egypt* 63B4
Gebel Halâl, Mt *Egypt* 63B3
Gebel Hamata, Mt *Egypt* 64C2
Gebel Katherina, Mt *Egypt* 62B4
Gebel Kharim, Mt *Egypt* 63B4
Gebel Libni, Mt *Egypt* 63B3
Gebel Maghâra, Mt *Egypt* 63B3
Gebel Sha'îra, Mt *Egypt* 63C4
Gebel Sinn Bishr, Mt *Egypt* 63B4
Gebel Yi'allaq, Mt *Egypt* 63B3
Gebés *Tunisia* 69E2
Gedad del Maiz *Mexico* 20C1
Gedaref *Sudan* 64C4
Gediz, R *Turk* 39F3
Gedser *Den* 40C2
Geel *Belg* 34C1
Geelong *Aust* 78B3
Geeveston *Aust* 78E3
Geidam *Nig* 69J3
Geikie, R *Can* 3H2
Geilenkirchen *W Germ* 34D1
Geita *Tanz* 70D4
Gejiu *China* 50A5
Gela *Italy* 38C3
Geldern *W Germ* 34D1
Gelibolu *Turk* 39F2
Gelidonya Burun *Turk* 62B2
Gelleana *Mexico* 20B1
Gelnhausen *W Germ* 34E1
Gelsenkirchen *W Germ* 34D1
Gelting *W Germ* 30F8
Gemas *Malay* 53C5
Gembloux *Belg* 34C1
Gembut *Nig* 69J4
Gemena *Zaïre* 70B3
Gemerek *Turk* 62C2
Gemlik *Turk* 62A1
Gemona *Italy* 38C1
Gemona del Friuli *Italy* 35E1
Gemsbok Nat Pk *Botswana* 72C2
Geneina *Sudan* 70C2
General Acha *Arg* 26C3
General Alvear, Buenos Aires *Arg* 26C3
General Alvear, Mendoza *Arg* 26B2
General Arenales *Arg* 26C2
General Belgrano *Arg* 26D3
General Belgrano, Base *Ant* 80F2
General Bernardo O'Higgins, Base *Ant* 80G2
General Capdevia *Arg* 26C1
General Conesa, Buenos Aires *Arg* 26D3
General Conesa, Rio Negro *Arg* 26C4
General Eugenio A Garay *Arg* 23D2
General Eugenio A Garay *Par* 24F8
General Grant Grove Section, Region *USA* 18C2
General Guido *Arg* 26D3
General La Madrid *Arg* 26C3
General Lavalle *Arg* 26D3
General Levalle *Arg* 26C2
General Madariaga *Arg* 26D3
General Manuel Belgrano, Mt *Arg* 23C3
General Paz, Buenos Aires *Arg* 26D3
General Paz, Corrientes *Arg* 26D1
General Pico *Arg* 26C3
General Pinto *Arg* 26C2
General Pirán *Arg* 26D3
General Roca *Arg* 23C5

General San Bolivar *Mexico* 20B1
General Santos *Phil* 55G9
General Viamonte *Arg* 26C3
General Villegas *Arg* 26C3
Genesee, R *USA* 11D2
Geneseo *USA* 11D2
Geneva = Genève
Geneva, Nebraska *USA* 15C1
Geneva, New York *USA* 12B1
Geneva,L of = LacLéman
Genève *Switz* 38B1
Genil, R *Spain* 37B2
Genoa = Genova
Genoa *Aust* 78C3
Genova *Italy* 38B2
Gent *Belg* 34B1
Genteng *Indon* 54C4
Genthin *E Germ* 40C2
Geokchay *USSR* 43H7
George *S Africa* 72C3
George, R *Can* 5M4
George,L *Aust* 78C2
George,L, Florida *USA* 13C3
George,L, New York *USA* 11E2
George Sd *NZ* 79A2
George Town *Aust* 78E3
Georgetown, California *USA* 18B1
Georgetown, Delaware *USA* 11D3
Georgetown *Guyana* 25G2
Georgetown, Kentucky *USA* 10C3
George Town *Malay* 53C4
Georgetown *St Vincent* 21N2
Georgetown, S Carolina *USA* 13D2
Georgetown, Texas *USA* 15C3
Georgetown *The Gambia* 68A3
George V Land, Region *Ant* 80G8
George West *USA* 15F4
Georgia, State *USA* 13C2
Georgian B *Can* 10C1
Georgia,Str of *Can* 3D4
Georgina, R *Aust* 76C3
Georgiu-Dezh *USSR* 43F5
Georgiyevsk *USSR* 43G7
Gera *E Germ* 40C2
Geraldine *NZ* 79B2
Geraldton *Aust* 76A3
Geraldton *Can* 7E2
Gerar, R *Israel* 63C3
Gérardmer *France* 34D2
Gerardsbergen *Belg* 34B1
Gerdine,Mt *USA* 4C3
Gerdova Peak, Mt *USA* 8J3
Gerik *Malay* 53C4
Gering *USA* 9B3
Gerlachovsky, Mt *Pol* 43C6
Germanson Lodge *Can* 3D2
Germiston *S Africa* 72D2
Gerolstein *W Germ* 34D1
Gerona *Spain* 37C1
Geseke *W Germ* 34E1
Gestro, R *Eth* 70E3
Getafe *Spain* 37B1
Gettysburg, Pennsylvania *USA* 12B3
Gettysburg, S Dakota *USA* 9C2
Getúlio Vargas *Brazil* 26E1
Geumpang *Indon* 54A2
Gevaş *Turk* 62D2
Gevgelija *Yugos* 39E2
Gex *France* 35B1
Ghabāghib *Syria* 63D2
Ghadamis *Libya* 68C1
Ghaem Shahr *Iran* 61C1
Ghāghara, R *India* 59B2
Ghana, Republic *Africa* 68B4
Ghanzi *Botswana* 72C1
Ghardaïa *Alg* 69C2
Gharyan *Libya* 67A1
Ghāt *Libya* 67A2
Ghazaouet *Alg* 69B1
Ghāziābād *India* 58D3
Ghazi Khan *Pak* 58C3
Ghazni *Afghan* 58B2
Gheorgheni *Rom* 39F1
Gheorghiu G Dei *Rom* 39F1
Ghubbat al Qamar, B *S Yemen* 65F3
Ghubbat Sawqirah, B *Oman* 65G3
Ghudamis *Alg* 66E4
Ghurian *Afghan* 61E2
Gialo *Libya* 67B2
Giamame *Somalia* 70E3
Giarre *Italy* 38D3
Gibbon *USA* 14C1
Gibeon *Namibia* 72B2
Gibraltar, Colony *SW Europe* 37A2
Gibraltar,Str of *Spain/Africa* 37A2
Gibson Desert *Aust* 76B3
Gibsons *Can* 16B1
Giddalūr *India* 60B1
Giddi P *Egypt* 63B3
Gien *France* 34B3
Giessen *W Germ* 40B2
Gifford *USA* 13C3
Gifu *Japan* 51D4
Gigha, I *Scot* 32C4
Giglio, I *Italy* 38C2
Gijon *Spain* 37A1
Gila, R *USA* 17D4
Gila Bend *USA* 17D4
Gila Bend Mts *USA* 17D4
Gilbert, R *Aust* 76D2
Gilbert Is *Pacific O* 77G1
Gilbert,Mt *Can* 3D3
Gildford *USA* 16D1
Gilé *Mozam* 71D5
Gilead, Region *Jordan* 63C2
Gilf Kebir Plat *Egypt* 67B2
Gilgandra *Aust* 78C2
Gilgit *Pak* 58C1
Gilgit, R *Pak* 58C1
Gilgunnia *Aust* 78C2
Gillam *Can* 5J4
Gilles, L *Aust* 78A2
Gillette *USA* 9A3
Gill I *Can* 3C3
Gills Rock *USA* 10B1
Gilman *USA* 10B2
Gilroy *USA* 18B2
Gimli *Can* 9C1
Gineifa *Egypt* 63B3
Gingindlovu *S Africa* 72E2
Gingoog *Phil* 55G9
Ginir *Eth* 70E3
Gióna, Mt *Greece* 39E3
Gippsland, Mts *Aust* 78C3
Girard *USA* 10C2
Girardot *Colombia* 24D3
Girdle Ness, Pen *Scot* 32D3
Giresun *Turk* 62C1
Girga *Egypt* 64B1
Gir Hills *India* 58C4
Giri, R *Zaïre* 70B3
Giridih *India* 59C3
Girishk *Afghan* 58A2
Giromagny *France* 34D3
Gironde, R *France* 36B2
Girvan *Scot* 32C4
Gisborne *NZ* 79C2
Gisors *France* 34A2
Gitega *Burundi* 70C4
Giuba,R = Juba,R
Giulia, Region *Italy* 35E2
Giurgiu *Rom* 39F2
Givet *Belg* 34C1
Gizhiga *USSR* 47S3
Gizycko *Pol* 41E2
Gjirokastër *Alb* 39E2
Gjoatlaven *Can* 4J3
Gjøvik *Nor* 30G6
Glace Bay *Can* 5M5
Glacial Mt *Can* 3C2
Glacier B *USA* 3A2
Glacier Bay Nat Mon *USA* 8L4
Glacier Nat Pk, *USA/Can USA* 3F4
Glacier Peak, Mt *USA* 16B1
Glacier Str *Can* 5K2
Gladstone, Queensland *Aust* 76E3
Gladstone, S Aust *Aust* 78A2
Gladstone, Tasmania *Aust* 78E3
Gladstone *USA* 10B1
Glama, Mt *Iceland* 30A1
Glåma, R *Nor* 30G6
Glan, R *W Germ* 34D2
Glarner, Mts *Switz* 35C1
Glarus *Switz* 35C1
Glasco *USA* 15C2
Glasgow, Kentucky *USA* 10B3
Glasgow, Montana *USA* 9A2
Glasgow *Scot* 32C4
Glassboro *USA* 12C3
Glass Mt *USA* 18C2
Glastonbury *Eng* 33D6
Glazov *USSR* 42J4
Gleisdorf *Austria* 40D3
Glen Afton *NZ* 79C1
Glen Burnie *USA* 12B3
Glencoe *S Africa* 72E2
Glendale, Arizona *USA* 17D4
Glendale, California *USA* 18C3
Glendive *USA* 9B2
Glendo Res *USA* 9B3
Glenhallen *USA* 8J3
Glen Innes *Aust* 78D1
Glenmorgan *Aust* 78C1
Glenreagh *Aust* 78D2
Glen Rock *USA* 12B3
Glen Rose *USA* 15C3
Glens Falls *USA* 12D1
Glenwood, Arkansas *USA* 15D3
Glenwood, Minnesota *USA* 9C2
Glenwood, New Mexico *USA* 14A3
Glenwood Springs *USA* 14A2
Glidden *USA* 10A1
Glittertind, Mt *Nor* 30F6
Gliwice *Pol* 41D2
Globe *USA* 17D4
Głogów *Pol* 40D2
Glomfjord *Nor* 30G5
Gloucester *Aust* 78D2
Gloucester *Eng* 33D6
Gloucester *USA* 12E1
Gloversville *USA* 12C1
Glubokoye *USSR* 41F1
Glukhov *USSR* 43E5
Gmünd *Austria* 40D3
Gmunden *Austria* 40C3
Gniezno *Pol* 41D2
Goabeg *Namibia* 72B2
Goa, Daman and Diu, Union Territory *India* 60A1
Goālpāra *India* 59D2
Goaso *Ghana* 69F4
Goba *Eth* 70D3
Gobabis *Namibia* 72B1
Gobernador Crespo *Arg* 26C2
Gobernador Duval *Arg* 26B3
Gobi, Desert *China/Mongolia* 50B1
Gobo *Japan* 52C4
Gobza, R *USSR* 41G1
Gochas *Namibia* 72B1
Godag *India* 60B1
Godāvari, R *India* 60C1
Goddard,Mt *USA* 18C2
Goderich *Can* 10C2
Godhavn *Greenland* 5N3
Godhra *India* 58C4
Godoy Cruz *Arg* 26B2
Gods L *Can* 5J4
Godthab *Greenland* 5N3
Godwin Austen = K2
Goffstown *USA* 12E1
Gogama *Can* 10C1
Gogora *Eth* 64C4
Goiandira *Brazil* 27C2
Goianésia *Brazil* 27C2
Goiânia *Brazil* 27C2
Goiás *Brazil* 27B2
Goiás, State *Brazil* 25J6
Goio-Erê *Brazil* 27B3
Gojab, R *Eth* 70D3
Gökçeada, I *Turk* 39F2
Goksu, R *Turk* 43F8
Göksun *Turk* 62C2
Gol, R *USSR* 47M5
Golāghāt *India* 59D2
Gölbaşi *Turk* 62C2
Gol'chikha *USSR* 46K2
Golconda *USA* 16C2
Gold *USA* 12B2
Gold Beach *USA* 16B2
Gold Coast *Aust* 78D1
Golden *Can* 3E3
Golden B *NZ* 79B2
Goldendale *USA* 16B1
Golden Gate, Chan *USA* 18A2
Golden Meadow *USA* 15D4
Goldfield *USA* 17C3
Gold Point *USA* 18D2
Gold River *Can* 3C4
Goldthwaite *USA* 14C3
Goleniów *Pol* 40C2
Goleta *USA* 18C3
Golfe d'Ajaccio, G *Corse* 38B2
Golfe de Gabes, G *Tunisia* 69E2
Golfe de Gascogne = Biscay,Bay of
Golfe de Hammamet, G *Tunisia* 69E1
Golfe de la Napoule, G *France* 35B3
Golfe de St Florent, G *Corse* 38B2
Golfe de St-Malo, B *France* 36B2
Golfe du Lion, G *France* 36C3
Golfo Corcovado, G *Chile* 23B6
Golfo de Almeira, G *Spain* 37B2
Golfo de Ancud, G *Chile* 23B6
Golfo de Batabano, G *Cuba* 19D2
Golfo de Batano, G *Cuba* 21A2
Golfo de Cadiz, G *Spain* 37A2
Golfo de Cagliari, G *Sardegna* 38B3
Golfo de California, G *Mexico* 19A1
Golfo de Chiriqui, G *Panama* 19D4
Golfo de Fonseca *Honduras* 19D3
Golfo de Guacanayabo, G *Cuba* 21B2
Golfo de Guayaquil, G *Ecuador* 24B4
Golfo del Darien, G *Colombia/Panama* 21B5
Golfo de los Mosquitos, G *Panama* 24B2
Golfo del Papagaya, G *Nic* 24A1
Golfo de Mazarrón, G *Spain* 37B2
Golfo de Nicoya, G *Costa Rica* 24A2
Golfo de Oristano, G *Sardegna* 38B3
Golfo de Panamá, G *Panama* 19E4
Golfo de Papagayo, G *Costa Rica* 19D3
Golfo de Paria, G *Ven* 21E4
Golfo de Paris, G *Ven* 24F1
Golfo de Penas, G *Chile* 23B7
Golfo de St Florent *Corse* 36D3
Golfo de San Jorge, G *Spain* 37C1
Golfo de Tehuantepec, G *Mexico* 19C3
Golfo de Torugas, G *Colombia* 24C3
Golfo de Uraba, G *Colombia* 24C2
Golfo de Valencia, G *Spain* 37C2
Golfo de Venezia, G *Italy* 35E2
Golfo de Venezuela, G *Ven* 21C4
Golfo di Genova, G *Italy* 38B2
Golfo di Policastro, G *Italy* 38D3
Golfo di Squillace, G *Italy* 38D3
Golfo di Taranto, G *Italy* 38D2
Golfo di Trieste, G *Italy* 35E2
Golfo di Venezia, G *Italy* 38C1
Golfo Dulce, G *Costa Rica* 19D4
Golfo San Jorge, G *Arg* 23C7
Golfo San Matías, G *Arg* 23D6
Golmud *China* 48C3
Golocha *Eth* 70E3
Golovin B *USA* 8F3
Golovnino *USSR* 51F3
Goma *Zaïre* 70C4
Gombe *Nig* 69J3
Gombi *Nig* 69J3
Gomel *USSR* 41G2
Gomera, I *Canary Is* 68A2
Gómez Palacio *Mexico* 19B2
Gonam, R *USSR* 47O4
Gonbad-e Kāvūs *Iran* 61D1
Gonda *India* 59B2
Gondal *India* 58C4
Gondar *Eth* 70D2
Gondia *India* 59B3
Gönen *Turk* 62A1
Gonen, R *Turk* 39F3
Goney *Irish Rep* 33B5
Gongbo'gyamba *China* 59D1
Gongga Shan, Mt *China* 50A4
Gonghe *China* 50A2
Gongogi, R *Brazil* 27D1
Gongola, State *Nig* 69J4
Gongola, R *Nig* 69J3
Gonzales, California *USA* 18B2
Gonzales, Texas *USA* 15C4
Gonzalez *Mexico* 20C1
Gonzalez Chaves *Arg* 26C3
Good Hope,C of *S Africa* 72B3
Good Hope Mt *Can* 3D3
Gooding *USA* 16D2
Goodland *USA* 14B2
Goodnews Bay *USA* 8F4
Goodooga, R *Aust* 78C1
Goole *Eng* 33E5
Goolgowi *Aust* 78C2
Goolwa *Aust* 78A3
Goomalling *Aust* 76A4
Goombalie *Aust* 78C2
Goomer *Aust* 78D1
Goomeri *Aust* 78D1
Goondiwindi *Aust* 78D1
Goose Bay *Can* 5N4
Goose Creek *USA* 13D2
Goose L *USA* 16B2
Gooty *India* 60B1
Goraka *PNG* 76D1
Gora Koyp, Mt *USSR* 42K3
Gora Munku Sardyk, Mt *USSR* 47L4
Gora Narodnaya, Mt *USSR* 42K3
Gora Pay-Yer, Mt *USSR* 42L2
Gora Telpos-Iz, Mt 42K3
Goražde *Yugos* 39D2
Gordon *USA* 8K2
Gordon L *Can* 3F2
Gordonsville *USA* 11D3
Goré *Chad* 70B3
Gore *Eth* 70D3
Gore *NZ* 79A3
Gore Topko, Mt *USSR* 47P4
Gorgān *Iran* 61C1
Gorgona, I *Italy* 35C3
Gorinchem *Neth* 34C1
Goris *USSR* 62E2
Gorizia *Italy* 38C1
Gorki, Belorusskaya S.S.R. *USSR* 41G2
Gorki, Rossiyskaya S.F.S.R. *USSR* 42M2
Gor'kiy *USSR* 46F4
Gor'kovskoye Vodokhranilishche, Res *USSR* 42G4
Gorlitz *E Germ* 40C2
Gorlovka *USSR* 43F6
Gorman *USA* 18C3
Gorna Orjahovica *Bulg* 39F2
Gorno-Altaysk *USSR* 48B1
Gorno Lopatina, Mt *USSR* 51E1
Gorno Medvezh'ya, Mt *USSR* 51D2
Gorno Oblachnaya, Mt *USSR* 51C3
Gorno Tardoki Yani, Mt *USSR* 51D2
Gornozavodsk *USSR* 51E2
Gornyy *USSR* 51D1
Goro Denezhkin Kamen', Mt *USSR* 42K3
Gorodets *USSR* 42G4
Gorodnya *USSR* 41G2
Gorodok, Belorusskaya S.S.R. *USSR* 41G1
Gorodok, Ukrainskaya S.S.R. *USSR* 41E3
Gorodok, Ukrainskaya S.S.R. *USSR* 41F3
Goroka *PNG* 49H7
Gorokhpur *India* 59B2
Gorong, I *Indon* 55D3
Gorongosa *Mozam* 71D5
Gorontalo *Indon* 55B2
Goroubi, R *U Volta* 69G3
Goro Yurma, Mt *USSR* 42L4
Gorutuba, R *Brazil* 27D2
Goryachinsk *USSR* 47M4
Gory Akkyr, Upland *USSR* 43J7
Gory Byrranga, Mts *USSR* 47L2
Goryn', R *USSR* 41F3
Gory Putorana, Mts *USSR* 47L1
Góry Świetokrzyskie, Upland *Pol* 41E2
Gory Tel'pos-iz', Mt *USSR* 46G3
Gorzow Wielkopolski *Pol* 30H8
Goshen *USA* 18C2
Goshogawara *Japan* 51E3
Gosku, R *Turk* 43F8
Gospić *Yugos* 38D2
Gostivar *Yugos* 39E2
Gostynin *Pol* 41D2
Göteborg *Sweden* 30G7
Gotel, Mts *Nig* 70B3
Gothenburg *USA* 14B1
Gotland, I *Sweden* 30H7
Gotō-retto, I *Japan* 51B5
Gotska Sandön, I *Sweden* 30H7
Gōtsu *Japan* 51C4
Gottwaldov *Czech* 41D3
Gouda *Neth* 34C1
Goudoumaria *Niger* 70B2
Gough I *Atlantic O* 73H7
Goulburn *Aust* 78C2
Goumbou *Mali* 68B3
Goundam *Mali* 68B3
Gouré *Niger* 70B2
Gourma Rharous *Mali* 68B3
Gournay-en-Bray *France* 34A2
Gouro *Chad* 70B2
Govenlock *Can* 16E1
Gove Pen *Aust* 49G8
Goverla, Mt *USSR* 43C6
Governador Valadares *Brazil* 27D2
Governador Virasoro *Arg* 26D1
Govind Ballabh Paht Sāgar, L *India* 59B3
Gowanda *USA* 12A1
Gowārān *Afghan* 58B3
Goya *Arg* 26D1
Goz-Beïda *Chad* 70C2
Gozo, I *Medit S* 38C3
Goz Regeb *Sudan* 64C3
Graaff-Reinet *S Africa* 72C3
Gracefield *Can* 11D1
Grado *Italy* 35E2
Grafton *Aust* 77E3
Grafton *Aust* 78D1
Grafton, N Dakota *USA* 9C2
Grafton, W Virginia *USA* 10C3
Graham, R *Can* 3D2
Graham I *Can* 3B3
Graham L *Can* 3F2
Graham,Mt *USA* 17E4
Grahamstown *S Africa* 72D3
Grajaú *Brazil* 25J5
Grajewo *Pol* 41E2
Grámmos, Mt *Greece/Alb* 39E2
Grampian, Region *Scot* 32D3
Grampian, Mts *Scot* 32C3

Granada Colombia 24D3
Granada Nic 24A1
Granada Spain 37B2
Granby Can 11E1
Granby USA 14A1
Gran Canaria, I Canary Is 68A2
Gran Chaco, Region Arg 23D3
Grand, R, Michigan USA 10B2
Grand, R, Missouri USA 15D1
Grand B Dominica 21Q2
Grand Bahama, I Bahamas 7F4
Grand Ballon, Mt France 34D3
Grand Bank Can 5N5
Grand Banks Atlantic O 73F1
Grand Bassam Ivory Coast 69F4
Grand Bérard, Mt France 35B2
Grand Canyon USA 17D3
Grand Canyon Nat Pk USA 17D3
Grand Cayman, I Caribbean 21A3
Grand Centre Can 3F3
Grand Coulee USA 16C1
Grande, R Arg 26B3
Grande, R, Bahia Brazil 25K6
Grande, R, M nas Gerais/São Paulo Brazil 27C2
Grande Cache Can 3E3
Grande Chartreuse, Region France 35A2
Grande Comore, I Comoros 71E5
Grande Prairie Can 3E2
Grande Prairie USA 15C3
Grand Erg de Bilma, Desert Region Niger 70B2
Grand erg Occidental, Mts Alg 68C1
Grand erg Oriental, Mts Alg 68C1
Grande Rivière de la Baleine, R Can 5L4
Grande Ronde, R USA 16C1
Gran Desierto USA 17D4
Grand Falls, New Brunswick Can 5M5
Grand Falls, Newfoundland Can 5N5
Grand Forks Can 16C1
Grand Forks USA 9C2
Grand Gorge USA 12C1
Grand Haven USA 10B2
Grand Island USA 14C1
Grand Isle USA 15E3
Grand Junction USA 14A2
Grand Marais USA 15D4
Grand Marais USA 10A1
Grand Mère Can 11E1
Grandola Port 37A2
Grand Rapids Can 4J4
Grand Rapids, Michigan USA 10B2
Grand Rapids, Minnesota USA 10A1
Grand St Bernard, P Italy/Switz 35B2
Grand Teton, Mt USA 6B2
Grand Teton Nat Pk USA 16D2
Grand Valley USA 14A2
Grandvilliers France 34A2
Grangeburg USA 19D1
Grangeville USA 16C1
Granite Peak, Mt, Montana USA 16E1
Granite Peak, Mt, Utah USA 17D2
Granollérs Spain 37C1
Gran Paradiso, Mt Italy 38B1
Gran Pilastro, Mt Austria/Italy 35D1
Grantham Eng 33E5
Grant,Mt USA 18C1
Grantown-on-Spey Scot 32D3
Grants USA 14A2
Grants Pass USA 16B2
Granville France 36B2
Granville USA 12D1
Granville L Can 4H4
Grão Mogol Brazil 27D2
Grapevine USA 18C3
Grapevine Mts USA 18D2
Graskop S Africa 72E1
Grasse France 36D3
Grassrange USA 16E1
Grass Valley USA 17B3
Gravelbourg Can 4H5
Gravelines France 34B1
Gravelotte S Africa 71D6
Gravenhurst Can 11D2
Grave Peak, Mt USA 16D1
Gravesend Aust 78D1
Gravina I USA 8M4
Gray France 35A1
Grayling USA 8F3
Grays Harbour, B USA 16B1
Grays L USA 16D2
Grayson USA 10C3

Grayville USA 10B3
Graz Austria 40D3
Great, R Jamaica 21H1
Great Abaco, I Bahamas 7F4
Great Australian Bight, G Aust 76B4
Great B, New Hampshire USA 12E1
Great B, New Jersey USA 12C3
Great Bahama Bank Bahamas 19E2
Great Barrier I NZ 79C1
Great Barrier Reef, Is Aust 76D2
Great Barrington USA 12D1
Great Basin USA 17C2
Great Bear, R Can 8O2
Great Bear L Can 4F3
Great Bend USA 14C2
Great Bitter L Egypt 63B3
Great Cacapon USA 12A3
Great Coco I Burma 60E2
Great Dividing Range, Mts Aust 76D3
Great Driffield Eng 33E4
Great Egg Harbour, B USA 12C3
Greater Antarctic Region Ant 80F10
Greater Antilles, Is Caribbean 21B2
Greater London, Metropolitan County Eng 33E6
Greater Manchester, Metropolitan County Eng 33D5
Great Exuma, I Bahamas 19E2
Great Falls USA 16D1
Great Fish, R S Africa 72D3
Great Glen, V Scot 32C3
Great Himalayan Range, Mts Asia 59C2
Great Inagua, I Bahamas 7F4
Great Karroo, Mts S Africa 72C3
Great Kei, R S Africa 72D3
Great L Aust 78E3
Great Namaland, Region Namibia 71B6
Great Nicobar, I Indian O 60E3
Great Ormes Head, C Wales 33D5
Great Pt USA 12E2
Great Ragged, I Bahamas 7F4
Great Ruaha, R Tanz 71D4
Great Sacandaga L USA 11E2
Great Salt L USA 16D2
Great Salt Lake Desert USA 16D2
Great Sand Sea Libya/Egypt 67B2
Great Sandy Desert Aust 76B3
Great Sandy Desert USA 6A2
Great Sandy I = Fraser I
Great Sitkin, I USA 8C6
Great Slave L Can 4G3
Great Smoky Mts USA 13C1
Great Smoky Mts Nat Pk USA 13C1
Great Snow Mt Can 3D2
Great South B USA 12D2
Great Tafelberg, Mt S Africa 72C3
Great Victoria Desert Aust 76B3
Great Wall China 50B2
Great Yarmouth Eng 33F5
Greco,C Cyprus 63C1
Greece, Republic Europe 39E3
Greece USA 11D2
Greeley USA 14B1
Greely Fjord Can 5K1
Green, R, Kentucky USA 10B3
Green, R, Utah USA 17D3
Green B USA 10B1
Green Bay USA 10B2
Greencastle, Indiana USA 10B3
Greencastle, Pennsylvania USA 12B3
Greene USA 12C1
Greeneville USA 13C1
Greenfield, California USA 18B2
Greenfield, California USA 18C3
Greenfield, Massachusetts USA 12D1
Greenfield, Wisconsin USA 10B2
Green Lake Can 3G3
Greenland, Dependency N Atlantic 5O2
Greenland Basin Greenland S 73H1
Greenland S Greenland 80B1
Greenock Scot 32C4
Greenport USA 12D2

Green River, Utah USA 17D3
Green River, Wyoming USA 16E2
Greensboro, Maryland USA 12C3
Greensboro, N Carolina USA 13D1
Greensburg, Kansas USA 14C2
Greensburg, Kentucky USA 10B3
Greensburg, Pennsylvania USA 11D2
Greenstone, Pt Scot 32C3
Greenup USA 10B3
Green Valley USA 17D4
Greenville, Alabama USA 13B2
Greenville Lib 68B4
Greenville, Mississippi USA 15D3
Greenville, N Carolina USA 13D1
Greenville, N Hampshire USA 12E1
Greenville, Ohio USA 10C2
Greenville, S Carolina USA 13C2
Greenville, Texas USA 15C3
Greenville,C Aust 49H8
Greenwich Eng 33F6
Greenwich USA 12D2
Greenwood, Delaware USA 12C3
Greenwood, Mississippi USA 15D3
Greenwood, S Carolina USA 13C2
Greers Ferry L USA 15D2
Gregory USA 9C3
Gregory,L Aust 78A1
Gregory Range, Mts Aust 76D2
Greifswald E Germ 40C2
Gremikha USSR 42F2
Grenå Den 40C1
Grenada USA 15E3
Grenada, I Caribbean 21E4
Grenadines,The, Is Caribbean 21E4
Grenfell Aust 78C2
Grenfell Can 3H3
Grenoble France 36D2
Grenville Grenada 21M2
Grenville,C Aust 76D2
Gresham USA 16B1
Gresik, Jawa Indon 54D4
Gresik, Sumatera Indon 54B3
Gretna USA 15D4
Grey, R NZ 79B2
Greybull USA 16E2
Grey Hunter Pk, Mt Can 8L3
Grey Is Can 5N4
Greylock,Mt USA 12D1
Greymouth NZ 79B2
Grey Range, Mts Aust 76D3
Greystones Irish Rep 33B5
Greytown S Africa 72E2
Griekwastad S Africa 72C2
Griffin USA 13C2
Griffith Aust 78C2
Grim,C Aust 76D5
Grimsby Can 11D2
Grimsby Eng 33E5
Grimsey, I Iceland 30B1
Grimshaw Can 3E2
Grimstad Nor 30F7
Grindelwald Switz 35C1
Grinnell USA 9D3
Grinnell Pen Can 5J2
Grise Fjord Can 5K2
Griva USSR 42J3
Grizzly Bear, Mt Can 8O2
Grobina USSR 30J7
Groblersdal S Africa 72D2
Gröbming Austria 35E1
Grodno USSR 41E2
Gromati R India 59B2
Groningen Neth 40B2
Groom USA 14B2
Groot, R S Africa 72C3
Groote Eylandt, I Aust 76C2
Grootfontein Namibia 71B5
Groot-Karasberge, Mts Namibia 72B2
Groot Laagte, R Botswana 72C1
Groot Vloer, Salt L S Africa 72C2
Gros Islet St Lucia 21P2
Grosser Feldberg, Mt W Germ 34E1
Grosseto Italy 38C2
Gross-Gerau W Germ 34E2
Grossglockner, Mt Austria 40C3
Gross Venediger, Mt Austria 35E1
Grosvenor,L USA 8G4
Gros Ventre Range, Mts USA 16D2
Groton USA 9C2
Groundhog, R Can 10C1

Grove Hill USA 13B2
Groveland USA 18B2
Grover City USA 18B3
Groveton USA 11E2
Groznyy USSR 43H7
Grudziadz Pol 41D2
Grünau Namibia 72B2
Grutness Scot 32E2
Gruzinskaya SSR, Republic USSR 43G7
Gryazi USSR 43G5
Gryazovets USSR 42F4
Grytviken South Georgia 23J8
Guacuí Brazil 27D3
Guadalajara Mexico 20B1
Guadalajara Spain 37B1
Guadalcanal, I Solomon Is 77E1
Guadalimar, R Spain 37B2
Guadalope, R Spain 37B1
Guadalqivir, R Spain 37B2
Guadalupe Mexico 19B2
Guadalupe USA 18B3
Guadalupe, I Mexico 2G6
Guadalupe, R USA 14C4
Guadalupe Nat Pk USA 14B3
Guadalupe Peak, Mt USA 14B3
Guadalupe Victoria Mexico 20B1
Guadarupe Mexico 20B1
Guadeloupe, I Caribbean 21E3
Guadian, R Spain 37B2
Guadiana, R Port 37A2
Guadiana, R Spain 37B2
Guadix Spain 37B2
Guaira Brazil 27B3
Guajará Mirim Brazil 24E6
Guajira,Pen de Colombia 24D1
Gualaceo Ecuador 24C4
Gualdo Tadino Italy 35E3
Gualeguay Arg 26D2
Gualeguaychú Arg 26D2
Guam, I Pacific O 49H5
Guamini Arg 26C3
Gua Musang Malay 53C5
Guanajuato Mexico 20B1
Guanajuato, State Mexico 20B1
Guanambi Brazil 27D1
Guanare Ven 24E2
Guandacol Arg 26B1
Guane Cuba 19D2
Guangdong, Province China 50C5
Guanghan China 50A3
Guanghua China 50C3
Guangmao Shan, Mt China 50A4
Guangnan China 50A5
Guangyuan China 50B3
Guangze China 50D4
Guangzhon China 50C5
Guangzhou China 44G4
Guanhães Brazil 27D2
Guania, R Colombia 24E3
Guanipa, R Ven 21E5
Guantánamo Cuba 21B2
Guanting Shuiku, Res China 50D1
Guanxi, Province China 50B5
Guan Xian China 50A3
Guapa Colombia 24C2
Guaporé Brazil 26E1
Guaporé, R Brazil 26E1
Guaporé, R Brazil/Bol 24F6
Guaquí Bol 24E7
Guará, R Brazil 27D1
Guarapuava Brazil 27B4
Guaraqueçaba Brazil 27C4
Guaratinguetá Brazil 27C3
Guarda Port 37A1
Guardafui,C Somalia 67E3
Guarda Mor Brazil 27C2
Guardia Chile 26B1
Guardia Mitre Arg 26C4
Guarita, R Brazil 26E1
Guasave Mexico 6C4
Guastalla Italy 35D2
Guatemala Guatemala 19C3
Guatemala, Republic C America 19C3
Guatraché Arg 26C3
Guavrare, R Colombia 24D3
Guaxupé Brazil 27C3
Guayaguayare Trinidad 21L1
Guayaquil Ecuador 24B4
Guaymas Mexico 19A2
Guayquiraro, R Arg 26D2
Guba Eth 70D3
Guba Zaïre 71C5
Guba Buorkhaya, B USSR 47P2
Guban, Region Somalia 70E3
Gubat Phil 55F8
Gubbio Italy 35E3
Gubin Pol 40C2
Gubio Nig 69J3
Güdür India 60B2
Guebwiller France 34D3
Guelma Alg 69D1

Guelpho Can 10C2
Guelta Zemmur Mor 68A2
Güemez Mexico 20C1
Guenabacoa Cuba 21A2
Guerara Alg 69C2
Guéréda Chad 70C2
Guéret France 36C2
Guernsey USA 9B3
Guernsey, I UK 36B2
Guerrero, State Mexico 20B2
Gughe, Mt Eth 70D3
Gugigu China 47O4
Guguan, I Pacific O 49H5
Guiargambone Aust 78C2
Guichón Urug 26D2
Guider Cam 69J4
Guidong China 50C4
Guiglo Ivory Coast 68B4
Guija Mozam 72E1
Gui Jiang, R China 50C5
Guildford Eng 33E6
Guilin China 50C4
Guillestre France 35B2
Guinan China 50A2
Guinda USA 18A1
Guinea, Republic Africa 68A3
Guinea Basin Atlantic O 73H4
Guinea-Bissau, Republic Africa 68A3
Guinea,G of W Africa 68C4
Güines Cuba 21A2
Guir, Well Mali 68B3
Guiranwala Pak 58C2
Guiratinga Brazil 27B2
Güiria Ven 24F1
Guise France 34B2
Guiuan Phil 55G8
Gui Xian China 50B5
Guiyang China 50B4
Guizhou, Province China 50B4
Gujarät, State India 58C4
Gujrat Pak 58C2
Gulbarga India 60B1
Gulbene USSR 41F1
Guledagudda India 60B1
Gulfport USA 13B2
Gulf,The S W Asia 56D3
Gulgong Aust 78C2
Gulian China 51A1
Gulin China 50B4
Gulkana USA 8J3
Gulkana, R USA 8J3
Gull L Can 3F3
Gull Lake Can 3G3
Gulu Uganda 70D3
Guluguba Aust 78C1
Gulung Chamah, Mt Malay 54F6
Gumel Nig 69H3
Gummersbach W Germ 34D1
Gummi Nig 69H3
Gumpla India 59B3
Guna India 58D4
Guna, Mt Eth 70D2
Gundagai Aust 78C3
Gungu Zaïre 70B4
Gunnedah Aust 78D2
Gunnison USA 14A2
Gunnison, R USA 14A2
Guntakal India 60B1
Guntersville USA 13B2
Guntersville L USA 13B2
Guntür India 60C1
Gunung Batu Putch, Mt Malay 53C5
Gunung Benom, Mt Malay 54G7
Gunung Besar, Mt Indon 54E3
Gunung Besar, Mt Malay 54F6
Gunung Besar, Mt Malay 54G7
Gunung Bulu, Mt Indon 54E2
Gunung Gedang, Mt Indon 54B3
Gunung Geureudong, Mt Indon 54A2
Gunung Kulabu, Mt Indon 54A2
Gunung Lawit, Mt Malay 54D2
Gunung Lawu, Mt Indon 54D4
Gunung Leuser, Mt Indon 54A2
Gunung Lokilalaka, Mt Indon 55B3
Gunung Mekongga, Mt Indon 55B3
Gunung Menyapa, Mt Indon 54E2
Gunung Niapa, Mt Indon 54E2
Gunung Ogoamas, Mt Indon 55B2
Gunung Patah, Mt Indon 54B3
Gunung Raung, Mt Indon 54D4
Gunung Resag, Mt Indon 54B3
Gunung Sarempaka, Mt Indon 54E3
Gunungsitoli Indon 54A2
Gunung Sumbing, Mt Indon 54D4

Gunung Tahan, Mt Malay 53C5
Gunung Talakmau, Mt Indon 54B2
Gunung Tapis, Mt Malay 54G7
Gunung Tokala, Mt Indon 55B3
Gunza Angola 71B5
Guoyang China 50D3
Guranda Ecuador 24C4
Gurara Nig 69H4
Gurdáspur India 58D2
Gurgaon India 58D3
Gurkha Nepal 59B2
Gurktaler Alpen, Mts Austria 35E1
Gurskoye USSR 51D1
Gürün Turk 62C2
Gurupi, R Brazil 25J4
Gurvan Sayhan Uul, Upland Mongolia 50A1
Gur'yev USSR 43J6
Gurzinskaya, Republic USSR 46F5
Gusau Nig 69H3
Gusev USSR 41E2
Gushan China 51A4
Gus'khrustalnyy USSR 42G4
Gustavus USA 8L4
Gustine USA 18B2
Guston USA 7E3
Gütersloh W Germ 40B2
Guthrie, Kentucky USA 10B3
Guthrie, Oklahoma USA 15C2
Guthrie, Texas USA 14B3
Gutiérrez Zamora Mexico 20C1
Guttenberg USA 9D3
Guyana, Republic S America 25G3
Guyana Basin Atlantic O 73F4
Guyang China 50C1
Guyenne, Region France 36B3
Guymon USA 14B2
Guyra Aust 78D2
Guyuan China 50B2
Guzar USSR 61F1
Gwa Burma 59D4
Gwabegar Aust 78C2
Gwadabawa Nig 69H3
Gwalior India 58D3
Gwanda Zim 72D1
Gwane Zaïre 70C3
Gwardar Pak 61E3
Gwelo Zim 66G9
Gwent, County Wales 33D6
Gweru Zim 71C5
Gwydir, R Aust 78C1
Gwynedd Wales 33D4
Gyangzê China 59C2
Gyaring Hu, L China 48C3
Gydanskiy Poluostrov, Pen USSR 46J2
Gyirong China 59C2
Gyldenløues Greenland 5O3
Gympie Aust 78D1
Gyöngyös Hung 41D3
Györ Hung 41D3

H

Ha'apai Group, Is Tonga 77H2
Haapajärvi Fin 30K6
Haapsalu USSR 42C4
Haarlem Neth 40A2
Haarstrang, Region W Germ 34D1
Habana Cuba 19D2
Habarüt Oman 65F3
Habbän S Yemen 65E4
Habiganj Bang 59D3
Habomai Shoto, I USSR 51F3
Hachijō-jima, I Japan 51D5
Hachiman Japan 52C3
Hachinohe Japan 51E3
Hachioji Japan 52C3
Hackettstown USA 12C2
Hack,Mt, Mt Aust 78A2
Hadbaram Oman 65G3
Haddington Scot 32D4
Haddon Corner Aust 78B1
Haddon Downs Aust 78B1
Hadejia Nig 69J3
Hadejia, R Nig 69H3
Hadera Israel 63C2
Hadiboh Socotra 65F4
Hadley B Can 4H2
Hadong S Korea 52A3
Hadong Vietnam 50B5
Haḍramawt, Region S Yemen 65E3
Hadsund Den 40C1
Haeju N Korea 51B4
Haeju-man, B N Korea 52A3
Haenam S Korea 52A4
Hafar al Bātin S Arabia 65E1
Haffners Bjerg, Mt Greenland 5M2
Hafir Sudan 64B3
Hafizabad Pak 58C2

Häflong India 59D2
Hafnafjörður Iceland 30A2
Hag'Abdullah Sudan 64B4
Hagemeister, I USA 8F4
Hagen W Germ 40B2
Hagerstown USA 12B3
Hagi Japan 52B4
Ha Giang Vietnam 50A5
Hagondange France 34D2
Haguenan France 34D2
Hagunia, Well Mor 68A2
Haha-jima, I Japan 48H4
Hah Xil Hu, L China 48C3
Haicheng China 51A3
Haifa Israel 63C2
Haifa,B of Israel 63C2
Hai He, R China 50D2
Haikang China 50C5
Haikou China 53E1
Ha'il S Arabia 64D1
Hailākāndi India 59D3
Hailar China 47N5
Hailong China 51B3
Hailun China 51B2
Hailuoto, I Fin 30J5
Hainan, I China 53D2
Haines USA 8L4
Haines Junction Can 8L3
Hainfeld Austria 40D3
Haiphong Vietnam 50B5
Haiti, Republic Caribbean 21C3
Haiwee Res USA 18D2
Haiya Sudan 70D2
Haiyan China 50A2
Haiyuan China 50B2
Haizhou Wan, B China 50D3
Hajdúböszörmény Hung 41E3
Hajfah Yemen 64D3
Hajiki-saki, Pt Japan 52C3
Haka Burma 59D3
Hakalau Hawaiian Is 18E5
Hakkâri Turk 62D2
Hakodate Japan 51E3
Hakui Japan 52C3
Haku-san, Mt Japan 52C3
Ḥalab Syria 43F8
Halabja Iraq 62E3
Halaib Sudan 70D1
Halba Leb 63D1
Halberstadt E Germ 40C2
Halcon,Mt Phil 55F8
Halden Nor 30G7
Haldia India 59C3
Haldwāni India 58D3
Halfway, R Can 3D2
Halifax Can 5M5
Halifax Eng 33E5
Halifax USA 11D3
Halkett,C USA 8H1
Halla-San, Mt S Korea 52A4
Hall Basin, Sd Can 5M1
Hall Beach Can 5K3
Halle Belg 34C1
Halle E Germ 40C2
Halley, Base Ant 80F1
Halleybury Can 11D1
Hall I USA 8D3
Halliday USA 9B2
Hallingdal, R Nor 30F6
Hallock USA 9C2
Hall Pen Can 5M3
Hall's Creek Aust 76B2
Hallstead USA 12C2
Halmahera, I Indon 55C2
Halmahera S Indon 55C3
Halmstad Sweden 30G7
Haltern W Germ 40B2
Haltia, Mt Nor 30J5
Haltwhistle Eng 32D4
Halul, I Qatar 65F1
Haluza, Hist Site Israel 63C3
Hamada Japan 52B4
Hamada de Tinrhert, Desert Region Alg 68C2
Hamada du Dra, Upland Alg 68B2
Hamadän Iran 61B2
Hamada Tounassine, Region Alg 68B2
Ḥamäh Syria 43F8
Hamamatsu Japan 52C4
Hamar Nor 30G6
Hama-Tombetsu Japan 52D1
Hambantota Sri Lanka 60C3
Hamburg, Arkansas USA 15D3
Hamburg, Iowa USA 15C1
Hamburg, New York USA 12A1
Hamburg, Pennsylvania USA 12C2
Hamburg W Germ 40B2
Hamden USA 12D2
Hämeeninna Fin 30J6
Hamersley Range, Mts Aust 76A3
Hamgyong Sanmaek, Mts N Korea 51B3
Hamhüng N Korea 51B3
Hami China 48C2

Hamidiyah Syria 63C1
Hamilton, Alabama USA 13B2
Hamilton Aust 78B3
Hamilton Can 11D2
Hamilton, Montana USA 16D1
Hamilton, New York USA 12C1
Hamilton NZ 79C1
Hamilton, Ohio USA 10C3
Hamilton Scot 32C4
Hamilton Inlet, B Can 5N4
Hamilton,Mt USA 18B2
Hamina Fin 30K6
Hamirpur India 59B2
Hamju N Korea 52A3
Hamm W Germ 40B2
Hammädah al Hamra, Upland Libya 67A2
Hammerdal Sweden 30H6
Hammerfest Nor 30J4
Hammond, Illinois USA 10B2
Hammond, Louisiana USA 15D3
Hammond, Montana USA 9B2
Hammonton USA 12C3
Hampden NZ 79B3
Hampshire, County Eng 33E6
Hampton, Arkansas USA 15D3
Hampton, Iowa USA 9D3
Hampton, New Hampshire USA 12E1
Hampton, Virginia USA 11D3
Hämün-e Jaz Mürian, L Iran 61D3
Hamun-i-Lora, Salt L Pak 58B3
Hamun-i Mashkel, Salt Plain Pak 61E3
Han, R S Korea 52A3
Hana Hawaiian Is 18E5
Hanalei Hawaiian Is 18E5
Hanamaki Japan 51E4
Hanau W Germ 34E1
Hancheng China 50C2
Hanchuan China 50C3
Hancock, Maryland USA 12B3
Hancock, Michigan USA 10B1
Hancock, New York USA 12C2
Handa Japan 52C4
Handan China 50C2
Handeni Tanz 70D4
Hanford USA 18C2
Hanggin Qi China 50B2
Hangö Fin 30J7
Hangzhou China 50E3
Hangzhou Wan, B China 50E3
Hanish, I Yemen 64D4
Hankinson USA 9C2
Hanksville USA 17D3
Hanmer Springs NZ 79B2
Hanna Can 3F3
Hannibal USA 15D2
Hannover W Germ 40B2
Hanöbukten, B Sweden 30G7
Hanoi Viet 53D1
Hanover S Africa 72C3
Hanover USA 12B3
Hanover, I Chile 23B8
Han Shui China 50B3
Han Shui, R China 50C3
Hänsi India 58D3
Hantay Mongolia 48D2
Hanzhong China 50B3
Häora India 59C3
Haparanda Sweden 30J5
Hapch'on S Korea 52A3
Hapevi Brazil 26D1
Häpoli India 59B2
Haql S Arabia 62C4
Harad Yemen 64D3
Haradh S Arabia 65E2
Hara Fanna Eth 70E3
Haraja S Arabia 64D3
Haramachi Japan 52D3
Harar Eth 70E3
Harare Zim 71D5
Harazé Chad 70C2
Harbin China 51B2
Harbor Beach USA 10C2
Harda India 58D4
Hardangerfjord, Inlet Nor 30F6
Hardin USA 9A2
Hardt, Region W Germ 34D2
Hardwicke B Aust 78A2
Hardy USA 15D2
Hargeysa Somalia 70E3
Har Hakippa, Mt Israel 63C3
Harhu, L China 48C3
Hari, R Indon 54B3
Harib Yemen 65E4
Harima-nada, B Japan 52B4
Harlan USA 10C3
Harlem USA 16E1
Harlingen Neth 40B2
Harlingen USA 15F4
Harlow Eng 33F6
Harlowtown USA 16E1
Har Meron, Mt Israel 63C2
Harney Basin USA 16C2
Harney L USA 16C2
Härnösand Sweden 30H6

Har Nuur, L Mongolia 47L5
Harper Lib 68B4
Harper L USA 18D3
Harper,Mt USA 8K3
Harpers Ferry USA 11D3
Har Ramon, Mt Israel 63C3
Harrät al 'Uwayrid, U. Region S Arabia 64C1
Harrät Kishb, Region S Arabia 64D2
Harrat Nawaäsif, Region S Arabia 64D2
Harrat Rahat, Region S Arabia 64D2
Harricanaw, R Can 5L4
Harriman USA 13C1
Harriman Res USA 12D1
Harrington USA 12C3
Harrington Harbour Can 5N4
Harris, District Scot 32B3
Harrisburg, Illinois USA 10B3
Harrisburg, Pennsylvania USA 12B2
Harrismith S Africa 72D2
Harrison B USA 8H1
Harrisonburg USA 11D3
Harrisonville USA 15D2
Harris,Sound of, Chan Scot 32B3
Harrisville USA 10C2
Harrogate Eng 33E4
Har Saggi, Mt Israel 63C3
Harstad Nor 30H5
Hart, R Can 8L3
Hartbees, R S Africa 72C2
Härteigen, Mt Nor 30F6
Hartford, Connecticut USA 12D2
Hartford, Michigan USA 10B2
Hartford, S Dakota USA 9C3
Hartkjølen, Mt Nor 30G6
Hart,L Aust 78A2
Hartland Can 11F1
Hartland Pt Eng 33C6
Hartlepool Eng 32E4
Hartley USA 14B2
Hartselle USA 13B2
Hartshorne USA 15C3
Hartwell Res USA 13C2
Hartz, R S Africa 72C2
Harut, R Afghan 61E2
Harvard,Mt USA 14A2
Harvey USA 9B2
Harwich Eng 33F6
Haryäna, State India 58D3
Häsä Jordan 63C3
Hasaheisa Sudan 64B4
Häsbaiya Leb 63C2
Haselmere Eng 33E6
Hashimoto Japan 52C4
Hashtpar Iran 61B1
Hashtrüd Iran 61B1
Häsik Oman 65G3
Haskell USA 14C3
Hassan India 60B2
Hasselt Belg 40B2
Hassi Inifel Alg 68C2
Hassi Mdakane, Well Alg 68B2
Hassi Messaoud Alg 68C1
Hassi R'mel Alg 69C2
Hassleholm Sweden 30G4
Hastings Aust 78C3
Hastings Eng 33F6
Hastings, Minnesota USA 9D3
Hastings, Nebraska USA 6D2
Hastings NZ 79C1
Hatchet L Can 3H2
Hatchie, R USA 13B1
Hatfield Aust 78B2
Hatham Inlet USA 8F2
Häthras India 58D3
Ha Tinh Viet 53D2
Hattah Aust 78B2
Hatteras,C USA 7F3
Hattiesburg USA 15E3
Hatvan Hung 41D3
Hau Bon Viet 53D3
Haud, Region Eth 70E3
Haugesund Nor 30F7
Hauhungaroa Range, Mts NZ 79C1
Haultain, R Can 3G2
Hauraki G NZ 79B1
Hauroko,L NZ 79A3
Hausstock, Mt Switz 35C1
Haut Atlas, Mts Mor 69A2
Haute Kotto, Region CAR 70C3
Haute-Marne, Department France 34C2
Haute-Saône, Department France 34C3
Hautes Fagnes, Mts Belg 34C1
Hauteville-Lompnès France 35A2
Hautmont Belg 34C1

Haut-Rhin, Department France 34D3
Hauts Plateaux, Mts Alg 69B2
Hauzdar Iran 61E2
Hauz Qala Afghan 58A2
Havana USA 10A2
Havana = Habana
Havankulam Sri Lanka 60B3
Havasu L USA 17D4
Havelock USA 13D2
Havelock North NZ 79C1
Haverfordwest West 33C6
Haverhill USA 12E1
Häveri India 60B2
Haverstraw USA 12D2
Havlíčkův Brod Czech 40D3
Havre Eng 16E1
Havre de Grace USA 12B3
Havre-St-Pierre Can 5M4
Havsa Turk 39F2
Hawaii Hawaiian Is 18E5
Hawaii Volcanoes Nat Pk Hawaiian Is 18E5
Hawal, R Nig 69J3
Hawea,L NZ 79A2
Hawera NZ 79B1
Hawi Hawaiian Is 18E5
Hawick Scot 32D4
Hawkdun Range, Mts NZ 79A2
Hawke B NZ 79C1
Hawke,C Aust 78D2
Hawker Aust 78A2
Hawley USA 12C2
Hawng Luk Burma 53B1
Hawr al Habbaniyah, L Iraq 62D3
Hawr al Hammär, L Iraq 62E3
Hawthorne USA 18C1
Hay Aust 78B2
Hay, R Can 4G3
Hayange France 34C2
Haycock USA 4B3
Hayden, Arizona USA 17D4
Hayden, Colorado USA 14A1
Hayes, R Can 5J4
Hayes Halvø, Region Greenland 5M2
Hayes,Mt USA 8J3
Haymarket USA 12B3
Haynin S Yemen 65E3
Hay River Can 4G3
Hays USA 14C2
Hays Yemen 64D4
Haysville USA 15C2
Hayward, California USA 18A2
Hayward, Wisconsin USA 10A1
Hazard USA 10C3
Hazäribäg India 59C3
Hazebrouck France 34B1
Hazelhurst USA 15D3
Hazel Str Can 4G2
Hazelton Can 4F4
Hazelton Mts Can 3C2
Hazen B USA 8E3
Hazen L Can 5L1
Hazeva Israel 63C3
Hazleton USA 12C2
Healdsburg USA 18A1
Healesville Aust 78C3
Healy USA 8J3
Heard I Indian O 74E7
Hearne USA 15C3
Hearst Can 7E2
Heart, R USA 9B2
Hebbronville USA 15F4
Hebei, Province China 50D2
Hebel Aust 78C1
Heber City USA 16D2
Hebgen L USA 16D2
Hebi China 50C2
Hebian China 50C2
Hebron Can 5M4
Hebron Israel 63C3
Hebron, N. Dakota USA 9B2
Hebron, Nebraska USA 15C1
Hecate Str Can 3B3
Heceta I USA 8M4
Hechi China 50B5
Hechingen W Germ 34E2
Hecla and Griper B Can 4G2
Hector,Mt NZ 79C2
Hede Sweden 30G6
Hedemora Sweden 30H6
He Devil Mt USA 16C1
Heerenveen Neth 40B2
Heerlen Neth 34C1
Hefa = Haifa
Hefei China 50D3
Hefeng China 50B4
Hegang China 51C2
Hegura-jima, I Japan 52C3
Heho Burma 59E3
Heiburg I Can 5J2
Heidan, R Jordan 63C3
Heide W Germ 40B2
Heidelberg, Cape Province S Africa 72C3
Heidelberg, Transvaal S Africa 72D2
Heidelberg W Germ 40B3

Heihe *China* 47D4
Heilbron *S Africa* 72D2
Heilbronn *W Germ* 40B3
Heiligenstadt *E Germ* 40C2
Heilongjiang, Province *China* 51B2
Heilong Jiang, R *China* 51A1
Heinola *Fin* 30K6
Hejiang *China* 50B4
Hekla, Mt *Iceland* 5R3
Hekou *Viet* 53C1
Hekou Yaozou Zizhixian *China* 50A5
Helan *China* 50B2
Helan Shan, Mt *China* 50B2
Helena, Arkansas *USA* 15D3
Helena, Montana *USA* 16D1
Helendale *USA* 18D3
Helen Reef, *Pacific O* 55D2
Helensburgh *Scot* 32C3
Heliopolis *Egypt* 63A3
Helleh, R *Iran* 61C3
Hellin *Spain* 37B2
Hells Canyon, R *USA* 16C1
Hellweg, Region *W Germ* 34D1
Helm *USA* 18B2
Helmand, R *Afghan* 61E2
Helmeringhausen *Namibia* 72B2
Helmond *Neth* 34C1
Helmsdale *Scot* 32D2
Helong *China* 51B3
Helsingborg *Sweden* 30G7
Helsingfors = Helsinki
Helsingør *Den* 40C1
Helsinki *Fin* 30J6
Helston *Eng* 33C6
Helwân *Egypt* 62B4
Hempstead *USA* 15C3
Hemse *Sweden* 30H7
Henan *China* 50A3
Henan, Province *China* 50C3
Hen and Chicken Is *NZ* 79B1
Henashi-zaki, C *Japan* 52C2
Henderson, Kentucky *USA* 10B3
Henderson, N. Carolina *USA* 13D1
Henderson, Nevada *USA* 17D3
Henderson, Texas *USA* 15D3
Hendersonville, N. Carolina *USA* 13C1
Hendersonville, Tennessee *USA* 13B1
Hendrik Verwoerd Dam *S Africa* 72D3
Heng-ch'un *Taiwan* 50E5
Hengduan Shan, Mts *China* 48C4
Hengelo *Neth* 40B2
Hengshan *China* 50B2
Hengshui *China* 50D2
Heng Xian *China* 53D1
Hengyang *China* 50C4
Henhoaha *Nicobar Is* 53A4
Henley-on-Thames *Eng* 33E6
Henlopen,C *USA* 12C3
Henniker *USA* 12E1
Henrietta *USA* 14C3
Henrietta Maria,C *Can* 5K4
Henrieville *USA* 17D3
Henryetta *USA* 15C2
Henry Kater Pen *Can* 5M3
Henties Bay *Namibia* 72A1
Hentiyn Nuruu, Mts *Mongolia* 48D2
Henzada *Burma* 53B2
Hepu *China* 50B5
Herat *Afghan* 61E2
Herbert *Can* 4H4
Herbert, I *USA* 8D5
Herbertville *NZ* 79C2
Herborn *W Germ* 34E1
Heredia *Costa Rica* 21A4
Hereford *Eng* 33D5
Hereford *USA* 14B3
Hereford & Worcester, County *Eng* 33D5
Herentals *Belg* 34C1
Héricourt *France* 35B1
Herington *USA* 15C2
Heriot *NZ* 79A3
Herisau *Switz* 35C1
Herkimer *USA* 12C1
Hermagor *Austria* 35E1
Herma Ness, Pen *Scot* 32E1
Hermanus *S Africa* 72B3
Hermidale *Aust* 78C2
Hermitage *NZ* 79B2
Hermit Is *PNG* 76D1
Hermon,Mt = Jebel ash Shaykh
Hermosillo *Mexico* 19A2
Hernandarias *Par* 27B4
Herndon *USA* 12B2
Herne *W Germ* 34D1
Herning *Den* 40B1
Herowābād *Iran* 61B1
Herradura *Arg* 27A4
Herrera *Arg* 26C1
Herrera del Duque *Spain* 37B2
Herschel I *Can* 8L2
Hershey *USA* 12B2
Hertford, County *Eng* 33E6
Herzliyya *Israel* 63C2
Hesbaye, Region *Belg* 34C1
Hesdin *France* 34A1
Heshui *China* 50B2
Hesperia *USA* 18D3
Hess, R *Can* 8M3
Hessen, State *W Germ* 40B2
Hetch Hetchy Res *USA* 18C2
Hettinger *USA* 9B2
Heweth, Oilfield *N Sea* 33F5
Hexham *Eng* 32D4
He Xian *China* 50C5
Heystekrand *S Africa* 72D2
Heyuan *China* 50C5
Heywood *Aust* 78B3
Heze *China* 50D2
Hialeah *USA* 13E4
Hibbing *USA* 9D2
Hickory *USA* 13C1
Hicks Bay *NZ* 79C1
Hicks,Pt *Aust* 78C3
Hico *USA* 15C3
Hidaka-sammyaku, Mts *Japan* 52D2
Hidalgo *Mexico* 20C1
Hidalgo, State *Mexico* 20C1
Hidalgo del Parral *Mexico* 19B2
Hidrolândia *Brazil* 27C2
Hierro, I *Canary Is* 68A2
Higashine *Japan* 52D3
Higashi-suidō, Str *Japan* 51B5
High Desert *USA* 16B2
High Island *USA* 15D4
Highland, Region *Scot* 32C2
Highland *USA* 18D3
Highland Peak, Mt *USA* 18C1
Highlands Falls *USA* 12C2
High Level *Can* 3E2
High Point *USA* 13C1
High Prairie *Can* 3E2
High River *Can* 4G4
Highrock L *Can* 3G2
High Springs *USA* 13C3
Hightstown *USA* 12C2
High Wycombe *Eng* 33E6
Hiiumaa, I *USSR* 30J7
Hiiumaa, I *USSR* 42C4
Hijaz, Region *S Arabia* 64C1
Hikigawa *Japan* 52C4
Hiko *USA* 17C3
Hikone *Japan* 52C3
Hikurangi *NZ* 79B1
Hildago *Mexico* 6C4
Hildago del Parral *Mexico* 6C4
Hildesheim *W Germ* 40B2
Hillaby,Mt *Barbados* 21Q2
Hill City *USA* 14C2
Hillerød *Den* 40C1
Hill Island L *Can* 3G1
Hillsboro, N. Dakota *USA* 9C2
Hillsboro, New Hampshire *USA* 12E1
Hillsboro, New Mexico *USA* 14A3
Hillsboro, Ohio *USA* 10C3
Hillsboro, Oregon *USA* 16B1
Hillsboro, Texas *USA* 15C3
Hillston *Aust* 78C2
Hillsville *USA* 10C3
Hillswick *Scot* 32E1
Hilo *Hawaiian Is* 18E5
Hilton *USA* 12B1
Hilvan *Turk* 62C2
Hilversum *Neth* 40B2
Himachal Pradesh, State *India* 58D2
Himalaya = Great Himalayan Range
Himalaya, Mts *Asia* 57G3
Himatnagar *India* 58C4
Himeji *Japan* 51C5
Him *Japan* 51D4
Hims *Syria* 43F9
Hinchinbrook Entrance *USA* 8J3
Hinchinbrook I *USA* 8J3
Hinckley, Minnesota *USA* 9D2
Hinckley Res *USA* 12C1
Hindaun *India* 58D3
Hindu Kush, Mts *Afghan* 58B1
Hindupur *India* 60B2
Hines Creek *Can* 3E2
Hinganghāt *India* 58D4
Hinggan Ling, Upland *China* 51B2
Hingol, R *Pak* 58B3
Hingoli *India* 58D5
Hinkley *USA* 18D3
Hinnøya, I *Nor* 30H5
Hinsdale *USA* 12D1
Hinton *Can* 3E3
Hinton *USA* 14C2
Hipolito Itrogoyen *Arg* 26B2
Hirado *Japan* 52A4
Hirado-shima, I *Japan* 52A4
Hirakud Res *India* 59B3
Hirfanli Baraji, Res *Turk* 62B2
Hirihar *India* 60B2
Hiroo *Japan* 52D2
Hirosaki *Japan* 51E3
Hiroshima *Japan* 51C5
Hirson *France* 34C2
Hirşova *Rom* 39F2
Hirtshals *Den* 40B1
Hisār *India* 58D3
Hisn al 'Abr *S Yemen* 65E3
Hispaniola, I *Caribbean* 21C3
Hisyah *Syria* 63D1
Hit *Iraq* 62D3
Hitachi *Japan* 51E4
Hitachi-Ota *Japan* 52D3
Hitchin *Eng* 33E6
Hitra, I *Nor* 30F6
Hiuchi-nada, B *Japan* 52B4
Hiwasa *Japan* 52B4
Hiyon, R *Israel* 63C3
Hjørring *Den* 40E1
Hka, R *Burma* 53B1
Ho *Ghana* 69G4
Hoa Binh *Viet* 53D1
Hoa Da *Viet* 53D3
Hobart *Aust* 78E3
Hobart *USA* 14C3
Hobbs *USA* 14B3
Hobro *Den* 40B1
Hobson L *Can* 3D3
Hobyo *Somalia* 67D4
Hochalm Spitze, Mt *Austria* 35E1
Hochgolling, Mt *Austria* 35E1
Ho Chi Minh = Saigon
Hochkonig, Mt *Austria* 40C3
Hochon *N Korea* 52A2
Hockenheim *W Germ* 34E2
Hockönig, Mt *Austria* 35E1
Hódmezö'hely *Hung* 39E1
Hodonin *Czech* 40D3
Hoek van Holland *Neth* 34C1
Hoengsŏng *S Korea* 52A3
Hoeryong *N Korea* 51B3
Hoeyang *N Korea* 52A3
Hof *W Germ* 40C2
Hofsjökull, Mts *Iceland* 30B2
Hōfu *Japan* 51C5
Hoggar, Upland *Alg* 68C2
Hohe Acht, Mt *W Germ* 34D1
Hohes Gras, Mts *W Germ* 34E1
Hohe Tauern, Mts *Austria* 35E1
Hohhot *China* 50C1
Höhn *Iceland* 5R3
Hoh Sai Hu, L *China* 48C3
Hoh Xil Shan, Mts *China* 57G2
Hoima *Uganda* 70D3
Hojāi *India* 59D2
Hojo *Japan* 52B4
Hokianga Harbour, B *NZ* 79B1
Hokitika *NZ* 79B2
Hokkaidō *Japan* 51E3
Hokmābād *Iran* 61D1
Hokota *Japan* 52D3
Holbrook *Aust* 78C3
Holbrook *USA* 17D4
Holden *USA* 17D3
Holdenville *USA* 15C2
Holdrege *USA* 14C1
Hole Narsipur *India* 60B2
Holetown *Barbados* 21Q2
Holguín *Cuba* 21B2
Holitika *NZ* 79B2
Holitna, R *USA* 8G3
Hollabrunn *Austria* 40D3
Holland *USA* 10B2
Hollidaysburg *USA* 12A2
Hollis *USA* 14C3
Hollister *USA* 18B2
Holly Springs *USA* 15E3
Hollywood, California *USA* 18C3
Hollywood, Florida *USA* 13E4
Holman Island *Can* 4G2
Holmsund *Sweden* 30J6
Holon *Israel* 63C2
Holstebro *Den* 40B1
Holstein *USA* 9C3
Holsteinborg *Greenland* 5N3
Holston, R *USA* 13C1
Holt *USA* 10C2
Holton *USA* 15C2
Holy Cross *USA* 8G3
Holyhead *Wales* 33C5
Holy I *Eng* 32E4
Holy I *Wales* 33C5
Holyoke, Colorado *USA* 14B1
Holyoke, Massachusetts *USA* 12D1
Holzminden *W Germ* 34E1
Homalin *Burma* 59D3
Homburg *W Germ* 34E1
Home B *Can* 5M3
Homer, Alaska *USA* 8H4
Homer, Louisiana *USA* 15D3
Homer Tunnel *NZ* 79A2
Homerville *USA* 13C2
Homestead *USA* 13E4
Homewood *USA* 13B2
Homnābād *India* 60B1
Homoine *Mozam* 71D6
Homs *Syria* 29J5
Hondeklip B *S Africa* 72B3
Hondo, New Mexico *USA* 14A3
Hondo, Texas *USA* 14C4
Hondo, R *Mexico* 19C3
Honduras, Republic *C America* 19D3
Honduras,G of *Honduras* 19D3
Hønefoss *Nor* 30G6
Honesdale *USA* 12C2
Honey L *USA* 17B2
Honfleur *France* 34A2
Hong = Nui Con Voi
Hong, R *Viet* 53C1
Hon Gai *Viet* 53D1
Hongchŏn *S Korea* 52A3
Hongguo *China* 50A4
Hong Hu, L *China* 50C4
Honghui *China* 50B2
Hongjiang *China* 50C4
Hong Kong, Colony *S E Asia* 50C5
Hongor *Mongolia* 48E2
Hongshui He, R *China* 50B5
Hongsong *S Korea* 52A3
Hongwon *N Korea* 52A3
Hongyuan *China* 50A3
Hongze Hu, L *China* 50D3
Honiara *Solomon Is* 77E1
Honjō *Japan* 52D3
Hon Khoai, I *Camb* 53C4
Hon Lan, I *Viet* 53D3
Honnigsvåg *Nor* 30K4
Honningsvåg *Nor* 42D1
Honokaa *Hawaiian Is* 18E5
Honolulu *Hawaiian Is* 18E5
Hon Panjang, I *Viet* 53C4
Honshu, I *Japan* 51D4
Hood,Mt *USA* 16B1
Hood River *USA* 16B1
Hooker *USA* 14B2
Hook Head, C *Irish Rep* 33B5
Hoonah *USA* 8L4
Hooper Bay *USA* 8E3
Hoopstad *S Africa* 72D2
Hoorn *Neth* 40A2
Hoosick Falls *USA* 12D1
Hoover Dam *USA* 6B3
Hope, Alaska *USA* 8J3
Hope, Arkansas *USA* 15D3
Hope *Can* 3D4
Hopedale *Can* 5M4
Hopen, I *Barents S* 46D2
Hopes Advance,C *Can* 5M3
Hopetoun *Aust* 78B3
Hopetown *S Africa* 72C2
Hopewell, Pennsylvania *USA* 12A2
Hopewell, Virginia *USA* 11D3
Hopkinsville *USA* 10B3
Hoquiam *USA* 16B1
Horasan *Turk* 62D2
Horb *W Germ* 34E2
Hordiyo *Somalia* 67E3
Horgen *Switz* 35C1
Horizon Depth *Pacific O* 75L6
Hormuz,Str of *Oman/ Iran* 65G1
Horn *Austria* 40D3
Horn, C *Iceland* 5Q3
Hornaday, R *Can* 8O2
Hornavan, L *Sweden* 30H5
Hornbeck *USA* 15D3
Hornbrook *USA* 16B2
Hornby *NZ* 79B2
Horndon *USA* 18C2
Hornell *USA* 12B1
Hornepayne *Can* 5K5
Horn I *USA* 13B2
Horn Mts *Can* 4F3
Hornsea *Eng* 33E5
Horn Uul, Mt *Mongolia* 50B1
Horqin-Youyi Qianqi *China* 51A2
Horqin Zuoyi *China* 51A3
Horqueta *Par* 23E2
Horseheads *USA* 12B1
Horsens *Den* 40C1
Horseshoe Bay *Can* 16B1
Horseshoe Bend *USA* 16C2
Horsham *Aust* 78B3
Horsham *Eng* 33E6
Horten *Nor* 30G7
Horton, R *Can* 8O2
Hose Mts *Malay* 54D2
Hoshab *Pak* 61E3
Hoshangābād *India* 58D4
Hoshiārpur *India* 58D2
Hosington *USA* 14C2
Hospet *India* 60B1
Hoste, I *Chile* 23C9
Hotan *China* 57F2
Hotazel *S Africa* 72C2
Hot Springs, Arkansas *USA* 15D3
Hot Springs, S. Dakota *USA* 9B3
Hottah *Can* 4G3
Hottentot Pt *Namibia* 72A2
Houdan *France* 34A2
Houghton *USA* 10B1
Houlton *USA* 11F1
Houma *China* 50C2
Houma *USA* 15D4
Houmet Essouq *Tunisia* 69E2
Houndé *U Volta* 69F3
Houqi *China* 51A3
Housatonic, R *USA* 12D2
Houston *Can* 3C3
Houston, Mississippi *USA* 15E3
Houston, Texas *USA* 15C4
Houtman, Is *Aust* 76A3
Houtzdale *USA* 12A2
Hovd *Mongolia* 48C2
Hövsgol Nuur, L *Mongolia* 48D1
Howard *Aust* 78D1
Howard City *USA* 10B2
Howard P *USA* 8G2
Howe,C *Aust* 78C3
Howe Sd *Can* 16B1
Howick *S Africa* 72E2
Howland *USA* 11F1
Höxter *W Germ* 34E1
Hoy, I *Scot* 32D2
Høyanger *Nor* 30F6
Hoyt Lakes *USA* 9D2
Hradeç-Králové *Czech* 40D2
Hranice *Czech* 41D3
Hron, R *Czech* 41D3
Hsin-chu *Taiwan* 50E5
Hsipaw *Burma* 59E3
Hsüeh Shan, Mt *Taiwan* 50E5
Hsuyong *S Korea* 52A4
Huab, R *Namibia* 72A1
Huachi *China* 50B2
Huacho *Peru* 24C6
Huade *China* 50C1
Huaibei *China* 50D3
Huaibin *China* 50D3
Huaide *China* 51A3
Huai He, R *China* 50D3
Huaihua *China* 50C4
Huaiji *China* 50C5
Huainan *China* 50D3
Hualapai Peak, Mt *USA* 17D3
Hualfin *Arg* 26B1
Hua-lien *Taiwan* 48F4
Huallaga, R *Peru* 24C5
Huallanca *Peru* 24C5
Huamachuco *Peru* 24C5
Huambo *Angola* 71B5
Huanan *China* 51C2
Huanay *Bol* 24E7
Huancabamba *Peru* 24C5
Huancavelica *Peru* 24C6
Huancayo *Peru* 24C6
Huangchuan *China* 50D3
Huange He, R *China* 50A3
Huang Hai = Yellow S
Huang He, R *China* 50D2
Huangling *China* 50B2
Huangliu *China* 53D2
Huangnihe *China* 51B3
Huangpi *China* 50C3
Huangshi *China* 50D3
Huanguelén *Arg* 26C3
Huangyan *China* 50E4
Huanren *China* 51B3
Huánuco *Peru* 24C5
Huanuni *Bol* 23C1
Huan Xian *China* 50B2
Huaráz *Peru* 24C5
Huarmey *Peru* 24C6
Huascarán, Mt *Peru* 24C5
Huasco *Chile* 26A1
Huasco, R *Chile* 26A1
Huatusco *Mexico* 20C2
Huauchinango *Mexico* 20C1
Huaunamota, R *Mexico* 20B1
Huautla *Mexico* 20C2
Hua Xian *China* 50C2
Huayapan, R *Mexico* 19B2
Hubei, Province *China* 50C3
Huben *Austria* 35E1
Hubli *India* 60B1
Hucal *Arg* 26C3
Huch'ang *N Korea* 51B3
Huddersfield *Eng* 33E5
Hudiksvall *Sweden* 30H6
Hudson, Florida *USA* 13C3
Hudson, Michigan *USA* 10C2
Hudson, New York *USA* 12D1
Hudson, R *USA* 12D1
Hudson B *Can* 5K4
Hudson Bay *Can* 4H4
Hudson Falls *USA* 12D1
Hudson's Hope *Can* 3D2
Hudson Str *Can* 5L3
Hue *Viet* 53D2
Huejuqvilla *Mexico* 20B1
Huejutla *Mexico* 20C1
Huelva *Spain* 37A2
Hueramo *Mexico* 20B2
Húercal Overa *Spain* 37B2

Huertecillas *Mexico* **20B1**
Huesca *Spain* **37B1**
Huexotla, Hist Site *Mexico* **20C2**
Hughenden *Aust* **76D3**
Hughes *USA* **8H2**
Hughes, R *Can* **3H2**
Hugli, R *India* **59C3**
Hugo *USA* **15C3**
Hugoton *USA* **14B2**
Hui'an *China* **50D4**
Huiarau Range, Mts *NZ* **79C1**
Huib Hochplato, Plat *Namibia* **72B2**
Hŭich'ŏn *N Korea* **51B3**
Huifa He, R *China* **51B3**
Huilai *China* **50D5**
Huili *China* **50A4**
Huillapima *Arg* **26B1**
Huimanguillo *Mexico* **20D2**
Huinan *China* **51B3**
Huinca Renancó *Arg* **26C2**
Huisne, R *France* **34A2**
Huixtla *Mexico* **19C3**
Huizache *Mexico* **20B1**
Huize *China* **50A4**
Huizhou *China* **50C5**
Hujuápan de Léon *Mexico* **20C2**
Hukawng Valley *Burma* **59E2**
Hulan *China* **51B2**
Hulayfah *S Arabia* **64D1**
Hulin *China* **51C2**
Hull *Can* **11D1**
Hull *Eng* **33E5**
Hull, I *Phoenix Is* **77H1**
Hulla, Mt *Colombia* **24C3**
Hultsfred *Sweden* **40D1**
Hulun Nur, L *China* **47N5**
Huma *China* **51B1**
Huma He, R *China* **51A1**
Humaita *Brazil* **24F5**
Humansdorp *S Africa* **72C3**
Humber, R *Eng* **33E5**
Humberside, County *Eng* **33E5**
Humboldt *Can* **4H4**
Humboldt, Iowa *USA* **9D3**
Humboldt, Tennessee *USA* **13B1**
Humboldt, R *USA* **16C2**
Humboldt B *USA* **16B2**
Humboldt Gletscher, Gl *Greenland* **5M2**
Humboldt L *USA* **17C3**
Humeburn *Aust* **78C1**
Hume,L *Aust* **78C3**
Humpata *Angola* **71B5**
Humphreys *USA* **18C2**
Humphreys,Mt, California *USA* **18C2**
Humphreys Peak, Mt, Arizona *USA* **17D3**
Húnaflóri, B *Iceland* **30A1**
Hunan, Province *China* **50C4**
Hunchun *China* **51C3**
Hundred Mile House *Can* **3D3**
Hunedoara *Rom* **39E1**
Hünfeld *W Germ* **34E1**
Hungary, Republic *Europe* **41D3**
Hungerford *Aust* **78B1**
Hŭngnam *N Korea* **51B4**
Hungry Horse Res *USA* **16D1**
Hunjiang *China* **51B3**
Hunsberge, Mts *Namibia* **72B2**
Hunsrück, Mts *W Germ* **34D2**
Hunter, R *Aust* **78D2**
Hunter I *Can* **3C3**
Hunter Is *Aust* **78E3**
Hunter,Mt *USA* **8H3**
Huntingburg *USA* **10B3**
Huntingdon *Eng* **33E5**
Huntingdon, Indiana *USA* **10B2**
Huntingdon, Pennsylvania *USA* **12A2**
Huntington *USA* **10C3**
Huntington Beach *USA* **18C4**
Huntington L *USA* **18C2**
Huntly *NZ* **79C1**
Huntly *Scot* **32D3**
Hunt,Mt *Can* **8N3**
Hunt Pen *Aust* **78A1**
Huntsville, Alabama *USA* **13B2**
Huntsville *Can* **11D1**
Huntsville, Texas *USA* **15C3**
Huolongmen *China* **51B2**
Huong Khe *Viet* **53D2**
Huon Peninsula, Pen *PNG* **49H7**
Huonville *Anst* **78E3**
Hurd,C *Can* **10C1**
Hurghada *Egypt* **64B1**
Hurley *USA* **10A1**
Huron, California *USA* **18B2**
Huron, S. Dakota *USA* **9C3**
Huron,L *USA/Can* **10C1**
Hurtado *Chile* **26A2**
Hurunui, R *NZ* **79B2**
Husavik *Iceland* **30B1**
Huşi *Rom* **39F1**
Huskvarna *Sweden* **30G7**
Huslia *USA* **8G2**
Husn *Jordan* **63C2**
Husum *W Germ* **40B2**
Hutchinson *USA* **15C2**
Hutton,Mt *Aust* **78C1**
Hutuo He, R *China* **50D2**
Huy *Belg* **34C1**
Huzhu *China* **50A2**
Hvar, I *Yugos* **38D2**
Hwadae *N Korea* **52A2**
Hwange *Zim* **71C5**
Hwange Nat Pk *Zim* **71C5**
Hwapyong *N Korea* **52A2**
Hyannis, Massachusetts *USA* **12E2**
Hyannis, Nebraska *USA* **9B3**
Hyaryas Nuur, L *Mongolia* **48C2**
Hydaburg *USA* **3B2**
Hyde Park *USA* **12D2**
Hyderābād *India* **60B1**
Hyderabad *Pak* **58B3**
Hyères *France* **35B3**
Hyhe *Can* **3E2**
Hyland, R *Can* **8N3**
Hyndman *USA* **12A3**
Hyndman Peak, Mt *USA* **6B2**
Hyrynsalmi *Fin* **42D3**
Hyūga *Japan* **51C5**
Hyvikää *Fin* **30J6**

I

Iaçu *Brazil* **25K6**
Ialomiţa, R *Rom* **39F2**
Iärpen *Sweden* **30G6**
Iaşi *Rom* **39F1**
Ibadan *Nig* **69G4**
Ibagué *Colombia* **24C3**
Ibar, R *Yugos* **39E2**
Ibarra *Ecuador* **24C3**
Ibb *Yemen* **64D4**
Ibi *Nig* **69H4**
Ibiá *Brazil* **27C2**
Ibicaraí *Brazil* **27E1**
Ibicui, R *Brazil* **26D1**
Ibicuy *Arg* **26D2**
Ibirubá *Brazil* **26E1**
Ibiza *Spain* **37C2**
Ibiza, I *Spain* **37C2**
Ibo *Mozam* **71E5**
Ibotirama *Brazil* **25K6**
'Ibri *Oman* **65G2**
Ica *Peru* **24C6**
Icá, R *Brazil* **24E4**
Icana *Brazil* **24E3**
Iceland, Republic *N Atlantic O* **30A1**
Ice Mt *Can* **3D3**
Icha *USSR* **47R4**
Ichalkaranji *India* **60A1**
Ichihara *Japan* **51E4**
Ichinomiya *Japan* **52C3**
Ichinoseki *Japan* **51E4**
Icy B *USA* **8K4**
Icy C *USA* **8F1**
Icy Str *USA* **3A2**
Ida, R *USSR* **47L4**
Idabell *USA* **15D3**
Ida Grove *USA* **9C3**
Idah *Nig* **69H4**
Idaho, State *USA* **16D2**
Idaho City *USA* **16C2**
Idaho Falls *USA* **16D2**
Idaho Springs *USA* **14A2**
Idanha *USA* **16B2**
Idar Oberstein *W Germ* **34D2**
Idehan Marzūg, Desert *Libya* **67A2**
Idehan Ubari, Desert *Libya* **67A2**
Idelés *Alg* **68C2**
Iderlym Gol, R *Mongolia* **48C2**
Idfu *Egypt* **64B2**
Ídhi Óros, Mt *Greece* **39E3**
Ídhra, I *Greece* **39E3**
Idiofa *Zaïre* **70B4**
Iditarod, R *USA* **8G3**
Idlib *Syria* **62C2**
Idrija *Yugos* **35E2**
Idritsa *USSR* **30K7**
Idutywa *S Africa* **72D3**
Ierápetra *Greece* **39F3**
Iesi *Italy* **35E3**
Ifakara *Tanz* **71D4**
Ifalik, I *Pacific* **49H6**
Ifanadiana *Madag* **71E6**
Ife *Nig* **69G4**
Iférouane *Niger* **68C3**
Igan *Malay* **54D2**
Igaranava *Brazil* **27C3**
Igarka *USSR* **46K3**
Igatimi *Par* **27A3**
Igbetti *Nig* **69G4**
Igdir *Iran* **62E2**
Iggesund *Sweden* **30H6**
Iglesia *Arg* **26B2**
Iglesias *Sardegna* **38B3**
Igloolik *Can* **5K3**
Ignace *Can* **7D2**
Iğneada Burun, Pt *Turk* **62A1**
Ignoitijala *Andaman Is* **60E2**
Igoumenítsa *Greece* **39E3**
Igra *USSR* **42J4**
Igrim *USSR* **42L3**
Iguala *Mexico* **20C2**
Iguape *Brazil* **23G2**
Iguatama *Brazil* **27C3**
Iguatemi *Brazil* **27B3**
Iguatemi, R *Brazil* **27A3**
Iguatu *Brazil* **25L5**
Iguéla *Gabon* **70A4**
Igumale *Nig* **69H4**
Ihiala *Nig* **69H4**
Ihosy *Madag* **71E6**
Iida *Japan* **51D4**
Iide-san, Mt *Japan* **52C3**
Iisalmi *Fin* **30K6**
Iizuka *Japan* **52B4**
Ijebulgbo *Nig* **69G4**
Ijebu Ode *Nig* **69G4**
Ijsselmeer, S *Neth* **40B2**
Ijuí *Brazil* **26E1**
Ijui, R *Brazil* **26D1**
Ikaría, I *Greece* **39F3**
Ikeda *Japan* **51E3**
Ikela *Zaïre* **70C4**
Ikerre *Nig* **69H4**
Ikhtiman *Bulg* **39E2**
Iki, I *Japan* **52A4**
Ikire *Nig* **69G4**
Ikolik,C *USA* **8H4**
Ikopa, R *Madag* **71E5**
Ila *Nig* **69G4**
Ilagan *Phil* **55F7**
Ilām *Iran* **61B2**
Ilanskiy *USSR* **48C1**
Ilanz *Switz* **35C1**
Ilaro *Nig* **69G4**
Île à la Crosse *Can* **3G2**
Île à la Crosse,L *Can* **3G2**
Ilebo *Zaire* **66G8**
Île De France, Region *France* **34B2**
Île de Jerba, I *Tunisia* **69E2**
Île de Noirmoutier, I *France* **36B2**
Ile de Ré, I *France* **36B2**
Île des Pins, I *Nouvelle Calédonie* **77F3**
Ile d'Orleans *Can* **11E1**
Ile d'Ouessant, I *France* **36A2**
Ile d'Yeu, I *France* **36B2**
Ilek, R *USSR* **43K5**
Ile María Cleofas, I *Mexico* **20A1**
Ile María Madre, I *Mexico* **20A1**
Ile María Magdalena *Mexico* **20A1**
Ile San Juanico, I *Mexico* **20A1**
Îles Bélèp *Nouvelle Calédonie* **77F2**
Îles Chesterfield *Nouvelle Calédonie* **77E2**
Îles de Horn, Is *Pacific O* **77H2**
Iles d'Hyleres, Is *France* **36D3**
Ilesha *Nig* **69G4**
Iles Kerkenna, Is *Tunisia* **69E2**
Ilfracombe *Eng* **33C6**
Ilgaz Dağları, Mts *Turk* **62B1**
Ilha Bazaruto, I *Mozam* **71D6**
Ilha Comprida, I *Brazil* **27C3**
Ilha de Boipeba, I *Brazil* **27E1**
Ilha De Maracá, I *Brazil* **25H3**
Ilha de Marajó, I *Brazil* **25H4**
Ilha de São Francisco, I *Brazil* **27C4**
Ilha de São Sebastião, I *Brazil* **27C3**
Ilha de Tinharé, I *Brazil* **27E1**
Ilha do Bananal, Region *Brazil* **25H6**
Ilha do Cardoso, I *Brazil* **27C4**
Ilha Grande, I *Brazil* **27D3**
Ilha Grande ou Sete Quedas, I *Brazil* **27B3**
Ilha Santo Amaro, I *Brazil* **27C3**
Ilhas Selvegens, I *Atlantic O* **68A2**
Ilhéus *Brazil* **25L6**
Iliamna L *USA* **8G4**
Iliamna V *USA* **8H3**
Iliers *France* **34A2**
Iligan *Phil* **55F9**
Ilim, R *USSR* **48D1**
Il'inskiy *USSR* **51E2**
Iliodhrómia, I *Greece* **39E3**
Ilion *USA* **12C1**
Illana B *Phil* **55F9**
Illapel *Chile* **26A2**
Illapel, R *Chile* **26A2**
Illéla *Niger* **68C3**
Iller, R *W Germ* **35D1**
Illescas *Mexico* **20B1**
Îlles Wallis, Is *Pacific O* **77H2**
Illiamna L *USA* **4C4**
Illinois, State *USA* **10B2**
Illinois, R *USA* **10A3**
Illizi *Alg* **68C2**
Ilo *Peru* **24D7**
Iloilo *Phil* **55F8**
Ilomantsi *Fin* **30L6**
Ilorin *Nig* **69G4**
Ilwaki *Indon* **55C4**
Il'yino *USSR* **41G1**
Imabari *Japan* **52B4**
Imalchi *Japan* **52C3**
Imari *Japan* **52A4**
Imatra *Fin* **42D3**
Imbituba *Brazil* **23G3**
Imbitura *Brazil* **27B4**
Imi *Eth* **70E3**
Imjin, R *N Korea* **52A3**
Imlay *USA* **16C2**
Immenstadt *W Germ* **35D1**
Imo, State *Nig* **69H4**
Imola *Italy* **38C2**
Imperatriz *Brazil* **25J5**
Imperia *Italy* **38B2**
Imperial *USA* **14B1**
Imperial V *USA* **17C4**
Impfondo *Congo* **70B3**
Imphāl *India* **59D3**
Imst *Austria* **35D1**
Imuruk L *USA* **8F2**
Ina *Japan* **52C3**
In Afahleleh, Well *Alg* **68C2**
Inamba-jima, I *Japan* **52C4**
In Amenas *Alg* **68C2**
Inari *Fin* **30K5**
Inarijärvi, L *Fin* **30K5**
Inawashiro-ko, L *Japan* **52D3**
In Belbel *Alg* **68C2**
Ince Burun, Pt *Turk* **43F7**
Incekum Burun, Pt *Turk* **62B2**
Inch'ŏn *S Korea* **51B4**
In Dagouber, Well *Mali* **68B2**
Indais, R *Brazil* **27C2**
Indals, R *Sweden* **30H6**
Indefatigable, Gasfield *N Sea* **33G5**
Independence, California *USA* **18C2**
Independence, Iowa *USA* **9D3**
Independence, Kansas *USA* **15C2**
Independence, Missouri *USA* **15D2**
Independence Mts *USA* **16C2**
Inderagiri, R *Indon* **54B3**
Inderborskiy *USSR* **43J6**
India, Federal Republic *Asia* **57F4**
Indiana, State *USA* **10B2**
Indiana *USA* **11D2**
Indian-Antarctic Basin *Indian O* **74F7**
Indian-Antarctic Ridge *Indian O* **74F7**
Indianapolis *USA* **10B3**
Indian Desert = Thar Desert
Indian Harbour *Can* **5N4**
Indian Head *Can* **3H3**
Indian O **74E5**
Indianola, Iowa *USA* **15D1**
Indianola, Mississippi *USA* **15D3**
Indianópolis *Brazil* **27C2**
Indian Springs *USA* **17C3**
Indiga *USSR* **42H2**
Indigirka, R *USSR* **47Q3**
Indo China, Region *S E Asia* **53D2**
Indonesia, Republic *S E Asia* **49F7**
Indore *India* **58D4**
Indramayu *Indon* **54C4**
Indre, R *France* **36C2**
Indus, R *Pak* **58B3**
Inebdu *Turk* **43E7**
In Ebeggi, Well *Alg* **68C2**
Inebolu *Turk* **62B1**
In Ecker *Alg* **68C2**
Inegöl *Turk* **62A1**
In Ezzane *Alg* **68D2**
Infante,C *S Africa* **72C3**
Ingal *Niger* **68C3**
Ingersoll *Can* **10C2**
Ingham *Aust* **76D2**
Inglefield Land, Region *Can* **5M2**
Inglewood *NZ* **79B1**
Inglewood, Queensland *Aust* **78D1**
Inglewood *USA* **18C4**
Inglewood, Victoria *Aust* **78B3**
Ingólfshöfði, I *Iceland* **30B2**
Ingolstadt *W Germ* **40C3**
Ingrāj Bāzār *India* **59C3**
In-Guezzam, Well *Alg* **68C3**
Inhaca, I *Mozam* **72E2**
Inhaca Pen *Mozam* **72E2**
Inhambane *Mozam* **71D6**
Inharrime *Mozam* **71D6**
Inhumas *Brazil* **27C2**
Inirida, R *Colombia* **24E3**
Inishowen, District *Irish Rep* **32B4**
Injune *Aust* **78C1**
Inklin *Can* **3B2**
Inklin, R *Can* **8M4**
Inland L *USA* **8G2**
Inn, R *Austria* **35D1**
Innamincka *Aust* **78B1**
Inner Mongolia, Autonomous Region *China* **48D2**
Innisfail *Aust* **76D2**
Innokent'yevskiy *USSR* **51E2**
Innoko, R *USA* **8G3**
Innsbruck *Austria* **40C3**
Inongo *Zaïre* **70B4**
Inoucdjouac *Can* **5L4**
Inowrocław *Pol* **41D2**
In Salah *Alg* **68C2**
Insil *S Korea* **52A3**
Inta *USSR* **42K2**
Interlaken *Switz* **35B1**
International Date Line **77H3**
International Falls *USA* **9D2**
Intiyaco *Arg* **26C1**
Intra *Italy* **35C2**
Intu *Indon* **54E3**
Inubo-saki, C *Japan* **52D3**
Inuvik *Can* **4E3**
Inveraray *Scot* **32C3**
Invercargill *NZ* **79A3**
Inverell *Aust* **78D1**
Invermere *Can* **3E3**
Inverness *Scot* **32C2**
Inverurie *Scot* **32D3**
Investigator Str *Aust* **78A3**
Inya *USSR* **48B1**
Inya, R *USSR* **47Q3**
Inyanga *Zim* **71D5**
Inyokern *USA* **18D3**
Inyo Mts *USA* **18C2**
Inzia, R *Zaïre* **70B4**
Ioánnina *Greece* **39E3**
Iola *USA* **15C2**
Iolotan *USSR* **61E1**
Iona, I *Scot* **32B3**
Iôna Nat Pk *Angola* **71B5**
Ione *USA* **16C1**
Ionian Is = Iónioi Nísoi
Ionian S *Italy/Greece* **39D3**
Iónioi Nísoi, Is *Greece* **39E3**
Ioniveyem, R *USSR* **8D2**
Íos, I *Greece* **39F3**
Iowa, State *USA* **9D3**
Iowa, R *USA* **9D3**
Iowa City *USA* **10A2**
Iowa Falls *USA* **9D3**
Ipameri *Brazil* **27C2**
Ipanema *Brazil* **27D2**
Ipatovo *USSR* **43G6**
Ipiales *Colombia* **24C3**
Ipiaú *Brazil* **27E1**
Ipiranga *Brazil* **27B4**
Ipoh *Malay* **53C5**
Iporá *Brazil* **25H7**
Ipsala *Turk* **39F2**
Ipswich *Aust* **78D1**
Ipswich *Eng* **33F5**
Ipswich *USA* **12E1**
Iput, R *USSR* **41G2**
Iquape *Brazil* **27C3**
Iquique *Chile* **23B2**
Iquitos *Peru* **24D4**
Irai *Brazil* **26E1**
Iráklion *Greece* **39F3**
Iran, Republic *S W Asia* **56D2**
Irānshahr *Iran* **61E3**
Irapuato *Mexico* **20B1**
Iraq, Republic *S W Asia* **62D3**
Irati *Brazil* **27B4**
Irā Wan, Watercourse *Libya* **67A2**
Irbid *Jordan* **63C2**
Irbit *USSR* **42L4**
Irbit *USSR* **46H4**
Ireland, Republic *NW Europe* **28E3**
Ireng, R *Guyana* **25G3**
Iri *S Korea* **51B4**
Irian Jaya, Province *Indon* **49G7**
Iriba *Chad* **70C2**
Iriga *Phil* **55F8**
Iringa *Tanz* **71D4**
Iriomote, I *Japan* **48F4**
Iriona *Honduras* **21A3**
Iriri, R *Brazil* **25H5**
Irish S *Eng/Irish Rep* **33C5**
Irkillik, R *USA* **8H2**
Irkutsk *USSR* **47M4**
Irlysh *USSR* **46J4**
Iron Knob *Aust* **78A2**
Iron Mountain *USA* **10B1**
Iron Range *Aust* **76D2**
Iron River *USA* **10B1**
Irontown *USA* **10C3**
Ironwood *USA* **10A1**
Iroquois Falls *Can* **7E2**
Iro-zaki, C *Japan* **52C4**
Irrawaddy, R *Burma* **59E4**

Irrawaddy,Mouths of the Burma 53A2
Irtysh, R USSR 46H4
Irun Spain 37B1
Irvine Scot 32C4
Irving USA 15C3
Isa Nig 69H3
Isabela Phil 55F9
Isabella Res USA 18C3
Isachsen Can 4H2
Isachsen,C Can 4H2
Ísafjörður Iceland 5Q3
Isahaya Japan 51C5
Isangi Zaïre 70C3
Isar, R W Germ 35D1
Isarco, R Italy 35D1
Isbister Scot 32E1
Ischgl Austria 35D1
Ischia, I Italy 38C2
Ise Japan 52C4
Iseo Italy 35D2
Isère, R France 35A2
Iserlohn W Germ 34D1
Isernia Italy 38C2
Ise-wan, B Japan 52C4
Iseyin Nig 69G4
Ishigaki, I Japan 48F4
Ishikari, R Japan 51E3
Ishikari-wan, B Japan 51E3
Ishim USSR 46H4
Ishim, R USSR 46H4
Ishinomaki Japan 51E4
Ishioka Japan 52D3
Ishkashim Afghan 58C1
Ishpeming USA 10B1
Isil'kul USSR 46J4
Isimu Indon 55B2
Isiolo Kenya 70D3
Isiro Zaïre 70C3
Iskenderun Turk 62C2
Iskenferun Körfezi, B Turk 62C2
İskilip Turk 62B1
Iskitim USSR 46K4
Iskur, R Bulg 39E2
Iskut, R Can/USA 8M4
Isla Mexico 20C2
Isla Apipe Grande Arg 26D1
Isla Beata Dom Rep 21C3
Isla Bermejo, I Arg 26C3
Isla Blanquilla Ven 21E4
Isla Coiba, I Panama 24B2
Isla de Cedros, I Mexico 6B4
Isla de Chiloé, I Chile 23B6
Isla de Cozumel, I Mexico 19D2
Isla de la Gorâve Cuba 21C3
Isla de la Juventud, I Cuba 21A2
Isla de las Lechiguanas, I Arg 26D2
Isla del Coco, I Costa Rica 2K8
Isla del Maiz, I Caribbean 19D3
Isla de Lobos, I Mexico 20C1
Isla de los Estados, I Arg 23D8
Isla de Marajó, I Brazil 22F4
Isla de Pascua, I Pacific O 75O6
Isla de Providencia, I Caribbean 21A4
Isla de San Andres, I Caribbean 21A4
Isla de Santa Catarina, I Brazil 23G3
Isla du Diable, I French Guiana 25H2
Isla Fernando de Noronha, I Brazil 25M4
Isla Grande de Tierra del Fuego, I Arg/Chile 23C8
Isla la Tortuga, I Ven 21D4
Islamabad Pak 58C2
Isla Magdalena, I Mexico 19A2
Isla Margarita Ven 21E4
Isla Mocha Chile 26A3
Islamorada USA 13E4
Island L Can 7D1
Island Lg Aust 78A2
Island Park USA 16D2
Islands,B of NZ 79B1
Isla Providencia, I Colombia 24B1
Isla Puná, I Ecuador 24B4
Isla San Ambrosia, I Pacific O 73D6
Isla San Felix, I Pacific O 73D6
Isla Santa Margarita, I Mexico 19A2
Isla Santa Maria, I Chile 26A3
Islas Baleares, Is Spain 37C2
Islas Canarias, Is Atlantic O 68A2
Islas Columbretes, Is Spain 37C2
Islas de la Bahia, Is Honduras 19D3
Islas del Maíz, Is Caribbean 21A4
Islas de Margarita, Is Ven 24F1
Islas Diego Ramírez, Is Chile 23C9
Islas Galapagos, Is Pacific O 24N
Islas Juan Fernandez, Is Pacific O 24Q
Islas los Roques, Is Ven 24E1
Islas Malvinas = Falkland Is
Islas Revilla Gigedo, Is Pacific O 75O4
Islas Wollaston Is Chile 23C9
Isla Tidra, I Maur 68A3
Isla Wellington, I Chile 23B7
Islay, I Scot 32B4
Isle, R France 36C2
Isle Amsterdam, I Indian O 74E6
Isle au Haut, I USA 11F2
Isle of Wight, I Eng 33E6
Isle Royale, I USA 10B1
Isle Royale Nat Pk USA 10B1
Isle St Paul, I Indian O 74E6
Îles Crozet, I Indian O 74D7
Îles de la Société Pacific O 75M5
Îles Gambier, Is Pacific O 75N6
Isles Glorieuses, Is Madag 71E5
Îles Kerguelen, Is Indian O 74E7
Îles Loyauté, Is Nouvelle Calédonie 77F3
Îles Marquises, Is Pacific O 75N5
Îles Tuamotu, Is Pacific O 75M5
Îles Tubai, Is Pacific O 75M6
Isleton USA 18B1
Ismâ'ilîya Egypt 62B3
Isna Egypt 64B1
Isoanala Madag 71E6
Isoka Zambia 71D5
Isola di Capraia, I Italy 35C3
Isola Egadi, I Italy 38C3
Isola Ponziane, I Italy 38C2
Isole Lipari, Is Italy 38C3
Isoles Tremiti, Is Italy 38D2
Isosaki Japan 52C3
Isparta Turk 62B2
Israel, Republic S W Asia 63C2
Isser, R Alg 37C2
Issoire France 36C2
Issoudun France 36C2
Is-sur-Tille France 35A1
Istanbul Turk 62A1
Istiáia Greece 39E3
Istmo de Tehuantepec, Isthmus Mexico 20D2
Istokpoga,L USA 13E4
Istra, Pen Yugos 38C1
Istranca Dağlari, Upland Turk 39F2
Itaberai Brazil 27C2
Itabira Brazil 27D2
Itabirito Brazil 27D3
Itabuna Brazil 27E1
Itacaré Brazil 27E1
Itacoatiara Brazil 25G4
Itacurubi del Rosario Par 27A3
Itagui Colombia 24C2
Itaituba Brazil 25G4
Itajai Brazil 23G3
Itajuba Brazil 27C3
Italy, Repubic Europe 38C2
Itamaraju Brazil 27E2
Itamarandiba Brazil 27D2
Itambacuri Brazil 27D2
Itambe Brazil 27D2
Itambé, Mt Brazil 27D2
Itänagar India 59D2
Itanhaém Brazil 27C3
Itanhém Brazil 27D2
Itanhém, R Brazil 27D2
Itaobím Brazil 27D2
Itapaci Brazil 27C1
Itapecerica Brazil 27C3
Itaperuna Brazil 27D3
Itapetinga Brazil 25K7
Itapetininga Brazil 27C3
Itapeva Brazil 27C3
Itapipoca Brazil 25L4
Itapuranga Brazil 27C2
Itaquari, R Brazil 27C1
Itaqui Brazil 26D1
Itarantim Brazil 27D2
Itararé Brazil 27C3
Itararé, R Brazil 27C3
Itaúna Brazil 27D3
Iténez, R Brazil/Bol 24F6
Ithaca USA 11D2
Ith Hills, Mts W Germ 34E1
Itimbiri, R Zaïre 70C3
Itinga Brazil 27D2
Itiquira, R Brazil 27A2
Itivdleq Greenland 5N3
Itjørdal Nor 30G6
Ito Japan 52C4
Itoigawa Japan 51D4
Iton, R France 34A2
Itonomas, R Bol 24F6
Itu Brazil 27C3
Itu Nig 69H4
Ituberá Brazil 27E1
Itumbiara Brazil 27C2
Iturama Brazil 27B2
Iturbe Arg 23C2
Iturbide Mexico 20C1
Iturutaba Brazil 27C2
Ituzzaingó Arg 26D1
Itzehoe W Germ 40E2
Iul'tin USSR 47T3
Iurga USSR 46K4
Ivacevichi USSR 41F2
Ivai, R Brazil 27B3
Ivalo Fin 30K5
Ivangrad Yugos 39D2
Ivanhoe Aust 78B2
Ivano USSR 46D5
Ivano-Frankovsk USSR 41E3
Ivanovo USSR 42G4
Ivdel' USSR 42L3
Ivindo, R Gabon 70B3
Ivinhema Brazil 27B3
Ivinhema, R Brazil 27B3
Ivohibe Madag 71E6
Ivongo Soanierana Madag 71E5
Ivory Coast, Republic Africa 68B4
Ivrea Italy 38B1
Ivujivik Can 5L3
Iwaki Japan 51E4
Iwaki, R Japan 52D2
Iwaki-san, Mt Japan 52D2
Iwakuni Japan 51C5
Iwamizawa Japan 52D2
Iwanai Japan 51E3
Iwo Nig 69G4
Iwo Jima, I Japan 48H4
Ixcuintla Mexico 20B1
Ixmiquilpa Mexico 20C1
Ixtapa Mexico 20B2
Ixtepec Mexico 20C2
Ixtlán Mexico 20B1
Iyo Japan 52B4
Iyo-nada, B Japan 52B4
Izhevsk USSR 46G4
Izhma USSR 42J2
Izhma, R USSR 42J2
Izigan,C USA 8E5
Izki Oman 65G2
Izmail USSR 41F3
İzmir Turk 62A2
İzmir Körfezi, B Turk 39F3
İzmit Turk 62A1
İznik Turk 62A1
Iznik Golü, L Turk 39F2
Izra' Syria 63D2
Izúcar de Matamoros Mexico 20C2
Izuhara Japan 52A4
Izumi-sano Japan 52C4
Izumo Japan 52B3
Izu-shotō, Is Japan 51D5
Izvestkovyy USSR 51C2

J

Jabal al Akhdar, Mts Libya 67B1
Jabal al 'Arab Syria 63D2
Jabal al Qara', Mts Oman 65F3
Jabal an Nuşayriyah, Mts Syria 63D1
Jabal as Sawdā, Mts Libya 67A2
Jabal az Zannah UAE 65F2
Jabal Halimah, Mt Syria/Leb 63D1
Jabal Mahrāt, Mts S Yemen 65F3
Jabalpur India 59B3
Jabal Shammar, Region S Arabia 64D1
Jabal Tuwayq, Mts S Arabia 65E2
Jablah Syria 63C1
Jablonec nad Nisou Czech 40D2
Jaboatão Brazil 25L5
Jaca Spain 37B1
Jacala Mexico 20C1
Jacareacanga Brazil 25G5
Jacarezinho Brazil 25H8
Jacarie Brazil 27C3
Jáchal Arg 23C4
Jaciara Brazil 27B2
Jacinto Brazil 27D2
Jackfish L Can 3G3
Jackman Station USA 11E1
Jacksboro USA 14C3
Jacks Mt USA 12B2
Jackson, Alabama USA 13B2
Jackson Aust 78C1
Jackson, California USA 18B1
Jackson, Michigan USA 10C2
Jackson, Minnesota USA 9D3
Jackson, Mississippi USA 15D3
Jackson, Missouri USA 10B3
Jackson, Ohio USA 10C3
Jackson, Tennessee USA 13B1
Jackson, Wyoming USA 16D2
Jackson,C NZ 79B2
Jackson Head, Pt NZ 79A2
Jackson L USA 16D2
Jacksonville, Arkansas USA 15D3
Jacksonville, Florida USA 13C2
Jacksonville, Illinois USA 10A3
Jacksonville, N Carolina USA 13D2
Jacksonville, Texas USA 15C3
Jacksonville Beach USA 13C2
Jacmel Haiti 21C3
Jacobabad Pak 58B3
Jacobina Brazil 25K6
Jacona Mexico 20B2
Jacui, R Brazil 26E1
Jädib S Yemen 65F3
Jadotville = Likasi
Jaén Peru 24C5
Jaén Spain 37B2
Jaffa = Tel Aviv Yafo
Jaffa,C Aust 78A3
Jaffna Sri Lanka 60B3
Jaffrey USA 12D1
Jagannathganj Ghat Bang 59C3
Jagdalpur India 60C1
Jagdaqi China 51A1
Jagin, R Iran 61D3
Jagtial India 60B1
Jaguaquara Brazil 27E1
Jaguarão Brazil 26E2
Jaguarão, R Brazil 26E2
Jaguarialva Brazil 27C3
Jagüé Arg 26B1
Jagüé, R Arg 26B1
Jahan Dāgh, Mt Iran 43H8
Jahrom Iran 61C3
Jailolo Indon 55C2
Jāina India 58D5
Jainca China 50A2
Jaipur India 58D3
Jaisalmer India 58C3
Jajarm Iran 61D1
Jajce Yugos 38D2
Jakarta Indon 54C4
Jakes Corner Can 3B1
Jakobshavn Greenland 5N3
Jakobstad Fin 30J6
Jal USA 14B3
Jalaca Mexico 20C2
Jalaid Qi China 51A2
Jalai-Kut Afghan 58B2
Jalapa Mexico 20C2
Jales Brazil 27B3
Jaleswar Nepal 59C2
Jalgaon India 58D4
Jalingo Nig 69J4
Jalisco, State Mexico 20A2
Jalón, R Spain 37B1
Jalo Oasis Libya 67B2
Jālor India 58C3
Jalostotitlan Mexico 20B1
Jalpāiguri India 59C2
Jalpan Mexico 20C1
Jama Ecuador 24B4
Jamaaré, R Nig 69H3
Jamaica, I Caribbean 21B3
Jamaica Chan Caribbean 21B3
Jamalpur Bang 59C3
Jambi Indon 54B3
Jambussar India 58C4
James, R, N. Dakota USA 9C2
James, R, Virginia USA 11D3
James B Can 5K4
Jameston USA 4J5
Jamestown Aust 78A2
Jamestown, N. Dakota USA 9C2
Jamestown, New York USA 11D2
Jamestown, Rhode Island USA 12E2
Jamestown S Africa 72D3
Jamiltepec Mexico 20C2
Jamkhandi India 60B1
Jammu India 58C2
Jammu and Kashmir, State India 58D2
Jamnagar India 58B4
Jampur Pak 58C3
Jämsä Fin 42C3
Jamshedpur India 59C3
Janakpur Nepal 59C2
Janaúba Brazil 27D2
Jandaq Iran 61C2
Jandowae Aust 78D1
Janesville USA 10B2
Jan Mayen, I Norwegian S 80B1
Januária Brazil 27D2
Jaora India 58D4
Japan, Empire E Asia 51
Japan,S of S E Asia 51C4
Japan Trench Pacific O 74J3
Japurá, R Brazil 24E4
Jarābulus Syria 62C2
Jaraguá Brazil 27C2
Jaraguari Brazil 27B3
Jarama, R Spain 37B1
Jarash Jordan 63C2
Jardim Brazil 27A3
Jardin, R Spain 37B2
Jardines de la Reina, Is Cuba 21B2
Jargalant = Hovd
Jari, R Brazil 25H3
Jaria Jhānjail Bang 59D2
Jarny France 34C2
Jarocin Pol 40D2
Jaroslaw Pol 41E2
Järpen Sweden 42A3
Jartai China 50B2
Jasdan India 58C4
Jasikan Ghana 69G4
Jāsk Iran 61D3
Jaslo Pol 41E3
Jason Is Falkland Is 23D8
Jasper, Alabama USA 13B2
Jasper, Arkansas USA 15D2
Jasper Can 3E3
Jasper, Florida USA 13C2
Jasper, Indiana USA 10B3
Jasper, Texas USA 15D3
Jasper Nat Pk Can 3E3
Jastrowie Pol 40D2
Jatai Brazil 27B2
Játiva Spain 37B2
Jatobá Brazil 25J4
Jau Brazil 27C3
Jauja Peru 24C6
Jaumave Mexico 20C1
Jaunpur India 59B2
Java = Jawa
Javadi Hills India 60B2
Javand Afghan 61E1
Javari = Yavari
Java S Indon 49D7
Java Trench Indon 76A2
Jawa, I Indon 54C4
Jayapura Indon 49H7
Jayrūd Syria 63D2
Jazá'ir Farasān, Is S Arabia 64D3
Jazirat Maşirah, I Oman 65G2
Jazminal Mexico 20B1
Jbel Ayachi, Mt Mor 69B2
Jbel Ouarkziz, Mts Mor 68B2
Jbel Sarhro, Mt Mor 68B1
Jeanerette USA 15D4
Jebba Nig 69G4
Jebel 'Abd al 'Aziz, Mt Syria 62D2
Jebel Abyad, Desert Region Sudan 70C2
Jebel Akhdar, Mt Oman 65G2
Jebel al Lawz, Mt S Arabia 62C4
Jebel ash Shaykh, Mt Syria 63C2
Jebel Asoteriba, Mt Sudan 70D1
Jebel az Zāwiyah, Upland Syria 63D1
Jebel Bāqir, Mt Jordan 63C4
Jebel Belaia, Mt Eth 64C4
Jebel Ed Dabab, Mt Jordan 63C3
Jebel el Ata'ita, Mt Jordan 63C3
Jebel el Harad, Mt Jordan 63C4
Jebel esh Sharqi, Mts Leb/Syria 62C3
Jebel Hamoyet, Mt Sudan 64C3
Jebel Hārūn, Mt Jordan 63C3
Jebel Ithriyat, Mt Jordan 63D3
Jebel Ja'lan, Mt Oman 65G2
Jebel Liban, Mts Leb 63C2
Jebel Ma'lūlā, Mt Syria 63D2
Jebel Marra, Mt Sudan 70C2
Jebel Mubrak, Mt Jordan 63C3
Jebel Mudeisisat, Mt Jordan 63D3
Jebel Oda, Mt Sudan 64C2
Jebel Qasr ed Deir, Mt Jordan 63C3
Jebel Qatim, Mt Jordan 63C4
Jebel Ram Jordan 63C4
Jebel Um ed Daraj, Mt Jordan 63C2
Jebel Um el Hashim, Mt Jordan 63C4
Jebel Um Ishrīn, Mt Jordan 63C4
Jebel Uweinat, Mt Sudan 70C1
Jedburgh Scot 32D4
Jedda = Jiddah
Jedrzejów Pol 41E2
Jefferson, Iowa USA 9D3
Jefferson, Texas USA 15D3
Jefferson, R USA 16D1
Jefferson City USA 7D3

Jefferson,Mt USA 6B3
Jeffersonville USA 10B3
Jega Nig 69G3
Jejui-Guazú, R Par 27A3
Jekabpils USSR 42D4
Jelena Gora Pol 40D2
Jelgava USSR 42C4
Jember Indon 54D4
Jemez Pueblo USA 14A2
Jena E Germ 40C2
Jenaja, I Indon 54C2
Jenbach Austria 35D1
Jendouba Tunisia 69D1
Jenin Israel 63C2
Jennings USA 15D3
Jennings, R Can 3B2
Jenseniky, Upland Czech 40D2
Jensen Nunatakker, Mt Greenland 5O3
Jens Munk, I Can 5K3
Jeparit Aust 78B3
Jequié Brazil 25L6
Jequital, R Brazil 27D2
Jequitinhonha Brazil 27D2
Jequitinhonha, R Brazil 25K7
Jerada Mor 69B2
Jerantut Malay 54G7
Jerez Mexico 20B1
Jerez de la Frontera Spain 37A2
Jerez de los Caballeros Spain 37A2
Jericho Israel 63C3
Jerilderie Aust 78C3
Jerome USA 16D2
Jersey, I UK 36B2
Jersey City USA 7F2
Jersey Shore USA 11D2
Jerseyville USA 10A3
Jerusalem Israel 62C3
Jervis B Aust 78D3
Jervis Inlet, Sd Can 3D3
Jesenice Yugos 38C1
Jessore Bang 59C3
Jesup USA 7E3
Jesus Carranza Mexico 20D2
Jesus Maria Arg 26C2
Jetmore USA 14C2
Jewett City USA 12E2
Jeypore India 60C1
Jezerce, Mt Alb 39D2
Jezioro Mamry, L Pol 41E2
Jezioro Śniardwy, L Pol 41E2
Jezzine Leb 63C2
Jhābua India 58C4
Jhālāwār India 58D4
Jhang Maghiana Pak 58C2
Jhānsi India 58D3
Jhārsuguda India 59B3
Jhelum Pak 58C2
Jhelum, R Pak 58C2
Jhunjhunūn India 58D3
Jiamusi China 51C2
Ji'an, Jiangxi China 50C4
Ji'an, Jilin China 51B3
Jiande China 50D4
Jiang'an China 50B4
Jiangbiancun China 50D4
Jiangcheng China 50A5
Jiang Jiang, R China 50B3
Jiangjin China 5B4
Jiangmen China 50C5
Jiangsu, Province China 50D3
Jiangxi, Province China 50C4
Jiangyou China 50A3
Jianping China 50D1
Jianshui China 50A5
Jian Xi, R China 50D4
Jianyang China 50D4
Jiaohe China 51B3
Jiaonan China 50E2
Jiao Xian China 50E2
Jiaozhou Wan, B China 50E2
Jiaozuo China 50C2
Jiaxiang China 50E3
Jiayin China 51C2
Jiayuguan China 48C3
Jiddah S Arabia 64C2
Jiddat Al Harāsis, Region Oman 65G3
Jiddat az Zawliyah, Region Oman 65G2
Jieshou China 50D3
Jiexiu China 50C2
Jigzhi China 50A3
Jihlava Czech 40D3
Ji'jel Alg 69D1
Jilib Somalia 70E3
Jilin China 51B3
Jilin, Province China 51B3
Jiliu He, R China 51A1
Jiloca, R Spain 37B1
Jiménez, Coahuila Mexico 14B4
Jiménez, Tamaulipas Mexico 20C1
Jimma Eth 70D3
Jinan China 50D2
Jind India 58D3
Jingbian China 50B2

Jingdezhen China 50D4
Jinghong China 53C1
Jingmen China 50C3
Jingning China 50B2
Jing Xiang China 50B4
Jinhua China 50D4
Jining, Nei Monggol China 50C1
Jining, Shandong China 50D2
Jinja Uganda 70D3
Jinping China 53C1
Jinsha Jiang, R China 50A4
Jinshi China 50C4
Jinxi China 50E1
Jin Xian China 50E2
Jinzhou China 50E1
Jiparaná, R Brazil 24F5
Jipijapa Ecuador 24B4
Jiquilpan Mexico 20B2
Jiroft Iran 61D3
Jishou China 50B4
Jisr ash Shughūr Syria 62C2
Jiu, R Rom 39E2
Jiujiang China 50D4
Jiulong China 50A4
Jiulong Jiang, R China 50D4
Jiutai China 51B3
Jiwani Pak 61E3
Jixi China 51C2
Jiza Jordan 63C3
Jīzan S Arabia 64D3
Joal Sen 68A3
João Monlevade Brazil 27D2
João Pessoa Brazil 25M5
João Pinheiro Brazil 25J7
João Pirheiro Brazil 27C2
Joboticabal Brazil 27C3
Jocoli Arg 26B2
Jodhpur India 58C3
Joensuu Fin 30K6
Joeuf France 34C2
Joffre,Mt Can 3E3
Jogbani India 59C2
Jog Falls India 60A2
Johannesburg S Africa 72D2
Johannesburg USA 17C3
Johan Pen Can 5L2
John Can 3E2
John, R USA 8H2
John Day USA 16C2
John Day, R USA 16B1
John H. Kerr Res USA 11D3
John Martin Res USA 14B2
John O'Groats Scot 32D2
John Redmond Res USA 15C2
Johnsonburg USA 12A2
Johnson City, New York USA 12C1
Johnson City, Tennessee USA 13C1
Johnston USA 13C2
Johnston Pt St Vincent 21N2
Johnstown, New York USA 12C1
Johnstown, Pennsylvania USA 11D2
Johor Bharu Malay 53C5
Joigny France 36C2
Joinville Brazil 23G3
Joinville France 34C2
Jok, R USSR 42J5
Jokkmokk Sweden 30H5
Jöl, Mts S Yemen 65E4
Jolfa Iran 43H8
Joliet USA 7E2
Joliette Can 5L5
Jolo Phil 55F9
Jolo, I Phil 55F9
Joma, Mt China 57H2
Jonava USSR 41E1
Jonè China 50A3
Jonesboro, Arkansas USA 7D3
Jonesboro, Arkansas USA 10A3
Jonesboro, Louisiana USA 15D3
Jones Sd Can 5K2
Joniškis USSR 41E1
Jönköping Sweden 30G7
Jonquière Can 11E1
Joplin USA 7D3
Jordan, Kingdom S W Asia 62C3
Jordan, Montana USA 9A2
Jordan, New York USA 12B1
Jordan, R Israel 63C2
Jordan Valley USA 16C2
Jordão, R Brazil 27B4
Jorhāt India 59D2
Jörn Sweden 42C2
Jorong Indon 54D3
Jørpeland Nor 30F7
Jos Nig 69H4
José Batlle y Ordoñez Urug 26E2
Jose Pañganiban Phil 55F8
José Pedro Varela Urug 26E2
Joseph Bonaparte G Aust 76B2
Joseph City USA 17D3

Josephine, Oilfield N Sea 32G3
Jos Plat Nig 69H4
Jotunheimen, Mt Nor 46B3
Jouai'ya Leb 63C2
Jounié Leb 63C2
Jowal India 59D2
Jowhar Somalia 70E3
Joy,Mt Can 8M3
Juàjeiro Brazil 25K5
Juan Aldama Mexico 20B1
Juan de Fuca,Str of USA/Can 4F5
Juan de Nova, I Mozam Chan 71E5
Juárez Arg 26D3
Juazeiro do Norte Brazil 25L5
Juba Sudan 70D3
Juba, R Somalia 70E3
Jubail Leb 63C1
Jubbah S Arabia 62D3
Jucar, R Spain 37B2
Juchatengo Mexico 20C2
Juchipila, R Mexico 20B1
Juchitán Mexico 20C2
Juchitlan Mexico 20B1
Judenburg Austria 40C3
Juilaca Peru 24D7
Juiling Shan, Hills China 50C4
Juiz de Fora Brazil 25K8
Jujuy, State Arg 23C2
Julesburg USA 14B1
Juli Peru 24E7
Julianatop, Mt Suriname 25G3
Julianehab Greenland 5O3
Jülich W Germ 34D1
Julijske Alpen, Mts Yugos 35E1
Júlio de Castilhos Brazil 26E1
Jullundur India 58D2
Jumla Nepal 59B2
Jum Suwwäna, Mt Jordan 63C3
Jünägadh India 58C4
Junan China 50D2
Junction, Texas USA 14C3
Junction, Utah USA 17D3
Junction City USA 6D3
Jundiaí Brazil 23G2
Juneau USA 4E4
Junee Aust 76D4
June Lake USA 18C2
Jungfrau, Mt Switz 38B1
Juniata, R USA 12B2
Junín Arg 23D4
Junin de los Andes Arg 26A3
Junipero Serra Peak, Mt USA 18B2
Junlian China 50A4
Juquiá Brazil 23G2
Jur, R Sudan 70C3
Jura I Scot 32C4
Jura, Mts France 36D2
Jura,Sound of, Chan Scot 32C3
Jurf ed Darāwish Jordan 63C3
Jürmala USSR 42C4
Juruá, R Brazil 24E4
Juruena, R Brazil 25G6
Jusheng China 51B2
Jüsiyah Syria 63D1
Justo Daract Arg 26B2
Jutai, R Brazil 24E4
Juticalpa Honduras 19D3
Jutland = Jylland
Jüymand Iran 61D2
Jylland, Pen Den 40B1
Jyväskyla Fin 30K6

K

K2, Mt China/India 57F2
Ka, R Nig 69H3
Kaakhka USSR 61D1
Kaapmuiden S Africa 72E2
Kabaena, I Indon 76B1
Kabala Sierra Leone 68A4
Kabale Rwanda 70D4
Kabalo Zaïre 70C4
Kabambare Zaïre 70C4
Kabarole Uganda 70D3
Kabba Nig 69H4
Kabia, I Indon 76B1
Kabinakagami L Can 10C1
Kabinda Zaïre 70C4
Kabir, R Syria 63C1
Kabir Kuh, Mts Iran 61B2
Kabompo Zambia 71C5
Kabompo, R Zambia 71C5
Kabongo Zaïre 71C4
Kabul Afghan 58B2
Kaburuang, I Indon 55C2
Kabushiya Sudan 64B3
Kachchh,G of India 58B4
Kachkanar USSR 42K4
Kachug USSR 47M4
Kadan Burma 53B3
Kadapongan, I Indon 54E3
Kadavu, I Fiji 7G2
Kadi India 58C4
Kadina Aust 78A2
Kadinhani Turk 62B2

Kadiri India 60B2
Kadiyevka USSR 43F6
Kadoka USA 9B3
Kadoma Zim 71C5
Kadugli Sudan 70C2
Kaduna Nig 69H3
Kaduna, State Nig 69H3
Kaduna, R Nig 69H3
Kadūr India 60B2
Kadusam, Mt China 59E2
Kadzherom USSR 42K3
Kaédi Maur 68A3
Kaena Pt Hawaiian Is 18E5
Kaesöng N Korea 51B4
Kafanchan Nig 69H4
Kaffrine Sen 68A3
Kafr Behum Syria 63D1
Kafr Sa'd Egypt 63A3
Kafr Saqv Egypt 63A3
Kafrün Bashūr Syria 63D1
Kafue Zambia 71C5
Kafue, R Zambia 71C5
Kafue Nat Pk Zambia 71C5
Kaga Japan 51D4
Kagalaska, I USA 8C6
Kagan USSR 46H6
Kağizman Turk 43G7
Kagmar Sudan 64B4
Kagoshima Japan 51C5
Kagul USSR 41F3
Kâhak Iran 61D1
Kahama Tanz 70D4
Kahan Pak 58B3
Kahayan, R Indon 54D3
Kahemba Zaïre 71B4
Kahler Asten, Mt W Germ 34E1
Kahnūj Iran 61D3
Kahoka USA 10A2
Kahoolawe, I Hawaiian Is 18E5
Kahramanmaraş Turk 62C2
Kahuku Pt Hawaiian Is 18E5
Kahului Hawaiian Is 18E5
Kaiapoi NZ 79B2
Kaibab Plat USA 17D3
Kaieteur Fall Guyana 25G2
Kaifeng China 50C3
Kaikohe NZ 79B1
Kaikoura NZ 77G5
Kaikoura Pen NZ 79B2
Kaikoura Range, Mts NZ 79B2
Kaili China 50B4
Kailua Hawaiian Is 18E5
Kaimana Indon 49G7
Kainan Japan 52C4
Kainji Res Nig 69G3
Kaipara Harbour, B NZ 79B1
Kaiping China 50C5
Kairouan Tunisia 69E1
Kaiser Peak, Mt USA 18C2
Kaiserslautern W Germ 36D2
Kaiserslautern W Germ 40B3
Kaishantun China 51B3
Kaisiadorys USSR 41F2
Kaitaia NZ 79B1
Kaitangata NZ 79A3
Kaithal India 58D3
Kaiwi Chan Hawaiian Is 18E5
Kai Xian China 50B3
Kaiyuan, Liaoning China 50A5
Kaiyuan, Yunnan China 51A3
Kaiyuh Mts USA 8G3
Kajaani Fin 30K6
Kajaki Afghan 58B2
Kajang Malay 54F7
Kajiado Kenya 70D4
Kajrān Afghan 58B2
Kaka Sudan 70D2
Kakabeka Falls Can 10B1
Kakamega Kenya 70D3
Kake Japan 52B4
Kake USA 8M4
Kakhonak USA 8H4
Kakhovskoye Vodokhranilishche, Res USSR 46E5
Kāki Iran 61C3
Kākināda India 60C1
Kakiska L Can 3E1
Kakogawa Japan 52B4
Kaktovik USA 8K1
Kakuda Japan 52D3
Kalaa El Khasba Tunisia 69D1
Kalabahi Indon 55B4
Kalabáka Greece 39E3
Kalabakan Malay 54E2
Kalabo Zambia 71C5
Kalach USSR 43G5
Kalach-na-Donu USSR 43G6
Kaladan, R Burma 59D3
Kalae, C Hawaiian Is 18E5
Kalahari Desert Botswana 71C6
Kalahari Gemsbok Nat Pk S Africa 72C2
Kalai-Mor USSR 61E1
Kalajoki Fin 42C3
Kalakan USSR 47N4
Kalakepen Indon 54A2
Kalam Pak 58C1

Kalámai Greece 39E3
Kalamazoo USA 7E2
Kalao, I Indon 55B4
Kalaotoa, I Indon 55B4
Kalapana Hawaiian Is 18E5
Kalarsh USSR 41F3
Kalat Pak 58B3
Kalaupapa Hawaiian Is 18E5
Kalbän Oman 65G2
Kalecik Turk 62B1
Kaledupa, I Indon 55B4
Kalembau, I Indon 54E3
Kalémié Zaïre 70C4
Kalevala USSR 42E2
Kalewa Burma 59D3
Kalgin I USA 8H3
Kalgoorlie Aust 76B4
Kali, R India 59B2
Kalianda Indon 54C4
Kalibo Phil 55F8
Kalima Zaïre 70C4
Kalimantan, Province Indon 54D3
Kálimnos, I Greece 39F3
Kálimpang India 59C2
Kaliningrad USSR 30J8
Kalinin USSR 42F4
Kaliningrad USSR 42B5
Kalinkovichi USSR 43D5
Kalinovka USSR 41F3
Kalispell USA 6B2
Kalisz Pol 41D2
Kaliua Tanz 70D4
Kalix Sweden 30J5
Kalkfeld Namibia 71B6
Kalkfontein Botswana 72C1
Kalkrand Namibia 72B1
Kallakoopah, R Aust 78A1
Kallávesi, L Fin 30K6
Kallonis Kólpos, B Greece 39F3
Kalluk USA 4C4
Kalmar Sweden 30H7
Kalmytskaya ASSR, Republic USSR 43H6
Kalocsa USA 10A2
Kalolio Indon 55B3
Kalomo Zambia 71C5
Kalona USA 10A2
Kalone Peak, Mt Can 3C3
Kalpeni, I India 60A2
Kälpi India 58D3
Kalskag USA 8F3
Kaltag USA 8G3
Kaluga USSR 42F5
Kalundborg Den 30G7
Kalush USSR 41E3
Kalyän India 60A1
Kalyandurg India 60B2
Kalyazin USSR 42F4
Kam, R Nig 69J4
Kama, R USSR 42J3
Kamaishi Japan 51E4
Kamalia Pak 58C2
Kamanawa Mts NZ 79C1
Kamanjab Namibia 71B5
Kamara China 47O4
Kamarãn, I Yemen 64D3
Kamat, Mt India 58D2
Kamban India 60B3
Kambarka USSR 42J4
Kambia Sierra Leone 68A4
Kamchatka, Pen USSR 47S4
Kamenets Podolskiy USSR 41F3
Kamenka USSR 42G5
Kamen-na-Obi USSR 46K4
Kamen' Rybolov USSR 51C3
Kamenskoya USSR 47S3
Kamensk-Ural'skiy USSR 42L4
Kamieskroon S Africa 72B3
Kamilukuak L Can 4H3
Kamina Zaïre 71C4
Kaminak L Can 5J3
Kaminoyama Japan 52D3
Kamloops Can 4F4
Kamo USSR 62E1
Kamogawa Japan 52D3
Kampala Uganda 70D3
Kampar Malay 53C5
Kampar, R Indon 54B2
Kampen Neth 40B2
Kamphaeng Phet Thai 53B2
Kampot Camb 53C3
Kampuchea = Cambodia
Kamsack Can 3H3
Kamsaptar Iran 61E3
Kamskoye Vodokhranilishche, Res USSR 42K4
Kāmthi India 58D4
Kamuchawie L Can 3H2
Kamyshin USSR 43H5
Kamyslov USSR 42L4
Kanaaupscow, R Can 5L4
Kanab USA 17D3
Kanaga, I USA 8C6
Kanal Yugos 35E1
Kananga Zaïre 70C4
Kanash USSR 42H4
Kanayama Japan 52C3

Kanazawa *Japan* 51D4
Kanbisha *USA* 4C3
Kanchipuram *India* 60B2
Kandahar *Afghan* 58B2
Kandalaksha *USSR* 46E3
Kandalakshskaya Guba, B *USSR* 30L5
Kandé *Togo* 69G4
Kandel, Mt *W Germ* 34D2
Kandi *Benin* 69G3
Kandos *Aust* 78C2
Kandy *Sri Lanka* 60C3
Kane *USA* 11D2
Kane Basin, B *Can* 5L1
Kanem, Desert Region *Chad* 70B2
Kaneohe *Hawaiian Is* 18E5
Kanevka *USSR* 42F2
Kanfanar *Yugos* 35E2
Kang *Botswana* 72C1
Kangaba *Mali* 68B3
Kangal *Turk* 62C2
Kangâmiut *Greenland* 5N3
Kangān *Iran* 61C3
Kangar *Malay* 53C4
Kangaroo I *Aust* 76C4
Kanga'tsiaq *Greenland* 5N3
Kangavar *Iran* 61B2
Kangbao *China* 50C1
Kangchenjunga, Mt *Nepal* 57G3
Kangding *China* 50A4
Kangerdlugssuaq, B *Greenland* 5P3
Kangerdlugssvatsaiq, B *Greenland* 5P3
Kangetet *Kenya* 70D3
Kanggye *N Korea* 51B3
Kangnŭng *S Korea* 51B4
Kango *Gabon* 70B3
Kangto, Mt *China* 48C4
Kang Xian *China* 50B3
Kanh Hung *Viet* 53D4
Kaniama *Zaïre* 71C4
Kani Giri *India* 60B1
Kanin Nos, Pt *USSR* 46F3
Kankaanpää *Fin* 30J6
Kankakee *USA* 10B2
Kankakee, R *USA* 10B2
Kankan *Guinea* 68B3
Kānker *India* 59B3
Kannapolis *USA* 13C1
Kanniyākuman *India* 60B3
Kano *Nig* 69H3
Kano, State *Nig* 69H3
Kano, R *Nig* 69H3
Kanorado *USA* 14B2
Kanoya *Japan* 51C5
Kānpur *India* 59B2
Kansas, State *USA* 6D3
Kansas, R *USA* 15C2
Kansas City *USA* 7D3
Kanshi *China* 50D5
Kansk *USSR* 48C1
Kansŏng *S Korea* 52A3
Kantchari *U Volta* 69G3
Kanthi *India* 59C3
Kantishna *USA* 8H3
Kantishna, R *USA* 8H3
Kanye *Botswana* 72D1
Kao-hsiung *Taiwan* 48E4
Kaoka Veld, Plain *Namibia* 71B5
Kaolack *Sen* 68A3
Kaoma *Zambia* 71C5
Kapaa *Hawaiian Is* 18E5
Kapaau *Hawaiian Is* 18E5
Kapanga *Zaïre* 71C4
Kap Cort Adelaer, C *Greenland* 5O3
Kap Dalton, C *Greenland* 5Q3
Kapellskär *Sweden* 30H7
Kap Farvel, C *Greenland* 5O3
Kap Gustav Holm, C *Greenland* 5P3
Kapiri *Zambia* 71C5
Kapit *Malay* 54D2
Kaplan *USA* 15D3
Kaplice *Czech* 40C3
Kapoe *Thai* 53B4
Kapona *Zaïre* 71C4
Kaposvár *Hung* 39D1
Kap Parry, C *Can* 5L2
Kap Ravn, C *Greenland* 5Q3
Kapsan *N Korea* 52A2
Kapsukas *USSR* 42C5
Kapuas, R *Indon* 54C3
Kapunda *Aust* 78A2
Kapurthala *India* 58D2
Kapuskasing *Can* 5K5
Kapuskasing, R *Can* 10C1
Kaputar, Mt *Aust* 78D2
Kapydzhik, Mt *USSR* 43H8
Kapyŏng *S Korea* 52A3
Kap York, C *Greenland* 5M2
Kara, R *Togo* 69G4
Karabük *Turk* 62B1
Karacabey *Turk* 39F2
Karachi *Pak* 58B4
Karad *India* 60A1
Kara Daglari, Mt *Turk* 43F7
Karadeniz Boğazi, Sd *Turk* 43D7
Karaftit *USSR* 48E1
Karaganda *USSR* 46J5
Karagayly *USSR* 46J5
Kāraikāl *India* 60B2
Karaj *Iran* 61C1
Karak *Jordan* 62C3
Karak *Malay* 54F7
Kara Kalpakskaya, Republic *USSR* 46G5
Karakax He, R *China* 58D1
Karakelong, I *Indon* 55C2
Karakoram, Mts *India* 58D1
Karakoram, P *India/China* 58D1
Karakoro, R *Maur/Sen* 68A3
Karakumskiy Kanal *USSR* 61E1
Karakumy, Desert *USSR* 46G6
Karama *Jordan* 63C3
Karama, R *Indon* 55A3
Karaman *Turk* 43E8
Karamay *China* 46K5
Karamea *NZ* 79B2
Karamea Bight, B *NZ* 79B2
Karanhk, R *Turk* 43E8
Kāranja *India* 58D4
Karapınar *Turk* 62B2
Kara S *USSR* 46J2
Karasburg *Namibia* 72B2
Karasjok *Nor* 30K5
Karasuk *USSR* 46J4
Karataş *Turk* 62C2
Kara Tau, Mts *USSR* 46H5
Karathuri *Burma* 53B3
Karatsu *Japan* 51B5
Karaul *USSR* 46K3
Karavostasi *Cyprus* 63B1
Karawanken, Mts *Austria* 35E1
Karāz *Iran* 61C3
Karbalā' *Iraq* 62D3
Karcag *Hung* 41E3
Kardhítsa *Greece* 39E3
Karel'skaya ASSR, Republic *USSR* 42E3
Karen *Andaman Is* 60E2
Karepino *USSR* 42K3
Karesvando *Sweden* 30J5
Karet, Desert Region *Maur* 68B2
Kargasok *USSR* 46K4
Kargopol' *USSR* 42F3
Karh, R *Turk* 43G8
Kari *Nig* 69J3
Kariba *Zim* 71C5
Kariba, L *Zim/Zambia* 71C5
Kariba Dam *Zim/Zambia* 71C5
Karibib *Namibia* 72B1
Karima *Sudan* 70D2
Karimata, I *Indon* 54C3
Karimganj *Bang* 59D3
Karīmnagar *India* 60B1
Karin *Somalia* 70E2
Karis *Fin* 30J6
Karishimbe, Mt *Zaïre* 70C4
Káristos *Greece* 39E3
Kārkal *India* 60A2
Karkar, I *PNG* 49H7
Karkheh, R *Iran* 61B2
Karkinitskiy Zaliv, B *USSR* 43E6
Karlik Shan, Mt *China* 47L5
Karlino *Pol* 40D2
Karl Marx Stadt *E Germ* 40C2
Karlobag *Yugos* 38D2
Karlovac *Yugos* 38D1
Karlovo *Bulg* 39E2
Karlovy Vary *Czech* 40C2
Karlshamn *Sweden* 30G7
Karlskoga *Sweden* 30G7
Karlskrona *Sweden* 30H7
Karlsruhe *W Germ* 40B3
Karlstad *Sweden* 30G7
Karlstad *USA* 9C2
Karluk *USA* 8H4
Karnafuli Res *Bang* 59D3
Karnal *India* 58D3
Karnataka, State *India* 60A1
Karnobat *Bulg* 39F2
Kärnten, Province *Austria* 35E1
Karoi *Zim* 71C5
Karonga *Malawi* 71D4
Karora *Sudan* 70D2
Karossa *Indon* 55A3
Kárpathos, I *Greece* 39F3
Karrats Fjord *Greenland* 5N2
Karree Berge *S Africa* 72C3
Kars *Turk* 43G7
Karsakpay *USSR* 46H4
Kārsava *USSR* 41F1
Karshi *USSR* 56E2
Karstula *Fin* 30J6
Kartaba *Leb* 63C1
Kartal *Turk* 39F2
Kartaly *USSR* 42L5
Karthaus *USA* 12A2
Kārūn, R *Iran* 61B2
Karwa *India* 59B2
Kārwār *India* 60A2
Karymskoye *USSR* 48E1
Kasai, R *Zaïre* 70B4
Kasaji *Zaïre* 71C5
Kasama *Zambia* 71D5
Kasanga *Tanz* 71D4
Kāsaragod *India* 60A2
Kasba L *Can* 4H3
Kasba Tadla *Mor* 69A2
Kasegaluk Lg *USA* 8F1
Kasempa *Zambia* 71C5
Kasenga *Zaïre* 71C5
Kasese *Uganda* 70D3
Kāshān *Iran* 61C2
Kashegelok *USA* 8G3
Kashi *China* 57F2
Kashima *Japan* 52B4
Kāshipur *India* 58D3
Kashiwazaki *Japan* 51D4
Kashmar *Iran* 61D1
Kashmir, State *India* 44E4
Kasimov *USSR* 42G5
Kasiruta, I *Indon* 55C3
Kaskaskia *USA* 10B3
Kasko *Fin* 30J6
Kasli *USSR* 42L4
Kaslo *Can* 4G5
Kasmere L *Can* 3H2
Kasonga *Zaïre* 70C4
Kasongo-Lunda *Zaïre* 71B4
Kásos, I *Greece* 39F3
Kaspiyskiy *USSR* 43H6
Kassala *Sudan* 70D2
Kassel *W Germ* 40B2
Kasserine *Tunisia* 69D1
Kassinga *Angola* 71B5
Kastamonou *Turk* 62B1
Kastélli *Greece* 39E3
Kastellorizon, I *Greece* 62A2
Kastoría *Greece* 39E2
Kástron *Greece* 39F3
Kasugai *Japan* 51D4
Kasumi *Japan* 52B3
Kasungu *Malawi* 71D5
Kasur *Pak* 58C2
Kataba *Zambia* 71C5
Katahdin,Mt *USA* 11F1
Katako-kombe *Zaïre* 70C4
Katalla *USA* 4D3
Katangli *USSR* 47Q4
Katanning *Aust* 76A4
Katchall, I *Indian O* 60E3
Kateríni *Greece* 39E2
Kates Needle, Mt *Can/USA* 4E4
Katha *Burma* 59E3
Katherine *Aust* 76C2
Kāthiāwār, Pen *India* 58C4
Kathib El Henu *Egypt* 63B3
Kathmandu *Nepal* 59C2
Kathua *India* 58D2
Katihār *India* 59C2
Katima Mulilo *Namibia* 71C5
Katmai,Mt *USA* 4C4
Katmai Nat Mon *USA* 8H4
Katni *India* 59B3
Katoomba *Aust* 78D2
Katowice *Pol* 41D2
Katrineholm *Sweden* 30H7
Katsina *Nig* 69H3
Katsina Ala *Nig* 69H4
Katsina Ala, R *Nig* 69H4
Katsuta *Japan* 52D3
Katsuura *Japan* 52D3
Katsuy *Japan* 52C3
Kattakurgan *USSR* 46H5
Kattegat, Str *Denmark/Sweden* 30G7
Katzenbuckel, Mt *W Germ* 34E2
Kau *Indon* 55C2
Kauai, I *Hawaiian Is* 18E5
Kauai Chan *Hawaiian Is* 18E5
Kaulakahi Chan *Hawaiian Is* 18E5
Kaunakaki *Hawaiian Is* 18E5
Kaunas *USSR* 42C5
Kaura Namoda *Nig* 69H3
Kautokeino *Nor* 30J5
Kavadarci *Yugos* 39E2
Kavajë *Alb* 39D2
Kavalerovo *USSR* 51D3
Kavali *India* 60B2
Kavála *Greece* 39E2
Kāvda *India* 58B4
Kavieng *PNG* 76E1
Kawagoe *Japan* 52C3
Kawaguchi *Japan* 52C3
Kawaihae *Hawaiian Is* 18E5
Kawakawa *NZ* 79B1
Kawambwa *Zambia* 71C4
Kawardha *India* 59B3
Kawartha Lakes *Can* 11D2
Kawasaki *Japan* 51D4
Kaweah, R *USA* 18C2
Kawerau *NZ* 79C1
Kawhia *NZ* 79B1
Kaya *U Volta* 69F3
Kayak I *USA* 8K4
Kayan, R *Indon* 54E2
Kāyankulam *India* 60B3
Kaycee *USA* 9A3
Kayeli *Indon* 55C3
Kayenta *USA* 17D3
Kayes *Mali* 68A3
Kayseri *Turk* 43F8
Kazach'ye *USSR* 47P2
Kazakh *USSR* 62E1
Kazakhskaya SSR, Republic *USSR* 46G5
Kazan' *USSR* 42H4
Kazanlük *Bulg* 39F2
Kazan Retto, Is *Japan* 48H4
Kazatin *USSR* 41F3
Kazbek, Mt *USSR* 43G7
Kāzerūn *Iran* 61C3
Kazhim *USSR* 42J3
Kazi Magomed *USSR* 62E1
Kazincbarcika *Hung* 41E3
Kazym, R *USSR* 42M3
Kazymskaya *USSR* 42M3
Kéa, I *Greece* 39E3
Kealaikahiki Chan *Hawaiian Is* 18E5
Kearney *USA* 6D2
Kearny *USA* 17D4
Keban Baraji, Res *Turk* 62C2
Kébémer *Sen* 68A3
Kebi, R *Chad* 69J4
Kebili *Tunisia* 69D2
Kebīr, R *Syria/Leb* 63D1
Kebrekaise, Mt *Sweden* 30H5
Kechika, R *Can* 3C2
Kecskemet *Hung* 41D3
Kedainiai *USSR* 41E1
Kedgwick *Can* 11F1
Kedong *China* 51B2
Kédougou *Sen* 68A3
Kedva *USSR* 42J3
Keechiga, R *Can* 8N4
Keele, R *Can* 8N3
Keele Pk, Mt *Can* 8M3
Keeler *USA* 17C3
Keene, California *USA* 18C3
Keene, New Hampshire *USA* 11E2
Keetmanshoop *Namibia* 72B2
Keewanee *USA* 10B2
Keewatin *Can* 9D2
Keewatin *USA* 10A1
Keewatin, Region *Can* 5J3
Kefallinía, I *Greece* 39E3
Kefamenanu *Indon* 55B4
Kefar Sava *Israel* 63C2
Keffi *Nig* 69H4
Keflavik *Iceland* 30A2
Keg River *Can* 4G4
Keheili *Sudan* 64B3
Kehsi Mansam *Burma* 53B1
Keith *Aust* 78B3
Keith *Scot* 32D3
Keith Arm, B *Can* 4F3
Kekertuk *Can* 5M3
Kekri *India* 58D3
Kelang *Malay* 53C5
Kelang, I *Indon* 55C3
Kelantan, R *Malay* 53C4
Kelibia *Tunisia* 69E1
Kelif *USSR* 58B1
Kelkit, R *Turk* 62C1
Kellé *Congo* 70B4
Keller L *Can* 8O3
Kellet,C *Can* 4F2
Kellogg *USA* 16C1
Kelloselka *Fin* 46D3
Kells *Irish Rep* 33B5
Kells Range, Hills *Scot* 32C4
Kelme *USSR* 41E1
Kelowna *Can* 4G5
Kelsey Bay *Can* 4F4
Kelso *Scot* 32D4
Kelso *USA* 16B1
Kelvington *Can* 3H3
Kem' *USSR* 46E3
Kem', R *USSR* 42E3
Ke Macina *Mali* 68B3
Kemano *Can* 3C3
Kemerovo *USSR* 46K4
Kemi *Fin* 30J5
Kemi, R *Fin* 30K5
Kemijärvi *Fin* 30K5
Kemmerer *USA* 16D2
Kempen, Region *Belg* 34C1
Kemp,L *USA* 14C3
Kemps Bay *Bahamas* 21B2
Kempsey *Aust* 78D2
Kempten *W Germ* 40C3
Kempt,L *Can* 11E1
Kenai *USA* 8H3
Kenai Mts *USA* 8H4
Kenai Pen *USA* 8H3
Kenamuke Swamp *Sudan* 70D3
Kendal *Eng* 33D4
Kendall *Aust* 78D2
Kendari *Indon* 76B1
Kendawangan *Indon* 54D3
Kendrāpāra *India* 59C3
Kendrick *USA* 16C1
Kenedy *USA* 15F4
Kenema *Sierra Leone* 68A4
Kenge *Zaïre* 70B4
Kengtung *Burma* 53B1
Kenhardt *S Africa* 72C2
Kéniéba *Mali* 68A3
Kenitra *Mor* 69A2
Kenka L *USA* 12B1
Kenmare *USA* 9B2
Kenna *USA* 14B3
Kennebec, R *USA* 11F1
Kennebunk *USA* 12E1
Kennedy *USA* 12A1
Kenner *USA* 15D4
Kennett *USA* 15E2
Kennett Square *USA* 12C3
Kennewick *USA* 16C1
Kenny Dam *Can* 4F4
Kenora *Can* 5J5
Kenosha *USA* 7E2
Kent, County *Eng* 33F6
Kent, Texas *USA* 14B3
Kent, Washington *USA* 16B1
Kentland *USA* 10B2
Kenton *USA* 10C2
Kent Pen *Can* 4H3
Kentucky, State *USA* 7E3
Kentucky, R *USA* 10C3
Kentucky L *USA* 7E3
Kentwood, Louisiana *USA* 15D3
Kentwood, Michigan *USA* 10B2
Kenya, Republic *Africa* 70D3
Kenya,Mt *Kenya* 70D4
Keokuk *USA* 10A2
Keonchi *India* 59B3
Keonjhargarh *India* 59C3
Kepaluan Tanimbar, Arch *Indon* 49G7
Keplavik *Iceland* 5Q3
Kepno *Pol* 41D2
Kepualuan Widi, Arch *Indon* 55C3
Kepulauan Alor, Arch *Indon* 55B4
Kepulauan Anambas, Arch *Indon* 54C2
Kepulauan Aru, Arch *Indon* 49G7
Kepulauan Babar, I *Indon* 76B1
Kepulauan Badas, Is *Indon* 54C2
Kepulauan Banda, Arch *Indon* 49G7
Kepulauan Banggai, I *Indon* 76B1
Kepulauan Barat Daya, Is *Indon* 76B1
Kepulauan Bunguran Seletan, Arch *Indon* 54C2
Kepulauan Gorong, Arch *Indon* 55D3
Kepulauan Kai, Arch *Indon* 49G7
Kepulauan Kawio, Arch *Indon* 55C2
Kepulauan Leti, I *Indon* 76B1
Kepulauan Lingga, Is *Indon* 54B3
Kepulauan Loloda, Arch *Indon* 55C2
Kepulauan Mentawi, Arch *Indon* 54A3
Kepulauan Nenusa, Arch *Indon* 55C2
Kepulauan Obi, Arch *Indon* 55C3
Kepulauan Riau, Arch *Indon* 54B2
Kepulauan Sabalana, Arch *Indon* 54E4
Kepulauan Sangihe, Arch *Indon* 55C2
Kepulauan Sermata, I *Indon* 76B1
Kepulauan Sula, I *Indon* 76B1
Kepulauan Talaud, Arch *Indon* 55C2
Kepulauan Tambelan, Is *Indon* 54C2
Kepulauan Tanimbar, I *Indon* 76C1
Kepulauan Togian, I *Indon* 76B1
Kepulauan Tukangbesi, Is *Indon* 76B1
Kepulauan Watubela, Arch *Indon* 55D3
Kepulauan Yef Fam, Arch *Indon* 55C3
Kepulaun Solor, Arch *Indon* 55B4
Kerala, State *India* 60B2
Kerang *Aust* 78B3
Kerava *Fin* 30J6
Kerbi, R *USSR* 51D1
Kerch' *USSR* 43F6
Kerchem'ya *USSR* 42J3
Kerema *PNG* 76D1
Keremeps *Can* 16C1
Keren *Eth* 70D2
Kerguelen Ridge *Indian O* 74E7
Kericho *Kenya* 70D4
Kerinci, Mt *Indon* 54B3

Kerio, R Kenya 70D3
Kerki USSR 56E2
Kérkira Greece 39D3
Kérkira, I Greece 39D3
Kermadec Is NZ 77H3
Kermadec Trench Pacific O 77H4
Kerman Iran 61D2
Kerman USA 18B2
Kermänshäh Iran 61B2
Kerme Körfezi, B Turk 39F3
Kermit USA 14B3
Kern, R USA 17C3
Kernville USA 18C3
Keros USSR 42J3
Kerrobert Can 3G3
Kerrville USA 14C3
Kershaw USA 13C2
Kertamulia Indon 54C3
Kerulen, R Mongolia 47N5
Kerzaz Alg 68B2
Keşan Turk 39F2
Kesennuma Japan 51E4
Keshan China 51B2
Kesir Daglari, Mt Turk 43G7
Kestenga USSR 30L5
Keswick Eng 33D4
Kéta Ghana 69G4
Ketapang Indon 54D3
Ketchikan USA 4E4
Ketia Niger 68C3
Keti Bandar Pak 58B4
Kétou Benin 69G4
Ketrzyn Pol 41E2
Kettering Eng 33E5
Kettering USA 10C3
Kettle, R Can 16C1
Kettleman City USA 18C2
Kettle River Range, Mts USA 16C1
Kettlestone B Can 5L3
Kevir-i Namak, Salt Flat Iran 61D2
Kewaunee USA 10B2
Keweenaw B USA 10B1
Keweenaw Pen USA 10B1
Key Harbour Can 10C1
Key Largo USA 13E4
Keyser USA 12A3
Key West USA 7E4
Kezhma USSR 47M4
K'félegháza Hung 39D1
Kgun L USA 8F3
Khabab Syria 63D2
Khabarovsk USSR 45H3
Khabur, R Syria 43G8
Khairpur Pak 58B3
Khairpur, Region Pak 58B3
Khakhea Botswana 72C1
Khalig El Tina, B Egypt 63B3
Khalīj Maşirah, B Oman 65G2
Khálki, I Greece 39F3
Khalkidhíki, Pen Greece 39E2
Khalkís Greece 39E3
Khal'mer-Yu USSR 42L2
Khalturin USSR 42H4
Khalūf Oman 65G2
Khambhät,G of India 58C4
Khāmgaon India 58D4
Khamir Yemen 64D3
Khamis Mushayt S Arabia 64D3
Kham Keut Laos 53C2
Khammam India 60C1
Khamsa Egypt 63B3
Khamseh, Mts Iran 61B1
Khan, R Laos 53C2
Khanabad Afghan 58B1
Khānaqīn Iraq 62E3
Khandwa India 58D4
Khanewal Pak 58C2
Khan ez Zabib Jordan 63D3
Khanh Hung Viet 53D4
Khaniá Greece 39E3
Khanpur Pak 58C3
Khān Shaykhūn Syria 63D1
Khanty-Mansiysk USSR 46H3
Khan Yunis Egypt 63C3
Khapalu India 58D1
Khapcheranga USSR 48D2
Kharabali USSR 43H6
Kharagpur India 59C3
Khārān Iran 61D3
Kharan Pak 58B3
Kharānaq Iran 61C2
Khārg, Is Iran 61C3
Khârga Oasis Egypt 67C2
Khargon India 58D4
Khar'Kov USSR 43F6
Kharlovka USSR 42F2
Kharmanli Bulg 39F2
Kharovsk USSR 42G4
Khartoum Sudan 70D2
Khartoum North Sudan 70D2
Khasan USSR 51C3
Khash Afghan 61E2
Khāsh Iran 61E3
Khash, R Afghan 61E2
Khashm el Girba Sudan 70D2
Khasi-Jaintia Hills India 59D2
Khaskovo Bulg 39F2
Khatanga USSR 47M2
Khatangskiy Zaliv, Estuary USSR 47N2
Khatyrka USSR 47T3
Khawsa Burma 53B3
Khaybar S Arabia 64C1
Khazzan an-Nasr, L Egypt 64B2
Khe Bo Viet 53C2
Khed Brahma India 58C4
Khemis Alg 37C2
Khemisset Mor 69A2
Khenchela Alg 69D1
Kherrata Alg 37D2
Kherson USSR 43E6
Khilok USSR 47N4
Khíos Greece 39F3
Khíos, I Greece 39F3
Khmel'nitskiy USSR 43D6
Khodorov USSR 41E3
Kholm Afghan 58B1
Kholm USSR 41G1
Kholmsk USSR 51E2
Khomas Hochland, Mts Namibia 72B1
Khong Laos 53D3
Khonj Iran 61C3
Khor USSR 51C2
Khor, R USSR 51D2
Khoramshahr Iran 61B2
Khōr Duwayhin, B UAE 65F2
Khorog USSR 58C1
Khorramābad Iran 61B2
Khosf Iran 61D2
Khost Pak 58B2
Khotin USSR 43D6
Khotol, Mt USA 8G3
Khouribga Mor 69A2
Khoyniku USSR 43D5
Khrebet Cherskogo, Mts USSR 47Q3
Khrebet Dzhagdy, Mts USSR 51B1
Khrebet Dzhugdzhur, Mts USSR 47P4
Khrebet Iskamen, Mts USSR 8C2
Khrebet Kopet Dag, Mts USSR 61D1
Khrebet Orulgan, Mts USSR 47O3
Khrebet Pay-khoy, Mts USSR 42L2
Khrebet Sikhote Alin', Mts USSR 51D2
Khrebet Tarbagatay, Mts USSR 57G1
Khrebet Tukuringra, Mts USSR 47O4
Khrebet Turana, Upland USSR 51C1
Khrysokhou B Cyprus 63B1
Khulga, R USSR 42L3
Khulna Bang 59C3
Khunjerab, P China/India 58D1
Khunsar Iran 61C2
Khurays S Arabia 65E1
Khurda India 59C3
Khurja India 58D3
Khūryan Mūryān, Is Oman 65G3
Khushab Pak 58C2
Khushnīyah Syria 63C2
Khust USSR 41E3
Khuwei Sudan 70C2
Khuzdar Pak 58B3
Khvāf Iran 61E2
Khvalynsk USSR 43H5
Khvor Iran 61D2
Khvormūj Iran 61C3
Khvoy Iran 43G8
Khwaja Muhammad, Mts Afghan 58C1
Khyber P Afghan/Pak 58C2
Kiambi Zaïre 71C4
Kiamichi, R USA 15C3
Kiana USA 8F2
Kibangou Congo 70B4
Kibaya Tanz 70D4
Kibombo Zaïre 70C4
Kibondo Tanz 70D4
Kibungu Rwanda 70D4
Kičevo Yugos 39E2
Kicking Horse P Can 4G4
Kidal Mali 68C3
Kidderminster Eng 33D5
Kidira Sen 68A3
Kidnappers,C NZ 79C1
Kiel W Germ 40C2
Kielce Pol 41E2
Kieler Bucht, B W Germ 40C2
Kiev = Kiyev
Kifab USSR 56E2
Kiffa Maur 68A3
Kigali Rwanda 66H8
Kigluaik Mts USA 8E3
Kigoma Tanz 70C4
Kiholo Hawaiian Is 18E5
Kii-sanchi, Mts Japan 52C4
Kii-suido, B Japan 51C5
Kikhchik USSR 47R4
Kikinda Yugos 39E1
Kikládhes, Is Greece 39E3
Kikon PNG 76D1
Kikonai Japan 52D2
Kikori PNG 49H7
Kikwit Zaïre 70B4
Kilauea Crater, Mt Hawaiian Is 18E5
Kilbuck Mts USA 4C3
Kilchu N Korea 51B3
Kilcoy Aust 78D1
Kildane, County Irish Rep 33B5
Kildare Irish Rep 33B5
Kilgore USA 15D3
Kilifi Kenya 70E4
Kilimanjaro, Mt Tanz 70D4
Kilindoni Tanz 71D4
Kilis Turk 62C2
Kiliya USSR 41F3
Kilkenny, County Irish Rep 33B5
Kilkenny Irish Rep 33B5
Kilkís Greece 39E2
Killarney Aust 78D1
Killarney Irish Rep 31B3
Killeen USA 15C3
Killik, R USA 8H2
Killin Scot 32C3
Killíni, Mt Greece 39E3
Kilmarnock Scot 32C4
Kil'mez USSR 42J4
Kilosa Tanz 71D4
Kilrush Irish Rep 31B3
Kilunga, R Nig 69J4
Kilwa Zaïre 71C4
Kilwa Kisiwani Tanz 71D4
Kilwa Kivinje Tanz 71D4
Kim, R Cam 69J4
Kimba Aust 78A2
Kimball USA 14B1
Kimball,Mt USA 8K3
Kimberley Can 3E4
Kimberley S Africa 72C2
Kimberley Plat Aust 76B2
Kimch'aek N Korea 51B3
Kimch'ŏn S Korea 51B4
Kimhae S Korea 52A3
Kími Greece 39E3
Kimje S Korea 52A3
Kimry USSR 42F4
Kimwha N Korea 52A3
Kinabalu, Mt Malay 54E1
Kinabatangan, R Malay 54E1
Kincardine Can 10C2
Kincolith Can 3C2
Kinder USA 15D3
Kindersley Can 3G3
Kindia Guinea 68A3
Kindu Zaïre 70C4
Kinel' USSR 42J5
Kineshma USSR 42G4
Kingaroy Aust 78D1
King City USA 17B3
Kingcome Inlet Can 4F4
King Cove USA 8F4
Kingfisher USA 15C2
King George Is Can 5L4
King I Aust 76D5
King I Can 3C3
Kingissepp USSR 42C4
King Leopold Range, Mts Aust 76B2
Kingman USA 6B3
Kingombe Zaïre 70C4
Kingoonya Aust 78A2
Kingsburg USA 18C2
Kings Canyon Nat Pk USA 17C3
Kingscote Aust 78A3
King Sd Aust 76B2
Kingsford USA 10B1
Kingsland USA 13C2
King's Lynn Eng 33F5
Kingsmill Group, Is Kiribati 77G1
Kings Park USA 12D2
Kings Peak, Mt USA 6B2
Kingsport USA 13C1
Kingston Aust 76C4
Kingston Can 5L5
Kingston Jamaica 19E3
Kingston, New York USA 11E2
Kingston NZ 79A3
Kingston, Pennsylvania USA 12C2
Kingstown St Vincent 21E4
Kingstown St Vincent 24F1
Kingsville USA 6D4
Kingussie Scot 32C3
King William I Can 4J3
King William's Town S Africa 72D3
Kinkala Congo 70B4
Kinna Sweden 30G7
Kinnairds Head, Pt Scot 32D3
Kinomoto Japan 52C3
Kinross Scot 32D3
Kinshasa Zaïre 70B4
Kinsley USA 14C2
Kinston USA 13D1
Kintap Indon 54E3
Kintyre, Pen Scot 32C4
Kinuso Can 3E2
Kinyeti, Mt Sudan 70D3
Kinzig, R W Germ 34E1
Kipahigan L Can 3H2
Kiparissía Greece 39E3
Kiparissiakós Kólpos, G Greece 39E3
Kipawa,L Can 11D1
Kipili Tanz 71D4
Kipnuk USA 8F4
Kippure, Mt Irish Rep 33B5
Kipushi Zaïre 71C5
Kirchheim W Germ 34E2
Kirensk USSR 47M4
Kirgizskaya SSR, Republic USSR 46J5
Kirgizskiy Khrebet, Mts USSR 57F1
Kiri Zaïre 70B4
Kiribati, Is Pacific O 77G1
Kırıkkale Turk 62B2
Kirishi USSR 42E4
Kirithar Range, Mts Pak 58B3
Kirkağaç Turk 39F3
Kirk Bulāg Dāgh, Mt Iran 43H8
Kirkby Eng 33D4
Kirkcaldy Scot 32D3
Kirkcudbright Scot 32C4
Kirkenes Nor 30K5
Kirkland Lake Can 5K5
Kırklareli Turk 62A1
Kirkpatrick,Mt Ant 80E
Kirksville USA 7D2
Kirkūk Iraq 62D2
Kirkwall Scot 32D2
Kirkwood USA 15D2
Kirkwood, R S Africa 72D3
Kirov USSR 42E5
Kirov USSR 42H4
Kirovabad USSR 43H7
Kirovakan USSR 62D1
Kirovgrad USSR 42K4
Kirovograd USSR 43E6
Kirovsk USSR 42E2
Kirovskiy, Kamchatka USSR 47R4
Kirovskiy, Primorskiykray USSR 51C2
Kirs USSR 42J4
Kirşehir Turk 62B2
Kiruna Sweden 40C2
Kiryū Japan 52C3
Kisangani Zaïre 70C3
Kisar, I Indon 55C4
Kisaran Indon 54A2
Kisarazu Japan 52C3
Kishanganj India 59C2
Kishangarh India 58C3
Kishinev USSR 43D6
Kishiwada Japan 52C4
Kisii Kenya 70D4
Kisiju Tanz 71D4
Kiska, I USA 8B6
Kiskunhalas Hung 41D3
Kislovodsk USSR 46F5
Kismaayo Somalia 70E4
Kiso-sammyaku, Mts Japan 52C3
Kissidougou Guinea 68B4
Kissimmee,L USA 13C3
Kississing L Can 3H2
Kisumu Kenya 70D4
Kisvárda Hung 41E3
Kita Mali 68B3
Kitab USSR 46H6
Kitakami Japan 52D3
Kitakami, R Japan 52D3
Kitakata Japan 52D3
Kita-Kyūshū Japan 51C5
Kitale Kenya 70D3
Kitalo, I Japan 48H4
Kitami Japan 51E3
Kitami-Esashi Japan 52D2
Kit Carson USA 14B2
Kitchener Can 5K5
Kitgum Uganda 70D3
Kíthira, I Greece 39E3
Kíthnos, I Greece 39E3
Kiti,C Cyprus 63B1
Kitimat Can 4F4
Kitnen, R Fin 30K5
Kitsuki Japan 52B4
Kittanning USA 11D2
Kittery USA 11E2
Kittilä Fin 30J5
Kitty Hawk USA 13D1
Kitunda Tanz 71D4
Kitwanga Can 8N4
Kitwe Zambia 71C5
Kitzbühel Austria 40C3
Kitzbühler Alpen, Mts Austria 35E1
Kitzingen W Germ 40C3
Kiumbi Zaïre 70C4
Kivalina USA 8F2
Kivercy USSR 41F2
Kivu,L Zaïre/Rwanda 70C4
Kiwalik USA 4B3
Kiyev USSR 43E5
Kiyevskoye Vodokhranilishche, Res USSR 41G2
Kizel USSR 42K4
Kizema USSR 42G3
Kizil, R Turk 62C2
Kizyl-Arvat USSR 56D2
Kizyl-Atrek USSR 43J8
Kladno Czech 40C2
Klagenfurt Austria 40C3
Klaipėda USSR 42C4
Klamath USA 6A2
Klamath, R USA 16B2
Klamath Falls USA 6A2
Klamath Mts USA 16B2
Klappan, R Can 3C2
Klatovy Czech 40C3
Klawak USA 8M4
Kleiat Leb 63C1
Kleinsee S Africa 72B2
Klerksdorp S Africa 72D2
Kletnya USSR 41G2
Kleve W Germ 34D1
Klimovichi USSR 41G2
Klin USSR 42F4
Klintehamn Sweden 41D1
Klintsy USSR 43E5
Klipplaat S Africa 72C3
Ključ Yugos 38D2
Kłodzko Pol 40D2
Klondike, R USA Can 8L3
Klondike, R USA/Can 8L3
Klondike Plat USA/Can 4D3
Klosterneuburg Austria 40D3
Kluane, R Can 8L3
Kluane L Can 8L3
Kluane Nat Pk Can 8L3
Kluczbork Pol 41D2
Klukwan USA 8L4
Klutina L USA 8J3
Knight I USA 8J3
Knighton Wales 33D5
Knin Yugos 38D2
Knob,C Aust 76A4
Knokke-Heist Belg 34B1
Knox,C Can 8M5
Knox Coast Ant 80G9
Knoxville, Iowa USA 9D3
Knoxville, Tennessee USA 7E3
Knud Ramsussens Land, Region Greenland 5O3
Knysna S Africa 72C3
Koba Indon 54C3
Kobbermirebugt Greenland 5O3
Kobe Japan 51D5
København Den 40C1
Kobiard Yugos 35E1
Koblenz W Germ 40B2
Koboldo USSR 51C1
Kobrin USSR 42C5
Kobroör, I Indon 49G7
Kobuk, R USA 8G2
Kočani Yugos 39E2
Kochang S Korea 52A3
Kŏch'ang S Korea 52A3
Ko Chang, I Thai 53C3
Koch Bihār India 59C2
Kochel W Germ 35D1
Kocher, R W Germ 34E2
Koch I Can 5L3
Kōchi Japan 51C5
Kodiak USA 8H4
Kodiak I USA 8H4
Kodikkarai India 60B2
Kodok Sudan 70D3
Kodomari-misaki, C Japan 52D2
Kodyma USSR 41F3
Koehn L USA 18D3
Koes Namibia 72B2
Koffiefontein S Africa 72D2
Koforidua Ghana 69F4
Kōfu Japan 51D4
Koga Japan 52C3
Køge Den 30G7
Kohat Pak 58C2
Koh-i-Baba, Mts Afghan 58B2
Koh-i-Hisar, Mts Afghan 58B1
Koh-i-Khurd, Mt Afghan 58B2
Kohima India 59D2
Koh-i-Mazar, Mt Afghan 58B1
Koh-i-Qaisar, Mt Afghan 61E2
Kohlu Pak 58B3
Kohtla Järve USSR 42D4
Kohung S Korea 52A4
Kohyon S Korea 52A4
Koide Japan 52C3
Koidern Can 8K3
Koihoa, Is Nicobar Is 53A4
Koin N Korea 52A2
Kōje-do, I S Korea 51B5
Ko-jima, I Japan 52C2
Kokchetav USSR 46H4
Kokemaki, L Fin 30J6
Kokkola Fin 30J6
Koko Nig 69G3
Kokoda PNG 76D1
Kokomo USA 10B2
Kokonau Indon 49G7

Kokpekty USSR 46K5
Koksan N Korea 52A3
Koksoak, R Can 5M4
Koksŏng S Korea 52A3
Kokstad S Africa 72D3
Ko Kut, I Thai 53C3
Kola USSR 42E2
Kolaka Indon 55B3
Ko Lanta, I Thai 53B4
Kolar India 60B2
Kolar Gold Fields India 60B2
Kolda Sen 68A3
Kolding Den 30F7
Kolendo USSR 51E1
Kolhāpur India 60A1
Koliganek USA 8G4
Kolín Czech 40D2
Köln W Germ 40B2
Koło Pol 41D2
Koloa Hawaiian Is 18E5
Kołobrzeg Pol 40D2
Kolokani Mali 68B3
Kolomna USSR 42F4
Kolomyya USSR 43D6
Kolono Indon 55B3
Kolonodale Indon 55B3
Kolpakovskiy USSR 47R4
Kolpashevo USSR 46K4
Kolpekty USSR 48B2
Kólpos Merabé lou, B Greece 39F3
Kólpos Singitikós, G Greece 39E2
Kólpos Strimonikós, G Greece 39E2
Kólpos Toronaíos, G Greece 39E2
Kolskiy Poluostrov, Pen USSR 42F2
Kolva, R USSR 42K2
Kolvereid Nor 30G6
Kolwezi Zaïre 71C5
Kolyma, R USSR 47R3
Kolymskaya Nizmennost, Lowland USSR 47R3
Kolymstoye Nagor'ye, Mts USSR 47S3
Kolyuchinskaya Guba, B USSR 8D2
Kom, Mt Bulg/Yugos 39E2
Koma Eth 70D3
Koma Japan 52D3
Komaduga Gana, R Nig 69J3
Komadugu Yobé, R Nig 69J3
Komaga take, Mt Japan 52D2
Komandorskiye Ostrova, I USSR 47S4
Komárno Czech 41D3
Komati, R S Africa 72E2
Komati Poort S Africa 72E2
Komatsu Japan 51D4
Komatsushima Japan 52B4
Kombissiri U Volta 69F3
Komi, Republic USSR 46G3
Kommunar USSR 48B1
Komodo, I Indon 55A4
Komoé, R Ivory Coast 69F4
Komoran, I Indon 49G7
Komoro Japan 52C3
Komotiní Greece 39F2
Kompasberg, Mt S Africa 72C3
Kompong Cham Camb 53D3
Kompong Chhnang, Mts Camb 53C3
Kompong Som Camb 53C3
Kompong Thom Camb 53D3
Kompong Trabek Camb 53D3
Komrat USSR 41F3
Komsberg, Mts S Africa 72C3
Komsomol'skiy USSR 42L2
Komsomol'sk na Amure USSR 47P4
Kona, R USSR 46H4
Kondagaon India 59B4
Kondoa Tanz 70D4
Kondon USSR 51D1
Kondopoga USSR 42E3
Kondukür India 60B1
Konergino USSR 8C2
Konevo USSR 42F3
Kong Christian IX Land, Region Greenland 5P3
Kong Frederik VI Kyst, Mts Greenland 5O3
Kongju S Korea 52A3
Kong Karls Land, Is Barents S 46D2
Kongkemul, Mt Indon 54E2
Kongolo Zaïre 70C4
Kongoussi U Volta 69F3
Kongsberg Den 30F7
Kongsvinger Nor 30G6
Königsberg = Kaliningrad
Königsee, L W Germ 35E1
Konin Pol 41D2
Konjic Yugos 39D2
Konongo Ghana 69F4
Konosha USSR 42G3
Konosu Japan 52C3
Konotop USSR 43E5
Konsk USSR 47L4
Końskie Pol 41E2
Konstanz W Germ 34E3
Kontagora Nig 69H3
Kontum Viet 53D3
Konus, Mt USSR 8B2
Konya Turk 43E8
Kootenay, L Can 16C1
Kootenay, R Can 3E4
Kopargaon India 58C5
Kópasker Iceland 5R3
Kópavogur Iceland 30A2
Koper Yugos 38C1
Kopet Dag, Mts Iran/USSR 56D2
Kopeysk USSR 42L4
Ko Phangan, I Thai 53C4
Ko Phuket, I Thai 53B4
Köping Sweden 30H7
Kopo-ri S Korea 52A3
Koppal India 60B1
Koprivnica Yugos 38D1
Korakskoye Nagor'ye, Mts USSR 47S3
Korangi Pak 58B4
Koraput India 60C1
Korba India 59B3
Korbach W Germ 40B2
Korbuk, R USA 4B3
Korçë Alb 39E2
Korčula, I Yugos 38D2
Korea B China/Korea 50E2
Korea Str S Korea/Japan 51B5
Korec USSR 41F2
Korf USSR 47S3
Körğlu Tepesi, Mt Turk 62B1
Korhogo Ivory Coast 68B4
Kori Creek India 58B4
Korinthiakós Kólpos, G Greece 39E3
Kórinthos Greece 39E3
Kōriyama Japan 51E4
Korkino USSR 42L5
Korkodon USSR 47R3
Korkodon, R USSR 47R3
Korkuteli Turk 62B2
Korla China 57G1
Kormakiti,C Cyprus 63B1
Kornat, I Yugos 38D2
Köroğlu Tepesi, Mt Turk 43E7
Korogwe Tanz 70D4
Koroit Aust 78B3
Koror, Palau Is Pacific O 49G6
Körös, R Hung 41E3
Korosten USSR 43D5
Korostyshev USSR 41F2
Koro Toro Chad 70B2
Korovin, I USA 8F4
Korsakov USSR 51E2
Korsør Den 30G7
Korti Sudan 64B3
Kortkeroz USSR 42J3
Kortrijk Belg 40A2
Koryong S Korea 52A3
Kós, I Greece 39F3
Kosa Belyaka, B USSR 8D2
Ko Samui, I Thai 53C4
Kosan N Korea 52A3
Koscierzyna Pol 41D2
Kosciusko USA 13B2
Kosciusko, Mt Aust 76D4
Kosciusko I USA 8M4
Koshikijima-retto, I Japan 51B5
Košice Czech 41E3
Kosma, R USSR 42J2
Kosong N Korea 51B4
Kosovska Mitrovica Yugos 39E2
Kossou, L Ivory Coast 68B4
Koster S Africa 72D2
Kosti Sudan 70D2
Kostopol' USSR 41F2
Kostroma USSR 42G4
Kostrzyn Pol 40C2
Kos'yu USSR 42K2
Koszalin Pol 30H8
Kota India 58D3
Kotaagung Indon 54B4
Kotabaharu Indon 54D3
Kotabaru Indon 54E3
Kota Bharu Malay 53C4
Kotabum Indon 54C3
Kot Addu Pak 58C2
Kota Kinabalu Malay 54E1
Kotamobagu Indon 55B2
Kotapad India 60C1
Kotapinang, I Indon 54F7
Kota Tinggi Malay 54G8
Kotel'nich USSR 42H4
Kotel'nikovo USSR 43G6
Kotka Fin 30K6
Kotlas USSR 42H3
Kotlik USA 8F3
Koton Karifi Nig 69H4
Kotor Yugos 39D2
Kotovsk USSR 43D6
Kotri Pak 58B3
Kötschach Austria 35E1
Kottagüdem India 60C1
Kottayam India 60B3
Kotto, R CAR 70C3
Kottūru India 60B2
Kotuy, R USSR 47L3
Kotzebue USA 8F2
Kotzebue Sd USA 4B3
Kouande Benin 69G3
Kouango CAR 70C3
Koudougou U Volta 69F3
Kougaberge, Mts S Africa 72C3
Koulamoutou Gabon 70B4
Koulikoro Mali 68B3
Koupéla U Volta 69F3
Kouri Mali 69F3
Kourou French Guiana 25H2
Kouroussa Guinea 68B3
Kousséri Cam 70B2
Kouvola Fin 30K6
Kovdor USSR 42D2
Kovel USSR 43C5
Kovno = Kaunas
Kovrov USSR 42G4
Kovylkino USSR 42G5
Kovzha, R USSR 42F3
Ko Way, I Thai 53C4
Kowloon Hong Kong 50C5
Kowŏn N Korea 52A3
Kowt-e-Ashrow Afghan 58B2
Köyceğiz Turk 62A2
Koyda USSR 42G2
Koydor USSR 30L5
Koyna Res India 60A1
Koynas USSR 42H3
Koyoa, I Indon 55C2
Koyuk USA 8F3
Koyuk, R USA 8F2
Koyukuk USA 8G3
Koyukuk, R USA 8G2
Kozan Turk 62C2
Kozańi Greece 39E2
Kozhikode = Calicut
Kozhim USSR 42K2
Koz'modemyansk USSR 42H4
Koztroma USSR 42G4
Kōzu-shima, I Japan 52C4
Kpandu Ghana 69G4
Kraai, R S Africa 72D3
Kragerø Nor 30F7
Kragujevac Yugos 39E2
Kra,Isthmus of Burma/Malay 53B3
Krakatau = Rakata
Krak des Chevaliers, Hist Site Syria 63D1
Kraków Pol 41D2
Kraljevo Yugos 39E2
Kramatorsk USSR 43F6
Kramfors Sweden 30H6
Kranj Yugos 38C1
Krapotkin USSR 43G6
Krasavino USSR 42H3
Krashnokamsk USSR 42K4
Krasino USSR 46G2
Kraśnik Pol 41E2
Krasnoarmeysk USSR 43H5
Krasnodar USSR 43F7
Krasnogorsk USSR 51E2
Krasnotur'insk USSR 42L4
Krasnoufimsk USSR 42K4
Krasnousol'-skiy USSR 42K5
Krasnovishersk USSR 42K3
Krasnovodsk USSR 43J7
Krasnoyarsk USSR 47K4
Krasnystaw Pol 41E2
Krasnyy Kut USSR 43H5
Krasnyy Luch USSR 43F6
Krasnyy Yar USSR 43H6
Kratie Camb 53D3
Kraulshavn Greenland 5N2
Krefeld W Germ 40B2
Kremenchug USSR 43E6
Kremenchugskoye Vodokhranilische, Res USSR 43E6
Kremenets USSR 41F2
Kremming USA 14A1
Krenitzin Is USA 8E5
Kribi Cam 70A3
Krichev USSR 42E5
Krimml Austria 35E1
Krinstinestad Fin 30J6
Krishna, R India 60B1
Krishnagiri India 60B2
Krishnangar India 59C3
Kristiansand Nor 30F7
Kristianstad Sweden 30G7
Kristiansund Nor 46B3
Kristineham Sweden 30G7
Kríti, I Greece 39E3
Krivoy Rog USSR 43E6
Krk, I Yugos 38C1
Krokodil, R S Africa 72D1
Kronotskaya Sopka, Mt USSR 47S4
Kronpris Frederik Bjerge, Mts Greenland 5P3
Kronshtadt USSR 30K7
Kroonstad S Africa 72D2
Kropotkin USSR 46F5
Kruger Nat Pk S Africa 72E1
Krugersdorp S Africa 72D2
Krui Indon 54B4
Kruje Alb 39D2
Krupki USSR 41F2
Krusenstern,C USA 8F2
Kruševac Yugos 39E2
Krustpils USSR 30K7
Kruzof I USA 8L4
Krym, Pen USSR 46E5
Krym, R USSR 43E7
Krymsk USSR 43F7
Krzyz Pol 40D2
Ksar El Boukhari Alg 69C1
Ksar el Kebir Mor 69A2
Kuala Indon 54A2
Kuala Dungun Malay 53C5
Kuala Kangsar Malay 54F6
Kuala Kelawang Malay 54G7
Kuala Kerai Malay 53C4
Kuala Kubu Baharu Malay 53C5
Kuala Lipis Malay 53C5
Kuala Lumpur Malay 53C5
Kuala Pilah Malay 54G7
Kuala Selangor Malay 54F7
Kualasimpang Indon 54A2
Kuala Trengganu Malay 53C4
Kuamut Malay 54E1
Kuandian China 51A3
Kuantan Malay 53C5
Kuba USSR 43H7
Kubar PNG 49H7
Kuching Malay 54D2
Kudat Malay 54E1
Kudus Indon 54D4
Kudymkar USSR 42J4
Kufstein Austria 40C3
Kugaluk, R Can 8M2
Kugmallit B Can 8M2
Kuhak Iran 61E3
Kuh Duren, Upland Iran 61D2
Kūh e Bazmān, Mt Iran 61D3
Kūh-e Dinar, Mt Iran 61C2
Kūh-e-Hazār Masjed, Mts Iran 61D1
Kūh-e Jebāl Barez, Mts Iran 61D3
Kūh-e Karkas, Mts Iran 61C2
Kūh-e Laleh Zar, Mt Iran 61D3
Kūh-e Sahand, Mt Iran 61B1
Kuh e Taftān, Mt Iran 61E3
Kūhhaye Alvand, Mts Iran 43H9
Kūhhaye Sabalan, Mts Iran 43H8
Kūhhā-ye Zāgros, Mts Iran 61B2
Kuhmo Fin 30K6
Kūhpāyeh Iran 61C2
Kūhpāyeh, Mt Iran 61D2
Kūh ye Bashākerd, Mts Iran 61D3
Kūh ye Sabalan, Mt Iran 61B1
Kuibis Namibia 72B2
Kuigillingok USA 4B4
Kuiseb, R Namibia 72B1
Kuiu I USA 8M4
Kujang N Korea 52A3
Kuji Japan 51E3
Kuju-san, Mt Japan 52B4
Kukaklek L USA 8G4
Kukës Alb 39E2
Kukpowruk, R USA 8F2
Kukup Malay 53C5
Kül, R Iran 61D3
Kula Turk 39F3
Kulai Malay 54G8
Kulakshi USSR 43K6
Kulal,Mt Kenya 70D3
Kulata Bulg 39E2
Kuldiga USSR 42C4
Kulim Malay 54F6
Kulov, R USSR 42G2
Kulpawn, R Ghana 69F3
Kul'sary USSR 43J6
Kulu India 58D2
Kulu Turk 62B2
Kululli Eth 64D4
Kulunda USSR 46J4
Kulwin Aust 78B2
Kuma, R USSR 43H7
Kumagaya Japan 52C3
Kumai Indon 54D3
Kumak USSR 43L5
Kumamoto Japan 51C5
Kumano Japan 52C4
Kumanovo Yugos 39E2
Kumara China 51B1
Kumasi Ghana 69F4
Kumba Cam 70A3
Kumbakonam India 60B2
Kumbo Cam 69J4
Kümch'ŏn N Korea 52A3
Kumdah S Arabia 65E2
Kumertau USSR 42K5
Kumgang N Korea 52A3
Kŭmhwa S Korea 51B4
Kumla Sweden 30H7
Kŭmnyŏng S Korea 52A4
Kŭmo-do, I S Korea 52A4
Kumon Range, Mts Burma 59E2
Kumta India 60A2
Kümüx China 57G1
Kunar, R Afghan 58C2
Kunda USSR 30K7
Kundla India 58C4
Kunduz Afghan 58B1
Kunene, R Angola 66F9
Kunghit, I Can 8M5
Kungsbacka Sweden 30G7
Kungur USSR 42K4
Kunhing Burma 53B1
Kunlun Shan, Mts China 57G2
Kunming China 50A4
Kunovat, R USSR 42M3
Kunsan S Korea 51B4
Kuopio Fin 30K6
Kupa, R Yugos 38D1
Kupang Indon 76B2
Kupiano PNG 76D2
Kupreanof I USA 8M4
Kupreanof Pt USA 8G4
Kupyansk USSR 43F6
Kuqa China 57G1
Kur, R USSR 51C2
Kura, R USSR 43H8
Kurabe Japan 52C3
Kurashiki Japan 51C5
Kurayoshi Japan 52B3
Kurdistan, Region Iran 61B1
Kŭrdzhali Bulg 39F2
Kure Japan 51C5
Kureyka, R USSR 47L3
Kurgan USSR 46H4
Kuria Muria Is = Khūryan Mūryān
Kurikka Fin 30J6
Kuril Is = Kuril'skoye Osrova
Kuril'sk USSR 51F2
Kuril'skiye Ostrova, Is USSR 47Q5
Kuril Trench Pacific O 74J2
Kurinskaya Kosa, Sand Spit USSR 43H8
Kurnool India 60B1
Kuroishi Japan 52D2
Kuroiso Japan 52D3
Kurow NZ 79B2
Kurri Kurri Aust 78D2
Kursk USSR 43F5
Kurskiy Zaliv, Lg USSR 41E1
Kuruktag, R China 48B2
Kuruman S Africa 72C2
Kuruman, R S Africa 72C2
Kurume Japan 51C5
Kurunegala Sri Lanka 60C3
Kuruntag, R China 46K5
Kur'ya USSR 42K3
Kusa USSR 42K4
Kuşadasi Körfezi, B Turk 39F3
Kus Golü, L Turk 39F2
Kushimoto Japan 51D5
Kushiro Japan 51E3
Kushka Afghan 61E1
Kushtia Bang 59C3
Kushum, R USSR 43J5
Kushva USSR 46H4
Kuskokwim, R USA 8F3
Kuskokwim B USA 8F4
Kuskokwim Mts USA 4C3
Kuskokwim Mts USA 8G3
Kusma Nepal 59B2
Kussharo-ko, L Japan 51E3
Kustanay USSR 46H4
Kütahya Turk 43D8
Kutai, R Indon 54E3
Kutaisi USSR 43G7
Kutchan Japan 52D2
Kutná Hora Czech 40D3
Kutno Pol 41D2
Kutu Zaïre 70B4
Kutubdia I Bang 59D3
Kutum Sudan 70C2
Kuusamo Fin 30K5
Kuvandyk USSR 43K5
Kuvbyshev USSR 29L3
Kuwait Kuwait 62E4
Kuwait, Sheikdom S W Asia 56C3
Kuwana Japan 52C3
Kuybyshev USSR 46G4
Kuybyshev USSR 46J4
Kuybyshevskoye Vodokhranilishche, Res USSR 42H5
Kuytun USSR 47M4
Kuzey Anadolu Daglari, Mts Turk 43F7
Kuznetsk USSR 43H5
Kuzomen USSR 42F2
Kvaenangen, Sd Nor 42C2
Kvichak USA 8G4
Kvichak, R USA 8G4
Kvichak B USA 8G4
Kvigtind, Mt Nor 30G5
Kvikkjokk Sweden 42B2
Kwale Kenya 70D4
Kwale Nig 69H4
Kwangju S Korea 51B4
Kwango, R Zaïre 70B4
Kwangyang S Korea 52A3

Kwanmo-bong, Mt *N Korea* 52A2
Kwara, State *Nig* 69H4
Kwekwe *Zim* 71C5
Kwethluk *USA* 8F3
Kwethluk, R *USA* 8F3
Kwidzyn *Pol* 41D2
Kwoka, Mt *Indon* 49G7
Kyabram *Aust* 78C3
Kyaikkami *Burma* 53B2
Kyaikto *Burma* 53B2
Kyakhta *USSR* 48D1
Kyancutta *Aust* 78A2
Kyaukme *Burma* 53B1
Kyauk-padaung *Burma* 53B1
Kyaukpyu *Burma* 53A2
Kyaukse *Burma* 59E3
Kychema *USSR* 42G2
Kyle *Can* 3G3
Kyle of Lochalsh *Scot* 31B2
Kyll, R *W Germ* 34D1
Kyneton *Aust* 78B3
Kyoga, L *Uganda* 70D3
Kyogle *Aust* 78D1
Kyŏngju *S Korea* 51B4
Kyongsang Sanmaek, Mts *S Korea* 52A3
Kyŏngsŏng *N Korea* 52A2
Kyonpyaw *Burma* 59E4
Kyoto *Japan* 51D4
Kyrenia *Cyprus* 63B1
Kyrta *USSR* 42K3
Kyshtym *USSR* 46H4
Kythrea *Cyprus* 63B1
Kyūshū, I *Japan* 51C5
Kyushu-Palau Ridge *Pacific O* 74H4
Kyustendil *Bulg* 39E2
Kyusyur *USSR* 47O2
Kyzyl *USSR* 48C1
Kyzylkum, Desert *USSR* 46H5
Kzyl Orda *USSR* 46H5

L

Laas Caanood *Somalia* 70E3
La Ascensíon *Mexico* 20C1
Laasphe *W Germ* 34E1
Laas Qoray *Somalia* 67D3
La Asunción *Ven* 24F1
La Banda *Arg* 26C1
La Barca *Mexico* 20B1
La Barge *USA* 16D2
Labasa *Fiji* 7G2
Labé *Guinea* 68A3
Labe, R *Czech* 40D2
Labelle *Can* 11E1
La Belle *USA* 13E4
Laberge,L *Can* 8L3
Labi *Brunei* 54D2
la Biche,L *Can* 3F3
Labinsk *USSR* 43G7
Labis *Malay* 54G7
Laboué *Leb* 63D1
Laboulaye *Arg* 26C2
Labrador, Region *Can* 5M4
Labrador City *Can* 5M4
Labrador S *Greenland/Can* 5N4
Lábrea *Brazil* 24F5
Labuan, I *Malay* 54E1
Labuha *Indon* 55C3
Labuhan *Indon* 54C4
Labuhanbajo *Indon* 55B4
Labuhanbatu *Indon* 54F7
Labuhanbilik *Indon* 54B2
Labutta *Burma* 53A2
Labytnangi *USSR* 42M2
La Capelle *France* 34B1
La Carlota *Arg* 26C2
La Carlota *Phil* 55F8
Lac Belot, L *Can* 8N2
Lac Bienville, L *Can* 5L4
Lac Brochet *Can* 3H2
Laccadive Is = Lakshadweep
Laccadive Is *India* 57F4
Lac d'Annecy, L *France* 35B2
Lac de Gras, L *Can* 4G3
Lac de Joux, L *Switz* 35B1
Lac de Neuchâtel, L *Switz* 35B1
Lac de Patzcuaro, L *Mexico* 20B2
Lac de Sayula, L *Mexico* 20B2
Lac des Bois, L *Can* 4F3
Lac des Milles Lacs, L *Can* 9D2
Lac du Bonnet *Can* 9C1
Lac du Bourget, L *France* 35A2
La Ceiba *Honduras* 19D3
Lacepede B *Aust* 78A3
La Châtre *France* 36C2
La Châtre-sur-le-Loir *France* 34A3
La-Chaux-de-Fonds *Switz* 35B1
Lachish, Hist Site *Israel* 63C3
Lachlan, R *Aust* 76D4
La Chorrera *Panama* 24C2
Lachute *Can* 11E1
La Ciotat *France* 35A3
La Ciudad *Mexico* 20A1
Lac Joseph, L *Can* 5M4
Lackawanna *USA* 11D2
Lac la Biche *Can* 4G4
Lac la Martre, L *Can* 4G3
Lac la Ronge, L *Can* 4H4
Lac L'eau Claire *Can* 5L4
Lac Léman, L *Switz/France* 38B1
Lac Manouane *Can* 5L4
Lac Manouane, L *Can* 7F1
Lac Maunoir, L *Can* 8N2
Lac Megantic *Can* 11E1
Lac Mistassini, L *Can* 5L4
La Cocha *Arg* 26B1
Lacombe *Can* 3F3
Laconia *USA* 11E2
La Coruña *Spain* 37A1
La Côte-St-André *France* 35A2
La Crosse *USA* 7D2
La Cruces *USA* 6C3
La Cruz *Arg* 26D1
La Cruz *Mexico* 20A1
Lac Seul, L *Can* 5J4
La Cygne *USA* 15D2
Ladākh Range *India* 58D2
Lādiz *Iran* 61E3
Lādnūn *India* 58C3
Ladong *China* 50B5
Ladozhskoye Ozero, L *USSR* 42E3
Lady Ann Str *Can* 5K2
Lady Barron *Aust* 78E3
Ladybrand *S Africa* 72D2
Ladysmith *Can* 3D4
Ladysmith *S Africa* 72D2
Ladysmith *USA* 10A1
Lae *PNG* 76D1
Laem Ngop *Thai* 53C3
Laesø, I *Den* 40C1
Lafayette, Colorado *USA* 14A2
Lafayette, Indiana *USA* 7E2
Lafayette, Louisiana *USA* 7D3
La Fène *France* 34B2
La-Ferté-Barnard *France* 34A2
La Ferté-St-Aubin *France* 34B2
La-Ferté-sous-Jouarre *France* 34B2
Lafia *Nig* 69H4
Lafiagi *Nig* 69H4
La Flèche *France* 36B2
La Galite, I *Tunisia* 69D1
Lagan, R *Sweden* 40C1
Lagarto *Brazil* 25L6
Laghouat *Alg* 69C2
Lagoa de Araruama *Brazil* 27D3
Lagoa de Castillos, L *Urug* 26E2
Lagoa de Rocha *Urug* 26E2
Lagoa dos Patos, Lg *Brazil* 23F4
Lagoa Feia *Brazil* 27D3
Lago Agrio *Ecuador* 24C4
Lagoa Juparanã, L *Brazil* 27D2
Lagoa Mandiore, L *Brazil* 27A2
Lagoa Mangueira, L *Brazil* 26E2
Lagoa mar Chiguita, L *Arg* 23D4
Lagoa Mirim, L *Urug/Brazil* 23F4
Lagoa Negra, L *Urug* 26E2
Lago Argentino, L *Arg* 23B8
Lagoa Uberaba, L *Brazil* 27A2
Lagoa Vermelha *Brazil* 26E1
Lago Buenos Aries, L *Arg* 23B7
Lago Cochrane, L *Chile/Arg* 23B7
Lago Colhué Huapi, L *Arg* 23C7
Lago de Chapala, L *Mexico* 19B2
Lago de Chiriqui, L *Panama* 24B2
Lago de Cuitzeo, L *Mexico* 20B2
Lago de la Laja, L *Chile* 23B5
Lago del Coghinas, L *Sardegna* 38B2
Lago de Maracaibo, L *Ven* 24D2
Lago de Nicaragua, L *Nic* 24A1
Lago de Perlas, L *Nic* 24B1
Lago de Santiaguillo, L *Mexico* 20B1
Lago di Bolsena, L *Italy* 38C2
Lago di Bracciano, L *Italy* 38C2
Lago di Como, L *Italy* 38B1
Lago d'Idro, L *Italy* 35D2
Lago di Garda, L *Italy* 38C1
Lago di Lecco, L *Italy* 35C2
Lago di Lugano, L *Italy* 35C2
Lago d'Iseo, L *Italy* 35D2
Lago d'Orta, L *Italy* 35C2
Lago General Carrera, L *Chile* 23B7
Lago Maggiore, L *Italy* 38B1
Lago Musters, L *Arg* 23C7
Lagon *France* 36B3
Lago Nahuel Haupi, L *Arg* 23B6
Lago O'Higgins, L *Chile* 23B7
Lago Omodeo, L *Sardegna* 38B2
Lago Poopó, L *Bol* 24E7
Lago Ranco, L *Chile* 23B6
Lago Rogaguado, L *Bol* 24E6
Lagos *Nig* 69G4
Lagos *Port* 37A2
Lagos, State *Nig* 69G4
Lago San Martin, L *Chile/Arg* 23B7
Lagos de Moreno *Mexico* 19B2
Lago Titicaca *Bol/Peru* 24E7
Lago Trasimeno, L *Italy* 35E3
La Goulette *Tunisia* 69E1
Lago Viedma, L *Arg* 23B7
La Grande *USA* 6B2
La Grande Rivière, R *Can* 5L4
Lagrange *Aust* 76B2
La Grange, Georgia *USA* 7E3
La Grange, Kentucky *USA* 10B3
La Grange, N Carolina *USA* 13D1
La Grange, Texas *USA* 15C4
La Gran Sabana, Mts *Ven* 24F2
La Grave *France* 35B2
Lagronño *Spain* 36B3
Laguna *USA* 14A3
Laguna Agua Brava *Mexico* 20A1
Laguna Aluminé, L *Arg* 26A3
Laguna Beach *USA* 17C4
Laguna Colorada Grande L *Arg* 26C3
Laguna de Bay, Lg *Phil* 55F8
Laguna de Caratasca, Lg *Honduras* 19D3
Laguna de Chiriqui, L *Panama* 19D4
Laguna de Guzmán, L *Mexico* 14A3
Laguna del Abra, L *Arg* 26C4
Laguna del Caimanero, L *Mexico* 20A1
Laguna de Managua, L *Nicaragua* 19D3
Laguna de Nicaragua, L *Nicaragua* 19D3
Laguna de Perlas, Lg *Nic* 21A4
Laguna de Pueblo Viejo, L *Mexico* 20C1
Laguna de Santa Maria, L *Mexico* 14A3
Laguna de Tamiahua, Lg *Mexico* 19C2
Laguna de Términos, Lg *Mexico* 19C3
Laguna de Yuriria, L *Mexico* 20B1
Laguna Iberá *Arg* 26D1
Laguna Itati, L *Arg* 26D1
Laguna le Altamira *Mexico* 20C1
Laguna Madre, Lg *Mexico* 19C2
Laguna Madre, Lg *USA* 15F4
Laguna Mar Chiquita, L *Arg* 26C2
Laguna Nahuel Huapi, L *Arg* 26A4
Laguna Nutauge, Lg *USSR* 8C2
Laguna Paiva *Arg* 26C2
Laguna Panguipulli, L *Chile* 26A3
Laguna Puyehue, L *Chile* 26A4
Laguna Ranco *Chile* 26A4
Laguna Repanco, L *Chile* 26A4
Laguna Salada, L *Mexico* 17C4
Laguna Seca *Mexico* 6C4
Laguna Superior, L *Mexico* 20C2
Laguna Tenkergynpil'gyn Lg *USSR* 8C2
Laguna Tortugas, L *Mexico* 20C1
Laguna Traful, L *Arg* 26A4
Laguna Trin, L *Arg* 26D1
Laguna Vankarem, Lg *USSR* 8C2
Laguna Veneta, Lg *Italy* 35E2
Laguna Villarrica, L *Chile* 26A3
Lagund Seca *Mexico* 20B1
Lahat *Indon* 54B3
Lahewa *Indon* 54A2
Lahia *Fin* 30J6
Lahij *S Yemen* 64D4
Lāhijān *Iran* 61C1
Lahn, R *W Germ* 34D1
Lahnstein *W Germ* 34D1
Lahore *Pak* 58C2
Lahr *France* 34D2
Lahti *Fin* 30K6
Iahud Datu *Malay* 54E1
La Huerta *Mexico* 20B2
Lai *Chad* 70B3
Laibin *China* 50B5
Lai Chau *Viet* 53C1
L'Aigle *France* 34A2
Laingsburg *S Africa* 72C3
Lairg *Scot* 32C2
Lais *Indon* 54B3
Lais *Phil* 55G9
Laiwui *Indon* 55C3
Laiyang *China* 50E2
Laizhou Wan, B *China* 50D2
Laja, R *Chile* 26A3
Lajeado *Brazil* 26E1
Lajes *Brazil* 23F3
La Jolla *USA* 18D4
La Junta *USA* 6C3
Lake Andes *USA* 9C3
Lake Cargelligo *Aust* 78C2
Lake Charles *USA* 7D3
Lake City, Florida *USA* 13C2
Lake City, Minnesota *USA* 9D3
Lake City, S Carolina *USA* 13D2
Lake District, Region *Eng* 33D4
Lake Elsinore *USA* 18D4
Lake Eyre Basin *Aust* 76C3
Lakefield *Can* 11D2
Lake Geneva *USA* 10B2
Lake George *USA* 12D1
Lake Harbour *Can* 5M3
Lake Havasu City *USA* 17D4
Lake Hughes *USA* 18C3
Lakehurst *USA* 12C2
Lake Isabella *USA* 18C3
Lake Jackson *USA* 15C4
Lake la Biche *Can* 3F3
Lakeland *USA* 13C3
Lake of the Woods *Can* 5J5
Lake Oswego *USA* 16B1
Lakeport *USA* 17B3
Lake Providence *USA* 15D3
Lake Pukaki *NZ* 79B2
Lakes Entrance *Aust* 78C3
Lakeshore *USA* 18C2
Lake Stewart *Aust* 78B1
Lake Traverse *Can* 11D1
Lakeview *USA* 6A2
Lakeview Mt *Can* 16B1
Lake Village *USA* 15D3
Lake Wales *USA* 13C3
Lakewood, California *USA* 18C4
Lakewood, Colorado *USA* 14A2
Lakewood, New Jersey *USA* 12C2
Lakewood, Ohio *USA* 10C2
Lake Worth *USA* 13E4
Lakhimpur *India* 59B2
Lakhpat *India* 58B4
Lakin *USA* 14B2
Lakki *Pak* 58C2
Lakonikós Kólpos, G *Greece* 39E3
Lakor, I *Indon* 55C4
Lakota *Ivory Coast* 68B4
Laksefjord, Inlet *Nor* 30K4
Lakselv *Nor* 30K4
Lakshadweep, Is *India* 60A2
La Laguna *Arg* 26C2
Lalibela *Eth* 64C4
La Libertad *Ecuador* 24B4
La Ligua *Chile* 26A2
Lalindi *Indon* 55B5
Lalindu, R *Indon* 55B3
La Linea *Spain* 37A2
Lalitpur *India* 58D4
Laloa *Indon* 55B3
La Loche *Can* 4H4
la Loche,L *Can* 3G2
La Loupe *France* 34A2
La Louvière *Belg* 34C1
La Luz *Nic* 21A4
La Madrid *Arg* 26B1
Lama Kara *Togo* 69G4
La Malbaie *Can* 5L5
La Malinche, Mt *Mexico* 20C2
La Mancha *Mexico* 20B1
La Mancha, Region *Spain* 37B2
Lamar, Colorado *USA* 6C3
Lamar, Missouri *USA* 15D2
Lamarque *Arg* 26B3
La Marque *USA* 15C4
Lambaréné *Gabon* 70B4
Lambayeque *Peru* 24B5
Lambert Gl *Ant* 80F10
Lamberts Bay *S Africa* 72B3
Lambertville *USA* 12C2
Lamblon,C *Can* 4F2
Lambro, R *Italy* 35C2
Lam Chi, R *Thai* 53C2
Lamego *Port* 37A1
La Meije, Mt *France* 35B2
La Merced *Arg* 26B1
La Merced *Peru* 24C6
Lamesa *USA* 14B3
La Mesa *USA* 17C4
Lamía *Greece* 39E3
Lammermuir Hills *Scot* 32D4
Lammhult *Sweden* 30G7
Lamon B *Phil* 55F8
Lamone, R *Italy* 35D2
Lamoni *USA* 15D1
Lamont, California *USA* 18C3
Lamont, Wyoming *USA* 9A3
Lamotrek, I *Pacific O* 49H6
Lamotte Beuvron *France* 34B3
La Moure *USA* 9C2
Lampasas *USA* 14C3
Lampeter *Wales* 33C5
Lamu *Kenya* 70E4
La Mure *France* 35A2
Lana *Italy* 35D1
Lanai, I *Hawaiian Is* 18E5
Lanai City *Hawaiian Is* 18E5
Lanark *Scot* 32D4
Lanbi, I *Burma* 53B3
Lancang, R *China* 53C1
Lancashire, County *Eng* 33D5
Lancaster, California *USA* 17C4
Lancaster *Eng* 33D4
Lancaster, Mississippi *USA* 15D1
Lancaster, New Hampshire *USA* 11E2
Lancaster, New York *USA* 12A1
Lancaster, Ohio *USA* 10C3
Lancaster, Pennsylvania *USA* 7F3
Lancaster, S Carolina *USA* 13C2
Lancaster Sd *Can* 5K2
Landak, R *Indon* 54C3
Landan *W Germ* 34E2
Landeck *Austria* 40C3
Lander *USA* 6C2
Landeta *Arg* 26C2
Landrum *USA* 13C1
Landsberg *W Germ* 40C3
Lands End, C *Can* 4F2
Land's End, Pt *Eng* 33C6
Landshut *W Germ* 40C3
Làndskrona *Sweden* 30G7
Lanett *USA* 13B2
La'nga Co, L *China* 59B1
Langdon *USA* 9C2
Langeb, Watercourse *Sudan* 64C3
Langeberg, Mt *S Africa* 72C2
Langenburg *Can* 3H3
Langenhagen *W Germ* 40B2
Langenthal *Switz* 35B1
Langholm *Scot* 32D4
Langjökull, Mts *Iceland* 30A2
Langkawi, I *Malay* 53B4
Langley *Can* 3D4
Langlo, R *Aust* 78C1
Langnau *Switz* 35B1
Langres *France* 36D2
langsa *Indon* 54A2
Lang Shan, Mts *China* 48D2
Lang Son *Viet* 53D1
Langtry *USA* 14B4
Languedoc, Region *France* 36C3
Lanigan *Can* 3G3
Lanin, Mt *Arg* 23B5
Lanoa,L, L *Phil* 55F9
Lansdale *USA* 12C2
Lansdowne House *Can* 5K4
Lansford *USA* 12C2
Lansing *USA* 7E2
Lanslebourg *France* 35B2
Lanzarote, I *Canary Is* 68A2
Lanzhou *China* 50A2
Lanzo Torinese *Italy* 35B2
Laoag *Phil* 55F7
Lao Cai *Viet* 53C1
Laoha He, R *China* 50D1
Laois, County *Irish Rep* 33B5
Laoise Port *Irish Rep* 33B5
Laoling *China* 52A2
Laon *France* 34B2
La Orova *Peru* 24C6
Laos, Republic *S E Asia* 53C2
Lapa *Brazil* 27C4
Lapalisse *France* 36C2
La Palma, I *Canary Is* 68A2
La Palmas *Panama* 24C2
La Paloma *Urug* 26E2
La Pampa, State *Arg* 26B3
La Panza Range, Mts *USA* 18B3
La Paragua *Ven* 24F2
La Paz *Arg* 23E4
La Paz *Arg* 26B2
La Paz *Bol* 24E7
La Paz *Mexico* 19A2
La Perouse, Str *USSR/Japan* 51E2
La Pesca *Mexico* 20C1
La Piedad *Mexico* 20B1
La Pine *USA* 16B2
Lapithos *Cyprus* 63B1

Laplace USA 15D3
la Placita Mexico 20B2
La Plant USA 9B2
La Plata Arg 23E4
La Plonge,L Can 3G2
La Porte USA 10B2
Laporte USA 12B2
Lappeenranta Fin 30K6
Lappland, Region Sweden/Fin 30H5
Laprida Arg 26C3
La Pryor USA 15F4
Laptev S USSR 47O2
Lapua Fin 30J6
La Puerta Arg 26B1
Lapu-Lapu Phil 55F8
La Punta Arg 26C1
La Purisma Mexico 6B4
Laqiya Arba'in, Well Sudan 70C1
La Quiaca Arg 23C2
L'Aquila Italy 38C2
Lar Iran 61C3
Larache Mor 69A1
Laragne France 35A2
Laramie USA 6C2
Laramie Mts USA 9A3
Laramie Range, Mts USA 6C2
Laranjeiras do Sul Brazil 27B4
Larantuka Indon 55B4
Larat, I Indon 55D4
Larca Spain 37B2
Laredo USA 6D4
Larestan, Region Iran 61C3
Largeau = Faya
L'Argentière France 35B2
Largo USA 13C3
Largs Scot 32C4
Lari Iran 61B1
Lariang, R Indon 55A3
La Rioja Arg 23C3
La Rioja, State Arg 23C3
Lárisa Greece 39E3
Larkana Pak 58B3
Larnaca Cyprus 62B3
Larnaca B Cyprus 63B1
Larne N Ire 32B4
Larned USA 14C2
La Robla Spain 37A1
La Roche-en-Ardenne Belg 34C1
La Rochelle France 36B2
La Roche-sur-Foron France 35B1
La Roche-sur-Yon France 36B2
La Roda Spain 37B2
La Romana Dom Rep 21D3
La Ronge Can 4H4
La Ronge,L Can 3H2
Larvik Nor 30G7
Lar'yak USSR 46J3
La Sabana Arg 26D1
La Sagra, Mt Spain 37B2
La Salle Can 11E1
La Salle USA 10B2
Las Animas USA 14B2
La Sarre Can 5L5
Las Avispas Arg 26C1
Las Cabras Chile 26A2
Lascano Urug 26E2
Lascombe Can 4G4
Las Cruces USA 14A3
La Selle, Mt Haiti 21C3
Lasengmia China 50B2
La Serena Chile 23B3
La Seyne France 35A3
Las Flores Arg 23E5
Lashe-Joveyn Afghan 61E2
Lashio Burma 53B1
La Sila, Mts Italy 38D3
Läsjerd Iran 61C1
Laskar Grah Afghan 58A2
Las Lajas Chile 26A3
Las Marismas, Marshland Spain 37A2
la Soledad Mexico 20B1
Lasolo Indon 55B3
Lasolo, R Indon 55B3
Las Palmas de Gran Canaria Canary Is 68A2
La Spezia Italy 38B2
Las Piedras Urug 26D2
Las Plumas Arg 23C6
Las Rosas Arg 26C2
Lassen Peak, Mt USA 16B2
Lassen Volcanic Nat Pk USA 16B2
Las Termas Arg 26C1
las Tinai Mexico 20C2
Las Tinajos Arg 26C1
Last Mountain L Can 3G3
Las Toscas Arg 26D1
Lastoursville Gabon 70B4
Lastovo, I Yugos 38D2
Las Tres Marias, Is Mexico 19B2
Las Varas Mexico 20A1
Las Varillas Arg 26C2
Las Vegas USA 6C3
Latakia = Al Lādhiqīyah
Latina Italy 38C2
La Toma Arg 26B2
La Tortuga, I Ven 24E1
La Trinidad Phil 55F7
Latrobe Aust 78E3
La Troya, R Arg 26B1
Latrun Israel 63C3
La Tuque Can 5L5
Lätür India 60B1
Latviyskaya SSR, Republic USSR 42C4
Lau Group, Is Fiji 77H2
Launceston Aust 76D5
Launceston Eng 33C6
La Unión Chile 23B6
La Union El Salvador 19D3
La Union Mexico 20B2
La Unión Peru 24C5
Laura Aust 76D2
Laurel, Delaware USA 11D3
Laurel, Maryland USA 12B3
Laurel, Mississippi USA 7E3
Laurel, Montana USA 16E1
Laurens USA 13C2
Laurie L Can 3H2
Laurinburg USA 13D2
Lausanne Switz 38B1
Laut, I Indon 54E3
Lautaro Chile 23B7
Lauterbach W Germ 34E1
Lauterecken W Germ 34D2
Lautoka, I Fiji 7G2
Laval Can 11E1
Laval France 36B2
Laveaga Peak, Mt USA 18B2
Laveno Italy 35C2
La Ventura Mexico 20B1
La Verá Par 27A4
Lavina USA 16E1
La Vôge, Region France 34C2
Lavras Brazil 25K8
Lavras do Sul Brazil 26E2
Lavrentiya USSR 8D2
Lavumisa Swaziland 72E2
Lawas Malay 54E2
Lawdar S Yemen 65E4
Lawele Indon 55B4
Lawksawk Burma 53B1
Lawra Ghana 69F3
Lawrence, Kansas USA 15C2
Lawrence, Massachusetts USA 11E2
Lawrence NZ 79A3
Lawrenceburg USA 13B1
Lawrenceville, Illinois USA 10B3
Lawrenceville, Pennsylvania USA 12B2
Lawton USA 6D3
Layla S Arabia 65E2
Laylo Sudan 70D3
La'youn Mor 68A2
Lazarev USSR 51E1
Lázaro Cárdenas Mexico 20B2
Laz Daua Somalia 67D3
Lazi Phil 55F9
Lazo USSR 51C3
Lead USA 6C2
Leader Can 3G3
Leadville USA 14A2
Leaf, R USA 13B2
Leakey USA 14C4
Leandro N Alem Arg 26D1
Leavenworth USA 15C2
Leba Pol 41D2
Lebanon, Kansas USA 14C2
Lebanon, Missouri USA 15D2
Lebanon, Oregon USA 16B2
Lebanon, Pennsylvania USA 11D2
Lebanon, Republic S W Asia 62C3
Lebanon, Tennessee USA 10B3
Lebec USA 18C3
Lebombo, Mts Mozam/S Africa/Swaziland 71D6
Lebork Pol 41D2
Le Bourg-d'Oisans France 35B2
Le Brassus Switz 35B1
Lebu Chile 23B5
Le Buet, Mt France 35B1
Le Cateau France 34B1
Lecce Italy 39D2
Lecco Italy 38B1
Lech, R Austria 35D1
Le Champ de Feu, Mt France 34D2
Lechtaler Alpen, Mts Austria 35D1
Le Creusot France 36C2
Ledbury Eng 33D5
Ledo India 59E2
Leduc Can 3F3
Lee USA 12D1
Leech L USA 9D2
Leeds Eng 31C3
Leek Eng 33D5
Leer W Germ 40B2
Leesburg, Florida USA 13C3
Leesburg, Virginia USA 12B3
Leesville USA 15D3
Leeton Aust 78C2
Leeugamka S Africa 72C3
Leeuwarden Neth 40B2
Leeuwin,C Aust 76A4
Lee Vining USA 18C2
Leeward Is Caribbean 21E3
Lefka Cyprus 63B1
Lefkara Cyprus 63B1
Lefkoniko Cyprus 63B1
Legazpi Phil 55F8
Legnago Italy 35D2
Legnica Pol 40D2
Le Grand-Luce France 34A3
Le Grand Veymont, Mt France 35A2
Legulzamo Colombia 24D4
Legvan Inlet Guyana 25G2
Leh India 58D2
Le Havre France 36C2
Lehi USA 17D2
Lehigh, R USA 12C2
Lehighton USA 12C2
Le Hohneck, Mt France 34D2
Leiah Pak 58C2
Leibnitz Austria 40D3
Leicester, County Eng 33E5
Leicester Eng 33E5
Leichhardt, R Aust 76C2
Leiden Neth 40A2
Leie, R Belg 34B1
Leigh Creek Aust 76C4
Leighton Buzzard Eng 33E6
Leine, R W Germ 40B2
Leinster, Region Irish Rep 33B5
Leipzig E Germ 40C2
Leiria Port 37A2
Leirvik Nor 30F7
Leiyang China 50C4
Leizhou Bandao, Pen China 50B5
Leizhou Wan, B China 50C5
Lek, R Neth 40A2
Lekemti Eth 70D3
Lekitobi Indon 55B3
Leksula Indon 55C3
Leland USA 15D3
Le Lavendou France 35B3
Lelija, Mt Yugos 39D2
Le Locle France 35B1
Le Lude France 34A3
Lema, R Mexico 20B1
Le Mans France 36C2
Le Mars USA 9C3
Lemhi Range, Mts USA 16D2
Lemieux Is Can 5M3
Lemmon USA 6C2
Lemmon,Mt USA 17D4
Lemon Bank, Oilfield N Sea 33G5
Lemoore USA 17C3
Lempdes France 36C2
Lemro, R Burma 59D3
Le Murge, Region Italy 38D2
Lena USSR 48D1
Lena, R USSR 47O3
Lend Austria 35E1
Lendery USSR 42E3
Lengshujiang China 50C4
Leninabad USSR 57E1
Leninakan USSR 46F5
Leningrad USSR 42E4
Leningradskaya, Base Ant 80F7
Leninogorsk, Tatar ASSR USSR 42J5
Leninogorsk USSR 48B1
Leninsk-Kuznetskiy USSR 46K4
Leninskoye USSR 51C2
Lenkoran' USSR 43H8
Lenne, R W Germ 34E1
Lenoir USA 13C1
Lenox USA 12D1
Lens France 34B1
Lensk USSR 47N3
Lentini Italy 38C3
Lenya, R Burma 53B3
Léo U Volta 69F3
Leoben Austria 38C1
Leominster Eng 33D5
Leominster USA 12E1
Leon Mexico 19B2
León Nic 24A1
Leon, Region Spain 37A1
León Spain 37A1
León, State Mexico 20C1
Leonardville Namibia 72B1
Leonarisso Cyprus 63C1
Leonidovo USSR 51E2
Leonora Aust 76B3
Leopoldina Brazil 27D3
Léopoldville = Kinshasa
Lepel USSR 42D5
Leper Belg 34B1
Leping China 50D4
Le Puy France 36C2
Léraba, R Ivory Coast 69F4
Léré Chad 70B3
Leribe Lesotho 72D2
Lerici Italy 35C2
Lérida Spain 37C1
Lermoos Austria 35D1
Léros, I Greece 39F3
Le Roy USA 12B1
Lerwick Scot 31C1
Les Andelys France 34A2
Les Arcs France 35B3
Les Cayes Haiti 21C3
Les Echelles France 35A2
Les Ecrins, Mt France 35B2
Les Escoumins Can 11F1
Leshan China 50A4
Leskovac Yugos 39E2
Les Landes, Region France 36B3
Leslie S Africa 72D2
Lesnoy USSR 42J4
Lesogorsk USSR 51E2
Lesosibirsk USSR 47L4
Lesotho, Kingdom S Africa 72D2
Lesozavodsk USSR 51C2
Les Sables-d'Olonne France 36B2
Lesser Antarctica, Region Ant 80E
Lesser Antilles, Is Caribbean 21D4
Lesser Slave L Can 3F2
Les Trois Evêchés, Mt France 35B2
Lésvos, I Greece 39F3
Leszno Pol 40D2
Letaba, R S Africa 72E1
Lethakeng Botswana 72D1
Letha Range, Mts Burma 59D3
Lethbridge Can 4G5
Lethem Guyana 25G3
Leti, I Indon 55C4
Letichev USSR 41F3
Let Oktyobr'ya USSR 47N4
Letong Indon 54C2
le Touquet-Paris-Plage France 33F6
Letpadan Burma 53B2
Le Tréport France 36C1
Leuk Switz 35B1
Leuven Belg 40A2
Levádhia Greece 39E3
Levanger Nor 30G6
Levanna, Mt Italy 35B2
Levanto Italy 35C2
Levelland USA 14B3
Levens France 35B3
Lévêque,C Aust 49F8
Leverkusen W Germ 34D1
Levice Czech 41D3
Levico Italy 35D2
Levin NZ 79C2
Lévis Can 5L5
Levittown USA 11E2
Lévka Óri, Mt Greece 39E3
Levkás Greece 39E3
Levkás, I Greece 39E3
Lévque,C Aust 76B2
Levski Bulg 39F2
Lewes Eng 33F6
Lewis USA 14C2
Lewis, I Scot 31B2
Lewisburg USA 12B2
Lewis P NZ 79B2
Lewis Range, Mts USA 6B2
Lewis Smith,L USA 13B2
Lewiston, Idaho USA 6B2
Lewiston, Maine USA 7F2
Lewistown, Montana USA 6C2
Lewistown, Pennsylvania USA 11D2
Lewisville USA 15D3
Lexington, Kentucky USA 7E3
Lexington, Missouri USA 15D2
Lexington, N Carolina USA 13C1
Lexington, Nebraska USA 14C1
Lexington, Virginia USA 11D3
Lexington Park USA 11D3
Leyte G Phil 55G8
Lezhe Alb 39D2
Lhasa China 57H2
Lhazê China 59C2
Lhokseumawe Indon 54A1
Lhozhag China 59D2
Lhunze China 48C4
Liancourt Rocks = Tok-do
Lianga Phil 55G9
Liangdang China 50B3
Lianjiang China 50C5
Lianping China 50C5
Lian Xian China 50C5
Lianyungang China 50D3
Liaoding Bandao, Pen China 50E1
Liaodong Wan, B China 50E1
Liao He, R China 50E1
Liaoning, Province China 50E1
Liaoyang China 50E1
Liaoyuan China 50E1
Liaoyuang China 51B3
Liard, R Can 4F3
Liard River Can 4F4
Liart France 34C2
Libby USA 16C1
Libenge Zaïre 70B3
Liberal USA 6C3
Liberec Czech 40C2
Liberia, Republic Africa 68A4
Liberty, Missouri USA 15D2
Liberty, New York USA 11E2
Liberty, Pennsylvania USA 12B2
Liberty, Texas USA 15D3
Libourne France 36B3
Libres Mexico 20C2
Libreville Gabon 70A3
Libya, Republic Africa 67A2
Libyan Desert Libya 67B2
Libyan Plat Egypt 67B1
Licata Italy 38C3
Lichfield Eng 33E5
Lichinga Mozam 71D5
Lichtenburg S Africa 72D2
Licking, R USA 10C3
Lick Observatory USA 18B2
Lida USA 18D2
Lida USSR 42D5
Lidköping Sweden 30G7
Lido di Ostia Italy 38C2
Liechtenstein, Principality Europe 38B1
Liège Belg 40B2
Lielupe, R USSR 41E1
Lienart Zaïre 70C3
Lienz Austria 40C3
Liepāja USSR 30J7
Liepāja USSR 42C4
Lier Belg 34C1
Liestal Switz 35B1
Liévre, R Can 11E1
Liezen Austria 40C3
Liffey, R Irish Rep 33B5
Lifford Irish Rep 32B4
Lifu, I Nouvelle Calédonie 77F3
Lightning Ridge Aust 78C1
Ligny-en-Barrois France 34C2
Ligonha, R Mozam 71D5
Liguria, Region Italy 35C2
Ligurian, S Italy 38B2
Lihir Group, Is PNG 77E1
Lihue Hawaiian Is 18E5
Likasi Zaïre 71C5
Likupang Indon 55C2
Lille France 36C1
Lillebonne France 34A2
Lillehammer Nor 30G6
Lillers France 34B1
Lillestøm Nor 30G6
Lillooet Can 3D3
Lillooet, R Can 3D3
Lilongwe Malawi 71D5
Liloy Phil 55F9
Lim, R Yugos 39D2
Lima Peru 24C6
Lima Spain 37A1
Lima USA 7E2
Lima Res USA 16D2
Limassol Cyprus 62B3
Limavady N Ire 32B4
Limay, R Arg 26B3
Limay Mahuida Arg 26B3
Limbe Malawi 71D5
Limbotto Indon 55B2
Limburg W Gem 40B2
Limeira Brazil 25J8
Limerick Irish Rep 31B3
Limfjorden, L Den 40B1
Limmen Bight, B Aust 76C2
Límnos, I Greece 39F3
Limoeiro Brazil 25L5
Limoges France 36C2
Limón Costa Rica 19D4
Limon USA 6C3
Limone Italy 35B2
Limousin, Region France 36C2
Limpopo, R Mozam 72E1
Linanes Mexico 20C1
Linapacan Str Phil 55E8
Linares Chile 23B5
Linares Mexico 6D4
Linares Spain 37B2
Lincang China 48C4
Lincoln Arg 23D4
Lincoln, California USA 15C1
Lincoln, County Eng 33E5
Lincoln Eng 33E5
Lincoln, Illinois USA 10B2
Lincoln, Maine USA 11F1
Lincoln, Nebraska USA 6D2
Lincoln, New Hampshire USA 11E2
Lincoln NZ 79B2
Lincoln USA 18B1
Lincoln, S Greenland 80A
Lincoln City USA 16B2
Lincoln Park USA 10C2
L'Incudina, Mt Corse 38B2
Lindau W Germ 40B3
Linden Guyana 25G2
Lindesnes, C Nor 30F7

Lindi *Tanz* **71D4**
Lindi, R *Zaïre* **70C3**
Lindley *S Africa* **72D2**
Lindos *Greece* **39F3**
Lindsay, California *USA* **18C2**
Lindsay *Can* **11D2**
Lindsay, Montana *USA* **9A2**
Line Is *Pacific O* **75M4**
Linfen *China* **50C2**
Lingao *China* **53D2**
Lingayen *Phil* **55F7**
Lingen *W Germ* **40B2**
Lingle *USA* **9B3**
Lingling *China* **50C4**
Lingshan *China* **50B5**
Lingshi *China* **50C2**
Linguère *Sen* **68A3**
Linhai, Heilongjiang *China* **51A1**
Linhai, Rhejiang *China* **50E4**
Linhares *Brazil* **25L7**
Linhe *China* **50B1**
Linjiang *China* **51B3**
Linköping *Sweden* **30H7**
Linkou *China* **51C2**
Linqing *China* **50D2**
Lins *Brazil* **27C3**
Lintao *China* **50A2**
Linthal *Switz* **35C1**
Linton *USA* **9B2**
Linxi *China* **48E2**
Linxia *China* **50A2**
Linz *Austria* **40C3**
Lipa *Phil* **55F8**
Lipari, I *Italy* **38C3**
Lipetsk *USSR* **43F5**
Lipova *Rom* **39E1**
Lippe, R *W Germ* **40B2**
Lippstadt *W Germ* **34E1**
Lira *Uganda* **70D3**
Liranga *Congo* **70B4**
Lisala *Zaïre* **70C3**
Lisboa *Port* **37A2**
Lisbon = Lisboa
Lisbon *USA* **9C2**
Lisburn *N Ire* **33B4**
Lisburne,C *USA* **8E2**
Lishui *China* **50D4**
Li Shui, R *China* **50C4**
Lisichansk *USSR* **43F6**
Lisieux *France* **36C2**
L'Isle-Adam *France* **34B2**
L'Isle-sur-le-Doubs *France* **35B1**
Lismore *Aust* **77E3**
Litang *China* **50B5**
Litani, R *Leb* **63C2**
Litani, R *Suriname* **25H3**
Litchfield, Illinois *USA* **10B3**
Litchfield, Minnesota *USA* **9D2**
Lithgow *Aust* **76E4**
Lititz *USA* **12B2**
Litke *USSR* **51E1**
Litovko *USSR* **51D2**
Litovskaya SSR, Republic *USSR* **42C4**
Little, R *USA* **15C3**
Little Abaco, I *Bahamas* **7F4**
Little Aden *S Yemen* **64D4**
Little Andaman, I *Andaman Is* **60E2**
Little Barrier I *NZ* **79C1**
Little Belt Mts *USA* **16D1**
Little Bitter L *Egypt* **63B3**
Little Bow, R *Can* **3F3**
Little Cayman, I *Caribbean* **19D3**
Little Egg Harbour, B *USA* **12C3**
Little Falls, Minnesota *USA* **9D2**
Little Falls, New York *USA* **12C1**
Littlefield *USA* **14B3**
Littlefork *USA* **9D2**
Little Fork, R *USA* **9D2**
Little Halibut Bank, Sand-bank *Scot* **32E2**
Little Inagua, I *Caribbean* **21C2**
Little Karroo, R *S Africa* **72C3**
Little Koniuji, I *USA* **8G4**
Little Lake *USA* **18D3**
Little Missouri, R *USA* **9B2**
Little Nicobar, I *Nicobar Is* **53A4**
Little Rock *USA* **7D3**
Littlerock *USA* **18D3**
Little Sitkin, I *USA* **8B6**
Little Smoky *Can* **3E3**
Little Smoky, R *Can* **3E3**
Littlestown *USA* **12B3**
Little Tanaga, I *USA* **8C6**
Littleton, Colorado *USA* **14A2**
Littleton, New Hampshire *USA* **11E2**
Liuhe *China* **51B3**
Liuzhou *China* **50B5**
Livanátais *Greece* **39E3**
Livāni *USSR* **41F1**
Livarot *France* **34A2**
Livengood *USA* **8J2**
Livenza, R *Italy* **35E2**
Live Oak *USA* **13C2**
Livermore *USA* **17B3**
Livermore,Mt *USA* **14B3**
Liverpool *Can* **5M5**
Liverpool *Eng* **33D5**
Liverpool B *Can* **4E2**
Liverpool B *Eng* **33D5**
Liverpool,C *Can* **5L2**
Liverpool Range, Mts *Aust* **78D2**
Livingston, Montana *USA* **6B2**
Livingston, Tennessee *USA* **13B1**
Livingston, Texas *USA* **15D3**
Livingstone = Maramba
Livingston,L *USA* **15C3**
Livno *Yugos* **38D2**
Livny *USSR* **43F5**
Livonia *USA* **10C2**
Livorno *Italy* **38C2**
Livramento do Brumado *Brazil* **27D1**
Liwale *Tanz* **71D4**
Lizard Pt *Eng* **33C7**
Ljubljana *Yugos* **38C1**
Ljungan, R *Sweden* **30G6**
Ljungby *Sweden* **30G7**
Ljusdal *Sweden* **30H6**
Ljusnan, R *Sweden* **42B3**
Llandeilo *Wales* **33D6**
Llandovery *Wales* **33D6**
Llandrindod Wells *Wales* **33D5**
Llandudno *Wales* **33D5**
Llanelli *Wales* **33C6**
Llangollen *Wales* **33D5**
Llano *USA* **14C3**
Llano, R *USA* **14C3**
Llano Estacado, Plat *USA* **6C3**
Llanos, Region *Colombia/Ven* **Z4D2**
Llanos de Chiquitos, Region *Bol* **24F7**
Llera *Mexico* **20C1**
Llerena *Spain* **37A2**
Lleyn, Pen *Wales* **33C5**
Llimsk *USSR* **47M4**
Llin *USSR* **47M4**
Llorin *Nigeria* **66E7**
Lloyd George,Mt *Can* **3D2**
Lloyd L *Can* **3G2**
Lloydminster *Can* **4H4**
Llullaillaco, Mt *Chile/Arg* **23C2**
Loa, R *Chile* **23C2**
Loan *France* **36C2**
Loange, R *Zaïre* **70B4**
Lobatse *Botswana* **72D2**
Lobaye, R *CAR* **70B3**
Loberia *Arg* **26D3**
Lobito *Angola* **71B5**
Lobos *Arg* **26D3**
Locano *Italy* **35B2**
Locarno *Switz* **35C1**
Loch Awe, L *Scot* **32C3**
Lochboisdale *Scot* **32B3**
Loch Bracadale, Inlet *Scot* **32B3**
Loch Broom, Estuary *Scot* **32C3**
Loch Doon, L *Scot* **32C4**
Loch Earn, L *Scot* **32C3**
Loch Eriboll, Inlet *Scot* **32C2**
Loch Ericht, L *Scot* **32C3**
Loches *France* **36C2**
Loch Etive, Inlet *Scot* **32C3**
Loch Ewe, Inlet *Scot* **32C3**
Loch Fyne, Inlet *Scot* **32C3**
Loch Hourn, Inlet *Scot* **32C3**
Loch Indaal, Inlet *Scot* **32B4**
Lochinver *Scot* **32C2**
Loch Katrine, L *Scot* **32C3**
Loch Leven, L *Scot* **32D3**
Loch Linnhe, Inlet *Scot* **32C3**
Loch Lochy, L *Scot* **32C3**
Loch Lomond, L *Scot* **32C3**
Loch Long, Inlet *Scot* **32C3**
Lochmaddy *Scot* **32B3**
Loch Maree, L *Scot* **32C3**
Loch Morar, L *Scot* **32C3**
Lochnagar, Mt *Scot* **32D3**
Loch Ness, L *Scot* **32C3**
Loch Rannoch, L *Scot* **32C3**
Loch Roag, Inlet *Scot* **32B2**
Lochsa, R *USA* **16C1**
Loch Sheil, L *Scot* **32C3**
Loch Shin, L *Scot* **32C2**
Loch Snizort, Inlet *Scot* **32B3**
Loch Sunart, Inlet *Scot* **32C3**
Loch Tay, L *Scot* **32C3**
Loch Torridon, Inlet *Scot* **32C3**
Lock *Aust* **78A2**
Lockerbie *Scot* **32D4**
Lock Haven *USA* **11D2**
Lockport *USA* **11D2**
Loc Ninh *Viet* **53D3**
Locri *Italy* **38D3**
Lod *Israel* **63C3**
Loddon, R *Aust* **78B3**
Lodeynoye Pole *USSR* **42E3**
Lodge Grass *USA* **16E1**
Lodhran *Pak* **58C3**
Lodi *Italy* **38B1**
Lodi *USA* **17B3**
Lodja *Zaïre* **70C4**
Lods *France* **35B1**
Lodwar *Kenya* **70D3**
Łódź *Pol* **41D2**
Loeriesfontein *S Africa* **72B3**
Lofer *Austria* **35E1**
Lofoten, Is *Nor* **30G5**
Logan, New Mexico *USA* **14B2**
Logan, Utah *USA* **6B2**
Logan,Mt *Can* **4D3**
Logan Mts *Can* **8N3**
Logansport, Indiana *USA* **10B2**
Logansport, Louisiana *USA* **15D3**
Loganton *USA* **12B2**
Logroño *Spain* **37B1**
Lohārdaga *India* **59B3**
Lohja *Fin* **30J6**
Lohr *W Germ* **34E2**
Loikaw *Burma* **53B2**
Loimaa *Fin* **30J6**
Loing, R *France* **34B2**
Loir, R *France* **36C2**
Loire, R *France* **36C2**
Loire et Cher, Department *France* **34A3**
Loiret, Department *France* **34B3**
Loja *Ecuador* **24C4**
Loja *Spain* **37B2**
Loji *Indon* **55C3**
Lokan Tekojärvi, Res *Fin* **30K5**
Lokeren *Belg* **34B1**
Lokitaung *Kenya* **70D3**
Loknya *USSR* **41F1**
Lokoja *Nig* **69H4**
Lokolo, R *Zaïre* **70C4**
Lokoro, R *Zaïre* **70C4**
Loks Land, I *Can* **5M3**
Lolland, I *Den* **40C2**
Loloda *Indon* **55C2**
Lolo P *USA* **16D1**
Lom *Bulg* **39E2**
Lom, R *Cam* **69J4**
Lomami, R *Zaïre* **71C4**
Loma Mts *Sierra Leone/Guinea* **68A4**
Lombagin *Indon* **55B2**
Lombardia, Region *Italy* **35C2**
Lomblen, I *Indon* **55B4**
Lombok, I *Indon* **54E4**
Lomé *Togo* **69G4**
Lomela *Zaïre* **70C4**
Lomela, R *Zaïre* **70C4**
Lomond, Oilfield *N Sea* **32G3**
Lomonosov *USSR* **42D4**
Lomont, Region *France* **35B1**
Lompoc *USA* **17B4**
Łomza *Pol* **41E2**
Lonāvale *India* **60A1**
Loncoche *Chile* **23B5**
London *Can* **5K5**
London *Eng* **33E6**
London *USA* **10C3**
Londonderry, County *N Ire* **32B4**
Londonderry *N Ire* **32B4**
Londonderry, I *Chile* **23B9**
Londonderry,C *Aust* **76B2**
Londres *Arg* **23C3**
Londrina *Brazil* **23F2**
Lone Mt *USA* **18D1**
Lone Pine *USA* **18C2**
Long, I *Bahamas* **7F4**
Long, I *PNG* **49H7**
Long Akah *Malay* **54D2**
Longarone *Italy* **35E1**
Longavi, Mt *Chile* **26A3**
Long B *Jamaica* **21H2**
Long B *USA* **13D2**
Long Beach, California *USA* **6B3**
Long Beach, New York *USA* **11E2**
Long Branch *USA* **11E2**
Longchuan *China* **50D5**
Long Creek *USA* **16C2**
Longford *Aust* **78E3**
Longford, County *Irish Rep* **33B5**
Longford *Irish Rep* **33B5**
Long Forties, Region *N Sea* **32E3**
Longhua *China* **50D1**
Long I *Can* **5L4**
Long I *PNG* **76D1**
Long I *USA* **7F2**
Long Island Sd *USA* **12D2**
Longjiang *China* **51A2**
Long L *Can* **10B1**
Long L *USA* **9B2**
Longlac *Can* **5K4**
Longlin *China* **50B5**
Longmont *USA* **6C2**
Longnawan *Indon* **54E2**
Longny *France* **34C2**
Long Prairie *USA* **9D2**
Longquimay *Chile* **23B5**
Longreach *Aust* **76D3**
Longshou Shan, Upland *China* **50A2**
Longs Peak, Mt *USA* **14A1**
Longtown *Eng* **32D4**
Longueuil *Can* **11E1**
Longuimay *Chile* **26A3**
Longuyon *France* **34C2**
Longview, Texas *USA* **7D3**
Longview, Washington *USA* **6A2**
Longwy *France* **36D2**
Longxi *China* **50A3**
Long Xuyen *Viet* **53D3**
Longyan *China* **50D4**
Longzhou *China* **50B5**
Lonigo *Italy* **35D2**
Lons-le-Saunier *France* **36D2**
Lookout,C *USA* **7F3**
Loolmalasin, Mt *Tanz* **70D4**
Loon, R *Can* **3E2**
Lop Buri *Thai* **53C3**
Lopez, C *Gabon* **70A4**
Lop Nur, L *China* **48C2**
Lora del Rio *Spain* **37A2**
Lorain *USA* **7E2**
Loralai *Pak* **58B2**
Lordegān *Iran* **61C2**
Lord Howe, I *Aust* **77E4**
Lord Howe Rise *Pacific O* **75K5**
Lord Mayor B *Can* **5J3**
Lordsburg *USA* **6C3**
Lorena *Brazil* **27C3**
Loreo *Italy* **35E2**
Loreto *Mexico* **20B1**
Lorient *France* **36B2**
Lorne *Aust* **78B3**
Lörrach *W Germ* **40B3**
Lorraine, Region *France* **36D2**
Los Alamos *USA* **6C3**
Los Andes *Chile* **26A2**
Los Angeles *Chile* **23B5**
Los Angeles *USA* **6B3**
Los Angeles Aqueduct *USA* **18C3**
Los Banos *USA* **17B3**
Los Cerrillos *Arg* **26B2**
Los Corchos *Mexico* **20A1**
Los Gatos *USA* **17B3**
Lošinj, I *Yugos* **38C2**
Los Juries *Arg* **26C1**
Los Lagos *Chile* **26A3**
Los Laiaderoz *Mexico* **20C1**
Los Loros *Chile* **26A1**
Los Luncas *USA* **14A3**
Los Menucos *Arg* **26B4**
Los Mochis *Mexico* **19B2**
Los Olivos *USA* **18B3**
Los Sauces *Chile* **26A3**
Losser *USSR* **42J3**
Lossiemouth *Scot* **32D3**
Los Telares *Arg* **26C1**
Los Testigos, Is *Ven* **21E4**
Lost Hills *USA* **18C3**
Lost Trail P *USA* **16D1**
Los Vilos *Chile* **23B4**
Lot, R *France* **36C3**
Lota *Chile* **26A3**
Lothian, Region *Scot* **32D4**
Lotikipi Plain *Sudan/Kenya* **70D3**
Loto *Zaïre* **70C4**
Lotsane, R *Botswana* **72D1**
Lötschberg Tunnel *Switz* **35B1**
Lotta, R *Fin USSR* **30K5**
Loudéac *France* **36B2**
Louga *Sen* **68A3**
Lough Allen, L *Irish Rep* **31B3**
Lough Boderg, L *Irish Rep* **33B5**
Loughborough *Eng* **33E5**
Lough Bouna, L *Irish Rep* **33B5**
Lough Carlingford, L *N Ire* **33B4**
Lough Conn, L *Irish Rep* **31B3**
Lough Corrib, L *Irish Rep* **31B3**
Lough Derg, L *Irish Rep* **31B3**
Lough Derravaragh, L *Irish Rep* **33B5**
Loughead I *Can* **4H2**
Lough Ennell, L *Irish Rep* **33B5**
Lough Erne, L *N Ire* **31B3**
Lough Foyle, Estuary *N Ire/Irish Rep* **31B2**
Lough Neagh, L *N Ire* **31B3**
Lough Oughter, L *Irish Rep* **33B4**
Lough Ree, L *Irish Rep* **31B3**
Lough Sheelin, L *Irish Rep* **33B5**
Lough Strangford, L *Irish Rep* **33C4**
Lough Swilly, Estuary *Irish Rep* **32B4**
Louhans *France* **35A1**
Louisa *USA* **10C3**
Louisa Reef, I *S E Asia* **54D1**
Louise, I *Can* **8M5**
Louise,L *USA* **8J3**
Louisiade Arch *Solomon Is* **77E2**
Louisiana, State *USA* **7D3**
Louis Trichardt *S Africa* **72D1**
Louisville, Georgia *USA* **13C2**
Louisville, Kentucky *USA* **7E3**
Louisville, Mississippi *USA* **13B2**
Loukhi *USSR* **42E2**
Lount L *Can* **9D1**
Loup, R *France* **35B3**
Loup, R *USA* **14C1**
Lourdes *France* **36B3**
Louth *Aust* **78C2**
Louth, County *Irish Rep* **33B5**
Louth *Eng* **33E5**
Louvain = Leuven
Louviers *France* **36C2**
Lovat, R *USSR* **42E4**
Lovech *Bulg* **39E2**
Loveland *USA* **14A1**
Loveland P *USA* **14A2**
Lovell *USA* **16E2**
Lovelock *USA* **17C2**
Lóvere *Italy* **38C1**
Lovington *USA* **14B3**
Lovozero *USSR* **42F2**
Low,C *Can* **5K3**
Lowell, Massachusetts *USA* **7F2**
Lowell, Oregon *USA* **16B2**
Lowell *USA* **12E1**
Lower Arrow L *Can* **16C1**
Lower Hutt *NZ* **79B2**
Lower Lake *USA* **18A1**
Lower Post *Can* **8N4**
Lower Red L *USA* **9C2**
Lower Seal,L *Can* **5L4**
Lowestoft *Eng* **33F5**
Łowicz *Pol* **41D2**
Loxton *Aust* **78B2**
Loxton *S Africa* **72C3**
Loyalsock Creek, R *USA* **12B2**
Loyd George,Mt *Can* **4F4**
Loznica *Yugos* **39D2**
loz Reyes *Mexico* **20B2**
Lozva, R *USSR* **46H3**
Luacano *Angola* **71C5**
Luachimo *Angola* **71C4**
Lualaba, R *Zaïre* **70C4**
Luampa *Zambia* **71C5**
Luân *Angola* **71C5**
Lu'an *China* **50D3**
Luanda *Angola* **71B4**
Luando, R *Angola* **71B5**
Luanginga, R *Angola* **71C5**
Luang Namtha *Laos* **53C1**
Luang Prabang *Laos* **53C2**
Luangue, R *Angola* **71B4**
Luangwa, R *Zambia* **71D5**
Luan He, R *China* **50D1**
Luanping *China* **50D1**
Luanshya *Zambia* **71C5**
Luapula, R *Zaïre* **71C5**
Luarca *Spain* **37A1**
Lubalo *Angola* **71B4**
L'uban *USSR* **41F2**
Lubang Is *Phil* **55F8**
Lubango *Angola* **71B5**
Lubbock *USA* **6C3**
Lübeck *W Germ* **40C2**
Lubefu *Zaïre* **70C4**
Lubefu, R *Zaïre* **70C4**
Lubero *Zaïre* **70C3**
Lubéron, R *France* **35A3**
Lubilash, R *Zaïre* **71C4**
Lublin *Pol* **41E2**
Lubny *USSR* **43E5**
Lubok Antu *Malay* **54D2**
Lubudi *Zaïre* **71C4**
Lubudi, R *Zaïre* **71C4**
Lubuklinggau *Indon* **54B3**
Lubumbashi *Zaïre* **71C5**
Lubutu *Zaïre* **70C4**
Lucas *Brazil* **27A1**
Lucban *Phil* **55F8**
Lucca *Italy* **38C2**
Luce, B *Scot* **32C4**
Lucedale *USA* **15E3**
Lucena *Phil* **55F8**
Lucenec *Czech* **41D3**
Lucerne = Luzern
Lucero *Mexico* **14A3**
Luchegorsk *USSR* **51C2**
Luchuan *China* **50C5**
Lucia *USA* **18B2**
Luckenwalde *E Germ* **40C2**
Luckhoff *S Africa* **72C2**
Lucknow *India* **59B2**
Lucusse *Angola* **71C5**
Lüda *China* **50E2**
Lüdenscheid *W Germ* **34D1**
Lüderitz *Namibia* **72B2**
Ludhiana *India* **58D2**
Ludington *USA* **10B2**
Ludlow, California *USA* **17C4**
Ludlow *Eng* **33D5**
Ludlow, Vermont *USA* **12D1**

Ludogorie, Upland *Bulg* 39F2
Ludowici *USA* 13C2
Luduş *Rom* 39E1
Ludvika *Sweden* 30H6
Ludwigsburg *W Germ* 40B3
Ludwigshafen *W Germ* 40B3
Ludwigslust *E Germ* 40C2
Luebo *Zaïre* 70C4
Luema, R *Zaïre* 70C4
Luembe, R *Angola* 71C4
Luena *Angola* 71B5
Luene, R *Angola* 71C5
Lüeyang *China* 50B3
Lufeng *China* 50D5
Lufkin *USA* 7D3
Luga *USSR* 42D4
Luga, R *USSR* 42D4
Lugano *Switz* 38B1
Lugela *Mozam* 71D5
Lugenda, R *Mozam* 71D5
Lugo *Italy* 35D2
Lugo *Spain* 37A1
Lugoj *Rom* 39E1
Luhuo *China* 50A3
Lui R *Angola* 71B4
Luiana *Angola* 71C5
Luiana, R *Angola* 71C5
Luichow Peninsula = Leizhou Bandao
Luino *Italy* 35C2
Luionga, R *Zaïre* 70B3
Luipan Shan, Upland *China* 50B2
Luiro, R *Fin* 42D2
Luishia *Zaïre* 71C5
Luixi *China* 48C4
Luiza *Zaïre* 71C4
Luján *Arg* 26B2
Luján *Arg* 26D2
Lujiang *China* 50D3
Lukenie, R *Zaïre* 70B4
Lukeville *USA* 17D4
Luki *USSR* 46E4
Lukolela *Zaïre* 70B4
Łuków *Pol* 41E2
Lukuga, R *Zaïre* 70C4
Lukulu *Zambia* 71C5
Lule, R *Sweden* 42C2
Luleå *Sweden* 30J5
Lüleburgaz *Turk* 39F2
Lüliang Shan, Mts *China* 50C2
Luling *USA* 15C4
Llullaillaco, Mt *Chile* 24E8
Lulonga, R *Zaïre* 70C3
Luluabourg = Kananga
Lumbala *Angola* 71C5
Lumberton *USA* 7F3
Lumbis *Indon* 54E2
Lumbovka *USSR* 42G2
Lumding *India* 59D2
Lumeje *Angola* 71C5
Lumsden *NZ* 79A3
Lund *Sweden* 30G7
Lundar *Can* 9C1
Lundazi *Zambia* 71D5
Lundi, R *Zim* 71D6
Lundy, I *Eng* 33C6
Lüneburg *W Germ* 40C2
Luneville *France* 34D2
Lunga, R *Zambia* 71C5
Lunglei *India* 59D3
Lungue Bungo, R *Angola* 71B5
Luninec *USSR* 41F2
Luning *USA* 18C1
Luobei *China* 51C2
Luobomo *Congo* 70B4
Luocheng *China* 50B5
Luoding *China* 50C5
Luohe *China* 50C3
Luo He, R, Henan *China* 50C3
Luo He, R, Shaanxi *China* 50B2
Luoxiao Shan, Hills *China* 50C4
Luoyang *China* 50C3
Luozi *Zaïre* 70B4
Lupane *Zim* 71C5
Lupilichi *Mozam* 71D5
Lu Qu = Tao He
Luque *Par* 23E3
Lure *France* 34D3
Lurgan *N Ire* 33B4
Lurio, R *Mozam* 71D5
Luristan, Region *Iran* 61B2
Lusaka *Zambia* 71C5
Lusambo *Zaïre* 70C4
Lushnjë *Alb* 39D2
Lushoto *Tanz* 70D4
Lushui *China* 48C4
Lüshun *China* 50E2
Lusk *USA* 9B3
Luton *Eng* 33E6
Lutsk *USSR* 43D5
Luuq *Somalia* 70E3
Luverne *USA* 9C3
Luvua, R *Zaïre* 71C4
Luwegu, R *Tanz* 71D4
Luwingu *Zambia* 71D5
Luwuk *Indon* 55B3
Luxembourg, Grand Duchy *N W Europe* 34D2
Luxembourg *Lux* 36D2
Luxeuil-les-Bains *France* 34D3
Luxi *China* 50A5
Luxor *Egypt* 67C2
Luza *USSR* 42H3
Luza, R *USSR* 42H3
Luzern *Switz* 38B1
Luzerne *USA* 12D1
Luzhai *China* 50B5
Luzhi *China* 50B4
Luzhou *China* 50B4
Luziânia *Brazil* 27C2
Luzon, I *Phil* 55F7
Luzon Str *Phil* 55F6
L'vov *USSR* 41E3
Lybster *Scot* 32D2
Lycksele *Sweden* 30H6
Lydenburg *S Africa* 71C6
Lyell I *Can* 3B3
Lyell,Mt *USA* 6B3
Lykens *USA* 12B2
Lyman *USA* 16D2
Lyme B *Eng* 33D6
Lyme Regis *Eng* 33D6
Lynchburg *USA* 7F3
Lyndhurst *Aust* 78A2
Lynn *USA* 11E2
Lynn Canal, Sd *USA* 3A2
Lynn Haven *USA* 13B2
Lynn Lake *Can* 3H2
Lynx L *Can* 4H3
Lyon *France* 36C2
Lyon Canal, Sd *USA* 8L4
Lyons, Georgia *USA* 13C2
Lyons, New York *USA* 12B1
Lyons, R *Aust* 76A3
Lys, R *Italy* 35B2
Lys'va *USSR* 42K4
Lyttelton *NZ* 79B2
Lytton *Can* 3D3
Lytton *USA* 18A1
Lyubeshov *USSR* 41F2
Lyublino *USSR* 42F4

M

Ma, R *Viet* 53C1
Ma'agan *Jordan* 63C2
Ma'alot Tarshiha *Israel* 63C2
Ma'an *Jordan* 62C3
Ma'anshan *China* 50D3
Ma'arrat an Nu'mān *Syria* 63D1
Maas, R *Neth* 34C1
Maaseik *Belg* 34C1
Maasin *Phil* 55F8
Maastricht *Belg* 40B2
Mabalane *Mozam* 72E1
Mabaruma *Guyana* 25G2
Mablethorpe *Eng* 33F5
Mabote *Mozam* 71D6
Mabrita *USSR* 41E2
M'adel *USSR* 41F2
Macaé *Brazil* 27D3
McAlester *USA* 6D3
McAllen *USA* 6D4
Macaloge *Mozam* 71D5
Macao, Dependency *China* 50C5
Macapá *Brazil* 25H3
Macarani *Brazil* 27D2
Macas *Ecuador* 24C4
Macaú *Brazil* 25L5
Macaúbas *Brazil* 27D1
M'Bari, R *CAR* 70C3
McBrice *Can* 3D3
McCall *USA* 16C2
McCamey *USA* 14B3
McCammon *USA* 16D2
McCarthy *USA* 8K3
McCauley I *Can* 3B3
Macclesfield *Eng* 33D5
McClintock B *Can* 5K1
McClintock Chan *Can* 4H2
McClure *USA* 12B2
McClure,L *USA* 18B2
McClure Str *Can* 4G2
McComb *USA* 15D3
McConaughy,L *USA* 14B1
McConnellsburg *USA* 12B3
McCook *USA* 6C2
Macculloch,C *Can* 5L2
McCusker,Mt *Can* 3D2
McDame *Can* 4F4
McDermitt *USA* 16C2
Macdonald, R *Can* 3F3
Mcdonald Peak, Mt *USA* 16D1
Macdonnell Ranges, Mts *Aust* 76C3
Macedo de Cavaleiros *Port* 37A1
Maceió *Brazil* 25L5
Macenta *Guinea* 68B4
Macerata *Italy* 38C2
Macfarlane, R *Can* 3G2
Macfarlane,L *Aust* 78A2
McGehee *USA* 15D3
McGill *USA* 17D3
McGrath *USA* 4C3
McGuire,Mt *USA* 16D1
Machaco *Brazil* 27C3
Machaíla *Mozam* 71D6
Machakos *Kenya* 70D4
Machala *Ecuador* 24C4
Machaze *Mozam* 71D6
Mācherla *India* 60B1
Machgharab *Leb* 63C2
Machias *USA* 11F2
Machilipatnam *India* 60C1
Machiques *Ven* 24D1
Machu-Picchu, Hist Site *Peru* 24D6
Macia *Mozam* 71D6
Macias Nguema = Fernando Poo
McIntosh *USA* 9B2
MacIntyre, R *Aust* 78C1
Mack *USA* 14A2
Mackay *Aust* 76D3
Mackay *USA* 16D2
Mackay,L *Aust* 76B3
McKean, I *Phoenix Is* 77H1
McKeesport *USA* 11D2
Mackenzie *Can* 3D2
Mackenzie, R *Can* 4F3
Mackenzie, Region *Can* 4F3
Mackenzie B *Can* 4E3
Mackenzie King I *Can* 4G2
Mackenzie Mts *Can* 4E3
Mackinac,Str of *USA* 10C1
Mackinaw City *USA* 10C1
McKinley,Mt *USA* 8H3
McKinney *USA* 15C3
Mackinson Inlet, B *Can* 5L2
McKittrick *USA* 18C3
Macksville *Aust* 78D2
Mclaoughlin,Mt *USA* 16B2
McLaughlin *USA* 9B2
Maclean *Aust* 78D1
Maclear *S Africa* 72D3
McLennan *Can* 4G4
McLeod, R *Can* 3E3
McLeod B *Can* 4G3
McLeod,L *Aust* 76A3
McLeod Lake *Can* 3D2
Macmillan, R *Can* 4E3
McMillan,L *USA* 14B3
Macmillan P *Can* 8M3
McMinnville, Oregon *USA* 16B1
McMinnville, Tennessee *USA* 13B1
McMurdo, Base *Ant* 80F7
McNamara,Mt *Can* 3C2
McNary *USA* 17E4
McNaughton L *Can* 3E3
Macomb *USA* 10A2
Macomer *Sardegna* 38B2
Macomia *Mozam* 71D5
Mâcon *France* 36C2
Macon, Georgia *USA* 7E3
Macon, Missouri *USA* 15D2
Macondo *Angola* 71C5
Macoun L *Can* 3H2
McPherson *USA* 15C2
Macquarie, Is *Aust* 74J7
Macquarie, R *Aust* 78C2
Macquarie Harbour, B *Aust* 78E3
Macquarie,L *Aust* 78D2
McRae *USA* 13C2
MacRobertsn Land, Region *Ant* 80F11
M'saken *Tunisia* 69E1
M'Sila *Alg* 69C1
McTavish Arm, B *Can* 4G3
Macumba, R *Aust* 78A1
Macunaga *Italy* 35C2
McVicar Arm, B *Can* 4F3
M'yaróvár *Hung* 40D3
Mada, R *Nig* 69H4
Mādabā *Jordan* 63C3
Madadi, Well *Chad* 70C2
Madagascar, I *Indian O* 66J9
Madagascar Basin *Indian O* 74D6
Madama *Niger* 70B1
Madang *PNG* 76D1
Madaoua *Niger* 68C3
Madaripur *Bang* 59D3
Madau *USSR* 61C1
Madawaska, R *Can* 11D1
Madaya *Burma* 59E3
Madeira, I *Atlantic O* 68A1
Madeira, R *Brazil* 22D4
Madeira, R *Brazil* 24F5
Madelia *USA* 9D3
Madera *Mexico* 19B2
Madera *USA* 17B3
Madgaon *India* 60A1
Madhubani *India* 59C2
Madhya Pradesh, State *India* 59B3
Madicine Bow Mts *USA* 14A1
Madikeri *India* 60B2
Madimba *Zaïre* 70B4
Madingo Kayes *Congo* 70B4
Madingou *Congo* 70B4
Madison, Indiana *USA* 7E3
Madison, Minnesota *USA* 9C2
Madison, Nebraska *USA* 9C3
Madison, S Dakota *USA* 9C3
Madison, Wisconsin *USA* 7E2
Madison, R *USA* 16D1
Madisonville, Kentucky *USA* 10B3
Madisonville, Texas *USA* 15C3
Madiun *Indon* 54D4
Mado Gashi *Kenya* 70D3
Madonna Di Campiglio *Italy* 35D1
Madras *India* 60C2
Madras *USA* 16B2
Madre de Dios, I *Chile* 23A8
Madre de Dios, R *Bol* 24E6
Madrid *Spain* 37B1
Madridejos *Spain* 37B2
Madura, I *Indon* 54D4
Madurai *India* 60B3
Maebashi *Japan* 52C3
Mae Khlong, R *Thai* 53B3
Mae Nam Lunang, R *Thai* 53B4
Mae Nam Mun, R *Thai* 53C2
Mae Nam Ping, R *Thai* 53B2
Maengsan *N Korea* 52A3
Maevatanana *Madag* 71E5
Maewo, I *Vanuatu* 77F2
Mafeking *S Africa* 72D2
Mafeteng *Lesotho* 72D2
Maffra *Aust* 78C3
Mafia, I *Tanz* 71D4
Mafra *Brazil* 23G3
Mafraq *Jordan* 62C3
Magadan *USSR* 47Q4
Magargué *Colombia* 24D2
Magaria *Niger* 69H3
Magdagachi *USSR* 51B1
Magdalena *Arg* 26D3
Magdalena *Mexico* 6B3
Magdalena *USA* 14A3
Magdalena, R *Colombia* 21C4
Magdalena,Mt *Malay* 54E2
Magdalene *Mexico* 19A1
Magdalen Is *Can* 5M5
Magdeburg *E Germ* 40C2
Magdelena, R *Colombia* 24D2
Magé *Brazil* 25K8
Magelang *Indon* 54D4
Maggia, R *Switz* 35C1
Maghâgha *Egypt* 62B4
Magherafelt *N Ire* 32B4
Maglie *Italy* 39D2
Magnitogorsk *USSR* 42K5
Magnolia *USA* 15D3
Mago *USSR* 51E1
Magoé *Mozam* 71D5
Magog *Can* 11E1
Magosal *Mexico* 20C1
Magra, R *Italy* 35C2
Magrath *Can* 3F3
Magruder Mt *USA* 18D2
Magude *Mozam* 72E2
Maguse River *Can* 5J3
Magwe *Burma* 53B1
Mahābād *Iran* 43H8
Mahabharat Range, Mts *Nepal* 59C2
Mahād *India* 60A1
Mahadeo Hills *India* 58D4
Mahaffey *USA* 12A2
Mahajanga *Madag* 71E5
Mahalapye *Botswana* 72D1
Mahānadi, R *India* 59B3
Mahanoro *Madag* 71E5
Mahanoy City *USA* 12B2
Maharashtra, State *India* 60A1
Māhāsamund *India* 59B3
Maha Sarakham *Thai* 53C2
Mahavavy, R *Madag* 71E5
Mahbūbnagar *India* 60B1
Mahdia *Tunisia* 69E1
Mahe *India* 60B2
Mahekar *India* 58D4
Mahéli, I *Comoros* 71E5
Mahendragarh *India* 59B3
Mahenge *Tanz* 71D4
Mahesāna *India* 58C4
Mahia Pen *NZ* 79C1
Mahnomen *USA* 9C2
Mahoba *India* 58D3
Mahón *Spain* 37C2
Mahony L *Can* 8N2
Mahrés *Tunisia* 69E2
Mahuva *India* 58C4
Maicao *Colombia* 24D1
Maîche *France* 35B1
Maichew *Eth* 64C4
Maidstone *Eng* 33F6
Maiduguri *Nig* 70B2
Maigomaj, R *Sweden* 42B3
Maihar *India* 59B3
Maijdi *Bang* 59D3
Mail Kyun, I *Burma* 53B3
Maimana *Afghan* 58A1
Main, R *W Germ* 34E2
Main Chan *Can* 10C1
Mai-Ndombe, L *Zaïre* 70B4
Maine, State *USA* 7G2
Maine, Region *France* 34A3
Mainé-Soroa *Niger* 69J3
Mainland, I *Scot* 32D2
Mainpuri *India* 58D3
Maintenon *France* 34A2
Maintirano *Madag* 71E5
Mainz *W Germ* 40B2
Maio, I *Cape Verde* 68A4
Maipó, Mt *Arg/Chile* 23C4
Maipú *Arg* 26D3
Maiquetía *Ven* 24E1
Maira, R *Italy* 35B2
Mairābāri *India* 59D2
Maiskhal I *Bang* 59D3
Maitland, New South Wales *Aust* 76E4
Maitland, S Australia *Aust* 78A2
Maiz *W Germ* 36D1
Maizuru *Japan* 51D4
Majene *Indon* 76A1
Majes, R *Peru* 24D7
Maji *Eth* 70D3
Majia He, R *China* 50D2
Majunga = Mahajanga
Makale *Eth* 70D2
Makale *Indon* 55A3
Makalo *Indon* 54B3
Makalu, Mt *China/Nepal* 59C2
Makarikha *USSR* 42K2
Makarov *USSR* 51E2
Makarska *Yugos* 38D2
Makaryev *USSR* 42G4
Makassar = Ujung Pandang
Makassar Str *Indon* 54E3
Makat *USSR* 43J6
Makeni *Sierra Leone* 68A4
Makeyevka *USSR* 43F6
Makgadikgadi, Salt Pan *Botswana* 71C6
Makhachkala *USSR* 43H7
Makharadze *USSR* 62D1
Makian, I *Indon* 55C2
Makindu *Kenya* 70D4
Makkah = Mecca
Makkovik *Can* 5N4
Makó *Hung* 41E3
Makokou *Gabon* 70B3
Makorako,Mt *NZ* 79C1
Makoua *Congo* 70B3
Makrāna *India* 58C3
Makran Coast Range, Mts *Pak* 58A3
Maksimovka *USSR* 51D2
Maksotag *Iran* 61E3
Maktar *Tunisia* 69D1
Mākū *Iran* 43G8
Makumbi *Zaïre* 70C4
Makurazaki *Japan* 51C5
Makurdi *Nig* 69H4
Makushin V *USA* 8E5
Malabang *Phil* 55F9
Malabar Coast *India* 60B2
Malabo *Bioko* 66E7
Malabrigo *Arg* 26D1
Malacca,Str of *S E Asia* 53C5
Malad City *USA* 16D2
Málaga *Colombia* 24D2
Malaga *Spain* 37B2
Malaga *USA* 14B3
Malaimbandy *Madag* 71E6
Malaita, I *Solomon Is* 77F1
Malakal *Sudan* 70D3
Malakand *Pak* 58C2
Malamala *Indon* 55B3
Malang *Indon* 54D4
Malange *Angola* 71B4
Malanville *Benin* 69G3
Mal Anyuy, R *USSR* 47S3
Mälaren, L *Sweden* 30H7
Malargüe *Arg* 26B3
Malartic *Can* 11D1
Malaspina Gl *USA* 8K4
Malatya *Turk* 43F8
Malawi, Republic *Africa* 71D5
Malawi,L = Nyasa,L
Malaya Sidima *USSR* 51D2
Malaybalay *Phil* 55G9
Malāyer *Iran* 61B2
Malaysia, Federation *S E Asia* 49D6
Malazgirt *Turk* 62D2
Malbork *Pol* 41D2
Malbrán *Arg* 26C1
Malchin *E Germ* 40C2
Malden *USA* 15E2
Maldives Is *Indian O* 57F5
Maldives Ridge *Indian O* 74E4
Maldon *Eng* 34A1
Maldonado *Urug* 23F4
Male *Italy* 35D1
Malegaon *India* 58C4
Malé Karpaty, Upland *Czech* 40D3
Malekula, I *Vanuatu* 77F2
Malema *Mozam* 71D5
Malen'ga *USSR* 42F2
Malesherbes *France* 34B2
Mālestān *Afghan* 58B2
Maleuz *USSR* 42K5
Malgomaj, L *Sweden* 30H5
Malha, Well *Sudan* 70C2

Malheur L *USA* **16C2**
Mali, Republic *Africa* **68B3**
Mali Hka, R *Burma* **59E2**
Malili *Indon* **55B3**
Malin *USSR* **41F2**
Malinau *Indon* **54E2**
Malindi *Kenya* **70E4**
Malines = Mechelen
Malin Head, Pt *Irish Rep* **31B2**
Malkala Range, Mts *India* **59B3**
Malkāpur *India* **58D4**
Malkara *Turk* **39F2**
Malko Tŭrnovo *Bulg* **39F2**
Mallaig *Scot* **32C3**
Mallawi *Egypt* **67C2**
Málles Venosta *Italy* **35D1**
Mallorca, I *Spain* **37C2**
Malm *Nor* **30G6**
Malmberget *Sweden* **30J5**
Malmédy *W Germ* **34D1**
Malmesbury *Eng* **33D6**
Malmesbury *S Africa* **72B3**
Malmö *Sweden* **30G7**
Malmyzh *USSR* **42H4**
Malolos *Phil* **55F8**
Malone *USA* **11E2**
Maloti Mts *Lesotho* **72D2**
Måløy *Nor* **30F6**
Malozemel'skaya Tundra, Plain *USSR* **42J2**
Mal Paso *Mexico* **20B1**
Malpaso *Mexico* **20D2**
Malpelo, I *Colombia* **22B3**
Malpo, R *Chile* **26A2**
Mālpura *India* **58D3**
Malta, Idaho *USA* **16D2**
Malta, Montana *USA* **6C2**
Malta, Chan *Malta/Italy* **38C3**
Malta, I *Medit S* **38C3**
Maltahöhe *Namibia* **72B1**
Malton *Eng* **33E4**
Malung *Sweden* **30G6**
Mālvan *India* **60A1**
Malvern *USA* **15D3**
Malvérnia *Mozam* **72E1**
Malwa Plat *India* **58D4**
Malyy Kavkaz, Mts *USSR* **46F5**
Malyy Uzen', R *USSR* **H6**
Mama *USSR* **47N4**
Mamadysh *USSR* **42J4**
Mambasa *Zaïre* **70C3**
Mamberamo, R *Aust* **76C1**
Mamberamo, R *Indon* **49G7**
Mambéré, R *CAR* **70B3**
Mamciju *Indon* **55A3**
Mamers *France* **34A2**
Mamfé *Cam* **70A3**
Mammoth *USA* **17D4**
Mammoth Cave Nat Pk *USA* **10B3**
Mammoth Pool Res *USA* **18C2**
Mamoré, R *Bol* **24E6**
Mamou *Guinea* **68A3**
Mampikony *Madag* **71E5**
Mampong *Ghana* **69F4**
Mamshit, Hist Site *Israel* **63C3**
Ma'mūl *Oman* **65G3**
Mamuno *Botswana* **72C1**
Man *Ivory Coast* **68B4**
Mana *Hawaiian Is* **18E5**
Manabo *Madag* **71E6**
Manacapuru *Brazil* **24F4**
Manacor *Spain* **37C2**
Manado *Indon* **55B2**
Managua *Nic* **24A1**
Manakara *Madag* **71E6**
Manam, I *PNG* **76D1**
Mananara *Madag* **71E5**
Mananjary *Madag* **71E6**
Manapouri *NZ* **79A3**
Manapouri,L *NZ* **79A3**
Manas *Bhutan* **59D2**
Manas *China* **57G1**
Manas Hu, L *China* **46K5**
Manaslu, Mt *Nepal* **59B2**
Manasquan *USA* **12C2**
Manaus *Brazil* **25G4**
Manavgat *Turk* **43E8**
Manbij *Syria* **62C2**
Manbilla Plat *Nig* **69J4**
Man,Calf of, I *Eng* **33C4**
Mancheral *India* **60B1**
Manchester, Connecticut *USA* **11E2**
Manchester *Eng* **33D5**
Manchester, Kentucky *USA* **10C3**
Manchester, New Hampshire *USA* **7F2**
Manchester, Pennsylvania *USA* **12B2**
Manchester, Tennessee *USA* **13B1**
Manchester, Vermont *USA* **12D1**
Manchuria, Hist Region *China* **51B2**
Mand, R *Iran* **61C3**
Manda *Tanz* **71D5**
Mandaguari *Brazil* **27B3**
Mandal *Nor* **30F7**
Mandalay *Burma* **53B1**
Mandalgovĭ *Mongolia* **48D2**
Mandal Ovoo *Mongolia* **50A1**
Mandalya Körfezi, B *Turk* **39F3**
Mandan *USA* **6C2**
Mandelona *USA* **10B2**
Mandera *Eth* **70E3**
Mandeville *Jamaica* **21B3**
Mandidzudzure *Zim* **71D5**
Mandimba *Mozam* **71D5**
Mandioli, I *Indon* **55C3**
Mandla *India* **59B3**
Mandritsara *Madag* **71E5**
Mandsaur *India* **58D4**
Manduria *Italy* **39D2**
Māndvi *India* **58B4**
Mandya *India* **60B2**
Manevichi *USSR* **41F2**
Manfalût *Egypt* **64B1**
Manfield *Eng* **33E5**
Manfredonia *Italy* **38D2**
Manga *Brazil* **27D1**
Manga *U Volta* **69F3**
Manga, Desert Region *Niger* **70B2**
Mangakino *NZ* **79C1**
Mangalia *Rom* **39F2**
Mangalmé *Chad* **70C2**
Mangalore *India* **60A2**
Manggar *Indon* **54C3**
Mangin Range, Mts *Burma* **59E3**
Mangnia *China* **48C3**
Mangoche *Malawi* **71D5**
Mangoky, R *Madag* **71E6**
Mangole, I *Indon* **55C3**
Māngral *India* **58B4**
Manguerinha *Brazil* **27B4**
Mangui *China* **47O4**
Mangum *USA* **14C3**
Manhattan *USA* **6D3**
Manhica *Mozam* **72E2**
Manhuacu *Brazil* **25K8**
Mania, R *Madag* **71E5**
Maniago *Italy* **35E1**
Manica *Mozam* **71D5**
Manicouagan, R *Can* **5M5**
Manicouagan Res *Can* **5M4**
Manifah *S Arabia* **65E1**
Manila *Phil* **55F8**
Manila *USA* **16E2**
Manilla *Aust* **78D2**
Maninian *Ivory Coast* **68B3**
Manipa, I *Indon* **55C3**
Manipur, State *India* **59D3**
Manipur, R *Burma* **59D3**
Manisa *Turk* **43D8**
Man,Isle of *Irish Sea* **31C3**
Manistee *USA* **10B2**
Manistee, R *USA* **10B2**
Manistique *USA* **10B1**
Manitoba, Province *Can* **4J4**
Manitoba,L *Can* **4J4**
Manito L *Can* **3G3**
Manitou *Can* **9C2**
Manitou Falls *Can* **9D1**
Manitou Is *USA* **10B1**
Manitoulin, I *Can* **5K5**
Manitou Springs *USA* **14B2**
Manitowik L *Can* **10C1**
Manitowoc *USA* **10B2**
Maniwaki *Can* **11D1**
Manizales *Colombia* **24C2**
Manja *Madag* **71E6**
Manjimup *Aust* **76A4**
Mānjra, R *India* **60B1**
Mankato *USA* **7D2**
Mankono *Ivory Coast* **68B4**
Manley Hot Springs *USA* **8H3**
Manly *NZ* **79B1**
Manmād *India* **58C4**
Manna *Indon* **54B3**
Mannahill *Aust* **78A2**
Mannar *Sri Lanka* **60B3**
Mannār,G of *India* **60B3**
Mannārgudi *India* **60B2**
Mannheim *W Germ* **40B3**
Manning *Can* **3E2**
Manning *USA* **13C2**
Mannum *Aust* **78A2**
Mano *Sierra Leone* **68A4**
Manokwari *Indon* **76C1**
Manono *Zaïre* **71C4**
Manoron *Burma* **53B3**
Manosque *France* **35A3**
Mano-wan, B *Japan* **52C3**
Manp'o *N Korea* **51B3**
Mānsa *India* **58D2**
Mansa *Zambia* **71C5**
Mansel I *Can* **5K3**
Mansfield, Arkansas *USA* **15D2**
Mansfield *Aust* **78C3**
Mansfield, Louisiana *USA* **15D3**
Mansfield, Massachusetts *USA* **12E1**
Mansfield, Ohio *USA* **7E2**
Mansfield, Pennsylvania *USA* **11D2**
Manso, R *Brazil* **27B2**
Manston *USA* **10A2**
Mansyu Deep *Pacific O* **49G5**
Mantalingajan,Mt *Phil* **55E9**
Mantap-san, Mt *N Korea* **52A2**
Mantaro, R *Peru* **24C6**
Manteca *USA* **18B2**
Manteo *USA* **13D1**
Mantes *France* **36C2**
Manti *USA* **17D3**
Mantova *Italy* **38C1**
Mantta *Fin* **30J6**
Manturovo *USSR* **42G4**
Manuel *Mexico* **20C1**
Manuel Benavides *Mexico* **14B4**
Manuel Ribas *Brazil* **27B3**
Manui, I *Indon* **55B3**
Manukan *Phil* **55F9**
Manukau *NZ* **77G4**
Manus, I *Pacific O* **49H7**
Manzanares *Spain* **37B2**
Manzanillo *Cuba* **19E2**
Manzanillo *Mexico* **19B3**
Manzhouli *USSR* **47N5**
Manzil *Jordan* **63D3**
Manzini *Swaziland* **71D6**
Mao *Chad* **70B2**
Maomao Shan, Mt *China* **50A2**
Maoming *China* **50C5**
Mapai *Mozam* **71D6**
Mapam Yumco, L *China* **59B1**
Mapia, Is *Pacific O* **49G6**
Maple Creek *Can* **4H5**
Mapulanguene *Mozam* **72E1**
Maputo *Mozam* **72E2**
Maputo, R *Mozam* **72E2**
Ma Qu = Huange He
Maqu *China* **50A3**
Maquan He, R *China* **59C2**
Maquela do Zombo *Angola* **70B4**
Maquinchao *Arg* **23C6**
Marabá *Brazil* **25J5**
Maracaibo *Ven* **24D1**
Maracaju *Brazil* **27A3**
Máracás *Brazil* **27D1**
Maracay *Ven* **24E1**
Marādah *Libya* **67A2**
Maradi *Niger* **68C3**
Marāgheh *Iran* **43H8**
Marakech *Mor* **28E5**
Maralal *Kenya* **70D3**
Maramasike, I *Solomon Is* **77F1**
Maramba *Zambia* **71C5**
Maran *Malay* **54G7**
Marana *USA* **17D4**
Marand *Iran* **43H8**
Maranhão, R *Brazil* **27C1**
Maranhõa, State *Brazil* **25J4**
Maranoa, R *Aust* **78C1**
Marañón, R *Peru* **24C4**
Maras *Turk* **43F8**
Marathon *Can* **5K5**
Marathon, Florida *USA* **13E4**
Marathon, New York *USA* **12B1**
Marathon, Texas *USA* **14B3**
Maratua, I *Indon* **54E2**
Maraú *Brazil* **27E1**
Maravatio *Mexico* **20B2**
Marawi *Phil* **55F9**
Marayes *Arg* **26B2**
Mar'ayt *S Yemen* **65F3**
Marbella *Spain* **37B2**
Marble Bar *Aust* **76A3**
Marble Canyon *USA* **17D3**
Marble Canyon *USA* **17D3**
Marble Hall *S Africa* **72D2**
Marblehead *USA* **12E1**
Marburg *W Germ* **40B2**
Marcelino Ramos *Brazil* **26E1**
Marche *Belg* **40B2**
Marche, Region *Italy* **35E3**
Marchean *Spain* **37A2**
Marche-en-Famenne *Belg* **34C1**
Marco *USA* **13E4**
Marcos Juárez *Arg* **26C2**
Marcus Baker,Mt *USA* **8J3**
Marcy,Mt *USA* **11E2**
Mar Dağlari, Mt *Turk* **43G8**
Mardan *Pak* **58C2**
Mar del Plata *Arg* **23E5**
Mardin *Turk* **43G8**
Maré, I *Nouvelle Calédonie* **77F3**
Mareb, R *Eth* **70D2**
Mareeba *Aust* **49H8**
Marfa *USA* **14B3**
Margaretville *USA* **12C1**
Margarita *Arg* **26C1**
Margate *Eng* **33F6**
Marghita *Rom* **39E1**
Maria I *Aust* **78E3**
Mariana, Is *Pacific O* **74J3**
Mariana Lake *Can* **3F2**
Marianas Trench *Pacific O* **74J4**
Mariāni *India* **59D2**
Marianna, Arkansas *USA* **15D3**
Marianna, Florida *USA* **13B2**
Maria Van Diemen,C *NZ* **7G4**
Mariazell *Austria* **40D3**
Ma'rib *Yemen* **65E3**
Maribor *Yugos* **38D1**
Marico, R *Botswana/S Africa* **72D1**
Maricopa *USA* **18C3**
Maricourt *Can* **5L3**
Maridi *Sudan* **70C3**
Marie Byrd Land, Region *Ant* **80F5**
Marie Galante, I *Caribbean* **21E3**
Mariehamn *Fin* **30H6**
Mariembourg *Belg* **34C1**
Marienburg *Suriname* **25H2**
Mariental *Namibia* **72B1**
Mariestad *Sweden* **30G7**
Marietta, Georgia *USA* **13C2**
Marietta, Ohio *USA* **10C3**
Marietta, Oklahoma *USA* **15C3**
Mariga, R *Nig* **69H3**
Marigot *Dominica* **21Q2**
Marilia *Brazil* **23G2**
Marimba *Angola* **71B4**
Marinduque, I *Phil* **55F8**
Marinette *USA* **7E2**
Maringá *Brazil* **23F2**
Maringa, R *Zaïre* **70C3**
Marion, Arkansas *USA* **15D2**
Marion, Illinois *USA* **10B3**
Marion, Indiana *USA* **7E2**
Marion, Ohio *USA* **7E2**
Marion, S Carolina *USA* **13D2**
Marion,L *USA* **7E3**
Marion Reef *Aust* **77E2**
Mariposa *USA* **17C3**
Mariposa, R *USA* **18B2**
Mariposa Res *USA* **18B2**
Marisa *Indon* **55B2**
Marista, R *Bulg* **43D7**
Mariyskaya ASSR, Republic *USSR* **42H4**
Marjayoun *Leb* **63C2**
Marjina Gorki *USSR* **41F2**
Marka *Jordan* **63C3**
Marka *Somalia* **70E3**
Markaryd *Sweden* **40C1**
Market Drayton *Eng* **33D5**
Market Harborough *Eng* **33E5**
Markham,Mt *Ant* **80E**
Markleeville *USA* **18C1**
Markovo *USSR* **47S3**
Marlboro, Massachusetts *USA* **12E1**
Marlboro, New Hampshire *USA* **12D1**
Marlborough *Aust* **76D3**
Marle *France* **34B2**
Marlin *USA* **15C3**
Marlow *USA* **12D1**
Marmande *France* **36C3**
Marmara Adi, I *Turk* **39F2**
Marmara,S of *Turk* **62A1**
Marmaris *Turk* **39F3**
Marmarth *USA* **9B2**
Marmet *USA* **10C3**
Marmion, L *Can* **9D2**
Marmolada, Mt *Italy* **38C1**
Marmot B *USA* **8H4**
Mar Muerto, Lg *Mexico* **20D2**
Marnay *France* **35A1**
Marne, Department *France* **34C2**
Marne, R *France* **34B2**
Maro *Chad* **70B3**
Maroantsetra *Madag* **71E5**
Marondera *Zim* **71D5**
Maroni, R *French Guiana* **25H3**
Maroochydore *Aust* **78D1**
Maros *Indon* **55A3**
Maroua *Cam* **70B2**
Marovoay *Madag* **71E5**
Marquesas Keys, Is *USA* **7E4**
Marquette *USA* **7E2**
Marquise *France* **34A1**
Marra, R *Aust* **78C2**
Marracuene *Mozam* **72E2**
Marrakech *Mor* **68B1**
Marree *Aust* **76C3**
Marrero *USA* **15D4**
Marromeu *Mozam* **71D5**
Marrupa *Mozam* **71D5**
Marsa Alam *Egypt* **64B1**
Marsabit *Kenya* **70D3**
Marsala *Italy* **38C3**
Marsberg *W Germ* **34E1**
Marseille *France* **36D3**
Marshall, Alaska *USA* **8F3**
Marshall, Illinois *USA* **10B3**
Marshall, Michigan *USA* **10C2**
Marshall, Minnesota *USA* **9C3**
Marshall, Missouri *USA* **15D2**
Marshall, Texas *USA* **7D3**
Marshall, Virginia *USA* **12B3**
Marshall Is *Pacific O* **75K4**
Marshalltown *USA* **9D3**
Marshfield, Missouri *USA* **15D2**
Marshfield, Wisconsin *USA* **10A2**
Marsh Harbour *Bahamas* **21B1**
Marsh I *USA* **15D4**
Marsh L *Can* **8M3**
Marta *Ecuador* **24B4**
Martaban,G of *Burma* **53B2**
Martapura *Indon* **54B3**
Martapura *Indon* **54D3**
Martha's Vineyard, I *USA* **11E2**
Martigny *Switz* **36D2**
Martin *Czech* **41D3**
Martin, S Dakota *USA* **9B3**
Martin, Tennessee *USA* **13B1**
Martinborough *NZ* **79C2**
Martín de Loyola *Arg* **26B3**
Martínez de la Torre *Mexico* **20C1**
Martinique, I *Caribbean* **21E4**
Martin,L *USA* **13B2**
Martin Pt *USA* **8K1**
Martinsburg *USA* **11D3**
Martins Ferry *USA* **10C2**
Martinsville *USA* **11D3**
Martin Vaz, I *Atlantic O* **73G5**
Martiques *France* **36D3**
Marton *NZ* **79C2**
Martos *Spain* **37B2**
Marudi *Malay* **54D2**
Maruf *Afghan* **58B2**
Marugame *Japan* **52B4**
Marvine,Mt, Mt *USA* **17D3**
Mārwār *India* **58C3**
Mary *USSR* **46H6**
Maryborough, Queensland *Aust* **77E3**
Maryborough, Victoria *Aust* **78B3**
Mary Henry,Mt *Can* **4F4**
Maryland, State *USA* **7F3**
Maryport *Eng* **32D4**
Marysville, California *USA* **17B3**
Marysville, Kansas *USA* **15C2**
Marysville, Washington *USA* **16B1**
Maryville, Iowa *USA* **7D2**
Maryville, Missouri *USA* **15D1**
Maryville, Tennessee *USA* **13C1**
Marzuq *Libya* **67A2**
Masabb Dumyât, C *Egypt* **63A3**
Masada = Mezada
Mas'adah *Syria* **63C2**
Masai Steppe, Upland *Tanz* **70D4**
Masaka *Uganda* **70D4**
Masally *USSR* **62E2**
Masamba *Indon* **55B3**
Masan *S Korea* **51B4**
Masasi *Tanz* **71D5**
Masaya *Nic* **19D3**
Masbate *Phil* **55F8**
Masbate, I *Phil* **55F8**
Mascara *Alg* **69C1**
Mascarene Ridge *Indian O* **74D5**
Mascota *Mexico* **20B1**
Mascote *Brazil* **27E2**
Masela, I *Indon* **55C4**
Maseru *Lesotho* **72D2**
Mashad *Iran* **44D4**
Mashaki *Afghan* **58B2**
Mashhad *Iran* **61D1**
Mashkel, R *Pak* **61E3**
Masi-Manimba *Zaïre* **70B4**
Masindi *Uganda* **70D3**
Masisi *Zaïre* **70C4**
Masjed Soleyman *Iran* **61B2**
Masoala, C *Madag* **71F5**
Mason, Nevada *USA* **18C1**
Mason, Texas *USA* **14C3**
Mason City *USA* **7D2**
Masqat *Oman* **65G2**
Mass, R *Neth* **40B2**
Massa *Italy* **38C2**
Massachusetts, State *USA* **7F2**
Massachusetts B *USA* **11E2**
Massachusetts Bay *USA* **11E2**
Massakori *Chad* **70B2**
Massa Marittima *Italy* **35D3**
Massangena *Mozam* **71D6**
Massawa *Eth* **70D2**
Massawa Chan *Eth* **64C3**
Massena *USA* **11E2**
Massénya *Chad* **70B2**
Masset *Can* **3B3**
Massey *Can* **10C1**
Massif Central, Mts *France* **36C2**
Massif de l'Ouarsenis, Mts *Alg* **69C1**
Massif de l'Adamaoua, Mts *Cam* **70B3**
Massif de la Hotte, Mts *Haiti* **21C3**
Massif de l'Isalo, Upland *Madag* **71E6**

Massif des Bongo, Upland *CAR* 70C3
Massif du Pelvoux, Mts *France* 36D2
Massif du Tsaratanana, Mt *Madag* 71E5
Massillon *USA* 10C2
Massina, Region *Mali* 68B3
Massinga *Mozam* 71D6
Massingir *Mozam* 72E1
Masteksay *USSR* 43J6
Masterton *NZ* 77G5
Masuda *Japan* 51C5
Maşyāf *Syria* 62C2
Matachewan *Can* 10C1
Matachie *Mexico* 14A4
Matadi *Zaïre* 70B4
Matagalpa *Nic* 24A1
Matagami *Can* 5L4
Matagorda B *USA* 6D4
Matagorda I *USA* 15F4
Matakana I *NZ* 79C1
Matala *Angola* 71B5
Matale *Sri Lanka* 60C3
Matam *Sen* 68A3
Matameye *Niger* 68C3
Matamoros *Mexico* 19C2
Ma'tan as Sarra, Well *Libya* 67B2
Matane *Can* 5M5
Mataró *Spain* 37C1
Matanzas *Cuba* 19D2
Matapédia, R *Can* 11F1
Mataquito, R *Chile* 26A2
Matara *Sri Lanka* 60C3
Mataram *Indon* 76A1
Matarani *Peru* 24D7
Mataripe *Brazil* 27E1
Matatiele *S Africa* 72D3
Mataura *NZ* 79A3
Matehuala *Mexico* 19B2
Matelica *Italy* 35E3
Matelot *Trinidad* 21L1
Matera *Italy* 38D2
Mátészalka *Hung* 41E3
Mateur *Tunisia* 69D1
Mather *USA* 18C2
Matheson *Can* 10C1
Mathis *USA* 15F4
Mathura *India* 58D3
Mati *Phil* 55G9
Matías Romero *Mexico* 20C2
Matisiri, I *Indon* 54E3
Matlock *Eng* 33E5
Matmata *Tunisia* 69D2
Mato Grosso *Brazil* 25G6
Mato Grosso, State *Brazil* 25G6
Mato Grosso do Sul, State *Brazil* 25G7
Matola *Mozam* 72E2
Matrah *Oman* 65G2
Matrei im Osttirol *Austria* 35E1
Matrûh *Egypt* 62A3
Matruh *Egypt* 67B1
Matsue *Japan* 51C4
Matsumae *Japan* 51E3
Matsumoto *Japan* 51D4
Matsusaka *Japan* 51D5
Matsuyama *Japan* 51C5
Mattagami, R *Can* 5K5
Mattawa *Can* 11D1
Matterhorn, Mt *Switz/ Italy* 38B1
Matterhorn, Mt *USA* 16C2
Matthew Town *Bahamas* 21C2
Mattituck *USA* 12D2
Mattoon *USA* 10B3
Matun *Afghan* 58B2
Matura B *Trinidad* 21L1
Maturin *Ven* 24F2
Mau *India* 59B2
Maúa *Mozam* 71D5
Maubeuge *France* 36C1
Maude *Aust* 78B2
Maud Seamount *Atlantic O* 73J8
Maui, I *Hawaiian Is* 18E5
Maule, R *Chile* 26A3
Maumee *USA* 10C2
Maumee, R *USA* 10C2
Maumere *Indon* 55B4
Maun *Botswana* 71C5
Mauna Kea, Mt *Hawaiian Is* 18E5
Mauna Loa, Mt *Hawaiian Is* 18E5
Maunoir,L *Can* 4F3
Maures, Mts *France* 35B3
Mauriac *France* 36C2
Mauritania, Republic *Africa* 68A2
Mauritius, I *Indian O* 66K10
Mauterndorf *Austria* 35E1
Mavinga *Angola* 71C5
Mavue *Mozam* 72E1
Mawlaik *Burma* 59D3
Mawson, Base *Ant* 80G10
Max *USA* 9B2
Maxaila *Mozam* 72E1
Maxcaltzin *Mexico* 20C1
Maya, I *Indon* 54C3
Maya, R *USSR* 47P4
Mayādīn *Syria* 62D2
Mayaguana, I *Bahamas* 7F4
Mayagüez *Puerto Rico* 21D3
Mayahi *Niger* 68C3
Mayama *Congo* 70B4
Mayamey *Iran* 61D1
Mayanobab *Indon* 55D4
Maybole *Scot* 32C4
May,C *USA* 7F3
Maydena *Aust* 78E3
Mayen *W Germ* 34D1
Mayenne *France* 36B2
Mayer *USA* 17D4
Mayerthorpe *Can* 3E3
Mayfa'ah *S Yemen* 65E4
Mayfield *USA* 10B3
Mayhill *USA* 14A3
Maykop *USSR* 43F7
Maymaneh *Afghan* 46H6
Maymyo *Burma* 53B1
Mayo *Can* 4E3
Mayo *USA* 12B3
Mayo Deo, R *Cam* 69J4
Mayon, Mt *Phil* 55F8
Mayor, Mt *Spain* 37C2
Mayor Buratovich *Arg* 26C3
Mayor I *NZ* 79C1
Mayor P Lagerenza *Par* 23D1
Mayotte, I *Indian O* 71E5
May Pen *Jamaica* 21H2
May Point,C *USA* 12C3
Mayrhofen *Austria* 35D1
Mayskiy *USSR* 51B1
Mays Landing *USA* 12C3
Mayson L *Can* 3G2
Maysville *USA* 10C3
Mayumba *Gabon* 70B4
Mayville *USA* 9C2
Maywood *USA* 14B1
Mazabuka *Zambia* 71C5
Mazaffarnagar *India* 58D3
Mazapil *Mexico* 20B1
Mazar *China* 58D1
Mazār *Jordan* 63C3
Mazara del Vallo *Italy* 38C3
Mazar-i-Sharif *Afghan* 58B1
Mazatlán *Mexico* 19B2
Mazeikiai *USSR* 42C4
Mazra *Jordan* 63C3
Mbabane *Swaziland* 71D6
Mbabo,Mt *Cam* 69J4
Mbaïki *CAR* 70B3
Mbala *Zambia* 71D4
Mbalabala *Zim* 71C6
Mbale *Uganda* 70D3
Mbalmayo *Cam* 70B3
Mbam, R *Cam* 70B3
Mbamba Bay *Tanz* 71D5
Mbandaka *Zaïre* 70B3
Mbanza Congo *Angola* 70B4
Mbanza-Ngungu *Zaïre* 70B4
Mbarara *Uganda* 70D4
Mbé *Cam* 69J4
Mbengwi *Cam* 69J4
Mbènza *Congo* 70B3
Mbére, R *Cam* 70B3
Mbeya *Tanz* 71D4
Mbinda *Congo* 70B4
Mbouda *Cam* 69J4
Mbout *Maur* 68A3
Mbuji-Mayi *Zaïre* 70C4
Mbuli, R *Nig* 69J3
Mbulu *Tanz* 70D4
Mburucuyá *Arg* 26D1
Mcherrah, Region *Alg* 68B2
Mchinji *Malawi* 71D5
Mdrak *Viet* 53D3
Meade *USA* 14B2
Meade, R *USA* 8G1
Mead,L *USA* 6B3
Meadow Lake *Can* 4H4
Meadville *USA* 10C2
Me-akan dake, Mt *Japan* 52D2
Mealy Mts *Can* 5N4
Meandarra *Aust* 78C1
Meander River *Can* 4G4
Meath *Irish Rep* 33B5
Meaux *France* 36C2
Mecca *S Arabia* 64C2
Mecca *USA* 17C4
Mechanicville *USA* 12D1
Mechelen *Belg* 40A2
Mecheria *Alg* 69B2
Mecklenburger Bucht, B *E Germ* 40C2
Meconta *Mozam* 71D5
Mecuburi *Mozam* 71D5
Mecufi *Mozam* 71E5
Mecula *Mozam* 71D5
Medan *Indon* 54A2
Medanos *Arg* 26C3
Médanos *Arg* 26D2
Médéa *Alg* 69C1
Medecine Bow Peak, Mt *USA* 14A1
Medecine Hat *Can* 3F3
Medellín *Colombia* 24C2
Medenine *Tunisia* 69E2
Medford *USA* 6A2
Medgidia *Rom* 39F2
Media Agua *Arg* 26B2
Mediaş *Rom* 39E1
Medical Lake *USA* 16C1
Medicine Bow *USA* 9A3
Medicine Bow Peak, Mt *USA* 9A3
Medicine Hat *Can* 4G5
Medicine Lodge *USA* 14C2
Medina *Brazil* 27D2
Medina, N Dakota *USA* 9C2
Medina, New York *USA* 12A1
Medina *S Arabia* 64C2
Medinaceli *Spain* 37B1
Medina del Campo *Spain* 37A1
Medina de Rio Seco *Spain* 37A1
Medina L *USA* 14C4
Medinipur *India* 59C3
Mediterranean S *Europe* 66E4
Medley *Can* 3G3
Mednogorsk *USSR* 43K5
Mêdog *China* 59E2
Medouneu *Gabon* 70B3
Medvedista, R *USSR* 43G5
Medvezh'i Ova, I *USSR* 47S2
Medvezh'yegorsk *USSR* 46E3
Meekatharra *Aust* 76A3
Meeker *USA* 14A1
Meerut *India* 58D3
Meeteetse *USA* 16E2
Mega *Eth* 70D3
Megalópolis *Greece* 39E3
Mégara *Greece* 39E3
Meghālaya, State *India* 59D2
Meghna, R *Bang* 59D3
Megido, Hist Site *Israel* 63C2
Mehaïguene, R *Alg* 69C2
Mehoryuk *USA* 8E3
Mehran, R *Iran* 61C3
Mehriz *Iran* 61C2
Meia Ponte, R *Brazil* 27C2
Meiganga *Cam* 70B3
Meiktila *Burma* 53B1
Meiringen *Switz* 35C1
Meishan *China* 50A4
Meissen *E Germ* 40C2
Mei Xian *China* 50D5
Meizhou *China* 50D5
Mejillones *Chile* 24D8
Mekambo *Gabon* 70B3
Meknès *Mor* 69A2
Mekong = Lancang
Mekong, R *Camb* 53D3
Mekrou, R *Benin* 69G3
Melaka *Malay* 53C5
Melanesia, Region *Pacific O* 74J5
Melawi, R *Indon* 54D3
Melbourne *Aust* 76D4
Melbourne *USA* 7E4
Melchor Múzquiz *Mexico* 6C4
Melfi *Chad* 70B2
Melfort *Can* 4H4
Melilla *N W Africa* 69B1
Melimoyu, Mt *Chile* 23B6
Melincué *Arg* 26C2
Melipilla *Chile* 26A2
Melita *Can* 9B2
Melitopol' *USSR* 43F6
Meliville Bugt, B *Greenland* 5M2
Mellègue, R *Tunisia* 69D1
Melli, R *Eth* 64D4
Melmoth *S Africa* 72E2
Melo *Arg* 26C2
Melo *Urug* 23F4
Melo, R *Brazil* 27A3
Melones Res *USA* 18B2
Melozitna, R *USA* 8H2
Melrose *USA* 9D2
Mels *Switz* 35C1
Melsungen *W Germ* 34E1
Melta,Mt *Malay* 54E1
Melton Mowbry *Eng* 33E5
Melun *France* 36C2
Melville *Can* 4H4
Melville,C *Dominica* 21Q2
Melville Hills, Mts *Can* 4F3
Melville I *Aust* 76C2
Melville I *Can* 4G2
Melville,L *Can* 5N4
Melville Pen *Can* 5K3
Memba *Mozam* 71E5
Memboro *Indon* 76A1
Memmingen *W Germ* 40C3
Mempawan *Indon* 54C2
Memphis, Tennessee *USA* 7E3
Memphis, Texas *USA* 14B3
Mena *USA* 15D3
Mena *USSR* 41G2
Menai Str *Wales* 33C5
Ménaka *Mali* 68C3
Menasha *USA* 10B2
Mencué *Arg* 26B4
Mendawai, R *Indon* 54D3
Mende *France* 36C3
Mendebo, Mts *Eth* 70D3
Mendenhall,C *USA* 8E4
Mendi *PNG* 76D1
Mendip Hills, Upland *Eng* 33D6
Mendocino,C *USA* 16B2
Mendocino Seascarp *Pacific O* 75M3
Mendota, California *USA* 18B2
Mendota, Illinois *USA* 10B2
Mendoza *Arg* 23C4
Mendoza, State *Arg* 23C5
Menemen *Turk* 39F3
Menen *Belg* 34B1
Mengcheng *China* 50D3
Menggala *Indon* 54C3
Menghai *China* 53B1
Mengla *China* 50A5
Menglian *China* 53B1
Mengzi *China* 50A5
Menindee *Aust* 76D4
Menindee L *Aust* 78B2
Meningie *Aust* 78A3
Menominee *USA* 10B1
Menomonee Falls *USA* 10B2
Menomonie *USA* 10A2
Menongue *Angola* 71B5
Menorca, I *Spain* 37C1
Mentasta Mts *USA* 8K3
Mentmore *USA* 14A2
Mentok *Indon* 54C3
Menton *France* 35B3
Mentor *USA* 10C2
Ménu *France* 34B2
Menyuan *China* 50A2
Menzelinsk *USSR* 42J4
Meppen *W Germ* 40B2
Mer *France* 34A3
Merah *Indon* 54E2
Meramec, R *USA* 15D2
Merano *Italy* 38C1
Merauke *Indon* 76D1
Merced *USA* 6A3
Merced, R *USA* 18B2
Mercedario, Mt *Chile* 23B4
Mercedes *Arg* 23C4
Mercedes, Buenos Aires *Arg* 23E4
Mercedes, Corrientes *Arg* 23E3
Mercedes *Urug* 23E4
Mercury B *NZ* 79C1
Mercury Is *NZ* 79C1
Mercy B *Can* 4F2
Mercy,C *Can* 5M3
Meredith,L *USA* 14B2
Meregh *Somalia* 70E3
Mergui *Burma* 53B3
Mergui Arch *Burma* 53B3
Mérida *Mexico* 19D2
Mérida *Spain* 37A2
Mérida *Ven* 24D2
Meridian *USA* 7E3
Merimbula *Aust* 78C3
Meringur *Aust* 78B2
Merkel *USA* 14B3
Merowe *Sudan* 70D2
Merredin *Aust* 76A4
Merrick, Mt *Scot* 32C4
Merrill *USA* 10B1
Merrillville *USA* 10B2
Merrimack, R *USA* 12E1
Merriman *USA* 9B3
Merritt *Can* 3D3
Merritt Island *USA* 13C3
Merriwa *Aust* 78D2
Mersa Fatma *Eth* 64D4
Mers el Kebir *Alg* 37B2
Mersey, R *Eng* 33D5
Merseyside, Metropolitan County *Eng* 33D5
Mersin *Turk* 43E8
Mersing *Malay* 53C5
Merta *India* 58C3
Merthyr Tydfil *Wales* 33D6
Mertola *Port* 37A2
Meru, Mt *Tanz* 70D4
Merzifon *Turk* 43F7
Merzig *W Germ* 34D2
Mesa *USA* 6B3
Mesa Verde Nat Pk *USA* 14A2
Meschede *W Germ* 34E1
Mescit Dağ, Mt *Turk* 62D1
Meshik *USA* 8G4
Meshra Er Req *Sudan* 70C3
Mesocco *Switz* 35C1
Mesolóngion *Greece* 39E3
Mesquite, Nevada *USA* 17D3
Mesquite, Texas *USA* 15C3
Messaad *Alg* 69C2
Messalo, R *Mozam* 71D5
Messina *Italy* 38D3
Messina *S Africa* 72D1
Messíni *Greece* 39E3
Messiniakós Kólpos, G *Greece* 39E3
Mesta = Néstos
Mesta, R *Bulg* 39E2
Mestre *Italy* 38C1
Meta, R *Colombia* 24D3
Meta, R *USSR* 42E4
Meta, R *Ven* 24E2
Meta Incognito Pen *Can* 5L3
Metairie *USA* 15D4
Metaline Falls *USA* 16C1
Metán *Arg* 23D3
Metangula *Mozam* 71D5
Metaponto *Italy* 38D2
Metauro, R *Italy* 35E3
Metemma *Eth* 64C4
Methil *Scot* 32D3
Methuen *USA* 12E1
Methven *NZ* 79B2
Metlakatla *USA* 8M4
Metlaoui *Tunisia* 69D2
Metropolis *USA* 10B3
Mettür *India* 60B2
Metz *France* 36D2
Metzingen *W Germ* 34E2
Meulaboh *Indon* 54A2
Meulan *France* 34A2
Meung-sur-Loire *France* 34A3
Meurthe, R *France* 34D2
Meurthe-et-Moselle, Department *France* 34D2
Meuse, Department *France* 34C2
Meuse, R *Belg* 34C1
Meuse, R *France* 36D2
Mexia *USA* 15C3
Mexicali *Mexico* 19A1
Mexican Hat *USA* 17E3
Mexico, Federal Republic *Central America* 19B2
México *Mexico* 19C3
México, State *Mexico* 20B2
Mexico *USA* 15D2
Mexico,G of *C America* 19C2
Meximieux *France* 35A2
Mezada, Hist Site *Israel* 63C3
Mezcala *Mexico* 20C2
Mezcalapa, R *Mexico* 20D2
Mezen' *USSR* 46F3
Mezen, R *USSR* 42H3
Mezha, R *USSR* 41G1
Mezhdusharskiy, I *USSR* 42J1
Mezquital *Mexico* 20B1
Mezquital, R *Mexico* 20B1
Mgachi *USSR* 51E1
Mhow *India* 58D4
Miahuatlán *Mexico* 20C2
Miami, Arizona *USA* 17D4
Miami, Florida *USA* 7E4
Miami, Oklahoma *USA* 15D2
Miami Beach *USA* 7E4
Miandowāb *Iran* 43H8
Miandrivazo *Madag* 71E5
Miāneh *Iran* 43H8
Mianwali *Pak* 58C2
Mianyang *China* 50A3
Mianyang *China* 50C3
Mianzhu *China* 50A3
Miaodao Qundao, Arch *China* 50E2
Miao Ling, Upland *China* 50B4
Miass *USSR* 42L5
Michalovce *Czech* 41E3
Michel *Can* 16D1
Miches *Dom Rep* 21D3
Michigan, State *USA* 7E2
Michigan City *USA* 10B2
Michigan,L *USA* 7E2
Michipicoten *Can* 10C1
Michipicoten I *Can* 5K5
Michoacan, State *Mexico* 20B2
Michunnsk *USSR* 46F4
Michurin *Bulg* 39F2
Michurinsk *USSR* 43G5
Micronesia, Region *Pacific O* 74J4
Midai, I *Indon* 54C2
Mid Atlantic Ridge *Atlantic O* 73F4
Middelburg *Neth* 34B1
Middle Alkali L *USA* 16B2
Middle America Trench *Pacific O* 75O4
Middle Andaman, I *Indian O* 60E2
Middleboro *USA* 12E2
Middleburg, Cape Province *S Africa* 72C3
Middleburg, Pennsylvania *USA* 12B2
Middleburg, Transvaal *S Africa* 72D2
Middleburg, Virginia *USA* 12B3
Middleburgh *USA* 12C1
Middlebury *USA* 11E2
Middlesboro *USA* 7E3
Middlesbrough *Eng* 33E4
Middletown, Connecticut *USA* 12D2
Middletown, Delaware *USA* 12C3
Middletown, New York *USA* 11E2
Middletown, Ohio *USA* 10C3

Middletown, Pennsylvania *USA* 12B2
Middleville *USA* 12C1
Midelt *Mor* 69B2
Mid Glamorgan, County *Wales* 33D6
Mīdī *Yemen* 64D3
Mid Indian Basin *Indian O* 74E5
Mid Indian Ridge *Indian O* 74E5
Midland *Can* 5L5
Midland, Michigan *USA* 10C2
Midland, Texas *USA* 6C3
Midongy Atsimo *Madag* 71E6
Mid Pacific Mts *Pacific O* 75K4
Midvale *USA* 16C2
Midway Is *Pacific O* 75L3
Midwest *USA* 9A3
Midwest City *USA* 15C2
Midyat *Turk* 62D2
Midžor, Mt *Yugos* 39E2
Mielec *Pol* 41E2
Miercurea-Ciuc *Rom* 39F1
Mieres *Spain* 37A1
Mifflintown *USA* 12B2
Miguel Auza *Mexico* 20B1
Miguihuana *Mexico* 20C1
Mihara *Japan* 52B4
Mijun Shuiku, Res *China* 50D1
Mikhayiovka *USSR* 46F4
Mikhaylovgrad *Bulg* 39E2
Mikhaylovka *USSR* 43G5
Mikhaylovskiy *USSR* 46J4
Mikhrot Timna *Israel* 63C4
Mikkeli *Fin* 30K6
Mikkwa, R *Can* 3F2
Míkonos, I *Greece* 39F3
Mikulov *Czech* 40D3
Mikumi *Tanz* 71D4
Mikun *USSR* 42J3
Mikuni-sammyaku, Mts *Japan* 51D4
Mikura-jima, I *Japan* 52C4
Milaca *USA* 9D2
Milagro *Ecuador* 24C4
Milan = Milano
Milan *USA* 13B1
Milana *Alg* 37C2
Milange *Mozam* 71D5
Milango, R *Indon* 55B2
Milano *Italy* 38B1
Milas *Turk* 43D8
Milbank *USA* 9C2
Mildura *Aust* 76D4
Mile *China* 50A5
Mileh Tharthār, L *Iraq* 62D3
Miles *Aust* 76E3
Miles City *USA* 6C2
Milford, Connecticut *USA* 12D2
Milford, Delaware *USA* 11D3
Milford, Massachusetts *USA* 11E2
Milford, Nebraska *USA* 15C1
Milford, New Hampshire *USA* 12E1
Milford, Pennsylvania *USA* 12C2
Milford, Utah *USA* 17D3
Milford Haven *Wales* 33C6
Milford Haven, Sd *Wales* 33C6
Milford L *USA* 15C2
Milford Sd *NZ* 79A2
Miliana *Alg* 69C1
Milk, R *USA* 9A2
Mil'Kovo *USSR* 47R4
Milk River *Can* 3F3
Millau *France* 36C3
Millbrook *USA* 12D2
Milledgeville *USA* 13C2
Mille Lacs, L *USA* 9D2
Miller *USA* 9C3
Miller,Mt *USA* 8K3
Millerovo *USSR* 43G6
Millersburg *USA* 12B2
Millers Creek *Aust* 78A1
Millers Falls *USA* 12D1
Millerton *USA* 12D2
Millerton L *USA* 18C2
Millicent *Aust* 78B3
Millington *USA* 13B1
Millinocket *USA* 11F1
Millmerran *Aust* 78D1
Millstätter See, L *Austria* 35E1
Milltown *Can* 11F1
Milltown *USA* 16D1
Mill Valley *USA* 18A2
Millville *USA* 11E3
Milne Land, I *Greenland* 5Q2
Milolii *Hawaiian Is* 18E5
Mílos, I *Greece* 39E3
Milparinka *Aust* 76D3
Milroy *USA* 12B2
Milton, Florida *USA* 13B2
Milton *NZ* 79A3
Milton, Pennsylvania *USA* 12B2
Milwaukee *USA* 7E2
Mimmaya *Japan* 52D2
Mina *USA* 18C1
Mina, R *Alg* 37C2
Mīnā' al Ahmadī *Kuwait* 62E4
Mīnāb *Iran* 61D3
Minahassa Pen *Indon* 55B2
Minaki *Can* 9D1
Minamata *Japan* 51C5
Minas *Indon* 54B2
Minas *Urug* 23E4
Minas Gerais, State *Brazil* 25J7
Minas Novas *Brazil* 27D2
Minatitlan *Mexico* 19C3
Minbu *Burma* 53A1
Minbya *Burma* 53A1
Mincha *Chile* 26A2
Minch,Little, Sd *Scot* 32B3
Minch,North, Sd *Scot* 32B2
Minch,The, Sd *Scot* 31B2
Minchumina,L *USA* 8H3
Mincio, R *Italy* 35D2
Mindanao, I *Phil* 55F9
Minden, Louisiana *USA* 15D3
Minden, Nevada *USA* 18C1
Minden *W Germ* 40B2
Mindona L *Aust* 78B2
Mindoro, I *Phil* 55F8
Mindoro Str *Phil* 55F8
Minehead *Eng* 33D6
Mineiros *Brazil* 25H7
Mineola *USA* 15C3
Mineral de Monte *Mexico* 20C1
Mineral Wells *USA* 14C3
Minersville *USA* 12B2
Mingary *Aust* 78B2
Mingechaurskoye Vodokhranilische, Res *USSR* 43H7
Mingshui *China* 51B2
Minhe *China* 50A2
Minialo *Italy* 35D3
Minicoy, I *India* 60A3
Min Jiang, R, Fujian *China* 50D4
Min Jiang, R, Sichuan *China* 50A4
Minkler *USA* 18C2
Minlaton *Aust* 78A2
Minle *China* 50A2
Minna *Nig* 69H4
Minneapolis *USA* 7D2
Minnedosa *Can* 4J4
Minnesota, State *USA* 7D2
Minnesota, R *USA* 9C3
Minnitaki L *Can* 9D2
Miño, R *Spain* 37A1
Minot *USA* 6C2
Minqin *China* 50A2
Min Shan, Upland *China* 50A3
Minsk *USSR* 42D5
Minsk Mazowiecki *Pol* 41E2
Minto *USA* 8J3
Minto Inlet, B *Can* 4G2
Minto,L *Can* 5L4
Minturn *USA* 14A2
Minusinsk *USSR* 48C1
Min Xian *China* 50A3
Minyael Qamn *Egypt* 63A3
Miquelon *Can* 5N5
Mirage L *USA* 18D3
Miraj *India* 60A1
Miramar *Arg* 23E5
Miram Shah *Pak* 58B2
Miranda, R *Brazil* 27A2
Miranda de Ebro *Spain* 37B1
Mirandia *Brazil* 27A3
Mirandola *Italy* 35D2
Mir Bachchen Küt *Afghan* 58B2
Mirbāt *Oman* 65F3
Mirebeau *France* 35A1
Mirecourt *France* 34C2
Miri *Malay* 54D2
Miri, Mt *Pak* 61E3
Mirik,C *Maur* 68A3
Mirinay, R *Arg* 26D1
Mirjāveh *Iran* 61E3
Mirna, R *Yugos* 35E2
Mirnoye *USSR* 47K3
Mirnyy *USSR* 47N3
Mirnyy, Base *Ant* 80G9
Miron L *Can* 3H2
Mironovka *USSR* 41G3
Mirpur *Pak* 58C2
Mirpur Khas *Pak* 58B3
Mirtoan S *Greece* 39E3
Miryang *S Korea* 51B4
Mirzāpur *India* 59B2
Misantla *Mexico* 20C2
Misgar *Pak* 58C1
Mishan *China* 51C2
Mishawaka *USA* 10B2
Misheguk Mt *USA* 8F2
Mi-shima, I *Japan* 52B4
Mishmi Hills *India* 59E2
Misima, I *Solomon Is* 77E2
Misiones, State *Arg* 23F3
Miskolc *Hung* 41E3
Mismīyah *Syria* 63D2
Misoöl, I *Indon* 49G7
Misow L *Can* 3H2
Misrātah *Libya* 67A1
Missinaibi, R *Can* 5K5
Missinaibi L *Can* 10C1
Missinipe *Can* 3H2
Mission, S Dakota *USA* 9B3
Mission, Texas *USA* 15F4
Mission City *Can* 16B1
Mississauga *Can* 11D2
Mississippi, State *USA* 7D3
Mississippi, R *USA* 7D3
Mississippi Delta *USA* 15E3
Missoula *USA* 6B2
Missour *Mor* 69B2
Missouri, State *USA* 7D3
Missouri, R *USA* 7D2
Missouri Valley *USA* 9C3
Mistassini,L *Can* 7F1
Misti, Mt *Peru* 24D7
Mitchell *Aust* 78C1
Mitchell *USA* 6D2
Mitchell, R *Aust* 76D2
Mitchell,Mt *USA* 7E3
Mitchell River *Aust* 49H8
Mit el Nasâra *Egypt* 63A3
Mît Ghamr *Egypt* 63A3
Mithankot *Pak* 58B3
Mitilíni *Greece* 39F3
Mitla *Mexico* 20C2
Mitla P *Egypt* 63B3
Mitre, I *Solomon Is* 77G2
Mitrofania I *USA* 8G4
Mittersill *Austria* 35E1
Mitu *Colombia* 24D3
Mitumbar, Mts *Zaïre* 70C4
Mitwaba *Zaïre* 71C4
Mitzic *Gabon* 70B3
Miura *Japan* 52C3
Mi Xian *China* 50C3
Miyake, I *Japan* 48G3
Miyake-jima, I *Japan* 52C4
Miyako, I *Japan* 48F4
Miyakonojō *Japan* 51C5
Miyazaki *Japan* 51C5
Miyazu *Japan* 52C3
Miyoshi *Japan* 51C5
Miyun *China* 50D1
Mi-zaki, Pt *Japan* 52D2
Mizan Teferi *Eth* 70D3
Mizdah *Libya* 67A1
Mizil *Rom* 39F1
Mizo Hills *India* 59D3
Mizoram, Union Territory *India* 59D3
Mizpe Ramon *Israel* 63C3
Mizuho, Base *Ant* 80F11
Mizusawa *Japan* 51E4
Mjolby *Sweden* 30H7
Mkushi *Zambia* 71C5
Mkuzi *S Africa* 72E2
Mladá Boleslav *Czech* 40C2
Mława *Pol* 41E2
Mljet, I *Yugos* 39D2
Mmabatho *S Africa* 72D2
Mnadi *India* 58D2
Moa, I *Indon* 55C4
Moa, R *Sierra Leone* 68A4
Moab, Region *Jordan* 63C3
Moab *USA* 6C3
Moamba *Mozam* 72E2
Moanda *Congo* 70B4
Moanda *Gabon* 70B4
Moba *Zaïre* 71C4
Mobara *Japan* 52D3
Mobaye *CAR* 70C3
Mobayi *Zaire* 70C3
Moberly *USA* 7D3
Mobile *USA* 7E3
Mobile B *USA* 7E3
Mobile Pt *USA* 13B2
Mobridge *USA* 6C2
Moçambique *Mozam* 71E5
Moçâmedes *Angola* 71B5
Moc Chau *Viet* 53C1
Mochudi *Botswana* 72D1
Mocimboa da Praia *Mozam* 71E5
Mocoa *Colombia* 24C3
Mococa *Brazil* 27C3
Mocoreta, R *Arg* 26D2
Moctezulma, R *Mexico* 20C1
Moctezuma *Mexico* 20B1
Mocuba *Mozam* 71D5
Modane *France* 35B2
Modder, R *S Africa* 72D2
Modena *Italy* 38C2
Moder, R *France* 34D2
Modesto *USA* 6A3
Modesto Res *USA* 18B2
Modica *Italy* 38C3
Mödling *Austria* 40D3
Moe *Aust* 76D4
Moesa, R *Switz* 35C1
Moffat *Scot* 32D4
Moga *India* 58D2
Mogadiscio *Somalia* 66J7
Mogaung *Burma* 59E2
Mogi das Cruzes *Brazil* 27C3
Mogilev *USSR* 42D5
Mogilev Podolskiy *USSR* 43D6
Mogi-Mirim *Brazil* 27C3
Mogincual *Mozam* 71E5
Moglev *USSR* 41G2
Mogliano *Italy* 35E2
Mogna *Arg* 26B2
Mogocha *USSR* 48E1
Mogochin *USSR* 46K4
Mogok *Burma* 59E3
Mogol, R *S Africa* 72D1
Moguer *Spain* 37A2
Mohaka, R *NZ* 79C1
Mohale's Hoek *Lesotho* 72D3
Mohall *USA* 9B2
Mohammadia *Alg* 69C1
Mohammedia *Mor* 69A2
Mohanganj *Bang* 59D3
Mohave,L *USA* 17D3
Mohawk *USA* 12C1
Mohawk, R *USA* 11E2
Mohican,C *USA* 8E3
Mohoro *Tanz* 71D4
Mointy *USSR* 46J5
Mo i Rana *Nor* 30G5
Moissac *France* 36C3
Mojave *USA* 17C3
Mojave, R *USA* 18D3
Mojave Desert *USA* 6B3
Mojokerto *Indon* 54D4
Mokada, Mt *Eth* 64C4
Mokama *India* 59C2
Mokau, R *NZ* 79B1
Mokelumne Aqueduct *USA* 18B1
Mokelumne Hill *USA* 18B1
Mokelumne North Fork, R *USA* 18B1
Mokhotlong *Lesotho* 72D2
Moknine *Tunisia* 69E1
Mokokchüng *India* 59D2
Mokolo *Cam* 70B2
Mokp'o *S Korea* 51B5
Moksha, R *USSR* 42G5
Molango *Mexico* 20C1
Moláoi *Greece* 39E3
Moldavskaya SSR, Republic *USSR* 43D6
Molde *Nor* 30F6
Moldoveanu, Mt *Rom* 39E1
Mole Nat Pk *Ghana* 69F4
Molepolole *Botswana* 72D1
Molesheim *France* 34D2
Molfetta *Italy* 38D2
Molina *Chile* 26A3
Möll, R *Austria* 35E1
Mollendo *Peru* 24D7
Molodechno *USSR* 42D5
Molodezhnaya, Base *Ant* 80G11
Molokai, I *Hawaiian Is* 18E5
Moloma, R *USSR* 42H4
Molong *Aust* 78C2
Molopo, R *S Africa/ Botswana* 72C2
Molounddu *Cam* 70B3
Molson L *Can* 6D1
Molucca S *Indon* 76B1
Moluccas, Is *Indon* 49F7
Moma *Mozam* 71D5
Mombaca *Brazil* 25K5
Mombasa *Kenya* 70D4
Mombetsu *Japan* 52D2
Mompono *Zaïre* 70C3
Mon, I *Den* 40C2
Monach, Is *Scot* 32B3
Monaco, Principality *Europe* 36D3
Monadhliath, Mts *Scot* 32C3
Monaghan, County *Irish Rep* 33B4
Monaghan *Irish Rep* 33B4
Monahans *USA* 14B3
Mona Pass *Caribbean* 21D3
Monarch Mt *Can* 3C3
Monarch P *USA* 14A2
Monashee Mts *Can* 4G4
Monastereven *Irish Rep* 31B3
Monbetsu *Japan* 52D2
Moncalieri *Italy* 35B2
Monção *Brazil* 25J4
Monchegorsk *USSR* 30L5
Mönchen-gladbach *W Germ* 40B2
Monclova *Mexico* 19B2
Moncton *Can* 5M5
Monctova *Mexico* 6C4
Mondego, R *Port* 37A1
Mondovi *Italy* 38B2
Moneague *Jamaica* 21H1
Monessen *USA* 11D2
Monett *USA* 15D2
Monfalcone *Italy* 38C1
Monforte de Lemos *Spain* 37A1
Monga *Zaïre* 70C3
Mongala, R *Zaïre* 70C3
Mongalla *Sudan* 70D3
Mong Cai *Viet* 53D1
Mongo *Chad* 70B2
Mongolia, Republic *Asia* 48C2
Mongu *Zambia* 71C5
Mönhhaan *Mongolia* 47N5
Monitor Range, Mts *USA* 17C3
Monkoto *Zaïre* 70C4
Monmouth *Eng* 33D6
Monmouth *USA* 10A2
Monmouth,Mt *Can* 3D3
Mono, R *Togo* 69G4
Mono L *USA* 17C3
Monopoli *Italy* 39D2
Monreal del Campo *Spain* 37B1
Monroe, Louisiana *USA* 15D3
Monroe, Michigan *USA* 10C2
Monroe, N Carolina *USA* 13C2
Monroe, Washington *USA* 16B1
Monroe, Wisconsin *USA* 10B2
Monroe City *USA* 15D2
Monrovia *Lib* 68A4
Monrovia *USA* 18D3
Mons *Belg* 40A2
Monselice *Italy* 35D2
Monson *USA* 12D1
Mönsterås *Sweden* 40D1
Montagne d'Ambre, Mt *Madag* 71E5
Montagnes des Ouled Naïl, Mts *Alg* 69C2
Montagu *S Africa* 72C3
Montague I *USA* 8J4
Montaigu *France* 36B2
Montallo, Mt *Italy* 38D3
Montana, State *USA* 6B2
Montañas de León, Mts *Spain* 37A1
Montargis *France* 36C2
Montauban *France* 36C3
Montauk *USA* 11E2
Montauk Pt *USA* 11E2
Montbard *France* 34C3
Montbéliard *France* 36D2
Mont Blanc, Mt *France/ Italy* 38B1
Montceau les Mines *France* 36C2
Montceny, Mt *Spain* 37C1
Mont Cinto, Mt *Corse* 36D3
Montcornet *France* 34C2
Mont d'Amain, Mt *France* 34A2
Mont-de-Marsin *France* 36B3
Montdidier *France* 36C2
Monteagudo *Bol* 24F7
Monte Alegre *Brazil* 25H4
Monte Amiata, Mt *Italy* 38C2
Monte Azul *Brazil* 27D2
Monte Baldo, Mt *Italy* 35D2
Montebello *Can* 11D1
Monte Bello Is *Aust* 76A3
Montebelluna *Italy* 35E2
Monte Carlo *France* 35B3
Monte Carmelo *Brazil* 27C2
Monte Caseros *Arg* 26D2
Montecatini *Italy* 35D3
Monte Catria, Mt *Italy* 35E3
Monte Cimone, Mt *Italy* 38C2
Monte Cinto, Mt *Corse* 38B2
Monte Coman *Arg* 26B2
Monte Corno, Mt *Italy* 38C2
Montecristi *Dom Rep* 21C3
Montecristo, I *Italy* 38C2
Monte Escobedo *Mexico* 20B1
Monte Falterona, Mt *Italy* 35D3
Monte Gargano, Mt *Italy* 38D2
Montego Bay *Jamaica* 21B3
Monte Grappa, Mt *Italy* 35D2
Monte Lesima, Mt *Italy* 35C2
Montélimar *France* 36C3
Montelindo, R *Par* 27A3
Monte Miletto, Mt *Italy* 38C2
Montemo-o-Novo *Port* 37A2
Montemorelos *Mexico* 19C2
Montenā *Colombia* 21B5
Montenegro, Region *Yugos* 39D2
Montengero *Brazil* 26E1
Monte Orsaro, Mt *Italy* 35C3
Monte Pascoal, Mt *Brazil* 27E2
Monte Patria *Chile* 26A2
Monte Pennino, Mt *Italy* 35E3
Monte Pississ, Mt *Arg* 26B1
Monte Pollino, Mt *Italy* 38D3
Monte Pramaggiore, Mt *Italy* 35E2
Montepuez *Mozam* 71D5
Montepulciano *Italy* 35D3
Montereau-Faut-Yonne *France* 34B2
Monterey, California *USA* 6A3
Monterey, Virginia *USA* 11D3
Monterey B *USA* 6A3
Montería *Colombia* 24C2
Montero *Bol* 24F7
Monte Rosa, Mt *Italy/ Switz* 35B2
Monterrey *Mexico* 19B2
Montes Claros *Brazil* 25K7
Montes de Toledo, Mts *Spain* 37B2
Montevarchi *Italy* 35D3
Montevideo *Urug* 23E4

Montevideo *USA* 9C3
Montevil *France* 33F6
Monte Viso, Mt *Italy* 38B2
Monte Vista *USA* 14A2
Montezuma *USA* 14B2
Montezuma Peak, Mt *USA* 18D2
Mont Gimie, Mt *St Lucia* 21P2
Montgomery, Alabama *USA* 7E3
Montgomery, Pennsylvania *USA* 12B2
Montgomery P *USA* 18C2
Mont Gréboun *Niger* 68C2
Montherme *France* 34C2
Monthey *Switz* 35B1
Monticello, Arkansas *USA* 15D3
Monticello, Iowa *USA* 10A2
Monticello, Minnesota *USA* 9D2
Monticello, New York *USA* 12C2
Monticello, Utah *USA* 6C3
Monti del Gennargentu, Mt *Sardegna* 38B2
Montier-en-Der *France* 34C2
Monti Lessini, Mts *Italy* 35D2
Monti Nebrodi, Mts *Italy* 38C3
Montivilliers *France* 34A2
Mont-Laurier *Can* 5L5
Montluçon *France* 36C2
Montmagny *Can* 5L5
Montmédy *France* 34C2
Montmirail *France* 34B2
Montmorency *Can* 11E1
Mont Mounier, Mt *France* 35B2
Montoro *Spain* 37B2
Montoursville *USA* 12B2
Mont Pelat, Mt *France* 36D3
Montpelier, Idaho *USA* 16D2
Montpelier, Ohio *USA* 10C2
Montpelier, Vermont *USA* 7F2
Montpellier *France* 36C3
Montréal *Can* 5L5
Montreal L *Can* 3G3
Montreal Lake *Can* 3G3
Montreuil *France* 36C1
Montreux *Switz* 38B1
Montrevel *France* 35A1
Mont Risoux, Mt *France* 35B1
Montrose, Colorado *USA* 6C3
Montrose, Pennsylvania *USA* 12C2
Montrose *Scot* 31C2
Montrose, Oilfield *N Sea* 32F3
Mont-St-Michel *France* 36B2
Monts des Ksour, Mts *Alg* 69B2
Monts des Ouled Neil, Mts *Alg* 37C3
Monts du Hodna, Mts *Alg* 37C2
Montserrat, I *Caribbean* 21E3
Mont Ventoux, Mt *France* 35A2
Monument Mt *USA* 8F2
Monument V *USA* 6B3
Monveda *Zaïre* 70C3
Monywa *Burma* 53B1
Monza *Italy* 38B1
Monze *Zambia* 71C5
Mooi, R *S Africa* 72E2
Mooi River *S Africa* 72D2
Moomba *Aust* 78B1
Moonbi Range, Mts *Aust* 78D2
Moonda L *Aust* 78B1
Moonie *Aust* 78D1
Moonie, R *Aust* 78C1
Moonta *Aust* 78A2
Moora *Aust* 76A4
Mooraberree *Aust* 78B1
Moorcroft *USA* 9B3
Moore,L *Aust* 76A3
Moorfoot Hills *Scot* 32D4
Moorhead *USA* 6D2
Moorpark *USA* 18C3
Moorreesburg *S Africa* 72B3
Moose, R *Can* 5K4
Moosehead L *USA* 11F1
Moose Jaw *Can* 4H4
Moose Lake *USA* 9D2
Moosomin *Can* 4H4
Moosonee *Can* 5K4
Moosup *USA* 12E2
Mopeia *Mozam* 71D5
Mopti *Mali* 68B3
Moquegua *Peru* 24D7
Mora *Cam* 69J3
Mora *Sweden* 30G6
Mora *USA* 9D2
Morada *Brazil* 25L5
Morādābād *India* 58D3
Morada Nova de Minas, L *Brazil* 27C2
Morafenobe *Madag* 71E5
Moramanga *Madag* 71E5
Moran *USA* 16D2
Morant Bay *Jamaica* 21J2
Morant Pt *Jamaica* 21J2
Moratuwa *Sri Lanka* 60B3
Morava, R *Austria/Czech* 40D3
Morava, R *Yugos* 39E2
Moraveh Tappeh *Iran* 61D1
Moray Firth, Estuary *Scot* 31C2
Morbegno *Italy* 35C1
Morbi *India* 58C4
Morcillo *Mexico* 20B1
Mor Dağ, Mt *Turk* 62D2
Morden *Can* 4J5
Mordovskaya ASSR, Republic *USSR* 42G5
Moreau, R *USA* 9B2
Morecambe *Eng* 33D4
Morecambe B *Eng* 33D4
Moree *Aust* 76D3
Morée *France* 34A3
Morehead *USA* 10C3
Morehead City *USA* 13D2
Mörel *Switz* 35C1
Morelia *Mexico* 19B3
Morelos *Mexico* 20B1
Morelos *Mexico* 20C1
Morelos, State *Mexico* 20C2
Morena *India* 58D3
Moresby I *Can* 4E4
Moreton I *Aust* 78D1
Moreuil *France* 34B2
Morez *France* 35B1
Morgan City *USA* 15D4
Morgan Hill *USA* 18B2
Morgan,Mt *USA* 18C2
Morganton *USA* 13C1
Morgantown *USA* 11D3
Morgenzon *S Africa* 72D2
Morges *Switz* 35B1
Morhange *France* 34D2
Mori *Japan* 51E3
Moriarty *USA* 14A3
Moriatio *Tobago* 21K1
Morice L *Can* 3C3
Morin Dawa *China* 51A2
Morinville *Can* 3F3
Morioka *Japan* 51E4
Morisset *Aust* 78D2
Morkoka, R *USSP* 47N3
Morlaix *France* 36B2
Morne Diablotin, Mt *Dominica* 21Q2
Morney *Aust* 78B1
Mornington, I *Aust* 76C2
Moro *Pak* 58B3
Morobe *PNG* 76D1
Morocco, Kingdom *Africa* 68B1
Moro G *Phil* 55F9
Morogoro *Tanz* 71D4
Moroleon *Mexico* 20B1
Morombe *Madag* 71E6
Morón *Cuba* 21B2
Morondava *Madag* 71E6
Moron de la Frontera *Spain* 37A2
Moroni *Comoros* 71E5
Morotai, I *Indon* 55C2
Moroto *Uganda* 70D3
Morozovsk *USSR* 43G6
Morpeth *Eng* 32E4
Morphou *Cyprus* 63B1
Morphou B *Cyprus* 63B1
Morrill *USA* 9B3
Morrilton *USA* 15D2
Morrinhos *Brazil* 27C2
Morrinsville *NZ* 79C1
Morris *Can* 9C2
Morris *USA* 9C2
Morristown, New Jersey *USA* 12C2
Morristown, New York *USA* 11D2
Morristown, Tennessee *USA* 13C1
Morrisville, New York *USA* 12C1
Morrisville, Pennsylvania *USA* 12C2
Morro Bay *USA* 18B3
Morro de Papanoa *Mexico* 20B2
Morro de Petatlán *Mexico* 20B2
Morrumbala *Mozam* 71D5
Morrumbene *Mozam* 71D6
Morshansk *USSR* 42G5
Mortagne-au-Perche *France* 34A2
Mortara *Italy* 35C2
Morteros *Arg* 26C2
Mortes = Manso
Mortes, R, Malo Grosso *Brazil* 25H6
Mortes, R, Minas Gerais *Brazil* 27D3
Mortlake *Aust* 78B3
Morton *USA* 14B3
Moruga *Trinidad* 21L1
Moruya *Aust* 78D3
Morven *Aust* 78C1
Morvern, Pen *Scot* 32C3
Morwell *Aust* 78C3
Morzhovoi B *USA* 8F4
Mosbach *W Germ* 34E2
Moscos Is *Burma* 53B3
Moscow = Moskva
Moscow, Idaho *USA* 16C1
Moscow, Pennsylvania *USA* 12C2
Mosel, R *W Germ* 40B2
Moselebe, R *Botswana* 72C2
Moselle, Department *France* 34D2
Moselle, R *France* 34D2
Moses Lake *USA* 16C1
Mosgiel *NZ* 79B3
Moshi *Tanz* 70D4
Mosinee *USA* 10B2
Mosjøen *Nor* 30G5
Moskal'vo *USSR* 47Q4
Moskva *USSR* 46E4
Mosquero *USA* 14B2
Mosquito, R *Brazil* 27D2
Moss *Nor* 30G7
Mossaka *Congo* 70B4
Mossâmedes = Moçâmedes
Mossel Bay *S Africa* 72C3
Mossendjo *Congo* 70B4
Mossgiel *Aust* 78B2
Mossoró *Brazil* 25L5
Most *Czech* 40C2
Mostaganem *Alg* 69C1
Mostar *Yugos* 39D2
Mostardos *Brazil* 26E2
Mosty *USSR* 41E2
Mosul *Iraq* 62D2
Motala *Sweden* 30G7
Motherwell *Scot* 32D4
Motihāri *India* 59B2
Motilla del Palancar *Spain* 37B2
Motloutse, R *Botswana* 72D1
Motovun *Yugos* 35E2
Motril *Spain* 37B2
Mott *USA* 9B2
Motueka *NZ* 79B2
Motueka, R *NZ* 79B2
Moudon *Switz* 35B1
Mouila *Gabon* 70B4
Moulamein *Aust* 78B2
Mould Bay *Can* 4G2
Moulins *France* 36C2
Moulmein *Burma* 53B2
Moulouya, R *Mor* 69B2
Moultrie *USA* 13C2
Moultrie,L *USA* 13D2
Mound City, Illinois *USA* 10B3
Mound City, Missouri *USA* 15C1
Moundou *Chad* 70B3
Moundsville *USA* 10C3
Mount Aigoual, Mt *France* 36C3
Mountain, R *Can* 8N2
Mountain Brook *USA* 13B2
Mountain Grove *USA* 15D2
Mountain Home, Arkansas *USA* 15D2
Mountain Home, Idaho *USA* 16C2
Mountain View *USA* 18A2
Mountain Village *USA* 8F3
Mount Airy, Maryland *USA* 12B3
Mount Airy, N Carolina *USA* 13C1
Mount Ayliff *S Africa* 72D3
Mount Carmel *USA* 12B2
Mount Desert I *USA* 11F2
Mount Dutton *Aust* 78A1
Mount Eba *Aust* 78A2
Mount Fletcher *S Africa* 72D3
Mount Gambier *Aust* 78B3
Mount Hagen *PNG* 76D1
Mount Holly *USA* 12C3
Mount Holly Springs *USA* 12B2
Mount Hope *Aust* 78A2
Mount Isa *Aust* 76C3
Mount Jackson *USA* 12A3
Mount Jewett *USA* 12A2
Mount Lofty Range, Mts *Aust* 78A2
Mount McKinley Nat Pk *USA* 8H3
Mount Magnet *Aust* 76A3
Mount Manara *Aust* 78B2
Mount Mézenc, Mt *France* 36C3
Mount Morgan *Aust* 76E3
Mount Morris *USA* 12B1
Mount Perry *Aust* 78D1
Mount Pleasant, Texas *USA* 15D3
Mount Pleasant, Utah *USA* 17D3
Mount Pocono *USA* 12C2
Mount Rainier Nat Pk *USA* 16B1
Mounts B *Eng* 33C6
Mount Shasta *USA* 16B2
Mount Union *USA* 12B2
Mount Vernon, Alabama *USA* 13B2
Mount Vernon, Illinois *USA* 10B3
Mount Vernon, Kentucky *USA* 15C3
Mount Vernon, Washington *USA* 16B1
Mourne Mts *N Ire* 33B4
Moussa Ali, Mt *Djibouti* 64D4
Moussoro *Chad* 70B2
Moustiers Ste Marie *France* 35B3
Mouth of the Indus *Pak* 58B4
Mouths of the Ganga *India/Bang* 59C3
Mouths of the Mekong *Viet* 53D4
Mouths of the Niger *Nigeria* 68C4
Moutier *Switz* 35B1
Moûtiers *France* 35B2
Moutong *Indon* 55B2
Mouydir, Mts *Alg* 68C2
Mouyondzi *Congo* 70B4
Mouzon *France* 34C2
Moyahua *Mexico* 20B1
Moyale *Kenya* 70D3
Moyamba *Sierra Leone* 68A4
Moyen Atlas, Mts *Mor* 69A2
Moyeni *Lesotho* 72D3
Moyero, R *USSR* 47M3
Moyo *Uganda* 70D3
Moyobamba *Peru* 24C5
Moyu *China* 58D1
Mozambique, Republic *Africa* 71D6
Mozambique Chan *Mozam/Madag* 71D6
Mozhga *USSR* 42J4
Mozyr *USSR* 43D5
Mozyr, R *USSR* 30K8
Mpanda *Tanz* 70D4
Mpika *Zambia* 71D5
Mporokosa *Zambia* 71D4
Mposhi *Zambia* 71C5
Mpulungu *Zambia* 71D4
Mpwapwa *Tanz* 70D4
Mstislavl' *USSR* 41G2
Mtsensk *USSR* 42F5
Mtubatuba *S Africa* 72E2
Mtwara *Tanz* 71E5
Muang Chainat *Thai* 53C2
Muang Chiang Rai *Thai* 53C2
Muang Kalasin *Thai* 53C2
Muang Khon Kaen *Thai* 53C2
Muang Lampang *Thai* 53B2
Muang Lamphun *Thai* 53B2
Muang Loei *Thai* 53C2
Muang Lom Sak *Thai* 53C2
Muang Nakhon Phanom *Thai* 53C2
Muang Nakhon Sawan *Thai* 53B2
Muang Nan *Thai* 53C2
Muang Phayao *Thai* 53C2
Muang Phetchabun *Thai* 53C2
Muang Phichit *Thai* 53C2
Muang Phitsanulok *Thai* 53C2
Muang Phrae *Thai* 53C2
Muang Roi Et *Thai* 53C2
Muang Sakon Nakhon *Thai* 53C2
Muang Samut Prakan *Thai* 53C3
Muang Uthai Thani *Thai* 53C2
Muang Yasothon *Thai* 53C2
Muar *Malay* 53C5
Muara *Brunei* 54D2
Muara *Indon* 54B3
Muaralakitan *Indon* 54B3
Muaratebo *Indon* 54B3
Muaratewah *Indon* 54E3
Muarenim *Indon* 54B3
Muaungmaya *Burma* 53A2
Mubende *Uganda* 70D3
Mubi *Nig* 69J3
Muchinga, Mts *Zambia* 71D5
Muck, I *Scot* 32B3
Muckadilla *Aust* 78C1
Mucuri *Brazil* 27E2
Mucuri, R *Brazil* 27D2
Mucusso *Angola* 71C5
Mudanjiang *China* 51B3
Mudayy *Oman* 65F3
Muddy Gap P *USA* 9A3
Mudgee *Aust* 78C2
Mud L *USA* 18D2
Mudon *Burma* 53B2
Mud'vuga *USSR* 42F3
Mue *Nouvelle Calédonie* 77F3
Mueda *Mozam* 71D5
Mufulira *Zambia* 71C5
Mufu Shan, Hills *China* 50C4
Mugadishu = Muqdisho
Mugadzhary, Mts *USSR* 43K6
Mughayra *S Arabia* 62C4
Muğla *Turk* 62A2
Mugodzhary, Mts *USSR* 46G5
Mugu *Nepal* 59B2
Muguaping *China* 50A3
Muhammad Qol *Sudan* 64C2
Muhaywir *Iraq* 62D3
Mühlacker *W Germ* 34E2
Mühldorf *W Germ* 40C3
Muhlhausen *E Germ* 40C2
Muhos *Fin* 30K6
Mui Bai Bung, C *Camb* 53C4
Muine Bheag *Irish Rep* 33B5
Mujimbeji *Zambia* 71C5
Mukachevo *USSR* 41E3
Mukah *Malay* 54D2
Mukawa *Japan* 52D2
Muko-jima, I *Japan* 48H4
Muktinath *Nepal* 59B2
Mukur *Afghan* 58B2
Mulan *China* 51B2
Mulberry *USA* 15D2
Mulchatna, R *USA* 8G3
Mulchén *Chile* 26A3
Mulde, R *E Germ* 40C2
Mule Creek *USA* 9B3
Muleshoe *USA* 14B3
Mulgrave I *Aust* 49H8
Mulhacén, Mt *Spain* 37B2
Mülheim *W Germ* 34D1
Mulhouse *France* 34D3
Muli *China* 50A4
Muling *China* 51C3
Muling He, R *China* 51C2
Mull, I *Scot* 32C3
Mullaitvu *Sri Lanka* 60C3
Mullaley *Aust* 78C2
Mullewa *Aust* 76A3
Müllheim *W Germ* 34D3
Mullica, R *USA* 12C3
Mullingar *Irish Rep* 33B5
Mull of Kintyre, Pt *Scot* 32C4
Mull of Oa, C *Scot* 32B4
Mullumbimby *Aust* 78D1
Mulobezi *Zambia* 71C5
Multan *Pak* 58C2
Muluku, Is *Indon* 55C3
Mumbwa *Zambia* 71C5
Mumra *USSR* 43H6
Muna, I *Indon* 55B4
München *W Germ* 40C3
Muncho, L *Can* 3C2
Munchŏn *N Korea* 52A3
Muncie *USA* 10B2
Munconnie,L *Aust* 78A1
Muncy *USA* 12B2
Münden *W Germ* 40B2
Mundubbera *Aust* 78D1
Mungallala *Aust* 78C1
Mungallala, R *Aust* 78C1
Mungbere *Zaïre* 70C3
Mungeli *India* 59B3
Munger *India* 59C2
Mungindi *Aust* 78C1
Munich = München
Munising *USA* 10B1
Muñoz Gomero, Pen *Chile* 23B8
Munroe L *Can* 3J2
Munsan *S Korea* 52A3
Münsingen *W Germ* 34E2
Munster *France* 34D2
Münster *Switz* 35C1
Münster *W Germ* 40B2
Münsterland, Region *W Germ* 34D1
Muntii Apuseni, Mts *Rom* 39E1
Muntii Călimanilor, Mts *Rom* 39E1
Muntii Carpaţii Meridionali, Mts *Rom* 39E1
Muntii Rodnei, Mts *Rom* 39E1
Muntii Zarandului, Mts *Rom* 39E1
Munzur Silsilesi, Mts *Turk* 62C2
Muomio *Fin* 46D3
Muong Khoua *Laos* 53C1
Muong Man *Viet* 53D3
Muong Nong *Laos* 53D2
Muong Ou Neua *Laos* 53C1
Muong Sai *Laos* 53C1
Muong Sen *Viet* 53C2
Muong Sing *Laos* 53C1
Muong Son *Laos* 53C1
Muonio *Fin* 30J5
Muonio, R *Sweden/Fin* 30J5
Muqaddam, Watercourse *Sudan* 64B3
Muqdisho *Somalia* 70E3
Mur, R *Austria* 38C1
Murakami *Japan* 51D4
Murallón, Mt *Chile/Arg* 23B7
Murashi *USSR* 42H4
Murat, R *Turk* 62D2
Muravera *Sardegna* 38B3
Murayama *Japan* 52D3
Murcanyo *Somalia* 65F4
Murcheh Khvort *Iran* 61C2
Murchison *NZ* 79B2
Murchison, R *Aust* 76A3
Murcia, Region *Spain* 37B2
Murcia *Spain* 37B2
Murdo *USA* 9B3

Mureş, R Rom 39E1
Muresui, R Rom 39E1
Murfreesboro USA 13B1
Murfreesboro USA 13D1
Murg, R W Germ 34E2
Murgab, R USSR 46H6
Murgha Kibzai Pak 58B2
Murgon Aust 78D1
Muri India 59C3
Muriaé Brazil 27D3
Muriege Angola 71C4
Murmansk USSR 42E2
Murom USSR 42G4
Muroran Japan 51E3
Muros Spain 37A1
Muroto Japan 51C5
Muroto-zaki, C Japan 52B4
Murphy, Idaho USA 16C2
Murphy, N Carolina USA 13C1
Murphys USA 18B1
Murray, Kentucky USA 10B3
Murray, Utah USA 16D2
Murray, R Aust 78B2
Murray, R Can 3D3
Murray Bridge Aust 78A3
Murray,L PNG 49H7
Murray,L USA 13C2
Murraysburg S Africa 72C3
Murray Seacarp Pacific O 75M3
Murrhardt W Germ 34E2
Murrumbidgee, R Aust 78B2
Murrumburrah Aust 78C2
Murrurundi Aust 78D2
Murten Switz 35B1
Murtoa Aust 78B3
Murupara NZ 79C1
Murwāra India 59B3
Murwillimbah Aust 78D1
Muş Turk 62D2
Musala, Mt Bulg 39E2
Musan N Korea 51B3
Musandam, Pen Oman 65G1
Muscat = Masqat
Muscat, Region Oman 65G2
Muscatine USA 9D3
Musgrave Range, Mts Aust 76C3
Mushie Zaïre 70B4
Muskeget Chan USA 12E2
Muskegon USA 10B2
Muskegon, R USA 10B2
Muskogee USA 15C2
Muskoka,L Can 11D2
Musmar Sudan 64C3
Musoma Tanz 70D4
Mussau, I PNG 76D1
Musselshell, R USA 16E1
Mussende Angola 71B5
Mussidan France 36C2
Mustafa-Kemalpasa Turk 39F2
Mustang Nepal 59B2
Musu-dan, C N Korea 52A2
Muswelibrook Aust 78D2
Mut Egypt 67B2
Mutarara Mozam 71D5
Mutare Zim 71D5
Mutis, Mt Indon 55B4
Mutnyy Materik USSR 42K2
Mutoko Zim 71D5
Mutsamudu Comoros 71E5
Mutshatsha Zaïre 71C5
Mutsu Japan 51E3
Mutsu-wan, B Japan 51E3
Mutunópolis Brazil 27C1
Mu Us Shamo, Desert China 50B2
Muxima Angola 71B4
Muya USSR 47N4
Muyezerskiy USSR 42E3
Muyinga Burundi 70D4
Muyumba Zaïre 71C4
Muyun Kum, Desert USSR 57E1
Muzaffarābād Pak 58C2
Muzaffargarh Pak 58C2
Muzaffarpur India 59C2
Muzhi USSR 46H3
Muzlag, Mt China 57G2
Muzon,C USA 3B3
Muztagala, Mt China 57F2
Mvuma Zim 71D5
Mwanza Tanz 70D4
Mwanza Zaïre 71C4
Mweka Zaïre 70C4
Mwene Ditu Zaïre 71C4
Mwenezi Zim 71D6
Mwenga Zaïre 70C4
Mweru, L Zambia 71C4
Mwinilunga Zambia 71C5
Myanaung Burma 59E4
Myingyan Burma 59E3
Myingyao Burma 53B1
Myinmoletkat, Mt Burma 53B3
Myinmu Burma 59E3
Myitkyina Burma 59E2
Myitta Burma 53B3
Myittha Burma 59E3
Mymensingh Bang 59D3
Myojin, I Japan 48G3
Myongchon N Korea 52A2
Myonggan N Korea 52A2
Myrdal Nor 30F6
Myrdalsjökur, Mts Iceland 30B2
Myrtle Beach USA 13D2
Myrtle Creek USA 16B2
Mys Chaplino, C USSR 47U3
Mys Chelyuskin, C USSR 47M2
Mys Chukotskiy, Pt USSR 8D3
Mys Dezhneva, Pt USSR 8E2
Mysen Nor 30G7
Mysiloborz Pol 40C2
Mys Kanin Nos, C USSR 42G2
Mys Kronotskiy, C USSR 47S4
Myślenice Pol 41D3
Mys Lopatka, C USSR 47R4
Mys Navarin, C USSR 47T3
Mys Nygchigen, Pt USSR 8D2
Mys Olyutorskiy, C USSR 47T3
Mysore India 60B2
Mys Sarych, C USSR 43E7
Mys Serdtse Kamen, Pt USSR 8D2
Mys Shelagskiy, C USSR 47T2
Mys Shmidta USSR 47T3
Mys Sivuchiy, C USSR 47S4
Mys Svyatoy Nos, C USSR 42F2
Mystic USA 12E2
Mys Tyub-Karagan, Pt USSR 43J7
Mys Yelizavety, C USSR 47Q4
Mys Zhelaniya, C USSR 46H2
My Tho Viet 53D3
Mytle Point USA 16B2
Mzimba Malawi 71D5
Mzuzú Malawi 71D5

N

Naalehu Hawaiian Is 18E5
Naantali Fin 30J6
Naas Irish Rep 33B5
Nabari Japan 52C4
Naberezhnyye Chelny USSR 42J4
Nabesna, R USA 8K3
Nabeul Tunisia 69E1
Nabileque, R Brazil 27A3
Nablus Israel 63C2
Nacala Mozam 71E5
Naches USA 16B1
Nachingwea Tanz 71D5
Nacimiento, R USA 18B3
Nacimiento Res USA 18B3
Nacogdoches USA 15D3
Nacondam, I Indian O 53A3
Nacozari Mexico 19B1
Nadel, Mt W Germ 34E1
Nadi Fiji 7G2
Nadiād India 58C4
Nador Mor 37B2
Nadūshan Iran 61C2
Nadvoitsy USSR 42E3
Nadvornaya USSR 41E3
Naestved Den 40C1
Nafoora Libya 67B2
Nagahama Japan 52B4
Naga Hills Burma 59E2
Nagai Japan 52C3
Nagal, I USA 8G5
Nāgāland, State India 59D2
Nagano Japan 51D4
Nagaoka Japan 51D4
Nāgappattinam India 60B2
Nagar Parkar Pak 58C4
Nagasaki Japan 51B5
Nagashima Japan 52C4
Nagato Japan 52B4
Nāgaur India 58C3
Nāgercoil India 60B3
Nagha Kalat Pak 58B3
Nagina India 58D3
Nagold W Germ 34E2
Nagoya Japan 51D4
Nāgpur India 58D4
Nagqu China 57H2
Nagykanizsa Hung 40D3
Nagykörös Hung 41D3
Naha Japan 48F4
Nahaimo Can 6A2
Nāhan India 58D2
Nahang, R Iran 61E3
Nahanni Butte Can 4F3
Nahanni Nat Pk Can 8N3
Nahanni Range, Mts Can 8O3
Nahariya Israel 63C2
Nahar Ouassel, R Alg 69C1
Nahāvand Iran 61B2
Nahe, R W Germ 34D2
Nahpu China 50D2
Nahuel Niyeu Arg 26B4
Naikliu Indon 55B4
Naimen Qi China 50E1
Nain Can 5M4
Nā'in Iran 61C2
Naini Tai India 58D3
Nainpur India 59B3
Nairn Scot 32D3
Nairobi Kenya 70D4
Najafābād Iran 61C2
Najd, Region S Arabia 64D1
Najin N Korea 51C3
Najrān S Arabia 64D3
Naju S Korea 52A3
Nakadori-jima Japan 52A4
Nakama Japan 52B4
Nakaminato Japan 51E4
Nakamura Japan 52B4
Nakano Japan 52C3
Nakano-shima, I Japan 52B3
Nakatsu Japan 51C5
Nakatsu-gawa Japan 52C3
Nakfa Eth 64C3
Nakhichevan USSR 43H8
Nakhl Egypt 63B4
Nakhodka USSR 51C3
Nakhon Pathom Thai 53C3
Nakhon Ratchasima Thai 53C3
Nakhon Si Thammarat Thai 53C4
Nakina, British Columbia Can 3B2
Nakina, Ontario Can 5K4
Nakina, R Can 3B2
Naknek USA 8G4
Naknek L USA 8G4
Nakrek USA 4C4
Nakskov Den 30G7
Naktong, R S Korea 52A3
Nakuru Kenya 70D4
Nakusp Can 3E3
Nal'chik USSR 43G7
Nalgonda India 60B1
Nallamala Range, Mts India 60B1
Naltia, Mt Nor/Fin 42C2
Nālūt Libya 67A1
Namaacha Mozam 72E2
Namak, L Iran 46G6
Namakzar-e Shadad, Salt Flat Iran 61D2
Namangan USSR 46J5
Namapa Mozam 71D5
Namaqualand, Region S Africa 71B7
Nambour Aust 78D1
Nambucca Heads Aust 78D2
Nam Can Viet 53D4
Namcha Barwa, Mt China 57H2
Nam Co, L China 57H2
Nam Dinh Viet 53D1
Nametil Mozam 71D5
Namew L Can 3H3
Namhae-do, I S Korea 51B5
Namib Desert Namibia 72A1
Namibia, Dependency Africa 71B6
Namlea Indon 55C3
Namling China 59C2
Namo Indon 55B3
Namoi, R Aust 78C2
Nampa Can 3E2
Nampa USA 16C2
Nampala Mali 68B3
Nam Phong Thai 53C2
Namp'o N Korea 51B4
Nampula Mozam 71D5
Namsos Nor 30G6
Namton Burma 53B1
Namtsy USSR 47O3
Namtu Burma 59E3
Namu Can 3C3
Namuno Mozam 71D5
Namur Belg 34C1
Namutoni Namibia 71B5
Namwŏn S Korea 51B4
Nanaimo Can 3D4
Nanam N Korea 51B3
Nanango Aust 78D1
Nanao Japan 51D4
Nanatsu-jima, I Japan 52C3
Nanbu China 50B3
Nancha China 51B2
Nanchang China 50D4
Nanchong China 50B3
Nancowry, I Indian O 60E3
Nancy France 36D2
Nanda Devi, Mt India 59B1
Nānded India 60B1
Nandewar Range, Mts Aust 78D2
Nandurbar India 58C4
Nandyāl India 60B1
Nanga Eboko Cam 70B3
Nangahale Indon 55B4
Nanga Parbat, Mt Pak 58C1
Nangapinoh Indon 54D3
Nangatayap Indon 54D3
Nangis France 34B2
Nangnim N Korea 52A2
Nangnim Sanmaek, Mts N Korea 51B3
Nang Xian China 59D2
Nangzhou China 45G4
Nanjangūd India 60B2
Nanjing China 50D3
Nanking = Nanjing
Nankoku Japan 52B4
Nan Ling, Region China 50C4
Nanliu, R China 53D1
Nanning China 50B5
Nanortalik Greenland 5O3
Nanpan Jiang, R China 50A5
Nānpāra India 59B2
Nanping China 50D4
Nansen Sd Can 5J1
Nansio Tanz 70D4
Nantes France 36B2
Nanticoke USA 12C2
Nanton Can 3F3
Nantong China 50E3
Nantua France 35A1
Nantucket USA 12E2
Nantucket I USA 12E2
Nantucket Sd USA 12E2
Nanty Glo USA 12A2
Nanumanga, I Tuvalu 77G1
Nanumea, I Tuvalu 77G1
Nanuque Brazil 27D2
Nanyang China 50C3
Nanyang Hu, L China 50D2
Nanyuki Kenya 70D3
Naoetsu Japan 51D4
Naokot Pak 58B4
Napa USA 18A1
Napaiskak USA 8F3
Napanee Can 11D2
Napas USSR 46K4
Napassoq Greenland 5N3
Nape Laos 53D2
Napier NZ 79C1
Naples = Napoli
Naples, Florida USA 13E4
Naples, New York USA 12B1
Naples, Texas USA 15D3
Napo China 50B5
Napo, R Peru/Ecuador 24D4
Napoleon USA 9C2
Napoli Italy 38C2
Naqadeh Iran 61B1
Naqb Ishtar Jordan 63C3
Nara Japan 52C4
Nara Mali 68B3
Naracoorte Aust 76D4
Naranjos Mexico 20C1
Narasarāopet India 60B1
Narathiwat Thai 53C4
Narayanganj Bang 59D3
Nārāyenpet India 60B1
Narbonne France 36C3
Narendranagar India 58D2
Nares Str Can 5L2
Narew, R Pol 41E2
Narita Japan 52D3
Narmada, R India 58C4
Nārnaul India 58D3
Naro Fominsk USSR 42F4
Narok Kenya 70D4
Narowal Pak 58C2
Narrabri Aust 76D4
Narran, L Aust 78C1
Narran, R Aust 78C1
Narrandera Aust 78C2
Narrogin Aust 76A4
Narromine Aust 78C2
Narrows USA 10C3
Narrowsburg USA 12C2
Narsimhapur India 58D4
Narsipatnam India 60C1
Narssalik Greenland 5O3
Narssaq Greenland 5O3
Narssarssuaq Greenland 5O3
Narubis Namibia 72B2
Narugo Japan 52D3
Naruto Japan 52B4
Narva USSR 42D4
Narvik Nor 30H5
Narwāna India 58D3
Nar'yan Mar USSR 42J2
Narylico Aust 78B1
Naryn USSR 46J5
Nasarawa Nig 69H4
Nasca Ridge Pacific O 73D5
Nashua USA 12E1
Nashville, Arkansas USA 15D3
Nashville, Tennessee USA 13B1
Našice Yugos 39D1
Nāsik India 58C4
Nasir Sudan 70D3
Nass, R Can 3C2
Nassau Bahamas 21B1
Nassau USA 12D1
Nasser,L Egypt 67C2
Nassian Ivory Coast 69F4
Nässjö Sweden 30G7
Nastapoka Is Can 5L4
Nata Botswana 71C6
Natal Brazil 25L5
Natal Indon 54A2
Natal, Province S Africa 72E2
Natal Basin Indian O 74C6
Natanz Iran 61C2
Natashquan Can 5M4
Natashquan, R Can 5M4
Natchez USA 15D3
Natchitoches USA 15D3
Nathalia Aust 78C3
Nathorsts Land, Region Greenland 5Q2
Nation, R Can 3D2
National City USA 17C4
National Republic of China = Taiwan
Natitingou Benin 69G3
Natori Japan 52D3
Natovl'a USSR 41F2
Natron, L Tanz 70D4
Naturaliste,C Aust 76A4
Nauders Austria 35D1
Nauen E Germ 40C2
Naugatuck USA 12D2
Naumburg E Germ 40C2
Naur Jordan 63C3
Nauru, I Pacific O 77F1
Naushki USSR 47M4
Naute Dam, Res Namibia 72B2
Nautla Mexico 20C1
Nauzad Afghan 61E2
Navajo Res USA 6C3
Navalmoral de la Mata Spain 37A2
Navarino, I Chile 23C9
Navarra, Province Spain 37B1
Navarro Arg 26D3
Navasota USA 15C3
Navasota, R USA 15C3
Navia, R Spain 37A1
Navidad Chile 26A2
Naviraí Brazil 27B3
Navlakhi India 58C4
Navlya USSR 43E5
Navojoa Mexico 19B2
Návpaktos Greece 39E3
Návplion Greece 39E3
Navrongo Ghana 69F3
Navsāri India 58C4
Nawá Syria 63D2
Nawāda India 59C3
Nawah Afghan 58B2
Nawrabshah Pak 58B3
Naxi China 50B4
Náxos, I Greece 39F3
Nayar Mexico 20B1
Nayarit, State Mexico 20A1
Nāy Band Iran 61C3
Nay Band Iran 61D2
Nayoro Japan 51E3
Nazaré Brazil 27E1
Nazareth Israel 63C2
Nazay France 36B2
Nazca Peru 24D6
Nazilli Turk 62A2
Nazimovo USSR 47L4
Nazko, R Can 3D3
Nazwa Oman 65G2
Nazyvayevsk USSR 46J4
Ndalatando Angola 71B4
Ndélé CAR 70C3
Ndendé Gabon 70B4
Ndende, I Solomon Is 77F2
N'Djamena Chad 70B2
Ndjolé Gabon 70B4
Ndola Zambia 71C5
Ndouci Ivory Coast 69F4
Neabul Aust 78C1
Neales, R Aust 78A1
Neápolis Greece 39E3
Near Is USA 8A6
Neath Wales 33D6
Nebine, R Aust 78C1
Nebit Dag USSR 46G6
Nebraska, State USA 6C2
Nebraska City USA 15C1
Nechako, R Can 3D3
Neches, R USA 15C3
Neckar, R W Germ 34E2
Necochea Arg 26D3
Nêdong China 59D2
Needles USA 17D4
Neenah USA 10B2
Neepawra Can 4J4
Neerpelt Belg 34C1
Nefta Tunisia 69D2
Neftegorsk USSR 51E1
Neftelensk USSR 47M4
Negelli Eth 70D3
Negev, Desert Israel 63C3
Negla, R Par 27A3
Negolu, Mt Rom 43C6
Negombo Sri Lanka 60B3
Negrais,C Burma 53A2
Negritos Peru 24B4
Negro, R, Amazonas Brazil 24F4
Negro, R Arg 26C4
Negro, R, Mato Grosso de Sul Brazil 27A2
Negro, R Par 27A3
Negro, R Urug 26D2
Negros, I Phil 55F8
Negru Voda Rom 39F2
Nehbāndan Iran 61E2
Nehe China 51A2
Neijiang China 50B4
Neillsville USA 10A2
Nei Monggol, Autononous Region China 50B1

Neira *Colombia* 24C3
Nejo *Eth* 70D3
Nelidovo *USSR* 42E4
Neligh *USA* 9C3
Nellore *India* 60B2
Nel'ma *USSR* 51D2
Nelson *Can* 3E4
Nelson *NZ* 79B2
Nelson, R *Can* 5J4
Nelson,C *Aust* 78B3
Nelson I *USA* 8F3
Nelspruit *S Africa* 72E2
Néma *Maur* 68B3
Nemagt Uul, Mt *Mongolia* 50A1
Neman, R *USSR* 41E1
Neman, R *USSR* 41F2
Nemilen, R *USSR* 51D1
Nemira, Mt *Rom* 39F1
Nemor He, R *China* 51B2
Nemours *France* 34B2
Nemuro *Japan* 51F3
Nen, R *China* 47O5
Nenagh *Irish Rep* 31B3
Nenana *USA* 8J3
Nenana, R *USA* 8J3
Nene, R *Eng* 33E5
Nenggiri, R *Malay* 54F6
Nenjiang *China* 51B2
Neodesha *USA* 15C2
Neosho *USA* 15D2
Nepa *USSR* 47M4
Nepal, Kingdom *Asia* 57G3
Nepalganj *Nepal* 59B2
Nephi *USA* 17D3
Neqarot, R *Israel* 63C3
Nequén, State *Arg* 26A3
Nerchinsk *USSR* 48E1
Neretva, R *Yugos* 39D2
Nero Deep *Pacific O* 49H5
Nes' *USSR* 42G2
Neskaupstaður *Iceland* 30C1
Nesle *France* 34B2
Nesleyville *Can* 5N5
Ness City *USA* 14C2
Nesselrode,Mt *Can* 3B2
Néstos, R *Greece* 39E2
Netanya *Israel* 63C2
Netcong *USA* 12C2
Netherlands, Kingdom *Europe* 40B2
Netherlands Antilles, Is *Caribbean* 2M7
Netrakona *Bang* 59D3
Nettling L *Can* 5L3
Neubrandenburg *E Germ* 40C2
Neuchâtel *Switz* 35B1
Neufchâteau *Belg* 34C2
Neufchâteau *France* 34C2
Neufchâtel *France* 36C2
Neufchâtel-en-Bray *France* 34A2
Neumünster *W Germ* 40B2
Neunkirchen *Austria* 38D1
Neunkirchen *W Germ* 34D2
Neuquén *Arg* 26B3
Neuquén, State *Arg* 23B6
Neuquén, R *Arg* 26B3
Neuruppin *E Germ* 40C2
Neuse, R *USA* 13D1
Neuss *W Germ* 34D1
Neustadt *W Germ* 40C2
Neustadt an der Weinstrasse *W Germ* 34E2
Neustadt im Schwarzwalk *W Germ* 34E3
Neustrelitz *E Germ* 40C2
Neuwied *W Germ* 34D1
Nevada, State *USA* 6B3
Nevada *USA* 15D2
Nevada de Chillán, Mts *Chile/Arg* 26A3
Nevada de Collima *Mexico* 20B2
Nevada de Toluca, Mt *Mexico* 20C2
Nevatim *Israel* 63C3
Nevel *USSR* 42D4
Nevel'sk *USSR* 51E2
Never *USSR* 51A1
Nevers *France* 36C2
Nevertire *Aust* 78C2
Nevis, I *Caribbean* 21E3
Nevis, R *USSR* 41F2
Nevşehir *Turk* 62B2
Nev'yansk *USSR* 42L4
New, R *USA* 10C3
Newala *Tanz* 71D5
New Albany, Indiana *USA* 10B3
New Albany, Mississippi *USA* 15E3
New Amsterdam *Guyana* 25G2
New Angledool *Aust* 78C1
Newark, Delaware *USA* 11D3
Newark, New Jersey *USA* 7F2
Newark, New York *USA* 12B1
Newark, Ohio *USA* 10C2
Newark-upon-Trent *Eng* 33E5
New Bedford *USA* 11E2
New Bella Bella *Can* 3C3
Newberg *USA* 16B1
New Bern *USA* 13D1
Newberry *USA* 13C2
New Bethesda *S Africa* 72C3
New Bight *Bahamas* 21B2
New Boston *USA* 10C3
New Braunfels *USA* 14C4
New Britain *USA* 12D2
New Britain, I *PNG* 76E1
New Britain Trench *PNG* 76E1
New Brunswick, Province *Can* 5M5
New Brunswick *USA* 12C2
Newburgh *USA* 12C2
Newbury *Eng* 33E6
Newburyport *USA* 12E1
New Canaan *USA* 12D2
Newcastle *Aust* 78D2
New Castle, Indiana *USA* 10B3
Newcastle *N Ire* 33C4
New Castle, Pennsylvania *USA* 10C2
Newcastle *S Africa* 72D2
Newcastle, Wyoming *USA* 9B3
Newcastle upon Tyne *Eng* 32E4
Newcastle Waters *Aust* 76C2
New Cuyama *USA* 18C3
New Delhi *India* 58D3
New England Range, Mts *Aust* 78D2
Newenham,C *USA* 8F4
Newfane *USA* 12A1
New Forest,The *Eng* 33E6
Newfoundland, Province *Can* 5M4
Newfoundland, I *Can* 5N5
Newfoundland Basin *Atlantic O* 73F2
New Franklin *USA* 15D2
New Galloway *Scot* 32C4
New Georgia, I *Solomon Is* 77E1
New Glasgow *Can* 5M5
New Guinea, I *S E Asia* 76D1
New Haifa *Sudan* 64C3
Newhalen *USA* 8H4
Newhall *USA* 18C3
New Hampshire, State *USA* 7F2
New Hampton *USA* 9D3
New Hanover *S Africa* 72E2
New Hanover, I *PNG* 76E1
Newhaven *Eng* 33F6
New Haven *USA* 11E2
New Hazelton *Can* 3C2
New Hebrides Trench *Pacific O* 77F3
New Iberia *USA* 15D3
New Ireland, I *PNG* 76E1
New Jersey, State *USA* 7F2
Newkirk *USA* 14B3
New Liskeard *Can* 5L5
New London *USA* 12D2
Newman *Aust* 76A3
Newman *USA* 18B2
Newmarket *Eng* 33F5
New Market *USA* 11D3
New Meadows *USA* 16C2
New Mexico, State *USA* 6C3
New Milford, Connecticut *USA* 12D2
New Milford, New York *USA* 12C2
Newnan *USA* 13C2
New Norfolk *Aust* 78E3
New Orleans *USA* 7D3
New Paltz *USA* 12C2
New Philadelphia *USA* 10C2
New Plymouth *NZ* 79B1
Newport, Arkansas *USA* 15D2
Newport *Eng* 33E6
Newport, Kentucky *USA* 10C3
Newport, New Hampshire *USA* 12D1
Newport, Oregon *USA* 16B2
Newport, Pennsylvania *USA* 12B2
Newport, Rhode Island *USA* 11E2
Newport, Vermont *USA* 11E2
Newport *Wales* 33D6
Newport, Washington *USA* 16C1
Newport Beach *USA* 18D4
Newport News *USA* 7F3
New Providence, I *Caribbean* 21B1
Newquay *Eng* 33C6
New Quebe Crater *Can* 5L3
New Ross *Irish Rep* 33B5
Newry *N Ire* 33B4
New Siberian Is = Novosibirskye Ostrova
New Smyrna Beach *USA* 13C3
New South Wales, State *Aust* 76D4
New Stuyahok *USA* 8G4
Newton, Iowa *USA* 9D3
Newton, Kansas *USA* 15C2
Newton, Massachusetts *USA* 12E1
Newton, Mississippi *USA* 15E3
Newton, New York *USA* 12C2
Newton Abbot *Eng* 33D6
Newton Stewart *N Ire* 32B4
Newton Stewart *Scot* 32C4
New Town *USA* 9B2
Newtown *Wales* 33D5
Newtownards *N Ire* 33C4
New Ulm *USA* 9D3
Newville *USA* 12B2
New Westminster *Can* 4F5
New York, State *USA* 7F2
New York *USA* 7F2
New Zealand, Dominion *SW Pacific O* 77G5
New Zealand Plat *Pacific O* 75K7
Neya *USSR* 42G4
Neyriz *Iran* 61C3
Neyshābūr *Iran* 61D1
Nezeto *Angola* 71B4
Nezhin *USSR* 43E5
Ngabé *Congo* 70B4
Ngadda *Nig* 69J3
Ngami, L *Botswana* 71C6
N'Gaoundéré *Cam* 69J4
Ngaruawahia *NZ* 79C1
Ngaruroro, R *NZ* 79C1
Ngauruhoe,Mt *NZ* 79C1
Ngo *Congo* 70B4
Ngoc Linh, Mt *Viet* 53D2
Ngoko, R *Cam* 70B3
Ngoring Hu, L *China* 48C3
Ngorongoro Crater *Tanz* 70D4
N'Gounié, R *Gabon* 70B4
Nguigmi *Niger* 70B2
Ngulu, I *Pacific O* 49G6
Nguru *Nig* 69J3
Nha Trang *Viet* 53D3
Nhecolandia *Brazil* 27A2
Nhill *Aust* 78B3
Nhlangano *Swaziland* 72E2
Nhommarath *Laos* 53D2
Nhulunbuy *Aust* 76C2
Niafounké *Mali* 68B3
Niagara *USA* 10B1
Niagara Falls *Can* 11D2
Niagara Falls *USA* 11D2
Niah *Malay* 54D2
Niakaramandougou *Ivory Coast* 68B4
Niamey *Niger* 68C3
Niangara *Zaïre* 70C3
Niangoloko *U Volta* 69F3
Nia Nia *Zaïre* 70C3
Nianzishan *China* 51A2
Nias, I *Indon* 54A2
Nicaragua, Republic *C America* 19D3
Nicastro *Italy* 38D3
Nice *France* 36D3
Nicholl's Town *Bahamas* 21B1
Nicholson *USA* 12C2
Nicobar Is *Indian O* 57H5
Nicosia *Cyprus* 63B1
Nicoya,Pen de *Costa Rica* 19D3
Nidda, R *W Germ* 34E1
Nidzica *Pol* 41E2
Niederbronn *France* 34D2
Niedere Tauern, Mts *Austria* 35E1
Niedersachsen, State *W Germ* 40B2
Niemba *Zaïre* 70C4
Nienburg *W Germ* 40B2
Niers, R *W Germ* 34D1
Niete,Mt *Lib* 68B4
Nieuw Amsterdam *Suriname* 25G2
Nieuw Nickeire *Suriname* 25G2
Nieuwoudtville *S Africa* 72B3
Nieuwpoort *Belg* 34B1
Nieves *Mexico* 20B1
Niğde *Turk* 62B2
Niger, Republic *Africa* 68C3
Niger, State *Nig* 69H4
Niger, R *Nig* 69H4
Nigeria, Federal Republic *Africa* 68C4
Nighthawk L *Can* 10C1
Nigríta *Greece* 39E2
Nihommatsu *Japan* 52D3
Niigata *Japan* 51D4
Niihama *Japan* 51C5
Nii-jima, I *Japan* 52C4
Niimi *Japan* 52B4
Niitsu *Japan* 51D4
Nijil *Jordan* 63C3
Nijmegen *Neth* 40B2
Nikel' *USSR* 42E2
Nikki *Benin* 69G3
Nikko *Japan* 51D4
Nikolayev *USSR* 43E6
Nikolayevsk *USSR* 43H6
Nikolayevsk-na-Amure *USSR* 47Q4
Nikol'sk, Penza *USSR* 42H5
Nikol'sk, RSFSR *USSR* 42H4
Nikolski *USA* 8E5
Nikopol *USSR* 43E6
Niksar *Turk* 62C1
Nīkshahr *Iran* 61E3
Nikšić *Yugos* 39D2
Nikunau, I *Kiribati* 77G1
Nila, I *Indon* 55C4
Nile, R *N E Africa* 56B3
Niles *USA* 10B2
Nilgiri Hills *India* 60B2
Niltepec *Mexico* 20D2
Nimach *India* 58C4
Nîmes *France* 36C3
Nimmitabel *Aust* 78C3
Nimule *Sudan* 70D3
Nine Degree Chan *Indian O* 57F5
Ninety-East Ridge *Indian O* 74F5
Ninety Mile Beach *Aust* 78C3
Ning'an *China* 51B3
Ningde *China* 50D4
Ningdu *China* 50D4
Ningjing Shan, Mts *China* 48C3
Ningming *China* 53D1
Ningnan *China* 50A4
Ningxia, Province *China* 50B2
Ning Xian *China* 50B2
Ninh Binh *Vietnam* 50B5
Ninigo Is *PNG* 76D1
Ninilchik *USA* 8H3
Nioaque *Brazil* 27A3
Niobrara *USA* 9B3
Niobrara, R *USA* 6D2
Nioki *Zaïre* 70B4
Nioro du Sahel *Mali* 68B3
Niort *France* 36B2
Nipawin *Can* 4H4
Nipigon *Can* 5K5
Nipigon B *Can* 10B1
Nipigon,L *Can* 5K5
Nipissing, R *Can* 5K5
Nipissing,L *Can* 10C1
Nipomo *USA* 18B3
Nipton *USA* 17C3
Niquelândia *Brazil* 27C1
Nirmal *India* 60B1
Nirmāli *India* 59C2
Niš *Yugos* 39E2
Nisāb *S Yemen* 65E4
Nishinoomote *Japan* 51C5
Nishino-shima, I *Japan* 48G4
Nishino-shima, I *Japan* 52B3
Nishi-suidō, Str *S Korea* 52A4
Nishiwaki *Japan* 52B4
Nisling, R *Can* 8L3
Nissan Is *PNG* 77E1
Nisutlin, R *Can* 8M3
Nitchequon *Can* 5L4
Niterói *Brazil* 25K8
Nith, R *Scot* 32D4
Nitibe *Indon* 55B4
Nitra *Czech* 41D3
Nitro *USA* 10C3
Niue, I *Pacific O* 77J2
Niulakita, I *Tuvalu* 77G2
Niut, Mt *Malay* 54D2
Niutao, I *Tuvalu* 77G1
Nivelles *Belg* 34C1
Nivernais, Region *France* 36C2
Nivskiy *USSR* 30L5
Nizāmābād *India* 60B1
Nizana, Hist Site *Israel* 63C3
Nizhneudinsk *USSR* 48C1
Nizhniye Sergi *USSR* 42K4
Nizhniy Lomov *USSR* 42G5
Nizhniy Odes *USSR* 42J3
Nizhniy Tagil *USSR* 46G4
Nizhnyaya, R *USSR* 47L3
Nizhnyaya Zolotitsa *USSR* 42G2
Nizip *Turk* 62C2
Nizmennost *USSR* 43E6
Njoko, R *Zambia* 71C5
Njombe *Tanz* 71D4
Nkambé *Cam* 70B3
Nkawkaw *Ghana* 69F4
Nkhata Bay *Malawi* 71D5
Nkongsamba *Cam* 70B3
N'Konni *Niger* 68C3
Noakhali *Bang* 59D3
Noatak *USA* 8F2
Noatak, R *USA* 8G2
Nobeoka *Japan* 51C5
Noboribetsu *Japan* 52D2
Nobres *Brazil* 27A1
Noce, R *Italy* 35D1
Nochistlán *Mexico* 20B1
Nochixtlán *Mexico* 20C2
Nocona *USA* 15C3
Nogales, Sonora *Mexico* 19A1
Nogales *USA* 17D4
Nogales, Veracruz *Mexico* 20C2
Nogara *Italy* 35D2
Nogata *Japan* 52B4
Nogent-en-Bassigny *France* 34C2
Nogent-le-Rotrou *France* 34A2
Nogent-sur-Seine *France* 34B2
Noginsk *USSR* 42F4
Nogliki *USSR* 51E1
Nogoyá *Arg* 26D2
Nogoyá, R *Arg* 26D2
Nohar *India* 58C3
Noheji *Japan* 52D2
Nojane *Botswana* 72C1
Nojima-zaki, C *Japan* 52C4
Nok Kundi *Pak* 61E3
Nokomis L *Can* 3H2
Nola *CAR* 70B3
Nolinsk *USSR* 42H4
Nomans Land, I *USA* 12E2
Nombre de Dioz *Mexico* 20B1
Nome *USA* 8E3
Nomeny *France* 34D2
Nomgon *Mongolia* 50B1
Nomo-saki, Pt *Japan* 52A4
Nonachol L *Can* 4H3
Nong'an *China* 51B3
Nong Khai *Thai* 53C2
Nongoma *S Africa* 72E2
Nonouti, I *Kiribati* 77G1
Nonsan *S Korea* 52A3
Noordoewer *Namibia* 72B2
Noorvik *USA* 8F2
Nootka Sd *Can* 3C4
Nopala *Mexico* 20C2
Noqui *Angola* 70B4
Noranda *Can* 5L5
Nord, Department *France* 34B1
Nordaustlandet, I *Barents S* 46D2
Nordegg *Can* 3E3
Nordfjord, Inlet *Nor* 30F6
Nordfriesische, Is *W Germ* 30F8
Nordhausen *E Germ* 40C2
Nordrhein Westfalen, State *W Germ* 40B2
Nordkapp, C *Nor* 30J4
Nordre *Greenland* 5N3
Nord Stronfjället, Mt *Sweden* 30G5
Nordvik *USSR* 47N2
Nore, R *Irish Rep* 33B5
Norfolk, County *Eng* 33F5
Norfolk, Nebraska *USA* 9C3
Norfolk, Virginia *USA* 11D3
Norfolk I *Aust* 77F3
Norfolk L *USA* 15D2
Norfolk Ridge *Pacific O* 75K5
Noril'sk *USSR* 47K3
Normal *USA* 10B2
Norman *USA* 15C2
Normandie, Region *France* 36B2
Norman,L *USA* 13C1
Normanton *Aust* 76D2
Norman Wells *Can* 8N2
Norne *USA* 4B3
Norra Storfjället, Mt *Sweden* 42B2
Norris L *USA* 13C1
Norristown *USA* 11D2
Norrköping *Sweden* 30H7
Norrsundet *Sweden* 30H6
Norrtälje *Sweden* 30H7
Norseman *Aust* 76B4
Norsk *USSR* 51C1
Nortelândia *Brazil* 27A1
North, S *N W Europe* 73J2
Northallerton *Eng* 33E4
Northam *Aust* 76A4
Northam *S Africa* 72D2
North American Basin *Atlantic O* 73E3
Northampton *Aust* 76A3
Northampton, County *Eng* 33E5
Northampton *Eng* 33E5
Northampton *USA* 11E2
North Andaman, I *Indian O* 60E2
North Arm, B *Can* 4G3
North Augusta *USA* 13C2
North Aulatsvik, I *Can* 5M4
North Battleford *Can* 3G3
North Bay *Can* 5L5
North Bend *USA* 16B2
North Berwick *Scot* 32D3
North Berwick *USA* 12E1
North,C *Can* 5M5
North C *NZ* 7G4
North C *USA* 8D5
North Canadian, R *USA* 14B2
North Carolina, State *USA* 7E3
North Cascade Nat Pk *USA* 16B1
North Chan *Can* 10C1
North Chan *Ire/Scot* 32C4
North Collins *USA* 12A1
North Dakota, State *USA* 6C2
North Downs *Eng* 33F6

North Downs, Upland
  Eng 34A1
North East USA 11D2
North East Atlantic Basin
  Atlantic O 73H1
Northeast C USA 8E3
Northern Ireland UK 31B3
Northern Light L Can 9D2
Northern Range, Mts
  Trinidad 21L1
Northern Territory Aust 76C2
North Esk, R Scot 32D3
Northfield,
  Massachusetts USA 12D1
Northfield, Minnesota
  USA 9D3
North Foreland Eng 33F6
North Foreland, Pt Eng 34A1
North Fork, R USA 8H3
North I NZ 79B1
North Korea, Republic S
  E Asia 51B4
North Land = Severnaya
  Zemlya
North Little Rock USA 15D3
North Loup, R USA 9B3
North Magnetic Pole
  Can 80B4
North Miami USA 13E4
North Miami Beach USA 13E4
North Nahanni, R Can 8O3
North Palisade, Mt USA 18C2
North Platte USA 14B1
North Platte, R USA 6C2
North Pole Arctic 80A
North Pt Barbados 21Q2
North Pt USA 10C1
North Raccoon, R USA 9D3
North Rona, I Scot 31B2
North Ronaldsay, I Scot 32D2
North Saskatchewan, R
  Can 3G3
North Sea N W Europe 31D2
North Seal Can 3H2
North Sentinel Andaman
  Is 60E2
North Slope USA 8J2
North Slope, Region
  USA 4D3
North Stradbroke, I Aust 78D1
North Syracuse USA 12B1
North Taranaki Bight, B
  NZ 79B1
North Tonawanda USA 12A1
North Truchas Peak, Mt
  USA 6C3
North Uist, I Scot 32B3
Northumberland, County
  Eng 32D4
Northumberland Is Aust 76E3
Northumberland Str Can 5M5
North Vancouver Can 16B1
Northville USA 12C1
North Walsham Eng 33F5
Northway USA 8K3
North West C Aust 76A3
North West Frontier,
  Province Pak 58C2
North West River Can 5M4
North West Territories
  Can 4G3
Northwood USA 9C2
North York Moors Nat
  Pk Eng 33E4
Norton, R USA 14C2
Norton B USA 8F3
Norton Sd USA 8F3
Norvegia,C Ant 80F1
Norwalk, Connecticut
  USA 12D2
Norwalk, Ohio USA 10C2
Norway, Kingdom
  Europe 30F6
Norway House Can 4J4
Norwegian B Can 5J2
Norwegian Basin
  Norewegian S 73H1
Norwegian S N W
  Europe 46B3
Norwich, Connecticut
  USA 12D2
Norwich Eng 33F5
Norwich, New York USA 12C1
Norwood, Massachusetts
  USA 12E1
Norwood, Ohio USA 10C3
Nos Emine, C Bulg 39F2
Noshiro Japan 51D3
Nos Kaliakra, C Bulg 39F2
Nosovaya USSR 42J2
Nosovka USSR 41G2
Noss, I Scot 32E1
Nossob, R Namibia 72B1
Nostråbäd Iran 61E3
Nosy Barren, I Madag 71E5
Nosy Bé, I Madag 71E5
Nosy Boraha, I Madag 71F5
Nosy Varika Madag 71E6
Notéc, R Pol 40D2
Notikeuin Can 4G4
Noto Italy 38D3

Notodden Nor 30F7
Noto-hantō, Pen Japan 52C3
Notre Dams B Can 5N5
Nottingham, County Eng 33E5
Nottingham Eng 33E5
Nottingham, I Can 5L3
Nottingham Island Can 5L3
Notukeu Creek, R Can 9A2
Nouadhibou Maur 68A2
Nouakchott Maur 68A3
Nouméa Nouvelle
  Calédonie 77F3
Nouna U Volta 69F3
Noupoort S Africa 72C3
Nouveau Comptoir Can 5L4
Nouvelle Anvers Zaïre 70B3
Nouvelle Calédonie, I S
  W Pacific O 77F3
Nova América Brazil 27C2
Nova Caipemba Angola 71B4
Nova Chaves Angola 71C5
Nova Esparança Brazil 27B3
Nova Friburgo Brazil 27D3
Nova Gaia Angola 71B5
Nova Granada Brazil 27C3
Nova Herizonte Brazil 27C3
Nova Lima Brazil 27D3
Nova Lisboa = Huambo
Nova Londrina Brazil 27B3
Nova Mambone Mozam 71D6
Novara Italy 35C2
Nova Roma Brazil 27C1
Nova Sagres Indon 55C4
Nova Scotia, Province
  Can 5M5
Novato USA 18A1
Nova Venécia Brazil 27D2
Novaya Kakhovka USSR 43E6
Novaya Zemlya, I
  Barents S 46G2
Nova Zagora Bulg 39F2
Nove Russas Brazil 25K4
Nové Zámky Czech 39D1
Novgorod USSR 42E4
Novigrad Yugos 35E2
Novikovo USSR 51E2
Novi Ligure Italy 35C2
Novillero Mexico 20A1
Novi Pazar Bulg 39F2
Novi Pazar Yugos 39E2
Novi Sad Yugos 39D1
Novoalekseyevka USSR 43K5
Novoanninskiy USSR 43G5
Novobureyskiy USSR 51C2
Novocherkassk USSR 43F6
Novodvinsk USSR 42G3
Novograd Volynskiy
  USSR 43D5
Novogrudok USSR 41F2
Novo Hamburgo Brazil 26E1
Novokazalinsk USSR 46H5
Novokuznetsk USSR 46K4
Novolazarevskaya, Base
  Ant 80F12
Novo Mesto Yugos 38D1
Novomirgorod USSR 41G3
Novomoskovsk USSR 42F5
Novo Redondo Angola 71B5
Novorossiysk USSR 43F7
Novorybnoye USSR 47M2
Novosibirsk USSR 46K4
Novosibirskye Ostrova, I
  USSR 47P2
Novotroitsk USSR 43K5
Ntvo Uzensk USSR 43H5
Novovolynsk USSR 41E2
Novo Vyatsk USSR 42H4
Novozybkov USSR 43E5
Novvy Port USSR 46J3
Novy Dwór Mazowiecki
  Pol 41E2
Novyy Lyalya USSR 42L4
Novyy Port USSR 42N2
Novyy Uzem USSR 43J7
Nowa Sól Pol 40D2
Nowata USA 15C2
Nowgong India 59D2
Nowitna, R USA 8H3
Nowra Aust 78D2
Now Shahr Iran 61C1
Nowshera Pak 58C2
Nowy Sącz Pol 41E3
Noyes I USA 8M4
Noyon France 34B2
Nsawam Ghana 69F4
Nsukka Nig 69H4
Nuanetsi Zim 72E1
Nuanetsi, R Zim 72E1
Nuatja Togo 69G4
Nuba, Mts Sudan 70D2
Nubian Desert Sudan 64B2
Nuble, R Chile 26A3
Nueces, R USA 6D4
Nueltin L Can 4J3
Nueva Casas Grandes
  Mexico 19B1
Nueva Germania Par 27A3
Nueva Gerona Cuba 21A2
Nueva Imperial Chile 26A3
Nueva Laredo Mexico 6C4
Nueva Palmira Urug 26D2

Nueva Rosita Mexico 19B2
Nuevitas Cuba 21B2
Nuevo, State Mexico 20B1
Nuevo Casas Grandes
  Mexico 19B1
Nuevo Ideal Mexico 20A1
Nuevo Laredo Mexico 19C2
Nugaal, Region Somalia 67D4
Nûgâtsiaq Greenland 5N2
Nugssuag, Pen
  Greenland 5N2
Nûgussuag, I Greenland 5N2
Nui, I Tuvalu 77G1
Nui Con Voi, R Vietnam 50A5
Nuits France 34C3
Nu Jiang, R China 59E2
Nukey Bluff, Mt Aust 78A2
Nukhayb Iraq 62D3
Nukufetau, I Tuvalu 77G1
Nukulaelae, I Tuvalu 77G1
Nukunon, I Tokelau Is 77H1
Nukus USSR 46G5
Nulato USA 8G3
Nullarbor Plain Aust 76B4
Numan Nig 69J4
Numata Japan 52C3
Numatinna, R Sudan 70C3
Numazu Japan 51D4
Numfoor, I Indon 49G7
Numurkah Aust 78C3
Nunapitchuk USA 8F3
Nunda USA 12A1
Nunivak I USA 8E3
Nunkun, Mt India 58D2
Nunligran USSR 8C3
Nuomin He, R China 51A1
Nuoro Sardegna 38B2
Nurābād Iran 61C2
Nure, R Italy 35C2
Nuriootpa Aust 78A2
Nuristan, Upland Afghan 58C1
Nurlat USSR 42J5
Nurmes Fin 30K6
Nürnberg W Germ 40C3
Nurri,Mt Aust 78C2
Nusa Tenggara, Is Indon 54E4
Nusa Tenggara Timor,
  Province Indon 55B4
Nusaybin Turk 62D2
Nushagak, R USA 8G4
Nushagak B USA 8G4
Nushagak Pen USA 8G4
Nushki Pak 58B3
Nutak Can 5M4
Nutzotin Mts USA 8K3
Nuwakot Nepal 59B2
Nuwara-Eliya Sri Lanka 60C3
Nuweveldreeks, Mts S
  Africa 72C3
Nuyukjuak Can 5L3
Nyack USA 12D2
Nyahururu Falls Kenya 70D3
Nyah West Aust 78B3
Nyai S Africa 4C3
Nyaingentanglha Shan,
  Mts China 48C3
Nyakabindi Tanz 70D4
Nyaksimvol' USSR 42L3
Nyala Sudan 70C2
Nyalam China 59C2
Nyamlell Sudan 70C3
Nyanda Zim 71D6
Nyandoma USSR 42G3
Nyanga, R Gabon 70B4
Nyang Qu China 59D2
Nyasa,L Malawi 66H9
Nyasa L Malawi/Mozam 71D5
Nyaunglebin Burma 53B2
Nyazepetrovsk USSR 42K4
Nyborg Den 30G7
Nybro Sweden 30H7
Nyda USSR 46J3
Nyeboes Land, Region
  Can 5M1
Nyeri Kenya 70D4
Nyimba Zambia 71D5
Nyingchi China 57H2
Nyíregyháza Hung 41E3
Nyiru,Mt Kenya 70D3
Nykarleby Fin 30J6
Nykøbing Den 30F7
Nykøbing Den 30G8
Nyköping Sweden 30H7
Nyl, R S Africa 72D1
Nylstroom S Africa 72D1
Nymagee Aust 78C2
Nynäshamn Sweden 30H7
Nyngan Aust 78C2
Nyon Switz 35B1
Nyong, R Cam 70B3
Nyongwol S Korea 52A3
Nyongwon N Korea 52A3
Nyons France 36D3
Nysa Pol 40D2
Nysh USSR 51E1
Nyssa USA 16C2
Nyukhcha USSR 42H3
Nyukzha, R USSR 48F1
Nyurba USSR 47N3

Nzega Tanz 70D4
Nzérékore Guinea 68B4
Nzi, R Ivory Coast 69F4

O

Oacoma USA 9C3
Oaggsimiut Greenland 5O3
Oahe,L USA 9B3
Oahe Res USA 6C2
Oahu, I Hawaiian Is 18E5
Oakbank Aust 78B2
Oakdale USA 18B2
Oakes USA 9C2
Oakey Aust 78D1
Oakland, California USA 17B3
Oakland, Nebraska USA 9C3
Oakland, Oregon USA 16B2
Oakland City USA 10B3
Oak Lawn USA 10B2
Oakley, California USA 18B2
Oakley, Kansas USA 14B2
Oak Ridge USA 13C1
Oakridge USA 16B2
Oakville Can 11D2
Oamaru NZ 79B3
Oasis, California USA 18D2
Oasis, Nevada USA 16D2
Oates Land, Region Ant 80F7
Oatlands Aust 78E3
Oaxaca Mexico 20C2
Oaxaca, State Mexico 20C2
Ob', R USSR 46J3
Obama Japan 52C3
Oban NZ 79A3
Oban Scot 32C3
Obanazawa Japan 52D3
Oban Hills Nig 69H4
Obeh Afghan 61E2
Oberammergau W Germ 35D1
Oberdrauburg Austria 35E1
Oberhausen W Germ 34D1
Oberlin USA 14B2
Obernburg W Germ 34E2
Oberstdorf W Germ 35D1
Obervellach Austria 35E1
Obi, I Indon 55C3
Obidos Brazil 25G4
Obihiro Japan 51E3
Obluch'ye USSR 51C2
Obo CAR 70C3
Obock Djibouti 70E2
Oborniki Pol 40D2
Oboyan USSR 43F5
O'Brien USA 16B2
Obshchiy Syrt, Mts
  USSR 43J5
Obskava Guba, B USSR 46J2
Obuasi Ghana 69F4
Ocala USA 13C3
Ocampo Mexico 20C1
Ocana Colombia 24D2
Ocaño Spain 37B2
Ocean C USA 8L4
Ocean City, Maryland
  USA 11D3
Ocean City, New Jersey
  USA 12C3
Ocean Falls Can 4F4
Ocean I = Banaba
Oceano USA 18B3
Oceanside USA 18D4
Ocean Springs USA 15E3
Ocher USSR 42J4
Ochil Hills Scot 32D3
Ochlockonee, R USA 13C2
Ocho Rios Jamaica 21H1
Ocmulgee, R USA 13C2
Oconee, R USA 13C2
Oconto USA 10B2
Ocotlán, Jalisco Mexico 20B1
Ocotlán, Oaxaca Mexico 20C2
Ocozocoautla Mexico 20D2
Oda Japan 69F4
Oda Japan 52B3
Ōdaejin N Korea 52A2
Ōðáðahraun, Region
  Iceland 30B2
Odate Japan 51E3
Odawara Japan 51D4
Odda Nor 30F6
Odem USA 15F4
Odemira Port 37A2
Ödemiş Turk 39F3
Odendaalsrus S Africa 72D2
Odense Den 30G7
Odenwald, Region W
  Germ 34E2
Oder, R Pol/E Germ 40C2
Oderzo Italy 35E2
Odessa, Texas USA 14B3
Odessa USSR 43E6
Odessa, Washington
  USA 16C1
Odienné Ivory Coast 68B4
Odra = Oder
Odra, R Pol 41D2
Oeiras Brazil 25K5
Oelrichs USA 9B3
Oelwein USA 9D3
Ofanto, R Italy 38D2

Ofaqim Israel 63C3
Offa Nig 69G4
Offaly, County Irish Rep 33B5
Offenbach W Germ 34E1
Offenburg W Germ 34D2
Ofunato Japan 52D3
Oga Japan 51D4
Ogaden, Region Eth 70E3
Ogaki Japan 51D4
Ogallala USA 14B1
Ogasawara Gunto, Is
  Japan 48H4
Ogbomosho Nig 69G4
Ogden, Iowa USA 9D3
Ogden, Utah USA 16D2
Ogden, Mt USA 3B2
Ogdensburg USA 11D2
Ogeechee, R USA 13C2
Ogilvie Can 8L2
Ogilvie Mts Can 4E3
Oglethorpe,Mt USA 13C2
Oglio, R Italy 35D2
Ognon, R France 35B1
Ogoja Nig 69H4
Ogoouê, R Gabon 70A4
Ogou, R Togo 69G4
Ogre USSR 41E1
Oguilet Khenachich, Well
  Mali 68B2
Ogulin Yugos 38D1
Ogun, State Nig 69G4
Ogunquit USA 12E1
Ohai NZ 79A3
Ohakune NZ 79C1
Ohata Japan 52D2
Ohau,L NZ 79A2
Ohio, State USA 7E2
Ohio, R USA 10B3
Ohm, R W Germ 34E1
Ohopoho Namibia 71B5
Ohre, R Czech 40C2
Ohrid Yugos 39E2
Ohridsko Jezero, L
  Yugos/Alb 39E2
Ohura NZ 79B1
Oiapoque French Guiana 25H3
Oijiaojing China 48C2
Oil City USA 11D2
Oildale USA 18C3
Oilian Shan, Mts China 47L6
Oise, Department France 34B2
Oise, R France 36C2
Oita Japan 51C5
Ojai USA 18C3
Ojinaga Mexico 19B2
Ojitlán Mexico 20C2
Ojiya Japan 52C3
Ojocaliente Mexico 20B1
Ojos del Salado, Mt Arg 23C3
Ojueloz Mexico 20B1
Oka, R USSR 42F5
Okahandja Namibia 72B1
Okanagan Falls Can 16C1
Okanagan L Can 3E3
Okanogan USA 16C1
Okanogan, R USA 16C1
Okanogan Range, Mts
  Can/USA 16B1
Okara Pak 58C2
Okasise Namibia 72B1
Okavango, R Namibia/
  Angola 71B5
Okavango Delta, Marsh
  Botswana 71C5
Okaya Japan 51D4
Okayama Japan 51C5
Okazaki Japan 52C4
Okeechobee USA 13E4
Okeechobee,L USA 13E4
Okefenokee Swamp
  USA 13C2
Okene Nig 69H4
Okha India 58B4
Okha USSR 51E1
Okhaldunga Nepal 59C2
Okhotsk USSR 47Q4
Okhotsk,S of =
  Okhotskoye More
Okinawa, I Japan 48F4
Okinawa gunto, Arch
  Japan 48F4
Oki-shoto, Is Japan 51C4
Okitipupa Nig 69G4
Oklahoma, State USA 6D3
Oklahoma City USA 15C2
Okmulgee USA 15C2
Okombahe Namibia 72B1
Okondja Gabon 70B4
Okoppe Japan 52D2
Okoyo Congo 70B4
Okpara, R Nig 69G4
Okstinden, Mt Nor 42A2
Oktyndan USSR 43K6
Oktyabr'sk USSR 43K6
Oktyabr'skiy, Amurskaya
  USSR 51B1
Oktyabr'skiy,
  Bashkirskaya USSR 42J5
Oktyabr'skiy, Kamchatka
  USSR 48J1
Oktyabr'skoye USSR 42M3

Okushiri-tō, I Japan 51D3
Okwa, R Botswana 72C1
Olafsvik Iceland 30A2
Olancha USA 18D2
Olanch Peak, Mt USA 18C2
Öland, I Sweden 30H7
Olary Aust 78B2
Olathe USA 15D2
Olavarría Arg 23D5
Olbia Sardegna 38B2
Olcott USA 12A1
Old Crow Can 8L2
Oldenburg, Niedersachsen W Germ 40B2
Oldenburg, Schleswig-Holstein W Germ 40C2
Old Forge USA 12C2
Oldham Eng 33D5
Old Harbor USA 8H4
Old Head of Kinsale, C Scot 31B3
Old Lyme USA 12D2
Olds Can 3F3
Old Town USA 11F2
Old Wives L Can 3G3
Olean USA 12A1
Olekma, R USSR 47O4
Olekminsk USSR 47N3
Olenegorsk USSR 42E2
Olenek USSR 47N3
Olenek, R USSR 47O2
Olevsk USSR 41F2
Ol'ga USSR 51D3
Olifants, R, Cape Province S Africa 72C3
Olifants, R Namibia 72B1
Olifants, R, Transvaal S Africa 72E1
Olifantshoek S Africa 72C2
Olimar, R Urug 26E2
Ólimbos, Mt Greece 39E2
Olímpia Brazil 27C3
Olinala Mexico 20C2
Olinda Brazil 25M5
Oliva Arg 26C2
Olivares, Mt Arg 23C4
Oliveira Brazil 27D3
Oliver Can 3E4
Oliver L Can 3H2
Olivia USA 9D3
Ollagüe Chile 23C2
Ollague Chile 24E8
Ollagüe, Mt Bol 23C2
Olney, Illinois USA 10B3
Olney, Texas USA 14C3
Olochi USSR 48F1
Olofstrom Sweden 30G7
Olombo Congo 70B4
Olomouc Czech 40D3
Olonets USSR 42E3
Olongapa Phil 55F8
Oloron ste Marie France 36B3
Olovyannaya USSR 48E1
Olpe W Germ 34D1
Olsztyn Pol 41E2
Olten Switz 35B1
Oltul, R Rom 39E2
Olympia USA 16B1
Olympic Nat Pk USA 16B1
Olympus = Ólimbos
Olympus,Mt Cyprus 63B1
Olympus,Mt USA 16B1
Omachi Japan 52C3
Omae-zaki, C Japan 52C4
Omagh N Ire 32B4
Omaha USA 15C1
Omak USA 16C1
Oman, Sultanate Arabian Pen 65G2
Oman,G of UAE 65G2
Omaruru Namibia 72B1
Omaruru, R Namibia 72A1
Oma-saki, C Japan 52D2
Omboué Gabon 70A4
Omdurman Sudan 70D2
Ometepec Mexico 20C2
Ominato Japan 52D2
Omineca, R Can 3C2
Omineca Mts Can 3C2
Omiya Japan 52C3
Ommaney,C USA 8M4
Ommanney B Can 4H2
Omo, R Eth 70D3
Omoku Nig 69H4
Omolay, R USSR 47P3
Omolon, R USSR 47R3
Omono, R Japan 52D3
Omsk USSR 46J4
Omu Japan 52D2
Omura Japan 51B5
Omuramba Eiseb, R Botswana 72C1
Omuta Japan 51C5
Omutninsk USSR 42J4
Onalaska USA 10A2
Onancock USA 11D3
Onang Indon 55A3
Onaping L Can 10C1
Onawa USA 9C3
Oncócua Angola 71B5
Ondangua Namibia 71B5
Ondava, R Czech 41E3
Ondo Nig 69G4
Ondo, State Nig 69G4
Öndörhaan Mongolia 48E2
One and Half Degree Chan Indian O 57F5
Onega USSR 46E3
Onega, R USSR 42F3
Oneida USA 12C1
Oneida L USA 12B1
O'Neill USA 9C3
Onekotan, I USSR 48J2
Onema Zaïre 70C4
Oneonta USA 12C1
Onezhskaya Guba, B USSR 42F2
Onezhskoye Ozero, L USSR 46E3
Ongers, R S Africa 72C3
Ongiva Angola 71B5
Ongjin N Korea 51B4
Ongniud Qi China 50D1
Ongole India 60C1
Onieda L USA 11D2
Onilahy, R Madag 71E6
Onitsha Nig 69H4
Onjüül Mongolia 48D2
Ono Japan 52C3
Onohara-jima, I Japan 52C4
Onomichi Japan 51C5
Onotoa, I Kiribati 77G1
Onslow Aust 76A3
Onslow B USA 13D2
Ontake-san, Mt Japan 52C3
Ontario, California USA 18D3
Ontario, Oregon USA 16C2
Ontario, Province Can 5J4
Ontario,L USA/Can 11D2
Onteniente Spain 37B2
Ontong Java Atoll Solomon Is 77E1
Onyang S Korea 52A3
Onyx USA 18C3
Oodnadatta Aust 76C3
Ooldea Aust 76C4
Oologah L USA 15C2
Oostende Belg 34B1
Oosterschelde, Estuary Neth 34B1
Ootacamund India 60B2
Ootsa L Can 3C3
Opal Mexico 20B1
Opala USSR 47R4
Opala Zaïre 70C4
Opanake Sri Lanka 60C3
Oparino USSR 42H4
Opava Czech 41D3
Opelika USA 13B2
Opelousas USA 15D3
Opheim USA 9A2
Ophir USA 8G3
Opochka USSR 41F1
Opole Pol 41D2
Oporto = Porto
Opotiki NZ 79C1
Opp USA 13B2
Oppdal Nor 30F6
Opunake NZ 79B1
Oradea Rom 39E1
Oraefajökull, Mts Iceland 30B2
Orai India 58D3
Oran Alg 69B1
Orán Arg 23D2
Orán Arg 24F8
Orang N Korea 52A2
Orange Aust 78C2
Orange, California USA 18D4
Orange France 36C3
Orange, Texas USA 15D3
Orange, R S Africa 72B2
Orangeburg USA 13C2
Orange City USA 9C3
Orange Free State, Province S Africa 72D2
Orange Park USA 13C2
Orangeville Can 10C2
Oranienburg E Germ 40C2
Oranje, R S Africa 72C2
Oranjemund Namibia 72B2
Orapa Botswana 72D1
Oras Phil 55G8
Orăştie Rom 39E1
Oravita Rom 39E1
Orbetello Italy 38C2
Orbisonia USA 12B2
Orbost Aust 78C3
Orchies France 34B1
Orco, R Italy 35B2
Orcutt USA 18B3
Ord USA 9C3
Ord, R Aust 76B2
Orderville USA 17D3
Ord,Mt Aust 76B2
Ordos, Desert China 47M6
Ordu Turk 62C1
Ordway USA 14B2
Ordzhonikidze USSR 43G7
Örebro Sweden 30H7
Oregon, State USA 6A2
Oregon USA 10C2
Oregon City USA 16B1
Oregrund Sweden 30H6
Orekhovo Zuyevo USSR 42F4
Orel USSR 43F5
Orem USA 17D2
Orenburg USSR 43J5
Orense Arg 26D3
Orense Spain 37A1
Oresund, Str Den/Sweden 40C1
Oreti, R NZ 79A3
Orgeyev USSR 41F3
Orhaneli, R Turk 39F3
Orhon Gol, R Mongolia 48D2
Oriental Mexico 20C2
Orientos Aust 78B1
Orihuela Spain 37B2
Orillia Can 11D2
Orinoco, R Ven 24F2
Oriskany Falls USA 12C1
Orissa, State India 59B3
Oristano Sardegna 38B3
Orivesi, L Fin 30K6
Oriximina Brazil 25G4
Orizaba Mexico 20C2
Orizona Brazil 27C2
Orkney, I Scot 32D2
Orlândia Brazil 27C3
Orlando USA 13C3
Orléanais, Region France 36C2
Orléans France 36C2
Orleans USA 12E2
Orlik USSR 47L4
Ormara Pak 61E3
Ormea Italy 35B2
Ormoc Phil 55F8
Ormond Beach USA 13C3
Ornain, R France 34C2
Ornans France 35B1
Orne, R France 36B2
Örnsköldsvik Sweden 30H6
Oro N Korea 52A2
Orocué Colombia 24D3
Orofino USA 16C1
Oron Israel 63C3
Orontes = 'Āşī
Oroqen Zizhiqi China 51A1
Oroquieta Phil 55F9
Orosháza Hung 41E3
Orotukan USSR 47R3
Oroville, California USA 17B3
Oroville, Washington USA 16C1
Ørsba Nor 30F6
Orsha USSR 41G2
Orsières Switz 35B1
Orsk USSR 46G4
Orthez France 36B3
Ortigueira Spain 37A1
Ortles, Mts Italy 35D1
Ortles, Mt Italy 36E2
Ortoire, R Trinidad 21L1
Ortonville USA 9C2
Oruro Bol 24E7
Osa USSR 42K4
Osage, Iowa USA 9D3
Osage, Wyoming USA 9B3
Osage, R USA 15D2
Osaka Japan 52C3
Osa,Pen de Costa Rica 19D4
Osbrov Stolbovoy, I USSR 47P2
Osceola, Arkansas USA 15E2
Osceola, Iowa USA 15D1
Osgood Mts USA 16C2
Oshamambe Japan 52D2
Oshawa Can 11D2
Ō-shima, I Japan 52C2
Ō-shima, I Japan 52C4
Oshkosh, Nebraska USA 14B1
Oshkosh, Wisconsin USA 10B2
Oshnoviyeh Iran 43H8
Oshogbo Nig 69G4
Oshosh USA 5K5
Oshwe Zaïre 70B4
Osijek Yugos 39D1
Osimo Italy 35E3
Osinniki USSR 46K5
Osipovichi USSR 41F2
Oskaloosa USA 15D1
Oskarshamn Sweden 42B4
Oslo Nor 30G6
Osmaniye Turk 62C2
Osnabrück W Germ 40B2
Osório Brazil 23F3
Osorno Chile 23B6
Osorno Spain 37B1
Osoyoos Can 16C1
Ospika, R Can 3D2
Ossa,Mt Aust 76D5
Ossé, R Nig 69H4
Osseo USA 10A2
Ossiacher See, L Austria 35E1
Ossining USA 12D2
Ossora USSR 47S4
Ostashkov USSR 42E4
Ostend = Oostende
Østerdalen, V Nor 30G6
Östersund Sweden 30G6
Östhammär Sweden 30H6
Ostia Italy 38C2
Ostiglia Italy 35D2
Ostrava Czech 41D3
Ostróda Pol 41D2
Ostroleka Pol 41E2
Ostrov USSR 42D4
Ostrova De-Longa, I USSR 47R2
Ostrova Petra, I USSR 47N2
Ostrov Arakamchechen, I USSR 8D3
Ostrov Balyy, I USSR 46J2
Ostrov Begicheva, I USSR 47N2
Ostrov Bel'kovskiy, I USSR 47P2
Ostrov Bennetta, I USSR 47R2
Ostrov Beringa, I USSR 47S4
Ostrov Bolshavik, I USSR 47M2
Ostrov Bol'shoy Lyakhovskiy, I USSR 47Q2
Ostrov Dolgiy, I USSR 42K2
Ostrov Faddeyevskiy, I USSR 47Q2
Ostrov Green Bell, I Barents S 46H1
Ostrov Hurup, I USSR 47Q5
Ostrov Iturup, I USSR 51F3
Ostrov Karaginskiy, I USSR 47S4
Ostrov Kolguyev, I USSR 42H2
Ostrov Komsomolets, I USSR 47L1
Ostrov Kotel'nyy, I USSR 47P2
Ostrov Kunashir, I USSR 51F3
Ostrov Malyy Lyalchovskiy, I USSR 47Q2
Ostrov Malyy Taymyr, I USSR 47M2
Ostrov Mechdusharskiy, I Barents S 46G2
Ostrov Mednyy, I USSR 47S4
Ostrov Novaya Sibir, I USSR 47R2
Ostrov Ogurchinskiy, I USSR 43J8
Ostrov Oktyabrskay Revolyutsii, I USSR 47L2
Ostrov Paramushir, I USSR 47R4
Ostrov Pioner, I USSR 47K2
Ostrov Rudol'fa, I Barents S 46G1
Ostrov Russkiy, I USSR 47L2
Ostrov Shmidta, I USSR 47L1
Ostrov Urup, I USSR 47Q5
Ostrov Ushakova, I USSR 46J1
Ostrov Vaygach, I USSR 46G2
Ostrov Vrangelya, I USSR 47T2
Ostrów Pol 41D2
Ostrowiec Pol 41E2
Ostrów Mazowiecka Pol 41E2
Ōsumi-kaikyō, Str Japan 51C5
Ōsumi-shotō, Is Japan 51C5
Osuna Spain 37A2
Oswego USA 11D2
Oswego USA 12B1
Oswego, R USA 12B1
Oswestry Eng 33D5
Oświęcim Pol 41D3
Ota Japan 52C3
Otago Pen NZ 79B3
Otaki NZ 79C2
Otaru Japan 51E3
Otavalo Ecuador 24C3
Otavi Namibia 71B5
Otawara Japan 52D3
Otego USA 12C1
Othello USA 16C1
Otherside, R Can 3G2
Óthris, Mt Greece 39E3
Oti, R Ghana 69G4
Otiki, R Nig 69G4
Otis, Colorado USA 14B1
Otis, Massachusetts USA 12D1
Otish Mts Can 7F1
Otisville USA 12C2
Otjimbingwe Namibia 72B1
Otjiwarongo Namibia 71B6
Otog Qi China 50B2
Otoineppu Japan 52D2
Otorohanga NZ 79C1
Otranto Italy 39D2
Otranto,Str of, Chan Italy/Alb 39D2
Otsego USA 10B2
Otsego L USA 12C1
Otsu Japan 52C3
Otta Nor 30F6
Otta, R Nor 30F7
Ottawa Can 11D1
Ottawa, Illinois USA 10B2
Ottawa, Kansas USA 15C2
Ottawa, R Can 11D1
Ottawa Is Can 5K4
Otter Rapids Can 5K4
Otto Fjord Can 5K1
Ottosdal S Africa 72D2
Ottumwa USA 10A2
Ottweiler W Germ 34D2
Otukpa Nig 69H4
Oturkpo Nig 69H4
Otusco Peru 24C5
Otway,C Aust 78B3
Otwock Pol 41E2
Ötz Austria 35D1
Otzal, Mts Austria 35D1
Ou, R Laos 53C1
Ouachita, R USA 15D3
Ouachita,L USA 15D3
Ouachita Mts USA 15D3
Ouadane Maur 68A2
Ouadda CAR 70C3
Ouaddai, Desert Region Chad 70C2
Ouagadougou U Volta 69F3
Ouahigouya U Volta 69F3
Ouaka CAR 70C3
Oualam Niger 68C3
Oualé, R U Volta 69G3
Ouallen Alg 68C2
Ouanda Djallé CAR 70C3
Ouanne, R France 34B3
Ouarane, Region Maur 68A2
Ouargla Alg 68C1
Ouarra, R CAR 70C3
Ouarzazate Mor 68B1
Ouassel, R Alg 37C2
Oubangui, R Congo 70B3
Oudenaarde Belg 34B1
Oudtshoorn S Africa 72C3
Oued Tlělat Alg 37B2
Oued Zem Mor 69A2
Ouellé Ivory Coast 69F4
Ouesso Congo 70B3
Ouezzane Mor 69A2
Ouham, R Chad 70B3
Ouidah Benin 69G4
Oujda Mor 69B2
Oulainen Fin 30J6
Oulu Fin 30K5
Oulu, R Fin 30K6
Oulujärvi, L Fin 30K6
Oum Chalouba Chad 70C2
Oum el Bouaghi Alg 69D1
Oumer Rbia, R Mor 69A2
Oum Hadjer Chad 70B2
Oum Haouach, Watercourse Chad 70C2
Ounas, R Fin 30K5
Ounasjoki, R Fin 42C2
Ounastunturi, Mt Fin 42C2
Ounianga Kebir Chad 70C2
Our, R W Germ 34D1
Ouray USA 14A2
Ource, R France 34C2
Ouricurí Brazil 25K5
Ourig, R France 34B2
Ourinhos Brazil 27C3
Ouro Prêto Brazil 27D3
Ourthe, R Belg 34C1
Ouse, R Eng 33E4
Ouse, R Eng 33F5
Outer Hebrides, Is Is 31B2
Outer Santa Barbara, Chan USA 18C4
Outjo Namibia 71B6
Outlook Can 3G3
Outokumpu Fin 30K6
Ouvèze, R France 35A2
Ouyen Aust 78B3
Ovada Italy 35C2
Ovalle Chile 26A2
Ovamboland, Region Namibia 71B5
Ova Solovetskiye, I USSR 42F2
Ova Tyuleni, Is USSR 43J7
Overton USA 17D3
Övertorneå Sweden 30J5
Ovid, Colorado USA 14B1
Ovid, New York USA 12B1
Oviedo Spain 37A1
Ovruch USSR 43D5
Ovsyanka USSR 47O4
Owaka NZ 79A3
Owasco L USA 12B1
Owase Japan 52C4
Owatonna USA 9D3
Owego USA 12B1
Owens, R USA 18C2
Owensboro USA 10B3
Owens L USA 18D2
Owen Sound Can 10C2
Owen Stanley Range, Mts PNG 76D1
Owerri Nig 69H4
Owl Creek Mts, Mts USA 16E2
Owo Nig 69H4
Owosso USA 10C2
Owyhee USA 16C2
Owyhee, R USA 16C2
Owyhee Mts USA 16C2
Oxampampa Peru 24C6
Oxbow Can 3H4
Oxelösund Sweden 30H7
Oxford, County Eng 33E6
Oxford Eng 33E5

Oxford, Massachusetts *USA* 12E1
Oxford, Mississippi *USA* 15E3
Oxford, New York *USA* 12C1
Oxnard *USA* 18C3
Oyama *Japan* 51D4
Oyen *Can* 3F3
Oyen *Gabon* 70B3
Oykel, R *Scot* 32C3
Oymyakon *USSR* 47Q3
Oyo *Nig* 69G4
Oyonnax *France* 35A1
Øyre *Nor* 30F6
Oyster B *Aust* 78E3
Ozamiz *Phil* 55F9
Ozarichi *USSR* 41F2
Ozark *USA* 13B2
Ozark Plat *USA* 15D2
Ozarks,L of the *USA* 15D2
Ózd *Hung* 41E3
Ozero Alakol, L *USSR* 46K5
Ozero Balkhash, L *USSR* 46J5
Ozero Baykal, L *USSR* 47M4
Ozero Bolon, L *USSR* 51D2
Ozero Bol'shoye Kizi, L *USSR* 51E1
Ozero Chany, L *USSR* 46J4
Ozero Chiya, L *USSR* 51E1
Ozero Chudskoye, L *USSR* 42D4
Ozero Chukchagirskoye, L *USSR* 51D1
Ozero Evoron, L *USSR* 47P4
Ozero Il'men, L *USSR* 42E4
Ozero Imandra, L *USSR* 30L5
Ozero Issyk Kul', L *USSR* 57F1
Ozero Khanka, L *USSR/China* 51C3
Ozero Kovdozero, L *USSR* 30L5
Ozero Kuyto, L *USSR* 42E2
Ozero Onezhskoye, L *USSR* 42F3
Ozero Orel', L *USSR* 51D1
Ozero Pyaozero, L *USSR* 42E2
Ozero Sevan, L *USSR* 43H7
Ozero Taymyr, L *USSR* 47M2
Ozero Tengiz, L *USSR* 46H4
Ozero Topozero, L *USSR* 42E2
Ozero Udyl', L *USSR* 51D1
Ozero Vygozero, L *USSR* 42F3
Ozero Zaysan *USSR* 46K5
Ozerskiy *USSR* 51E2
Ozona *USA* 14B3
Ozuluama *Mexico* 20C1

P

Paarl *S Africa* 72B3
Pabbay, I *Scot* 32B3
Pabianice *Pol* 41D2
Pabna *Bang* 59C3
Pabrade *USSR* 41F2
Pacasmayo *Peru* 24C5
Pacheca *Brazil* 26E2
Pacheco *Mexico* 20B1
Pachuca *Mexico* 20C1
Pacific *USA* 18B1
Pacific-Antarctic Ridge *Pacific O* 75N7
Pacific Grove *USA* 18B2
Pacific O 75G8
Pacitan *Indon* 54D4
Pacuí, R *Brazil* 27D2
Padang *Indon* 54B3
Padang *Indon* 55B4
Padangpanjang *Indon* 54B3
Padangsidempuan *Indon* 54A2
Padany *USSR* 42E3
Paderborn *W Germ* 40B2
Padlei *Can* 4J3
Padma, R *Bang* 59D3
Padova *Italy* 35D2
Padre I *USA* 6D4
Padstow *Eng* 33C6
Padthaway *Aust* 78B3
Padua = Padova
Paducah, Kentucky *USA* 10B3
Paducah, Texas *USA* 14B3
Padunskoye More, L *USSR* 30L5
Paegam *N Korea* 52A2
Paengnyŏng-do, I *S Korea* 51A4
Paeroa *NZ* 79C1
Pafuri *Mozam* 72E1
Pag, I *Yugos* 38C2
Pagadian *Phil* 55F9
Pagai Seletan, I *Indon* 54B3
Pagai Utara, I *Indon* 54B3
Pagalu, I *Eq Guinea* 68C4
Pagan, I *Pacific O* 49H5
Pagatan *Indon* 54E3
Page *USA* 17D3
Pago Mission *Aust* 49F8
Pagondhas *Greece* 39F3
Pagosa Springs *USA* 14A2
Pahala *Hawaiian Is* 18E5
Pahiatua *NZ* 79C2
Pahoa *Hawaiian Is* 18E5
Pahokee *USA* 13E4
Pai, R *Nig* 69J4
Päijänna, L *Fin* 30K6
Paillaco *Chile* 26A4
Pailola Chan *Hawaiian Is* 18E5
Painesville *USA* 10C2
Painted Desert *USA* 17D3
Paintsville *USA* 10C3
Paisley *Scot* 32C4
Paita *Peru* 24B5
Pajala *Sweden* 30J5
Pajeti *Indon* 55B4
Pakistan, Republic *Asia* 56E3
Pak Lay *Laos* 53C2
Pakokku *Burma* 59E3
Pakowki L *Can* 3F3
Pakrac *Yugos* 38D1
Paks *Hung* 39D1
Pak Sane *Laos* 53C2
Pakse *Laos* 53D2
Pakwach *Uganda* 70D3
Pala *Chad* 70B3
Palagruža, I *Yugos* 38D2
Palaiseau *France* 34B2
Palala, R *S Africa* 72D1
Palalankwe *Andaman Is* 60E2
Palana *USSR* 47R4
Palangkaraya *Indon* 54D3
Palani *India* 60B2
Palanpur *India* 58C4
Palapye *Botswana* 72D1
Palatka *USA* 13C3
Palau Is *Pacific O* 49G6
Palaw *Burma* 53B3
Palawan, I *Phil* 55E9
Palawan Pass *Phil* 55E9
Palayankottai *India* 60B3
Paldiski *USSR* 30J7
Paleleh *Indon* 55B2
Palembang *Indon* 54B3
Palencia *Spain* 37B1
Paleokhorio *Cyprus* 63B1
Palermo *Italy* 38C3
Palestine, Region *Israel* 63C3
Palestine *USA* 15C3
Paletwa *Burma* 59D3
Pālghāt *India* 60B2
Pāli *India* 58C3
Palimé *Togo* 69G4
Palin,Mt *Malay* 54E1
Palisade *USA* 14A2
Pālitāna *India* 58C4
Palk Str *India/Sri Lanka* 60B3
Pallasovka *USSR* 43H5
Pallastunturi, Mt *Fin* 30J5
Palliser B *NZ* 79B2
Palliser,C *NZ* 79C2
Palma *Mozam* 71E5
Palma de Mallorca *Spain* 37C2
Palmares *Brazil* 25L5
Palmares do Sul *Brazil* 26E2
Palmar Sur *Costa Rica* 21A5
Palmas *Brazil* 27B4
Palmas,C *Lib* 68B4
Palmas de Monte Alto *Brazil* 27D1
Palma Soriano *Cuba* 21B2
Palm Bay *USA* 13C3
Palm Beach *USA* 13E4
Palmdale *USA* 18C3
Palmeira *Brazil* 27C4
Palmeira dos Indos *Brazil* 25L5
Palmer *USA* 8J3
Palmer, Base *Ant* 80G3
Palmer Arch *Ant* 80G3
Palmer Land, Region *Ant* 80F3
Palmerston *NZ* 79B3
Palmerston North *NZ* 79C2
Palmerton *USA* 12C2
Palmetto *USA* 13E4
Palmi *Italy* 38D3
Palmiera das Missões *Brazil* 26E1
Palmillas *Mexico* 20C1
Palmira *Colombia* 24C3
Palm Is *Aust* 76D2
Palm Springs *USA* 17C4
Palmyra, Missouri *USA* 10A3
Palmyra, New York *USA* 12B1
Palmyra, Pennsylvania *USA* 12B2
Palmyras Pt *India* 59C3
Palo Alto *USA* 18A2
Paloh *Indon* 54C2
Paloích *Sudan* 70D2
Palomares *Mexico* 20C2
Palomar Mt *USA* 17C4
Palopo *Indon* 55B3
Palu *Indon* 55A3
Palu *Turk* 62C2
Palwal *India* 58D3
Palyavaam, R *USSR* 8B2
Pama *U Volta* 69G3
Pamekasan *Indon* 54D4
Pameungpeuk *Indon* 54C4
Pamiers *France* 36C3
Pamir, Mts *China* 57F2
Pamir, R *USSR* 46J6
Pamlico, R *USA* 13D1
Pamlico Sd *USA* 13D1
Pampa *USA* 14B2
Pampa de la Salinas, Salt pan *Arg* 26B2
Pampa de la Varita, Plain *Arg* 26B3
Pampanua *Indon* 55B3
Pampeiro *Brazil* 26D2
Pamplona *Colombia* 24D2
Pamplona *Spain* 37B1
Pana *USA* 10B3
Panaca *USA* 17D3
Panagyurishte *Bulg* 39E2
Panaji *India* 60A1
Panamá *Panama* 24C2
Panama, Republic *C America* 24B2
Panama Canal *Panama* 21B5
Panama City *USA* 13B2
Panamint Range, Mts *USA* 17C3
Panamint V *USA* 18D2
Panaro, R *Italy* 35D2
Panay, I *Phil* 55F8
Pancevo *Yugos* 39E2
Pandan *Phil* 55F8
Pandharpur *India* 60B1
Pandie Pandie *Aust* 78A1
Panevežys *USSR* 41E1
Panfilov *USSR* 46K5
Pang, R *Burma* 53B1
Pangani *Tanz* 70D4
Pangani, R *Tanz* 70D4
Pangi *Zaïre* 70C4
Pangkajene *Indon* 55A3
Pangkalpinang *Indon* 54C3
Pangnirtung *Can* 5M3
Pangtara *Burma* 53B1
Panguitch *USA* 17D3
Pangutaran Group, Is *Phil* 55F9
Panhandle *USA* 14B2
Panipat *India* 58D3
Panjao *Afghan* 58B2
Panjgur *Pak* 61E3
Pankof,C *USA* 8F5
Pankshin *Nig* 69H4
P'anmunjŏm *N Korea* 51B4
Panna *India* 59B3
Panorama *Brazil* 27B3
Pantanal de São Lourenço, Swamp *Brazil* 27A2
Pantanal do Rio Negro, Swamp *Brazil* 27A2
Pantanal do Taquari, Swamp *Brazil* 27A2
Pantar, I *Indon* 55B4
Pantelleria, I *Medit S* 38C3
Pantepec *Mexico* 20C1
Panuco *Mexico* 20C1
Pánuco, R *Mexico* 20C1
Pan Xian *China* 50A4
Paola *Italy* 38D3
Paola *USA* 15D2
Paoli *USA* 10B3
Papa *Hung* 40D3
Papaikou *Hawaiian Is* 18E5
Papakura *NZ* 79B1
Papaloapan, R *Mexico* 20C2
Papantla *Mexico* 20C1
Papa Stour, I *Scot* 32E1
Papatoetoe *NZ* 79B1
Papa Westray, I *Scot* 32D2
Paphos *Cyprus* 63B1
Papua,G of *PNG* 76D1
Papua New Guinea, Republic *S E Asia* 76D1
Papudo *Chile* 26A2
Papun *Burma* 53B2
Para, State *Brazil* 25H4
Pará, R *Brazil* 25J4
Paraburdoo *Aust* 76A3
Paracas,Pen de *Peru* 24C6
Paracatu *Brazil* 27C2
Paracatu, R *Brazil* 27C2
Paracel Is *S E Asia* 53E2
Parachilna *Aust* 78A2
Parachinar *Pak* 58C2
Paracin *Yugos* 39E2
Pará de Minas *Brazil* 27D2
Paradise, California *USA* 17B3
Paradise, Nevada *USA* 17D3
Paradise Peak, Mt *USA* 18D1
Paragould *USA* 15D2
Paraguá, R *Bol* 24F6
Paragua, R *Ven* 24F2
Paraguaçu, R *Brazil* 27D1
Paraguai, R *Brazil* 25G7
Paraguari *Par* 27A4
Paraguay, Republic *S America* 23E2
Paraguay, R *Par* 23E2
Paraiba, State *Brazil* 25L5
Paraíba do Sul, R *Brazil* 27D3
Paraiso *Mexico* 20D2
Parakou *Benin* 69G4
Parakylia *Aust* 78A2
Paramakkudi *India* 60B3
Paramaribo *Suriname* 25G2
Paramirim *Brazil* 27D1
Paramushir, I *USSR* 48J1
Paraná *Brazil* 27B3
Paraná, State *Brazil* 23F2
Paraná *Urug* 26C2
Paraná, R *Arg* 23E4
Paranã, R *Brazil* 25J6
Paranaguá *Brazil* 27C4
Paranaiba *Brazil* 27B2
Paranaiba, R *Brazil* 27B2
Paranapanema, R *Brazil* 27B3
Paranavai *Brazil* 27B3
Parang *Phil* 55F9
Paraope, R *Brazil* 27D2
Paraparaumu *NZ* 79B2
Paratinga *Brazil* 27D1
Parbhani *India* 60B1
Parc National d'Arly *U Volta* 69G3
Parc National de la Komoé *Ivory Coast* 69F4
Parc National de la Pendjari *Benin* 69G3
Parcs Nationaux du W *Benin* 69G3
Pardes Hanna *Israel* 63C2
Pardo *Arg* 26D3
Pardo, R, Bahia *Brazil* 27E2
Pardo, R, Mato Grosso do Sul *Brazil* 27B3
Pardo, R, Minas Gerais *Brazil* 27C2
Pardo, R, Sao Paulo *Brazil* 27C3
Pardubice *Czech* 40D2
Parece Vela, Reef *Pacific O* 48G4
Parecis *Brazil* 27A1
Parent *Can* 7F2
Parent,L *Can* 11D1
Parepare *Indon* 55A3
Parepare *Indon* 76A1
Parera *Arg* 26C3
Pariaman *Indon* 54B3
Paria,Pen de *Ven* 24F1
Parigi *Indon* 55B3
Parika *Guyana* 25G2
Paris *France* 36C2
Paris, Kentucky *USA* 10C3
Paris, Tennessee *USA* 13B1
Paris, Texas *USA* 15C3
Parker *USA* 17D4
Parkersburg *USA* 10C3
Parkes *Aust* 78C2
Parkesburg *USA* 12C3
Park Falls *USA* 10A1
Parkfield *USA* 18B3
Park Forest *USA* 10B2
Park Rapids *USA* 9C2
Parkston *USA* 9C3
Parksville *Can* 16B1
Park Valley *USA* 16D2
Parlākimidi *India* 60C1
Parli *India* 60B1
Parma *Italy* 35D2
Parma *USA* 10C2
Parnaiba *Brazil* 25K4
Parnaiba, R *Brazil* 25K4
Párnon Óros, Mts *Greece* 39E3
Pärnu *USSR* 42C4
Paro *Bhutan* 59C2
Paroo, R *Aust* 78B1
Paroo Channel, R *Aust* 78B2
Paropamisus, Mts *Afghan* 61E2
Páros, I *Greece* 39F3
Parowan *USA* 17D3
Parpaillon, Mts *France* 35B2
Parral *Chile* 26A3
Parramatta *Aust* 78D2
Parras *Mexico* 6C4
Parry B *Can* 5K3
Parry,C *Can* 8O1
Parry Is *Can* 4G2
Parry Pen *Can* 8O2
Parry Sd *Can* 5L5
Parry Sound *Can* 10C1
Parsberg *W Germ* 40C3
Parsnip, R *Can* 4F4
Parsons, Kansas *USA* 15C2
Parsons, West Virginia *USA* 11D3
Parthenay *France* 36B2
Partinico *Italy* 38C3
Partizansk *USSR* 51C3
Paru, R *Brazil* 25H4
Páruco *Mexico* 20A1
Parvatipuram *India* 60C1
Parys *S Africa* 72D2
Pasadena, Texas *USA* 15C4
Pasadena *USA* 18C3
Pasangkayu *Indon* 55A3
Pasarwajo *Indon* 55B4
Pasawing *Burma* 53B2
Pascagoula *USA* 15E3
Paşcani *Rom* 39F1
Pasco *USA* 16C1
Pas-de-Calais, Department *France* 34B1
Pasewalk *W Germ* 30G8
Pasfield L *Can* 3G2
Pashū'iyeh *Iran* 61D3
Pasley,C *Aust* 76B4
Pasni *Pak* 61E3
Paso de los Libres *Arg* 26D1
Paso de los Toros *Urug* 23E4
Paso Limay *Arg* 23B6
Paso Robles *USA* 18B3
Pasquia Hills *Can* 3H3
Passaic *USA* 12C2
Passau *W Germ* 40C3
Passo de los Libres *Arg* 23E3
Passo del Toro, Mt *Mexico* 20B1
Passo di Stelvio, Mt *Italy* 35D1
Passo di Tonale *Italy* 35D1
Passo Fundo *Brazil* 26E1
Passos *Brazil* 27C3
Passy *France* 35B2
Pastaza, R *Peru* 24C4
Pasteur *Arg* 26C3
Pas,The *Can* 4H4
Pasto *Colombia* 24C3
Pastol B *USA* 8F3
Pasubio, Mt *Italy* 35D2
Pasuruan *Indon* 54D4
Pasvalys *USSR* 41E1
Pātan *India* 58C4
Patan *Nepal* 59C2
Patchewollock *Aust* 78B3
Patea *NZ* 79B1
Patea, R *NZ* 79B2
Paterno *Italy* 38C3
Paterson *USA* 12C2
Paterson Inlet, B *NZ* 79A3
Pathankot *India* 58D2
Pathfinder Res *USA* 9A3
Patiāla *India* 58D2
Pativilca *Peru* 24C6
Pátmos, I *Greece* 39F3
Patna *India* 59C2
Patnos *Turk* 62D2
Patos *Brazil* 25L5
Patos de Minas *Brazil* 27C2
Patquia *Arg* 26B2
Pátrai *Greece* 39E3
Patrasuy *USSR* 42L3
Patrocinio *Brazil* 27C2
Patta, I *Kenya* 70E4
Pattallasang *Indon* 55A4
Pattani *Thai* 53C4
Patterson, California *USA* 18B2
Patterson, Louisiana *USA* 15D4
Patterson,Mt *Can* 8M3
Patterson Mt *USA* 18C2
Patton *USA* 12A2
Pattullo,Mt *Can* 3C2
Patu *Brazil* 25L5
Patuakhali *Bang* 59D3
Patuca, R *Honduras* 19D3
Patzcuaro *Mexico* 20B2
Pau *France* 36B3
Paulatuk *Can* 8O2
Paulistana *Brazil* 25K5
Paulpietersburg *S Africa* 72E2
Pauls Valley *USA* 15C3
Paungde *Burma* 53B2
Pauri *India* 58D2
Pauskie *Nor* 30H5
Pavão *Brazil* 27D2
Pavia *Italy* 35C2
Pavlodar *USSR* 46J4
Pavlof V *USA* 8F4
Pavlov B *USA* 8F4
Pavlovich *USSR* 47O4
Pavlovka *USSR* 42K4
Pavlovo *USSR* 42G4
Pavlovsk *USSR* 43G5
Pavullo nel Frigano *Italy* 35D2
Pawan, R *Indon* 54D3
Pawhuska *USA* 15C2
Paw Paw *USA* 12A3
Pawtucket *USA* 12E2
Paxton *USA* 14B1
Payakumbuh *Indon* 54B3
Payerne *Switz* 35B1
Payette *USA* 16C2
Payne,L *Can* 5L4
Paynesville *USA* 9D2
Paysandu *Urug* 26D2
Pays d'Auge, Region *France* 34A2
Pays-de-Bray, Region *France* 34A2
Pays de Caux, Region *France* 34A2
Pays d'Ouche, Region *France* 34A2
Pazardzhik *Bulg* 39E2
Pazin *Yugos* 35E2
Peace, R *Can* 3E2
Peace, R *USA* 13E4
Peace River *Can* 3E2
Peach Springs *USA* 17D3
Peak District Nat Pk *Eng* 33E5
Peake, R *Aust* 78A1
Peaked Mt *USA* 11F1
Peak Hill *Aust* 78C2
Peak Mandala, Mt *Indon* 49G7
Peak,The, Mt *Eng* 33E5
Peale,Mt *USA* 17E3
Pearl, R *USA* 15D3
Pearl City *Hawaiian Is* 18E5

Pearl Harbour *Hawaiian Is* 18E5
Pearsall *USA* 15F4
Pearston *S Africa* 72D3
Peary Chan *Can* 4H2
Pebane *Mozam* 71D5
Peć *Yugos* 39E2
Peçanha *Brazil* 27D2
Pecan Island *USA* 15D4
Pechenga *USSR* 30L5
Pechora *USSR* 42K2
Pechora, R *USSR* 42J2
Pechorskaya Guba, G *USSR* 42J2
Pechorskoye More, S *USSR* 42J2
Pecoraro, Mt *Italy* 38D3
Pecos *USA* 14B3
Pecos, R *USA* 14B3
Pécs *Hung* 41D3
Pedang Endau *Malay* 54G7
Pedhoulas *Cyprus* 63B1
Pedirka *Aust* 78A1
Pedra Azul *Brazil* 27D2
Pedregulho *Brazil* 27C3
Pedro Cays, Is *Caribbean* 21B3
Pedro de Valdivia *Chile* 23C2
Pedro Gomes *Brazil* 27B2
Pedro Juan Caballero *Par* 27A3
Pedro Luro *Arg* 26C3
Pedro Mentova *Mexico* 20C1
Pedro,Pt *Sri Lanka* 60C3
Pedro R Fernandez *Arg* 26D1
Peebinga *Aust* 78B2
Peebles *Scot* 32D4
Pee Dee, R *USA* 13D2
Peekskill *USA* 12D2
Peel *Eng* 33C4
Peel, R *Can* 8M2
Peel Sd *Can* 4J2
Peensylvania, State *USA* 7F2
Peera Peera Poolanna, L *Aust* 78A1
Peerless L *Can* 3F2
Peg Arfak, Mt *Indon* 49G7
Pegasus B *NZ* 79B2
Pegtmel', R *USSR* 8B2
Pegu *Burma* 59E4
Pegunungan Barisan, Mts *Indon* 54B3
Pegunungan Iran, Mts *Malay Indon* 54D2
Pegunungan Maoke, Mts *Indon* 76C1
Pegunungan Meratus, Mts *Indon* 54E3
Pegunungan Muller, Mts *Indon* 54D2
Pegunungan Schwanet, Mts *Indon* 54D3
Pegunungan T gapuluh, Mts *Indon* 54B3
Pegu Yoma, Mts *Burma* 53B2
Pehuajó *Arg* 26C3
Peixe, R, Mato Grosso *Brazil* 27B1
Peixe, R, Sao Paulo *Brazil* 27B3
Pei Xian *China* 50D3
Pekalongan *Indon* 54C4
Pekan *Malay* 53C5
Pekanbaru *Indon* 54B2
Pekin *USA* 10B2
Peking = Beijing
Pelabohan Kelang *Malay* 53C5
Pelagie Is *Mediterranean S* 69E1
Pelau Pelau Bob, Is *Indon* 55C3
Pelau Pelau Kangean, Is *Indon* 54E4
Pelau Pelau Karimunjawa Arch *Indon* 54D4
Pelau Pelau Maisel, Is *Indon* 55C4
Pelau Pelau Penyu, Is *Indon* 55C4
Pelau Pelau Postilyon, Is *Indon* 54E4
Pelau Pelau Salabangka, Is *Indon* 55B3
Peleaga, Mt *Rom* 39E1
Peleduy *USSR* 47N4
Pelee I *Can* 10C2
Peleng, I *Indon* 76B1
Pelican *USA* 8L4
Pelican L *USA* 9D2
Pelican Pt *S Africa* 72A1
Pellegrini *Arg* 26C3
Pello *Fin* 30J5
Pelly, R *Can* 8M3
Pelly Bay *Can* 5J3
Pelly Crossing *Can* 8L3
Pelly Mts *Can* 8M3
Pelotas *Brazil* 26E2
Pelotas, R *Brazil* 23F3
Pelusium, Hist Site *Egypt* 63B3
Pelvoux, Region *France* 35B2
Pelym, R *USSR* 42L3
Pemalang *Indon* 54C4
Pematang *Indon* 54B3
Pematangsiantar *Indon* 54A2
Pemba *Mozam* 71E5
Pemba, I *Tanz* 70D4
Pemberton *Can* 3D3
Pembina *USA* 9C2
Pembina, R *Can* 3E3
Pembroke *Can* 11D1
Pembroke *USA* 13C2
Pembroke *Wales* 33C6
Pemuco *Chile* 26A3
Penacook *USA* 12E1
Penambo Range, Mts *Malay* 54E2
Penápolis *Brazil* 27B3
Peñarroya *Spain* 37A2
Penarroya, Mt *Spain* 37B1
Peña Trevina, Mt *Spain* 37A1
Pende, R *Chad* 70B3
Pendelton,Mt *Can* 8N4
Pendjari, R *Benin* 69G3
Pendleton *USA* 16C1
Pend Oreille, R *USA* 16C1
Penedo *Brazil* 25L6
Penganga, R *India* 58D5
P'eng hu Lieh tao, Is *Taiwan* 50D5
Penglai *China* 50E2
Pengshui *China* 50B4
Pengunungan Maoke, Mts *Indon* 49G7
Península de la Guajiri, Pen *Colombia* 21C4
Península de Paria, Pen *Ven* 21E4
Peninsular Malaysia *Malay* 53C5
Penjamo *Mexico* 20B1
Pennabilli *Italy* 35E3
Penner, R *India* 60B2
Pennine Chain, Mts *Eng* 32D4
Penns Grove *USA* 12C3
Pennsylvania, State *USA* 7F2
Penn Yan *USA* 12B1
Penny Highlands, Mts *Can* 5M3
Penobscot, R *USA* 11F1
Penobscot B *USA* 11F2
Penola *Aust* 78B3
Penong *Aust* 76C4
Penonomé *Panama* 21A5
Penrith *Eng* 33D4
Pensacola *USA* 13B2
Pensacola Mts *Ant* 80E
Pensiangan *Malay* 54E2
Pentecost, I *Vanuatu* 77F2
Penticton *Can* 3E4
Pentland Firth, Chan *Scot* 32D2
Pentland Hills *Scot* 32D4
Penza *USSR* 42H5
Penzance *Eng* 33C6
Penzhina, R *USSR* 47S3
Penzhinskaya Guba, B *USSR* 47S3
Peoria *USA* 10B2
Perabumulih *Indon* 54B3
Perak, R *Malay* 53C5
Perawang *Indon* 54B2
Perdido, R *Brazil* 27A3
Pereira *Colombia* 24C3
Pereira Barreto *Brazil* 27B3
Perelazovskiy *USSR* 43G6
Perenosa B *USA* 8H4
Pereyaslav *USSR* 41G2
Pereyaslavka *USSR* 51D2
Pergamino *Arg* 26C2
Pergola *Italy* 35E3
Peribonca, R *Can* 5L4
Perim, I *S Yemen* 64D4
Périgueux *France* 36C2
Perlas Arch de, Is *Panama* 19E4
Perm' *USSR* 42K4
Pernambuco = Recife
Pernambuco, State *Brazil* 25L5
Pernatty Lg *Aust* 78A2
Pernik *Bulg* 39E2
Péronne *France* 34B2
Perote *Mexico* 20C2
Perpignan *France* 36C3
Perris *USA* 18D4
Perry, Florida *USA* 13C2
Perry, Georgia *USA* 13C2
Perry, New York *USA* 12A1
Perry, Oklahoma *USA* 15C2
Perry River *Can* 4H3
Perrysburg *USA* 10C2
Perryton *USA* 14B2
Perryville, Alaska *USA* 8G4
Perryville, Missour *USA* 15E2
Perth *Aust* 76A4
Perth *Can* 11D2
Perth *Scot* 32D3
Perth Amboy *USA* 12C2
Pertuis *France* 35A3
Peru, Republic *S America* 24D6
Peru *USA* 10B2
Peru Basin *Pacific O* 75P5
Peru-Chile Trench *Pacific O* 73E6
Perugia *Italy* 38C2
Perugorria *Arg* 26D1
Perušic *Yugos* 38D2
Pervari *Turk* 62D2
Pervomaysk, RSFSR *USSR* 42G5
Pervomaysk, Ukraine SSR *USSR* 43E6
Pervoural'sk *USSR* 42K4
Pesaro *Italy* 35E3
Pescadero *USA* 18A2
Pescadores = P'eng-hu Lieh-tao
Pescara *Italy* 38C2
Peschiera *Italy* 35D2
Pescia *Italy* 35D3
Peshawar *Pak* 58C2
Peshkopi *Alb* 39E2
Peshtigo *USA* 10B1
Pestovo *USSR* 42F4
Petah Tiqwa *Israel* 63C2
Petaluma *USA* 17B3
Pétange *Lux* 34C2
Petatlán *Mexico* 20B2
Petauke *Zambia* 71D5
Petenwell L *USA* 10B2
Peterborough *Aust* 78A2
Peterborough *Can* 11D2
Peterborough *Eng* 33E5
Peterborough *USA* 12E1
Peterhead *Scot* 32E3
Petermann Gletscher, Gl *Greenland* 5M1
Petermann Range, Mts *Aust* 76B3
Peteroa, Mt *Chile/Arg* 23B5
Peter Pond L *Can* 3G2
Petersburg, Alaska *USA* 8M4
Petersburg, Virginia *USA* 11D3
Petitot, R *Can* 3E2
Petlād *India* 58C4
Petlalcingo *Mexico* 20C2
Peto *Mexico* 19D2
Petomskoye Nagor'ye, Upland *USSR* 47N4
Petorca *Chile* 26A2
Petoskey *USA* 10C1
Petra, Hist Site *Jordan* 63C3
Petral, Base *Ant* 80G2
Petrified Forest Nat Pk *USA* 17E3
Petrolina *Brazil* 25K5
Petropavlovsk *USSR* 46H4
Petropavlovsk-Kamchatskiy *USSR* 48J1
Petrópolis *Brazil* 27D3
Petrovadovsk *USSR* 46E3
Petrovsk *USSR* 43H5
Petrovsk Zabaykal'skiy *USSR* 48D1
Petrozavodsk *USSR* 42E3
Petrus *S Africa* 72D2
Petrusburg *S Africa* 72D2
Petrusville *S Africa* 72C3
Pevek *USSR* 47T3
Peza, R *USSR* 42H2
Pfälzer Wald, Region *W Germ* 34D2
Pforzheim *W Germ* 40B3
Phagwara *India* 58D2
Phalaborwa *S Africa* 72E1
Phalodi *India* 58C3
Phalsbourg *France* 34D2
Phaltan *India* 60A1
Phangnga *Thai* 53B4
Phanom Dang, Mts *Camb* 53C3
Phan Rang *Viet* 53D3
Phan Thiet *Viet* 53D3
Pharr *USA* 15F4
Phelps L *Can* 3H2
Phelps L *USA* 13D1
Phenix City *USA* 13B2
Phet Buri *Thai* 53B3
Phiafay *Laos* 53D3
Philadelphia, Mississippi *USA* 15E3
Philadelphia, Pennsylvania *USA* 12C2
Philip *USA* 9B3
Philippeville = Skikda
Philippeville *Belg* 34C1
Philippine S *Pacific O* 49F5
Philippines, Republic *S E Asia* 49F5
Philippine Trench *Pacific O* 74H4
Philippolis *S Africa* 72D3
Philipsburg, Montana *USA* 16D1
Philipsburg, Pennsylvania *USA* 11D2
Philip Smith Mts *USA* 8J2
Philipstown *S Africa* 72C3
Phillipine S *Phil* 55F7
Phillips B *Can* 5K1
Phillipsburg, Kansas *USA* 14C2
Phillipsburg, New Jersey *USA* 12C2
Philpots Pen *Can* 5K2
Phnom Penh *Camb* 53C3
Phoenix, Arizona *USA* 17D4
Phoenix, New York *USA* 12B1
Phoenix, Is *Pacific O* 77H1
Phoenixville *USA* 12C2
Phong Saly *Laos* 53C1
Phu Bia, Mt *Laos* 53C2
Phu Cuong *Viet* 53D3
Phuket *Thai* 53B4
Phulbāni *India* 59B3
Phu Miang, Mt *Thai* 53C2
Phu Set, Mt *Laos* 53D2
Phu Tho *Viet* 53D1
Phu Vinh *Viet* 53D4
Phyäselkä, L *Fin* 30K6
Piacenza *Italy* 35C2
Pialba *Aust* 78D1
Pian, R *Aust* 78C2
Pianoro *Italy* 35D2
Pianosa, I *Italy* 38C2
Pianosa, I *Italy* 38D2
Piaseczno *Pol* 41E2
Piata *Brazil* 27D1
Piatra-Neamţ *Rom* 39F1
Piaui, State *Brazil* 25K5
Piave *Italy* 35E2
Piave, R *Italy* 35E1
Pibor, R *Sudan* 70D3
Pibor Post *Sudan* 70D3
Picardie, Region *France* 34B2
Picayune *USA* 15E3
Pic de Rochebrune, Mt *France* 35B2
Pichilemu *Chile* 26A2
Pichi Mahuida *Arg* 26C3
Pichucalco *Mexico* 20D2
Pickering *Eng* 33E4
Pickle Lake *Can* 5J4
Pico, I *Açores* 68A1
Pico Bernina, Mt *Switz* 35C1
Pico Bolivar, Mt *Ven* 21C5
Pico de Anito, Mt *Spain* 37C1
Pico del Infiernillo, Mt *Mexico* 19B3
Pico Duarte, Mt *Dom Rep* 21C3
Picos *Brazil* 25K5
Picos de Europa, Mt *Spain* 37B1
Picton *Aust* 78D2
Picton *NZ* 79B2
Pic Toussidé, Mt *Chad* 70B1
Picún Leufú, R *Arg* 26A3
Piedade *Brazil* 27C3
Piedra *USA* 18C2
Piedra de Aguila *Arg* 26B4
Piedras Blancas,Pt *USA* 18B3
Piedras Negras *Mexico* 19B2
Pie I *Can* 10B1
Pieksämäki *Fin* 30K6
Pielinen, L *Fin* 30K6
Piemonte, Region *Italy* 35B2
Pienaarsrivier *S Africa* 72D2
Pierre *USA* 9B3
Pieštany *Czech* 41D3
Pietermaritzburg *S Africa* 72E2
Pietersburg *S Africa* 72D1
Pietrasanta *Italy* 35D3
Piet Retief *S Africa* 72E2
Pietrosu, Mt *Rom* 43C6
Pietrosul, Mt *Rom* 39F1
Pieve di Cadore *Italy* 35E1
Pigailoe, I *Pacific O* 49H6
Pigeon L *Can* 3F3
Piggott *USA* 15D2
Pigüé *Arg* 26C3
Pijijapan *Mexico* 20D2
Pikangikum L *Can* 5J4
Pikes Peak *USA* 14A2
Piketberg *S Africa* 72B3
Pikeville *USA* 10C3
Pikintaleq *Greenland* 5O3
Pik Kommunizma, Mt *USSR* 57F2
Pikounda *Congo* 70B3
Pik Pobedy, Mt *China/USSR* 57G1
Pila *Arg* 26D3
Pila *Pol* 40D2
Pilar *Par* 23E3
Pilcomayo, R *Arg/Par* 23D2
Pilgrim's Rest *S Africa* 72E1
Pilibhit *India* 58D3
Pilica, R *Pol* 41D2
Pillar,C *Aust* 78E3
Pílos *Greece* 39E3
Pilot Knob Mt *USA* 16C1
Pilot Peak, Mt *USA* 18D1
Pilot Point *USA* 8G4
Pilot Station *USA* 8F3
Pilottown *USA* 15E3
Pimenta *Brazil* 25G4
Pinang, I *Malay* 53C4
Pinar del Rio *Cuba* 21A2
Pinas *Arg* 26B2
Pinche *Belg* 34C1
Pincher Creek *Can* 3F3
Pindaré, R *Brazil* 25J4
Píndhos, Mts *Greece* 39E3
Pine Bluff *USA* 15D3
Pine Bluffs *USA* 14B1
Pine City *USA* 9D2
Pine Creek *Aust* 76C2
Pine Creek, R *USA* 12B2
Pinecrest *USA* 18C1
Pinedale, California *USA* 18C2
Pinedale, Wyoming *USA* 16E2
Pine Falls *Can* 9C1
Pine Flat Res *USA* 18C2
Pinega *USSR* 42G3
Pinega, R *USSR* 42H3
Pine Grove *USA* 12B2
Pine Hills *USA* 13C3
Pinehouse L *Can* 3G2
Pinehurst *USA* 13D1
Pine I *USA* 13E4
Pineland *USA* 15D3
Pinellas Park *USA* 13C3
Pine Mt *USA* 18B3
Pine Point *Can* 3F1
Pine Ridge *USA* 9B3
Pinerolo *Italy* 35B2
Pines,Lo'the *USA* 15D3
Pineville *USA* 15D3
Pingdingshan *China* 50C3
Pingguo *China* 50B5
Pingliang *China* 50B2
Pingluo *China* 50B2
Pingtan Dao, I *China* 50D4
P'ing tung *Taiwan* 50E5
Pingwu *China* 50A3
Pingxiang, Guangxi *China* 50B5
Pingxiang, Jiangxi *China* 50C4
Pinheiro *Brazil* 25J4
Pinheiro Machado *Brazil* 26E2
Pini, I *Indon* 54A2
Piniós, R *Greece* 39E3
Pinjang *Indon* 55B2
Pinjarra *Aust* 76A4
Pink Mountain *Can* 3D2
Pinnaroo *Aust* 78B3
Pinos,I de, I = Islas de la Juventud
Pinos,Mt *USA* 18C3
Pinos,Pt *USA* 17B3
Pinotepa Nacional *Mexico* 20C2
Pinrang *Indon* 55A3
Pinsk *USSR* 43D5
Pinto *Arg* 26C1
Pinyug *USSR* 42H3
Pioche *USA* 17D3
Piombino *Italy* 38C2
Pioneer Mts *USA* 16D1
Pionerskiy *USSR* 42L3
Piórsá *Iceland* 5Q3
Piotroków Trybunalski *Pol* 41D2
Piper, Oilfield *N Sea* 32F2
Piper Peak, Mt *USA* 18D2
Pipestone *USA* 9C3
Pipinas *Arg* 26D3
Pipmuacan Res *Can* 7F2
Pipmudcan, Res *Can* 5M4
Piqua *USA* 10C2
Piquiri, R *Brazil* 27B4
Piracanjuba *Brazil* 27C2
Piracicaba *Brazil* 27C3
Piraçununga *Brazil* 27C3
Pirai do Sul *Brazil* 27C3
Piraiévs *Greece* 39E3
Pirajui *Brazil* 27C3
Piran *Yugos* 35E2
Piranhas *Brazil* 27B2
Pirapora *Brazil* 27D2
Piratina, R *Brazil* 26D1
Piratini, R *Brazil* 26E2
Pirdop *Bulg* 39E2
Pirenópolis *Brazil* 27C2
Pires do Rio *Brazil* 27C2
Pírgos *Greece* 39E3
Pirineos = Pyrénées
Pirineos, Mts *Spain* 36B3
Piripiri *Brazil* 25K4
Pirmasens *W Germ* 34D2
Pirot *Yugos* 39E2
Pir Panjāl Range, Mts *Pak* 58C2
Piru *Indon* 55C3
Piru Creek, R *USA* 18C3
Pisa *Italy* 35D3
Pisco *Peru* 24C6
Piseco *USA* 12C1
Písek *Czech* 40C3
Pishin *Pak* 58B2
Pismo Beach *USA* 18B3
Pissis, Mt *Arg* 23C3
Pistoia *Italy* 35D3
Pisuerga, R *Spain* 37B1
Pit, R *USA* 16B2
Pitalito *Colombia* 24C3
Pitanga *Brazil* 27B3
Pitcairn, I *Pacific O* 75N6
Pite, R *Sweden* 30H5
Piteå *Sweden* 30J5
Piteşti *Rom* 39E2
Pit Gorodok *USSR* 47L4
Pithiviers *France* 34B2
Pitkyaranta *USSR* 42E3
Pitlochry *Scot* 32D3

Pitlyar *USSR* 42M2
Pitrutquén *Chile* 26A3
Pitt, I *NZ* 77H5
Pitt I *Can* 3C3
Pittsburg, California *USA* 18B1
Pittsburg, Kansas *USA* 15D2
Pittsburgh *USA* 11D2
Pittsfield, Illinois *USA* 10A3
Pittsfield, Massachusetts *USA* 12D1
Pittston *USA* 12C2
Pittsworth *Aust* 78D1
Piute Peak, Mt *USA* 18C3
Piuthan *Nepal* 59B2
Pivan' *USSR* 51D1
Pixley *USA* 18C3
Pizzo Redorta, Mt *Italy* 35D1
Pjórsá *Iceland* 30B2
Pjura *Peru* 24B5
Placentia B *Can* 5N5
Placerville *USA* 18B1
Plaine d'Alsace, Plain *France* 34D2
Plaine des Flandres, Plain *France/Belg* 34B1
Plaine du Tidikelt, Desert Region 68C2
Plaine Lorraine, Region *France* 34C2
Plains *USA* 14B2
Plainview, Nebraska *USA* 9C3
Plainview, Texas *USA* 14B3
Planada *USA* 18B2
Planalto de Mato Grosso Plat *Brazil* 25H7
Planalto do Borborema, Plat *Brazil* 25L5
Planalto do Mato Grosso Mts *Brazil* 24B1
Planet Deep *PNG* 77E1
Plankinton *USA* 9C3
Plano *USA* 15C3
Plantation *USA* 13E4
Plant City *USA* 13C3
Plasencia *Spain* 37A1
Plast *USSR* 42L5
Plastun *USSR* 51D3
Plateau, State *Nig* 69H4
Plateau de Dadango *Togo* 69G3
Plateau de Langres, Plat *France* 34C3
Plateau De St Christol, Region *France* 35A2
Plateau du Tademait *Alg* 68C2
Plateau Lorrain, Plat *France* 34D2
Plateaux de Limousin, Plat *France* 36C2
Plateaux du Sersou, Plat *Alg* 37C2
Plato *Colombia* 21C5
Plato Ustyurt, Plat *USSR* 46G5
Platres *Cyprus* 63B1
Platte *USA* 9C3
Platte, R *USA* 14B1
Platteville *USA* 10A2
Plattsburgh *USA* 11E2
Plattsmouth *USA* 15C1
Plauen *E Germ* 40C2
Plavsk *USSR* 42F5
Playa Azul *Mexico* 20B2
Playas *Ecuador* 24B4
Playa Vincente *Mexico* 20C2
Plaza de Moro Almanzor, Mt *Spain* 37A1
Pleasanton, California *USA* 18B2
Pleasanton, Texas *USA* 15F4
Pleasantville *USA* 12C3
Pleasure Ridge Park *USA* 10B3
Pleiku *Viet* 53D3
Plenty,B of *NZ* 79C1
Plentywood *USA* 9B2
Pleszew *Pol* 41D2
Pletipi,L *Can* 5L4
Pleven *Bulg* 39E2
Plevlja *Yugos* 39D2
Plezetsk *USSR* 42F3
Ploče *Yugos* 39D2
Płock *Pol* 41D2
Ploërmel *France* 36B2
Ploieşti *Rom* 39F2
Plombières-les-Bains *France* 34D3
Płońsk *Pol* 42C5
Plovdiv *Bulg* 39E2
Plummer *USA* 16C1
Plummer,Mt *USA* 8G3
Plumtree *Zim* 71C6
Plymouth, California *USA* 18B1
Plymouth *Eng* 33C6
Plymouth, Indiana *USA* 10B2
Plymouth, Massachusetts *USA* 12E2
Plymouth, Pennsylvania *USA* 12C2
Plymouth B *USA* 12E2
Plymouth Sd *Eng* 33C6
Plynlimon, Mt *Wales* 33D5
Plzeň *Czech* 40C3
Pniewy *Pol* 40D2
Pô *U Volta* 69F3
Po, R *Italy* 35E2
Pobé *Benin* 69G4
Pobedino *USSR* 51E2
Pocatello *USA* 16D2
Pochutla *Mexico* 20C2
Poções *Brazil* 27D1
Pocomoke City *USA* 11D3
Poconé *Brazil* 27A2
Pocos de Caldas *Brazil* 27C3
Po di Volano, R *Italy* 35D2
Podkamennaya Tunguska, R *USSR* 47L3
Podolsk *USSR* 42F4
Podol'skaya Vozvyshennost', Upland *USSR* 41F3
Podporozh'ye *USSR* 42E3
Podyuga *USSR* 42G3
Pofadder *S Africa* 72B2
Poggibonsi *Italy* 35D3
Poghdar *Afghan* 58A2
Pogranichnyy *USSR* 51C3
Poh *Indon* 55B3
P'ohang *S Korea* 51B4
Poinsett,C *Ant* 80G9
Point *Aust* 78C2
Pointe-à-Pitre *Guadeloupe* 21E3
Pointe de Barfleur, Pt *France* 36B2
Pointe Noire *Congo* 70B4
Pointe Pongara, Pt *Gabon* 70A3
Point Fairy *Aust* 78B3
Point Fortin *Trinidad* 21L1
Point Hope *USA* 8E2
Point L *Can* 4G3
Point Lay *USA* 8F2
Point Pleasant, New Jersey *USA* 12C2
Point Pleasant, W Virginia *USA* 10C3
Point St Bernard, Mt *France* 35B2
Poison *USA* 3F4
Poitiers *France* 36C2
Poitou, Region *France* 36B2
Poix *France* 34A2
Pokaran *India* 58C3
Pokataroo *Aust* 78C1
Pokhara *Nepal* 59B2
Pokrovsk *USSR* 47O3
Polacca *USA* 17D3
Poland, Republic *Europe* 41D2
Poland *USA* 12C1
Polath *Turk* 43E8
Polatli *Turk* 62B2
Poleang *Indon* 55B3
Polewali *Indon* 55A3
Poli *Cam* 69J4
Poligny *France* 35A1
Poliny Osipenko *USSR* 47P4
Polis *Cyprus* 63B1
Políyiros *Greece* 39E2
Pollāchi *India* 60B2
Polollo Is *Phil* 55F8
Polonnye *USSR* 41F2
Polotsk *USSR* 41F1
Polson *USA* 16D1
Poltava *USSR* 43E6
Pölten *Austria* 38D1
Polunochoye *USSR* 42K3
Poluostrov Kanin, Pen *USSR* 42G2
Poluostrov Mangyshiak, Pen *USSR* 43J7
Poluostrov Rybachiy, Pen *USSR* 30L5
Poluostrov Taymyr, Pen *USSR* 47L2
Poluostrov Yamal, Pen *USSR* 46J2
Polvadera *USA* 14A3
Polyarnyy, Murmansk *USSR* 42E2
Polyarnyy, Yakutskaya *USSR* 47Q2
Polyarnyy Ural, Mts *USSR* 42L2
Polynesia, Region *Pacific O* 75L4
Pomabamba *Peru* 24C5
Pomba, R *Brazil* 27D3
Pomona *USA* 18D3
Pomona Res *USA* 15C2
Pompano Beach *USA* 13E4
Pompton Lake *USA* 12C2
Ponca City *USA* 15C2
Ponce *Puerto Rico* 21D3
Ponce de Leon B *USA* 13E4
Pondicherry *India* 60B2
Pond Inlet *Can* 5L2
Ponferrade *Spain* 37A1
Pongo, R *Sudan* 70C3
Pongola, R *S Africa* 72E2
Ponnāni *India* 60B2
Ponnyadoung Range, Mts *Burma* 59D3
Ponoka *Can* 3F3
Ponoy *USSR* 46F3
Ponoy, R *USSR* 42G2
Pons *France* 36B2
Ponta da Baleia, Pt *Brazil* 27E2
Ponta Delgada *Açores* 68A1
Ponta do Mutá, Pt *Brazil* 27E1
Ponta do Padrão, Pt *Angola* 70B4
Ponta dos Búzios, Pt *Brazil* 27D3
Ponta Grossa *Brazil* 27B4
Pontailler-sur-Saône *France* 35A1
Pontal *Brazil* 27C3
Pont-à-Mousson *France* 34C2
Ponta Pora *Brazil* 27A3
Pontarlier *France* 36D2
Pontassieve *Italy* 35D3
Pontchartrain,L *USA* 15D3
Pont d'Ain *France* 35A1
Ponte de Pedra *Brazil* 27A1
Pontedera *Italy* 38C2
Ponte Lecca *Corse* 38B2
Pontevedra *Spain* 37A1
Pontiac, Illinois *USA* 10B2
Pontiac, Michigan *USA* 10C2
Pontianak *Indon* 54C3
Pontivy *France* 36B2
Pontoise *France* 34B2
Pontotoc *USA* 15E3
Pontremoli *Italy* 35C2
Pont-sur-Yonne *France* 34B2
Pontypool *Wales* 33D6
Pontypridd *Wales* 33D6
Poole *Eng* 33E6
Poona = Pune
Pooncarie *Aust* 78B2
Poopelloe,L, L *Aust* 78B2
Poorman *USA* 8G3
Popayán *Colombia* 24C3
Poperinge *Belg* 34B1
Popilta L *Aust* 78B2
Poplar *USA* 9A2
Poplar, R *USA* 3G4
Poplar Bluff *USA* 15D2
Poplarville *USA* 15E3
Popndetta *PNG* 76D1
Popocatepetl, Mt *Mexico* 20C2
Popof, I *USA* 8F4
Popokabaka *Zaïre* 70B4
Popondetta *PNG* 49H7
Popovo *Bulg* 39F2
Poraiba, R *Brazil* 27C3
Porangatu *Brazil* 27C1
Porbandar *India* 58B4
Porcher I *Can* 3B3
Porcos, R *Brazil* 27C1
Porcupine, R *USA/Can* 8K2
Porcupine Hills *Can* 3H3
Pordenone *Italy* 35E2
Poreč *Yugos* 38C1
Porecatu *Brazil* 27B3
Pori *Fin* 30J6
Porirua *NZ* 79B2
Porjus *Sweden* 30H5
Poronay, R *USSR* 51E1
Poronaysk *USSR* 51E2
Porosozero *USSR* 42E3
Porrentruy *Switz* 35B1
Porretta *Italy* 35D3
Porsangen, Inlet *Nor* 30K4
Porsgrunn *Nor* 30F7
Portadown *N Ire* 33B4
Portage *USA* 10B2
Portage La Prairie *Can* 9C2
Portal *USA* 9B2
Port Alberni *Can* 3D4
Portalegre *Port* 37A2
Portales *USA* 14B3
Port Alfred *Can* 5L5
Port Alfred *S Africa* 72D3
Port Alice *Can* 3C3
Port Allegany *USA* 12A2
Port Allen *USA* 15D3
Port Angeles *USA* 16B1
Port Antonio *Jamaica* 21B3
Portarlington *Irish Rep* 33B5
Port Arthur *USA* 15D4
Port Askaig *Scot* 32B4
Port-Audemer *France* 34A2
Port Augusta *Aust* 78A2
Port-au-Prince *Haiti* 21C3
Port Austin *USA* 10C2
Port Blair *Andaman Is* 60E2
Port Campbell *Aust* 78B3
Port Canning *India* 59C3
Port Cartier *Can* 5M5
Port Chalmers *NZ* 79B3
Port Charlotte *USA* 13E4
Port Chester *USA* 12D2
Port Clements *Can* 3B3
Port Colborne *Can* 11D2
Port Credit *Can* 11D2
Port Davey *Aust* 78E3
Port-de-Paix *Haiti* 21C3
Port Dickson *Malay* 53C5
Port Edward *S Africa* 72E3
Porteirinha *Brazil* 27D2
Port Elgin *Can* 10C2
Port Elizabeth *S Africa* 72D3
Port Ellen *Scot* 32B4
Porter Pt *St Vincent* 21N2
Porterville *USA* 18C2
Port Fairy *Aust* 76D4
Port Gentil *Gabon* 70A4
Port Gibson *USA* 15D3
Port Graham *USA* 8H4
Port Hammond *Can* 16B1
Port Harcourt *Nigeria* 66E7
Port Hardy *Can* 3C3
Port Hawkesbury *Can* 5M5
Port Hedland *Aust* 76A3
Port Heiden = Meshik
Porthmadog *Wales* 33C5
Port Hope Simpson *Can* 5N4
Port Hueneme *USA* 18C3
Port Huron *USA* 10C2
Portimão *Port* 37A2
Port Jackson, B *Aust* 78D2
Port Jefferson *USA* 12D2
Port Jervis *USA* 12C2
Port Kembla *Aust* 78D2
Portland, Indiana *USA* 10C2
Portland, Maine *USA* 11E2
Portland, New South Wales *Aust* 78C2
Portland, Oregon *USA* 16B1
Portland, Victoria *Aust* 78B3
Portland Bight, B *Jamaica* 21H2
Portland Bill, Pt *Eng* 33D6
Portland,C *Aust* 78E3
Portland Canal, Sd *USA/Can* 8M4
Portland I *NZ* 79C1
Portland Pt *Jamaica* 21H2
Portland Sd *USA* 3B2
Port Laoise *Irish Rep* 31B3
Port Lavaca *USA* 15F4
Port-l'Evêque *France* 34A2
Port Lincoln *Aust* 78A2
Port Loko *Sierra Leone* 68A4
Port Louis *Mauritius* 71F6
Port MacDonnell *Aust* 78B3
Port McNeill *Can* 3C3
Port Macquarie *Aust* 78D2
Port Matilda *USA* 12A2
Port Moller *USA* 8F4
Port Moresby *PNG* 76D1
Port Nolloth *S Africa* 72B2
Port Norris *USA* 12C3
Port-Nouveau-Québec *Can* 5M4
Port Novo *Benin* 66E7
Porto *Port* 37A1
Pôrto Alegre *Brazil* 23F4
Porto Alexandre *Angola* 71B5
Porto Armuelles *Panama* 21A5
Pôrto Artur *Brazil* 27A1
Pôrto 15 de Novembro *Brazil* 27B3
Pôrto dos Meinacos *Brazil* 27B1
Pôrto E Cunha *Brazil* 23F2
Pôrto Esperança *Brazil* 27A2
Portoferraio *Italy* 38C2
Port of Spain *Trinidad* 21E4
Portogruaro *Italy* 35E2
Porto Jofre *Brazil* 27A2
Porto Lucena *Brazil* 26D1
Portomaggiore *Italy* 35D2
Porto Mendez *Brazil* 27B3
Porto Murtinho *Brazil* 27A3
Porto Novo *Benin* 69G4
Port Orchard *USA* 16B1
Porto Recanati *Italy* 35E3
Port Orford *USA* 16B2
Porto Santo, I *Medeira* 68A1
Porto São José *Brazil* 27B3
Pôrto Seguro *Brazil* 25L7
Porto Torres *Sardegna* 38B2
Porto União *Brazil* 27B4
Porto Vecchio *Corse* 38B2
Pôrto Velho *Brazil* 24F5
Port Pegasus, B *NZ* 79A3
Port Phillip B *Aust* 78B3
Port Pirie *Aust* 78A2
Port Radium *Can* 8P2
Portree *Scot* 32B3
Port Renfrew *Can* 16B1
Port Royal *Jamaica* 21J2
Port Royal Sd *USA* 13C2
Portrush *N Ire* 32B4
Port Said *Egypt* 63B3
Port St Joe *USA* 13B3
Port St Johns *S Africa* 72D3
Port Saunders *Can* 5N4
Port Shepstone *S Africa* 72E3
Port Simpson *Can* 3B3
Portsmouth *Dominica* 21Q2
Portsmouth *Eng* 33E6
Portsmouth, New Hampshire *USA* 12E1
Portsmouth, Ohio *USA* 10C3
Portsmouth, Virginia *USA* 11D3
Port Stephens, B *Aust* 78D2
Port Sudan *Sudan* 70D2
Port Sulphur *USA* 15E3
Porttipahdan Tekojärvi, Res *Fin* 30K5
Portugal, Republic *Europe* 37A2
Portville *USA* 12A1
Port Washington *USA* 10B2
Port Weld *Malay* 53C5
Porvenir *Bol* 24E6
Posadas *Arg* 23E3
Posadas *Spain* 37A2
Poschiavo *Switz* 35D1
Posheim Pen *Can* 5K2
Poshinok *USSR* 41G2
Posht-e Badam *Iran* 61D2
Poso *Indon* 55B3
Posŏng *S Korea* 52A4
Posse *Brazil* 27C1
Post *USA* 14B3
Postavy *USSR* 41F1
Post Clinton *USA* 10C2
Poste-de-la-Baleine *Can* 5L4
Postmasburg *S Africa* 72C2
Postojna *Yugos* 38C1
Pos'yet *USSR* 51C3
Pota *Indon* 55B4
Potchetstroom *S Africa* 72D2
Poteau *USA* 15D2
Potenza *Italy* 38D2
Potgietersrus *S Africa* 72D1
Poth *USA* 14C4
Poti *USSR* 43G7
Potiskum *Nig* 69J3
Potlatch *USA* 16C1
Potloer, Mt *S Africa* 72C3
Pot Mt *USA* 16C1
Potomac, R *USA* 11D3
Potomac South Branch, R *USA* 12A3
Potosi *Bol* 24E7
Potrerillos *Chile* 23C3
Potsdam *E Germ* 40C2
Potter *USA* 14B1
Pottstown *USA* 12C2
Pottsville *USA* 12B2
Poughkeepsie *USA* 12D2
Pouso Alegre *Brazil* 27C3
Poverty B *NZ* 79C1
Povonets *USSR* 42F3
Povorino *USSR* 43G5
Povungnituk *Can* 5L4
Powder, R *USA* 9A2
Powder River *USA* 9A3
Powell *USA* 16E2
Powell Creek *Aust* 76C2
Powell,L *USA* 17D3
Powell River *Can* 3D4
Power, R *USA* 6C2
Powys, County *Wales* 33D5
Poxoréo *Brazil* 27B2
Poyang Hu, L *China* 50D4
Poyarkovo *USSR* 51B2
Pozantı *Turk* 62C2
Poza Rica *Mexico* 20C1
Poznań *Pol* 40D2
Pozo Colorado *Par* 23E2
Poz Poluy *USSR* 42M2
Pozzuoli *Italy* 38C2
Pra, R *Ghana* 69F4
Prachin Buri *Thai* 53C3
Prachuap Khiri Khan *Thai* 53B3
Praděd, Mt *Czech* 40D2
Pradelles *France* 36C3
Prado *Brazil* 27E2
Prague = Praha
Praha *Czech* 40C2
Praia *Cape Verde* 68A4
Praia Rica *Brazil* 27A1
Prainha *Brazil* 24F5
Prairie Dog Town Fork, R *USA* 14B3
Prairie du Chien *USA* 10A2
Prairie Village *USA* 15D2
Prakhon Chai *Thai* 53C3
Prata *Brazil* 27C2
Prata, R *Brazil* 27C2
Prates = Dongsha Qundao
Prato *Italy* 35D3
Pratomagno, Mt *Italy* 35D3
Prattsville *USA* 12C1
Prattville *USA* 13B2
Prawle Pt *Eng* 36B1
Praya *Indon* 54E4
Predazzo *Italy* 35D1
Predivinsk *USSR* 47L4
Predporozhnyy *USSR* 47Q3
Pregolyu, R *USSR* 41E2
Prek Kak *Camb* 53D3
Prentice *USA* 10A1
Prenzlau *E Germ* 40C2
Preparis I *Burma* 60E2
Preparis North Chan *Burma* 53A2
Preparis South Chan *Burma* 53A3
Přerov *Czech* 40D3
Presa de les Adjuntas *Mexico* 20C1

Presa del Infiernillo *Mexico* 20B2
Presa de Salto Grande *Urug* 26D2
Presa Netzahualcóyotl *Mexico* 20D2
Prescott, Arizona *USA* 17D4
Prescott, Arkansas *USA* 15D3
Prescott *Can* 11D2
Presho *USA* 9B3
Presidencia Roque Sáenz Peña *Arg* 23D3
Presidente Epitácio *Brazil* 27B3
Presidente Frei, Base *Ant* 80G2
Presidente Migúel Aleman, L *Mexico* 20C2
Presidente Murtinho *Brazil* 27B2
Presidente Prudente *Brazil* 27B3
Presidenté Vargas *Brazil* 25H8
Presidente Venceslau *Brazil* 27B3
Presidio *USA* 14B4
Presidio, R *Mexico* 20A1
Prešov *Czech* 41E3
Prespansko Jezero, L *Yugos* 39E2
Presque Isle *USA* 11F1
Prestea *Ghana* 69F4
Preston *Eng* 33D5
Preston, Idaho *USA* 6B2
Preston, Minnesota *USA* 9D3
Preston, Missouri *USA* 15D2
Prestwick *Scot* 32C4
Prêto *Brazil* 25J8
Prêto, R *Brazil* 27C2
Pretoria *S Africa* 72D2
Preveza *Greece* 39E3
Prey Veng *Camb* 53D3
Pribilof Is *USA* 8E4
Price *USA* 17D3
Price I *Can* 3C3
Prichard *USA* 13B2
Prichernomorskaya Nizmennost', Lowland *USSR* 43E6
Prickly Pt *Grenada* 21M2
Pridneprovskaya Vozvyshennost', Upland *USSR* 41F3
Priekule *USSR* 41E1
Prieska *S Africa* 72C2
Priest L *USA* 16C1
Priest River *USA* 16C1
Prikaspiyskaya Nizmennost', Region *USSR* 43H6
Prilep *Yugos* 39E2
Priluki *USSR* 43E5
Primero, R *Arg* 26C2
Primorsk *USSR* 30K6
Primorsko-Akhtarsk *USSR* 43F6
Primrose L *Can* 3G3
Prince Albert *Can* 3G3
Prince Albert *S Africa* 72C3
Prince Albert,C *Can* 4F2
Prince Albert Nat Pk *Can* 3G3
Prince Albert Pen *Can* 4G2
Prince Albert Sd *Can* 4G2
Prince Charles I *Can* 5L3
Prince Charles Mts *Ant* 80G10
Prince Edward, I *Indian O* 74C7
Prince Edward I *Can* 5M5
Prince George *Can* 3D3
Prince Gustaf Adolp, S *Can* 4H2
Prince of Wales,C *USA* 8E2
Prince of Wales I *Aust* 49H8
Prince of Wales I *Can* 4H2
Prince of Wales I *USA* 3B2
Prince of Wales Str *Can* 4G2
Prince Patrick I *Can* 4F2
Prince Regent Inlet, Str *Can* 5J2
Prince Rupert *Can* 3B3
Princess Charlotte B *Aust* 76D2
Princess Royal I *Can* 3C3
Princes Town *Trinidad* 21L1
Princeton *Can* 3D4
Princeton, Illinois *USA* 10B2
Princeton, Kentucky *USA* 10B3
Princeton, Missouri *USA* 15D1
Princeton, New Jersey *USA* 12C2
Princeton, W Virginia *USA* 10C3
Prince William *USA* 4D3
Prince William Sd *USA* 8J3
Principe, I *W Africa* 68C4
Prineville *USA* 16B2
Pringle,Mt *USA* 8J2
Prins Christian Sund, Sd *Greenland* 5O3
Prinsesse Astric Kyst, Region *Ant* 80F12
Prinsesse Ragnhild Kyst, Region *Ant* 80F12
Prins Karls Forland, I *Barents S* 46C2
Prinzapolca *Nic* 19D3
Priozerzk *USSR* 42E3
Pripyat, R *USSR* 30K8
Pripyat', R *USSR* 41F2
Priština *Yugos* 39E2
Pritzwalk *E Germ* 40C2
Privolzhskaya Vozvyshennost', Upland *USSR* 42G5
Prizren *Yugos* 39E2
Probolinggo *Indon* 54D4
Procatello *USA* 4G5
Proctor *USA* 9D2
Proddatūr *India* 60B2
Progreso *Mexico* 19D2
Progress *USSR* 51B2
Project City *USA* 16B2
Prokhladnyy *USSR* 43G7
Prokop'yevsk *USSR* 46K4
Proletarskaya *USSR* 43G6
Proliv Dmitriya Lapteva, Str *USSR* 47P2
Proliv Karskiye Vorota, Str *USSR* 46G2
Proliv Longa, Str *USSR* 47T2
Proliv Vilritskago, Str *USSR* 47L2
Prome *Burma* 59E4
Promissão *Brazil* 27A2
Pronya, R *USSR* 41G2
Prophet, R *Can* 3D2
Propriá *Brazil* 25L6
Prospect, New York *USA* 12C1
Prospect, Oregon *USA* 16B2
Prosperine *Aust* 76D3
Prostějov *Czech* 40D3
Prøven *Greenland* 5N2
Provence, Region *France* 36D3
Providence *USA* 12E2
Provideniya *USSR* 47U3
Provincetown *USA* 12E1
Provins *France* 34B2
Provo *USA* 17D2
Provost *Can* 3F3
Prudentópolis *Brazil* 27B4
Prudhoe B *USA* 8J1
Prudhoe Bay *USA* 8J1
Prudhoe Land *Greenland* 5M2
Pruszkow *Pol* 41E2
Prut, R *Rom/USSR* 41F3
Prutul, R *USSR* 43D6
Pruzhany *USSR* 41E2
Pryor *USA* 15C2
Przemys'l *Pol* 41E3
Psará, I *Greece* 39F3
Pskov *USSR* 42D4
Ptich, R *USSR* 41F2
Ptolemaïs *Greece* 39E2
Puan *S Korea* 52A3
Pucallpa *Peru* 24D5
Pucheng *China* 50D4
Pucón *Chile* 26A3
Pudasjärvi *Fin* 30K5
Pudozh *USSR* 42F3
Pudukkottai *India* 60B2
Puebai de Trives *Spain* 37A1
Puebla *Mexico* 20C2
Puebla, State *Mexico* 20C2
Puebla de Sanabria *Spain* 37A1
Pueblo *USA* 14B2
Puelches *Arg* 26B3
Puelén *Arg* 26B3
Puenta Ixbapa *Mexico* 20B2
Puente del Inca *Arg* 26B2
Puerta Aguja *Peru* 24B5
Puerta Coles *Peru* 24D7
Puerta de los Llanos *Arg* 26B2
Puerta de Mita *Mexico* 20A1
Puerta do Calcanhar, Pt *Brazil* 25L5
Puerta do Oro, Pt *S Africa* 72E2
Puerta Galera *Mexico* 20C2
Puerta Gallinas *Colombia* 24D1
Puerta Maldonado Pt *Mexico* 20C2
Puerta Mariato *Panama* 24B2
Puerta Médanosa, Pt *Arg* 23C7
Puerta Mongrove *Mexico* 20B2
Puerta Roca Partida *Mexico* 20C2
Puerta San Blas, Pt *Panama* 19E4
Puerta San Telmo *Mexico* 20B2
Puerto Adela *Brazil* 27B3
Puerto Aisén *Chile* 23B7
Puerto Angel *Mexico* 20C2
Puerto Armuelles *Panama* 19D4
Puerto Artur *Brazil* 25G6
Puerto Asis *Colombia* 24C3
Puerto Ayacucho *Ven* 24E2
Puerto Barrios *Guatemala* 19D3
Puerto Berrio *Colombia* 24D2
Puerto Cabello *Ven* 24E1
Puerto Cabezas *Nic* 19D3
Puerto Carreño *Ven* 24E2
Puerto Casado *Brazil* 27A3
Puerto Cavezas *Nic* 24B1
Puerto Cooper *Brazil* 27A3
Puerto Cortes *Costa Rica* 19D4
Puerto Cortés *Honduras* 19D3
Puerto del Rosario *Canary Is* 68A2
Puerto E Cunha *Brazil* 25H8
Puerto Escondido *Mexico* 20C2
Puerto Fijo *Ven* 24D1
Puerto Franco *Brazil* 25J5
Puerto Guarani *Brazil* 27A3
Puerto Heath *Bol* 24E6
Puerto Juarez *Mexico* 19D2
Puerto la Cruz *Ven* 24F1
Puertollano *Spain* 37B2
Puerto Lopez *Colombia* 21C4
Puerto Madryn *Arg* 23D6
Puerto Maldonado *Peru* 24E6
Puerto Marquéz *Mexico* 20C2
Puerto Montt *Chile* 23B6
Puerto Moritt *Chile* 22C7
Puerto Murtinho *Brazil* 25G8
Puerto Natales *Chile* 23B8
Puerto Peñasco *Mexico* 19A1
Puerto Pinasco *Brazil* 27A3
Puerto Pirámides *Arg* 23D6
Puerto Plata *Dom Rep* 21C3
Puerto Princesa *Phil* 55E9
Puerto Rico *Colombia* 24C3
Puerto Rico, I *Caribbean* 21D3
Puerto Rico Trench *Caribbean* 21D3
Puerto San Juan de Lima *Mexico* 20B2
Puerto Santanga *Brazil* 25H4
Puerto Sastre *Brazil* 27A3
Puerto Suárez *Bol* 23E1
Puerto Vallarta *Mexico* 20A1
Puerto Varas *Chile* 23B6
Puerto Villarroel *Bol* 24F7
Pugachev *USSR* 43H5
Pugal *India* 58C3
Puigcerdá *Spain* 37C1
Pujŏn *N Korea* 52A2
Pujŏn Res *N Korea* 52A2
Pukaki,L, L *NZ* 79B2
Pukchin *N Korea* 52A2
Pukch'ŏng *N Korea* 51B3
Pukekobe *NZ* 79B1
Puketeraki Range, Mts *NZ* 79B2
Puksoozero *USSR* 42G3
Pula *Yugos* 38C2
Pulaski, New York *USA* 11D2
Pulaski, Tennessee *USA* 13B1
Pulaski, Virginia *USA* 10C3
Pulau Kolepom, I *Indon* 49G7
Pulau Pulau Asia, Is *Indon* 55D2
Pulau Pulau Ayu, Is *Indon* 55D2
Pulau Pulau Banyak, Arch *Indon* 54A2
Pulau Pulau Batu, Is *Indon* 54A3
Pulau Pulau Kangean, Is *Indon* 76A1
Pulau Pulau Macan, Is *Indon* 76B1
Pulau Pulau Pisang, Is *Indon* 55D3
Pulautelo *Indon* 54A3
Pulawy *Pol* 41E2
Pulicat,L *India* 60C2
Pul-i-Khumri *Afghan* 58B1
Puliyangudi *India* 60B3
Pullendorf *W Germ* 34E3
Pullman *USA* 16C1
Pulo Anna Merir, I *Pacific I* 49G6
Pulog,Mt *Phil* 55F7
Pulozero *USSR* 30L5
Pultusk *Pol* 41E2
Puna de Atacama *Arg* 23C3
Punakha *Bhutan* 59C2
Punch *Pak* 58C2
Punda Milia *S Africa* 72E1
Pune *India* 60A1
Punéper *Mexico* 20B2
Pungsan *N Korea* 52A2
Pungso *N Korea* 52A2
Punia *Zaïre* 70C4
Punitaqui *Chile* 26A2
Punjab, Province *Pak* 58C2
Punjab, State *India* 58D2
Puno *Peru* 24D7
Punta Abreojos, Pt *Mexico* 19A2
Punta Alice, Pt *Italy* 38D3
Punta Alta *Arg* 26C3
Punta Arenas *Chile* 23B8
Punta Baja, Pt *Mexico* 19A2
Punta Bermeja, Pt *Arg* 26C4
Punta Curaumilla, Pt *Chile* 26A2
Punta da Marca, Pt *Angola* 71B5
Punta de Barra Falsa, Pt *Mozam* 71D6
Punta del Este *Urug* 26E2
Punta di Portofino, Pt *Italy* 35C2
Punta Eugenia, Pt *Mexico* 19A2
Punta Galera *Chile* 26A3
Punta Gorda *Belize* 19D3
Punta Gorda *USA* 13E4
Punta Lavapié, Pt *Chile* 26A3
Punta Lengua de Vaca, Pt *Chile* 26A2
Punta Licosa, Pt *Italy* 38C2
Punta Norte, Pt *Arg* 26D3
Punta Piedras, Pt *Arg* 26D3
Punta Poroto, Pt *Chile* 26A1
Punta Rasa, Pt *Arg* 26C4
Puntarenas *Costa Rica* 24B1
Punta Rubia, Pt *Arg* 26C4
Punta San Antonia, Pt *Mexico* 6B4
Punta Sur *Arg* 26D3
Punta Topocalma *Chile* 26A2
Puntjak Ranakah, Mt *Indon* 55B4
Punxsutawney *USA* 12A2
Puper *Indon* 55D3
Puqi *China* 50C4
Purcell *USA* 15C2
Purcell Mt *USA* 8G2
Purcell Mts *Can* 3E3
Purén *Chile* 26A3
Purgatoire, R *USA* 14B2
Puri *India* 59C3
Pūrna *India* 60B1
Pūrnia *India* 59C2
Pursat *Camb* 53C3
Puruandro *Mexico* 20B1
Purus, R *Brazil* 24F4
Purvis *USA* 15E3
Purwokerto *Indon* 54C4
Purworejo *Indon* 54D4
Pusad *India* 58D5
Pusan *S Korea* 51B4
Pushakhta *USSR* 42F3
Pushkin *USSR* 42E4
Pustochka *USSR* 41F1
Putaendo *Chile* 26A2
Putao *Burma* 59E2
Putaruru *NZ* 79C1
Putian *China* 50D4
Putnam *USA* 12E2
Putney *USA* 12D1
Puttalam *Sri Lanka* 60B3
Puttgarden *W Germ* 40C2
Putumayo, R *Ecuador* 24C4
Putussibau *Indon* 54D2
Puulavesl, L *Fin* 30K6
Puyallup *USA* 16B1
Puy de Sancy, Mt *France* 36C2
Puyehue *Chile* 26A4
Puysegur Pt *NZ* 79A3
Pweto *Zaïre* 71C4
Pwllheli *Wales* 33C5
Pyalma *USSR* 42F3
Pyapon *Burma* 53B2
Pyasina, R *USSR* 47K2
Pyatigorsk *USSR* 43G7
Pyinmana *Burma* 59E4
Pyŏktong *N Korea* 52A2
Pyonggang *N Korea* 52A3
Pyŏnggok-dong *S Korea* 52A3
P'Yŏngsann *N Korea* 52A3
P'yongt'aek *S Korea* 52A3
P'yŏngyang *N Korea* 51B4
Pyramid Hill *Aust* 78B3
Pyramid L *USA* 17C2
Pyramid,Mt *NZ* 79A2
Pyrénées, Mts *France* 36B3
Pytalovo *USSR* 41F1
Pyu *Burma* 53B2

Q

Qabatiya *Israel* 63C2
Qabr Hūd *S Yemen* 65E3
Qā'el Hafira, Mud Flats *Jordan* 63D3
Qa'el Jinz, Mud Flats *Jordan* 63D3
Qaidam Pendi, Salt Flat *China* 48C3
Qaisar *Afghan* 61E1
Qa Khanna, Salt Marsh *Jordan* 63D2
Qala Adras Kand *Afghan* 61E2
Qala'en Nahl *Sudan* 70D2
Qala Nau *Afghan* 61E2
Qalat *Afghan* 58B2
Qal'at al Hisn *Syria* 63D1
Qal'at al Marqab, Hist Site 63C1
Qal'at Bishah *S Arabia* 64D2
Qal'at Sālih *Iraq* 62E3
Qamdo *China* 48C3
Qara *Egypt* 67B2
Qareh Dāgh, Mts *Iran* 43H8
Qare Shīrīn *Iran* 61B2
Qaryat al Ulyā *S Arabia* 65E1
Qasr el Kharana *Jordan* 63D3
Qasr-e-Qand *Iran* 61E3
Qasr Farafra *Egypt* 67B2
Qaṭana *Syria* 63D2
Qatar, Emirate *Arabian Pen* 65F1
Qatrāna *Jordan* 63D3
Qattāra Depression *Egypt* 67B2
Qāyen *Iran* 61D2
Qazvīn *Iran* 61C1
Qena *Egypt* 64B1
Qeydār *Iran* 61B1
Qeys, I *Iran* 61C3
Qezel Owzan, R *Iran* 43H8
Qian'an *China* 51A3
Qian Gorlos *China* 51A2
Qian Jiang, R *China* 50B5
Qian Shan, Upland *China* 50E1
Qidong *China* 50E3
Qijiang *China* 50B4
Qila Ladgasht *Pak* 61E3
Qila Saifullah *Pak* 58B2
Qilian *China* 50A2
Qilian Shan *China* 48C3
Qin'an *China* 50B3
Qingdao *China* 50E2
Qinggang *China* 51B2
Qinghai, Province *China* 50A2
Qinghai Hu, L *China* 48C3
Qinghai Hu, L *China* 50A2
Qinghai Hu, L *China* 50A2
Qingjiang, Jiangsu *China* 50D3
Qingjiang, Jiangxi *China* 50D4
Qing Jiang, R *China* 50B3
Qingshuihe *China* 50C2
Qingshui He, R *China* 50B2
Qingtonxia *China* 50B2
Qingyang *China* 50B2
Qingyuan, Liaoning *China* 51B3
Qingyuan, Zhejiang *China* 50D4
Qing Zang, Upland *China* 57G2
Qingzhou *China* 50B5
Qingzhou *China* 53D1
Qinhuangdao *China* 50D2
Qin Ling, Mts *China* 50B3
Qionghai *China* 53E2
Qionglai Shan, Upland *China* 50A3
Qiongzhou Haixia, Str *China* 53D1
Qiqihar *China* 51A2
Qiryat Ata *Israel* 63C2
Qiryat Gat *Israel* 63C3
Qiryat Shemona *Israel* 63C2
Qiryat Yam *Israel* 63C2
Qishn *S Yemen* 65F3
Qishon, R *Israel* 63C2
Qishran, I *S Arabia* 64C2
Qitai *China* 47K5
Qitaihe *China* 51C2
Qixing He, R *China* 51C2
Qiyang *China* 50C4
Qog Qi *China* 50B1
Qolleh-ye-Damavand, Mt *Iran* 43J8
Qolleh-ye Damavand, Mt *Iran* 61C1
Qom *Iran* 61C2
Qomisheh *Iran* 61C2
Qomolangma Feng, Mt = Everest,Mt
Qornet es Saouda, Mt *Leb* 63D1
Qôrnoq *Greenland* 5N3
Qorveh *Iran* 61B1
Qotābad *Iran* 61D3
Qotúr, R *Iran* 43H8
Quabbin Res *USA* 12D1
Quaggablat *S Africa* 72C2
Quakertown *USA* 12C2
Quam Phu Quoc, I *Viet* 53C3
Quanah *USA* 14C3
Quang Ngai *Viet* 53D2
Quang Tri *Viet* 53D2
Quan Long *Viet* 53D4
Quanzhou, Fujian *China* 50D5
Quanzhou, Guangxi *China* 50C4
Qu'Appelle *Can* 9B1
Qu' Appelle, R *Can* 4H4
Quarai, R *Urug* 26D2
Quaral *Brazil* 26D2
Quarayyāt *Oman* 65G2
Quardho *Somalia* 67D4
Quarkoye *U Volta* 69F3
Quartzsite *USA* 17D4
Quatsino Sd *Can* 3C3
Quchan *Iran* 61D1
Queanbeyan *Aust* 78C3
Québec *Can* 11E1
Quebec, Province *Can* 5L4

Quebra-Anzol, R *Brazil* 27C2
Quebracho *Urug* 26D2
Quedas do Iguaçu
 Brazil/Arg 23F3
Queen Anne *USA* 12B3
Queen Bess,Mt *Can* 3C3
Queen Charlotte *Can* 3B3
Queen Charlotte Is *Can* 3B3
Queen Charlotte Sd *Can* 3C3
Queen Charlotte Str *Can* 3C3
Queen Elizabeth Is *Can* 4H1
Queen Mary Land,
 Region *Ant* 80G9
Queen Maud G *Can* 4H3
Queen Maud Mts *Ant* 80E
Queens, Borough, New
 York *USA* 12D2
Queens, Chan *Can* 4J2
Queens Ch *Aust* 49F8
Queenscliff *Aust* 78B3
Queensland, State *Aust* 76D3
Queenstown *Aust* 78E3
Queenstown *NZ* 79A3
Queenstown *S Africa* 72D3
Queenstown *USA* 12B3
Quela *Angola* 71B4
Quelimane *Mozam* 71D5
Quemado *USA* 14A3
Quémé, R *Benin* 69G4
Quemoquemú *Arg* 26C3
Quensel L *Can* 3D3
Quequén *Arg* 26D3
Quequén, R *Arg* 26D3
Querétaro *Mexico* 20B1
Queretaro, State *Mexico* 20B1
Quesnel *Can* 3D3
Quetta *Pak* 58B2
Quezaltenango
 Guatemala 19C3
Queziot *Israel* 63C3
Quezon City *Phil* 55F8
Quibala *Angola* 71B5
Quibaxe *Angola* 71B4
Quibdó *Colombia* 24C2
Quiberon *France* 36B2
Quicama Nat Pk *Angola* 71B4
Quiindy *Par* 27A4
Quijing *China* 50A4
Quilima *Chile* 26A2
Quilino *Arg* 26C2
Quillabamba *Peru* 24D6
Quillacollo *Bol* 24E7
Quillan *France* 36C3
Quill L *Can* 4H4
Quill Lakes *Can* 3H3
Quillota *Chile* 26A2
Quilon *India* 60B3
Quilpie *Aust* 78B1
Quilpué *Chile* 26A2
Quimbele *Angola* 71B4
Quimili *Arg* 26C1
Quimper *France* 36B2
Quimperlé *France* 36B2
Quincy, California *USA* 17B3
Quincy, Illinois *USA* 10A3
Quincy, Massachusetts
 USA 12E1
Quines *Arg* 26B2
Quinhagak *USA* 8F4
Qui Nhon *Viet* 53D3
Quintanar de la Orden
 Spain 37B2
Quintero *Chile* 26A2
Quinto, R *Arg* 26C2
Quirihue *Chile* 26A3
Quirima *Angola* 71B5
Quirindi *Aust* 78D2
Quissanga *Mozam* 71E5
Quissico *Mozam* 71D6
Quito *Ecuador* 24C4
Quixadá *Brazil* 25L4
Qumbu *S Africa* 72D3
Quorn *Aust* 78A2
Qus *Egypt* 64B1
Quşayir *Oman* 65F4
Quseir *Egypt* 64B1
Qutdligssat *Greenland* 5N3
Quthing = Moyeni
Qu Xian, Sichuan *China* 50B3
Qu Xian, Zhejiang *China* 50D4
Quynh Luu *Viet* 53D2
Quzhou *China* 50C2
Qüzü *China* 59D2

R

Raahe *Fin* 30J6
Raasay, I *Scot* 32B3
Raasay,Sound of, Chan
 Scot 32B3
Raas Caseyr, C *Somalia* 65F4
Rab, I *Yugos* 38C2
Raba *Indon* 54E4
Rába, R *Hung* 40D3
Rabak *Sudan* 64B4
Rabat *Mor* 69A2
Rabaul *PNG* 76E1
Rabba *Jordan* 63C3
Rabbit Lake *Can* 3H2
Rabigh *S Arabia* 64C2
Racconigi *Italy* 35B2

Race,C *Can* 5N5
Race Pt *USA* 12E1
Rachaya *Leb* 63C2
Rachel, Mt *W Germ* 40C3
Rach Gia *Viet* 53D3
Racine *USA* 10B2
Radã' *Yemen* 64D4
Radcliff *USA* 10B3
Radford *USA* 10C3
Radhanpur *India* 58C4
Radix,Pt *Trinidad* 21L1
Radom *Pol* 41E2
Radomsko *Pol* 41D2
Radomyshl' *USSR* 41F2
Radstadt *Austria* 35E1
Radviliškis *USSR* 41E1
Radville *Can* 3H4
Rae *Can* 4G3
Rãe Bareli *India* 59B2
Rae Isthmus *Can* 5K3
Rae L *Can* 4G3
Raetihi *NZ* 79C1
Rafaela *Arg* 26C2
Rafah *Egypt* 63C3
Rafai *CAR* 70C3
Rafhã Al Jumaymah *S
 Arabia* 62D3
Rafsanjän *Iran* 61D2
Raga *Sudan* 70C3
Ragged Pt *Barbados* 21Q2
Raguba *Libya* 67A2
Ragusa *Italy* 38C3
Raha *Indon* 55B3
Rahad, R *Sudan* 64C4
Raheita *Eth* 64D4
Rahimyar Khan *Pak* 58C3
Rãhjerd *Iran* 61C2
Raíces *Arg* 26D2
Rãichur *India* 60B1
Raigarh *India* 59B3
Rainbow *Aust* 78B3
Rainbow City *USA* 13B2
Rainbow Lake *Can* 3E2
Rainier *USA* 16B1
Rainier,Mt *USA* 16B1
Rainy, R *USA* 9D2
Rainy L *Can* 9D2
Rainy P *USA* 8H3
Rainy River *Can* 9D2
Raipur *India* 59B3
Rãjahmundry *India* 60C1
Rajang, R *Malay* 54D2
Rajanpur *Pak* 58C3
Rãjapãlaiyam *India* 60B3
Rãjasthan, State *India* 58C3
Rãjgarh *India* 58D3
Rãjgarh, State *India* 58D4
Rãjkot *India* 58C4
Rãjmahãl Hills *India* 59C3
Raj Nãndgaon *India* 59B3
Rãjpipla *India* 58C4
Rajshahi *Bang* 59C3
Rajur *India* 58D4
Rakaia, R *NZ* 79B2
Rakata, I *Indon* 54C4
Raka Zangbo, R *China* 57G3
Rakhov *USSR* 41E3
Rakhshan, R *Pak* 61E3
Rakhyüt *Oman* 65F3
Rakops *Botswana* 72C1
Rakov *USSR* 41F2
Raleigh *USA* 13D1
Ralny L *Can* 5J5
Ram *Jordan* 63C4
Rama *Israel* 63C2
Ramallah *Israel* 63C3
Rãmanãthapuram *India* 60B3
Ramapo Deep *Pacific
 Oc* 48H3
Ramat Gan *Israel* 63C2
Rambervillers *France* 34D2
Rambouillet *France* 34A2
Rãmgarh, Bihar *India* 59C3
Rãmgarh, Rajasthan
 India 58C3
Rãmhormoz *Iran* 61B2
Ramla *Israel* 63C3
Ramlat Al Wahibah,
 Region *Oman* 65G2
Ramlat as Sab'atayn,
 Region *S Yemen* 65E3
Ramona *USA* 17C4
Rãmpur *India* 58D3
Rãmpura *India* 58D4
Ramree, I *Burma* 59D4
Rãmsar *Iran* 43J8
Ramsey *Eng* 33C4
Ramsey *USA* 12C2
Ramsey I *Wales* 33C6
Ramsgate *Eng* 33F6
Ramtha *Jordan* 63D2
Ramu, R *PNG* 76D1
Ranau *Malay* 54E1
Rancagua *Chile* 26A2
Rancheria, R *Can* 3B1
Ranchester *USA* 9A3
Rãnchi *India* 59C3
Rãnchi Plat *India* 59B3
Ratherow *E Germ* 40C2
Rathlin, I *N Ire* 32B4
Randfontein *S Africa* 72D2

Randolph, New York
 USA 12A1
Randolph, Vermont *USA* 11E2
Randsburg *USA* 18D3
Ranfurly *NZ* 79B3
Rangamati *Bang* 59D3
Rangely *USA* 14A1
Rangiora *NZ* 79B2
Rangitaiki, R *NZ* 79C1
Rangitate, R *NZ* 79B2
Rangitikei, R *NZ* 79C1
Rangoon *Burma* 53B2
Rangpur *India* 59C2
Rani India 60B2
Ranibennur *India* 60B2
Ranier,Mt, Mt *USA* 6A2
Rãniganj *India* 59C3
Rankins Springs *Aust* 78C2
Ranklin Inlet *Can* 5J3
Rann of Kachchh, Flood
 Area *India* 58B4
Ranong *Thai* 53B4
Rantauparapat *Indon* 54A2
Rantepao *Indon* 55A3
Rantoul *USA* 10B2
Ranuro, R *Brazil* 27B1
Raohe *China* 51C2
Raon-l'Etape *France* 34D2
Raoul, I *NZ* 77H3
Rapallo *Italy* 35C2
Rapel, R *Chile* 26A2
Raper,C *Can* 5M3
Rapid City *USA* 9B3
Rapid River *USA* 10B1
Rappahannock, R *USA* 11D3
Rappang *Indon* 55A3
Rapperswil *Switz* 35C1
Raritan B *USA* 12C2
Ras Abü Dâra, C *Egypt* 64C2
Ra's Abu Madd, C *S
 Arabia* 64C2
Ras Abu Shagara, C
 Sudan 64C2
Ra's al 'Ayn *Syria* 62D2
Ra's al Hadd, C *Oman* 65G2
Ras al Kaimah *UAE* 65G1
Ra's al Kalb, C *S Yemen* 65E4
Ras-al-Kuh, C *Iran* 65G1
Ra's al Madrakah, C
 Oman 65G3
Ras Andadda, C *Eth* 64D3
Ra's ash Sharbatãt, C
 Oman 65G3
Ra's Asis, C *Sudan* 64C3
Ra's at Tarfã, C *S Arabia* 64D3
Ra's az Zawr, C *S Arabia* 65E1
Rãs Bânas, C *Egypt* 64C2
Ras Burûn, C *Egypt* 63B3
Ras Dashan, Mt *Eth* 64C4
Ra's Duqm *Oman* 65G3
Ra's-e-Barkan, Pt *Iran* 61B2
Ra's-e-Fasteh, C *Iran* 61E3
Râs el Barr, C *Egypt* 63A3
Râs el Kenâyis, Pt *Egypt* 62A3
Ras el Nafas, Mt *Egypt* 63C4
Râs El Sudr, C *Egypt* 63B4
Ras en Naqb, Upland
 Jordan 63C4
Ra's Fartak, C *S Yemen* 65F3
Râs Ghârib *Egypt* 64B1
Rashad *Sudan* 70D2
Ras Hadarba, C *Egypt* 64C2
Rashãdîya *Jordan* 63C3
Rashîd *Egypt* 62B3
Rasht *Iran* 61B1
Ra's ibn Hâni, C *Syria* 63C1
Ra's Jaddi, C *Pak* 61E3
Ra's Jibish, C *Oman* 65G2
Râs Kasar, C *Sudan* 64C3
Ras Khanzira, C *Somalia* 70E2
Ras Koh, Mt *Pak* 58B3
Râs Matarma, C *Egypt* 63B4
Ra's Momi, C *Socotra* 65F4
Râs Muhammad, C
 Egypt 64B1
Ras Nouadhibou, C
 Maur 68A2
Ra's Nuh, C *Pak* 61E3
Ra's Ormara, C *Pak* 61E3
Ra's Sharwayn, C *S
 Yemen* 65F3
Rasshua, I *USSR* 48J2
Ra's Shu'ab, C *Socotra* 65F4
Rass Kaboudia, Pt
 Tunisia 69E1
Rasskazovo *USSR* 43G5
Ra's Tanãqib, C *S Arabia* 65E1
Ra's Tannürah *S Arabia* 65F1
Rastatt *W Germ* 40B3
Ra's 'Tsa, C *Yemen* 64D3
Ras Uarc = Cabo Tres
 Foreas
Ras Um Seisaban, Mt
 Jordan 63C4
Ras Xaafuun, C *Somalia* 67E3
Ratangarh *India* 58C3
Rath *India* 58D3
Rat I *USA* 8B6

Rat Is *USA* 8B6
Ratlãm *India* 58C4
Ratnãgiri *India* 60A1
Ratnapura *Sri Lanka* 60C3
Ratno *USSR* 41E2
Raton *USA* 14B2
Rattenberg *Austria* 35D1
Rättvik *Sweden* 30H6
Ratz, Mt *Can* 3B2
Rau, I *Indon* 55C2
Raub *Malay* 54F7
Rauch *Arg* 26D3
Raukumara Range, Mts
 NZ 79C1
Raul Soares *Brazil* 27D3
Rauma *Fin* 30J6
Raurkela *India* 59B3
Ravânsar *Iran* 61B2
Rävar *Iran* 61D2
Rava Russkaya *USSR* 41E2
Ravena *USA* 12D1
Ravenna *Italy* 35E2
Ravensburg *W Germ* 40B3
Ravenshoe *Aust* 76D2
Ravi, R *Pak* 58C2
Rãvndiz *Iraq* 41F2
Rawalpindi *Pak* 58C2
Rawãndiz *Iraq* 43G3
Rawicz *Pol* 40D2
Rawlinna *Aust* 76B4
Rawlins *USA* 6C2
Rawson *Arg* 23D6
Rawu *China* 59E2
Raya, Mt *Indon* 54D3
Rãyadurg *India* 60B2
Rãyagada *India* 60C1
Raychikhinsk *USSR* 51B2
Raydah *Yemen* 64D3
Räyen *Iran* 61D3
Raymond, California
 USA 18C2
Raymond *Can* 16D1
Raymond, New
 Hampshire *USA* 12E1
Raymond, Washington
 USA 16B1
Raymond Terrace *Aust* 78D2
Raymondville *USA* 15F4
Ray Mts *USA* 8H2
Rayon *Mexico* 20C1
Raysüt *Oman* 65F3
Razan *Iran* 61B1
Razdel'naya *USSR* 41G3
Razdol'noye *USSR* 51C3
Razgrad *Bulg* 39F2
Razim, L *Rom* 39F2
Reading *Eng* 33E6
Reading *USA* 12C2
Read Island *Can* 4G3
Readsboro *USA* 12D1
Real de Padre *Arg* 26B2
Realicó *Arg* 26C3
Rebecca, Well *Libya* 67B2
Rebiana Sand Sea *Libya* 67B2
Reboly *USSR* 30L6
Rebun-tō, I *Japan* 51E2
Recherche,Arch of the,
 Is *Aust* 76B4
Rechitsa *USSR* 41G2
Recife *Brazil* 25M5
Recife,C *S Africa* 72D3
Recifes da Pedra Grande
 Arch *Brazil* 27E2
Récifs D'Entrecasteaux
 Nouvelle Calédonie 77F2
Recklinghausen *W Germ* 34D1
Reconquista *Arg* 26D1
Recreo *Arg* 26C1
Red, R *Can/USA* 9C2
Red, R *USA* 15D3
Redang, I *Malay* 53C4
Red Bank, New Jersey
 USA 12C2
Red Bank, Tennessee
 USA 13B1
Redberry L *Can* 3G3
Red Bluff *USA* 17B2
Red Bluff L *USA* 14B3
Redcar *Eng* 33E4
Redcliff *Can* 3F3
Redcliffe *Aust* 78D1
Red Cliffs *Aust* 78B2
Red Cloud *USA* 14C1
Red Deer *Can* 3F3
Red Deer, R *Can* 3F3
Red Deer, R,
 Saskatchewan *Can* 3H3
Red Deer L *Can* 3H3
Redding *USA* 16B2
Redfield *USA* 9C3
Red Hills *USA* 14C2
Red L *USA* 7D2
Red Lake *Can* 5J4
Red Lake, R *USA* 9C2
Redlands *USA* 18D3
Red Lion *USA* 12B3
Red Lodge *USA* 16E1
Redmond *USA* 16B2

Red Mountain *USA* 18D3
Red Oak *USA* 15C1
Redon *France* 36B2
Redondo Beach *USA* 18C4
Redoubt V *USA* 8H3
Red River Delta *Vietnam* 50B5
Red Sea *Africa/Arabian
 Pen* 56B3
Redstone, R *Can* 8N3
Redwater *Can* 3F3
Redwater, R *USA* 3G4
Red Wing *USA* 9D3
Redwood City *USA* 18A2
Redwood Falls *USA* 9C3
Reed City *USA* 10B2
Reedley *USA* 18C2
Reedsport *USA* 16B2
Reedville *USA* 11D3
Reefton *NZ* 79B2
Refahiye *Turk* 62C2
Refugio *USA* 15F4
Regência *Brazil* 27E2
Regensburg *W Germ* 40C3
Reggane *Alg* 68C2
Reggio di Calabria *Italy* 38D3
Reggio Nell'Emilia *Italy* 35D2
Reghin *Rom* 39E1
Regina *Can* 3H3
Registan, Region *Afghan* 61E2
Regocijo *Mexico* 20A1
Rehoboth *Namibia* 72B1
Rehoboth Beach *USA* 11D3
Rehovot *Israel* 63C3
Reicito *Ven* 24E1
Reidsville *USA* 13D1
Reigate *Eng* 33E6
Reims *France* 34B2
Reinbeck *USA* 9D3
Reindeer, R *Can* 3H2
Reindeer L *Can* 3H2
Reinosa *Spain* 37B1
Reisterstown *USA* 12B3
Reitz *S Africa* 72D2
Reliance *Can* 4H3
Reliance *USA* 16E2
Relizane *Alg* 69C1
Remarkable,Mt *Aust* 78A2
Rembang *Indon* 54D4
Remeshk *Iran* 61D3
Remiremont *France* 34D2
Remscheid *W Germ* 34D1
Remsen *USA* 12C1
Rémuzat *France* 35A2
Rend L *USA* 10B3
Rendsburg *W Germ* 40B2
Renfrew *Can* 11D1
Rengat *Indon* 54B3
Rengo *Chile* 26A2
Reni *USSR* 41F3
Renk *Sudan* 70D2
Renland, Pen *Greenland* 5Q2
Renmark *Aust* 78B2
Rennell, I *Solomon Is* 77F2
Rennes *France* 36B2
Reno *USA* 17C3
Reno, R *Italy* 35D2
Renovo *USA* 12B2
Rensselaer *USA* 12D1
Renton *USA* 16B1
Reo *Indon* 55B4
Réo *Upper Volta* 69F3
Repetek *USSR* 61E1
Repki *USSR* 41G2
Reprêsa de Furnas, Dam
 Brazil 27C3
Reprêsa Três Marias,
 Dam *Brazil* 27C2
Republic *USA* 16C1
Republican, R *USA* 14C1
Republic of Ireland *NW
 Europe* 31B3
Repulse Bay *Can* 5K3
Rergus Falls *USA* 9C2
Réservoir Baskatong, Res
 Can 11D1
Réservoir Cabonga, Res
 Can 11D1
Réservoir Decelles, Res
 Can 11D1
Réservoir Dozois, Res
 Can 11D1
Réservoire Cabonga, Res
 Can 5L5
Réservoire Gouin, Res
 Can 5L5
Réservoire Manicouagan,
 Res *Can* 7G1
Reshteh-ye Alborz, Mts
 Iran 61C1
Reshui *China* 50A2
Resistencia *Arg* 23E3
Resita *Rom* 39E1
Resolute *Can* 5J2
Resolution I *NZ* 79A3
Resolution Island *Can* 5M3
Ressano Garcia *Mozam* 72E2
Restinga Seca *Brazil* 26E1
Retamito *Arg* 26B2
Rethel *France* 34C2
Réthimnon *Greece* 39E3
Reunion, I *Indian O* 74D6

Reus Spain 37C1
Reuss, R Switz 35C1
Reutlingen W Germ 34E2
Reutte Austria 35D1
Revda USSR 42L5
Revelstoke Can 3E3
Revillagigedo, Is Mexico 19A3
Revillagigedo I USA 8M4
Revin France 34C2
Revivim Israel 63C3
Rewa India 59B3
Rewari India 58D3
Rexburg USA 16D2
Reykjavik Iceland 30A2
Reynoldsville USA 12A2
Reynosa Mexico 19C2
Rezé France 36B2
Rezekne USSR 41F1
Rezh USSR 42L4
Rhätikon, Mts Austria/
    Switz 35C1
Rhazir, Republic Leb 63C1
Rheda Wiedenbrück W
    Germ 34E1
Rhein, R W Europe 40B2
Rheine W Germ 40B2
Rheinfelden Switz 35B1
Rheinland Pfalz, Region
    W Germ 36D2
Rheinwaldhorn, Mt Switz 35C1
Rhine = Rhein
Rhinebeck USA 12D2
Rhinelander USA 10B1
Rho Italy 35C2
Rhode Island, State USA 11E2
Rhode Island Sd USA 12E2
Rhodes = Ródhos
Rhodes Drift, Ford S
    Africa 72D1
Rhodes Peak, Mt USA 16D1
Rhône, R France 36C3
Rhyl Wales 33D5
Riachão do Jacuipe
    Brazil 25L6
Ria de Arosa, B Spain 37A1
Ria de Betanzos, B Spain 37A1
Ria de Corcubion, B
    Spain 37A1
Ria de Lage, B Spain 37A1
Ria de Sta Marta, B
    Spain 37A1
Ria de Vigo, B Spain 37A1
Riasi Pak 58C2
Ribadeo Spain 37A1
Ribas do Rio Pardo
    Brazil 27B3
Ribauè Mozam 71D5
Ribble, R Eng 33D5
Ribeira Brazil 27C3
Ribeirão Prêto Brazil 27C3
Riberalta Bol 24E6
Riccione Italy 35E3
Rice L Can 11D2
Rice Lake USA 10A1
Richao de Santana Brazil 27D1
Richard's Bay S Africa 72E2
Richards I Can 8L2
Richardson USA 15C3
Richardson, R Can 3F2
Richardson Mts Can 8L2
Richfield USA 17D3
Richfield Springs USA 12C1
Richgrove USA 18C3
Richland USA 16C1
Richlands USA 10C3
Richmond, California
    USA 18A2
Richmond, Cape
    Province S Africa 72C3
Richmond, Kentucky
    USA 10C3
Richmond, Natal S
    Africa 72E2
Richmond, New South
    Wales Aust 78D2
Richmond NZ 79B2
Richmond, Queensland
    Aust 76D3
Richmond, Virginia USA 11D3
Richmond Range, Mts
    NZ 79B2
Richmondville USA 12C1
Rideau, L Can 11D2
Ridgeland USA 13C2
Ridgway USA 12A2
Riding Mountain Nat Pk
    Can 9B1
Riecito Ven 21D4
Rienza, R Italy 35D1
Riesa E Germ 40C2
Riesco, I Chile 23B8
Riet, R S Africa 72C2
Rieti Italy 38C2
Riez France 35B3
Rif, Mts Mor 37B2
Rifle USA 14A2
Riga USSR 41E1
Riga, G of USSR 42C4
Rigān Iran 61D3
Rigby USA 16D2
Riggins USA 16C1

Rigolet Can 5N4
Riihimaki Fin 30J6
Rijeka Yugos 38C1
Rikuzen-Tanaka Japan 52D3
Rima, R Nig 69H3
Rimbey Can 3F3
Rimbo Sweden 30H7
Rimini Italy 35E2
Rîmnicu Sârat Rom 39F1
Rîmnicu Vîlcea Rom 39E1
Rimouski Can 7G2
Rincón de Romos
    Mexico 20B1
Ringkøbing Den 30F7
Rinihue Chile 26A3
Rinja, I Indon 55A4
Rio Benito Eq Guinea 70A3
Rio Branco Brazil 24E5
Rio Branco Urug 25E2
Rio Branco do Sul Brazil 27C4
Rio Bravo Mexico 15F4
Rio Bravo del Norte, R
    USA/Mexico 19B1
Rio Brilhante Brazil 27B3
Rio Bueno Chile 26A4
Riochacha Colombia 24D1
Rio Claro Brazil 27C3
Rio Claro Trinidad 21L1
Rio Colorado Arg 26C3
Rio Cuarto Arg 26C2
Rio de Jacuipe Brazil 25L6
Rio de Janeiro Brazil 27D3
Rio de Janeiro, State
    Brazil 27D3
Rio de la Plata, Estuary
    Arg/Urug 26D2
Rio Gallegos Arg 23C8
Rio Grande Arg 23C8
Rio Grande Brazil 26E2
Rio Grande Mexico 20B1
Rio Grande Nic 21A4
Rio Grande, R Nicaragua 19D3
Rio Grande, R USA/
    Mexico 19B2
Rio Grande City USA 15F4
Rio Grande de Santiago
    Mexico 20B1
Rio Grande do Norte,
    State Brazil 25L5
Rio Grande do Sul, State
    Brazil 26E1
Rio Grande Rise Atlantic
    O 73G6
Riohacha Colombia 21C4
Riom France 36C2
Riombamba Ecuador 24C4
Rio Mulatos Bol 24E7
Rio Negro Brazil 27C4
Rio Negro, State Arg 26B4
Rio Pardo Brazil 23F3
Rio Tercero Arg 26C2
Rio Theodore Roosevelt,
    R Brazil 24F6
Rio Turbio Arg 23B8
Riou L Can 3G2
Rio Verde Brazil 27B2
Rio Verde Mexico 20B1
Rio Verde de Mato
    Grosso Brazil 27B2
Ripley, Ohio USA 10C3
Ripley, Tennessee USA 13B1
Ripley, West Virginia
    USA 10C3
Ripon Eng 33E4
Ripon USA 18B2
Rishiri-tō, I Japan 51E2
Rishon le Zion Israel 63C3
Rising Sun USA 12B3
Risle, R France 34A2
Risør Nor 30F7
Ritchie's Arch Andaman
    Is 60E2
Ritenberk Greenland 5N2
Ritter,Mt USA 18C2
Ritzville USA 16C1
Rivadavia Arg 26B2
Rivadavia Chile 26A1
Rivadavia Gonzalez
    Moreno Arg 26C3
Riva de Garda Italy 35D2
Rivas Nic 24A1
Rivera Arg 26C3
Rivera Urug 26D2
Riverbank USA 18B2
River Cess Lib 68B4
Riverdale USA 18C2
Riverhead USA 12D2
Riverina Aust 78B3
Rivers, State Nig 69H4
Riversdale NZ 79A3
Riversdale S Africa 72C3
Riverside USA 18D4
Rivers Inlet Can 3C3
Riverton NZ 79A3
Riverton USA 16E2
Rives France 35A2
Riviera Beach USA 13E4
Rivière aux Feuilles, R
    Can 5L4
Rivière de la Baleine, R
    Can 5M4

Riviére-du-Loup Can 11F1
Rivière du Petit
    Mècatina, R Can 5M4
Rivigny-sur-Ornain
    France 34C2
Riwon N Korea 52A2
Riyadh S Arabia 65E2
Rize Turk 62D1
Rizhao China 50D2
Rizhskiy Zaliv = Riga,G
    of
Rizokaipaso Cyprus 63C1
Rjukan Nor 30F7
Roanes Pen Can 5K2
Roanne France 36C2
Roanoke, Alabama USA 13B2
Roanoke, Virginia USA 11D3
Roanoke, R USA 11D3
Roanoke Rapids USA 13D1
Roan Plat USA 17D3
Roberts USA 16D2
Roberts Creek Mt USA 17C3
Robertsforz Sweden 30J6
Robert S Kerr Res USA 15D2
Robertson S Africa 72B3
Robertsport Lib 68A4
Roberval Can 5L5
Robinvale Aust 78B2
Roblin Can 3H3
Robson,Mt Can 3E3
Robstown USA 15F4
Roca Partida, I Mexico 19A3
Rocas, I Atlantic O 73G5
Rocas, I Brazil 25M4
Rocca San Casciano
    Italy 35D2
Rocha Urug 26E2
Rochdale Eng 33D5
Rochedo Brazil 27B2
Rochefort France 36B2
Rochelle USA 10B2
Rocher River Can 4G3
Rochester Aust 78B3
Rochester Can 5L5
Rochester Eng 33F6
Rochester, Minnesota
    USA 9D3
Rochester, New
    Hampshire USA 12E1
Rochester, New York
    USA 12B1
Rock, R Can 3C1
Rock, R USA 10B2
Rockford USA 10B2
Rockglen Can 3G4
Rock Hill USA 13C2
Rockingham USA 13D2
Rock Island USA 10A2
Rockland USA 10B1
Rockledge USA 13C3
Rockport USA 15F4
Rock Rapids USA 9C3
Rock River USA 9A3
Rock Springs, Montana
    USA 9A2
Rocksprings, Texas USA 14B3
Rock Springs, Wyoming
    USA 16E2
Rocks Pt NZ 79B2
Rock,The Aust 78C3
Rockville, Connecticut
    USA 12D2
Rockville, Indiana USA 10B3
Rockville, Maryland USA 12B3
Rockwood USA 11F1
Rocky Ford USA 14B2
Rocky Island L Can 10C1
Rocky Mount USA 13D1
Rocky Mountain House
    Can 3F3
Rocky Mountain Nat Pk
    USA 14A1
Rocky Mts Can/USA 6B1
Rocky Pt USA 8F3
Rødbyhavn Den 30G8
Rødbyhavn Den 40C2
Rodeo Arg 26B2
Rodez France 36C3
Ródhos Greece 39F3
Ródhos, I Greece 39F3
Rodi Garganico Italy 38D2
Rodopi Planina, Mts
    Bulg 39E2
Roebourne Aust 76A3
Roedtan S Africa 72D1
Roer, R Neth 34D1
Roermond Neth 34C1
Roeselare Belg 34B1
Roes Welcome Sd Can 5K3
Rogachev USSR 41F2
Rogers USA 15D2
Rogers City USA 10C1
Rogers L USA 18D3
Rogers,Mt USA 10C3
Rogerson USA 16D2
Roggeveldberge, Mts S
    Africa 72B3
Rogue, R USA 16B2
Rohn Pak 58B3
Rohtak India 58D3

Roja USSR 41E1
Rolândia Brazil 27B3
Rolla Can 15D2
Rollins USA 16D1
Roma Aust 78C1
Roma Italy 38C2
Romagna, Region Italy 35D2
Romagnano Italy 35C2
Romain,C USA 13D2
Roman Rom 39F1
Romanche Gap Atlantic
    O 73H4
Romang, I Indon 55C4
Romania, Republic E
    Europe 43C6
Romano,C USA 13E4
Romans sur Isère France 36D2
Romanzof,C USA 8E3
Romanzof Mts USA 8K2
Romblon Phil 55F8
Rome = Roma
Rome, Georgia USA 13B2
Rome, New York USA 12C1
Rome USA 11D2
Romilly-sur-Seine France 36C2
Rommani Mor 69A2
Rompin Malay 54G7
Rompin, R Malay 54G7
Ronco Italy 35D2
Ronda Spain 37A2
Rondônia Brazil 24F6
Rondônia, State Brazil 24F6
Rondonópolis Brazil 27B2
Rong'an China 50B4
Rongchang China 50B4
Rongcheng China 50E2
Rongjiang China 50B4
Rong Jiang, R China 50B4
Rongklang Range, Mts
    Burma 53A1
Rønne Denmark 30G7
Ronneby Sweden 30H7
Ronne Ice Shelf Ant 80F2
Ronse Belg 34B1
Ronthieu, Region France 34A1
Roof Butte, Mt USA 6C3
Roorkee India 58D3
Roosendaal Neth 34C1
Roosevelt USA 17D2
Roosevelt I Ant 80E
Roosevelt,Mt Can 3C2
Root, R Can 8O3
Root, R USA 9D3
Roper, R Aust 76C2
Roquevaire France 35A3
Roraima, State Brazil 24F3
Roraima, Mt Ven 24F2
Røros Nor 30G6
Røros Nor 42A3
Rorschach Switz 35C1
Rørvik Nor 30G6
Ros', R USSR 41G3
Rosalie Dominica 21Q2
Rosamond USA 18C3
Rosamond L USA 18C3
Rosamorada Mexico 20A1
Rosario Arg 26C2
Rosário Brazil 25K4
Rosario Mexico 20A1
Rosario Par 27A3
Rosario Urug 26D2
Rosario del Tala Arg 26D2
Rosário do Sul Brazil 26E2
Rosário Oeste Brazil 27A1
Roscoe USA 12C2
Roscoff France 36B2
Roscommon Irish Rep 31B3
Roscrea Irish Rep 33B5
Roseau Dominica 21E3
Rosebery Aust 78E3
Rosebud USA 9A2
Roseburg USA 16B2
Rosenberg USA 15C4
Rosenheim W Germ 40C3
Rosetown Can 3G3
Roseville USA 18B1
Rosiorii de Verde Rom 39E2
Roskilde Den 30G7
Roslavl' USSR 42E5
Roslyatino USSR 42G4
Ross NZ 79B2
Ross, R Can 8M3
Rossan, Pt Irish Rep 31B3
Rossano Italy 38D3
Roseselare Belg 34B1
Roes Welcome Sd Can 5K3
Ross Ice Shelf Ant 80E
Rosseau L, L Can 11D1
Rossel, I Solomon Is 77E2
Ross Ice Shelf Ant 80E
Rossiyskaya S.F.S.R.,
    Republic USSR 42E4
Ross L USA 16B1
Rossland Can 3E4
Rosslare Irish Rep 33B5
Rosso Maur 68A3
Ross-on-Wye Eng 33D6

Rossosh USSR 43F6
Ross River Can 4E3
Ross S Ant 80F6
Rostâq Iran 61C3
Rosthern Can 3G3
Rostock E Germ 40C2
Rostov USSR 42F4
Rostov-na-Donu USSR 43F6
Roswell, Georgia USA 13C2
Roswell, New Mexico
    USA 14B3
Rota Pacific O 49H5
Rotenburg, Hessen W
    Germ 34E1
Rotenburg,
    Niedersachsen W
    Germ 40B2
Rothaar-Geb, Region W
    Germ 34E1
Rothera, Base Ant 80G3
Rotherham Eng 33E5
Rothesay Scot 32C4
Roti, I Indon 55B5
Roto Aust 78C2
Rotoiti,L NZ 79B2
Rotoroa,L NZ 79B2
Rotorua NZ 79C1
Rotorua,L NZ 79C1
Rottenburg W Germ 34E2
Rotterdam Neth 40A2
Rottweil W Germ 34E2
Rotuma, I Fiji 77G2
Roubaix France 34B1
Rouen France 36C2
Rough, Oilfield N Sea 33F5
Roulers = Roeselare
Round I Mauritius 71F6
Round Mountain USA 18D1
Round Mt Aust 78D2
Roundup USA 16E1
Rousay, I Scot 32D2
Roussillon, Region
    France 36C3
Rouxville S Africa 72D3
Rouyn Can 11D1
Rovaniemi Fin 30K5
Rovereto Italy 35D2
Rovigo Italy 35D2
Rovinj Yugos 38C1
Rovno USSR 43D5
Row'an Iran 61B1
Rowena Aust 78C1
Rowley I Can 5L3
Rowley Shoals Aust 76A2
Roxas, Palawan Phil 55E8
Roxas, Panay Phil 55F8
Roxboro USA 13D1
Roxburgh NZ 79A3
Roy USA 16E1
Royal Canal Irish Rep 33B5
Royal Leamington Spa
    Eng 33E5
Royal Oak USA 1^C2
Royal Tunbridge Wells
    Eng 33F6
Royan France 36B2
Roye France 34B2
Royston Eng 33E5
Rožňava Czech 41E3
Rozoy France 34B2
Rtishchevo USSR 43G5
Rt Kamenjak, C Yugos 35E2
Ruaha Nat Pk Tanz 71D4
Ruahine Range, Mts NZ 79C1
Ruapehu,Mt NZ 79C1
Rub al Khāli, Desert S
    Arabia 65D3
Rubha Hunish Scot 32B3
Rubinéia Brazil 27B3
Rubtsoysk USSR 46K4
Ruby USA 8G3
Ruby Mts USA 17C2
Rudan Iran 61D3
Rudbar Afghan 61E2
Rudbär Iran 61B1
Rudnaya Pristan' USSR 51D3
Rudnya USSR 41G2
Rudnyy USSR 51C3
Rudoka Planina, Mt
    Yugos 39E2
Rudolf,L Kenya/Eth 70D3
Rudong China 50E3
Rudyard USA 10C1
Rue France 34A1
Rufa'a Sudan 64B4
Ruffec France 36C2
Rufiji, R Tanz 71D4
Rufino Arg 26C2
Rufisque Sen 68A3
Rufunsa Zambia 71C5
Rugby Eng 33E5
Rugby USA 9B2
Rügen, I E Germ 30G8
Ruhr, R W Germ 34D1
Ruhr, R W Germ 40B2
Ruijin China 50D4
Rujen, Mt Bulg/Yugos 39E2
Rukwa, L Tanz 71D4
Rum, I Scot 32B3
Ruma Yugos 39D1
Rumāh S Arabia 65E1

Rumbek *Sudan* 70C3
Rum Cay, I *Caribbean* 21C2
Rumford *USA* 11E2
Rumilly *France* 35A2
Rum Jungle *Aust* 76C2
Rumoi *Japan* 52D2
Rumphi *Malawi* 71D5
Runanga *NZ* 79B2
Runaway,C *NZ* 79C1
Rundu *Namibia* 71B5
Rungwa *Tanz* 71D4
Rungwa, R *Tanz* 71D4
Rungwe, Mt *Tanz* 71D4
Ruoqiang *China* 57G2
Ruo Shui, R *China* 48D2
Rupat, I *Indon* 54F7
Rupea *Rom* 39F1
Rupert *USA* 16D2
Rupert, R *Can* 5L4
Rur, R *W Germ* 34D1
Rurrenabaque *Bol* 24E6
Rusape *Zim* 71D5
Ruse *Bulg* 39F2
Rushville, Illinois *USA* 10A2
Rushville, Nebraska *USA* 9B3
Rushworth *Aust* 78B3
Rusk *USA* 15C3
Ruskin *USA* 13E4
Russel L *Can* 3H2
Russell *Can* 3H3
Russell *NZ* 79B1
Russell *USA* 14C2
Russellville, Alabama *USA* 13B2
Russellville, Arkansas *USA* 15D2
Russellville, Kentucky *USA* 10B3
Russian, R *USA* 17B3
Russian Socialist Federated Soviet Rep *USSR* 42C5
Rustavi *USSR* 62E1
Rustenburg *S Africa* 72D2
Ruston *USA* 15D3
Rutana *Burundi* 70C4
Ruteng *Indon* 55B4
Rutenga *Zim* 72E1
Ruth *USA* 17C3
Rüthen *W Germ* 34E1
Rutla *Mexico* 20C2
Rutland *USA* 11E2
Rutland, I *Andaman Is* 60E2
Rutog *China* 58D2
Ruvu = Pangani
Ruvuma, R *Tanz/Mozam* 71E5
Ruwenzori Range, Mts *Uganda/Zaïre* 70D3
Ruya, R *Zim* 71D5
Ružomberok *Czech* 41D3
Rwanda, Republic *Africa* 70C4
Ryazan' *USSR* 42F5
Ryazhsk *USSR* 42G5
Rybinsk *USSR* 42F4
Rybinskoye Vodokhranilishche, Res *USSR* 42F4
Rybnitsa *USSR* 41F3
Rycroft *Can* 3E2
Ryde *Eng* 33E6
Rye *Eng* 33F6
Rye Patch Res *USA* 16C2
Ryl'sk *USSR* 43E5
Ryn Peskt, Desert *USSR* 43H6
Ryoju *S Korea* 52A3
Ryōtsu *Japan* 51D4
Ryskany *USSR* 41F3
Ryūkyū Retto, Arch *Japan* 48F4
Rzeszów *Pol* 41E2
Rzhev *USSR* 42E4

S

Sa'ādatābād *Iran* 61C2
Saad el Aali, Dam *Egypt* 64B2
Saale, R *E Germ* 40C2
Saanen *Switz* 35B1
Saar, R *W Germ* 34D2
Saarbrücken *W Germ* 34D2
Saarburg *W Germ* 34D2
Saaremaa, I *USSR* 30J7
Saarland, State *W Germ* 34D2
Saarlouis *W Germ* 34D2
Saavedra *Arg* 26C3
Saba'a *Egypt* 63B3
Šabac *Yugos* 39D2
Sabadell *Spain* 37C1
Sabae *Japan* 52C3
Sabah, State *Malay* 54E1
Sabak,C *USA* 8A6
Sabal *Indon* 55B3
Sabanalarga *Colombia* 21C4
Sabang *Indon* 54A1
Sabang *Indon* 55A2
Sabari, R *India* 60C1
Sabastiya *Israel* 63C2
Sabaya *Bol* 24E7
Sab'Bi'ār *Syria* 62C3
Sabderat *Eth* 64C3
Sabhā *Jordan* 63D2
Sabhā *Libya* 67A2
Sabi, R *Zim* 71D6
Sabie, R *S Africa* 72E2
Sabinas *Mexico* 19B2
Sabinas Hidalgo *Mexico* 19B2
Sabine, R *USA* 15C3
Sabine L *USA* 15D4
Sabkhat Maṭṭī, Salt Marsh *UAE* 65F2
Sabkhet El Bardawîl, Lg *Egypt* 63B3
Sablayan *Phil* 55F8
Sable,C *Can* 5M5
Sable,C *USA* 13E4
Sable I *Can* 5M5
Sabzevār *Iran* 61D1
Sacajawea Peak *USA* 16C1
Sacandaga Res *USA* 12C1
Sac City *USA* 9D3
Sachigo, R *Can* 7D1
Sach'on *S Korea* 52A3
Sachs Harbour *Can* 4F2
Sacile *Italy* 35E2
Säckingen *W Germ* 35B1
Saco, Maine *USA* 11E2
Saco, Montana *USA* 9A2
Sacramento *USA* 18B1
Sacramento, Mts *USA* 6C3
Sacramento, R *USA* 18B1
Sacramento, V *USA* 17B2
Sacramento Mts *USA* 14A3
Sa'dah *Yemen* 64D3
Sadanski *Bulg* 39E2
Sadh *Oman* 65G3
Sadiya *India* 59E2
Sado, R *Port* 37A2
Sado-shima, I *Japan* 51D4
Sādri *India* 58C3
Safad = Zefat
Safed Koh, Mts *Afghan* 58A2
Safer *Afghan* 61E2
Saffle *Sweden* 30G7
Safford *USA* 17E4
Safi *Jordan* 62C3
Safi *Mor* 69A2
Safidabeh *Iran* 61E2
Şāfītā *Syria* 63D1
Safonovo *USSR* 41G1
Safwān *Iraq* 62E3
Saga *China* 59C2
Saga *Japan* 52B4
Sagaing *Burma* 53B1
Sagami-nada, B *Japan* 52C4
Sāgar *India* 58D4
Sagavanirktok, R *USA* 8J2
Sag Harbor *USA* 12D2
Saginaw *USA* 10C2
Saginaw B *USA* 10C2
Saglek B *Can* 5M4
Saglouc *Can* 5L3
Sagō-ri *S Korea* 52A3
Saguache *USA* 14A2
Sagua de Tánamo *Cuba* 21B2
Sagua la Grande *Cuba* 21B2
Saguenay, R *Can* 5L5
Sagunto *Spain* 37B2
Sahāb *Jordan* 63D3
Sahagún *Spain* 37A1
Sahara, Desert *N Africa* 68C2
Saharanpur *India* 58D3
Sahiwal *Pak* 58C2
Şahrā al Hijārah, Desert Region *Iraq* 62D3
Sahra esh Sharqiya, Desert Region *Egypt* 64B1
Sahuayo *Mexico* 20B1
Sahyun, Hist Site *Syria* 63D1
Saibai I *Aust* 76D1
Saïda *Alg* 69C2
Säida *Leb* 63C2
Sa'idabad *Iran* 61D3
Saidia *Mor* 37B2
Saidpur *India* 59C2
Saidu *Pak* 58C2
Saigō *Japan* 52B3
Saigon *Viet* 53D3
Saiha *India* 59D3
Saihan Tal *China* 48E2
Saijo *Japan* 52B4
Saiki *Japan* 51C5
Saimaa, L *Fin* 42D3
Sain Alto *Mexico* 20B1
Saindak *Pak* 61E3
St Abb's Head, Pt *Scot* 32D4
St Albans *Eng* 33E6
St Albans, Vermont *USA* 11E2
St Albans, West Virginia *USA* 10C3
St Albans Head, C *Eng* 33D6
St Albert *Can* 3F3
St Amand-les-Eaux *France* 34B1
St Amand-Mont Rond *France* 36C2
St-Amour *France* 35A1
St André, C *Madag* 71E5
St-André-de-l'Eure *France* 34A2
St Andrew B *USA* 13B3
St Andrews *Scot* 32D3
St Andrew Sd *USA* 13C2
Ste Anne *Can* 9C2
Ste Anne de Beaupré *Can* 11E1
St Ann's Bay *Jamaica* 21H1
St Anthony *Can* 5N4
St Anthony *USA* 16D2
St Arnaud *Aust* 78B3
St Augustine *USA* 13C3
St Austell *Eng* 33C6
St-Avold *France* 34D2
St Bees Head, Pt *Eng* 33D4
St Boniface *Can* 9C2
St-Bonnet *France* 35B2
St Brides B *Wales* 33C6
St-Brieuc *France* 36B2
St-Calais *France* 34A3
St Catharines *Can* 11D2
St Catherine,Mt *Grenada* 21M2
St Catherines I *USA* 13C2
St Catherines Pt *Eng* 33E6
St Chamond *France* 36C2
St Charles, Idaho *USA* 16D2
St Charles, Missouri *USA* 15D2
St Clair *USA* 10C2
St Clair,L *USA/Can* 10C2
St Clair Shores *USA* 10C2
St Claud *France* 36D2
St Cloud *USA* 9D2
Ste Croix *Switz* 35B1
St Croix, I *Caribbean* 21E3
St Croix, R *USA* 10A1
St Croix, R *USA/Can* 11F1
St Croix Falls *USA* 10A1
St Davids Head, Pt *Wales* 33C6
St Denis *France* 34B2
St Denis *Réunion* 71F6
St-Dié *France* 34D2
St Dizier *France* 34C2
St Elias,Mt *USA* 8K3
St Elias Mts *Can* 8L3
Saintes *France* 36B2
St Étienne *France* 36C2
St Étienne-de-Tinée *France* 35B2
St-Félicien *Can* 11E1
St-Florentin *France* 34B2
St Francis *USA* 14B2
St Francis, R *USA* 15D2
St Francis B *S Africa* 72C3
St Francis,C *S Africa* 72C3
St Gallen *Switz* 35C1
St-Gaudens *France* 36C3
St George *Aust* 78C1
St George, South Carolina *USA* 13C2
St George, Utah *USA* 17D3
St George, I, Alaska *USA* 8E4
St George I, Florida *USA* 13C3
St Georgen im Schwarzwald *W Germ* 34E2
St George,Pt *USA* 16B2
St-Georges *Can* 11E1
St George's *Grenada* 21E4
St Georges Chan *Irish Rep/Wales* 33B5
St Georges Chan *PNG* 77E1
St Germain-du-Bois *France* 35A1
St German-en-laye *France* 34A2
St-Gervais *France* 35B2
St Gotthard, P *Switz* 35C1
St Govans Head, Pt *Wales* 33C6
St Helena *USA* 18A1
St Helena, I *Atlantic O* 73H5
St Helena B *S Africa* 72B3
St Helena Sd *USA* 13C2
St Helens *Aust* 78E3
St Helens *Eng* 33D5
St Helens *USA* 16B1
St Helens,Mt *USA* 16B1
St Helier *Jersey* 36B2
St Hippolyte *France* 35B1
St-Hubert *Belg* 34C1
St-Hyacinthe *Can* 5L5
St Ignace *USA* 10C1
St Ignace I *Can* 10B1
St Ives *Eng* 33C6
St James, Minnesota *USA* 9D3
St James, Missouri *USA* 15D2
St James,C *Can* 3B3
St Jean *Can* 11E1
St Jean-d'Angely *France* 36B2
St-Jean-de-Losne *France* 35A1
St-Jean-de-Maurienne *France* 35B2
St-Jean,L *Can* 11E1
St-Jérôme *Can* 11E1
St Joe *USA* 16C1
St Johann im Pongau *Austria* 35E1
Saint John *Can* 5M5
St John, R *USA Can* 11F1
St Johns, Arizona *USA* 17E4
St John's *Can* 5N5
St Johns, Michigan *USA* 10C2
St Johns, R *USA* 13C3
St Johnsbury *USA* 11E2
St Johnsville *USA* 12C1
St-Joseph *Can* 11E1
St Joseph, Louisiana *USA* 15D3
St Joseph, Michigan *USA* 10B2
St Joseph, Missouri *USA* 15D2
St Joseph *Trinidad* 21L1
St Joseph, R *USA* 10C2
St Joseph I *Can* 10C1
St Joseph I *USA* 15F4
St Joseph,L *Can* 5J4
St Julien *France* 35B1
St-Junien *France* 36C2
St-Just-en-Chaussée *France* 34B2
St Kilda, I *Scot* 32A3
St Kitts, I *Caribbean* 21E3
St-Laurent *France* 35A1
St Lawrence, R *Can* 5M5
Saint Lawrence,G of *Can* 5M5
St Lawrence I *USA* 8D3
St Lawrence Seaway *Can/USA* 11D2
St Leonard *Can* 11F1
St Lô *France* 36B2
St Louis *Can* 3G3
St Louis *Sen* 68A3
St Louis *USA* 10A3
St-Loup-sur-Semou *France* 34D3
St Lucia, I *Caribbean* 21E4
St Lucia,L *S Africa* 72E2
St Magnus, B *Scot* 32E1
St Malo *France* 36B2
St Marcellin *France* 35A2
Ste Marie, C *Madag* 71E6
Ste-Marie-aux-Mines *France* 34D2
St Maries *USA* 16C1
St Martin, I *Caribbean* 21E3
St-Martin-Vésubie *France* 35B2
St Mary,Mt *PNG* 76D1
St Mary Peak, Mt *Aust* 78A2
St Marys *Aust* 78E3
St Marys *USA* 11D2
St Marys, I *UK* 33B7
St Marys, R *USA* 13C2
Saint Mathias Group, Is *PNG* 76E1
St Matthew I *USA* 8D3
St Maurice, R *Can* 11E1
St-Maximin *France* 35A3
Ste-Menehould *France* 34C2
St Michael *USA* 8F3
St Michaels *USA* 12B3
St-Michel *France* 35B2
St-Mihiel *France* 34C2
St Moritz *Switz* 35C1
St-Nazaire *France* 36B2
St-Niklaas *Belg* 34C1
St-Omer *France* 34B1
St Pascal *Can* 11F1
St Paul *Can* 3F3
St Paul, Minnesota *USA* 9D3
St Paul, Nebraska *USA* 14C1
St Paul, I *USA* 8D4
St Paul, R *Lib* 68A4
St Paul,C *Ghana* 69G4
St Peter *USA* 9D3
St Petersburg *USA* 13C3
St Pierre *Can* 5N5
St Pierre,L *Can* 11E1
St-Pol-Sur-Ternoise *France* 34B1
St Pölten *Austria* 40D3
St Quentin *France* 34B2
St Raphaël *France* 36D3
St Sébastien, C *Madag* 71E5
St-Siméon *Can* 11F1
St Simons I *USA* 13C2
St Stephen *USA* 13C2
Ste Thérèse,L *Can* 8O3
St Thomas *Can* 10C2
St-Tropez *France* 35B3
St Truiden *Belg* 34C1
St-Valéry-en-Caux *France* 34A2
St-Valéry-sur-Somme *France* 34A1
St Vincent *USA* 9C2
St Vincent, C *Madag* 71E6
St Vincent, I *Caribbean* 21E4
St Vincent,G *Aust* 78A2
St-Vith *W Germ* 34D1
St Wendel *W Germ* 34D2
Saipan, I *Pacific O* 49H5
Saiydabad *Afghan* 58B2
Sajama, Mt *Bol* 24E7
Sak, R *S Africa* 72C3
Sakai *Japan* 51D5
Sakaidi *Japan* 52B4
Sakaiminato *Japan* 52B3
Sakākah *S Arabia* 62D3
Sakakawea,L *USA* 9B2
Sakami,L *Can* 7F1
Sakania *Zaïre* 71C5
Sakaraha *Madag* 71E6
Sakarya, R *Turk* 43E7
Sakasleja *USSR* 41E1
Sakata *Japan* 51D4
Saketél *Benin* 69G4
Sakhalin, I *USSR* 51E1
Sakhalinskiy Zaliv, B *USSR* 51E1
Sakishima gunto, Is *Japan* 48F4
Sakrivier *S Africa* 72C3
Sal, I *Cape Verde* 68A4
Sal, R *USSR* 43G6
Sala *Sweden* 30H7
Saladas *Arg* 26D1
Saladillo *Arg* 26D3
Saladillo, R *Arg* 26C2
Salado, R, Buenos Aires *Arg* 26D3
Salado, R, Mendoza/San Luis *Arg* 26B3
Salado, R, Sante Fe *Arg* 23D3
Salaga *Ghana* 69F4
Sala Hintoun *Camb* 53C3
Salal *Chad* 70B2
Şalālah *Oman* 65F3
Salamanca *Chile* 26A2
Salamanca *Mexico* 20B1
Salamanca *Spain* 37A1
Salamanca *USA* 12A1
Salamat, R *Chad* 70B3
Salamaua *PNG* 49H7
Salamis, Hist Site *Cyprus* 63B1
Salamonica *USA* 11D2
Salang *Indon* 54E2
Salangen *Nor* 30H5
Salar de Arizaro *Arg* 23C2
Salar de Atacama, Salt Pan *Chile* 23C2
Salar de Coipasa, Salt Pan *Bol* 24E7
Salar de Uyuni, Salt Pan *Bol* 24E8
Salasomaggiore *Italy* 35C2
Salavat *USSR* 42K5
Salawati, I *Indon* 76C1
Salayar *Indon* 55B4
Sala y Gomez, I *Pacific O* 75O6
Salazar *Arg* 26C3
Salbris *France* 36C2
Salcha, R *USA* 8J3
Saldanha *S Africa* 72B3
Saldhad *Syria* 63D2
Saldungaray *Arg* 26C3
Saldus *USSR* 41E1
Sale *Aust* 78C3
Salé *Mor* 69A2
Salebabu, I *Indon* 55C2
Salekhard *USSR* 42M2
Salem, Illinois *USA* 10B3
Salem *India* 60B2
Salem, Massachusetts *USA* 12E1
Salem, New Jersey *USA* 12C3
Salem, New York *USA* 12D1
Salem, Oregon *USA* 16B2
Salem, Virginia *USA* 10C3
Salembu Besar, I *Indon* 54D4
Salen *Sweden* 30G6
Salerno *Italy* 38C2
Salford *Eng* 33D5
Salgót *Hung* 39D1
Salgótarjan *Hung* 41D3
Salgueiro *Brazil* 25L5
Salida *USA* 14A2
Salihli *Turk* 39F3
Salima *Malawi* 71D5
Salimaa, L *Fin* 30K6
Salina, Kansas *USA* 15C2
Salina, Utah *USA* 17D3
Salina, I *Italy* 38C3
Salina Cruz *Mexico* 20C2
Salina de Arizato *Arg* 24E8
Salina Grande, Salt pan *Arg* 26B3
Salina Gualicho, Salt pan *Arg* 26B4
Salina La Antigua, Salt pan *Arg* 26B2
Salinas *Brazil* 27D2
Salinas *Mexico* 20B1
Salinas *USA* 18B2
Salinas, R *USA* 18B2
Salinas de Llancaneb, Salt Pan *Arg* 26B3
Salinas Grandes, Salt Pan *Arg* 26C1
Salinas Peak, Mt *USA* 14A3
Saline, R, Arkansas *USA* 15D3
Saline, R, Kansas *USA* 14B2
Salines,Pt *Grenada* 21M2
Saline V *USA* 18D2
Salinópolis *Brazil* 25J4
Salins *France* 35A1
Salisbury = Harare
Salisbury *Eng* 33E6
Salisbury, Maryland *USA* 11D3
Salisbury, North Carolina *USA* 13C1
Salisbury I *Can* 5L3
Salisbury Plain *Eng* 33E6
Salla *Fin* 30K5
Salladillo, R *Arg* 26C1
Sallanches *France* 35B2
Sallisaw *USA* 15D2

Sallyana *Nepal* 59B2
Salmas *Iran* 61A1
Salmi *USSR* 30L6
Salmo *Can* 16C1
Salmon *USA* 16D1
Salmon, R *USA* 16C1
Salmon Arm *Can* 3E3
Salmon River Mts *USA* 16C1
Salo *Fin* 30J6
Salò *Italy* 35D2
Salon-de-Provence *France* 36D3
Salonica = Thessaloníki
Salonta *Rom* 39E1
Salpausselkä, Region *Fin* 30K6
Salsacate *Arg* 26B2
Sal'sk *USSR* 43G6
Salt *Jordan* 63C2
Salt, R *S Africa* 72C3
Salt, R *USA* 17D4
Salta *Arg* 23C2
Salta, State *Arg* 23C2
Saltillo *Mexico* 19B2
Salt Lake City *USA* 16D2
Salto *Arg* 26C2
Salto *Urug* 26D2
Salto Angostura, Waterfall *Colombia* 24D3
Salto da Divisa *Brazil* 27E2
Salto das Sete Quedas *Brazil* 27B3
Salto del Angel, Waterfall *Ven* 24F2
Salto del Guaira, Waterfall *Brazil* 23E2
Salto Grande, Waterfall *Colombia* 24D4
Salton S *USA* 17C4
Saltos do Iguaçu, Waterfall *Arg* 27B4
Salt Range, Mts *Pak* 58C2
Salt River *Jamaica* 21H2
Saluda *USA* 13C2
Salue Timpaus, Str *Indon* 55B3
Salūr *India* 60C1
Saluzzo *Italy* 35B2
Salvador *Brazil* 25L6
Salvador,L *USA* 15D4
Salvatierra *Mexico* 20B1
Salwah *Qatar* 65F2
Salween, R *Burma* 53B1
Sal'yany *USSR* 43H8
Salyersville *USA* 10C3
Salzach, R *Austria* 35E1
Salzburg *Austria* 40C3
Salzburg, Province *Austria* 35E1
Salzgitter *W Germ* 40C2
Salzkammergut, Mts *Austria* 35E1
Salzwedel *E Germ* 40C2
Samagaltay *USSR* 48C1
Samales Group, Is *Phil* 55F9
Samaná *Dom Rep* 21D3
Samandaği *Turk* 62C2
Samangan *Afghan* 58B1
Samani *Japan* 52D2
Samannûd *Egypt* 63A3
Samar, I *Phil* 55G8
Samarai *PNG* 76E2
Samarinda *Indon* 54E3
Samarkand *USSR* 56E2
Sāmarrā' *Iraq* 62D3
Samar S *Phil* 55F8
Sambalpur *India* 59B3
Sambas *Indon* 54C2
Sambava *Madag* 71F5
Sambhal *India* 58D3
Samboja *Indon* 54E3
Sambor *USSR* 41E3
Sambre, R *France* 34B1
Samch'ŏk *S Korea* 51B4
Samch'ŏnp'o *S Korea* 52A4
Samdŭng *N Korea* 52A3
Same *Tanz* 70D4
Samedan *Switz* 35C1
Samer *France* 34A1
Samfya *Zambia* 71C5
Samnah, I *S Yemen* 65F4
Samka *Burma* 53B1
Sam Neua *Laos* 53C1
Samoan Is *Pacific O* 77H2
Sámos, I *Greece* 39F3
Samosir, I *Indon* 54A2
Samothráki, I *Greece* 39F2
Sampacho *Arg* 26C2
Sampaga *Indon* 55A3
Sampara, R *Indon* 55B3
Sampit *Indon* 54D3
Sampit, R *Indon* 54D3
Sam Rayburn Res *USA* 15D3
Samrong *Camb* 53C3
Samsø, I *Den* 40C1
Samsu *N Korea* 52A2
Samsun *Turk* 62C1
Samulaki *Indon* 55D4
San *Mali* 69F3
San, R *Camb* 53D3
San, R *Pol* 41E2
Şan'ā' *Yemen* 64D3
Sanaga, R *Cam* 70B3
San Agustín *Arg* 23C4
San Agustin,C *Phil* 55G9
Sanak I *USA* 8F5
Sanana *Indon* 55C3
Sanana, I *Indon* 55C3
Sanandaj *Iran* 61B1
San Andreas *USA* 18B1
San Andres Mts *USA* 14A3
San Andrés Tuxtla *Mexico* 19C3
San Angelo *USA* 14B3
San Antioco *Sardegna* 38B3
San Antioco, I *Medit S* 38B3
San Antonio *Arg* 26C1
San Antonio *Chile* 26A2
San Antonio, New Mexico *USA* 14A3
San Antonio *Phil* 55F7
San Antonio, Texas *USA* 14C4
San Antonio, R, California *USA* 18B2
San Antonio, R, Texas *USA* 15F4
San Antonio Abad *Spain* 37C2
San Antonio,C *Cuba* 19D2
San Antonio de Bravo *Mexico* 14B3
San Antonio de los Banos *Cuba* 21A2
San Antonio Este *Arg* 26C4
San Antonio,Mt *USA* 18D3
San Antonio Oeste *Arg* 26B4
San Antonio Res *USA* 18B3
San Ardo *USA* 18B2
San Augustin *Arg* 26D3
San Augustin de Valle Fértil *Arg* 26B2
Sanawad *India* 58D4
San Bartolo *Mexico* 20B1
San Benedicto, I *Mexico* 19A3
San Benito *USA* 15F4
San Benito, R *USA* 18B2
San Benito Mt *USA* 18B2
San Bernardino *USA* 18D3
San Bernardo *Chile* 26A2
San Bernardo Mts *USA* 17C4
San Blas *Mexico* 20A1
San Blas,C *USA* 13B3
San Carlos *Chile* 26A3
San Carlos *Mexico* 20C1
San Carlos *Nic* 24B1
San Carlos *Phil* 55F7
San Carlos *Urug* 26E2
San Carlos *USA* 17D4
San Carlos de Bariloche *Arg* 23B6
San-chung *Taiwan* 48F4
Sanchursk *USSR* 42H4
San Clemente *Chile* 26A3
San Clemente *USA* 18D4
San Clemente I *USA* 17C4
San Cristóbal *Arg* 26C2
San Cristóbal *Mexico* 19C3
San Cristóbal *Ven* 24D2
San Cristobal, I *Solomon Is* 77F2
Sancti Spíritus *Cuba* 19E2
Sand, R *S Africa* 72D1
Sanda *Indon* 54D3
Sandakan *Malay* 54E1
San Daniele del Friuli *Italy* 35E1
Sanday, I *Scot* 32D2
Sanderson *USA* 14B3
Sandfly L *Can* 3G2
San Diego *USA* 17C4
Sandikli *Turk* 62B2
Sandila *India* 59B2
Sand L *Can* 3J2
Sandnes *Nor* 30F7
Sandnessjøen *Nor* 30G5
Sandø *Faroes* 30D3
Sandoa *Zaïre* 71C4
Sandomierz *Pol* 41E2
San Donà di Piave *Italy* 35E2
Sandoway *Burma* 59D4
Sand Point *USA* 8F4
Sandpoint *USA* 16C1
Sandrio *Italy* 36D2
Sandspit *Can* 3B3
Sand Springs *USA* 15C2
Sandstone *Aust* 76A3
Sandstone *USA* 9D2
Sandu *China* 50C4
Sandusky *USA* 10C2
Sandviken *Sweden* 30H6
Sandwich *USA* 12E2
Sandy Bay *Can* 3H2
Sandy L *Can* 5J4
San Elcano *Arg* 26C2
San Estanislao *Par* 27A3
San Felipe, Baja Cal *Mexico* 6B3
San Felipe *Chile* 26A2
San Felipe, Guanajuato *Mexico* 20B1
San Felipe *Ven* 21D4
San Feliu de Guixols *Spain* 37C1
San Felix, I *Pacific O* 22B6
San Fernando *Chile* 26A2
San Fernando *Mexico* 20C1
San Fernando *Phil* 55F7
San Fernando *Phil* 55F7
San Fernando *Spain* 37A2
San Fernando *Trinidad* 21E4
San Fernando *USA* 18C3
San Fernando *Ven* 24E2
San Fernando, R *Mexico* 20C1
Sanford, Florida *USA* 13C3
Sanford, Maine *USA* 11E2
Sanford, N Carolina *USA* 13D1
Sanford *USA* 7E4
Sanford,Mt *USA* 8K3
San Francisco *Arg* 26C2
San Francisco *Dom Rep* 21C3
San Francisco *USA* 18A2
San Francisco B *USA* 18A2
San Francisco del Oro *Mexico* 19B2
San Francisco del Rincon *Mexico* 20B1
San Gabriel Mts *USA* 18D3
Sangamner *India* 58C5
Sangamon, R *USA* 10B3
Sangan, I *Pacific O* 49H5
Sangar *USSR* 47O3
Sangāreddi *India* 60B1
Sangeang, I *Indon* 54E4
Sanger *USA* 18C2
Sanggan He, R *China* 50C2
Sanggau *Indon* 54D2
Sangha, R *Congo* 70B3
Sanghar *Pak* 58B3
Sangihe, I *Indon* 55C2
San Giorgio di Nogaro *Italy* 35E2
Sangkhla Buri *Thai* 53B3
Sangkulirang *Indon* 54E2
Sāngli *India* 60A1
Sangmélima *Cam* 70B3
San Gorgonio Mt *USA* 6B3
Sangre de Cristo, Mts *USA* 14A2
San Gregorio *Arg* 26C2
San Gregorio *Urug* 26D2
San Gregorio *USA* 18A2
Sangrūr *India* 58D2
Sangutane, R *Mozam* 72E1
Sanico *Arg* 26A4
San Ignacio *Arg* 23E3
San Isidro *Phil* 55F8
San Jacinto *Colombia* 24D2
San Jacinto Peak, Mt *USA* 17C4
San Javier *Chile* 26A3
San Javier, Misiones *Arg* 26D1
San Javier, Sante Fe *Arg* 26D2
San Javier, R *Arg* 26D1
Sanjō, I *Japan* 51D4
San João del Rei *Brazil* 23H2
San Joaquin, R *USA* 18B2
San Joaquin Valley *USA* 18B2
San Jon *USA* 14B2
San José *Costa Rica* 24B1
San José *Guatemala* 19C3
San Jose, Luzon *Phil* 55F7
San Jose, Mindoro *Phil* 55F8
San Jose *USA* 18B2
San José, I *Mexico* 6B4
San José de Chiquitos *Bol* 24F7
San José de Feliciano *Arg* 26D2
San José de Jachal *Arg* 26B2
San José de la Dormida *Arg* 26C2
San José de la Mariquina *Chile* 26A3
San José del Cabo *Mexico* 6C4
San José de Mayo *Urug* 26D2
San José de Raices *Mexico* 20B1
San José do Rio Prêto *Brazil* 23G2
San Joseé del Cabo *Mexico* 19B2
Sanju *S Korea* 52A3
San Juan *Arg* 26B2
San Juan *Puerto Rico* 21D3
San Juan, State *Arg* 26B2
San Juan *Trinidad* 21L1
San Juan *USA* 18B3
San Juan *Ven* 24E2
San Juan, Mt *Cuba* 21B2
San Juan, Mts *USA* 6C3
San Juan, R *Arg* 26B2
San Juan, R, California *USA* 18B3
San Juan, R *Mexico* 20C2
San Juan, R *Nicaragua/Costa Rica* 19D3
San Juan, R, Utah *USA* 17D3
San Juan Bautista *Mexico* 20C2
San Juan Bautista *Par* 23E3
San Juan Bautista *USA* 18B2
San Juan del Norte *Nic* 19D3
San Juan de los Cayos *Ven* 21D4
San Juan de loz Lagoz *Mexico* 20B1
San Juan del Rio *Mexico* 20B1
San Juan del Sur *Nicaragua* 19D3
San Juan Evangelista *Mexico* 20C2
San Juan Is *USA* 16B1
San Juan Mts *USA* 14A2
San Juan Tepozcolula *Mexico* 20C2
San Julián *Arg* 23C7
San Justo *Arg* 26C2
Sankuru, R *Zaïre* 70C4
San Leandro *USA* 18A2
San Leopoldo *Brazil* 26E1
San Lorenzo *Arg* 26C2
San Lorenzo *Colombia* 24C3
San Lorenzo *Ecuador* 22C3
San Lucas *USA* 18B2
San Luis *Arg* 26B2
San Luis, State *Arg* 26B2
San Luis *USA* 17D4
San Luis de la Paz *Mexico* 20B1
San Luis del Palma *Arg* 26D1
San Luis Obispo *USA* 18B3
San Luis Obispo B *USA* 18B3
San Luis Potosi *Mexico* 20B1
San Luis Potosi, State *Mexico* 20B1
San Luis Res *USA* 18B2
Sanluri *Sardegna* 38B3
San Magallanes *Mexico* 20D2
San Maigualida, Mts *Ven* 24E2
San Manuel *Arg* 26D3
San Marcos *Chile* 26A2
San Marcos *Mexico* 20C2
San Marcos *USA* 15C4
San Marino, Republic *Europe* 35E3
San Martin, Catamarca *Arg* 26B1
San Martin, Mendoza *Arg* 26B2
San Martin, Base *Ant* 80G3
San Martin de los Andes *Arg* 26A4
San Martino di Castroza *Italy* 35D2
San Martin Tuxmelucan *Mexico* 20C2
San Mateo *USA* 18A2
San Matias *Brazil* 25G7
Sanmenxia *China* 50C3
San Miguel *El Salvador* 19D3
San Miguel *USA* 18B3
San Miguel, I *USA* 18B3
San Miguel del Allende *Mexico* 20B1
San Miguel del Monte *Arg* 26D3
San Miguel de Tucumán *Arg* 23C3
Sanming *China* 50D4
San Nicolas, I *USA* 6B3
San Nicolás de los Arroyos *Arg* 26C2
Sannieshof *S Africa* 72D2
Sanniquellie *Lib* 68B4
Sanok *Pol* 41E3
San Onofore *Colombia* 21B5
San Onofre *USA* 18D4
San Pablo *Phil* 55F8
San Pablo B *USA* 18A1
San Pedro, Buenos Aires *Arg* 26D2
San Pédro *Ivory Coast* 68B4
San Pedro, Jujuy *Arg* 23D2
San Pedro *Par* 23E2
San Pedro, R *USA* 17D4
San Pedro Chan *USA* 18C4
San Pedro de los Colonias *Mexico* 6C4
San Pedro Sula *Honduras* 19D3
San Pietro, I *Medit S* 38B3
San Quintin *Mexico* 19A1
San Rafael *Arg* 26B2
San Rafael *USA* 18A2
San Rafael Mts *USA* 18C3
San Remo *Italy* 35B3
San Saba, R *USA* 14C3
San Salvador *Arg* 26D2
San Salvador *El Salvador* 22B2
San Salvador *Mexico* 20B1
San Salvador, I *Caribbean* 21C2
San Salvador de Jujuy *Arg* 23C2
Sansanné-Mango *Togo* 69G3
San Sebastian *Spain* 37B1
Sansepolcro *Italy* 35E3
San Severo *Italy* 38D2
San Simeon *USA* 18B3
Santa *Vanuatu* 77F2
Santa Ana *Bol* 24E7
Santa Ana *Guatemala* 19C3
Santa Ana *USA* 18D4
Santa Ana Mts *USA* 18D4
Santa Anna *USA* 14C3
Santa Bárbara *Chile* 26A3
Santa Barbara *Mexico* 19B2
Santa Barbara *USA* 18C3
Santa Barbara, I *USA* 18C4
Santa Barbara Chan *USA* 18B3
Santa Barbara Res *USA* 18C3
Santa Catalina *USA* 6B3
Santa Catalina, I *USA* 18C4
Santa Catalina,G of *USA* 18C4
Santa Catarina, State *Brazil* 23F3
Santa Clara *Cuba* 21B2
Santa Clara *USA* 18B2
Santa Clara, R *USA* 18C3
Santa Cruz *Arg* 23C8
Santa Cruz *Bol* 24F7
Santa Cruz *Chile* 26A2
Santa Cruz *Phil* 55F8
Santa Cruz, State *Arg* 23B7
Santa Cruz *USA* 18A2
Santa Cruz, I *USA* 18C4
Santa Cruz, Is *Solomon Is* 77F2
Santa Cruz, R *USA* 17D4
Santa Cruz Cabrália *Brazil* 27E2
Santa Cruz Chan *USA* 18C3
Santa Cruz de la Palma *Canary Is* 68A2
Santa Cruz del Sur *Cuba* 21B2
Santa Cruz de Tenerife *Canary Is* 68A2
Santa Cruz do Cuando *Angola* 71C5
Santa Cruz do Rio Pardo *Brazil* 27C3
Santa Cruz do Sul *Brazil* 26E1
Santa Cruz Mts *USA* 18A2
Santa Elena *Arg* 26D2
Santa Elena *Ven* 24F3
Santa Fe *Arg* 26C2
Santa Fe, State *Arg* 26C2
Santa Fe *USA* 14A2
Santa Helena de Goiás *Brazil* 27B2
Santai *China* 50B3
Santa Inés, I *Chile* 23B8
Santa Isabel, La Pampa *Arg* 26B3
Santa Isabel, Sante Fe *Arg* 26C2
Santa Isabel, I *Solomon Is* 77E1
Santa Lucia *Urug* 26D2
Santa Lucia *USA* 18B2
Santa Lucia Range, Mts *USA* 17B3
Santa Luzia, I *Cape Verde* 68A4
Santa Margarita *Arg* 26C1
Santa Margarita *USA* 18B3
Santa Margarita, I *Mexico* 6B4
Santa Margarita, R *USA* 18D4
Santa Margherita *Italy* 35C2
Santa Maria *Brazil* 26E1
Santa Maria *Colombia* 21C4
Santa Maria *USA* 18B3
Santa Maria, I *Açores* 68A1
Santa Maria, R *Brazil* 26E2
Santa Maria, R, Chihuahua *Mexico* 14A3
Santa Maria, R, Queretaro *Mexico* 20C1
Santa Maria da Vitória *Brazil* 27D1
Santa Maria del Rio *Mexico* 20B1
Santa Marta *Colombia* 24D1
Santa Monica *USA* 18C3
Santa Monica B *USA* 18C4
Santana *Brazil* 27D1
Santana do Livramento *Brazil* 26D2
Santander *Colombia* 24C3
Santander *Spain* 37B1
Santañy *Spain* 37C2
Santa Paula *USA* 18C3
Santa Porto Helena *Brazil* 27B3
Santa Quitéria *Brazil* 25K4
Santarcangelo di Romagna *Italy* 35E2
Santarem *Brazil* 25H4
Santarém *Port* 37A2
Santa Rita do Araguaia *Brazil* 27B2
Santa Rosa *Brazil* 26E1
Santa Rosa, California *USA* 18A1
Santa Rosa *Honduras* 19D3
Santa Rosa, La Pampa *Arg* 26C3
Santa Rosa, Mendoza *Arg* 26B2
Santa Rosa, New Mexico *USA* 14B3
Santa Rosa, San Luis *Arg* 26B2
Santa Rosa, I *USA* 18B3
Santa Rosalía *Mexico* 19A2

Santa Rosa Range, Mts *USA* 16C2
Santa Sylvina *Arg* 26C1
Santa Talhada *Brazil* 25L5
Santa Teresa *Brazil* 27D2
Santa Teresa di Gallura *Sardegna* 38B2
Santa Vitoria do Palmar *Brazil* 26E2
Santa Ynez, R *USA* 18B3
Santa Ynez Mts *USA* 18B3
Santee, R *USA* 13D2
Santerno, R *Italy* 35D2
Santhia *Italy* 35C2
Santiago *Chile* 26A2
Santiago *Dom Rep* 21C3
Santiago *Mexico* 20A1
Santiago *Panama* 24B2
Santiago *Phil* 55F7
Santiago, R *Peru* 24C4
Santiago de Compostela *Spain* 37A1
Santiago de Cuba *Cuba* 21B2
Santiago del Estero *Arg* 26C1
Santiago del Estero, State *Arg* 23D3
Santiago Peak, Mt *USA* 18D4
Santo, State *Brazil* 25K7
Santo Anastatácio *Brazil* 27B3
Santo Angelo *Brazil* 26E1
Santo Antão, I *Cape Verde* 68A4
Santo Antonio da Platina *Brazil* 27B3
Santo Antônio de Jesus *Brazil* 27E1
Santo Antônio do Leverger *Brazil* 27A2
Santo Dominco *Mexico* 20B1
Santo Domingo *Dom Rep* 21D3
Santos *Brazil* 23G2
Santos *Brazil* 27C3
Santos Dumont *Brazil* 27D3
Santo Tomas *Mexico* 17C4
Santo Tomé *Arg* 26D1
San Valentin, Mt *Chile* 23B7
San Vicente *Chile* 26A2
San Vicente *Mexico* 20B1
San Vito al Tagliamento *Italy* 35E2
Sanza Pomba *Angola* 71B4
São Borja *Brazil* 26D1
São Carlos *Brazil* 27C3
São Domingos *Brazil* 27C1
São Félix, Mato Grosso *Brazil* 25H5
São Fidélis *Brazil* 27D3
São Francisco *Brazil* 27D2
São Francisco, R *Brazil* 25L5
São Francisco de Assis *Brazil* 26D1
São Francisco do Sul *Brazil* 23G3
São Gabriel *Brazil* 26E2
São Gotardo *Brazil* 27C2
Sao Hill *Tanz* 71D4
São João da Barra *Brazil* 27D3
São João da Boa Vista *Brazil* 27C3
São João d'Aliança *Brazil* 27C1
São João da Ponte *Brazil* 27D2
São João del Rei *Brazil* 27D3
São João do Paraíso *Brazil* 27D2
São Joaquim da Barra *Brazil* 27C3
São Jorge, I *Açores* 68A1
São José do Norte *Brazil* 26E2
São José do Rio Prêto *Brazil* 27C3
São José dos Campos *Brazil* 27C3
São José dos Pinhais *Brazil* 27C4
São Lourenço, R *Brazil* 27A2
São Lourenço do Sul *Brazil* 26E2
São Luis *Brazil* 25K4
Sao Luis Gonzaga *Brazil* 26E1
São Marcos, R *Brazil* 27C2
São Maria do Suaçui *Brazil* 27D2
São Mateus *Brazil* 27E2
São Mateus, R *Brazil* 27D2
São Miguel, I *Açores* 68A1
São Miguel de Araguaia *Brazil* 27B1
Saône, R *France* 36C2
São Nicolau, I *Cape Verde* 68A4
São Onofre, R *Brazil* 27D1
São Paulo *Brazil* 27C3
São Paulo, State *Brazil* 27B3
São Pedro do Sul *Brazil* 26E1
São Pedro e São Paulo, Is *Brazil* 22H3
São Raimundo Nonato *Brazil* 25K5
São Romão *Brazil* 27C2
São Sebastia do Paraiso *Brazil* 27C3
São Sepé *Brazil* 26E2
São Simão, Goias *Brazil* 27B2
São Simão, Sao Paulo *Brazil* 27C3
São Tiago, I *Cape Verde* 68A4
São Tomé, I *W Africa* 68C4
São Tomé and Principe, Republic *W Africa* 68C4
Saoura, Watercourse *Alg* 68B2
Saouriuiná, R *Brazil* 27A1
São Vicente *Brazil* 27C3
São Vincente, I *Cape Verde* 68A4
Sápai *Greece* 39F2
Saparua *Indon* 55C3
Sape *Indon* 54E4
Sapele *Nig* 69H4
Sapporo *Japan* 51E3
Sapri *Italy* 38D2
Saprsborg *Nor* 30G7
Sapulpa *USA* 15C2
Saqqez *Iran* 61B1
Saquenay, R *Can* 7F2
Sarāb *Iran* 43H8
Sarafa *USSR* 39F1
Sarajevo *Yugos* 39D2
Sarakhs *Iran* 61E1
Saraktash *USSR* 43K5
Sarala *USSR* 47K4
Saranac L *USA* 11E2
Saranac Lake *USA* 11E2
Sarandë *Alb* 39E3
Sarandi *Brazil* 26E1
Sarandi del Yi *Urug* 26D2
Sarandi Grande *Urug* 26D2
Sarangani Is *Phil* 55G9
Saranpaul' *USSR* 42L3
Saransk *USSR* 42H5
Saranza *Italy* 35C2
Sara Peak, Mt *Nig* 69H4
Sarapul *USSR* 42J4
Sarasota *USA* 13E4
Saratoga *USA* 9A3
Saratoga Springs *USA* 12D1
Saratok *Malay* 54D2
Saratov *USSR* 43H5
Saratovskoye Vodokhranilishche, Res *USSR* 43H5
Sarawak, State *Malay* 45G5
Saraykoy *Turk* 62A2
Sarbāz *Iran* 61E3
Sarbisheh *Iran* 61D2
Sarca, R *Italy* 35D1
Sardalais *Libya* 67A2
Sar Dasht *Iran* 61B1
Sardegna, I *Medit S* 38B2
Sardinia = Sardegna
Sarektjåkkå, Mt *Sweden* 30H5
Sarenga *Eth* 64C4
Sargodha *Pak* 58C2
Sarh *Chad* 70B3
Sārī *Iran* 61C1
Sarida, R *Isreal* 63C2
Sarikamiş *Turk* 62D1
Sarina *Aust* 76D3
Sarine, R *Switz* 35B1
Sar-i-Pul *Afghan* 58B1
Sarir *Libya* 67B2
Sarir Tibesti, Desert *Libya* 67A2
Sariwŏn *N Korea* 51B4
Sark, I *UK* 36B2
Şarkişla *Turk* 62C2
Sarmi *Indon* 49G7
Sarmiento *Arg* 23C7
Särna *Sweden* 30G6
Sarnen *Switz* 35C1
Sarnia *Can* 10C2
Sarny *USSR* 41F2
Saroaq *Greenland* 5N2
Sarobi *Afghan* 58B2
Sarolangun *Indon* 54B3
Saronikós Kólpos, G *Greece* 39E3
Saronno *Italy* 35C2
Saros Körfezi, B *Turk* 39F2
Saroto *USSR* 42M2
Sarralbe *France* 34D2
Sarrebourg *France* 34D2
Sarreguemines *France* 34D2
Sarre-Union *France* 34D2
Sarrion *Spain* 37B1
Sartanahu *Pak* 58B3
Sartène *Corse* 38B2
Sarthe, Department *France* 34A3
Sarthe, R *France* 36B2
Sārūt *Syria* 63D1
Sarvan *Iran* 61E3
Sarykamys *USSR* 43J6
Sarysu, R *USSR* 46H5
Sasarām *India* 59B3
Sasebo *Japan* 51B5
Saskatchewan, Province *Can* 4H4
Saskatchewan, R *Can* 4H4
Saskatoon *Can* 3G3
Saskylakh *USSR* 47N2
Sasolburg *S Africa* 72D2
Sasovo *USSR* 42G5
Sassandra *Ivory Coast* 68B4
Sassandra, R *Ivory Coast* 68B4
Sassari *Sardegna* 38B2
Sassnitz *E Germ* 40C2
Sassuolo *Italy* 35D2
Sastre *Arg* 26C2
Sasuna *Japan* 52A4
Sātāra *India* 60A1
Satellite B *Can* 4G2
Satengar, Is *Indon* 54E4
Säter *Sweden* 30H6
Satilla, R *USA* 13C2
Satka *USSR* 42K4
Satluj, R *India* 58D2
Satna *India* 59B3
Sātpura Range, Mts *India* 58C4
Satu Mare *Rom* 39E1
Satu Mare *Rom* 43C6
Sauce *Arg* 26D2
Sauda *Nor* 30F7
Saudi Arabia, Kingdom *Arabian Pen* 56C3
Sauer, R *W Germ/Lux* 34D2
Sauerland, Region *W Germ* 34D1
Sauðárkrókur *Iceland* 30B1
Saugatuck *USA* 10B2
Saugerties *USA* 12D1
Saugstad,Mt *Can* 3C3
Sauk Center *USA* 9D2
Sauk City *USA* 10B2
Sault Sainte Marie *Can* 5K5
Sault Ste Marie *Can* 10C1
Sault Ste Marie *USA* 10C1
Saumlaki *Indon* 49G7
Saumur *France* 36B2
Saurimo *Angola* 71C4
Sauteurs *Grenada* 21M2
Sava, R *Yugos* 39D2
Saval'i, I *Western Samoa* 77H2
Savalou *Benin* 69G4
Savan, R *Iran* 43H9
Savannah, Georgia *USA* 13C2
Savannah, Tennessee *USA* 13B1
Savannah, R *USA* 13C2
Savannakhet *Laos* 53C2
Savanna la Mar *Jamaica* 21B3
Savant Lake *Can* 5J4
Savarane *Laos* 53D2
Savé *Benin* 69G4
Save, R *Mozam* 71D6
Sāveh *Iran* 61C2
Saverne *France* 34D2
Savigliano *Italy* 35B2
Savigny *France* 34B2
Savinskiy *USSR* 42F3
Savio, R *Italy* 35E3
Savoie, Region *France* 36D2
Savona *Italy* 35C2
Savonlinna *Fin* 30K6
Savoonga *USA* 8D3
Savudrija Rtič, Pt *Yugos* 35E2
Savukoski *Fin* 30K5
Savu S *Indon* 55B4
Saw *Burma* 53A1
Sawai *Indon* 55C3
Sawai Mādhopur *India* 58D3
Sawang *Indon* 54B2
Sawankhalok *Thai* 53C2
Sawara *Japan* 52D3
Sawatch Mts *USA* 14A2
Sawknah *Libya* 67A2
Sawtooth Mt *USA* 8J2
Sawtooth Range, Mts *USA* 16C2
Sawu, I *Indon* 76B2
Saxton *USA* 12A2
Say *Niger* 69G3
Sayghan *Afghan* 58B1
Sayhandulaan *Mongolia* 50B1
Sayh Hajmah *Oman* 65G3
Sayhūt *S Yemen* 65F2
Saykhin *USSR* 43H6
Saynshand *Mongolia* 48D2
Sayre, Oklahoma *USA* 14C2
Sayre, Pennsylvania *USA* 12B2
Sayula *Mexico* 20C2
Sayulita *Mexico* 20A1
Say-Utes *USSR* 43J7
Sayville *USA* 12D2
Sayward *Can* 3C3
Sázava, R *Czech* 40C3
Sbisseb, R *Alg* 37C2
Scafell Pike, Mt *Eng* 33D4
Scalloway *Scot* 32E1
Scapa Flow, Sd *Scot* 32D2
Scarborough *Can* 11D2
Scarborough *Eng* 33E4
Scarborough *Tobago* 21E4
Scarp, I *Scot* 32B2
Schaffhausen *Switz* 38B1
Scharding *Austria* 40C3
Scharteberg, Mt *W Germ* 34D1
Schefferville *Can* 5M4
Schelde, R *Belg* 34B1
Schell Creek Range, Mts *USA* 17D3
Schenectady *USA* 12D1
Schertz *USA* 14C4
Schiedam *Neth* 34C1
Schio *Italy* 35D2
Schleiden *W Germ* 34D1
Schleswig *W Germ* 40B2
Schleswig Holstein, State *W Germ* 40B2
Schoharie *USA* 12C1
Schouten Is *PNG* 76D1
Schramberg *W Germ* 34E2
Schreiber *Can* 5K5
Schurz *USA* 17C3
Schuykill Haven *USA* 12B2
Schuylkill, R *USA* 12C2
Schwabische Alb, Upland *W Germ* 40B3
Schwarzrand, R *Namibia* 72B2
Schwarzwald, Mts *W Germ* 34E2
Schwarzwald, Upland *W Germ* 40B3
Schwatka Mts *USA* 8G2
Schwaz *Austria* 35D1
Schweinfurt *W Germ* 40C2
Schweizer Reneke *S Africa* 72D2
Schwerin *E Germ* 40C2
Schwyz *Switz* 35C1
Sciacca *Italy* 38C3
Scilly Isles, Is *UK* 33B7
Scioto, R *USA* 10C3
Scobey *USA* 9A2
Scone *Aust* 78D2
Scoresby Sd *Greenland* 5Q2
Scotia Ridge *Atlantic O* 73F7
Scotia S *Atlantic O* 73F7
Scotland, Country *U K* 32C3
Scott, Base *Ant* 80F7
Scottburgh *S Africa* 72E3
Scott,C *Can* 3C3
Scott City *USA* 14B2
Scott I *Ant* 80G6
Scott Inlet, B *Can* 5L2
Scott L *Can* 3G2
Scott,Mt *USA* 16B2
Scott Reef *Timor S* 76B2
Scottsbluff *USA* 9B3
Scottsboro *USA* 13B2
Scottsdale *Aust* 78E3
Scottsdale *USA* 17D4
Scranton *USA* 12C2
Scribner *USA* 9C3
Scuol *Switz* 35D1
Scutari = Shkodër
Seacow *S Africa* 72C3
Seal, R *Can* 4J4
Sea Lake *Aust* 78B3
Searchlight *USA* 17D3
Searcy *USA* 15D2
Searles *USA* 18D3
Seaside, California *USA* 18B2
Seaside, Oregon *USA* 16B1
Seaside Park *USA* 12C3
Seattle *USA* 16B1
Seba *Indon* 55B5
Sebago L, L *USA* 11E2
Sebanga *Indon* 54B2
Sebastopol *USA* 18A1
Sebez *USSR* 41F1
Seboanook L *USA* 11F1
Sebring *USA* 13E4
Secchia, R *Italy* 35D2
Secretary I *NZ* 79A3
Sedalia *USA* 15D2
Sedan *France* 34C2
Sedanka, I *USA* 8E5
Seddonville *NZ* 79B2
Sede Boqer *Israel* 63C3
Sederot *Israel* 63C3
Sédhiou *Sen* 68A3
Sedom *Israel* 63C3
Sedona *USA* 17D4
Seeheim *Namibia* 72B2
Seelig,Mt *Ant* 80E
Sées *France* 34A2
Sefrou *Mor* 69B2
Sefton,Mt *NZ* 79B2
Segamat *Malay* 53C5
Segezha *USSR* 42E3
Segorbe *Spain* 37B2
Ségou *Mali* 68B3
Segovia = Coco
Segovia *Spain* 37B1
Segre, R *Spain* 37C1
Seguam, I *USA* 8D6
Seguam Pass *USA* 8D6
Séguéla *Ivory Coast* 68B4
Seguia el Hamra, Watercourse *Mor* 68A2
Seguin *USA* 15C4
Segundo, R *Arg* 26C2
Seguntur *Indon* 54E2
Segura, R *Spain* 37B2
Sehwan *Pak* 58B3
Seiling *USA* 14C2
Seille, R *France* 34D2
Seinäjoki *Fin* 30J6
Seine, R *Can* 9D2
Seine, R *France* 36C2
Seine-et-Marne, Department *France* 34B2
Seine-Maritime, Department *France* 34A2
Sekenke *Tanz* 70D4
Selah *USA* 16B1
Selaru, I *Indon* 49G7
Selat Alas, Str *Indon* 54E4
Selat Bangka, Str *Indon* 54C3
Selat Berhala, B *Indon* 54B3
Selat Dampier, Str *Indon* 49G7
Selat Gaspar, Str *Indon* 54C3
Selat Lombok, Str *Indon* 54E4
Selat Mentawi, Str *Indon* 54A3
Selat Sape, Str *Indon* 54E4
Selat Sumba, Str *Indon* 55B4
Selat Sunda, Str *Indon* 54C4
Selat Wetar, Chan *Indon* 55C4
Selawati, I *Indon* 55D3
Selawik *USA* 8F2
Selawik, R *USA* 8G2
Selawik L *USA* 8F2
Selby *Eng* 33E5
Selby *USA* 9B2
Selçuk *Turk* 39F3
Seldovia *USA* 8H4
Selebi Pikwe *Botswana* 72D1
Selemdzha, R *USSR* 51C1
Selemdzhinsk *USSR* 51C1
Selennyakh, R *USSR* 47Q3
Selestat *France* 34D2
Selfoss *Iceland* 5Q3
Selfridge *USA* 9B2
Selima Oasis *Sudan* 70C1
Selizharovo *USSR* 41G1
Selkirk *Can* 4J4
Selkirk *Scot* 32D4
Selkirk Mts *Can* 3E3
Selma, Alabama *USA* 13B2
Selma, California *USA* 18C2
Selmer *USA* 13B1
Selongey *France* 35A1
Selouane *Mor* 37B2
Selous,Mt *Can* 8M3
Selta Karimata, Str *Indon* 54C3
Selva *Arg* 26C1
Selvas, Region *Brazil* 24D5
Selway *USA* 16C1
Selwyn *Aust* 76D3
Selwyn L *Can* 3H1
Selwyn Mts *Can* 4E3
Semarang *Indon* 54D4
Semenov *USSR* 42G4
Semichi Is *USA* 8A5
Semidi Is *USA* 8G4
Semiluki *USSR* 43F5
Seminoe Res *USA* 9A3
Seminole, Oklahoma *USA* 15C2
Seminole, Texas *USA* 14B3
Seminole,L *USA* 13C2
Semipalatinsk *USSR* 46K4
Semirara Is *Phil* 55F8
Semirom *Iran* 61C2
Semisopochnoi, I *USA* 8B6
Semitau *Indon* 54D2
Semnān *Iran* 61C1
Semois, R *Belg* 34C2
Sempoala, Hist Site *Mexico* 20C2
Semporna *Malay* 54E2
Sena Madureira *Brazil* 24E5
Senanga *Zambia* 71C5
Senatobia *USA* 15E3
Sendai, Honshū *Japan* 51E4
Sendai, Kyūshū *Japan* 51C5
Sendwha *India* 58D4
Seneca Falls *USA* 12B1
Seneca L *USA* 12B1
Senecu *Mexico* 14A3
Senegal, Republic *Africa* 68A3
Sénégal, R *Maur Sen* 68A3
Senekal *S Africa* 72D2
Sengkang *Indon* 55B3
Senhor do Bonfim *Brazil* 25L6
Senigallia *Italy* 38C2
Senj *Yugos* 38D2
Senkaku Gunto, Is *Japan* 48F4
Senlin Shan, Mt *China* 51C3
Senlis *France* 34B2
Sennar *Sudan* 70D2
Senneterre *Can* 5L5
Senones *France* 34D2
Sens *France* 34B2
Senta *Yugos* 39D1
Sentery *Zaïre* 70C4
Sentinel Peak, Mt *Can* 3D3
Seoni *India* 58D4
Seoul = Soul
Separation Pt *NZ* 79B2
Sep'o *N Korea* 52A3
Sepone *Laos* 53D2
Sepotuba, R *Brazil* 27A2
Sept-Iles *Can* 5M4
Séquédine *Niger* 70B1
Sequoia Nat Pk *USA* 18C2
Serai *Syria* 63C1
Seram, I *Indon* 55C3
Serang *Indon* 54C4
Serasan, I *Indon* 54C2

Serbia, Region *Yugos*	39D2	Serra Pacaraima, Mts		Shakopee *USA*	9D3	Shendam *Nig*	69H4
Serchio, R *Italy*	35D2	*Brazil/Ven*	24F3	Shakotan-misaki, C		Shendi *Sudan*	64B3
Serdobsk *USSR*	43G5	Serra Perima, Mts *Brazil*	24F3	*Japan*	52D2	Shenkursk *USSR*	42G3
Serein, R *France*	34B3	Serra Tumucumaque		Shaktoolik *USA*	8F3	Shenmu *China*	50C2
Seremban *Malay*	53C5	*Brazil*	25H3	Shamary *USSR*	42K4	Shenyang *China*	50E1
Serengeti Nat Pk *Tanz*	70D4	Serre, R *France*	34B2	Shambe *Sudan*	70D3	Shenzhen *China*	50C5
Serenje *Zambia*	71D5	Serres *France*	35A2	Shamokin *USA*	12B2	Sheopur *India*	58D3
Seret, R *USSR*	41F3	Serrezuela *Arg*	26B2	Shamrock *USA*	14B2	Sheperdstown *USA*	12B3
Sergach *USSR*	42H4	Serrinha *Brazil*	25L6	Shandaken *USA*	12C1	Shepetovka *USSR*	41F2
Sergeyevka *USSR*	51C3	Serrmilik *Greenland*	5P3	Shandon *USA*	18B3	Shepparton *Aust*	78C3
Sergino *USSR*	46H3	Serro *Brazil*	27D2	Shandong, Province		Sheppey,I of *Eng*	34A1
Sergipe, State *Brazil*	25L6	Sertenópolis *Brazil*	27B3	*China*	50D2	Sherard,C *Can*	5K2
Seria *Brunei*	54D2	Sêrtar *China*	50A3	Shangchuan Dao, I		Sherborne *Eng*	33D6
Serian *Malay*	54D2	Serua, I *Indon*	55D4	*China*	50C5	Sherbro I *Sierra Leone*	68A4
Sérifos, I *Greece*	39E3	Serule *Botswana*	72D1	Shangdu *China*	50C1	Sherbrooke *Can*	11E1
Serio, R *Italy*	35C2	Seruwai *Indon*	54A2	Shanghai *China*	50E3	Sherburne *USA*	12C1
Serir Calanscio, Desert		Seruvan, R *Indon*	54D3	Shangnan *China*	50C3	Shereik *Sudan*	64B3
Libya	67B2	Seryshevo *USSR*	51B1	Shangombo *Zambia*	71C5	Shergarh *India*	58C3
Sermaize-les-Bains		Seseganaga L *Can*	9D1	Shangra *China*	50D4	Sheridan, Arkansas *USA*	15D3
France	34C2	Sesfontein *Namibia*	71B5	Shangsi *China*	50B5	Sheridan, Wyoming *USA*	9A3
Sernovodsk *USSR*	42J5	Sesheke *Zambia*	71C5	Shang Xian *China*	50C3	Sherman *USA*	15C3
Serov *USSR*	46H4	Sestriere *Italy*	35B2	Shangzhi *China*	51B2	Sherridon *Can*	3H2
Serowe *Botswana*	72D1	Sestri Levante *Italy*	35C2	Shannon, R *Irish Rep*	31B3	s-Hertogenbosh *Neth*	40B2
Serpa *Port*	37A2	Setana *Japan*	51D3	Shannon L *Can*	3H2	Sheslay *Can*	8M4
Serpukhov *USSR*	42F5	Sète *France*	35C3	Shanqiu *China*	50D3	Sheslay, R *Can*	3B2
Serra Amamba *Par*	27A3	Sete Lagoas *Brazil*	27D2	Shansonggang *China*	51B3	Shetland, Is *Scot*	31C1
Serra Azul *Brazil*	27B1	Sétif *Alg*	69D1	Shantarskiye Ostrova, I		Shevchenko *USSR*	43J7
Serra da Canastra, Mts		Setit, R *Sudan*	64C4	*USSR*	48G1	Shevli, R *USSR*	51C1
Brazil	27C3	Seto *Japan*	52C3	Shantou *China*	50D5	Sheyenne *USA*	9C2
Serra da Estrela, Mts		Seto Naikai, S *Japan*	52B4	Shanxi, Province *China*	50C2	Sheyenne, R *USA*	9C2
Port	37A1	Settat *Mor*	69A2	Shan Xian *China*	50D3	Sheyk Sho'eyb, I *Iran*	61C3
Serra da Mantiqueira,		Settle *Eng*	33D4	Shaoguan *China*	50C5	Shiashkotan, I *USSR*	48J2
Mts *Brazil*	27C3	Settler *Can*	4G4	Shaoxing *China*	50E4	Shibarghan *Afghan*	58B1
Serra da Mombuca *Brazil*	27B2	Sêtúbal *Port*	37A2	Shaoyang *China*	50C4	Shibata *Japan*	51D4
Serra das Furnas, Mts		Seurre *France*	35A1	Shapinsay, I *Scot*	32D2	Shibeli, R *Eth*	70E3
Brazil	27B2	Sevastopol' *USSR*	43E7	Shaqqa *Syria*	63D2	Shibetsu *Japan*	52D2
Serra de Arrajas, Mts		Severn, R *Can*	5K4	Shaqqat aj Kharitah,		Shibin el Kom *Egypt*	67C1
Brazil	27C1	Severn, R *Eng*	33D5	Region *S Arabia*	65E3	Shibîn el Qanâtir *Egypt*	63A3
Serra de Fartura, Mts		Severnaya Dvina, R		Shaqra' *S Arabia*	65E1	Shibukawa *Japan*	52C3
Brazil	27B4	*USSR*	42G3	Shaqrā' *S Yemen*	65E4	Shickshinny *USA*	12B2
Se ra de Maracaju, Mts		Severnaya Zemlya, I		Sharawrah *S Arabia*	65E3	Shijiazhuang *China*	50C2
Brazil	27A3	*USSR*	47M1	Shari *Japan*	52D2	Shika, R *USSR*	51A1
Se ra de São Jeronimo		Severnyy Sos'va, R		Sharifābād *Iran*	61D1	Shikarpur *Pak*	58B3
Brazil	27A2	*USSR*	42L3	Sharjah *UAE*	65G1	Shikoku, I *Japan*	45H4
Serra do Boqairao, Mts		Severnyy Ural, Mts		Shark B *Aust*	76A3	Shikoku-sanchi, Mts	
Brazil	26D1	*USSR*	42K3	Sharlauk *USSR*	61D1	*Japan*	52B4
Serra do Cabral, Mt		Severo-Baykalskoye		Sharon,Plain of *Israel*	63C2	Shikotsu-ko, L *Japan*	52D2
Brazil	27D2	Nagorye, Mts *USSR*	47M4	Sharpsburg *USA*	12B3	Shilega *USSR*	42G3
Serra do Cachimbo, Mts		Severo Donets *USSR*	43F6	Sharya *USSR*	42H4	Shiliguri *India*	59C2
Brazil	25G5	Severodvinsk *USSR*	42F3	Shashamanna *Eth*	70D3	Shilka *USSR*	48E1
Serra do Caiapó, Mts		Severo Sos'va, R *USSR*	46H3	Shashani, R *Zim*	72D1	Shilka, R *USSR*	48E1
Brazil	27B2	Severoural'sk *USSR*	42L3	Shashe, R *Botswana*	72D1	Shillington *USA*	12C2
Serra do Canguçu, Mts		Sevier, R *USA*	17D3	Shashi *China*	50C3	Shillong *India*	59D2
Brazil	26E2	Sevier Desert *USA*	17D3	Shashone Mts *USA*	6B3	Shilovo *USSR*	42G5
Serra do Cantu, Mts		Sevier L *USA*	17D3	Shasta L *USA*	16B2	Shimabara *Japan*	52B4
Brazil	27B3	Seville *Spain*	37A2	Shasta,Mt *USA*	16B2	Shimada *Japan*	52C4
Serra do Caparaó, Mts		Seville = Sevilla		Shathah at Tahtā *Syria*	63D1	Shimanovsk *USSR*	51B1
Brazil	27D3	Sevlievo *Bulg*	39F2	Shatt al Gharrat, R *Iraq*	62E3	Shimizu *Japan*	51D4
Serra do Chifre *Brazil*	25K7	Sewa, R *Sierra Leone*	68A4	Shaubak *Jordan*	63C3	Shimoda *Japan*	52C4
Serra do Espinhaço, Mts		Seward, Alaska *USA*	8J3	Shaunavon *Can*	3G4	Shimoga *Japan*	60B2
Brazil	27D2	Seward, Nebraska *USA*	15C1	Shaver L *USA*	18C2	Shimonoseki *Japan*	51C5
Serra do Espinilho, Mts		Seward Pen *USA*	8E2	Shawangunk Mt *USA*	12C2	Shinano, R *Japan*	52C3
Brazil	26D1	Sexsmith *Can*	3E2	Shawano *USA*	10B2	Shinās *Oman*	65G2
Serra do Jibão, Mts		Seychelles, Is *Indian O*	66K8	Shawinigan *Can*	11E1	Shinglehouse *USA*	12A2
Brazil	27C2	Seyðisfjörður *Iceland*	30C1	Shawnee, Oklahoma		Shingü *Japan*	51D5
Serra do Mar, Mts *Brazil*	27C3	Seyðisfjörður *Iceland*	30C1	*USA*	15C2	Shinjō *Japan*	52D3
Serra do Mirante, Mts		Seyhan *Turk*	62C2	Shawnee, Wyoming *USA*	9A3	Shinminato *Japan*	51D4
Brazil	27B3	Seym, R *USSR*	43F5	Sha Xian *China*	50D4	Shinshär *Syria*	63D1
Ser a do Navio *Brazil*	25H3	Seymohan *USSR*	47R3	Shay Gap *Aust*	76B3	Shinyanga *Tanz*	70D4
Ser a do Paranapiacaba,		Seymour *Aust*	78C3	Shaykh Miskin *Syria*	63D2	Shiogama *Japan*	51E4
Mts *Brazil*	27C3	Seymour, Connecticut		Shaykh 'Uthmān *S*		Shiono-misaki, C *Japan*	52C4
Serra do Ramalho, Mts		*USA*	12D2	*Yemen*	64D4	Shiping *China*	50A5
Brazil	27D1	Seymour, Indiana *USA*	10B3	Shchigry *USSR*	43F5	Shippensburg *USA*	12B2
Serra do Roncador, Mts		Seymour, Texas *USA*	14C3	Shchors *USSR*	43E5	Shiprock *USA*	14A2
Brazil	27B1	Seyne *France*	35B2	Shchuchinsk *USSR*	46J4	Shiqāq al Ma'ātif,	
Serra dos Caiabis, Mts		Sežana *Yugos*	35E2	Sheboygan *USA*	10B2	Region *S Yemen*	65E3
Brazil	25G6	Sézanne *France*	34B2	Shebshi, Mts *Nig*	70B3	Shiquan *China*	50B3
Serra dos Dourados, Mts		Sfax *Tunisia*	69E2	Shebunino *USSR*	51E2	Shirakawa *Japan*	52D3
Brazil	27B3	Sfînto Gheorghe *Rom*	39F1	Sheenjek, R *USA*	8K2	Shirane-san, Mt *Japan*	52C3
Serra do Sincora, Mts		's-Gravenhage *Neth*	40A2	Sheep Haven, Estuary		Shirani-san, Mt *Japan*	52C3
Brazil	27D1	Shaanxi, Province *China*	50B3	*Irish Rep*	32B4	Shiraz *Iran*	61C3
Serra dos Parecis, Mts		Shabunda *Zaïre*	70C4	Sheerness *Eng*	33F6	Shirbîn *Egypt*	63A3
Brazil	24F6	Shache *China*	57F2	Shefar'am *Israel*	63C2	Shiriya-saki, C *Japan*	52D2
Serra dos Pilões, Mts		Shackleton Ice Shelf *Ant*	80G9	Sheffield, Alabama *USA*	13B2	Shir Küh *Iran*	61C2
Brazil	27C2	Shadadkot *Pak*	58B3	Sheffield *Eng*	33E5	Shirotori *Japan*	52C3
Serra do Taquaral, Mts		Shādhām, R *Iran*	61C2	Sheffield, Pennsylvania		Shirvān *Iran*	61D1
Brazil	27B2	Shafter *USA*	18C3	*USA*	12A2	Shishaldin V *USA*	8F5
Serra Dourada, Mts		Shaftesbury *Eng*	33D6	Sheffield, Texas *USA*	14B3	Shishmaref *USA*	8E2
Brazil	27B2	Shagamu *Nig*	69G4	Shekhupura *Pak*	58C2	Shishmaref Inlet *USA*	8E2
Serra Dourada, Mts		Shag Rocks, Is *South*		Shelagyote Peak, Mt		Shishmaref *USA*	4B3
Brazil	27C1	*Georgia*	23J8	*Can*	3C2	Shitanjing *China*	50B2
Serra Encantadas, Mts		Shāhabād *Iran*	61B2	Shelburne Falls *USA*	12D1	Shively *USA*	10B3
Brazil	26E2	Shah Alam *Malay*	54F7	Shelby, Michigan *USA*	10B2	Shivpuri *India*	58D3
Serra Formosa, Mts		Shahbē *Syria*	63D2	Shelby, Montana *USA*	16D1	Shivta, Hist Site *Israel*	63C3
Brazil	25G6	Shahdap *Iran*	61D2	Shelby, N Carolina *USA*	13C1	Shivwits Plat *USA*	17D3
Serra Geral, Mts, Bahia		Shahdol *India*	59B3	Shelbyville, Indiana *USA*	10B3	Shiwa Ngandu *Zambia*	71D5
Brazil	27D2	Shāhin Dezh *Iran*	61B1	Shelbyville, Tennessee		Shiyan *China*	50C3
Serra Geral, Mts, Parona		Shāh Küh *Iran*	61D2	*USA*	13B1	Shizuishan *China*	50B2
Brazil	27B4	Shahrak *Afghan*	61E2	Sheldon *USA*	9C3	Shizuoka *Japan*	52C3
Serra Geral de Goiás,		Shahr-e *Iran*	61D2	Sheldon,Mt *Can*	8M3	Shkodër *Alb*	39D2
Mts *Brazil*	27C1	Shahresa = Qomisheh		Shelikof Str *USA*	8H4	Shkov *USSR*	41G2
Serra Geral do Parana,		Shahr Kord *Iran*	61C2	Shellbrook *Can*	3G3	Shoalhaven, R *Aust*	78D2
Mts *Brazil*	27C2	Shahsavär *Iran*	43J8	Shelley *USA*	16D2	Shobara *Japan*	52B4
Sérrai *Greece*	39E2	Shaim *USSR*	42L3	Shellharbour *Aust*	78D2	Shoranür *India*	60B2
Serrana Bank, Is		Shājābād *India*	60B1	Shelter Pt *NZ*	79A3	Shorāpur *India*	60B1
Caribbean	19D3	Shājahānpur *India*	58C3	Shelton *USA*	16B1	Shoshone, California	
Serrana de Cuenca, Mts		Shājāpur *India*	58D4	Shemakha *USSR*	62E1	*USA*	17C3
Spain	37B1	Shakhtersk *USSR*	51E2	Shenandoah *USA*	15C1	Shoshone, Idaho *USA*	16D2
Serranias del Burro, Mts		Shakhty *USSR*	43G6	Shenandoah, R *USA*	11D3	Shoshone, R *USA*	16E2
Mexico	14B4	Shakhun'ya *USSR*	42H4	Shenandoah Mt *USA*	12A3	Shoshone L *USA*	16D2
Serranópolis *Brazil*	27B2	Shaki *Nig*	69G4	Shenandoah Nat Pk *USA*	11D3	Shoshone Mts *USA*	17C3
						Shoshoni *USA*	16E2
						Shostka *USSR*	43E5
						Showak *Sudan*	64C4
						Show Low *USA*	17D4
						Shreveport *USA*	15D3
						Shrewsbury *Eng*	33D5
						Shropshire, County *Eng*	33D5
						Shuangcheng *China*	51B2
						Shuanglia *China*	50E1
						Shuangyashan *China*	51C2
						Shubar kuduk *USSR*	43K6
						Shublik Mts *USA*	8J2
						Shuga *USSR*	42N2
						Shu He, R *China*	50D2
						Shuicheng *China*	50A4
						Shujaabad *Pak*	58C3
						Shujālpur *India*	58D4
						Shulan *China*	51B3
						Shule He *China*	48C2
						Shumagin Is *USA*	8G5
						Shumen *Bulg*	39F2
						Shumerlya *USSR*	42H4
						Shuncheng *China*	50D4
						Shungnak *USA*	8G2
						Shuo Xian *China*	50C2
						Shür Gaz *Iran*	61D3
						Shurugwi *Zim*	71C5
						Shuswap L *Can*	3E3
						Shuya *USSR*	42G4
						Shuyak I *USA*	8H4
						Shwebo *Burma*	59E3
						Shwegyin *Burma*	53B2
						Shweli, R *Burma*	59E3
						Siahan Range, Mts *Pak*	61E3
						Siah Koh, Mts *Afghan*	58A2
						Sialkot *Pak*	58C2
						Sian = Xi'an	
						Siarao, I *Phil*	55G9
						Siaton *Phil*	55F9
						Siau, I *Indon*	55C2
						Šiauliai *USSR*	41E1
						Sibay *USSR*	46G4
						Sibayi L *S Africa*	72E2
						Šibenik *Yugos*	38D2
						Siberut, I *Indon*	54A3
						Sibi *Pak*	58B3
						Sibirskoye *USSR*	48D1
						Sibirtsevo *USSR*	51C3
						Sibiti *Congo*	70B4
						Sibiti, R *Tanz*	70D4
						Sibiu *Rom*	39E1
						Sibley *USA*	9C3
						Siboa *Indon*	55A2
						Sibolga *Indon*	54A2
						Sibsāgar *India*	59D2
						Sibu *Malay*	54D2
						Sibuguay B *Phil*	55F9
						Sibut *CAR*	70B3
						Sibutu Pass *Malay/Phil*	54E1
						Sibuyan, I *Phil*	55F8
						Sibuyan S *Phil*	55F8
						Sichuan, Province *China*	50A3
						Sicilia, I *Medit S*	38C3
						Sicilian, Chan *Italy/*	
						Tunisia	38C3
						Sicily = Sicilia	
						Sicuari *Peru*	24D6
						Siddhapur *India*	58C4
						Siddipet *India*	60B1
						Sidhi *India*	59B3
						Sidi Barrani *Egypt*	67B1
						Sidi bel Abbès *Alg*	69B1
						Sidi Kacem *Mor*	69A2
						Sidlaw Hills *Scot*	32D3
						Sidley,Mt *Ant*	80F5
						Sidney *Can*	16B1
						Sidney, Montana *USA*	9B2
						Sidney, Nebraska *USA*	14B1
						Sidney, New York *USA*	12C1
						Sidney, Ohio *USA*	10C2
						Sidney Lanier,L *USA*	13C2
						Sidon = Säida	
						Sidrolândia *Brazil*	27B3
						Siedlce *Pol*	41E2
						Sieg, R *W Germ*	34D1
						Siegburg *W Germ*	34D1
						Siegen *W Germ*	34D1
						Sielle, R *France*	35A1
						Siem Reap *Camb*	53C3
						Siena *Italy*	38C2
						Siene, R *France*	34C3
						Sierpc *Pol*	41D2
						Sierra Andrés Tuxtla	
						Mexico	20C2
						Sierra Auca Mahuida,	
						Mts *Arg*	26B3
						Sierra Blanca *USA*	14A3
						Sierra Blanca, Mts *Arg*	26B4
						Sierra Colorada *Arg*	26B4
						Sierra de Albarracin, Mts	
						Spain	37B1
						Sierra de Alcaraz, Mts	
						Spain	37B2
						Sierra de Ancasti, Mts	
						Arg	26B1
						Sierra de Cordoba, Mts	
						Arg	26B2
						Sierra de Famantina, Mts	
						Arg	26B1
						Sierra de Gredos, Mts	
						Spain	37A1

Sierra de Guadalupe, Mts *Spain* 37A2
Sierra de Guadarrama, Mts *Spain* 37B1
Sierra de Guara, Mts *Spain* 37B1
Sierra de Gudar, Mts *Spain* 37B1
Sierra de Juárez *Mexico* 20C2
Sierra de la Ventana, Mts *Arg* 26C3
Sierra del Codi, Mts *Spain* 37C1
Sierra del Imán, Mts *Arg* 26D1
Sierra del Morro, Mt *Arg* 26B2
Sierra del Nevado, Mts *Arg* 26B3
Sierra de los Alamitos, Mts *Mexico* 19B2
Sierra de los Filabres *Spain* 37B2
Sierra de los Huicholes *Mexico* 20B1
Sierra de Miahuatlán *Mexico* 20C2
Sierra de Morones, Mts *Mexico* 20B1
Sierra de Ronda, Mts *Spain* 37A2
Sierra de San Luis, Mts *Arg* 26B2
Sierra de Segura, Mts *Spain* 37B2
Sierra de Tamaulipas *Mexico* 20C1
Sierra de Urbion, Mts *Spain* 37B1
Sierra de Uspallata, Mts *Arg* 26B2
Sierra de Valasco, Mts *Arg* 26B1
Sierra de Valle Fértil, Mts *Arg* 26B2
Sierra de Zacatécas, Mts *Mexico* 20B1
Sierra de Zongolica *Mexico* 20C2
Sierra Grande, Mts *Arg* 26C2
Sierra Leone, Republic *Africa* 68A4
Sierra Leone,C *Sierra Leone* 68A4
Sierra Madre, Mts *Phil* 55F7
Sierra Madre del Sur, Mts *Mexico* 20B2
Sierra Madre Mts *USA* 18B3
Sierra Madre Occidental, Mts *Mexico* 19B2
Sierra Madre Oriental, Mts *Mexico* 20B1
Sierra Malanzan, Mts *Arg* 26B2
Sierra Mojada *Mexico* 6C4
Sierra Morena, Mts *Spain* 37A2
Sierra Nevada, Mts *Spain* 37B2
Sierra Nevada, Mts *USA* 17B3
Sierra Nevada de santa Marta, Mts *Colombia* 24D1
Sierra Pié de Palo, Mts *Arg* 26B2
Sierra Vista *USA* 17D4
Sierre *Switz* 35B1
Siete Puntas, R *Par* 27A3
Sífnos, I *Greece* 39E3
Sig *Alg* 69B1
Sig *USSR* 42E2
Sigep *Indon* 54A3
Sighet *Rom* 41E3
Sighisoara *Rom* 39E1
Sigli *Indon* 54A1
Siglufjörður *Iceland* 30B1
Sigmaringen *W Germ* 34E2
Siguatepeque *Honduras* 24A1
Sigüenza *Spain* 37B1
Siguiri *Guinea* 68B3
Sihora *India* 58D4
Siirt *Turk* 62D2
Sikai Hu, L *China* 48C3
Sikanni, R *Can* 3D2
Sikar *India* 58D3
Sikaram, Mt *Afghan* 58B2
Sikasso *Mali* 68B3
Sikeli *Indon* 55B4
Sikeston *USA* 15E2
Síkinos, I *Greece* 39F3
Sikionía *Greece* 39E3
Sikkim, State *India* 59C2
Siktyakh *USSR* 47O2
Sil, R *Spain* 37A1
Silandro *Italy* 35D1
Silao *Mexico* 20B1
Silay *Phil* 55F8
Silchar *India* 59D3
Silet *Alg* 68C2
Silgarhi *Nepal* 59B2
Silifke *Turk* 62B2
Silinfah *Syria* 63D1
Siling Co, L *China* 57G2
Silistra *Bulg* 39F2
Siljan, L *Sweden* 42A3
Silkeborg *Den* 30F7
Sillian *Austria* 35E1
Siloam Springs *USA* 15D2
Silsbee *USA* 15D3
Siltou, Well *Chad* 70B2
Šilute *USSR* 41E1
Silvan *Turk* 62D2
Silvania *Brazil* 27C2
Silvassa *India* 58C4
Silver Bay *USA* 9D2
Silver City, Nevada *USA* 17C3
Silver City, New Mexico *USA* 14A3
Silver Lake *USA* 16B2
Silver Peak Range, Mts *USA* 18D2
Silver Spring *USA* 12B3
Silverthrone Mt *Can* 3C3
Silverton *Aust* 78B2
Silverton *USA* 14A2
Silvretta, Mts *Austria/Switz* 35D1
Simanggang *Malay* 54D2
Simao *China* 53C1
Simard,L *Can* 11D1
Simareh, R *Iran* 61B2
Simav *Turk* 39F3
Simav, R *Turk* 39F3
Simcoe,L *Can* 11D2
Simeohof, I *USA* 8G5
Simeulue, I *Indon* 54A2
Simferopol' *USSR* 43E7
Sími, I *Greece* 39F3
Simikot *Nepal* 59B2
Simla *India* 58D2
Simla *USA* 14B2
Simmern *W Germ* 34D1
Simmler *USA* 18C3
Simonstown *S Africa* 72B3
Simoon Sound *Can* 3C3
Simplon, Mt *Switz* 36D2
Simplon, P *Switz* 35C1
Simpson,C *USA* 4C2
Simpson Desert *Aust* 76C3
Simpson L *Can* 8N2
Simpson Peak, Mt *Can* 3B2
Simpson Pen *Can* 5K3
Simrishamn *Sweden* 30G7
Simushir, I *USSR* 48J2
Sinabang *Indon* 54A2
Sinadogo *Somalia* 70E3
Sinai, Pen *Egypt* 62B4
Sinaloa, State *Mexico* 20A1
Sinalunga *Italy* 35D3
Sincelejo *Colombia* 24C2
Sinclair,L *USA* 13C2
Sind *Pak* 58B3
Sind, R *India* 58D3
Sindirği *Turk* 39F3
Sindri *India* 59C3
Sinegorsk *USSR* 51E2
Sines *Port* 37A2
Singa *Sudan* 70D2
Singapore, Republic *S E Asia* 53C5
Singapore,Str of *S E Asia* 53C5
Singaraja *Indon* 54E4
Singen *W Germ* 34E3
Singida *Tanz* 70D4
Singkaling Hkamti *Burma* 59E2
Singkawang *Indon* 54C2
Singleton *Aust* 78D2
Singtep, I *Indon* 54B3
Singu *Burma* 53B1
Singuédeze, R *Mozam* 72E1
Sin'gye *N Korea* 52A3
Sinhŭng *N Korea* 52A2
Siniscola *Sardgena* 38B2
Sinjai *Indon* 55B4
Sinjár *Iraq* 62D2
Sinkai Hills, Mts *Afghan* 58B2
Sinkat *Sudan* 64C3
Sinkiang, Autonomous Region 57G1
Sinn, R *W Germ* 34E1
Sinnamary *French Guiana* 25H2
Sinnyong *S Korea* 52A3
Sinop *Turk* 62C1
Sinpa *N Korea* 52A2
Sinp'o *N Korea* 52A2
Sinp'yong *N Korea* 52A3
Sintana *Rom* 39E1
Sintang *Indon* 54D2
Sinton *USA* 15F4
Sintra *Port* 37A2
Sinú, R *Colombia* 24C2
Sinŭiju *N Korea* 51A3
Siofok *Hung* 41D3
Sion *Switz* 35B1
Sioux City *USA* 9C3
Sioux Falls *USA* 9C3
Sioux Lookout *Can* 9D1
Sipalay *Phil* 55F9
Siparia *Trinidad* 21L1
Siping *China* 51A3
Siple, Base *Ant* 80F3
Siple I *Ant* 80F5
Sipocot *Phil* 55F8
Sipora *Indon* 54A3
Sipsey, R *USA* 13B2
Siqueros *Mexico* 20A1
Siquijor, I *Phil* 55F9
Sira *India* 60B2
Siracusa *Italy* 38D3
Sirajganj *Bang* 59C3
Sir Alexander,Mt *Can* 3D3
Sirba, R *U Volta* 69G3
Sir Banī Yās, I *UAE* 65F2
Sir Edward Pellew Group Is *Aust* 76C2
Siret, R *Rom* 39F1
Sir James McBrien,Mt *Can* 8N3
Sir Kālahasti *India* 60B2
Sir Laurier,Mt *Can* 3E3
Şirnak *Turk* 62D2
Sirohi *India* 58C4
Sironcha *India* 60C1
Sironj *India* 58D4
Síros, I *Greece* 39E3
Sirretta Peak, Mt *USA* 18C3
Sirri, I *Iran* 61C3
Sirsa *India* 58C3
Sir Sandford,Mt *Can* 3E3
Sirsi *India* 60A2
Sirt *Libya* 67A1
Sirte Desert *Libya* 67A1
Sirte,G of *Libya* 67A1
Sisak *Yugos* 38D1
Sisaket *Thai* 53C2
Sisophon *Camb* 53C3
Sisquoc *USA* 18B3
Sisquoc, R *USA* 18C3
Sisseton *USA* 9C2
Sissili, R *U Volta* 69F3
Sissonne *France* 34B2
Sistan, Region *Iran/Afghan* 61E2
Sisteron *France* 36D3
Sistig Khem *USSR* 47L4
Sitāpur *India* 59B2
Sitía *Greece* 39F3
Sitio d'Abadia *Brazil* 27C1
Sitka *USA* 4E4
Sitkalidak I *USA* 8H4
Sitkinak, I *USA* 8H4
Sittang, R *Burma* 53B2
Sittard *Neth* 34C1
Sittwe *Burma* 59D3
Situbondo *Indon* 54D4
Sivaki *USSR* 51B1
Sivas *Turk* 62C2
Siverek *Turk* 62C2
Sivrihisar *Turk* 62B2
Siwa *Egypt* 67B2
Siwalik Range, Mts *India* 58D2
Siwalik Range, Mts *Nepal* 59B2
Siya *USSR* 42G3
Siyang *China* 50D3
Sjaelland, I *Den* 40C1
Skagen *Den* 30G7
Skagerrak, Str *Nor/Den* 30F7
Skagit, R *USA* 16B1
Skagit Mt *Can* 16B1
Skagway *USA* 4E4
Skaneateles *USA* 12B1
Skaneateles L *USA* 12B1
Skara *Sweden* 30G7
Skarzysko-Kamlenna *Pol* 41E2
Skeena, R *Can* 4F4
Skeena Mts *Can* 3C2
Skeenjek, R *USA* 4D3
Skegness *Eng* 33F5
Skellefte, R *Sweden* 42B2
Skellefteå *Sweden* 30J6
Skíathos, I *Greece* 39E3
Skidegate *Can* 4E4
Skiemiewice *Pol* 41E2
Skien *Nor* 30F7
Skikda *Alg* 69D1
Skikoku, I *Japan* 51C5
Skipton *Eng* 33E5
Skíros, I *Greece* 39E3
Skive *Den* 30F7
Skjern *Den* 40B1
Skjoldungen *Greenland* 5O3
Skokie *USA* 10B2
Skópelos, I *Greece* 39E3
Skopje *Yugos* 39E2
Skövde *Sweden* 30G7
Skovorodino *USSR* 47O4
Skowhegan *USA* 11F2
Skukuza *S Africa* 72E1
Skwentna *USA* 4C3
Skwierzyna *Pol* 40D2
Skye, I *Scot* 31B2
Slagelse *Den* 30G7
Slaney, R *Irish Rep* 33B5
Slatina *Rom* 39E2
Slaung *Indon* 54D4
Slav Brod *Yugos* 39D1
Slave, R *Can* 4G3
Slave Lake *Can* 3F2
Slavgorod, Belorusskoya *USSR* 41G2
Slavgorod, Rossiyskaya *USSR* 46J4
Slavuta *USSR* 41F2
Slavyansk *USSR* 43F6
Sleat,Sound of, Chan *Scot* 32C3
Sleetmute *USA* 8G3
Sleeve Bloom, Mts *Irish Rep* 33B5
Slidell *USA* 15E3
Slide Mt *USA* 12C2
Sligo *Irish Rep* 31B3
Sligo, B *Irish Rep* 31B3
Sliven *Bulg* 39F2
Sloan *USA* 17C3
Slobozia *Rom* 39F2
Slocan *Can* 3E4
Slonim *USSR* 41F2
Slough *Eng* 33E6
Slough, R *USA* 18B2
Slovensko, Region *Czech* 41D3
Slubice *Pol* 40C2
Sluch', R *USSR* 41F2
Sludyanka *USSR* 48D1
Slupsk *Pol* 40D2
Slutsk *USSR* 41F2
Slutsk, R *USSR* 41F2
Slyne Head, Pt *Irish Rep* 31A3
Slyudvanka *USSR* 47M4
Smallwood Res *Can* 5M4
Smara *Mor* 68A2
Smederevo *Yugos* 39E2
Smederevska Palanka *Yugos* 39E2
Smela *USSR* 43E6
Smethport *USA* 12A2
Smidovich *USSR* 51C2
Smirnykh *USSR* 51E2
Smith *Can* 3F2
Smith *USA* 18C1
Smith Arm, B *Can* 8O2
Smith B *USA* 8H1
Smithers *Can* 3C3
Smithfield, N Carolina *USA* 13D1
Smithfield *S Africa* 72D3
Smithfield, Utah *USA* 16D2
Smith I *Can* 5L3
Smith River *Can* 3C2
Smith Sd *Can* 3C3
Smiths Falls *Can* 11D2
Smithton *Aust* 78E3
Smoky, R *Can* 3E2
Smoky, R *USA* 14B2
Smoky C *Aust* 78D2
Smoky Hills *USA* 14C2
Smoky Lake *Can* 3F3
Smoky Mts *USA* 16D2
Smøla, I *Nor* 30F6
Smolensk *USSR* 42E5
Smólikas, Mt *Greece* 39E2
Smolyan *Bulg* 39E2
Smooky, R *Can* 3E2
Smoothstone L *Can* 3G3
Smorgon' *USSR* 41F2
Smyrna, Delaware *USA* 12C3
Smyrna, Georgia *USA* 13C2
Snaefell, Mt *Eng* 33C4
Snafell, Mt *Iceland* 30B2
Snake *USA* 16C1
Snake, R *USA* 16D2
Snake River Canyon *USA* 6B2
Snake River Plain *USA* 16D2
Snares, Is *NZ* 77F5
Sneek *Neth* 40B2
Snelling *USA* 18B2
Sněžka, Mt *Pol/Czech* 40D2
Snøhetta, Mt *Nor* 30F6
Snohomish *USA* 16B1
Snoqualmie P *USA* 16B1
Snoul *Camb* 53D3
Snowbird L *Can* 3H1
Snowdon, Mt *Wales* 33C5
Snowdonia Nat Pk *Wales* 33C5
Snowdrift *Can* 4G3
Snowflake *USA* 17D4
Snow Lake *Can* 4H4
Snow Shoe *USA* 12B2
Snowtown *Aust* 78A2
Snowville *USA* 16D2
Snowy Mts *Aust* 78C3
Snyder *USA* 14B3
Soan-kundo, I *S Korea* 51B5
Sobaek Sanmaek, Mts *S Korea* 52A3
Sobat, R *Sudan* 70D3
Sobral *Brazil* 25K4
Sochaczew *Pol* 41E2
Sochi *USSR* 43F7
Sŏch'on *S Korea* 52A3
Socorro *USA* 14A3
Socorro, I *Mexico* 19A3
Socos *Chile* 26A2
Socotra, I *S Yemen* 65F4
Soda L *USA* 18C3
Sodankylä *Fin* 30K5
Soda Springs *USA* 16D2
Soddo *Eth* 70D3
Soderhamn *Sweden* 30H6
Södertälje *Sweden* 30H7
Sodiri *Sudan* 70C2
Sodus Point *USA* 12B1
Soë *Indon* 55B4
Soest *W Germ* 34E1
Sofala *Mozam* 71D5
Sofanovo *USSR* 42H2
Sofia = Sofiya
Sofiya *Bulg* 39E2
Sofiysk *USSR* 51C1
Sofporog *USSR* 42E2
Sofu Gan, I *Japan* 48H4
Sogamoso *Colombia* 24D2
Sogda *USSR* 51C1
Sognefjorden, Inlet *Nor* 30F6
Sŏgwi-ri *S Korea* 52A4
Sog Xian *China* 57H2
Sohâg *Egypt* 64B1
Sohano *PNG* 77E1
Sohipat *India* 58D3
Soignies *Belg* 34B1
Soissons *France* 34B2
Sojat *India* 58C3
Sŏjosŏn-man, B *N Korea* 51A4
Sokcho *S Korea* 52A3
Söke *Turk* 62A2
Sokodé *Togo* 69G4
Sokol *USSR* 42F4
Sokołka *Pol* 41E2
Sokolo *Mali* 68B3
Søkongens Øy, I *Greenland* 5Q3
Sokota *Eth* 70D2
Sokoto *Nig* 69H3
Sokoto, State *Nig* 69H3
Sokoto, R *Nig* 69G3
Solander I *NZ* 79A3
Solano *Phil* 55F7
Solapur *India* 60B1
Solar, I *Indon* 55B4
Solbad Hall *Austria* 35D1
Sölden *Austria* 35D1
Soldotna *USA* 8H3
Soledad *Colombia* 21C4
Soledad *USA* 18B2
Soledade *Brazil* 26E1
Solent, Sd *Eng* 33E6
Solesmes *France* 34B1
Soligorsk *USSR* 41F2
Solikamsk *USSR* 42K4
Solimões *Peru* 24D4
Solingen *W Germ* 34D1
Solitaire *Namibia* 72B1
Sol'Itesk *USSR* 46G4
Sollefteå *Sweden* 30H6
Solliès-Pont *France* 35B3
Solling, Region *W Germ* 34E1
Sol'lletsk *USSR* 43J5
Solnenechnyy *USSR* 51D1
Sologne, R *France* 34A3
Solok *Indon* 54B3
Solomon Is *Pacific O* 77E1
Solon Springs *USA* 10A1
Solothurn *Switz* 35B1
Solov'yevsk *USSR* 51A1
Soltau *W Germ* 30F8
Solvang *USA* 18B3
Solvay *USA* 12B1
Solway Firth, Estuary *Scot/Eng* 32D4
Solwezi *Zambia* 71C5
Sōma *Japan* 52D3
Soma *Turk* 39F3
Somalia, Republic *E Africa* 56C5
Somali Basin *Indian O* 74D4
Sombor *Yugos* 39D1
Sombrero Chan *Indian O* 60E3
Sombretete *Mexico* 20B1
Somerset *Aust* 76D2
Somerset, County *Eng* 33D6
Somerset, Kentucky *USA* 10C3
Somerset, Massachusetts *USA* 12E2
Somerset, Pennsylvania *USA* 11D2
Somerset East *S Africa* 72D3
Somerset I *Can* 5J2
Somerset Res *USA* 12D1
Somers Point *USA* 12C3
Somersworth *USA* 12E1
Somerville *USA* 12C2
Somerville Res *USA* 15C3
Somes, R *Rom* 39E1
Somme, Department *France* 34B2
Somme, R *France* 34B2
Sommesous *France* 34C2
Somoto *Nic* 24A1
Son, R *India* 59B3
Sŏnch'ŏn *N Korea* 51A4
Sondags, R *S Africa* 72D3
Sønderborg *Den* 30F8
Søndre Strømfjord *Greenland* 5N3
Søndre Upernavik *Greenland* 4N2
Sondrio *Italy* 35C1
Song Ba, R *Viet* 53D3
Song Cau *Viet* 53D3
Sŏngch'on *N Korea* 52A3
Songea *Tanz* 71D5
Songgan *N Korea* 52A2
Songhua Jiang, R *China* 51B2

Songjiang China	50E3	Southern Alps, Mts NZ	79A2	Spessart, Region W Germ
Songjŏng S Korea	52A3	Southend Can	3H2	
Songkhla Thai	53C4	Southend-on-Sea Eng	33F6	

Songjiang China 50E3
Songjŏng S Korea 52A3
Songkhla Thai 53C4
Songnim N Korea 51B4
Song Pahang, R Malay 53C5
Songpan China 50A3
Songsan-ni S Korea 52A4
Sonhue Hu, L China 51B3
Sonid Youqi China 50C1
Son La Viet 53C1
Sonmiani Pak 58B3
Sonmiani Bay Pak 58B3
Sonoita Mexico 17D4
Sonoma USA 18A1
Sonora, California USA 18B2
Sonora, State Mexico 17D4
Sonora, Texas USA 14B3
Sonora, R Mexico 19A2
Sonoran Desert USA 6B3
Sonora P USA 18C1
Sonsonate El Salvador 19D3
Sonsorol, I Pacific O 49G6
Soo Canals USA/Can 7E2
Sooke Can 3D4
Sopot Pol 41D2
Sopron Hung 40D3
Soquel USA 18B2
Sora Italy 38C2
Sored, R Israel 63C3
Sorel Can 11E1
Sorell Aust 78E3
Soresina Italy 35C2
Sorgun Turk 62C2
Soria Spain 37B1
Sørkjosen Nor 30J5
Sørksop, I Barents S 46C2
Sor Mertvyy Kultuk, Plain USSR 43J6
Sorocaba Brazil 27C3
Sorochinsk USSR 42J5
Soroi, I Pacific O 49H6
Soroki USSR 41F3
Soroma-ko, L Japan 52D2
Sorong Indon 49G7
Sorong, Province Indon 55D3
Soroti Uganda 70D3
Sørøya, I Nor 30J4
Sorrento Italy 38C2
Sorsatunturi, Mt Fin 30K5
Sorsele Sweden 30H5
Sorsele Sweden 42B2
Sorsogon Phil 55F8
Sortavala USSR 42E3
Sŏsan S Korea 51B4
Sosnowiec Pol 41D2
Sospel France 35B3
Sos'va USSR 46H4
Sota, R Benin 69G3
Soto la Manna Mexico 20C1
Souanké Congo 70B3
Soubré Ivory Coast 68B4
Souderton USA 12C2
Soufrière St Lucia 21P2
Soufrière, V St Vincent 21N2
Souillac France 36C3
Souk Ahras Alg 69D1
Souk Larbat Gharb Mor 69A2
Soul S Korea 51B4
Soummam, R Alg 37C2
Sour = Tyr
Sources, Mt aux Lesotho 72D2
Souris Can 9B2
Souris, R Can/USA 9B2
Sousa Brazil 25L5
Sousse Tunisia 69E1
South Africa, Republic Africa 71C7
Southampton Can 10C2
Southampton Eng 33E6
Southampton USA 12D2
Southampton I Can 5K3
South Andaman, I Indian C 60E2
South Atlantic O 22G7
South Aulatsivik I Can 5M4
South Australia, State Aust 76C3
South Australian Basin Indian O 74H6
Southaven USA 15E3
South Baldy, Mt USA 14A3
South Bay USA 13E4
South Baymouth Can 10C1
South Bend, Indiana USA 10B2
South Bend, Washington USA 16B1
South Boston USA 11D3
Southbridge USA 12E1
South Cape = Ka Lae
South Carolina, State USA 7E3
South China S S E Asia 49E5
South Dakota, State USA 6C2
South Deerfield USA 12D1
South Downs Eng 33E6
South East C Aust 78E3
South East C USA 8E3
South East Pacific Basin Pacific O 75O7

Southern Alps, Mts NZ 79A2
Southend Can 3H2
Southend-on-Sea Eng 33F6
Southern Alps, Mts NZ 77F5
Southern Cross Aust 76A4
Southern Indian L Can 4J4
Southern Pines USA 13D1
Southfield Jamaica 21H2
South Fiji Basin Pacific O 75K6
South Foreland, Pt Eng 33F6
South Fork USA 14A2
South Fork, R, Alaska USA 8H3
South Fork, R, California USA 18B1
South Fork American, R USA 18B1
South Fork Kern, R USA 18C3
South Georgia, I S Atlantic O 22G9
South Glamorgan, County Wales 33D6
South Haven USA 10B2
South Henik L Can 4J3
South Hill USA 11D3
South Honshu Reige Pacific O 74J3
South I NZ 79A2
Southington USA 12D2
South Korea, Republic S E Asia 51B4
South Lake Tahoe USA 17B3
South Madagascar Ridge Indian O 74D6
South Magnetic Pole Ant 80GB
South Miami USA 13E4
South Mt USA 12B3
South Nahanni, R Can 4F3
South Negril Pt Jamaica 21G1
South Orkney, Is Atlantic O 73F8
South Pacific O 22B5
South Platte, R USA 14B1
South Pole Ant 80E
South Porcupine Can 10C1
Southport Eng 33D5
South Pt Barbados 21Q2
South River USA 12C2
South Ronaldsay, I Scot 32D2
South Sandwich Trench Atlantic O 73G7
South San Francisco USA 18A2
South Saskatchewan, R Can 3G3
South Saskatchewan, R Can 4H4
South Shields Eng 32E4
South Taranaki Bight, B NZ 79B1
South Uist, I Scot 32B3
South West Africa = Namibia
South West C Aust 76D5
Southwest C USA 8D3
South West Indian Ridge Indian O 74D6
South West Pacifc Bas'n Pacific O 75M6
South West Peru Ridge Pacific O 73D5
South Yemen, Republic Arabian Pen 56D3
South Yorkshire. County Eng 33E5
Soutpansberg, Mts S Africa 72D1
Sovetsk, R.S.F.SR USSR 41E1
Sovetsk, RSFSR USSR 42H4
Sovetskaya Gavan' USSR 51E2
Sovetskiy USSR 42L3
Sôya-misaki, C Japan 52D1
Soyo Congo Angola 71B4
Sozh, R USSR 42E5
Sozn, R USSR 41G2
Spa Belg 34C1
Spain, Kingdom 37
Spalato = Split
Spalding Eng 33E5
Spanish, R Can 10C1
Spanish Fork USA 17D2
Spanish Town Jamaica 21B3
Sparks USA 17C3
Sparta USA 10A2
Spartanburg USA 13C2
Spartí Greece 39E3
Spassk Dal'niy USSR 51C3
Spearfish USA 9B3
Spearman USA 14B2
Speightstown Barbados 21Q2
Spenard USA 8J3
Spencer, Indiana USA 10B3
Spencer, Iowa USA 9C3
Spencer Bay Can 5J3
Spencer, C Aust 78A3
Spencer G Aust 78A2
Spencer I Can 5L3
Spenser Mts NZ 79B2
Sperrin, Mts N Ire 32B4

Spessart, Region W Germ 34E2
Spey, R Scot 32D3
Speyer W Germ 40B3
Speyside Tobago 21K1
Spiez Switz 35B1
Spike Mt USA 8K2
Spilimbergo Italy 35E1
Spirir Lake USA 16C1
Spirit River Can 4G4
Spitsbergen = Svalbard
Spitsbergen, I Barents S 46C2
Spittal Austria 40C3
Spittal an der Drau Austria 35E1
Spjelkavik Nor 30F6
Split Yugos 38D2
Splügen Switz 35C1
Spokane USA 16C1
Spooner USA 10A1
Sporádhes, Is Greece 39F3
Spray USA 16C2
Spree, R E Germ 40C2
Springbok S Africa 72B2
Springdale USA 15D2
Springer USA 14B2
Springerville USA 17E4
Springfield, Colorado USA 14B2
Springfield, Illinois USA 10B3
Springfield, Massachusetts USA 12D1
Springfield, Minnesota USA 9D3
Springfield, Missouri USA 15D2
Springfield, Ohio USA 10C3
Springfield, Oregon USA 16B2
Springfield, Tennessee USA 13B1
Springfield, Vermont USA 11E2
Springfontein S Africa 72D3
Spring Mts USA 17C3
Springs S Africa 72D2
Springville, New York USA 12A1
Springville, Utah USA 17D2
Springwater USA 12B1
Spruce Mt USA 16D2
Spurn Head, C Eng 33F5
Spurn Head, Pt Eng 31D3
Spuzzum Can 16B1
Squamish Can 3D4
Sredhekolymsk USSR 47R3
Sredinnyy Khrebet, Mts USSR 47S4
Sredne-Russkaya Vozvyshennost, Upland USSR 42F5
Sredne Sibirskoye Ploskogorve, Tableland USSR 47M3
Sredniy Ural, Mts USSR 42K4
Srepok, R Camb 53D3
Sretensk USSR 48E1
Sre Umbell Camb 53C3
Srikakulam India 60C1
Sri Lanka, Republic S Asia 57G5
Srinagar Pak 58C2
Srivardhan India 60A1
Sroda Pol 40D2
Stack Skerry, I Scot 32C2
Stade W Germ 40B2
Staffa, I Scot 32B3
Stafford, County Eng 33D5
Stafford Eng 33D5
Stafford Springs USA 12D2
Stalingrad = Volgograd
Stalin,Mt Can 3D2
Stallberg, Mt S Africa 72B3
Stallworthy,C Can 5J1
Stalowa Wola Pol 41E2
Stamford, Connecticut USA 12D2
Stamford, New York USA 12C1
Stamford, Texas USA 14C3
Stampriet Namibia 72B1
Standerton S Africa 72D2
Standish USA 10C2
Stanford USA 16D1
Stanger S Africa 72E2
Stanislaus, R USA 18B2
Stanke Dimitrov Bulg 39E2
Stanley Aust 78E3
Stanley Falkland Is 23E8
Stanley, Idaho USA 16D2
Stanley, N Dakota USA 9B2
Stanley Res India 60B2
Stanleyville = Kisangani
Stann Creek Belize 19D3
Stanovoy Khrebet, Mts USSR 48F1
Stans Switz 35C1
Stanthorpe Aust 78D1
Stanton Banks, Sandbank Scot 32B3
Stapleton USA 14B1
Starachowice Pol 41E2

Stara Planiná, Mts Bulg 39E2
Staraya Russa USSR 42E4
Stara Zagora Bulg 39F2
Stargard Pol 40D2
Starkville USA 15E3
Starnberg W Germ 40C3
Starogard Gdanski Pol 41D2
Starokonstantinov USSR 41F3
Start Pt Eng 33D6
Staryy Oskol USSR 43F5
State College USA 12B2
Staten I USA 12C2
Statesboro USA 13C2
Statesville USA 13C1
Staunton USA 11D3
Stavanger Nor 30F7
Stavelot Belg 34C1
Stavropol' USSR 43G6
Stavropol' USSR 43G6
Stawell Aust 78B3
Stawno Pol 40D2
Stayton USA 16B2
Steamboat Springs USA 14A1
Stebbins USA 8F3
Steele,Mt Can 8K3
Steelton USA 12B2
Steen, R Can 3E2
Steen River Can 3E2
Steens Mt USA 16C2
Steenstrups Gletscher, Gl Greenland 5N2
Stefansson I Can 4H2
Stegi Swaziland 72E2
Steinach Austria 35D1
Steinbach Can 9C2
Steinkier Nor 30G6
Steinkjer Nor 42A3
Steinkopf S Africa 72B2
Stein Mt Can 3D3
Stella S Africa 72C2
Stellenbosch S Africa 72B3
Stemaco Mexico 20C2
Stenay France 34C2
Stendal E Germ 40C2
Stepanakert USSR 43H8
Stephen Can 9C2
Stephens,C NZ 79B2
Stephens Creek Aust 78B2
Stephenson USA 10B1
Stephens Pass USA 8M4
Stephenville Can 5N5
Stephenville USA 14C3
Stepovak B USA 8F4
Sterkstroom S Africa 72D3
Sterling, Colorado USA 14B1
Sterling, Illinois USA 10B2
Sterling, Kansas USA 14C2
Sterling, N Dakota USA 9B2
Sterling City USA 14B3
Sterling Heights USA 10C2
Sterlitamak USSR 42K5
Stettler Can 3F3
Steubenville USA 10C2
Stevens Point USA 10B2
Stevens Village USA 4D3
Stewart Can 3C2
Stewart USA 17C3
Stewart, R Can 8L3
Stewart Crossing Can 8L3
Stewart I NZ 79A3
Stewart Is Solomon Is 77F1
Stewart River Can 4E3
Stewartstown USA 12B3
Stewartville USA 9D3
Steyn S Africa 72D2
Steynsburg S Africa 72D3
Steytlerville S Africa 72C3
Stia Italy 35D3
Stika USA 8L4
Stikine, R Can 3B2
Stikine Ranges, Mts Can 8M4
Stillwater, Minnesota USA 9D2
Stillwater, Oklahoma USA 15C2
Stillwater Range, Mts USA 17C3
Stinett USA 14B2
Stirling Aust 78A2
Stirling Scot 32D3
Stockach W Germ 34E3
Stockbridge USA 12D1
Stockerau Austria 40D3
Stockholm Sweden 30H7
Stockport Eng 33D5
Stockton, California USA 18B2
Stockton Eng 33E4
Stockton, Kansas USA 14C2
Stockton L USA 15D2
Stoke-on-Trent Eng 33D5
Stokkseyri Iceland 30A2
Stokmarknes Nor 30G5
Stolbtsy USSR 30K8
Stolin USSR 41F2
Stone Harbour USA 12C3
Stonehaven Scot 32D3
Stonewall USA 15C3
Stony, R USA 8H3
Stony L Can 3J2
Storavan, L Sweden 30H5

Støren Nor 30G6
Storm B Aust 78E3
Storm Lake USA 9C3
Stornoway Scot 32B2
Storozhinets USSR 41F3
Storrs USA 12D2
Storsjön, L Sweden 30G6
Storuman Sweden 30H5
Story USA 9A3
Stoughton Can 3H4
Stoughton USA 12E1
Stour, R Eng 34A1
Stowmarket Eng 33F5
Stoyba USSR 51C1
Strablane N Ire 32B4
Strahan Aust 78E3
Stralsund E Germ 40C2
Strand S Africa 72B3
Stranda Nor 30F6
Strängnäs Sweden 30H7
Stranraer Scot 32C4
Strasbourg France 36D2
Strasburg USA 11D3
Stratford, California USA 18C2
Stratford Can 10C2
Stratford, Connecticut USA 12D2
Stratford NZ 79B1
Stratford, Texas USA 14B2
Stratford-on-Avon Eng 33E5
Strathalbyn Aust 78A3
Strathclyde, Region Scot 32C4
Strathmore Can 3F3
Stratton USA 11E1
Streator USA 10B2
Stresa Italy 35C2
Stretto de Messina, Str Italy/Sicily 38D3
Stroboli, I Italy 38D3
Stroeder Arg 26C4
Strømfjord Greenland 5N3
Stromness Scot 32D2
Strømø Faroes 30D3
Stromsburg USA 15C1
Stromsund Sweden 30H6
Ströms Vattudal, L Sweden 30G6
Stronsay, I Scot 32D2
Stroud Eng 33D6
Stroudsburg USA 12C2
Struma, R Bulg 39E2
Strumble Head, Pt Wales 33C5
Strumica Yugos 39E2
Stryy USSR 41E3
Stryy, R USSR 41E3
Strzelecki Creek, R Aust 78B1
Stuart, Florida USA 13E4
Stuart, Nebraska USA 9C3
Stuart, R Can 3D3
Stuart I USA 8F3
Stuart L Can 3D3
Stubaier Alpen, Mts Austria 35D1
Stubice Pol 30H8
Stuch, R USSR 43D5
Stung Sen Camb 53D3
Stung Treng Camb 53D3
Stura, R Italy 38B2
Sturge I Ant 80G7
Sturgeon Bay USA 10B2
Sturgeon Falls Can 11D1
Sturgeon L Can 9D1
Sturgis, Kentucky USA 10B3
Sturgis, Michigan USA 10B2
Sturgis, S Dakota USA 9B3
Sturt Creek, R Aust 76B2
Sturt Desert Aust 78B1
Stutterheim S Africa 72D3
Stuttgart W Germ 15D3
Stuttgart W Germ 40B3
Stykkishólmur Iceland 30A1
Styr, R USSR 41F2
Suaçuí Grande, R Brazil 27D2
Suakin Sudan 64C3
Suan N Korea 52A3
Su-ao Taiwan 50E5
Suardi Arg 26C2
Subi, I Indon 54C2
Subotica Yugos 39D1
Suceava Rom 43D6
Suchixtepec Mexico 20C2
Sucre Bol 24E7
Sucuriú, R Brazil 27B2
Sudan, Republic Africa 70C2
Sudbury Can 10C1
Sudbury Eng 33F5
Sudd, Swamp Sudan 70C3
Suddie Guyana 25G2
Sudr Egypt 63B4
Sue, R Sudan 70C3
Suemez I USA 8M4
Suerdrup Is Can 4H2
Suez Egypt 62B4
Suez Canal Egypt 62B3
Suez,G of Egypt 62B4
Suffern USA 12C2
Suffolk, County Eng 33F5
Suffolk USA 11D3
Sugarloaf Mt USA 11E2
Sugarloaf Pt Aust 78D2
Suggi L Can 3H3

Sugoy, R USSR	47R3	Sun Valley USA	16D2	Swartberge, Mts S		Tafasaset, Watercourse		Talkha Egypt	63A3
Suhār Oman	65G2	Sunwu China	51B2	Africa	72C3	Alg	68C2	Talladega USA	13B2
Sühbaatar Mongolia	48D1	Sunyani Ghana	69F4	Swartruggens S Africa	72D2	Taff, R Wales	33D6	Tall 'Afar Iraq	62D2
Sui Pak	58B3	Suojarvi USSR	42E3	Swatow		Tafila Jordan	63C3	Tallahassee USA	13C2
Suibin China	51C2	Suŏ-nada, B Japan	52B4	Swaziland, Kingdom S		Taft USA	18C3	Tallard France	35B2
Suide China	50C2	Suonejoki Fin	30K6	Africa	72E2	Tagant, Region Maur	68A3	Tall Bisah Syria	63D1
Suifenhe China	51C3	Supaul India	59C2	Sweden, Kingdom N		Tagaung Burma	59E3	Tallinn USSR	42C4
Suihua China	51B2	Superior, Arizona USA	17D4	Europe	30G7	Tagbilaran Phil	55F9	Tall Kalakh Syria	62C3
Suileng China	51B2	Superior, Nebraska USA	15C1	Swedru Ghana	69F4	Tagish L Can	3B2	Tallulah USA	15D3
Suining China	50B3	Superior, Wisconsin		Sweet Home USA	16B2	Tagliamento, R Italy	35E1	Tal'menka USSR	48B1
Suippes France	34C2	USA	10A1	Sweetwater USA	14B3	Taguenout Hagguerete,		Tal'noye USSR	43E6
Suir, R Irish Rep	31B3	Superior,L USA/Can	10B1	Sweetwater, R USA	9A3	Well Maur	68B2	Talpaki USSR	41E2
Sui Xian China	50C3	Suphan Buri Thai	53C3	Swellendam S Africa	72C3	Tagula, I Solomon Is	77E2	Taltal Chile	23B3
Suizhong China	50E1	Süphan Dağ Turk	62D2	Świdnica Pol	40D2	Tagum Phil	55G9	Talwood Aust	78C1
Sujāngarth India	58C3	Supiori, I Indon	49G7	Swidwin Pol	40D2	Tagus = Tejo		Tama USA	9D3
Sukabumi Indon	54C4	Supu Indon	55C2	Świebodzin Pol	40D2	Tahat, Mt Alg	68C2	Tamabo Range, Mts	
Sukadana, Borneo Indon	54D3	Suq 'Abs Yemen	64D3	Swiecie Pol	41D2	Tahiti, I Pacific O	75M5	Malay	54E2
Sukadana, Sumatra		Suq ash Suyukh Iraq	62E3	Swift Current Can	3G3	Tahlab, R Iran	61E3	Tamale Ghana	69F4
Indon	54C4	Suqaylibiyah Syria	63D1	Swift Current Creek, R		Tahlequah USA	15C2	Tamanrasset Alg	68C2
Sukagawa Japan	51E4	Suqian China	50D3	Can	9A1	Tahoe City USA	17B3	Tamanrasset,	
Sukaraya Indon	54D3	Suqutra = Socotra		Swift River Can	3B1	Tahoe,L USA	17B3	Watercourse Alg	68C2
Sukhinichi Shchekino		Sūr Oman	65G2	Swindon Eng	33E6	Tahoka USA	14B3	Tamaqua USA	12C2
USSR	42F5	Surabaya Indon	54D4	Świnoujście Pol	40C2	Tahoua Niger	68C3	Tamatave = Toamasina	
Sukhona, R USSR	42G4	Suraga-wan, B Japan	52C4	Switzerland, Federal		Tahta Egypt	64B1	Tamazula, Durango	
Sukhumi USSR	43G7	Surakarta Indon	54D4	Republic Europe	36D2	Tahulandang, I Indon	55C2	Mexico	20A1
Sukkertoppen Greenland	5N3	Sūrān Syria	63D1	Swords Irish Rep	33B5	Tahuna Indon	55C2	Tamazula, Jalisco	
Sukkertoppen, L		Surar, R USSR	42H5	Syderø Faroes	30D3	Tai'an China	50D2	Mexico	20B2
Greenland	5N3	Surat Aust	78C1	Sydney Aust	78D2	Taibus Qi China	50D1	Tamazunchale Mexico	20C1
Sukkozero USSR	30L6	Sürat India	58C4	Sydney Can	5M5	T'ai-chung Taiwan	50E5	Tambacounda Sen	68A3
Sukkur Pak	58B3	Süratgarh India	58C3	Sydney L Can	9D1	Taieri, R NZ	79B3	Tambores Urug	26D2
Sukma India	60C1	Surat Thani Thai	53B4	Syktyvakar USSR	42H3	Taihang Shan China	50C2	Tambov USSR	43G5
Sukpay, R USSR	51D2	Surendranagar India	58C4	Sylacauga USA	13B2	Taihape NZ	79C1	Tambre, R Spain	37A1
Sukses Namibia	71B6	Surf City USA	12C3	Sylarna, Mt Sweden	30G6	Tai Hu, L China	50E3	Tambu Indon	55B3
Sukumo Japan	52B4	Suriãpet India	60B1	Sylhet Bang	59D3	Taiki Japan	52D2	Tambura Sudan	70C3
Sukunka, R Can	3D2	Sürich Switz	36D2	Sylt, I W Germ	40B1	Tailai China	51A2	Tamega, R Port	37A1
Sula, R USSR	43F5	Surigao Phil	55G9	Sylvania USA	10C2	Taileleo Indon	54A3	Tamiahua Mexico	20C1
Sulaiman Range, Mts		Surin Thai	53C3	Sylvia,Mt Can	3D2	Tailem Bend Aust	78A3	Tamil Nādu, State India	60B2
Pak	58B3	Surinam, Republic		Symon Mexico	20B1	Tain Scot	32C3	Tamis, R Rom	39E1
Sula Sgeir, I Scot	32B2	Sur,Pt USA	18B2	Syowa, Base Ant	80G11	T'ai-nan Taiwan	50E5	Tam Ky Viet	53D2
Sulawesi, I Indon	55B3	Surrey, County Eng	33E6	Syracuse = Siracusa		Taiobeiras Brazil	27D2	Tampa USA	13C3
Sulawesi Sulatan, Prov		Sursee Switz	35C1	Syracuse, Kansas USA	14B2	T'ai pei Taiwan	50E5	Tampa B USA	13E4
Indon	55B3	Surtsey, I Iceland	30A2	Syracuse, New York		Taiping Malay	53C5	Tampere Fin	30J6
Sulawesi Tengah, Prov		Surulangan Indon	54B3	USA	12B1	Taira Japan	52D3	Tampico Mexico	20C1
Indon	55B3	Susa Italy	35B2	Syracuse USA	11D2	Tais Indon	54B3	Tampin Malay	54G7
Sulawesi Tenggara, Prov		Susaki Japan	52B4	Syrdal'ya, R USSR	46H5	Taisha Japan	52B3	Tamsagbulag Mongolia	48E2
Indon	55B3	Susanville USA	17B2	Syria, Republic S W Asia	62C2	Taitao,Pen de Chile	23B7	Tamsweg Austria	35E1
Sulawesi Utara, Prov		Süsch Switz	35D1	Sysert' USSR	42K4	T'ai-tung Taiwan	50E5	Tamu Burma	59D3
Indon	55B3	Susitna, R USA	8J3	Syzran' USSR	42H5	Taivelkoski Fin	30K5	Tamuis Mexico	20C1
Sulaymāniyah Iraq	62E3	Susquehanna USA	12C2	Szczecin Pol	40C2	Taiwan, Republic China	48F4	Tamworth Aust	78D2
Suleja Nig	69H4	Susquehanna, R USA	12B3	Szczecinek Pol	40D2	Taiwan Haixia =		Tamworth Eng	33E5
Sule Skerry, I Scot	32C2	Sussex USA	12C2	Szczytno Pol	41E2	Formosa Str		Tana Nor	30K4
Sulina Rom	39F1	Sussex West Eng	33E6	Szeged Hung	41E3	Taiyiba Jordan	63C3	Tana, L Eth	42D1
Sulitjelma Nor	30H5	Sustut Peak, Mt Can	3C2	Székesfehérvár Hung	41D3	Taiyuan China	50C2	Tana, R Kenya	70D2
Sullana Peru	24B4	Sutherland S Africa	72C3	Szekszard Hung	41D3	Taizhou China	50D3	Tana, R Nor/Fin	70E4
Sullivan USA	15D2	Sutherland USA	14B1	Szolnok Hung	41D3	Ta 'izz Yemen	64D4	Tanabe Japan	30K5
Sullivan Bay Can	3C3	Sutlej, R Pak	58C2	Szombathely Hung	40D3	Tajo, R Spain	37B1	Tanafjord, Inlet Nor	52C4
Sullivan L Can	3F3	Sutter Creek USA	17B3	Szprotawa Pol	40D2	Tak Thai	53B2	Tanaga, I USA	30K4
Sully-sur-Loire France	34B3	Sutton USA	10C3			Takada Japan	51D4	Tanahgrogot Indon	8C6
Sulmona Italy	38C2	Suttsu Japan	52D2	**T**		Takahashi Japan	52B4	Tanahjampea, I Indon	54E3
Sulphur, Louisiana USA	15D3	Sutwik I USA	8G4			Takaka NZ	79B2	Tanahmerah Indon	55B4
Sulphur, Oklahoma USA	15C3	Suva Fiji	7G2	Tabankulu S Africa	72D3	Takamatsu Japan	51C5	Tanakeke, I Indon	49G7
Sulphur Springs USA	15C3	Suwa Japan	51D4	Tabar Is PNG	76E1	Takaoka Japan	51D4	Tanana USA	55A4
Sultan Dağlari, Mts Turk	43E8	Suwałki Pol	41E2	Tabas Iran	61D2	Takapuna NZ	79B1	Tanana, R USA	8H2
Sultânpur India	59B2	Suwannee, R USA	13C3	Tabasco Mexico	20B1	Takasaki Japan	51D4	Tananarive =	8J3
Sulu Arch Phil	55F9	Suweilih Jordan	63C2	Tabasco, State Mexico	20D2	Takayama Japan	52C3	Antananarivo	
Sulu S Philip	49E6	Suwŏn S Korea	51B4	Tabatinga Brazil	24E4	Takazie, R Eth	64C4	Tananga Pass USA	8C6
Sulz W Germ	34E2	Su Xian China	50D3	Tabelbala Alg	68B2	Takefu Japan	51D4	Tanaro, R Italy	35C2
Sumampa Arg	23D3	Suzaka Japan	52C3	Tabeng Camb	53C3	Takeo Camb	53C3	Tanch'ŏn N Korea	51B3
Sumatera, I Indon	54A2	Suzhou China	50E3	Taber Can	3F3	Takeo Japan	52B4	Tandaho Eth	70E2
Sumba, I Indon	55B4	Suzu Japan	51D4	Tablas, I Phil	55F8	Take-shima = Tok-do		Tandil Arg	26D3
Sumbawa, I Indon	54E4	Suzuka Japan	52C4	Table Mt S Africa	72B3	Takestān Iran	61B1	Tandjong Datu, Pt Indon	54C2
Sumbawa Besar Indon	54E4	Suzu-misaki, C Japan	52C3	Table Mt USA	8K2	Taketa Japan	52B4	Tandjung d'Urville, C	
Sumbawanga Tanz	71D4	Svalbard, Is Barents S	46C2	Table Rock Res USA	15D2	Takikawa Japan	52D2	Indon	49G7
Sumburgh Head, Pt Scot	32E2	Svalyava USSR	41E3	Taboali Indon	54C3	Takingeun Indon	54A2	Tandjung Jambuair, C	
Sumenep Indon	54D4	Svartenhuk Halvø,		Tábor Czech	40C3	Takinoue Japan	52D2	Indon	54A1
Sumgait USSR	43H7	Region Greenland	4N2	Tabora Tanz	70D4	Takjvak L Can	4G3	Tandjung Layar, C Indon	54E3
Sumisu, I Japan	48H3	Svartisen, Mt Nor	30G5	Tabory USSR	42L4	Takkaze, R Eth	70D2	Tandjung Lumut, C	
Summerland Can	3E4	Svay Rieng Camb	53D3	Tabou Ivory Coast	68B4	Takla L Can	3C2	Indon	54C3
Summer Str USA	3B2	Sveg Sweden	30G6	Taboursouk Tunisia	69D1	Takla Landing Can	3C2	Tandjung Mangkalihet, C	
Summit Lake Can	4F4	Svendborg Den	30G7	Tabriz Iran	61B1	Takslesluk L USA	8F3	Indon	54E2
Summits Mt USA	17C3	Sverdlovsk USSR	46H4	Tabūk S Arabia	62C4	Taku, R Can	3B2	Tandjung Sambar, C	
Sumner,L NZ	79B2	Sverdrup Chan Can	5J1	Tacámbaro Mexico	20B2	Taku Arm, R Can	8M3	Indon	54D3
Sumoto Japan	52B4	Svetlaya USSR	51D2	Tacheng China	57G1	Taku Gl USA	3B2	Tandjung Sirik, C Malay	54D2
Sumter USA	13C2	Svetlogorsk USSR	41E2	Tacloban Phil	55G8	Takum Nig	69J4	Tandjung Vals, C Indon	49G7
Sumy USSR	43E5	Svetogorsk Fin	30K6	Tacna Peru	24D7	Tala Mexico	20B1	Tando Adam Pak	58B3
Sun, R USA	16D1	Svetozarevo Yugos	39E2	Tacna USA	17D4	Talabanya Hung	41D3	Tando Muhammad Khan	
Sunagawa Japan	52D2	Svilengrad Bulg	39F2	Tacoma USA	6A2	Talaga Indon	55C3	Pak	58B3
Sunan N Korea	52A3	Svir' USSR	41F2	Taconic Range USA	12D1	Talagang Pak	58C2	Tandou L Aust	78B2
Sunbury USA	12B2	Svit, R USSR	42E3	Tacuan, R Urug	26E2	Talagante Chile	26A2	Tāndūr India	60B1
Sunchales Arg	26C2	Švitavy Czech	40D3	Tacuarembó Urug	26D2	Talaimannar Sri Lanka	60B3	Taneatua NZ	79C1
Suncho Corral Arg	26C1	Svobodnyy USSR	51B1	Tacuati Par	27A3	Talak, Desert, Region		Tanega-shima, I Japan	51C5
Sunch'ŏn N Korea	51B4	Svolvaer Nor	30G5	Tadjoura Djibouti	70E2	Niger	68C3	Tanen Range, Mts	
Sunch'ŏn S Korea	51B5	Swain Reefs Aust	77E3	Tadjoura,G of Djibouti	64D4	Talasea PNG	76E1	Burma/Thai	53B2
Sundance USA	9B3	Swains, I American		Tadoussac Can	11F1	Talata Egypt	63B3	Tanezrouft, Desert	
Sundargarh India	59B3	Samoa	77H2	Tädpatri India	60B2	Talavera de la Reina		Region Alg	68B2
Sunderbans, Swamp		Swainsboro USA	13C2	Tadzhen USSR	46H6	Spain	37A1	Tang Iran	61D3
India	59C3	Swakop, R Namibia	72B1	Tadzhikskaya SSR,		Talca Chile	26A3	Tanga Tanz	70D4
Sunderland Eng	32E4	Swakopmund Namibia	72A1	Republic USSR	57E2	Talcahuano Chile	26A3	Tanga Is PNG	77E1
Sundre Can	3F3	Swale, R Eng	33E4	Taebaek Sanmaek, Mts		Tãlcher India	59C3	Tanganrog USSR	43F6
Sundridge Can	11D1	Swallow Reef, I S E Asia	54D1	S Korea	51B4	Talden USSR	51A1	Tanganyika,L Tanz/Zaïre	70C4
Sundsvaall Sweden	30H6	Swämihalli India	60B2	Taech'on S Korea	52A3	Taldy Kurgan USSR	57F1	Tanger Mor	69A1
Sungaianyar Indon	54E3	Swan, I Honduras	19D3	Taedong, R N Korea	52A3	Taligan Afghan	58B1	Tanggula Shan, Mts	
Sungaisalak Indon	54B3	Swanage Eng	33E6	Taegang-got, Pen N		Tali Post Sudan	70D3	China	57H2
Sungai Siput Malay	54F6	Swan Hill Aust	78B3	Korea	52A3	Taliwang Indon	54E4	Tangier = Tanger	
Sungei Petani Malay	54F6	Swan Hills Can	3E3	Taegu S Korea	51B4	Talkeetna USA	8H3	Tangjin S Korea	52A3
Sungguminasa Indon	55A4	Swan Hills, Mts Can	3E3	Taehŭksan, I S Korea	51B5	Talkeetna Mts USA	8J3	Tangkak Malay	54G7
Sunnyside USA	16C1	Swan I Caribbean	21A3	Taehung N Korea	52A2			Tangra Yumco, L China	57G2
Sunnyvale USA	17B3	Swan River Can	4H4	Taejön S Korea	51B4				
Sun Prairie USA	10B2	Swansea Wales	33D6	Taesek Dampar, L Malay	54G7				
Suntar USSR	47N3	Swansea B Wales	33D6	Tafalla Spain	37B1				
Suntsar Pak	61E3								

Tangshan *China* 50D2
Tangub *Phil* 55F9
Tanguy *USSR* 48D1
Tangwang He, R *China* 51B2
Tangyuan *China* 51B2
Tanjay *Phil* 55F9
Tanjong Bugel, C *Indon* 54D4
Tanjong Cangkuang, C *Indon* 54C4
Tanjong Malim *Malay* 54F7
Tanjong Puting, C *Indon* 54D3
Tanjong Selatan, C *Indon* 54D3
Tanjung *Indon* 54E3
Tanjungbalai *Indon* 54A2
Tanjungbaliha *Indon* 55C3
Tanjung Jabung, Pt *Indon* 54B3
Tanjung Karossa *Indon* 55A4
Tanjung Manimbaya, Pt *Indon* 55A2
Tanjungpandan *Indon* 54C3
Tanjung Priok *Indon* 54C4
Tanjungredeb *Indon* 54E2
Tanjung Selatan, Pt *Indon* 76A1
Tanjungselor *Indon* 54E2
Tanjung Torawitan, C *Indon* 55B2
Tanjung Vals, Pt *Indon* 76C1
Tank *Pak* 58C2
Tanna, I *Vanuatu* 77F2
Tannu Ola, Mts *USSR* 48C1
Tano, R *Ghana* 69F4
Tanout *Niger* 68C3
Tanquián *Mexico* 20C1
Tan-shui *Taiwan* 50E4
Tansing *Nepal* 59B2
Tanta *Egypt* 67C1
Tan-Tan *Mor* 68A2
Tanunak *USA* 4B3
Tanyang *S Korea* 52A3
Tanzania, Republic *Africa* 70D4
Tao'an *China* 51A2
Tao'er He, R *China* 51A2
Tao He, R *China* 50A3
Taolañaro *Madag* 71E6
Taole *China* 50B2
Taos *USA* 14A2
Taounate *Mor* 69B2
Taourirt *Mor* 69B2
Tapa *USSR* 42D4
Tapachula *Mexico* 19C3
Tapah *Malay* 54F6
Tapajós, R *Brazil* 25G4
Tapaktuan *Indon* 54A2
Tapalquén *Arg* 26C3
Tapan *Indon* 54B3
Tapanatepec *Mexico* 20D2
Tapanui *NZ* 79A3
Tapauá, R *Brazil* 24E5
Tapes *Brazil* 26E2
Tapi, R *India* 58D4
Taplejung *Nepal* 59C2
Tapoa, R *U Volta* 69G3
Tappahannock *USA* 11D3
Tapuaeniku, Mt *NZ* 79B2
Tapuaritinga *Brazil* 27C3
Tapul Group, Is *Phil* 55F9
Tapurucuara *Brazil* 24F4
Taquari, R *Brazil* 27B2
Tara *Aust* 78D1
Tara *USSR* 46J4
Tara, R *USSR* 46J4
Tara, R *Yugos* 39D2
Taraba, R *Nig* 69J4
Tarabuco *Bol* 24F7
Tarābulus = Tripoli
Taracón *Spain* 37B1
Taradale *NZ* 79C1
Tarakan *Indon* 54E2
Taramana *Indon* 55B4
Taransay, I *Scot* 32B3
Taranto *Italy* 38D2
Tarapoto *Peru* 24C5
Tarare *France* 36C2
Tararua Range, Mts *NZ* 79C2
Tarasovo *USSR* 42H2
Tarat *Alg* 68C2
Tarawera *NZ* 79C1
Tarazona *Spain* 37B1
Tarbat Ness, Pen *Scot* 32D3
Tarbela Res *Pak* 58C2
Tarbert, Strathclyde *Scot* 32C4
Tarbert, Western Isles *Scot* 32B3
Tarbes *France* 36B3
Tarboro *USA* 13D1
Tarcoola *Aust* 76C4
Tarcoon *Aust* 78C2
Taree *Aust* 78D2
Tarfaya *Mor* 68A2
Targhee P *USA* 16D2
Tarhūnah *Libya* 67A1
Tarif *UAE* 65F2
Tarija *Bol* 24F8
Tarikere *India* 60B2
Tarīm *S Yemen* 65E3
Tarime *Tanz* 70D4
Tarim He, R *China* 57G1
Tarim Pendi, Basin *China* 57G2
Tarin Kut *Afghan* 58B2
Tarkastad *S Africa* 72D3
Tarkio *USA* 15C1
Tarkwa *Ghana* 69F4
Tarlac *Phil* 55F7
Tarma *Peru* 24C6
Tarn, R *France* 36C3
Tarnobrzeg *Pol* 41E2
Tarnów *Pol* 41E3
Taro, R *Italy* 35C2
Taroom *Aust* 76D3
Tarragona *Spain* 37C1
Tarraleah *Aust* 78E3
Tarrasa *Spain* 37C1
Tarrytown *USA* 12D2
Tarsus *Turk* 62B2
Tartan, Oilfield *N Sea* 32E2
Tartaro, R *Italy* 35D2
Tartarskaya ASSR, Republic *USSR* 42H4
Tartu *USSR* 42D4
Tartūs *Syria* 62C3
Tarumirim *Brazil* 27D2
Tarutung *Indon* 54A2
Tarvisio *Italy* 35E1
Taschereau *Can* 11D1
Tashauz *USSR* 56D1
Tashigang *Bhutan* 59D2
Tashkent *USSR* 57E1
Tashkepri *USSR* 61E1
Tashtagol *USSR* 46K4
Tashtyp *USSR* 47L4
Tasikmalaya *Indon* 54C4
Tasil *Syria* 63C2
Tasiussaq *Greenland* 5N2
Tasker, Well *Niger* 70B2
Tasman B *NZ* 79B2
Tasmania, I *Aust* 76D5
Tasman Mts *NZ* 79B2
Tasman Pen *Aust* 78E3
Tasman S *NZ Aust* 77E4
Taşova *Turk* 62C1
Tassili du Hoggar, Desert, Region *Alg* 68C2
Tassili N'jjer, Desert, Region *Alg* 68C2
Tata *Mor* 68B2
Tataouine *Tunisia* 69E2
Tatarsk *USSR* 46J4
Tatarskiy Proliv, Str *USSR* 51E2
Tateyama *Japan* 52C3
Tathlina L *Can* 3E1
Tathlith *S Arabia* 64D3
Tatitlek *USA* 8J3
Tatla Lake *Can* 3D3
Tatry, Mts *Pol/Czech* 41D3
Tatsuno *Japan* 52B4
Tatta *Pak* 58B4
Tatuí *Brazil* 27C3
Tatum *USA* 14B3
Tatvan *Turk* 62D2
Ta'u, I *American Samoa* 77H2
Tauá *Brazil* 25K5
Taubaté *Brazil* 27C3
Taufstein, Mt *W Germ* 34E1
Taumarunui *NZ* 79C1
Taung *S Africa* 72C2
Taungdwingyi *Burma* 53B2
Taung-gyi *Burma* 53B1
Taungup *Burma* 53A2
Taunsa *Pak* 58C2
Taunton *Eng* 33D6
Taunton *USA* 12E2
Taunus, Region *W Germ* 34E1
Taupo *NZ* 79C1
Taupo,L *NZ* 79C1
Taurage *USSR* 41E1
Tauranga *NZ* 79C1
Tauranga Harbour, B *NZ* 79C1
Tauroa Pt *NZ* 79B1
Tavda, R *USSR* 29M3
Taveuni, I *Fiji* 77H2
Tavira *Port* 37A2
Tavistock *Eng* 33C6
Tavoy *Burma* 53B3
Tavoy Pt *Burma* 53B3
Tavşanli *Turk* 62A2
Tawa *NZ* 79B2
Tawakoni,L *USA* 15C3
Tawas City *USA* 10C2
Tawau *Malay* 54E2
Taweisha *Sudan* 70C2
Tawitawi, I *Phil* 55F9
Tawitawi Group, Is *Phil* 55F9
Taxco *Mexico* 20C2
Taxcoco *Mexico* 20C2
Tay, R *Scot* 32D3
Tayan *Indon* 54D3
Taylor, Alaska *USA* 8F2
Taylor *Can* 3D2
Taylor, Michigan *USA* 10C2
Taylor, Texas *USA* 15C3
Taylor,Mt *USA* 14A2
Taylorville *USA* 10B3
Taymā' *S Arabia* 64C1
Taymura, R *USSR* 47L3
Tay Ninh *Viet* 53D3
Tayolita *Mexico* 20A1
Tayshet *USSR* 47L4
Tayshir *Mongolia* 48C2
Tayside, Region *Scot* 32D3
Taytay *Phil* 55E8
Tayyebāt *Iran* 61E2
Taza *Mor* 69B2
Tazawako *Japan* 52D3
Tazawa-ko, L *Japan* 52D3
Tazerbo, Region *Libya* 67B2
Tazin L *Can* 3G2
Tazlina L *USA* 8J3
Tazovskiy *USSR* 46J3
Tbilisi *USSR* 43G7
Tchaourou *Benin* 69G4
Tchibanga *Gabon* 70B4
Tchigai,Plat du *Niger* 70B1
Tchin Tabaradene *Niger* 68C3
Tcholliré *Cam* 70B3
Tczew *Pol* 41D2
Teacapán *Mexico* 20A1
Te Anau *NZ* 79A3
Te Anua,L *NZ* 79A3
Te Aroha *NZ* 79C1
Te Awamutu *NZ* 79C1
Tébessa *Alg* 69D1
Tebingtinggi *Indon* 54A2
Teboman *Mexico* 20B2
Tecailtlán *Mexico* 20B2
Tecate *Mexico* 17C4
Tecclotlán *Mexico* 20B1
Techa, R *USSR* 42L4
Tećpan *Mexico* 20B2
Tecuala *Mexico* 20A1
Tecuci *Rom* 39F1
Tecumseh *USA* 15C1
Tedzhen *USSR* 56E2
Tedzhen, R *USSR* 46H6
Tees, R *Eng* 33E4
Tefé *Brazil* 24F4
Tegal *Indon* 54C4
Tegineneng *Indon* 54C4
Tegucigalpa *Honduras* 19D3
Tehachapi *USA* 18C3
Tehachapi Mts *USA* 18C3
Tehachapi P *USA* 17C3
Tehek L *Can* 4J3
Tehoru *Indon* 55C3
Tehrān *Iran* 61C1
Tehuacán *Mexico* 20C2
Tehuantepec *Mexico* 20C2
Tehuitzingo *Mexico* 20C2
Teifi, R *Wales* 33C5
Tejo, R *Port* 37A2
Tejon P *USA* 18C3
Tejupilco *Mexico* 20B2
Tekamah *USA* 9C3
Tekapo,L *NZ* 79B2
Tekeli *USSR* 57F1
Tekirdağ *Turk* 62A1
Tekir Dağlari, Mts *Turk* 39F2
Teknaf *Bang* 59D3
Teku *Indon* 55B3
Te Kuiti *NZ* 79C1
Tela *Honduras* 19D3
Telavi *USSR* 43H7
Tel Aviv Yafo *Israel* 63C2
Telegraph Creek *Can* 3B2
Telén *Arg* 26B3
Telescope Peak, Mt *USA* 17C3
Teles Pires, R *Brazil* 25G5
Telfs *Austria* 35D1
Teli *USSR* 47K4
Telkalakh *Syria* 43F9
Tell el Meise, Mt *Jordan* 63C3
Teller *USA* 8E2
Tellicherry *India* 60B2
Telok Anson *Malay* 53C5
Tělok Buli, B *Indon* 55C2
Tělok Darvel *Malay* 54E2
Tělok Dondo, B *Indon* 55B2
Tělok Flamingo, B *Indon* 49G7
Tělok Kau, B *Indon* 55C2
Tělok Kumai, B *Indon* 54D3
Tělok Labuk, B *Malay* 54E1
Tělok Pelabuanratu, B *Indon* 54C4
Tělok Saleh, B *Indon* 54E4
Tělok Sampit, B *Indon* 54D3
Tělok Sukadona, B *Indon* 54C3
Teloloapán *Mexico* 20C2
Telšiai *USSR* 41E1
Telukbatang *Indon* 54D3
Teluk Berau, B *Indon* 49G7
Telukbetung *Indom* 54C4
Teluk Bone, B *Indon* 55B3
Teluk Cendrawasih, B *Indon* 49G7
Telukdalam *Indon* 54A2
Teluk Mandar, B *Indon* 55A3
Teluk Tolo, B *Indon* 55B3
Teluk Tomini, B *Indon* 55B3
Těluk Weda, B *Indon* 55C2
Tema *Ghana* 69F4
Temagami,L *Can* 10C1
Temascal *Mexico* 20C2
Tembesi, R *Indon* 54B3
Tembilahan *Indon* 54B3
Temblador *Ven* 21E5
Temblor Range, Mts *USA* 18B3
Temerloh *Malay* 53C5
Temir *USSR* 46G5
Temirtau *USSR* 46J4
Temiscaming *Can* 11D1
Témiscouata,L *Can* 11F1
Temora *Aust* 78C2
Tempe *USA* 17D4
Temple *USA* 15C3
Templemore *Irish Rep* 33B5
Templeton *USA* 18B3
Tempoal *Mexico* 20C1
Temuco *Chile* 26A3
Temuka *NZ* 79B2
Tena *Ecuador* 24C4
Tenāli *India* 60C1
Tenancingo *Mexico* 20C2
Tenasserim *Burma* 53B3
Tenby *Wales* 33C6
Tenco, R *Par* 23D2
Tendaho *Eth* 64D4
Tende *France* 35B2
Tende, P *Italy* 35B2
Ten Degree Chan *Indian O* 60E3
Tendrara *Mor* 69B2
Ténéré, Desert Region *Niger* 70B2
Tenerife, I *Canary Is* 68A2
Ténès *Alg* 69C1
Tenessee P *USA* 14A2
Teng, R *Burma* 53B1
Tenggarong *Indon* 54E3
Tengger Shamo, Desert *China* 50A2
Tenkāsi *India* 60B3
Tenke *Zaïre* 71C5
Tenkodogo *U Volta* 69F3
Tenna, R *Italy* 35E3
Tennant Creek *Aust* 76C2
Tennessee, State *USA* 7E3
Tennessee, R *USA* 15E2
Teno *Chile* 26A2
Tenom *Malay* 54E1
Tenosique *Mexico* 19C3
Tensift, R *Mor* 69A2
Tentena *Indon* 55B3
Tenterfield *Aust* 78D1
Ten Thousand Is *USA* 13E4
Teocaltiche *Mexico* 20B1
Teófilo Otôni *Brazil* 27D2
Teotihiucan, Hist Site *Mexico* 20C2
Teotitlan *Mexico* 20C2
Tepa *Indon* 55C4
Tepatitlan *Mexico* 20B1
Tepehuanes *Mexico* 19B2
Tepeji *Mexico* 20C2
Tepic *Mexico* 20B1
Teplice *Czech* 40C2
Te Puke *NZ* 79C1
Tequila *Mexico* 20B1
Tequistepec *Mexico* 20C2
Ter, R *Spain* 37C1
Téra *Niger* 68C3
Teradomari *Japan* 52C3
Teramo *Italy* 38C2
Terceira, I *Açores* 68A1
Tereboviya *USSR* 41F3
Terenoz *Brazil* 27B2
Teresina *Brazil* 25K5
Teresópolis *Brazil* 27D3
Teressa, I *Indian O* 60E3
Teriang *Malay* 54G7
Terme *Turk* 62C1
Termez *USSR* 56E2
Termoli *Italy* 38C2
Ternate *Indon* 55C2
Terney *USSR* 51D3
Terni *Italy* 38C2
Ternopol *USSR* 41F3
Terra Bella *USA* 18C3
Terrace *Can* 3C3
Terrace Bay *Can* 10B1
Terracina *Italy* 38C2
Terrafirma *S Africa* 71C6
Terre Adélie, Region *Ant* 80G8
Terre Bonne B *USA* 15D4
Terre Haute *USA* 10B3
Terrell *USA* 15C3
Terry *USA* 9A2
Terschelling, I *Neth* 40B2
Teruel *Spain* 37B1
Teshekpuk *USA* 4C2
Teshekpuk L *USA* 8H1
Teshi, R *Nig* 69G4
Teshikaga *Japan* 52D2
Teshio, R *Japan* 51E3
Teshio dake, Mt *Japan* 52D2
Tesiyn Gol, Mts *Mongolia* 48C2
Teslin *Can* 8M3
Teslin, R *Can* 8M4
Teslin L *Can* 8M3
Teslyn Gol, R *Mongolia* 47L5
Tessalit *Mali* 68C2
Tessaoua *Niger* 68C3
Tessaout, R *Mor* 69A2
Tessenei *Eth* 64C3
Tete *Mozam* 71D5
Tetela *Mexico* 20B2
Teterev, R *USSR* 41F2
Teton, R *USA* 16D1
Teton Range, Mts *USA* 16D2
Tetouan *Mor* 69A1
Tetyushi *USSR* 42H4
Teuco, R *Arg* 24F8
Teúl de Gonzalez Ortega *Mexico* 20B1
Teun, I *Indon* 55C4
Teuri-tō, I *Japan* 52D2
Tevere, R *Italy* 38C2
Teviot, R *Scot* 32D4
Tevriz *USSR* 46J4
Te Waewae B *NZ* 79A3
Tewah *Indon* 54D3
Tewantin *Aust* 78D1
Têwo *China* 50A3
Texarkana *USA* 15D3
Texarkana,L *USA* 15D3
Texas *Aust* 78D1
Texas, State *USA* 6C3
Texas City *USA* 15D4
Texel, I *Neth* 40A2
Texhoma *USA* 14B2
Texoma,L *USA* 15C3
Teyateyaneng *Lesotho* 72D2
Teyuarah *Afghan* 58A2
Teziutlán *Mexico* 20C2
Tezouro *Brazil* 27B2
Tezpur *India* 59D2
Tha *Laos* 53C1
Thabana Ntlenyana, Mt *Lesotho* 72D2
Thaba Putsoa, Mt *Lesotho* 72D2
Thabazimbi *S Africa* 72D1
Thagyettaw *Burma* 53B3
Thai Binh *Viet* 53D1
Thailand, Kingdom *S E Asia* 53C2
Thailand,G of *Thai* 53C3
Thai Nguyen *Viet* 53D1
Thakhek *Laos* 53D2
Thal *Pak* 58C2
Thale Luang, L *Thai* 53C4
Thallon *Aust* 78C1
Thamarit *Oman* 65F3
Thames *NZ* 79C1
Thames, R *Eng* 33F6
Thamūd *S Yemen* 65E3
Thāne *India* 60A1
Thanh Hoah *Viet* 53D2
Thanjavur *India* 60B2
Thann *France* 34D3
Thar Desert *India* 58C3
Thargomindah *Aust* 78B1
Tharrawaddy *Burma* 59E4
Thásos, I *Greece* 39E2
Thaton *Burma* 53B2
Thayetmyo *Burma* 53A2
Thazi *Burma* 59E3
The Dalles *USA* 4F5
Thedford *USA* 9B3
The Gulf *S W Asia* 65F1
Thekulthili L *Can* 3G1
Thelon, R *Can* 4H3
The Naze *Eng* 34A1
Theodore *Aust* 76E3
Theodore Roosevelt L *USA* 17D4
Thermaïkós Kólpos, G *Greece* 39E2
Thermopolis *USA* 16E2
Thesiger B *Can* 4F2
Thessalon *Can* 10C1
Thessaloníki *Greece* 39E2
Thetford *Eng* 33F5
Thetford Mines *Can* 11E1
Theunissen *S Africa* 72D2
Thibodaux *USA* 15D4
Thicket Portage *Can* 4J4
Thief River Falls *USA* 9C2
Thielsen,Mt *USA* 16B2
Thiers *France* 36C2
Thiès *Sen* 68A3
Thika *Kenya* 70D4
Thimphu *Bhutan* 59C2
Thionville *France* 36D2
Thíra, I *Greece* 39F3
Thirsk *Eng* 33E4
Thisted *Den* 30F7
Thívai *Greece* 39E3
Thiviers *France* 36C2
Thoa *Can* 3G1
Thomas A Eddison,L *USA* 18C2
Thomaston, Georgia *USA* 13C2
Thomaston, Maine *USA* 11F2
Thomastown *Irish Rep* 33B5
Thomasville, Alabama *USA* 13B2
Thomasville, Georgia *USA* 13C2
Thomasville, N Carolina *USA* 13D1
Thom Bay *Can* 5J2
Thompson *Can* 4J4
Thompson *USA* 15D1
Thompson Falls *USA* 16C1
Thompson Landing *Can* 4G3
Thompson R *Can* 3D3
Thompsonville *USA* 12D2
Thomson *USA* 13C2

Thomson, R *Aust* 76D3
Thon Buri *Thai* 53C3
Thongwa *Burma* 53B2
Thonon-les-Bains *France* 35B1
Thoreau *USA* 14A2
Thornhill *Scot* 32D4
Thouars *France* 36B2
Thousand Is *Can/USA* 11D2
Three Forks *USA* 16D1
Three Hills *Can* 3F3
Three Kings Is *NZ* 7G4
Three Lakes *USA* 10B1
Three Pagodas P *Thai* 53B2
Three Rivers, California *USA* 18C2
Three Rivers, Michigan *USA* 10B2
Three Rivers, Texas *USA* 15F4
Three Sisters, Mt *USA* 16B2
Thule *Greenland* 5M2
Thun *Switz* 35B1
Thunder Bay *Can* 10B1
Thunder Mt *USA* 8F2
Thuner See, L *Switz* 35B1
Thung Song *Thai* 53B4
Thur, R *Switz* 35C1
Thüringen Wald, Upland *E Germ* 40C2
Thurles *Irish Rep* 33B5
Thursday I *Aust* 49H8
Thurso *Scot* 32D2
Thurston I *Ant* 80F4
Thusis *Switz* 35C1
Thylungra *Aust* 78B1
Tiandong *China* 50B5
Tian'e *China* 50B5
Tianjin *China* 50D2
Tianlin *China* 50B5
Tianqiaoling *China* 51B3
Tiân Shan, Mts *C Asia* 57G1
Tianshui *China* 50B3
Tianzhu *China* 50A2
Tiaret *Alg* 69C1
Tibagi, R *Brazil* 27B3
Tibati *Cam* 69J4
Tiberias *Israel* 63C2
Tiberias,L *Israel* 63C2
Tiber,R = Tevere,R
Tiber Res *USA* 16D1
Tibesti, Mountain Region *Chad* 70B1
Tibet, Autonomous Region *China* 57G2
Tibooburra *Aust* 78B1
Tibrikot *Nepal* 59B2
Tiburón, I *Mexico* 19A2
Tichitt *Maur* 68B3
Tichla *Mor* 68A2
Ticino, R *Italy/Switz* 35C2
Ticonderoga *USA* 11E2
Ticul *Mexico* 19D2
Tidjikja *Maur* 68A3
Tiefencastel *Switz* 35C1
Tiel *Neth* 34C1
Tieli *China* 51B2
Tieling *China* 51A3
Tielt *Belg* 34B1
Tienen *Belg* 34C1
Tiengen *W Germ* 34E3
Tien Shan, Mts *USSR/China* 46J5
Tientsin *China* 50D2
Tierp *Sweden* 30H6
Tierra Amarilla *Chile* 26A1
Tierra Amarilla *USA* 14A2
Tierra Blanca *Mexico* 20C2
Tierra Colorada *Mexico* 20C2
Tierra del Fuego, Territory *Arg* 23C8
Tierra del Fuego, I *Chile/Arg* 22C9
Tietê *Brazil* 27C3
Tiete, R *Brazil* 27B3
Tiffin *USA* 10C2
Tifton *USA* 13C2
Tifu *Indon* 55C3
Tigalda, I *USA* 8F5
Tigil *USSR* 47R4
Tignere *Cam* 69J4
Tigre, R *Peru* 24C4
Tigre, R *Ven* 24F2
Tigris, R *Iraq* 62E3
Tihuatlán *Mexico* 20C1
Tijuana *Mexico* 17C4
Tikamgarh *India* 58D4
Tikhin *USSR* 42E4
Tikhoretsk *USSR* 43G6
Tikopia, I *Solomon Is* 77F2
Tikrit *Iraq* 62D3
Tiksi *USSR* 47O2
Tilamuta *Indon* 55B2
Tilburg *Neth* 34C1
Tilbury *Eng* 33F6
Tilcara *Arg* 23C2
Tilcha *Aust* 78B1
Tilin *Burma* 53A1
Tillabéri *Niger* 68C3
Tillamook *USA* 16B1
Tillanchong, I *Indian O* 60E3
Tillia *Niger* 68C3
Tílos, I *Greece* 39F3
Tilpa *Aust* 78B2
Tiluá *Colombia* 24C3
Timanskiv Kryazh, Mts *USSR* 42H2
Timaru *NZ* 79B2
Timashevsk *USSR* 43F6
Timbákion *Greece* 39E3
Timbalier B *USA* 15D4
Timbédra *Maur* 68B3
Timbuktu = Tombouctou
Timétrine Monts, Mts *Mali* 68B3
Timia *Niger* 68C3
Timimoun *Alg* 68C2
Timişoara *Rom* 39E1
Timmins *Can* 10C1
Timor, I *Indon* 76B1
Timor S *Aust/Indon* 76B2
Timote *Arg* 26C3
Timsâh,L *Egypt* 63B3
Tims Ford L *USA* 13B1
Tinaca Pt *Phil* 55G9
Tinaco *Ven* 21D5
Tindivanam *India* 60B2
Tindouf *Alg* 68B2
Tinée, R *France* 35B2
Tinemaha Res *USA* 18C2
Tinfouchy *Alg* 68B2
Tin Fouye *Alg* 68C2
Tingmerkpuk Mt *USA* 8F2
Tingmiarmiut *Greenland* 5O3
Tingo Maria *Peru* 24C5
Tingrela *Ivory Coast* 68B3
Tingri *China* 59C2
Tinian *Pacific O* 49H5
Tinogasta *Arg* 26B1
Tínos, I *Greece* 39F3
Tinsukia *India* 59E2
Tintagel Head, Pt *Eng* 33C6
Tin Tarabine, Watercourse *Alg* 68C2
Tintinara *Aust* 78B3
Tin Zaouaten *Alg* 68C2
Tioga *USA* 9B2
Tioga, R *USA* 12B2
Tioga P *USA* 18C2
Tioman, I *Malay* 53C5
Tione *Italy* 35D1
Tioughnioga, R *USA* 12B1
Tipperary, County *Irish Rep* 33B5
Tipperary *Irish Rep* 31B3
Tipton, California *USA* 18C2
Tipton, Missouri *USA* 15D2
Tiptūr *India* 60B2
Tiquicheo *Mexico* 20B2
Tiranë *Alb* 39D2
Tirano *Italy* 35D1
Tiraspol *USSR* 43D6
Tir'at el Ismâilîya, Canal *Egypt* 63A3
Tirchchirāppalli *India* 60B2
Tire *Turk* 39F3
Tirebolu *Turk* 62C1
Tiree, I *Scot* 32B3
Tîrgovişte *Rom* 39F2
Tîrgu Jiu *Rom* 39E1
Tîrgu Mureş *Rom* 39E1
Tirich Mir, Mt *Pak* 58C1
Tiris, Region *Mor* 68A2
Tirlyanskiy *USSR* 42K5
Tîrnăveni *Rom* 39E1
Tírnavos *Greece* 39E3
Tirodi *India* 58D4
Tirol, Province *Austria* 35D1
Tirso, R *Sardegna* 38B2
Tiruchchendūr *India* 60B3
Tirunelveli *India* 60B3
Tirupati *India* 60B2
Tiruppattūr *India* 60B2
Tiruppur *India* 60B2
Tiruvannamalai *India* 60B2
Tisdale *Can* 3H3
Tishomingo *USA* 15C3
Tisiyah *Syria* 63D2
Tisza, R *Hung* 41E3
Titlagarh *India* 59B3
Titograd *Yugos* 39D2
Titovo Užice *Yugos* 39D2
Titov Veles *Yugos* 39E2
Titule *Zaïre* 70C3
Titusville *USA* 13C3
Tiverton *Eng* 33D6
Tivoli *Italy* 38C2
Tixtla *Mexico* 20C2
Tiyeglow *Somalia* 70E3
Tizayuca *Mexico* 20C2
Tizimin *Mexico* 19D2
Tizi Ouzou *Alg* 69C1
Tiznit *Mor* 68B2
Tizpan el Alto *Mexico* 20B1
Tlacolula *Mexico* 20C2
Tlacotalpan *Mexico* 20C2
Tlalchana *Mexico* 20B2
Tlalnepantla *Mexico* 20C2
Tlalpan *Mexico* 20C2
Tlaltenago *Mexico* 20B1
Tlancualpicán *Mexico* 20C2
Tlapa *Mexico* 20C2
Tlapacoyan *Mexico* 20C2
Tlaquepaque *Mexico* 20B1
Tlaxcala *Mexico* 20C2
Tlaxcala, State *Mexico* 20C2
Tlaxiaco *Mexico* 20C2
Tlell *Can* 8M5
Tlemcem *Alg* 69B2
Toamasina *Madag* 71E5
Toay *Arg* 26C3
Toba *Japan* 52C4
Toba and Kakar Ranges, Mts *Pak* 58B2
Tobago, I *Caribbean* 21E4
Toba Inlet, Sd *Can* 3D3
Tobelo *Indon* 55C2
Tobermory *Can* 10C1
Tobermory *Scot* 32B3
Tobi, I *Pacific O* 49G6
Tobin L *Can* 3H3
Tobin,Mt *USA* 17C2
Tōbi-shima, I *Japan* 52C3
Tobol, R *USSR* 46H4
Toboli *Indon* 55B3
Tobol'sk *USSR* 46H4
Tobruk = Tubruq
Tobseda *USSR* 42J2
Tocantins, R *Brazil* 25J4
Toccoa *USA* 13C2
Toce, R *Italy* 35C1
Tocopilla *Chile* 23B2
Tocorpuri *Bol* 23C2
Tocorpuri, Mt *Chile* 24E8
Tocuyo, R *Ven* 24E1
Toda *India* 58D3
Todeli *Indon* 55B3
Tödi, Mt *Switz* 35C1
Todong *S Korea* 52B3
Todos Santos *Mexico* 6B4
Tofield *Can* 3F3
Tofino *Can* 3C4
Tofua, I *Tonga* 77H2
Togiak *USA* 8F4
Togiak B *USA* 8F4
Togian, I *Indon* 55B3
Togni *Sudan* 64C3
Togo, Republic *Africa* 69G4
Togtoh *China* 50C1
Tohamiyam *Sudan* 64C3
Tohatchi *USA* 14A2
Tojo *Indon* 55B3
Tok *USA* 8K3
Tokachi, R *Japan* 51E3
Tokamachi *Japan* 52C3
Tokar *Sudan* 64C3
Tokara Retto, Arch *Japan* 48F4
Tokat *Turk* 62C1
Tŏkchŏk-kundo, Arch *S Korea* 51B4
Tok-do, I *S Korea* 52B3
Tokelau, Is *Pacific O* 77H1
Tokmak *USSR* 57F1
Tokomaru Bay *NZ* 79C1
Toku, R *Can/USA* 8M4
Tokung *Indon* 54D3
Tokuno, I *Japan* 48F4
Tokur *USSR* 51C1
Tokushima *Japan* 51C5
Tokuyama *Japan* 52B4
Tōkyō *Japan* 51D4
Tolaga Bay *NZ* 79C1
Toledo *Brazil* 25H8
Toledo *Chile* 26A1
Toledo *Spain* 37B2
Toledo *USA* 10C2
Toledo Bend Res *USA* 15D3
Tolentino *Italy* 35E3
Toliara *Madag* 71E6
Tolima *Colombia* 24C2
Toliman *Mexico* 20C1
Tolitoli *Indon* 55B2
Tolmezzo *Italy* 35E1
Tolmin *Yugos* 35E1
Tolocin *USSR* 41F2
Tolosa *Spain* 37B1
Tolsan-do, I *S Korea* 52A4
Toltén *Chile* 26A3
Toltén, R *Chile* 26A3
Toluca *Mexico* 20C2
Tol'yati *USSR* 42H5
Tom, R *USSR* 51C1
Tomah *USA* 10A2
Tomahawk *USA* 10B1
Tomakomai *Japan* 51E3
Tomani *Malay* 54E2
Tomari *USSR* 51E2
Tomaszów Mazowiecka *Pol* 41E2
Tomatlán *Mexico* 20A2
Tombigbee, R *USA* 13B2
Tomboco *Angola* 71B4
Tomboli *Indon* 55B3
Tombos *Brazil* 27D3
Tombouctou *Mali* 68B3
Tombstone *USA* 17E4
Tomburke *S Africa* 72D1
Tomé *Chile* 26A3
Tomelloso *Spain* 37B2
Tomer *Port* 37A2
Tomie *Japan* 52A4
Tomini *Indon* 55B2
Tomkinson Range, Mts *Aust* 76B3
Tommot *USSR* 47O4
Tomorrit, Mt *Alb* 39E2
Tomsk *USSR* 46K4
Toms River *USA* 12C3
Tonalá *Mexico* 19C3
Tonasket *USA* 16C1
Tonawanda *USA* 11D2
Tondano *Indon* 55C2
Tonga, Is *Pacific O* 77H3
Tongaat *S Africa* 72E2
Tongatapu, I *Tonga* 77H3
Tongatapu Group, Is *Tonga* 77H3
Tonga Trench *Pacific O* 77H3
Tongbei *China* 51B2
Tongchang *N Korea* 52A2
Tongcheng *China* 50D3
Tongchuan *China* 50B2
Tongde *China* 50A2
Tongeren *Belg* 34C1
Tonggu Jiao, I *China* 53E2
Tonghai *China* 50A5
Tonghe *China* 51B2
Tonghua *China* 51B3
Tongjiang *China* 51C2
Tongjosŏn-man *N Korea* 51B4
Tongkin,G of *Viet/China* 53D1
Tonglia *China* 50E1
Tongling *China* 50D3
Tongnae *S Korea* 52A3
Tongo *Aust* 78B2
Tongoy *Chile* 26A2
Tongren, Guizhou *China* 50B4
Tongren, Qinghai *China* 50A2
Tongsa *Bhutan* 59D2
Tongta *Burma* 53B1
Tongtian He, R *China* 48C3
Tongue *Scot* 32C2
Tongue, R *USA* 9A2
Tong Xian *China* 50D2
Tongxin *China* 50B2
Tongyu *China* 51A3
Tongzi *China* 50B4
Tonhil *Mongolia* 47L5
Tonich *Mexico* 6C4
Tonj *Sudan* 70C3
Tonk *India* 58D3
Tonkawa *USA* 15C2
Tonle Sap, L *Camb* 53C3
Tonnerre *France* 34C3
Tono *Japan* 52D3
Tonopah *USA* 17C3
Tonsina *USA* 8J3
Tooele *USA* 16D2
Toogoolawah *Aust* 78D1
Toompine *Aust* 78B1
Toowoomba *Aust* 78D1
Topaz L *USA* 18C1
Topeka *USA* 15C2
Topolobampo *Mexico* 6C4
Toppenish *USA* 16B1
Toppock *USA* 17D4
Torbali *Turk* 39F3
Torbat-e-Heydariyeh *Iran* 61D1
Torbat-e Jām *Iran* 61E1
Torbay *Eng* 33D6
Torbert,Mt *USA* 8H3
Tordesillas *Spain* 37A1
Torgau *E Germ* 40C2
Torhout *Belg* 34B1
Tori *Eth* 70D3
Tori, I *Japan* 48H3
Torino *Italy* 35B2
Torit *Sudan* 70D3
Torixoreu *Brazil* 27B2
Tormes, R *Spain* 37A1
Tornado Mt *Can* 3F3
Torne, L *Sweden* 30J5
Torneträsk *Sweden* 30H5
Torngat, Mts *Can* 5M4
Tornio *Fin* 30J5
Tornquist *Arg* 26C3
Torobuku *Indon* 55B3
Torodi *Niger* 69G3
Torom, R *USSR* 51D1
Toronto *Can* 11D2
Toropets *USSR* 42E4
Tororo *Uganda* 70D3
Toros Dağlari, Mts *Turk* 62B2
Torquato Severo *Brazil* 26E2
Torrance *USA* 18C4
Torrão *Port* 37A2
Torreblanca *Spain* 37C1
Torre del Greco *Italy* 38C2
Torrelavega *Spain* 37B1
Torremolinos *Spain* 37B2
Torrens,L *Aust* 78A2
Torrent *Arg* 26D1
Torreón *Mexico* 19B2
Torre Pellice *Italy* 35B2
Torres Is *Vanuatu* 77F2
Torres Str *Aust* 76D2
Torres Vedras *Port* 37A2
Torrington, Connecticut *USA* 12D2
Torrington, Wyoming *USA* 9B3
Torrón *Mexico* 6C4
Torshavn *Faroes* 30D3
Tortona *Italy* 35C2
Tortosa *Spain* 37C1
Torūd *Iran* 61D1
Toruń *Pol* 41D2
Tory, I *Irish Rep* 31B2
Torzhok *USSR* 42E4
Tosa *Japan* 52B4
Tosa-shimizu *Japan* 51C5
Tosa-wan, B *Japan* 51C5
Toscana, Region *Italy* 35D3
To-shima, I *Japan* 52C4
Tosmo *USSR* 30L7
Tosno *USSR* 42E4
Tostado *Arg* 26C1
Tosu *Japan* 52B4
Tosya *Turk* 62B1
Totala *Indon* 55B3
Tot'ma *USSR* 42G3
Totnes *Eng* 33D6
Totness *Suriname* 25G2
Totolapan *Mexico* 20C2
Totona *Spain* 37B2
Totoral *Chile* 26A1
Totoralejos *Arg* 26C1
Tottenham *Aust* 78C2
Tottori *Japan* 51C4
Touba *Ivory Coast* 68B4
Touba *Sen* 68A3
Toubkal, Mt *Mor* 68B1
Toucy *France* 34B3
Tougan *U Volta* 69F3
Tôuggourt *Alg* 69D2
Tougué *Guinea* 68A3
Toul *France* 34C2
Toulon *France* 36D3
Toulouse *France* 36C3
Toumodi *Ivory Coast* 68B4
Toungoo *Burma* 53B2
Tourcoing *France* 34B1
Tourine *Maur* 68A2
Tournai *Belg* 34B1
Tourouvre *France* 34A2
Tours *France* 36C2
Touws, R *S Africa* 72C3
Towada *Japan* 51E3
Towada-ko, L *Japan* 51E3
Towanda *USA* 12B2
Towne P *USA* 18D2
Towner *USA* 9B2
Townsend *USA* 16D1
Townsville *Aust* 76D2
Towraghondi *Afghan* 61E1
Towson *USA* 12B3
Towy, R *Wales* 33D6
Toyah *USA* 14B3
Toya-ko, L *Japan* 52D2
Toyama *Japan* 51D4
Toyama-wan, B *Japan* 52C3
Toygunen *USSR* 8D2
Toyohashi *Japan* 52C4
Toyonaka *Japan* 52C4
Toyooka *Japan* 52B3
Toyota *Japan* 51D4
Tozeur *Tunisia* 69D2
Traben-Trarbach *W Germ* 34D2
Trabzon *Turk* 62C1
Tracy, California *USA* 18B2
Tracy, Minnesota *USA* 9C3
Traiguén *Chile* 26A3
Trail *Can* 3E4
Tralee *Irish Rep* 31B3
Tramore *Irish Rep* 33B5
Tranås *Sweden* 30G7
Trang *Thai* 53B4
Trangan, I *Indon* 49G7
Trangie *Aust* 78C2
Tranqueras *Urug* 26D2
Transalaskan Pipeline *USA* 8J2
Transantarctic Mts *Ant* 80E
Transcona *Can* 9C2
Transkei, Self-governing homeland *S Africa* 72D3
Transvaal, Province *S Africa* 72D1
Transylvanian Alps = Muntii Carpaţii Meridionali
Trapani *Italy* 38C3
Traralgon *Aust* 78C3
Trarza, Region *Maur* 68A3
Trat *Thai* 53C3
Travaillant L *Can* 8M2
Traveller's, L *Aust* 78B2
Travemünde *W Germ* 40C2
Traverse City *USA* 10B2
Traverse Peak, Mt *USA* 8G2
Travers,Mt *NZ* 79B2
Travis,L *USA* 14C3
Trebbia, R *Italy* 35C2
Třebíč *Czech* 40D3
Trebinje *Yugos* 39D2
Trebon *Czech* 40C3
Treinta y Tres *Urug* 26E2
Trelew *Arg* 23C6
Trelleborg *Sweden* 30G7
Tremadog B *Wales* 33C5
Tremblant,Mt *Can* 11E1
Trembleur L *Can* 3D3
Tremont *USA* 12B2

Tremonton *USA* 16D2
Trenčin *Czech* 41D3
Trenque Lauquén *Arg* 26C3
Trent, R *Eng* 33E5
Trentino, Region *Italy* 35D1
Trento *Italy* 35D1
Trenton *Can* 11D2
Trenton, Missouri *USA* 15D1
Trenton, New Jersey *USA* 12C2
Trepassey *Can* 5N5
Tres Arroyos *Arg* 26C3
Tres Corações *Brazil* 27C3
Três Lagoas *Brazil* 23F2
Tres Lomas *Arg* 26C3
Tres Passos *Brazil* 26E1
Tres Picos *Mexico* 20D2
Tres Pinos *USA* 18B2
Três Rios *Brazil* 27D3
Trets *France* 35A3
Treviglio *Italy* 35C2
Treviso *Italy* 35E2
Treysa *W Germ* 34E1
Trezzo *Italy* 35C2
Tribune *USA* 14B2
Trichūr *India* 60B2
Trida *Aust* 78C2
Trier *W Germ* 34D2
Trieste *Italy* 38C1
Triglav, Mt *Yugos* 35E1
Trikomo *Cyprus* 63B1
Trim *Irish Rep* 33B5
Trincomalee *Sri Lanka* 60C3
Trinidad *Bol* 24F6
Trinidad *Urug* 26D2
Trinidad *USA* 14B2
Trinidad, I *Arg* 26C3
Trinidad, I *Caribbean* 21E4
Trinidade, I *Atlantic O* 73G6
Trinidad & Tobago, Is Republic *Caribbean* 21E4
Trinity *USA* 15C3
Trinity, R *USA* 6D3
Trinity B *Can* 5N5
Trinity Is *USA* 8H4
Trion *USA* 13B2
Triora *Italy* 35B2
Tripoli *Leb* 63C1
Tripoli *Libya* 67A1
Trípolis *Greece* 39E3
Tripura, State *India* 59D3
Tristan da Cunha, Is *Atlantic O* 73H6
Trivandrum *India* 60B3
Trnava *Czech* 41D3
Trobriand Is *PNG* 76E1
Trois Pistoles *Can* 11F1
Trois-Riviéres *Can* 11E1
Troitsk *USSR* 46H4
Troitsko Pechorsk *USSR* 42K3
Troitskoye *USSR* 51D2
Troitzk *USSR* 42L5
Trollhättan *Sweden* 30G7
Trollheimen, Mt *Nor* 30F6
Tromelin, I *Indian O* 66K9
Trompsburg *S Africa* 72D3
Tromsø *Nor* 30H5
Trona *USA* 18D3
Trondheim *Nor* 30G6
Trondheimfjord, Inlet *Nor* 30G6
Troödos Range, Mts *Cyprus* 63B1
Troon *Scot* 32C4
Tropic of Cancer 73J3
Tropic of Capricorn 73K6
Troudenni *Mali* 68B2
Trout, R *Can* 3D1
Trout L, Northwest Territories *Can* 3D1
Trout L, Ontario *Can* 5J4
Trout Peak, Mt *USA* 16E2
Trout Run *USA* 12B2
Trouville-sur-Mer *France* 34A2
Troy, Alabama *USA* 13B2
Troy, Montana *USA* 16C1
Troy, New York *USA* 12D1
Troy, Ohio *USA* 10C2
Troy, Pennsylvania *USA* 12B2
Troyan *Bulg* 39E2
Troyes *France* 34C2
Troy Peak, Mt *USA* 17C3
Trucial Coast, Region *UAE* 65F2
Truckee, R *USA* 17B3
Trujillo *Honduras* 19D3
Trujillo *Peru* 24C5
Trujillo *Spain* 37A2
Trujillo *Ven* 24D2
Trumbull,Mt *USA* 17D3
Trundle *Aust* 78C2
Truro *Can* 5M5
Truro *Eng* 33C6
Trust Territories of the Pacific Is *Pacific O* 49G6
Trutch *Can* 3D2
Truth or Consequences *USA* 14A3
Tsagaan Nuur, L *Mongolia* 48C2
Tsagan-Tologoy *USSR* 48C1
Tsaratanana *Madag* 71E5
Tsau *Botswana* 71C6
Tsavo *Kenya* 70D4
Tsavo Nat Pk *Kenya* 70D4
Tschida,L *USA* 9B2
Tselinograd *USSR* 46J4
Tses *Namibia* 72B2
Tsetserleg *Mongolia* 48C2
Tsetserleg *Mongolia* 48D2
Tsévié *Togo* 69G4
Tshabong *Botswana* 72C2
Tshane *Botswana* 72C1
Tshela *Zaïre* 70B4
Tshibala *Zaïre* 71C4
Tshikapa *Zaïre* 70C4
Tshuapa, R *Zaïre* 70C4
Tsihombe *Madag* 71E6
Tsimlyanskoye Vodokhranilishche, Res *USSR* 43G6
Tsinan = Jinan
Tsingtao = Qingdao
Tsiroanomandidy *Madag* 71E5
Tsitsutl Peak, Mt *Can* 3C3
Tsna, R *USSR* 41F2
Tsogt Ovoo *Mongolia* 50B1
Tsomo *S Africa* 72D3
Tsu *Japan* 52C4
Tsubata *Japan* 52C3
Tsuchira *Japan* 51E4
Tsugaru-kaikyō, Str *Japan* 51E3
Tsumeb *Namibia* 71B5
Tsumis *Namibia* 71B6
Tsunugi *Japan* 52C3
Tsuruga *Japan* 51D4
Tsuruoka *Japan* 51D4
Tsushima *Japan* 52C3
Tsushima, I *Japan* 51B5
Tsushima-Kaikyō = Korea Str
Tsuyama *Japan* 51C4
Tua, R *Port* 37A1
Tuangku, I *Indon* 54A2
Tuapse *USSR* 43F7
Tuatapere *NZ* 79A3
Tuba City *USA* 17D3
Tubarão *Brazil* 23G3
Tubas *Israel* 63C2
Tubbataha Reefs, Is *Phil* 55E9
Tübingen *W Germ* 40B3
Tubruq *Libya* 67B1
Tuckerton *USA* 12C3
Tucson *USA* 17D4
Tucumán, State *Arg* 23C3
Tucumcari *USA* 14B2
Tucunuco *Arg* 26B2
Tucupita *Ven* 24F2
Tudela *Spain* 37B1
Tudenet L *Can* 8N2
Tudmur *Syria* 62C3
Tuerto *Arg* 26C2
Tugela, R *S Africa* 72E2
Tuggerah, L *Aust* 78D2
Tugidak, I *USA* 8H4
Tuguegarao *Phil* 55F7
Tugur *USSR* 47P4
Tugur, R *USSR* 51D1
Tuhai He, R *China* 50D2
Tui, R *U Volta* 69F3
Tuktoyaktuk *Can* 8M2
Tukums *USSR* 41E1
Tukuyu *Tanz* 71D4
Tukzar *Afghan* 58B1
Tula *Mexico* 20C1
Tula *USSR* 42F5
Tulancingo *Mexico* 20C1
Tulangbawang, R *Indon* 54B3
Tulare *USA* 18C2
Tulare Lake Bed *USA* 18C2
Tularosa *USA* 14A3
Tulcán *Colombia* 24C3
Tulcea *Rom* 43D7
Tul'chin *USSR* 41F3
Tule, R *USA* 18C2
Tuli *Zim* 71C6
Tuli, R *Zim* 72D1
Tulia *USA* 14B3
Tulik V *USA* 8E5
Tulkarm *Israel* 63C2
Tullahoma *USA* 13B1
Tullarnore *Irish Rep* 33B5
Tulle *France* 36C2
Tullins *France* 35A2
Tullos *USA* 15D3
Tullow *Irish Rep* 33B5
Tully *USA* 12B1
Tulsa *USA* 15C2
Tulūl ash Shāmiyah, Desert Region *Syria/S Arabia* 62C3
Tulun *USSR* 47M4
Tulungagung *Indon* 54D4
Tumaco *Colombia* 24C3
Tumany *USSR* 47R3
Tumbarumba *Aust* 78C3
Tumbes *Ecuador* 24B4
Tumby Bay *Aust* 78A2
Tumen *China* 51B3
Tumkūr *India* 60B2
Tump *Pak* 61E3
Tumpat *Malay* 53C4
Tumsar *India* 58D4
Tumu *Ghana* 69F3
Tumut *Aust* 78C3
Tumut, R *Aust* 78C3
Tunapuna *Trinidad* 21L1
Tunceli *Turk* 62C2
Tunduma *Zambia* 71D4
Tunduru *Tanz* 71D5
Tundzha, R *Bulg* 39F2
Tungabhadra, R *India* 60B1
Tung-Chiang *Taiwan* 48E4
Tungnafellsjökull, Mts *Iceland* 30B2
Tungsten *Can* 8N3
Tunguska, R *USSR* 47M3
Tuni *India* 60C1
Tunis *Tunisia* 69E1
Tunisia, Republic *N Africa* 66E4
Tunja *Colombia* 24D2
Tunkhannock *USA* 12C2
Tuntutuliak *USA* 8F3
Tununak *USA* 8F3
Tunuyán *Arg* 26B2
Tunuyán, R *Arg* 26B2
Tunxi *China* 50D4
Tuolumne Meadows *USA* 18C2
Tupã *Brazil* 27B3
Tupaciguara *Brazil* 27C2
Tupancireta *Brazil* 26E1
Tupelo *USA* 15E3
Tupik *USSR* 41G1
Tupiza *Bol* 24E8
Tupman *USA* 18C3
Tupper Lake *USA* 11E2
Tupungato *Arg* 26B2
Tupungato, Mt *Arg* 23C4
Tura *India* 59D2
Tura *USSR* 47M3
Tura, R *USSR* 42L4
Turabah *S Arabia* 64D2
Turán *Iran* 61D1
Turan *USSR* 47L4
Turayf *S Arabia* 62C3
Turbat *Pak* 61E3
Turbo *Colombia* 24C2
Turda *Rom* 39E1
Turfan Depression *China* 46K5
Turgay *USSR* 46H4
Turgen Uul, Mt *Mongolia* 47L5
Turgutlu *Turk* 62A2
Turhal *Turk* 62C1
Türi *USSR* 30K7
Turia, R *Spain* 37B2
Turin = Torino
Turinsk *USSR* 42L4
Turiy Rog *USSR* 51C2
Turkestan, Region *C Asia* 56E1
Turkestan *USSR* 57E1
Turkey, Republic *W Asia* 62C2
Turkmenskaya, SSR, Republic *USSR* 56D1
Turkmenskiy Zaliv, B *USSR* 61C1
Turks Is *Caribbean* 21C2
Turku *Fin* 30J6
Turkwel, R *Kenya* 70D3
Turlock *USA* 18B2
Turlock L *USA* 18B2
Turnagain, R *Can* 3C2
Turnagain,C *NZ* 79C2
Turneffe I *Belize* 19D3
Turners Falls *USA* 12D1
Turnhout *Belg* 34C1
Turnor L *Can* 3G2
Turnu Măgurele *Rom* 39E2
Turnu-Severin *Rom* 39E2
Turpan *China* 47K5
Turquino, Mt *Cuba* 21B2
Turtkul' *USSR* 56E1
Turtle Creek Res *USA* 15C2
Turtle L *Can* 3G3
Turukhansk *USSR* 47K3
Turuntayevo *USSR* 48D1
Turvo, R, Goias *Brazil* 27B2
Turvo, R, São Paulo *Brazil* 27C3
Tur'ya, R *USSR* 41E2
Tuscaloosa *USA* 15E3
Tuscany = Toscana
Tuscarora Mt *USA* 12B2
Tuscola, Illinois *USA* 10B3
Tuscola, Texas *USA* 14C3
Tuscumbia *USA* 13B2
Tusharík *Iran* 61D2
Tussey Mt *USA* 12A2
Tuticorin *India* 60B3
Tutrakan *Bulg* 39F2
Tuttlingen *W Germ* 40B3
Tutuila, I *American Samoa* 77H2
Tututepec *Mexico* 20C2
Tuul Gol, R *Mongolia* 48D2
Tuvalu, Is *Pacific O* 77G1
Tuvinskaya, Republic *USSR* 47L4
Tuwayilel Haj, Mt *Jordan* 63C4
Tuwwal *S Arabia* 64C2
Tuxpan, Jalisco *Mexico* 20B2
Tuxpan, Nayarit *Mexico* 20A1
Tuxpan, Veracruz *Mexico* 20C1
Tuxtepec *Mexico* 20C2
Tuxtla Gutiérrez *Mexico* 19C3
Túy *Spain* 37A1
Tuya, R *Can* 3B2
Tuy Hoa *Viet* 53D3
Tuz Gölü, Salt L *Turk* 62B2
Tuz Khurmātū *Iraq* 62D3
Tuzla *Yugos* 39D2
Tweed, R *Scot/Eng* 32D4
Tweed Heads *Aust* 78D1
Tweedsmuir Hills *Scot* 32D4
Twentynine Palms *USA* 17C4
Twillingate *Can* 5N5
Twin Bridges *USA* 16D1
Twin Buttes Res *USA* 14B3
Twin Falls *USA* 16D2
Twins,The, Mt *NZ* 79B2
Twitchell Res *USA* 18B3
Two Harbors *USA* 10A1
Two Medicine, R *USA* 16D1
Two Rivers *USA* 10B2
Tygda *USSR* 47O4
Tyler *USA* 15C3
Tymovskoye *USSR* 51E1
Tynda *USSR* 48F1
Tyne, R *Eng* 32E4
Tyne and Wear, Metropolitan County *Eng* 32E4
Tynemouth *Eng* 32E4
Tynset *Nor* 30G6
Tyonek *USA* 8H4
Tyr *Leb* 63C2
Tyre = Tyr
Tyrma *USSR* 51C1
Tyrma, R *USSR* 51C1
Tyrone, County *N Ire* 32B4
Tyrone, New Mexico *USA* 14A3
Tyrone, Pennsylvania *USA* 12A2
Tyrrell,L *Aust* 78B3
Tyrrhenian S *Italy* 38C2
Tyumen' *USSR* 46H4
Tyung, R *USSR* 47O3
Tywyn *Wales* 33C5
Tzaneen *S Africa* 72E1
Tzoumérka, Mt *Greece* 39E3

U

Uarsciek *Somalia* 70E3
Ubá *Brazil* 27D3
Ubaí *Brazil* 27D2
Ubaitaba *Brazil* 27E1
Ubangi, R *CAR* 70B3
Ubaye, R *France* 35B2
Ube *Japan* 52B4
Ubeda *Spain* 37B2
Ubekendt Ejland, I *Greenland* 5N2
Uberaba *Brazil* 27C2
Uberlândia *Brazil* 27C2
Ubon Ratchathani *Thai* 53D2
Ubort, R *USSR* 41F2
Ubundi *Zaïre* 70C4
Ucayali, R *Peru* 24D5
Uch *Pak* 58C3
Uchiura-wan, B *Japan* 51E3
Uchur, R *USSR* 47P4
Ucluelet *Can* 16A1
Uda, R *USSR* 48C1
Udaipur *India* 58C4
Udaipur Garhi *Nepal* 59C2
Udaquoila *Arg* 26D3
Uddevalla *Sweden* 30G7
Uddjaur, L *Sweden* 30H5
Udgir *India* 60B1
Udhampur *India* 58D2
Udine *Italy* 35E1
Udmurtskaya, ASSR, Republic *USSR* 42J4
Udon Thani *Thai* 53C2
Udskaya Guba, B *USSR* 47P4
Udskoye *USSR* 51C1
Udupi *India* 60A2
Udzha *USSR* 47N2
Ueda *Japan* 52C3
Uele, R *Zaïre* 70C3
Uelen *USSR* 47U3
Uelzen *W Germ* 40C2
Uere, R *Zaïre* 70C3
Ufa *USSR* 42K5
Ufa, R *USSR* 42K4
Ugab, R *Namibia* 71B6
Ugaila, R *Tanz* 70D4
Ugak B *USA* 8H4
Uganda, Republic *Africa* 70D3
Ugashik B *USA* 8G4
Ugashik L *USA* 8G4
Ugine *France* 35B2
'Uglat as Suqūr *S Arabia* 64D1
Uglegorsk *USSR* 51E2
Uglich *USSR* 42F4
Uglovoye *USSR* 51C3
Ugra, R *USSR* 42F5
Uig *Scot* 32B3
Uige *Angola* 71B4
Uijŏngbu *S Korea* 52A3
Uil *USSR* 43J6
Uinta Mts *USA* 16D2
Uiryŏng *S Korea* 52A3
Uisŏng *S Korea* 52A3
Uitenhage *S Africa* 72D3
Ujfehértó *Hung* 41E3
Uji *Japan* 52C4
Ujiji *Tanz* 70C4
Ujina *Chile* 23C2
Ujjain *India* 58D4
Ujung *Indon* 55B4
Ujung Pandang *Indon* 76A1
Ukerewe, I *Tanz* 70D4
Ukhla *USSR* 29L2
Ukhrul *India* 59D2
Ukhta *USSR* 42J3
Ukiah, California *USA* 17B3
Ukiah, Oregon *USA* 16C1
Ukiah *USA* 6A3
Ukmerge *USSR* 41E1
Ukrainskaya, Republic *USSR* 43D6
Uku-jima, I *Japan* 52A4
Ulaanbaatar *Mongolia* 48D2
Ulaangom *Mongolia* 48C2
Ulaan Uul *Mongolia* 50C1
Ulangar Hu, L *China* 57G1
Ulansuhai Nur, L *China* 5B1
Ulan Ude *USSR* 48D1
Ulan Ul Hu, L *China* 48C3
Ulapes *Arg* 26B2
Ul'beya, R *USSR* 47Q3
Ulchin *S Korea* 51B4
Ulcinj *Yugos* 39D2
Uldz *Mongolia* 48E2
Uliastay *Mongolia* 48C2
Ulla *USSR* 41F1
Ulladulla *Aust* 78D3
Ullapool *Scot* 32C3
Ullsfjorden, Inlet *Nor* 30H5
Ullswater, L *Eng* 33D4
Ullung-do, I *S Korea* 51C4
Ulm *W Germ* 40C3
Uloowaranie,L *Aust* 78A1
Ulsan *S Korea* 51B4
Ulster, Region *N Ire* 33B4
Ulu *Indon* 55C2
Ulungur He, R *China* 46K5
Ulungur Hu, L *China* 46K5
Ulva, I *Scot* 32B3
Ulverston *Eng* 33D4
Ulverstone *Aust* 78E3
Ulya, R *USSR* 47Q4
Ulyanovka *USSR* 41G3
Ul'yanovsk *USSR* 42H5
Ulysses *USA* 14B2
Uman *USSR* 43E6
Umanak *Greenland* 5N2
Umaria *India* 59B3
Umarkot *Pak* 58B3
Umaroona,L *Aust* 78A1
Umatilla *USA* 16C1
Umba *USSR* 42E2
Umba, R *Tanz* 70D4
Umbertide *Italy* 35E3
Umboi I *PNG* 76D1
Ume, R *Sweden* 30H6
Umea *Sweden* 30J6
Umfolozi, R *S Africa* 72E2
Umiat *USA* 8H2
Umkomaas, R *S Africa* 72E3
Umm al Qaiwain *UAE* 65G1
Umm as Samim, Salt Marsh *Oman* 65G2
Umm Bell *Sudan* 70C2
Umm Hagar *Eth* 70D2
Umm Inderaba *Sudan* 64B3
Umm Keddada *Sudan* 70C2
Umm Lajj *S Arabia* 64C1
Umm Ruwaba *Sudan* 70D2
Umm Sa'id *Qatar* 65F2
Umm Saiyala *Sudan* 64B4
Umnaiti, R *Zim* 71C5
Umnak I *USA* 8E5
Umpqua, R *USA* 16B2
Umred *India* 58D4
Umtali *Zim* 66H9
Umtata *S Africa* 72D3
Umuarama *Brazil* 27B3
Umzimkulu *S Africa* 72D3
Umzimkulu, R *S Africa* 72E3
Umzimvubu, R *S Africa* 72D3
Umzingwane, R *Zim* 72D1
Una *Brazil* 27E2
Una, R *Yugos* 38D1
Unadilla *USA* 12C1
Unadilla, R *USA* 12C1
Unai *Brazil* 27C2
Unalakleet *USA* 8F3
Unalaska, I *USA* 8E5
Unayzah *S Arabia* 64D1
Uncasville *USA* 12D2
Uncompahgre Plat *USA* 14A2
Underberg *S Africa* 72D2
Underwood *USA* 9B2
Unecha *USSR* 42E5
Uneisa *Jordan* 63C3
Unga, I *USA* 8G4

Ungava B *Can* 5M4
União de Vitória *Brazil* 23F3
Unimak Bight *USA* 8F5
Unimak I *USA* 8F5
Unimak Pass *USA* 8E5
Unión *Arg* 26B3
Union, Missouri *USA* 15D2
Union, S Carolina *USA* 13C2
Union City, Pennsylvania *USA* 11D2
Union City, Tennessee *USA* 13B1
Uniondale *S Africa* 72C3
Union of Soviet Socialist Reps *Asia* 44D3
Union Springs *USA* 13B2
Uniontown *USA* 11D3
United Arab Emirates *Arabian Pen* 65F2
United Kingdom, Kingdom *W Europe* 28E3
United States of America 2H4
United States Range, Mts *Can* 5K1
Unity *Can* 3G3
Unity *USA* 16C2
University Park *USA* 14A3
Unna *W Germ* 34D1
Unnão *India* 59B2
Unsan *N Korea* 52A2
Unst, I *Scot* 32E1
Unuana, I *Indon* 55B3
Unuk, R *USA* 3B2
Ünye *Turk* 62C1
Unzha, R *USSR* 42G4
Upata *Ven* 24F2
Upemba Nat Pk *Zaïre* 71C4
Upernavik *Greenland* 5N2
Upington *S Africa* 72C2
Upland *USA* 18D3
Upolu, I *Western Samoa* 77H2
Upper Arlington *USA* 10C2
Upper Arrow L *Can* 3E3
Upper Hutt *NZ* 79C2
Upper Klamath L *USA* 16B2
Upper L *USA* 16B2
Upper Laugh Erne, L *N Ire* 33B4
Upper Manzanilla *Trinidad* 21L1
Upper Red L *USA* 9D2
Upper Seal,L *Can* 5L4
Upperville *USA* 12B3
Upper Volta, Republic *Africa* 68B3
Uppsala *Sweden* 30H7
Upsala *Can* 9D2
Upton *USA* 9B3
Urad Qianqi *China* 50B1
Urairah *S Arabia* 65E1
Urakawa *Japan* 52D2
Ural, R *USSR* 43J5
Uralla *Aust* 78D2
Ural'sk *USSR* 43J5
Uralskiy Khrebet, Mts *USSR* 46G4
Urandi *Brazil* 27D1
Uranium City *Can* 4H4
Urapunga *Aust* 49G8
Uravan *USA* 14A2
Urawa *Japan* 52C3
Uray *USSR* 42L3
Urbana, Illinois *USA* 10B2
Urbana, Ohio *USA* 10C2
Urbino *Italy* 35E3
Ure, R *Eng* 33D4
Uren' *USSR* 42H4
Urfa *Turk* 62C2
Urgal *USSR* 51C1
Urgench *USSR* 56E1
Urgun *Afghan* 58B2
Urkan, R *USSR* 51B1
Urla *Turk* 39F3
Urma *USSR* 51C1
Urmi, R *USSR* 51C2
Uromi *Nig* 69H4
Uroševac *Yugos* 39E2
Uruaçu *Brazil* 25J6
Uruacu *Brazil* 27C1
Uruapan *Mexico* 20B2
Urucuia, R *Brazil* 27C2
Uruguai, R *Brazil* 26E1
Uruguaiana *Brazil* 26D1
Uruguay, Republic *S America* 23E4
Uruguay, R *Urug* 23E4
Urumīyeh *Iran* 61B1
Ürümqi *China* 57G1
Urup, I *USSR* 48J2
'Urūq al Awārik, Region *S Arabia* 65E3
Urusha *USSR* 51A1
Uruzgan *Afghan* 58B2
Uryū-ko, L *Japan* 52D2
Uryupinsk *USSR* 43G5
Urzhum *USSR* 42J4
Urziceni *Rom* 39F2
Usa *China* 57G1
Usa *Japan* 52B4
Usa, R *USSR* 42L2
Uşak *Turk* 62A2
Usakos *Namibia* 72B1
Ushashi *Tanz* 70D4
Ush Tobe *USSR* 46J5
Ushuaia *Arg* 23C8
Ushumun *USSR* 47O4
Usk, R *Wales* 33D6
Üsküdar *Turk* 62A1
Uslar *W Germ* 34E1
Usogorsk *USSR* 42H3
Usol'ye Sibirskoye *USSR* 47M4
Uspallata *Arg* 26B2
Ussuri, R *USSR* 51C2
Ussuriysk *USSR* 51C3
Ust'Belaya *USSR* 47T3
Ust'Bol'sheretsk *USSR* 47R4
Uster *Switz* 35C1
Ustica, I *Italy* 38C3
Ústi nad Labem *Czech* 40C2
Ust'Ishim *USSR* 46J4
Ustka *Pol* 40D2
Ust'Kamchatsk *USSR* 47S4
Ust'-Kamenogorsk *USSR* 46K5
Ust'Kara *USSR* 42L2
Ust Karabula *USSR* 47L4
Ust'Katav *USSR* 42K4
Ust'-Kut *USSR* 47M4
Ust Labinsk *USSR* 43F6
Ust'Maya *USSR* 47P3
Ust'Nem *USSR* 42K3
Ust'Nera *USSR* 47Q3
Ust'Nyukzha *USSR* 47N4
Ust'Ordynskiy *USSR* 47M4
Ust'Tsil'ma *USSR* 42J2
Ust'Umal'ta *USSR* 47P4
Ust'ya, R *USSR* 42G3
Ust' Yuribey *USSR* 42M2
Usuki *Japan* 52B4
Usumacinta, R *Guatemala/Mexico* 19C3
Usutu, R *Swaziland* 72E2
Usvyaty *USSR* 41G1
Utah, State *USA* 6B3
Utah L *USA* 17D2
Utara, I *Indon* 55C2
Utena *USSR* 41F1
Uthal *Pak* 58B3
Utica *USA* 12C1
Utiel *Spain* 37B2
Utikuma L *Can* 3E2
Utrecht *Neth* 40B2
Utrecht *S Africa* 72E2
Utrera *Spain* 37A2
Utsjoki *Fin* 30K5
Utsunomiya *Japan* 51D4
Uttaradit *Thai* 53C2
Uttar Pradesh, State *India* 59B2
Utucuia, R *Brazil* 27C2
Utukok, R *USA* 8F2
Uval *USSR* 46H4
Uvéa, I *Nouvelle Calédonie* 77F3
Uvinza *Tanz* 70D4
Uvira *Zaïre* 70C4
Uvkusigssat *Greenland* 5N2
Uvlade *USA* 14C4
Uvsikaupunki *Fin* 30J6
Uvs Nuur, L *China* 48C1
Uwajima *Japan* 51C5
Uwak *Indon* 54A2
Uxin Qi *China* 50B2
Uyandina *USSR* 47Q3
Uyar *USSR* 47L4
Uyuni *Bol* 24E8
Uyûn Mûsa, Well *Egypt* 63B4
Uzbekskaya, S.S.R., Republic *USSR* 56E1
Uzerche *France* 36C2
Uzh, R *USSR* 41F2
Uzhgorod *USSR* 41E3
Uzlovaya *USSR* 42F5
Uzunköprü *Turk* 62A1

V

Vaal, R *S Africa* 72C2
Vaal Dam, Res *S Africa* 72D2
Vaalwater *S Africa* 72D1
Vaasa *Fin* 30J6
Vác *Hung* 41D3
Vacaria *Brazil* 23F3
Vacaria, R, Mato Grosso Do Sul *Brazil* 27B3
Vacaria, R, Minas Gerais *Brazil* 27D2
Va Castell *Arg* 26B1
Vacaville *USA* 17B3
Vacca,C *S Africa* 72C3
Vadodara *India* 58C4
Vadsø *Nor* 30K4
Vaduz *Leichtenstein* 35C1
Vaga, R *USSR* 42G3
Va Gesell *Arg* 23E5
Vågø *Faroes* 30D3
Váh, R *Czech* 41D3
Vahel *Israel* 63C3
Vaigai, R *India* 60B2
Vaitupu, I *Tuvalu* 77G1
Val *USSR* 51E1
Vâlcea *Rom* 43C6
Valcheta *Arg* 23C6
Valdagno *Italy* 35D2
Valday *USSR* 42E4
Valdayskaya Vozvyshennost', Upland *USSR* 42E4
Val de la Pascua *Ven* 24E2
Valdepeñas *Spain* 37B2
Valdez *USA* 8J3
Valdivia *Chile* 26A3
Val d'oise, Department *France* 34B2
Val-d'Or *Can* 11D1
Valdosta *USA* 13C2
Vale *USA* 16C2
Valemount *Can* 3E3
Valença, Bahia *Brazil* 27E1
Valença, Rio de Janeiro *Brazil* 27D3
Valence *France* 36C3
Valencia, Region *Spain* 37B2
Valencia *Spain* 37B2
Valencia *Ven* 24E1
Valencia de Alcantara *Spain* 37A2
Valenciennes *France* 34B1
Valentine, Nebraska *USA* 9B3
Valentine, Texas *USA* 14B3
Valenza *Italy* 35C2
Valera *Ven* 24D2
Valga *USSR* 30K7
Valikiyo *USSR* 46E4
Valjevo *Yugos* 39D2
Valkeakoski *Fin* 30J6
Valla de Sannago *Mexico* 20B1
Valladolid *Mexico* 19D2
Valladolid *Spain* 37A1
Valle d'Aosta, Region *Italy* 35B2
Valle de la Pascua *Ven* 21D5
Valle d'Isére *France* 35B2
Valledupar *Colombia* 24D1
Vallée de l'Azaouak, V *Niger* 68C3
Vallée Tilemis, V *Mali* 68C3
Valle Grande *Bol* 24F7
Vallejo *USA* 18A1
Vallenar *Chile* 26A1
Valle Pegueno, V *Brazil* 27D1
Valletta *Malta* 69E1
Valley City *USA* 9C2
Valley Falls *USA* 16B2
Valleyfield *Can* 11E1
Valleyview *Can* 3E2
Valli di Comacchio, Lg *Italy* 35E2
Valls *Spain* 37C1
Val Marie *Can* 3G4
Valmiera *USSR* 41F1
Valparaiso *Brazil* 27B3
Valparaiso *Chile* 26A2
Valparaiso *Mexico* 20B1
Valparaiso *USA* 13B2
Vals, R *S Africa* 72D2
Valsād *India* 58C4
Valuyki *USSR* 43F5
Valverde del Camino *Spain* 37A2
Vammala *Fin* 30J6
Van *Turk* 62D2
Vanavara *USSR* 47M3
Van Buren, Arkansas *USA* 15D2
Van Buren, Maine *USA* 11F1
Vancouleurs *France* 34C2
Vancouver *Can* 3D4
Vancouver *USA* 16B1
Vancouver,C *USA* 8E3
Vancouver I *Can* 4F5
Vancouver,Mt *Can* 8L3
Vandalia, Illinois *USA* 10B3
Vandalia, Ohio *USA* 10C3
Vanderhoof *Can* 3D3
Van Diemen,C *Aust* 49G8
Van Diemen G *Aust* 76C2
Vanegas *Mexico* 20B1
Vänern, L *Sweden* 30G7
Vänersborg *Sweden* 30G7
Van Etten *USA* 12B1
Vangaindrano *Madag* 71E6
Van Gölü, Salt L *Turk* 62D2
Vang Vieng *Laos* 53C2
Van Horn *USA* 14B3
Vanier *Can* 11D1
Vanikoto, I *Solomon Is* 77F2
Vanino *USSR* 51E2
Vankarem *USSR* 47U3
Vännäs *Sweden* 30H6
Vannes *France* 36B2
Vanoise, Mts *France* 35B2
Vanrhynsdorp *S Africa* 72B3
Vansittart I *Can* 5K3
Vanua Lava, I *Vanuatu* 77F2
Vanua Levu, I *Fiji* 77G2
Vanuatu, Is *Pacific O* 75K5
Van Wert *USA* 10C2
Vanwyksvlei *S Africa* 72C3
Var, R *France* 35B2
Vara, R *Italy* 35C2
Varallo *Italy* 35C2
Varāmīn *Iran* 61C1
Vārānasi *India* 59B2
Varandey *USSR* 42K2
Varangerfjord, Inlet *Nor* 30K4
Varangerhalvøya, Pen *Nor* 30L4
Varazdin *Yugos* 38D1
Varazze *Italy* 35C2
Varberg *Sweden* 30G7
Varde *Den* 30F7
Vardø *Nor* 30L4
Varéna *USSR* 41E2
Varenna *Italy* 35C2
Varese *Italy* 35C2
Varginha *Brazil* 27C3
Varkaus *Fin* 30K6
Varna *Bulg* 39F2
Värnamo *Sweden* 30G7
Varnek *USSR* 42K2
Varnville *USA* 13C2
Várzea da Palma *Brazil* 27D2
Varzi *Italy* 35C2
Vasconcelos *Brazil* 26E2
Vascongadas, Region *Spain* 37B1
Vāshir *Afghan* 61E2
Vashka, R *USSR* 42H3
Vasil'Kov *USSR* 43E5
Vassar *USA* 10C2
Västerås *Sweden* 30H7
Västervik *Sweden* 30H7
Vasto *Italy* 38C2
Vatnajökull, Mts *Iceland* 30B2
Vatneyri *Iceland* 30A1
Vatra Dornei *Rom* 39F1
Vättern, L *Sweden* 30G7
Vaughn *USA* 14A3
Va Unión *Arg* 26B1
Va Unión, Coahuila *Mexico* 15F4
Va Union, Durango *Mexico* 20B1
Va Union, Sinaloa *Mexico* 20A1
Vaupés, R *Colombia* 24D3
Vauxhall *Can* 3F3
Vava'u Group, Is *Tonga* 77H2
Vavunija *Sri Lanka* 60C3
Växjö *Sweden* 30G7
Vedia *Arg* 26C2
Vega *USA* 14B2
Vega, I *Nor* 30G5
Vega Pt *USA* 8B6
Vegreville *Can* 3F3
Vejer de la Frontera *Spain* 37A2
Vejle *Den* 30F7
Velázquez *Urug* 26E2
Velddrif *S Africa* 72B3
Velebit, Mts *Yugos* 38D2
Velenje *Yugos* 38D1
Velhas, R *Brazil* 27D2
Velikaya, R, Rossiyskaya *USSR* 47T3
Velikaya, R, RSFSR *USSR* 41F1
Velikaya, R *USSR* 30K7
Velikaya Kema *USSR* 51D2
Velikiye Luki *USSR* 42E4
Velikiy Ustyug *USSR* 42H3
Veliko Tŭrnovo *Bulg* 39F2
Vélingara *Sen* 68A3
Velizh *USSR* 41G1
Vella Lavella, I *Solomon Is* 77E1
Vellore *India* 60B2
Velmerstat, Mt *W Germ* 34E1
Vel'sk *USSR* 42G3
Velva *USA* 9B2
Vembanad L *India* 60B3
Vemor'ye *USSR* 51E2
Venado Tuerto *Arg* 23D4
Vençeslau Braz *Brazil* 27C3
Vendeuvre-sur-Barse *France* 34C2
Vendôme *France* 36C2
Venetie *USA* 8J2
Veneto, Region *Italy* 35D2
Venezia *Italy* 35E2
Venezia, Region *Italy* 35E2
Venezuela, Republic *S America* 24E2
Vengurla *India* 60A1
Veniaminof V *USA* 8G4
Venice = Venezia
Venkatagiri *India* 60B2
Venlo *Neth* 40B2
Venta, R *USSR* 41E1
Ventersburg *S Africa* 72D2
Ventspils *USSR* 41E1
Ventuari, R *Ven* 24E3
Ventura *USA* 18C3
Vepsovskaya Vozvyshennost', Upland *USSR* 42E3
Vera *Arg* 26C1
Vera *Spain* 37B2
Veracruz *Mexico* 20C2
Veracruz, State *Mexico* 20C1
Verāval *India* 58C4
Verbania *Italy* 35C2
Vercelli *Italy* 35C2
Vercors, Plat *France* 35A2
Vérde, R *Brazil* 27A1
Verde, R, Goias *Brazil* 27B2
Verde, R, Jalisco *Mexico* 20B1
Verde, R, Mato Grosso do Sul *Brazil* 27B2
Verde, R, Oaxaca *Mexico* 20C2
Verde, R *USA* 17D4
Verde,C = Cap Vert
Verde Grande, R *Brazil* 27D2
Verde,Pen *Arg* 26C3
Verdon, R *France* 36D3
Verdun *France* 34C2
Verdun-sur-le-Doubs *France* 35A1
Vereeniging *S Africa* 72D2
Vereshchagino *USSR* 42J4
Vereshchagino *USSR* 46K3
Verga,C *Guinea* 68A3
Vergara *Arg* 26D3
Vergara *Urug* 26E2
Vergato *Italy* 35D2
Verin *Spain* 37A1
Verissimo Sarmento *Angola* 71C4
Verkh Angara, R *USSR* 47N4
Verkheimbatskoye *USSR* 46K3
Verkhneural'sk *USSR* 42K5
Verkhnevilyuysk *USSR* 47O3
Verkhnyaya Toyma *USSR* 42H3
Verkhoyansk *USSR* 47P3
Verkhoyanskiy Khrebet, Mts *USSR* 47O3
Verkola *USSR* 42H3
Vermelho, R *Brazil* 27B2
Vermenton *France* 34B3
Vermilion *Can* 3F3
Vermilion Bay *Can* 9D2
Vermillion *USA* 9C3
Vermillion L *USA* 9D2
Vermont, State *USA* 7F2
Vernal *USA* 16E2
Vernalis *USA* 18B2
Verneuil *France* 34A2
Verneuk Pan, Salt L *S Africa* 72C3
Vernon *Can* 3E3
Vernon *France* 34A2
Vernon *USA* 14C3
Vero Beach *USA* 13E4
Verola *Greece* 39E2
Verolanuova *Italy* 35D2
Verona *Italy* 35D2
Verónica *Arg* 26D3
Versailles *France* 34B2
Verulam *S Africa* 72E2
Verviers *Belg* 34C1
Vervins *France* 34B2
Veselinovo *USSR* 41G3
Vesle, R *France* 34C2
Vesoul *France* 36D2
Vesterålen, Is *Nor* 30G5
Vestfjorden, Inlet *Nor* 30G5
Vestmannaeyjar *Iceland* 30A2
Vesuvio, Mt *Italy* 38C2
Veszprém *Hung* 41D3
Vetlanda *Sweden* 30H7
Vetluga, R *USSR* 42G4
Veurne *Belg* 34B1
Vevey *Switz* 35B1
Vexin, Region *France* 34B2
Veynes *France* 35A2
Vézelise *France* 34C2
Viana do Castelo *Port* 37A1
Viareggio *Italy* 35D3
Viborg *Den* 30F7
Vibo Valentia *Italy* 38D3
Vibraye *France* 34A2
Vice-commodoro Marambio, Base *Ant* 80G2
Vicenza *Italy* 38C1
Vich *Spain* 37C1
Vichada, R *Colombia* 24E3
Vichuga *USSR* 42G4
Vichy *France* 36C2
Vicksburg *USA* 15D3
Vicosa *Brazil* 27D3
Victor Harbor *Aust* 76C4
Victoria *Arg* 26C2
Victoria *Cam* 70A3
Victoria *Can* 3D4
Victoria *Chile* 26A3
Victoria *Hong Kong* 50C5
Victoria *Malay* 54E1
Victoria, State *Aust* 78B3
Victoria *USA* 15F4
Victoria, R *Aust* 76C2
Victoria, State *Aust* 76D4
Victoria de las Tunas *Cuba* 21B2
Victoria Falls *Zambia/Zim* 71C5
Victoria I *Can* 4G2
Victoria,L *Aust* 78B2
Victoria,L *C Africa* 70D4
Victoria Land, Region *Ant* 80F7
Victoria,Mt *Burma* 59D3

Victoria,Mt *PNG* 49H7
Victoria Nile, R *Uganda* 70D3
Victoria Range, Mts *NZ* 79B2
Victoria River Downs *Aust* 76C2
Victoria Str *Can* 4H3
Victoriaville *Can* 11E1
Victoria West *S Africa* 72C3
Victorica *Arg* 26B3
Victorville *USA* 17C4
Vicuña *Chile* 26A2
Vicuña Mackenna *Arg* 26C2
Vidalia *USA* 13C2
Videle *Rom* 39F2
Vidin *Bulg* 39E2
Vidisha *India* 58D4
Vidzy *USSR* 41F1
Viedma *Arg* 23D6
Viéjo *Costa Rica* 21A4
Viella *Spain* 37C1
Vienna = Wien
Vienna, Illinois *USA* 10B3
Vienna, W Virginia *USA* 10C3
Vienne *France* 36C2
Vienne, R *France* 36C2
Vientiane *Laos* 53C2
Vierwaldstätter See, L *Switz* 35C1
Vierzon *France* 36C2
Vieste *Italy* 38D2
Vietnam, Republic *S E Asia* 49D5
Vietri *Viet* 53D1
Vieux Fort *St Lucia* 21P2
Vif *France* 35A2
Vigan *Phil* 55F7
Vigevan *Italy* 35C2
Vignemale, Mt *France* 36B3
Vigo *Spain* 37A1
Vijayawāda *India* 60C1
Vijosë, R *Alb* 39D2
Vik *Iceland* 30B2
Vikhren, Mt *Bulg* 39E2
Viking *Can* 3F3
Viking North, Oilfield *N Sea* 33G5
Viking South, Oilfield *N Sea* 33G5
Vikna, I *Nor* 30G6
Vila da Maganja *Mozam* 71D5
Vila de Manatuto *Indon* 55C4
Vila de Salazar *Indon* 55C4
Vila Machado *Mozam* 71D5
Vilanculos *Mozam* 71D6
Vila Real *Port* 37A1
Vila Vasco da Gama *Mozam* 71D5
Vila Velha *Brazil* 27D3
Vilelas *Arg* 26C1
Vileyka *USSR* 41F2
Vilhelmina *Sweden* 30H6
Vilhena *Brazil* 25G6
Viljandi *USSR* 42D4
Viljoenskroon *S Africa* 72D2
Vilkovo *USSR* 41F3
Villa Ahumada *Mexico* 14A3
Villa Angela *Arg* 26C1
Villa Atamisqui *Arg* 26C1
Villa Atuel *Arg* 26B2
Villaba *Spain* 37A1
Villa Carranza *Mexico* 20B2
Villach *Austria* 38C1
Villa Colon *Arg* 26B2
Villa Constitución *Arg* 26C2
Villa de Cos *Mexico* 20B1
Villa de Maria *Arg* 26C1
Villa de Reyes *Mexico* 20B1
Villa Dolores *Arg* 26B2
Villa Flores *Mexico* 20D2
Villafranca d Verona *Italy* 35D2
Villa General Mitre *Arg* 26C2
Villa General Roca *Arg* 26B2
Villa Gesell *Arg* 26D3
Villagran *Mexico* 20C1
Villaguay *Arg* 26D2
Villa Guillermina *Arg* 26D1
Villa Hayes *Par* 27A4
Villahermosa *Mexico* 19C3
Villa Hidalgo *Mexico* 20B1
Villa Huidobro *Arg* 26C2
Villa Iris *Arg* 26C3
Villa Maria *Arg* 26C2
Villa Montes *Bol* 24F8
Villa Neuva *Mexico* 20B1
Villa Nova de Gaia *Port* 37A1
Villanueva de la Serena *Spain* 37A2
Villanueva-y-Geltrú *Spain* 37C1
Villa Ojo de Agua *Arg* 26C1
Villa Regina *Arg* 26B3
Villarreal *Spain* 37B2
Villarica *Chile* 26A3
Villarrica *Par* 23E3
Villarrobledo *Spain* 37B2
Villa San José *Arg* 26D2
Villa San Martin *Arg* 26C1
Villa Valeria *Arg* 26C2
Villavicencio *Colombia* 24D3
Villefranche *France* 36C2
Ville-Marie *Can* 5L5
Villena *Spain* 37B2
Villeneuve-St-Georges *France* 34B2
Villeneuve-sur-Lot *France* 36C3
Villeneuve-sur-Yonne *France* 34B2
Ville Platte *USA* 15D3
Villers-Cotterêts *France* 34B2
Villeurbanne *France* 36C2
Villiers *S Africa* 72D2
Villingen-Schwenningen *W Germ* 34E2
Villupuram *India* 60B2
Vilnius *USSR* 41F2
Vilyuy *USSR* 47N3
Vilyuysk *USSR* 47O3
Vimoutiers *France* 34A2
Vina, R *Cam* 69J4
Viña del Mar *Chile* 26A2
Vinaroz *Spain* 37C1
Vincennes *USA* 10B3
Vinchina *Arg* 26B1
Vindel, R *Sweden* 30H5
Vindhya Range, Mts *India* 58D4
Vineland *USA* 12C3
Vineyard Haven *USA* 12E2
Vinh *Viet* 53D2
Vinh Cam Ranh, B *Viet* 53D3
Vinh Loi *Viet* 53D4
Vinh Long *Viet* 53D3
Vinita *USA* 15C2
Vinkovci *Yugos* 39D1
Vinnitsa *USSR* 41F3
Vinson Massif, Upland *Ant* 80F3
Vinton *USA* 9D3
Vioolsdrift *S Africa* 72B2
Vipiteno *Italy* 35D1
Viqueque *Indon* 55C4
Virac *Phil* 55F8
Virddhāchalam *India* 60B2
Virden *Can* 9B2
Virei *Angola* 71B5
Virgem da Lapa *Brazil* 27D2
Virgin, R *USA* 17D3
Virginia *S Africa* 72D2
Virginia, State *USA* 7F3
Virginia *USA* 9D2
Virginia Beach *USA* 11D3
Virginia City *USA* 17C3
Virgin Is *Caribbean* 21E3
Viroqua *USA* 10A2
Virovitica *Yugos* 38D1
Virton *Belg* 34C2
Virudunagar *India* 60B3
Vis, I *Yugos* 38D2
Visalia *USA* 18C2
Visayan S *Phil* 55F8
Visby *Sweden* 30H7
Viscount Melville Sd *Can* 4H2
Višegrad *Yugos* 39D2
Viseu *Port* 37A1
Vishākhapatnam *India* 60C1
Vishera, R *USSR* 42K3
Visp *Switz* 35B1
Vissingen *Neth* 36C1
Vista *USA* 17C4
Vistula = Wisla
Vitavia, R *Czech* 40C3
Vite *India* 60A1
Vitebsk *USSR* 41G1
Viterbo *Italy* 38C2
Vitigudino *Spain* 37A1
Viti Levu, I *Fiji* 7G2
Vitim, R *USSR* 47N4
Vitora *Spain* 37B1
Vitoria *Brazil* 25L8
Vitoria da Conquista *Brazil* 25K6
Vitré *France* 36B2
Vitry-le-Francois *France* 34C2
Vittangi *Sweden* 30J5
Vittel *France* 34C2
Vittoria *Italy* 38C3
Vittorio Veneto *Italy* 35E2
Vityaz Depth *Pacific O* 48J2
Vivero *Spain* 37A1
Viv, R *USSR* 47L3
Vivorata *Arg* 26D3
Vizhne-Angarsk *USSR* 47N4
Vizianagaram *India* 60C1
Vizille *France* 35A2
Vizinga *USSR* 42J3
Vladeasa, Mt *Rom* 39E1
Vladimir *USSR* 46F4
Vladimir Volynskiy *USSR* 41E2
Vladivostok *USSR* 51C3
Vlieland, I *Neth* 40A2
Vlissingen *Neth* 34B1
Vlorë *Alb* 39D2
Vöcklabruck *Austria* 40C3
Vodnjan *Yugos* 35E2
Voeune Sai *Camb* 53D3
Vogel Peak, Mt *Nig* 69J4
Vogelsberg, Region *W Germ* 34E1
Voghera *Italy* 35C2
Vohibinany *Madag* 71E5
Vohimarina *Madag* 71F5
Voi *Kenya* 70D4
Voinjama *Lib* 68B4
Voiron *France* 36D2
Volborg *USA* 9A2
Volcán Baru, Mt *Panama* 21A5
Volcán Citlaltepetl, Mt *Mexico* 20C2
Volcán Lullaillaco, Mt *Chile* 24E8
Volcáno Copahue, Mt *Chile* 26A3
Volcáno Dumuyo, Mt *Arg* 26A3
Volcano Is = Kazan Retto
Volcáno Lanin, Mt *Arg* 26A3
Volcán Ollagüe, Mt *Chile* 24E8
Volcáno Llaima, Mt *Chile* 26A3
Volcáno Malpo, Mt *Arg* 26B2
Volcáno Peteroa, Mt *Chile* 26A3
Volcáno Tromen, V *Arg* 26B3
Volcáno Villarrica, Mt *Chile* 26A3
Volcán Paracutin, Mt *Mexico* 20B2
Volcán Puraće, Mt *Colombia* 24C3
Volcán Tinquiririca, Mt *Chile/Arg* 26A2
Volchansk *USSR* 42K4
Volga, R *USSR* 43H6
Volgodonsk *USSR* 43G6
Volgograd *USSR* 43G6
Volgogradskoye Vodokhranilishche, Res *USSR* 43H5
Volkhov *USSR* 42E4
Volkhov, R *USSR* 42E4
Volkovysk *USSR* 41E2
Volksrust *S Africa* 72D2
Volochanka *USSR* 47L1
Vologda *USSR* 42G4
Volognes *France* 36B2
Vólos *Greece* 39E3
Vol'sk *USSR* 43H5
Volta *USA* 18B2
Volta, R *Ghana* 69G4
Volta Blanche, R *U Volta* 69F3
Volta,L *Ghana* 69F4
Volta Noire, R *U Volta* 69F3
Volta Redonda *Brazil* 27D3
Volta Rouge, R *U Volta* 69F3
Volterra *Italy* 35D3
Voltri *Italy* 35C2
Volynskiy *USSR* 43D5
Volzhskiy *USSR* 43G6
Von Frank Mt *USA* 8H3
Vonguda *USSR* 42F3
Vopnafjörður *Iceland* 5R3
Voralberg, Province *Austria* 35C1
Vorder Rhein, R *Switz* 35C1
Vordingborg *Den* 40C1
Voriái, I *Greece* 43C8
Vorkuta *USSR* 46H3
Vorma, R *Nor* 30G6
Voronezh *USSR* 43F5
Voron'ya, R *USSR* 30M5
Voroshilovgrad *USSR* 43F6
Võru *USSR* 30K7
Vosges, Department *France* 34D2
Vosges, Mts *France* 36D2
Voshnyy Saytocan, Mts *USSR* 48C1
Voss *Nor* 30F6
Vostchnyy *USSR* 51E2
Vostochnyy *USSR* 51E1
Vostochnyy Sayan, Mts *USSR* 47L4
Vostok, Base *Ant* 80F9
Votkinsk *USSR* 42J4
Vouziers *France* 34C2
Voves *France* 34A2
Voyageurs Nat Pk *USA* 9D2
Voy Vozh *USSR* 42K3
Voznesensk *USSR* 43E6
Vozvyshennost' Karabil', Desert Region *USSR* 61E1
Vranje *Yugos* 39E2
Vratsa *Bulg* 39E2
Vrbas *Yugos* 39D1
Vrbas, R *Yugos* 38D2
Vrbovsko *Yugos* 38C1
Vrede *S Africa* 72D2
Vredendal *S Africa* 72B3
Vreed en Hoop *Guyana* 25G2
Vrhnika *Yugos* 35F2
Vršac *Yugos* 39E1
Vrtoče *Yugos* 38D2
Vryburg *S Africa* 72C2
Vryheid *S Africa* 72E2
Vsevidof,Mt *USA* 8E5
Vukovar *Yugos* 39D1
Vuktyl' *USSR* 42K3
Vulcan *Can* 3F3
Vulcano, I *Italy* 38C3
Vung Tau *Viet* 53D3
Vuollerim *Sweden* 30J5
Vyartsilya *USSR* 42E3
Vyatka, R *USSR* 42J4
Vyazemskiy *USSR* 51C2
Vyaz'ma *USSR* 42E4
Vyazniki *USSR* 42G4
Vyborg *USSR* 42D3
Vym, R *USSR* 42J3
Vyrnwy, R *Wales* 33D5
Vyshiy Volochek *USSR* 42E4
Vyškov *Czech* 40D3
Vysokogornyy *USSR* 51D1
Vytegra *USSR* 42F3

W

Wa *Ghana* 69F3
Waal, R *Neth* 34C1
Wabach *USA* 7E3
Wabasca *Can* 3F2
Wabasca, R *Can* 4G4
Wabasca L *Can* 3F2
Wabash *USA* 10B2
Wabash, R *USA* 10B3
Wabatongushi L *Can* 10C1
Wabowden *Can* 4J4
Wabush *Can* 5M4
Waccasassa B *USA* 13C3
Wachusett Res *USA* 12E1
Waco *USA* 15C3
Wad *Pak* 58B3
Waddān *Libya* 67A2
Waddington,Mt *Can* 4F4
Wadena *Can* 3H3
Wadena *USA* 9C2
Wadi Abu 'Amūd, V *Jordan* 63D3
Wadi Abu Tarfa, V *Egypt* 63B4
Wadi ad Dawāsin, Watercourse *S Arabia* 64D2
Wadi Adhanah, Watercourse *Yemen* 65E3
Wadi al Amilhayt, Watercourse *Oman* 65F3
Wadi al Bātin, Watercourse *Iraq* 62E4
Wadi al Ghudāf, Watercourse *Iraq* 62D3
Wadi al Harir, V *Syria* 63D2
Wadi al Masilāh, Watercourse *S Yemen* 65F3
Wadi al Mirah, Watercourse *S Arabia/Iraq* 62D3
Wadi al Ubayyid, Watercourse *Iraq* 62D3
Wadi Aman, Watercourse *S Yemen* 65F3
Wadi 'Araba, V *Israel* 63C3
Wadi Ar'ar, Watercourse *S Arabia* 62D3
Wadi as Hsabā', Watercourse *S Arabia* 65E2
Wadi as Sirhān, V *Jordan/S Arabia* 62C3
Wadi ath Thamhar, R *Iraq* 43G8
Wadi az Zaydi, V *Syria* 63D2
Wadi Bishah, Watercourse *S Arabia* 64D2
Wadi edh Dhab'i, V *Jordan* 63D3
Wadi el'Aqaba, V *Egypt* 63C4
Wadi el 'Arish, V *Egypt* 63B3
Wadi el Brûk, V *Egypt* 63B3
Wadi el Gafa, V *Egypt* 63A3
Wadi el Ghadaf, V *Jordan* 63D3
Wadi el Hasa, V *Jordan* 63C3
Wadi el Higayib, V *Egypt* 63B3
Wadi el Janab, V *Jordan* 63D3
Wadi el Jeib, V *Israel/Jordan* 63C3
Wadi el Khush Shah, V *Jordan* 63D4
Wadi el Milk, Watercourse *Sudan* 70C2
Wadi el Natrun, Watercourse *Egypt* 62A3
Wadi el Saheira, V *Egypt* 63B4
Wadi el Sîq *Egypt* 63B4
Wadi es Sir *Jordan* 63C3
Wadi Fidan, V *Jordan* 63C3
Wadi Habawnāh, Watercourse *S Arabia* 64D3
Wadi Haifa *Sudan* 64B2
Wadi Hareidin, V *Egypt* 63C3
Wadi Hasana, V *Egypt* 63B3
Wadi Hawrān, R *Iraq* 62D3
Wadi Howa, Watercourse *Sudan* 70C2
Wadi Ibra, Watercourse *Sudan* 70C2
Wadi Jawf, Watercourse *Yemen* 65E3
Wadi Luhfi, Watercourse *Jordan* 63D2
Wadi Makhay, Watercourse *S Yemen* 65E3
Wadi Mawr, Watercourse *Yemen* 64D3
Wadi Mugshin, Watercourse *Oman* 65F3
Wadi Mujib, V *Jordan* 63C3
Wādi Mūsa *Jordan* 63C3
Wadi Ouena, Watercourse *Egypt* 64B1
Wadi Qa'ash Shubyk, V *Jordan* 63D4
Wadi Qināb, Watercourse *S Yemen* 65F3
Wadi Qîtaiya, V *Egypt* 63C3
Wadi Ranyah, Watercourse *S Arabia* 64D2
Wadi Ratiyah, V *Jordan* 63D4
Wadi Ruweila, V *Jordan* 63D4
Wadi Sha'it, Watercourse *Egypt* 64B2
Wadi Shihan, Watercourse *Oman* 65F3
Wadi Tathlith, Watercourse *S Arabia* 64D2
Wadi Turabah, Watercourse *S Arabia* 64D2
Wadi Ugeiqa, V *Jordan* 63C3
Wad Medani *Sudan* 70D2
Waegwan *S Korea* 52A3
Wafra *Kuwait* 62E4
Wageningen *Neth* 34C1
Wager B *Can* 5K3
Wager Bay *Can* 5J3
Wagga Wagga *Aust* 78C3
Wagin *Aust* 76A4
Wagner *USA* 9C3
Waha *Indon* 55C3
Waha *Libya* 67A2
Wahaiwa *Hawaiian Is* 18E5
Wahoo *USA* 15C1
Wahpeton *USA* 9C2
Wai *India* 60A1
Waialua *Hawaiian Is* 18E5
Waiau *NZ* 79B2
Waiau, R *NZ* 79A3
Waiau, R *NZ* 79B2
Waigama *Indon* 55C3
Waigeo, I *Indon* 49G6
Waihi *NZ* 79C1
Waikabubak *Indon* 55A4
Waikaremoana,L *NZ* 79C1
Waikato, R *NZ* 79C1
Waikelo *Indon* 55A4
Waikerie *Aust* 78A2
Waikouaiti *NZ* 79B3
Wailuku *Hawaiian Is* 18E5
Waimakariri, R *NZ* 79B2
Waimate *NZ* 79B2
Waimea *Hawaiian Is* 18E5
Waingapu *Indon* 76B1
Wainwright *Can* 3F3
Wainwright *USA* 8F1
Waipara *NZ* 79B2
Waipukurau *NZ* 79C2
Wairarapa,L *NZ* 79C2
Wairau, R *NZ* 79B2
Wairoa *NZ* 79C1
Wairoa, R *NZ* 79C1
Waitaki, R *NZ* 79B2
Waitara *NZ* 79B1
Waitomo *NZ* 79C1
Waiuku *NZ* 79B1
Wajima *Japan* 52C3
Wajir *Kenya* 70E3
Wakasa-wan, B *Japan* 52C3
Wakatipu,L *NZ* 79A3
Wakaw *Can* 3G3
Wakayama *Japan* 51D5
Wa Keeney *USA* 14C2
Wakefield *Eng* 33E5
Wakefield *Jamaica* 21H1
Wakefield, Michigan *USA* 10B1
Wakefield, Rhode Island *USA* 12E2
Wakema *Burma* 53B2
Wakkanai *Japan* 51E2
Wakool, R *Aust* 78B3
Wakre *Indon* 55D3
Walbrzych *Pol* 40D2
Walcha *Aust* 78D2
Walcz *Pol* 40D2
Waldbröl *W Germ* 34D1
Walden *USA* 12C2
Waldia *Eth* 70E2
Waldshut *W Germ* 34E3
Wales, Country *U K* 33D5
Wales *USA* 8E2
Wales I *Can* 5K3
Walewale *Ghana* 69F3
Walgett *Aust* 78C2
Walgreen Coast, Region *Ant* 80F4
Walikale *Zaïre* 70C4
Walker *USA* 9D2
Walker L *USA* 18C1
Walker Pass *USA* 18C3
Walkerton *Can* 10C2
Wall *USA* 9B3
Wallace *USA* 16C1
Wallaroo *Aust* 78A2
Walla Walla *Aust* 78C3
Walla Walla *USA* 16C1
Walldürn *W Germ* 34E2

Wallingford *USA* 12D2
Wallis and Futuna, Is *Pacific O* 75K5
Wallowa *USA* 16C1
Wallowa Mts, Mts *USA* 16C1
Wallumbilla *Aust* 78C1
Walnut Ridge *USA* 15D2
Walouru *NZ* 79C1
Walpole *USA* 12D1
Walsall *Eng* 33E5
Walsenburg *USA* 14B2
Walsenburgh *USA* 6C3
Walterboro *USA* 13C2
Walter F George Res *USA* 13B2
Walters *USA* 14C3
Waltham *USA* 12E1
Walton *USA* 12C1
Walvis Bay *Namibia* 66F9
Walvis Bay *S Africa* 72A1
Walvis Ridge *Atlantic O* 73J6
Wamba *Nig* 69H4
Wamba, R *Zaïre* 70B4
Wamego *USA* 15C2
Wamsasi *Indon* 55C3
Wamsutter *USA* 16E2
Wana *Pak* 58B2
Wanaaring *Aust* 78B1
Wanaka *NZ* 79A2
Wanaka,L *NZ* 79A2
Wanapitei L *Can* 10C1
Wanda Shan, Upland *China* 51C2
Wando *S Korea* 52A4
Wandoan *Aust* 78C1
Wanganella *Aust* 78B3
Wanganui *NZ* 77G4
Wanganui *NZ* 79B1
Wanganui, R *NZ* 79C1
Wangaratta *Aust* 78C3
Wangiwangi, I *Indon* 55B4
Wangkui *China* 51B2
Wango Fitini *Ivory Coast* 69F4
Wangqing *China* 51B3
Wankie *Zim* 66G9
Wanle Weyne *Somalia* 70E3
Wanning *China* 53E2
Wanpaca *USA* 10B2
Wanparti *India* 60B1
Wanxian *China* 50B3
Wanyuan *China* 50B3
Wapawekka L *Can* 3H3
Wapiti, R *Can* 3E3
Wappapello,L *USA* 15D2
Wappingers Falls *USA* 12D2
Wapsipinicon, R *USA* 9D3
Wara Nat Pk *Cam* 69J3
Warangal *India* 60B1
Waratah *Aust* 78E3
Waratah B *Aust* 78C3
Warburg *W Germ* 34E1
Warburton *Aust* 78C3
Warburton, R *Aust* 78A1
Ward, R *Aust* 78C1
Warden *S Africa* 72D2
Warder *Eth* 70E3
Wardha *India* 58D4
Ward,Mt *NZ* 79A3
Ware *Can* 3C2
Ware *USA* 12D1
Wareham *USA* 12E2
Warendorf *W Germ* 34D1
Warialda *Aust* 78D1
Warin Chamrap *Thai* 53D2
Warmbad *Namibia* 72B2
Warmbad *S Africa* 71C6
Warminster *USA* 12C2
Warm Springs *USA* 17C3
Warnemünde *E Germ* 40C2
Warner Mts *USA* 16B2
Warner Robins *USA* 13C2
Warracknabeal *Aust* 78B3
Warrandirinna,L *Aust* 78A1
Warrego, R *Aust* 76D3
Warren, Arkansas *USA* 15D3
Warren *Aust* 78C2
Warren, Massachusetts *USA* 12E2
Warren, Minnesota *USA* 9C2
Warren, Ohio *USA* 10C2
Warren, Pennsylvania *USA* 11D2
Warrenpoint *N Ire* 33B4
Warrensburg *USA* 15D2
Warrenton *S Africa* 72C2
Warrenton *USA* 11D3
Warri *Nig* 69H4
Warrina *Aust* 78A1
Warrington *Eng* 33D5
Warrington *USA* 13B2
Warrnambool *Aust* 78B3
Warroad *USA* 9C2
Warsaw = Warszawa
Warsaw *USA* 12A1
Warszawa *Pol* 41E2
Warta, R *Pol* 41D2
Warwick *Aust* 78D1
Warwick, County *Eng* 33E5
Warwick *Eng* 33E5
Warwick, New York *USA* 12C2
Warwick, Rhode Island *USA* 12E2
Wasatch Range, Mts *USA* 17D3
Wasbank *S Africa* 72E2
Wasco *USA* 18C3
Waseca *USA* 9D3
Wasekamio L *Can* 3G2
Washap *Pak* 61E3
Washburn *USA* 10A1
Washburn L *Can* 4H2
Washburn,Mt *USA* 16D2
Wāshīm *India* 58D4
Washington, District of Columbia *USA* 7F3
Washington, Georgia *USA* 13C2
Washington, Indiana *USA* 10B3
Washington, Iowa *USA* 9D3
Washington, Missouri *USA* 15D2
Washington, N Carolina *USA* 13D1
Washington, New Jersey *USA* 12C2
Washington, Pennsylvania *USA* 10C2
Washington, State *USA* 6A2
Washington, Utah *USA* 17D3
Washington Court House *USA* 10C3
Washington Land *Can* 5M1
Washington,Mt *USA* 11E2
Washita, R *USA* 14C2
Wash,The *Eng* 33F5
Washuk *Pak* 58A3
Wasilla *USA* 8J3
Waspán *Nic* 21A4
Wassuk Range, Mts *USA* 18C1
Wassy *France* 34C2
Watampone *Indon* 55B3
Watansoppeng *Indon* 55A3
Waterberge, Mts *S Africa* 72D3
Waterbury *USA* 12D2
Waterbury L *Can* 3H2
Waterford, County *Irish Rep* 33B5
Waterford *Irish Rep* 31B3
Waterford Harbour *Irish Rep* 33B5
Waterloo *Belg* 34C1
Waterloo *USA* 9D3
Watersmeet *USA* 10B1
Waterton-Glacier International Peace Park *USA* 16D1
Watertown, New York *USA* 11D2
Watertown, S Dakota *USA* 9C3
Watertown, Wisconsin *USA* 10B2
Waterval-Boven *S Africa* 72E2
Waterville, Maine *USA* 11F2
Waterville, New York *USA* 12C1
Watervliet *USA* 12D1
Waterways *Can* 4G4
Watford *Eng* 33E6
Watford City *USA* 9B2
Watkins Bjerge, Mt *Greenland* 5Q3
Watkins Glen *USA* 12B1
Watonga *USA* 14C2
Watrous *Can* 6C1
Watrous *USA* 14B2
Watsa *Zaïre* 70C3
Watson Lake *Can* 8N3
Watsonville *USA* 18B2
Watt,Mt *Can* 3E2
Watukancoa *Indon* 55B3
Wau *PNG* 49H7
Wau *Sudan* 70C3
Waua *Can* 5K5
Wauchope *Aust* 78D2
Wauchula *USA* 13E4
Waukegan *USA* 10B2
Waukesha *USA* 10B2
Waupun *USA* 10B2
Waurika *USA* 15C3
Wausau *USA* 10B2
Wauwatosa *USA* 10B2
Wave Hill *Aust* 76C2
Waverey, R *Eng* 33F5
Waverly, Iowa *USA* 9D3
Waverly, New York *USA* 12B1
Waverly, Ohio *USA* 10C3
Wavre *Belg* 34C1
Wawa *Can* 10C1
Wawa *Nig* 69G4
Wāw Al Kabīr *Libya* 67A2
Wāw an Nāmūs, Well *Libya* 67A2
Wawona *USA* 18C2
Waxahachie *USA* 15C3
Wayabula *Indon* 55C2
Waycross *USA* 13C2
Wayne *USA* 9C3
Waynesboro, Georgia *USA* 13C2
Waynesboro, Mississippi *USA* 15E3
Waynesboro, Pennsylvania *USA* 12B3
Waynesboro, Virginia *USA* 11D3
Waynesville, Missouri *USA* 15D2
Waynesville, N Carolina *USA* 13C1
Wazi Khwa *Afghan* 58B2
Weald,The, Upland *Eng* 33F6
Wear, R *Eng* 32D4
Weatherford, Oklahoma *USA* 14C2
Weatherford, Texas *USA* 15C3
Weaverville *USA* 16B2
Webbwood *Can* 10C1
Webster, New York *USA* 12B1
Webster, S Dakota *USA* 9C2
Webster *USA* 12E1
Webster City, Massachusetts *USA* 9D3
Webster Groves *USA* 10A3
Weda *Indon* 55C2
Weddell I *Falkland Is* 23D8
Weddell S *Ant* 80G2
Wedge Mt *Can* 3D3
Weed *USA* 16B2
Weedville *USA* 12A2
Weenen *S Africa* 72E2
Wee Waa *Aust* 78C2
Weichang *China* 50D1
Weiden *W Germ* 40C3
Weifang *China* 50D2
Weihai *China* 50E2
Wei He, R, Henan *China* 50C3
Wei He, R, Shaanxi *China* 50C2
Weilmoringle *Aust* 78C1
Weinheim *W Germ* 34E2
Weining *China* 50A4
Weipa *Aust* 76D2
Weirton *USA* 10C2
Weiser *USA* 16C2
Weishan Hu, L *China* 50D3
Weissenfels *E Germ* 40C2
Weiss L *USA* 13B2
Weitzel L *Can* 3G2
Welch *USA* 10C3
Weldon *USA* 18C3
Welkom *S Africa* 72D2
Welland *Can* 11D2
Welland, R *Eng* 33E5
Wellesley Is *Aust* 76C2
Wellesley L *Can* 8L3
Wellfleet *USA* 12E2
Wellingborough *Eng* 33E5
Wellington *Aust* 78C2
Wellington, Colorado *USA* 14B1
Wellington, Kansas *USA* 15C2
Wellington, Nevada *USA* 18C1
Wellington *NZ* 79B2
Wellington *S Africa* 72B3
Wellington, Texas *USA* 14B3
Wellington Chan *Can* 5J2
Wells *Can* 3D3
Wells *Eng* 33D6
Wells, Nevada *USA* 16D2
Wells, New York *USA* 12C1
Wellsboro *USA* 12B2
Wellsford *NZ* 79B1
Wells,L *Aust* 76B3
Wellsville *USA* 12B1
Wels *Austria* 40C3
Welshpool *Wales* 33D5
Wembley *Can* 3E2
Wenatchee *USA* 16B1
Wenatchee, R *USA* 16C1
Wenchi *Ghana* 69F4
Wenden *China* 50E2
Wendover *USA* 16D2
Wenling *China* 50E4
Wenshan *China* 50A5
Wenthaggi *Aust* 76D4
Wentworth *Aust* 78B2
Wentzel L *Can* 3F2
Wen Xian *China* 50A3
Wenzhou *China* 50E4
Wenzhu *China* 50C4
Wepener *S Africa* 72D2
Werda *Botswana* 72C2
Wernecke Mts *Can* 8L2
Werra, R *E Germ* 40C2
Werris Creek *Aust* 78D2
Wesel *W Germ* 34D1
Wesel *W Germ* 40B2
Weser, R *W Germ* 40B2
Weskan *USA* 14B2
Weslaco *USA* 15F4
Wessel Is *Aust* 76C2
Wesser, R *W Germ* 34E1
Wesserbergland, Region *W Germ* 34E1
Wessington Spring *USA* 9C3
West Allis *USA* 10B2
West Australian Basin *Indian O* 74F5
West Australian Ridge *Indian O* 74F6
West B *USA* 15E3
West Bengal, State *India* 59C3
West Branch Delaware, R *USA* 12C1
West Branch Susquehanna, R *USA* 12A2
West Bromwich *Eng* 33E5
Westbrook *USA* 11E2
Westby *USA* 10A2
West Chester *USA* 12C3
Westend *USA* 18D3
Westerburg *W Germ* 34D1
Westerland *W Germ* 40B2
Westerly *USA* 12E2
Western Australia, State *Aust* 76B3
Western Ghats, Mts *India* 60A1
Western Isles *Scot* 32B3
Western Sahara, Region *Mor* 68A2
Western Samoa, Is *Pacific O* 77H2
Westerschelde, Estuary *Neth* 34B1
Westerwald, Region *W Germ* 34D1
Westfalen, Region *W Germ* 36D1
West Falkland, I *Falkland Is* 23D8
Westfield, Massachusetts *USA* 12D1
Westfield, New York *USA* 11D2
Westfield, Pennsylvania *USA* 12B2
West Frankfort *USA* 10B3
Westgate *Aust* 78C1
West Germany, Federal Republic *Europe* 40B2
West Glamorgan, County *Wales* 33D6
West Grand L *USA* 11F1
West Indies, Is *Caribbean S* 73E4
West Liberty *USA* 10C3
Westlock *Can* 3F3
West Lorne *Can* 10C2
Westmeath, County *Irish Rep* 33B5
West Memphis *USA* 15D2
West Midlands, County *Eng* 33E5
Westminster *Eng* 33E6
Westminster, Maryland *USA* 12B3
Westminster, S Carolina *USA* 13C2
West Nicholson *Zim* 72D1
Weston *Malay* 54E1
Weston *USA* 10C3
Weston-super-Mare *Eng* 33D6
West Palm Beach *USA* 13E4
West Plains *USA* 15D2
West Point, California *USA* 18B1
West Point, Mississippi *USA* 15E3
West Point, Nebraska *USA* 9C3
West Point, New York *USA* 12D2
West Point, Mt *USA* 8K3
Westport *NZ* 79B2
Westray, I *Scot* 31C2
West Road, R *Can* 3D3
West Side, Oilfield *N Sea* 33F5
West Virginia, State *USA* 7E3
West Walker *USA* 18C1
West Wyalong *Aust* 78C2
West Yellowstone *USA* 16D2
West Yorkshire, County *Eng* 33E5
Wetar, I *Indon* 55C4
Wetaskiwin *Can* 3F3
Wete *Tanz* 70D4
Wetter, R *W Germ* 34E1
Wetzlar *W Germ* 34E1
Wevok = Cape Lisburne
Wewak *PNG* 76D1
Wewoka *USA* 15C2
Wexford, County *Irish Rep* 33B5
Wexford *Irish Rep* 33B5
Weyburn *Can* 4H5
Weymouth *Eng* 33D6
Weymouth *USA* 12E1
Whakatane *NZ* 79C1
Whakatane, R *NZ* 79C1
Whalsay, I *Scot* 32E1
Whangarei *NZ* 79B1
Wharfe, R *Eng* 33E5
Wharton *USA* 15C4
Whataroa *NZ* 79B2
Wheatland *USA* 9A3
Wheaton, Maryland *USA* 12B3
Wheaton, Minnesota *USA* 9C2
Wheeler, R *Can* 3G2
Wheeler Peak, Mt, Nevada *USA* 17D3
Wheeler Peak, Mt, New Mexico *USA* 14A2
Wheeler Ridge *USA* 18C3
Wheeling *USA* 10C2
Whistler *Can* 3D4
Whitby *Can* 11D2
Whitby *Eng* 33E4
White, R, Arkansas *USA* 15D2
White, R *Can* 8K3
White, R, Colorado *USA* 14A1
White, R, Indiana *USA* 10B3
White, R, S Dakota *USA* 9B3
White B *Can* 5N4
White Butte, Mt *USA* 9B2
White Cliffs *Aust* 78B2
White Coomb, Mt *Scot* 31C2
Whitecourt *Can* 3E3
Whitefish *USA* 16D1
Whitefish Pt *USA* 10B1
Whitegull L *Can* 5M4
Whitehall, New York *USA* 11E2
Whitehall, Pennsylvania *USA* 12C2
Whitehall, Wisconsin *USA* 10A2
Whitehaven *Eng* 33D4
Whitehorse *Can* 8L3
White I *NZ* 79C1
White L *USA* 15D4
Whitemark *Aust* 78E3
White Mountain Peak, Mt *USA* 17C3
White Mountain Peak, Mt *USA* 18C2
White Mts, Alaska *USA* 8J2
White Mts, California *USA* 18C2
White Mts, New Hampshire *USA* 11E2
White Nile = Bahr el Abiad
White Nile, R *Sudan* 70D2
White Plains *USA* 12D2
White River *Can* 5K5
White River *USA* 9B3
White River Junction *USA* 11E2
White S = Beloye More
Whitesail L *Can* 3C3
White Salmon *USA* 16B1
Whitesand, R *Can* 3H3
White Sulphur Springs *USA* 16D1
Whiteville *USA* 13D2
White Volta, R *Ghana* 69F4
Whitewater *USA* 10B2
Whitewood *Can* 3H3
Whithorn *Scot* 32C4
Whitmire *USA* 13C2
Whitney,Mt *USA* 18C2
Whittier, Alaska *USA* 8J3
Whittier, California *USA* 18C4
Wholdia L *Can* 4H3
Whyalla *Aust* 78A2
Wiarton *Can* 10C2
Wiawso *Ghana* 69F4
Wibaux *USA* 9B2
Wichita *USA* 15C2
Wichita, R *USA* 14C3
Wichita Falls *USA* 14C3
Wichita Mts *USA* 14C3
Wick *Scot* 32D2
Wickenburg *USA* 17D4
Wicklow, County *Irish Rep* 33B5
Wicklow *Irish Rep* 33B5
Wicklow, Mts *Irish Rep* 33B5
Widgeegoara, R *Aust* 78C1
Wied, R *W Germ* 34D1
Wielun *Pol* 41D2
Wien *Austria* 40D3
Wiener Neustadt *Austria* 40D3
Wieprz, R *Pol* 41E2
Wiesbaden *W Germ* 34E1
Wiese, R *W Germ* 34D3
Wigan *Eng* 33D5
Wiggins *USA* 15E3
Wigtown *Scot* 32C4
Wigtown B *Scot* 32C4
Wil *Switz* 35C1
Wilbur *USA* 16C1
Wilcannia *Aust* 78B2
Wildcat Peak, Mt *USA* 17C3
Wildhorn, Mt *Switz* 35B1
Wild Horse *Can* 3F3
Wildspitze, Mt *Austria* 35D1
Wildwood, Florida *USA* 13C3
Wildwood, New Jersey *USA* 12C3
Wiley *USA* 14B2
Wilge, R *S Africa* 72D2
Wilhelm,Mt *PNG* 76D1
Wilhelmshaven *W Germ* 40B2
Wilkes-Barre *USA* 12C2
Wilkes Land *Ant* 80F8

Wilkie *Can* 3G3
Willamette, R *USA* 16B2
Willandra, R *Aust* 78B2
Willapa B *USA* 16B1
Willcox *USA* 17E4
Willemstad *Curaçao* 21D4
William, R *Can* 3G2
William Creek *Aust* 78A1
William,Mt *Aust* 78B3
Williams, Arizona *USA* 17D3
Williams, California *USA* 17B3
Williamsburg *USA* 11D3
Williams Lake *Can* 3D3
Williamson *USA* 10C3
Williamsport *USA* 12B2
Williamston *USA* 13D1
Williamstown, Massachusetts *USA* 12D1
Williamstown, W Virginia *USA* 10C3
Willimantic *USA* 12D2
Willingboro *USA* 12C2
Willingdon,Mt *Can* 3E3
Willis Group, Is *Aust* 76E2
Williston, Florida *USA* 13C3
Williston, N Dakota *USA* 9B2
Williston *S Africa* 72C3
Williston L *Can* 3D2
Willmar *USA* 9C2
Willoughby,C *Aust* 78A3
Willow, R *Can* 3D3
Willow Bunch *Can* 9A2
Willowmore *S Africa* 72C3
Willow Ranch *USA* 16B2
Willows *USA* 17B3
Willow Springs *USA* 15D2
Wilmington *Aust* 78A2
Wilmington, Delaware *USA* 12C3
Wilmington, N Carolina *USA* 13D2
Wilmington, Vermont *USA* 12D1
Wilnona *USA* 5J5
Wilson, Kansas *USA* 14C2
Wilson, N Carolina *USA* 13D1
Wilson, New York *USA* 12A1
Wilson *USA* 7F3
Wilson, L *USA* 14C2
Wilson, R *Aust* 78B1
Wilson,C *Can* 5K3
Wilson,Mt, California *USA* 18C3
Wilson,Mt, Colorado *USA* 14A2
Wilson,Mt, Oregon *USA* 16B1
Wilsons Promontory, Pen *Aust* 78C3
Wiltshire, County *Eng* 33E6
Wiltz *Lux* 34C2
Wiluna *Aust* 76B3
Winamac *USA* 10B2
Winburg *S Africa* 72D2
Winchendon *USA* 12D1
Winchester *Can* 11D1
Winchester *Eng* 33E6
Winchester, Kentucky *USA* 10C3
Winchester, New Hampshire *USA* 12D1
Winchester, Virginia *USA* 11D3
Wind, R *USA* 16E2
Windber *USA* 12A2
Wind Cave Nat Pk *USA* 9B3
Windermere *Eng* 33D4
Windhoek *Namibia* 72B1
Windom *USA* 9C3
Windorah *Aust* 76D3
Wind River Range, Mts *USA* 16E2
Windsor *Aust* 78D2
Windsor, Connecticut *USA* 12D2
Windsor *Eng* 33E6
Windsor, N Carolina *USA* 13D1
Windsor, Nova Scotia *Can* 5M5
Windsor, Ontario *Can* 10C2
Windsor, Quebec *Can* 11E1
Windsor Forest *USA* 13C2
Windsor Locks *USA* 12D2
Windward Is *Caribbean* 21E4
Windward Pass *Caribbean* 21C3
Winefred L *Can* 3F2
Winfield, Alabama *USA* 13B2
Winfield, Kansas *USA* 15C2
Wingham *Aust* 78D2
Winifreda *Arg* 26C3
Winisk, R *Can* 5K4
Winisk L *Can* 5K4
Winkana *Burma* 53B2
Winlock *USA* 16B1
Winneba *Ghana* 69F4
Winnebago *USA* 9D3
Winnebago,L *USA* 10B2
Winnemucca *USA* 16C2
Winner *USA* 9C3
Winnfield *USA* 15D3
Winnibigoshish L *USA* 9D2
Winnipeg *Can* 4J4
Winnipeg, R *Can* 9C1
Winnipeg,L *Can* 4J4
Winnipegosis *Can* 4J4
Winnipesaukee,L *USA* 11E2
Winona, Minnesota *USA* 9D3
Winona, Mississippi *USA* 15E3
Winooski *USA* 11E2
Winslow *USA* 17D4
Winsted *USA* 12D2
Winston-Salem *USA* 13C1
Wintera *USA* 18B1
Winterberg *W Germ* 34E1
Winter Garden *USA* 13C3
Winter Park *USA* 13C3
Winterswijk *Neth* 34D1
Winterthur *Switz* 35C1
Winthrop *USA* 9D3
Winton *Aust* 76D3
Winton *NZ* 79A3
Wisbech *Eng* 33F5
Wisconsin, State *USA* 7E2
Wisconsin, R *USA* 10A2
Wisconsin Dells *USA* 10B2
Wisconsin Rapids *USA* 5K5
Wiseman *USA* 8H2
Wisla, R *Pol* 41D2
Wismar *E Germ* 40C2
Wissembourg *France* 34D2
Witagron *Suriname* 25G2
Witbank *S Africa* 72D2
Witchita Falls *USA* 6D3
Witham, R *Eng* 33E5
Withernsea *Eng* 33F5
Witney *Eng* 33E6
Witten *W Germ* 34D1
Wittenberg *E Germ* 40C2
Wittenoom *Aust* 76A3
Wittlich *W Germ* 34D1
Witvlei *Namibia* 72B1
Wladyslawowo *Pol* 41D2
Włocławek *Pol* 41D2
Włodawa *Pol* 41E2
Wodonga *Aust* 78C3
Wohlen *Switz* 35C1
Wokam *Indon* 49G7
Woking *Eng* 33E6
Wolcott *USA* 12B1
Woleai, I *Pacific O* 49H6
Wolf, R *USA* 10B1
Wolfach *W Germ* 34E2
Wolf Creek *USA* 16B2
Wolf Creek P *USA* 14A2
Wolf L *Can* 3B1
Wolf Point *USA* 9A2
Wolfsberg *Austria* 40C3
Wolfsburg *W Germ* 40C2
Wollaston L *Can* 3H2
Wollaston Lake *Can* 3H2
Wollaston Pen *Can* 4G3
Wollongong *Aust* 78D2
Wolmaransstad *S Africa* 72D2
Wolow *Pol* 40D2
Wolowaru *Indon* 55B4
Wolseley *Aust* 78B3
Wolverhampton *Eng* 33D5
Womelsdorf *USA* 12B2
Wondai *Aust* 78D1
Wŏnju *S Korea* 51B4
Wonominta, R *Aust* 78B2
Wonowon *Can* 3D2
Wŏnsan *N Korea* 51B4
Wonthaggi *Aust* 78C3
Woocalla *Aust* 78A2
Woodbine *USA* 12C3
Woodbridge *USA* 11D3
Wood Buffalo Nat Pk *Can* 3F2
Woodburn *Aust* 78D1
Woodburn *USA* 16B1
Woodbury *USA* 12C3
Woodchopper *USA* 8K2
Woodfords *USA* 18C1
Wood L *Can* 3H2
Woodlake *USA* 18C2
Woodland, California *USA* 17B3
Woodland, Washington *USA* 16B1
Woodlark, I *PNG* 77E1
Woodmera *Aust* 76C4
Woodroffe,Mt *Aust* 76C3
Woods,L of the *Can* 9D2
Woodstock, Illinois *USA* 10B2
Woodstock, New Brunswick *Can* 11F1
Woodstock, Ontario *Can* 10C2
Woodstock, Virginia *USA* 12A3
Woodstown *USA* 12C3
Woodville *NZ* 79C2
Woodville *USA* 15D3
Woodward *USA* 14C2
Woomera *Aust* 78A2
Woonsocket *USA* 11E2
Wooster *USA* 10C2
Worcester *Eng* 33D5
Worcester *S Africa* 72B3
Worcester *USA* 12E1
Wörgl *Austria* 35E1
Workington *Eng* 33D4
Worland *USA* 16E2
Worms *W Germ* 34E2
Worms Head, Pt *Wales* 33C6
Worthing *Eng* 33E6
Worthington *USA* 9C3
Wounded Knee *USA* 9B3
Wowoni, I *Indon* 55B3
Wrangell *USA* 8M4
Wrangell,C *USA* 8A5
Wrangell I *USA* 8M4
Wrangell Mts *USA* 8K3
Wrath,C *Scot* 31B2
Wray *USA* 14B1
Wrexham *Wales* 33D5
Wrightson *USA* 17D4
Wrightsville *USA* 13C2
Wrightwood *USA* 18D3
Wrigley *Can* 4F3
Wrocław *Pol* 40D2
Wrzésnia *Pol* 41D2
Wuchang *China* 51B3
Wuchuan *China* 53E1
Wuda *China* 50E2
Wuday'ah *S Arabia* 65E3
Wudil *Nig* 69H3
Wuding He, R *China* 50C2
Wudu *China* 50A3
Wugang *China* 50C4
Wuhai *China* 50B2
Wuhan *China* 50C3
Wuhu *China* 50D3
Wuhua *China* 50D5
Wüjang *China* 58D2
Wujia He, R *China* 50B1
Wu Jiang, R *China* 50B4
Wukari *Nig* 69H4
Wuliaru, I *Indon* 55D4
Wuling Shan, Mts *China* 50B4
Wum *Cam* 69J4
Wumeng Shan, Upland *China* 50A4
Wuntho *Burma* 59E3
Wuppertal *W Germ* 34D1
Wuqi *China* 50B2
Wuqing *China* 50D2
Würzburg *W Germ* 40B3
Wurzen *E Germ* 40C2
Wusuli Jiang, R *China* 51C2
Wutai Shan, Mt *China* 50C2
Wuvulu, I *Pacific O* 49H7
Wuwei *China* 50A2
Wuxi *China* 50E3
Wuxing *China* 50E3
Wuyang *China* 50C2
Wuyiling *China* 51B2
Wuyi Shan, Mts *China* 50D4
Wuyuan *China* 50B1
Wuyur He, R *China* 51B2
Wuzhi Shan, Mts *China* 53D2
Wuzhong *China* 50B2
Wuzhou *China* 50C5
Wyandotte *USA* 10C2
Wyandra *Aust* 78C1
Wye, R *Eng* 33D6
Wylye, R *Eng* 33D6
Wymondham *Eng* 33F5
Wyndham *Aust* 76B2
Wynne *USA* 15D2
Wynniatt B *Can* 4G2
Wynyard *Aust* 78E3
Wynyard *Can* 3H3
Wyoming, State *USA* 6C2
Wyoming *USA* 10B2
Wyoming Peak, Mt *USA* 16D2
Wyoming Range, Mts *USA* 16D2
Wyong *Aust* 78D2
Wytheville *USA* 10C3

X

Xaidulla *China* 58D1
Xai Moron He, R *China* 50D1
Xai Xai *Mozam* 72E2
Xaltinguis *Mexico* 20C2
Xangongo *Angola* 71B5
Xanten *W Germ* 34D1
Xánthi *Greece* 39E2
Xau,L, L *Botswana* 72C1
Xenia *USA* 10C3
Xiaguan *China* 48C4
Xiahe *China* 50A2
Xiamen *China* 50D5
Xi'an *China* 50B3
Xianfeng *China* 50B4
Xiangfan *China* 50C3
Xiang Jiang, R *China* 50C4
Xiangtan, Province *China* 50C4
Xianning *China* 50C4
Xianyang *China* 50B3
Xiao'ergou *China* 51A2
Xiao Shui, R *China* 50C4
Xiapu *China* 50D4
Xichang *China* 50A4
Xicoténcatl *Mexico* 20C1
Xicotepec *Mexico* 20C1
Xieng Khouang *Laos* 53C2
Xifeng *China* 50B4
Xigazê *China* 59C2
Xi He, R *China* 50A1
Xiji *China* 50B2
Xi Jiang, R *China* 50C5
Xiliao He, R *China* 50E1
Xilin *China* 50B5
Xilitla *Mexico* 20C1
Xinfeng *China* 50D4
Xinghe *China* 50C1
Xingkai Hu, L *China/USSR* 51C2
Xingning *China* 50D5
Xingren *China* 50B4
Xingtai *China* 50C2
Xingu, R *Brazil* 25H4
Xingxingxia *China* 48C2
Xingyi *China* 50A4
Xinhan *China* 51B3
Xining *China* 50A2
Xinjin, Liaoning *China* 50E2
Xinjin, Sichuan *China* 50A3
Xinkai He, R *China* 51A3
Xinwen *China* 50D2
Xin Xian *China* 50C2
Xinxiang *China* 50C2
Xinyang *China* 50C3
Xinyi, Guangdong *China* 50C5
Xinyi, Jiangsu *China* 50D3
Xi Ujimqin Qi *China* 50D1
Xiuyan *China* 51A3
Xochimilco *Mexico* 20C2
Xuancheng *China* 50D3
Xuanhan *China* 50B3
Xuanhua *China* 50D1
Xuanwei *China* 50A4
Xuchang *China* 50C3
Xuddur *Somalia* 70E3
Xunhua *China* 50A2
Xun Jiang, R *China* 50C5
Xunke *China* 51B2
Xunwu *China* 50D5
Xupu *China* 50C4
Xuwen *China* 53D2
Xuwen *China* 53E1
Xuyong *China* 50B4
Xuzhou *China* 50D3

Y

Ya'an *China* 50A4
Yaapeet *Aust* 78B3
Yabassi *Cam* 70B3
Yablochnyy *USSR* 51E2
Yablonovyy Khrebet, Mts *USSR* 48D1
Yabrūd *Syria* 63D2
Yachats *USA* 16B2
Yacuiba *Bol* 24F8
Yādgīr *India* 60B1
Yafran *Libya* 67A1
Yagishiri-tō, I *Japan* 52D2
Yagotin *USSR* 41G2
Yaguari, R *Urug* 26D2
Yaguaron, R *Urug* 26E2
Yahualica *Mexico* 20B1
Yahuma *Zaïre* 70C3
Yaita *Japan* 52C3
Yaizu *Japan* 52C4
Yajiang *China* 50A4
Yakima *USA* 16B1
Yakima, R *USA* 16B1
Yako *U Volta* 69F3
Yakoma *Zaïre* 70C3
Yakujima-kaikyō, Str *Japan* 51C5
Yakumo *Japan* 51E3
Yaku-shima, I *Japan* 51C5
Yakutat *USA* 8L4
Yakutat B *USA* 8L4
Yakutsk *USSR* 47O3
Yakutskaya ASSR, Republic *USSR* 47N3
Yala *Thai* 53C4
Yalalag *Mexico* 20C2
Yale *Can* 16B1
Yalinga *CAR* 70C3
Yallourn *Aust* 78C3
Yalong, R *China* 48C3
Yalong Jiang, R *China* 50A4
Yalova *Turk* 39F2
Yalta *USSR* 43E7
Yalu He, R *China* 51A2
Yalu Jiang, R *China* 51B3
Yamada *Japan* 52D3
Yamagata *Japan* 51D4
Yamaguchi *Japan* 51C5
Yamal, Pen 42M2
Yamarovka *USSR* 48E1
Yamba, New S Wales *Aust* 78D1
Yamba, S Australia *Aust* 78B2
Yambio *Sudan* 70C3
Yambol *Bulg* 39F2
Yamdena, I *Indon* 55D4
Yamethin *Burma* 59E3
Yam Kinneret = Tiberias,L
Yamma Yamma,L *Aust* 78B1
Yampa, R *USA* 14A1
Yamsk *USSR* 47R4
Yamuna, R *India* 58D3
Yamzho Yumco, L *China* 59D2
Yana, R *USSR* 47P3
Yanac *Aust* 78B3
Yanagawa *Japan* 52B4
Yanam *India* 60C1
Yan'an *China* 50B2
Yanbu'al Bahr *S Arabia* 64C2
Yancannia *Aust* 78B2
Yancheng *China* 50E3
Yanchi *China* 50B2
Yandama, R *Aust* 78B1
Yangambi *Zaïre* 70C3
Yanggi *China* 48B2
Yanggu *S Korea* 52A3
Yang He, R *China* 50C1
Yangjiang *China* 50C5
Yangquan *China* 50C2
Yangsan *S Korea* 52A3
Yangshan *China* 50C5
Yangtze Gorges *China* 50C3
Yangtze,Mouths of the *China* 50E3
Yangyang *S Korea* 52A3
Yangzhou *China* 50D3
Yanhe *China* 50B4
Yanji *China* 51B3
Yanko *Aust* 78C3
Yankskiy Zaliv, B *USSR* 47P2
Yankton *USA* 9C3
Yanqqi *China* 57G1
Yan Shan, Hills 50D1
Yantabulla *Aust* 78B1
Yantai *China* 50E2
Yanzhou *China* 50D2
Yaoundé *Cam* 70B3
Yapen, I *Indon* 49G7
Yapeyú *Arg* 26D1
Yap Is *Pacific O* 49G6
Yaqui, R *Mexico* 19B2
Yaransk *USSR* 42H4
Yarenga *USSR* 42H3
Yarensk *USSR* 42H3
Yargon, R *Israel* 63C2
Yari, R *Colombia* 24D3
Yariga-dake, Mt *Japan* 51D4
Yarkant He, R *China* 57F2
Yarlung Zangbo Jiang, R *China* 59D2
Yarmin *Yemen* 64D4
Yarmouth *Can* 5M5
Yarmūk, R *Syria/Jordan* 63C2
Yaroslavl' *USSR* 42F4
Yarram *Aust* 78C3
Yarraman *Aust* 78D1
Yarrawonga *Aust* 78C3
Yar Sale *USSR* 42N2
Yartsevo *USSR* 42E4
Yartsevo *USSR* 47L3
Yarumal *Colombia* 24C2
Yasawa Group, Is *Fiji* 7G2
Yashi *Nig* 69H3
Yashikera *Nig* 69G4
Yashkul' *USSR* 43G6
Yasin *Pak* 58C1
Yasinya *USSR* 41E3
Yasnyy *USSR* 51B1
Yass *Aust* 78C2
Yass, R *Aust* 78C2
Yasugi *Japan* 52B3
Yates Center *USA* 15C2
Yathkyed L *Can* 4J3
Yatolema *Zaïre* 70C3
Yatsushiro *Japan* 51C5
Yatta *Israel* 63C3
Yavari *Peru* 24D4
Yavatmāl *India* 58D4
Yawatahama *Japan* 51C5
Ya Xian *China* 53D2
Yazd *Iran* 61C2
Yazd-e Khvāst *Iran* 61C2
Yazoo, R *USA* 15D3
Yazoo City *USA* 15D3
Ye *Burma* 53B2
Yedintsy *USSR* 41F3
Yeelanna *Aust* 78A2
Yefremov *USSR* 42F5
Yegorlyk, R *USSR* 43G6
Yei *Sudan* 70D3
Yeji *Ghana* 69F4
Yekaterinoslavka *USSR* 51B1
Yelets *USSR* 43F5
Yell, I *Scot* 31C1
Yellandu *India* 60C1
Yellow = Huang He
Yellowhead P *Can* 6B1
Yellowknife *Can* 4G3
Yellowmead P *Can* 4G4
Yellow Mt *Aust* 78C2
Yellow S *China/Korea* 45H4
Yellow Sea *China/Korea* 48F3
Yellowstone, R *USA* 6C2
Yellowstone L *USA* 16D2
Yellowstone Nat Pk *USA* 16D2
Yel'nya *USSR* 41G2
Yel'sk *USSR* 41F2
Yelverton B *Can* 5K1
Yelwa *Nig* 69G3
Yemen, Republic *Arabian Pen* 56D3
Yen Bai *Viet* 53C1
Yendi *Ghana* 69F4
Yengan *Burma* 53B1
Yenisey, R *USSR* 46K3

Yeniseysk *USSR* 47L4
Yeniseyskiy Kryazh,
Ridge *USSR* 47L3
Yeniseyskiy Zai, B *USSR* 46J2
Yentna, R *USA* 8H3
Yeo, R *Eng* 33D6
Yeoval *Aust* 78C2
Yeovil *Eng* 33D6
Yerbogachen *USSR* 47M3
Yerevan *USSR* 43G7
Yerington *USA* 17C3
Yermitsa *USSR* 42J2
Yermo *USA* 17C4
Yerofey *USSR* 47O4
Yerofey-Pavlovich *USSR* 51A1
Yeroham *Israel* 63C3
Yeropol *USSR* 47S3
Yershov *USSR* 43H5
Yerushalayim =
Jerusalem
Yeşil, R *Turk* 62C1
Yessey *USSR* 47M3
Yesud Hama'ala *Israel* 63C2
Yetman *Aust* 78D1
Yetti *Maur* 68B2
Yeu *Burma* 59E3
Yevlakh *USSR* 43H7
Yevpatoriya *USSR* 43E6
Ye Xian *China* 50E2
Yeysk *USSR* 43F6
Yi, R *Urug* 26D2
Yialousa *Cyprus* 63C1
Yi'an *China* 51B2
Yiannitsá *Greece* 39E2
Yibin *China* 50A4
Yichang *China* 50C3
Yichun *China* 51B2
Yijun *China* 50B2
Yıldızeli *Turk* 62C2
Yilehuli Shan, Upland
China 51A1
Yiliang *China* 50A5
Yinchuan *China* 50B2
Ying He, R *China* 50D3
Yingkou *China* 50E1
Yingshan, Hubei *China* 50D3
Yingshan, Sichuan *China* 50B3
Yingtan *China* 50D4
Yining *China* 57G1
Yin Shan, Upland *China* 50B1
Yirga Alem *Eth* 70D3
Yirol *Sudan* 70D3
Yirshi *China* 47N5
Yishan *China* 50B5
Yishui *China* 50D2
Yíthion *Greece* 39E3
Yitulihe *China* 51A1
Yivieska *Fin* 30J6
Yiyang *China* 50C4
Yli-Kitka, L *Fin* 42D2
Ylilornio *Sweden* 30J5
Ylivieska *Fin* 42C3
Yoakum *USA* 15C4
Yogope *Mexico* 20C2
Yogyakarta *Indon* 54D4
Yoho Nat Pk *Can* 3E3
Yokadouma *Cam* 70B3
Yokkaichi *Japan* 52C4
Yoko *Cam* 69J4
Yokobori *Japan* 52D3
Yokohama *Japan* 52C3
Yokosuka *Japan* 52C3
Yokote *Japan* 52D3
Yola *Nig* 69J4
Yonago *Japan* 51C4
Yonan *N Korea* 52A3
Yonezawa *Japan* 51E4
Yongam *S Korea* 52A4
Yong'an *China* 50D4
Yongchang *China* 50A2
Yŏngch'on *S Korea* 51B4
Yongchuan *China* 50B4
Yŏngchŭng-man, I *N
Korea* 52A3
Yongdeng *China* 50A2
Yongding *China* 50D5
Yongding He, R *China* 50D2
Yŏngdŏk *S Korea* 51B4
Yŏnggwang *S Korea* 52A3
Yŏnghŭng *N Korea* 51B4
Yŏngil-man, B *S Korea* 52A3
Yongji *China* 51B3
Yongju *S Korea* 51B4
Yongning *China* 50B2
Yong Peng *Malay* 54G7
Yŏngsanp'o *S Korea* 52A3
Yŏngyang *S Korea* 52A3
Yonkers *USA* 12D2
Yonne, Department
France 34B3
Yonne, R *France* 36C2
York *Eng* 33E5
York, Nebraska *USA* 15C1
York, Pennsylvania *USA* 12B3
York,C *Aust* 76D2
Yorke Pen *Aust* 78A2
Yorketown *Aust* 78A3
York Factory *Can* 5J4
York Sd *Aust* 49F8
Yorkshire Dales Nat Pk
Eng 33D4

Yorkshire Moors,
Moorland *Eng* 31C3
Yorkshire Wolds, Upland
Eng 33E4
Yorkton *Can* 3H3
Yorktown *USA* 11D3
York Village *USA* 12E1
Yorton *Can* 6C1
Yorubaland Plat *Nig* 69G4
Yosemite L *USA* 18B2
Yosemite Nat Pk *USA* 18C1
Yoshii, R *Japan* 52B4
Yoshino, R *Japan* 52B4
Yoshkar Ola *USSR* 42H4
Yŏsu *S Korea* 51B5
Yotvata *Israel* 63C4
Youghal *Irish Rep* 31B3
You Jiang, R *China* 50B5
Young *Aust* 78C2
Young *Urug* 26D2
Young Range, Mts *NZ* 79A2
Youngstown *Can* 3F3
Youngstown, New York
USA 12A1
Youngstown, Ohio *USA* 10C2
Yountville *USA* 18A1
Youssoufia *Mor* 69A2
Youyang *China* 50B4
Youyi *China* 51A2
Yozgat *Turk* 62B2
Ypané, R *Par* 27A3
Yreka *USA* 16B2
Ystad *Sweden* 30G7
Ystwyth, R *Wales* 33D5
Ythan, R *Scot* 32D3
Yuan Jiang, R, Hunan
China 50C4
Yuan Jiang, R, Yunnan
China 50A5
Yuanmu *China* 50A4
Yuanping *China* 50C2
Yuba City *USA* 17B3
Yūbari *Japan* 51E3
Yubi,C *Mor* 68A2
Yucatan, Pen *Mexico* 19D3
Yucatan Chan *Mexico/
Cuba* 19D2
Yucca *USA* 17D4
Yuci *China* 50C2
Yudi Shan, Mt *China* 51A1
Yudoma, R *USSR* 47P4
Yudu *China* 50D4
Yuexi *China* 50A4
Yueyang *China* 50C4
Yugorskiy Poluostrov,
Pen *USSR* 42L2
Yugoslavia, Federal
Republic *Europe* 39D2
Yu Jiang, R *China* 50B5
Yukon, R *USA/Can* 8G3
Yukon Territory *Can* 4E3
Yulin, Guangdong *China* 53E1
Yulin, Guangxi *China* 50C5
Yulin, Shaanxi *China* 50B2
Yuma *USA* 17D4
Yumen *China* 48C3
Yunan *China* 50D2
Yunaska, I *USA* 8D5
Yungay *Chile* 26A3
Yunkai Dashan, Hills
China 50C5
Yunta *Aust* 78A2
Yunxi *China* 50C3
Yun Xian *China* 50C3
Yunyang *China* 50B3
Yurimaguas *Peru* 24C5
Yu Shan, Mt *Taiwan* 50E5
Yushkozero *USSR* 42E3
Yushu, Jilin *China* 51B3
Yushu, Tibet *China* 57H2
Yuty *Par* 27A4
Yuxi *China* 50A5
Yuzawa *Japan* 52D3
Yuzh Bug, R *USSR* 41F3
Yuzhno-Kuril'sk *USSR* 51F3
Yuzhno-Sakhalinsk *USSR* 51E2
Yuzh Ural, Mts *USSR* 42K5
Yvelines, Department
France 34A2
Yverdon *Switz* 35B1
Yvetot *France* 34A2

Z

Zaandam *Neth* 40A2
Zabakalskiy *USSR* 47M4
Zab al Asfal, R *Iraq* 43G8
Žáb al Babir, R *Iraq* 62D2
Žáb as Şaghir, R *Iraq* 62D2
Zabaykal'sk *USSR* 48E2
Zabid *Yemen* 64D4
Žábol *Iran* 61E2
Zabreh *Czech* 40D3
Zabrze *Pol* 41D2
Zacapu *Mexico* 20B2
Zacatecas *Mexico* 20B1
Zacatecas, State *Mexico* 20B1
Zacatepec, Morelos
Mexico 20C2
Zacatepec, Oaxaca
Mexico 20C2

Zacatlan *Mexico* 20C2
Zacoalco *Mexico* 20B1
Zacualtipan *Mexico* 20C1
Zadar *Yugos* 38D2
Zadetkyi, I *Burma* 53B3
Zafra *Spain* 37A2
Zagazig *Egypt* 67C1
Zagora *Mor* 68B1
Zagorsk *USSR* 42F4
Zagreb *Yugos* 38D1
Zagros Mts = Kūhhā-ye
Zagros
Zāhedān *Iran* 61E3
Zahle *Leb* 63C2
Zahrez Chergui,
Marshland *Alg* 37C2
Zainsk *USSR* 42J4
Zaïre, Republic *Africa* 70C4
Zaïre, R *Zaïre/Congo* 70B4
Zaječar *Yugos* 39E2
Zakamensk *USSR* 48D1
Zakataly *USSR* 43H7
Zakhmet *USSR* 61E1
Zakho *Iraq* 62D2
Zákinthos, I *Greece* 39E3
Zakopane *Pol* 41D3
Zalaegerszeg *Hung* 40D3
Zalău *Rom* 39E1
Zalew Szczeciński, Lg
Pol 40C2
Zalim *S Arabia* 64D2
Zalingei *Sudan* 70C2
Zaliv Akademii, B *USSR* 47P4
Zaliv Aniva, B *USSR* 51E2
Zaliv Faddeya, B *USSR* 47M2
Zaliv Kara-Bogaz-Gol, B
USSR 43J7
Zaliv Kresta, B *USSR* 8C2
Zaliv Petra Velikogo, B
USSR 51C3
Zaliv Shelekhova, B
USSR 47R3
Zaliv Turpeniya, B *USSR* 51E2
Zamakh *S Yemen* 65E3
Zambesi, R *Mozam* 66H9
Zambezi *Zambia* 71C5
Zambezi, R *Zambia* 71C5
Zambia, Republic *Africa* 71C5
Zamboanga *Phil* 55F9
Zamboanga Pen *Phil* 55F9
Zambrów *Pol* 41E2
Zamfara, R *Nig* 69H3
Zamora *Ecuador* 24C4
Zamora *Mexico* 20B2
Zamora *Spain* 37A1
Zamora *USA* 18B1
Zamość *Pol* 41E2
Zamtang *China* 50A3
Zanaga *Congo* 70B4
Zanatepec *Mexico* 20D2
Záncara, R *Spain* 37B2
Zanda *China* 58D2
Zanesville *USA* 10C3
Zangla *India* 58D2
Zanjān *Iran* 61B1
Zanjitas *Arg* 26B2
Zanjon, R *Arg* 26B2
Zanzibar *Tanz* 70D4
Zanzibar, I *Tanz* 70D4
Zaouatanlaz *Alg* 68C2
Zaozhuang *China* 50D3
Zap, R *Turk* 62D2
Zapadnaja Dvina, R
USSR 30K7
Zapadno Dvina *USSR* 41G1
Zapadno Dvina, R *USSR* 41E1
Zapadno-Sakhalinskiy,
Mts *USSR* 51E1
Zapadno-Sibirskaya
Nizmennost', Lowland
USSR 46H3
Zapadnyy Sayan, Mts
USSR 47L4
Zapala *Arg* 26A3
Zapata *USA* 15F4
Zapolyarnyy *USSR* 42E2
Zaporozh'ye *USSR* 43F6
Zara *Turk* 62C2
Zaragoza *Mexico* 20B1
Zaragoza *Spain* 37B1
Zarand *Iran* 61C1
Zarand *Iran* 61D2
Zaranj *Afghan* 61E2
Zarara *Ven* 24E2
Zarasai *USSR* 41F1
Zárate *Arg* 26D2
Zard Kuh, Mt *Iran* 61B2
Zarembo I *USA* 8M4
Zarghun Shahr *Afghan* 58B2
Zargun, Mt *Pak* 58B2
Zaria *Nig* 69H3
Zarqa *Jordan* 62C3
Zarqa, R *Jordan* 63C2
Zaruma *Ecuador* 24C4
Zary *Pol* 40D2
Zarzis *Tunisia* 69E2
Zāskār, Mts *India* 58D2
Zāskār, R *India* 58D2
Zastron *S Africa* 72D3
Zatara, R *Jordan* 63D2

Zatoka Gdańska =
Gdańsk,G of
Zavety Il'icha *USSR* 51E2
Zavitinsk *USSR* 51B1
Zavü *China* 59E2
Zawiercie *Pol* 41D2
Zawilah *Libya* 67A2
Zayarsk *USSR* 47M4
Zaysan *USSR* 46K5
Zaysan *USSR* 57G1
Zayü, Mt *China* 48C4
Zduńska Wola *Pol* 41D2
Zeebrugge *Belg* 34B1
Zeelim *Israel* 63C3
Zeerust *S Africa* 72D2
Zefat *Israel* 63C2
Zegueren, Watercourse
Mali 68C3
Zeila *Somalia* 70E2
Zeitz *E Germ* 40C2
Zekog *China* 50A2
Zelenoborskiy *USSR* 42E2
Zelenodol'sk *USSR* 42H4
Zelenogorsk *USSR* 30K6
Zell *Austria* 35D1
Zell *W Germ* 35B1
Zell am See *Austria* 35E1
Zelten *Libya* 67A2
Zemio *CAR* 70C3
Zemlya Aleksandry, I
Barents S 46F1
Zemlya Frantsa Josifa, Is
Barents S 46F2
Zemlya Georga, I
Barents S 46F1
Zemlya Vil'cheka, I
Barents S 46H1
Zenifim, R *Israel* 63C3
Zenning *China* 50B4
Zergoun, R *Alg* 69C2
Zermatt *Switz* 35B1
Zestafoni *USSR* 43G7
Zevgari,C *Cyprus* 63B1
Zeya *USSR* 47O4
Zeya, R *USSR* 51B1
Zeya, Res *USSR* 47O4
Zeya Resevoir *USSR* 48F1
Zézere, R *Port* 37A1
Zghorta *Leb* 63C1
Zgierz *Pol* 41D2
Zhanggguangcai Ling, Mts
China 51B3
Zhangjiakou *China* 50D1
Zhangping *China* 50D4
Zhangwei He, R *China* 50D2
Zhangwu *China* 50E1
Zhangye *China* 50A2
Zhangzhou *China* 50D5
Zhanyi *China* 50A4
Zhaodong *China* 51B2
Zhaoqing *China* 50C5
Zhaotong *China* 50A4
Zhaoyang Hu, L *China* 50D2
Zhaoyuan *China* 51A2
Zharkamys *USSR* 43K6
Zharkovskiy *USSR* 41G1
Zhashkov *USSR* 41G3
Zhatay *USSR* 47O3
Zhdanov *USSR* 43F6
Zhejiang, Province *China* 50D4
Zheleznodorozhnyy
USSR 42J3
Zhengou *China* 44G4
Zhengzhou *China* 50C3
Zhenjiang *China* 50D3
Zhenlai *China* 51A2
Zhenxiong *China* 50A4
Zhenyuan *China* 50B4
Zherdevka *USSR* 43G5
Zhicheng *China* 50C3
Zhigalovo *USSR* 48D1
Zhigansk *USSR* 47O3
Zhijin *China* 50B4
Zhitkovichi *USSR* 41F2
Zhitomir *USSR* 41F2
Zhlobin *USSR* 41G2
Zhmerinka *USSR* 41F3
Zhob *Pak* 58B2
Zhodino *USSR* 41F2
Zhongba *China* 59B2
Zhongning *China* 50B2
Zhongshan *China* 50C5
Zhongwei *China* 50B2
Zhougdian *China* 48C4
Zhoushan Quandao,
Arch *China* 50E3
Zhovten' *USSR* 41G3
Zhuanghe *China* 50E2
Zhugqu *China* 50A3
Zhushan *China* 50C3
Zhuzhou *China* 50C4
Zibo *China* 50D2
Ziel,Mt *Aust* 76C3
Zielona Gora *Pol* 40D2
Zifta *Egypt* 63A3
Zigaing *Burma* 53A1
Zigong *China* 50A4
Ziguinchor *Sen* 68A3
Zihuatanejo *Mexico* 20B2
Zikhron Ya'aqov *Israel* 63C2

Žilina *Czech* 41D3
Ziller, R *Austria* 35D1
Zillertaler Alpen, Mts
Austria 35D1
Zilupe *USSR* 41F1
Zima *USSR* 47M4
Zimapan *Mexico* 20C1
Zimatlan *Mexico* 20C2
Zimbabwe, Republic
Africa 72D1
Zin, R *Israel* 63C3
Zinacatepec *Mexico* 20C2
Zinapécuaro *Mexico* 20B2
Zinder *Niger* 68C3
Ziniaré *U Volta* 69F3
Zion Nat Pk *USA* 18D3
Zi Shui *China* 50C4
Zitácuaro *Mexico* 20B2
Zittau *E Germ* 40C2
Ziya He, R *China* 50D2
Ziyang *China* 50A3
Zlatoust *USSR* 42K4
Zmeinogorsk *USSR* 46K4
Znin *Pol* 41D2
Znoimo *Czech* 40D3
Zoekmekuar *S Africa* 72D1
Zofinger *Switz* 35B1
Zoigê *China* 50A3
Zolochev *USSR* 41F3
Zolotonosha *USSR* 41G3
Zomba *Malawi* 71D5
Zongo *Zaïre* 70B3
Zonguldak *Turk* 62B1
Zorzor *Lib* 68B4
Zouerate *Maur* 68A2
Zrenjanin *Yugos* 39E1
Zug *Switz* 35C1
Zugdidi *USSR* 43G7
Zugspitze, Mt *W Germ* 35D1
Zújar, R *Spain* 37A2
Zumbo *Mozam* 71D5
Zumbrota *USA* 9D3
Zumpango *Mexico* 20C2
Zungeru *Nig* 69H4
Zuni *USA* 14A2
Zuni Mts *USA* 14A2
Zunyi *China* 50B4
Zuo, R *China* 53D1
Zuo Jiang, R *China* 50B5
Zürich *Switz* 35C1
Zürichsee, L *Switz* 35C1
Zuru *Nig* 69H3
Zuwärah *Libya* 67A1
Zuyevka *USSR* 42J4
Zvenigorodka *USSR* 41G3
Zvishavane *Zim* 71C6
Zvolen *Czech* 41D3
Zvornik *Yugos* 39D2
Zvoron, L *USSR* 51D1
Zweibrücken *W Germ* 34D2
Zweisimmen *Switz* 35B1
Zwickau *E Germ* 40C2
Zwolle *Neth* 40B2
Zyrardów *Pol* 41E2
Zyryanka *USSR* 47R3
Zyryanovsk *USSR* 46K5
Żywiec *Pol* 41D3
Zyyi *Cyprus* 63B1

This map and others like it were used by sailors in the 16th century as sailing and harbour guides. It contains information gathered from generations of harbour pilots and sailors.

Georgio Calapoda:
Portolan chart of Europe, 1560.